1/15175

The Fabulous Ego

THE

QUADRANGLE

FABULOUS EGO

ABSOLUTE POWER IN HISTORY

MILTON KLONSKY

THE NEW YORK TIMES BOOK CO.

ACKNOWLEDGMENTS

Illustrations
"The Death of Sardanapalus," Eugène Delacroix, The Louvre Museum, Paris.
Justinian and Theodora; Ivan the Terrible; Akbar the Great; Charles I; Louis XV; Catherine the Great,
New York Public Library Picture Collection.
The Grand Signor, Metropolitan Museum of Art, Rogers Fund 1944.
Napoleon I, The Bodley Head, London.

Text
Reprinted by permission of the publisher and The Loeb Classical Library from *Scriptores Historiae
Augustae*, Vol II, translated by D. Magie, Cambridge, Mass.: Harvard University Press, 1924.
Reprinted by permission of The Folio Society Ltd., London: excerpts from *At the Court of the Borgias, the
Diary of John Burchard*. Translated by Geoffrey Parker, 1963.
Reprinted by permission of the American Oriental Society, New Haven, Conn.: excerpts from Derk Bodie,
Statesman, Patriot, and General.
Reprinted by permission from The Asia Society, Inc., New York, N.Y.: excerpts from *Recollections on the
Customs of Cambodia* by Chou Ta-kuan.
Reprinted by permission from The Bodley Head, London: excerpts from *The St. Helena Journal of General
Baron Gourgaud (1815–1818)* edited by Norman Edwards and translated by Sidney Gillard.
Reprinted by permission of Oxford University Press, Delhi, India: excerpts from *The Commentary of Father
Monserrate*. Translated by J. S. Hoyland and annotated by S. N. Banerjee.
Reprinted by permission of Penguin Books Ltd., London: excerpts from *Procopius: The Secret History*.
Edited and translated by G. A. Williamson, © G. A. Williamson, 1966.

Designed by: Al Burkhardt

Library of Congress Cataloging in Publication Data

Klonsky, Milton, comp.
  The fabulous ego.

  CONTENTS: Sardanapalus (c. 800 B.C.).—Shih Huang Ti
(259–210 B.C.).—Elagabalus (204–222). [etc.]
  1. Kings and rulers—Biography. 2. Despotism.
I. Title.
D107.K55   909 [B]   74-77951
ISBN 0-8129-0490-7

Personae

In Memoriam S.K.

Siehe, wir lieben nicht, wie die Blumen, aus einem einzigen Jahr; uns steigt, wo wir lieben, unvordenklicher Saft in die Arme.

Prologue

The waking have one common world, but the sleeping turn aside each into a world of his own.

(Heraclitus, *Fr. 95*)

But if history (as has been said) is a nightmare from which mankind has not yet awakened, then the royal personae in this book are spectres that still haunt us. Each in his time, from the Assyrian king Sardanapalus across a span of almost 2500 years to Napoleon, was once the collective "I" of a whole people, self-enclosed in a world of his own. Assembled here side by side, however, on the same stage of the Theatrum Mundi, these one-of-a-kind and once-upon-a-time exalted egos seem weirdly anomalous, as if, somehow, a cyclops and a valkyrie, an abominable snowman, a golem, a giant sloth, a faust and a manticore, a miching malecho, a three-headed cerberus, a cockatrice and a pterodactyl were to be caged and exhibited together. And yet, in a way that makes them paradoxically no less fabulous and even rarer, they were also, of course, certifiably real, fixed like ourselves in the one common world of facts and dates.

The ancestral prototypes of these monarchs first made their appearance in Egypt and Mesopotamia, China and India, about the middle of the 4th millennium B.C., at that turning point when mankind at last became self-conscious and emerged from the *Urdummheit* of savagery and myth. Their reign thus began at the beginning of civilization and recorded history. As successors to the magic-working shamans and priest-kings of the aboriginal hunting tribes, they represented an entirely new type of ruler set above their subjects by divine right. In ancient Egypt, for instance, where the pharaoh was worshiped as a god incarnate, he focused within his own essential and collective Self, or *ka*, the convergence of heaven and earth on which both the right order of the cosmos and the salvation of the people depended. As described by the Jungian mythologist Erich Neumann, in his psychoanalytic study of *The Origins and History of Consciousness*:

> The immortal soul of the divine king Osiris becomes the immortal soul of each and every Egyptian, even as Christ the Saviour becomes the Christ-soul of every Christian, the self within us. In the same way the function of the chief, which is to will and decide, becomes the model for all subsequent acts of free will in the ego

vii

of the individual; and the law-making function, originally attributed to God . . .
has in modern man become the inner court of conscience.

Likewise, the lugals of Sumer and Akkad, the deva-rajahs of India, the Sons
of Heaven of China, if not godlings themselves on earth, were at least the
sacred stewards of the gods in heaven, and in their hands were placed the
keys of both kingdoms. The time of their world-wide emergence also served
as the seed-time of the great religious and ethical creeds of mankind. But
even when, in later ages, the institution of kingship became more and more
secular and profane, kings themselves in their own persons were still hedged
about with a noumenal awe and dread derived from that past.

From our own vantage point, here and now, as twentieth-century
egalitarian groundlings, we look back up at their royal highness in
astonishment, with a kind of cubist double take—seeing them first as time-
and flesh-bound mortal creatures on a level with ourselves, then once again
in altitudo as kings, at the topmost plane of being, capable of enacting in
reality what we can indulge only in dreams or daydreams. The prophetic
18th century social philosopher Giambattista Vico, in his *Scienza Nuova*,
envisioned the gods and heroes of mythology as "imaginative universals"
(*generi fantastici*), the symbols of collective representations, or "poetical
characters"; but in the course of time, by a further turn and turn about the
moebius curve, or mortal coil, of the *commodius vicus,* the roles of these
"poetical characters" were later assumed by the great kings of history. Such
transcendent figures as, say, Tamerlane or Harun al-Rashid or Ivan the
Terrible, taken out of their historical milieux, still exist in the imagination
on the same scale as Hamlet or Don Quixote or Oedipus, removed from
their literary contexts. They are, in that sense, timeless. But even within the
parenthetical arcs of birth and death—(204–222) or (764–809) or (1533–
1584) or whenever—as the "observed of all observers," these royal personae
seemed to their own subjects then as they do to people today to have
performed rather than lived their lives.

A similar observation may no doubt be made about any of us in our
multifarious public and private roles:

> All the world's a stage
> And all the men and women merely players;
> They have their exits and their entrances;
> And one man in his time plays many parts . . .

as Shakespeare put it, wearing the mask of Jacques in *As You Like It*. The
Globe Theatre itself, which was to the Theatrum Mundi as microcosm to
macrocosm, had as its emblem a figure of Atlas holding up the earth, to
which was affixed the motto: *Totus mundus agit histrionem.* And concerning
this motto, incidentally, there has been preserved (in a collection of poetic
oddments by Ben Jonson entitled *Farrago*) an extemporaneous crossfire in
rhyme between Jonson and Shakespeare, perhaps after both had quaffed a
few cups of canary at the Mermaid:

Jonson
If, but stage actors, all the world displays,
Where shall we find spectators of their plays?

Shakespeare
Little, or much, of what we see, we do;
We are both actors and spectators too.

—with the sole exception, it may be, of kings, who were never permitted to shed the heavy regalia of their selves as roles and escape into anonymity.

From the start, the lack of any clearly defined boundary between the two literary realms, history and drama, has resulted in much critical dispute as to territorial rights. In his *Poetics*, written around 335 B.C., Aristotle was the first to attempt to draw the line. "The difference between the poet and the historian," he wrote then, "lies not in the one composing verse and the other prose—you might put the work of Herodotus into verse, and it would still be a species of history for all that; the difference really consists in this, that one relates what has happened, and the other what may happen. Poetry, therefore, is higher and more philosophical than history: for poetry expresses the universal, history the particular." Yet Aristotle, though no less the great philosopher for all that, was essentially unhistorical, regarding as universally true what was so only for his own particular time and place. Since then the relationship between history and drama has undergone a profound reversal (or *peripeteia,* as he called it), for it is now history that has grown increasingly more abstract, while drama—especially in the modern forms of the novel and the movies—has based itself instead upon the absurd and anarchic unpredictability of the quotidian. Compare, for instance, Anton Chekhov's *The Cherry Orchard* with Spengler's *Decline of the West,* or the science-fiction movie *2001* with the metaphysical speculations of Teilhard de Chardin.

But then, as we know, there are infra-history, history qua history, and History. At the bottom of the heap lie the annals, anecdotes, memoirs, diaries, letters, public documents, TV interviews and Nixonian tapes (comparable to the *churingas,* minutely detailed memorials, made by savage tribes) that preserve a record of events in their radical contingency, the "sound and fury" made by successive generations before shuffling off the coil. Rising from this mishmash, in higher and higher tiers of abstraction, with the specific history of this subsumed under the generic history of that, is the idealized History of philosophers and theologians.

In the course of a famous controversy with Jean-Paul Sartre on the nature of history, the anthropologist Claude Lévi-Strauss once described these various hierarchies in his *The Savage Mind*: "History," he wrote, "is a discontinuous set of domains of history, each of which is defined by a characteristic frequency and by a differential coding of *before* and *after*. . . . It is not only fallacious but contradictory to conceive of the historical process as a continuous development, beginning with prehistory coded in tens or hundreds of millennia, then adopting the scale of millennia when it gets to the 4th or 3rd millennium, and continuing as history in centuries interlarded, at the pleasure of each author, with slices of annual history within the century, day to day history within the year or even hourly history within the day." Thus, according to Lévi-Strauss, the minutiae of everyday events noted by the clock, and of interest only to the private individual, would belong to one set of domains; national events signified by dates such as 1776, 1865, 1917, say, to another; and events of universal importance, such as the discovery of fire, the domestication of animals, the invention of writing, and so forth, in so far as they can be dated, to still another. The false assumption that all these incommensurable and discontinuous sets may somehow form a single continuous "history," he concludes, has arisen through a misleading analogy with our own psychic development, whereby we change in time yet retain self-identity, so that "historical knowledge appears to affirm the evidence of inner sense."

But all analogies, carried too far, may be misleading . . . which in turn leads us back to where we began.

Confronted by Lévi-Strauss' maze of "sets," on which a multiplicity of seemingly unrelated scenes, so to speak, with multitudinous characters are/were taking place in a multidimensional space-time, the historian must "make" history in about the same way a tragic poet (*poein*, to make or construct) in Aristotle's Athens once made tragedy. To avoid an infinite regress, he first has to fix the chronological limits of his chosen domain of "*before* . . . and *after*," just as a dramatist must devise his plot with a beginning, middle, and end. The characters and scenes of the Theatrum Mundi are of course real, belonging to our so-called "common world," but the action imitated by the historian must also *seem* real, with one event following another by necessary consequence, and not, as they so often are in life, by accidental collision and collusion. ("Of all plots," said Aristotle, "the episodic are the worst. . . . There is a great difference between a thing happening *propter hoc* and *post hoc*.") Events that might possibly have been regarded by the historical spectator as hardly worth his notice, going on somewhere in the wings, or as a piece of business in the background, or even behind the scenes, will then be revealed, in the plot devised by the historian, to have been of crucial importance after all.

So then, as co-producers, Clio, the muse of poetic tragedy, and Melpomene, the muse of history, have joined

> Reason, in itself confounded,
> Saw division grow together,
> To themselves yet either neither
> Simple were so well compounded
>
> That it cried, How true a twain
> Seemeth this concordant one!

—like Shakespeare's "co-supremes" in *The Phoenix & The Turtle*—and conspired to present the royal personae in this book. Most of the memoirs, diaries, and biographical accounts in which they appear were written either by contemporaries who observed them in action close up or else by near contemporaries who were still close enough in time to obtain intimately detailed descriptions of their lives and exploits. What has thereby been lost in historical perspective is gained in dramatic immediacy. This is of course the sort of history with which Aristotle was familiar (and Lévi-Strauss calls "infra-" or "low-powered" history), wherein chance, whether "mere" or "sheer," and also fact, whether "plain" or "hard," predominate. Yet every other sort, of whatever domain or degree of abstraction, must ultimately be based upon it. There may be, as Hamlet remarked to Horatio, "a destiny that shapes our ends" (teleological, not anatomical), but Cleopatra still pokes her incalculable nose, one-sixteenth of an inch more or less—yet in effect as vast as the proboscis of Florida—into all the foreordained, because preconceived, systems and cycles of history *in saecula saeculorum* elaborated by marxist determinists and mystical eschatologists.

So far, noses aside, eye hath not seen nor ear heard enough of the plot for anyone to guess The End. "The series of men," thought Pascal, in one of his most visionary *Pensées*, "may be considered a single man, living forever and continuously learning." And, in that sense, our cast of "poetical characters," as the exalted egos of now vanished supremacies (*"L'état, c'est moi,"* soliloquized Louis XIV), may also be said to have enacted in their own brief lives episodes of a psychohistorical drama of mankind. Here again, however, the unreconstructed author of *The Savage Mind* would reject as metaphysical hocus-pocus any such attempt to equate (as he puts it) "the notion of history and the notion of humanity . . . with the unavowed aim of making historicity the last refuge of a transcendental humanism: as if men could regain the illusion of liberty on the plane of the 'we' merely by giving up the 'I's that are too obviously wanting in consistency." Yet if it be an illusion, and nothing but, it is one that began with the original symbolical anthropos, Adam, and will most likely terminate with the apotheosis of Everyman at some forever futuristic Teilhardian omega point. In which case (just to bring this prologue around as well), Heraclitus' "common world," which has been fractured by time into a myriad of opposing and mutually exclusive *Weltanschauungs,* may not, it seems, lie beneath the sun of the waking but under the lid, in the depths of the "collective unconscious," one for all and all for one, of the sleeping.

After that peripeteia, we can only conclude by offering some explanation of the criterion employed to select the royal personae for this book. Each not only had to be of world importance, rising above his/her time and place, but the literary works in which they appear also had to have sufficient stature to be worthy of their presence. The choice having been thus narrowed, the fifteen anointed ones might be said to have presented themselves by divine right. Genghis Khan, perhaps, might have been

substituted for Tamerlane, or Nero for Elagabalus, or Charlemagne for
Harun al-Rashid; but then, in my judgment, the psychohistorical design of
the book, its own plot, would have been weakened. Many of those in the
cast, at least as embodied in their current political avatars, still make their
presence felt on the world scene: e.g., the Emperor Shih Huang Ti in
peasant costume disguised as Chairman Mao; or Czar Ivan the Terrible
sporting a false "cockroach moustache" as Comrade Stalin; or King
Charles I, impeached by Parliament in 1649 for "high crimes and
misdemeanors," saluting an American flag in his lapel as President Nixon.
Furthermore, since these viconian kings are conceived as "poetical characters," the symbols of collective representations, and exhibit in their own
essential humours a wide range of perennial human types, they are
manifestly present even in the contemporary U.S.A. Our stampeding herds
of chauvinist pigs and liberated sows, for instance, might discern their
ancestral features, hugely aggrandized, in the Grand Signor and Catherine
the Great; likewise our back-slapping and -stabbing, conniving and bribing
politicians and bureaucrats have their prototype in the Borgia Pope
Alexander VI; likewise those gangs of adolescent bluebeards and thrill-killers, such as the Zebras and Charles Manson & Co., have theirs in
Elagabalus; and also, though this might come as a surprise, even our legions
of turned-off and turned-on hipsters nowadays might find their cult imago
in that cool king Louis XV. Lord Acton's old saw about absolute power
corrupting absolutely (which he cribbed, by the way, from a description by
Herodotus of the Persian monarch Cambyses the Great) would apply as
well to anyone's or Everyman's imagination, where we are all equally
absolute. Accordingly, we observe ourselves in these royal personae "whose
actions [as Shakespeare remarked] are our dreams."

Much of the material for *The Fabulous Ego*, even when available in
English, has had to be exhumed from the vaults of Rare Book Rooms. The
biographies of Shih Huang Ti and Harun al-Rashid, for instance, have been
put together and, for the most part, translated into English for the first time;
though why this should be so, since the works containing them are regarded
as classics of Chinese and Arabic literature, must remain one of those
quirks of the inscrutable West that have always baffled the East. Finally, in
editing and condensing the original texts I have tried to preserve as much as
possible of their pith and stylistic flavor. Only spelling and punctuation
have been changed to conform with modern usage. Throughout I have
supplied subtitles, narrative bridges, and necessary factual information, this
last usually enclosed in brackets within the text; which has enabled me to
avoid the excessive use of footnotes, that fussy undergrowth crawling up the
pages of most tomes of history in dense patches of miniscule type, requiring
a third eye on the point of the chin to be read with ease. *The Fabulous Ego*,
it goes without saying, is not intended primarily for scholars, nor even for
lawyers and accountants, but for what used to be called the Common
Reader (though not so common nowadays), who might deem it a royal
privilege to enter into these presences.

Sardanapalus

Painting by Eugene Delacroix, Louvre, Paris.

Oh, thou wouldst have me doubtless set up edicts:
"Obey the king—contribute to his treasure—
Recruit his phalanx—spill your blood at bidding—
Fall down and worship, or get up and toil."
Or thus: "Sardanapalus on this spot
Slew fifty thousand of his enemies.
These are their sepulchres, and this his trophy."
I leave these things to conquerors; enough
For me, if I can make my subjects feel
The weight of human misery less, and glide
Ungroaning to the tomb: I take no license
Which I deny to them. We are all men.

> Lord Byron, *Sardanapalus*

Το begin with, did he ever exist? *The strange story of Sardanapalus was first related by the Greek historian Ctesias, who practiced medicine as royal physician to Artaxerxes II (404–358 B.C.) at the Persian court then in Babylon, where he had access to the national archives. His book, the* Persika, *which survives only in fragments, is the source of all subsequent accounts of the last Assyrian monarch.*

Ctesias probably derived the name Sardanapalus itself from a corruption of Ashurdaninpal, son of Shalmaneser II, whose reign ended with the fall of Nineveh in 823 B.C. He also, it seems, copied various traits of his character from the luxury-loving Ashurbanipal (referred to in the Bible, Ezra 4:10, as "the great and noble Asnappar"), who ruled Assyria from 668 to 625 B.C. And finally, he must have taken the account of his spectacular suicide from that of Shamash-shum-ukin, the brother of Ashurbanipal, who, after the failure of a palace revolt, burned himself alive together with his whole family to avoid falling into the king's hands.

As for the supposed effeminacy of Sardanapalus, the Persian conquerors of the Assyrian empire would be expected to make such jibes at the expense of their once fearsome overlords. It may be, too, that Ctesias conceived the tale of Sardanapalus's confinement in his harem out of an obscure recollection of the savage customs that once prevailed in the lands of Sheba, Benin, and Ethiopia (as described by Sir James Frazer in The Golden Bough), where the kings were under a taboo never to leave the palace on pain of being stoned to death. The last king of Assyria also has his counterpart in the last emperor of the Shang dynasty in China around 1100 B.C. (though Ctesias could never have heard of that), named Chou Hsin, who is supposed to have set fire to his palace and perished in the flames after losing his throne.

So, then, resurrecting and piecing together all these membra disjecta, like the scattered limbs of the Egyptian nature god Osiris, miraculously he reappears. Not quite historic yet not entirely mythic, sufficiently either to make him neither, but both at once, he has the same chimerical existence as an Agamemnon or Samson or Aeneas, what the philosopher Giambattista Vico would have dubbed a "poetical character." As such, in Byron's tragedy Sardanapalus, he transmits his famous testament to future ages:

> Why, those few lines contain the history
> Of all things human: hear—"Sardanapalus,
> The king, and son of Anacyndaraxes,
> In one day built Anchialus and Tarsus.
> Eat, drink, and love: the rest's not worth a fillip."

It was after reading Byron's play, incidentally, that the young Delacroix painted his The Death of Sardanapalus, about which picture his friend and admirer Baudelaire remarked that "it contains some very beautiful women, bright and shining and pink. . . . And Sardanapalus himself was as beautiful as a woman." Thus, the embers of that imaginary fire first lit by Ctesias to kindle the funeral pyre of a perhaps nonexistent king still glow in the noosphere.

The biography of Sardanapalus that follows, scarcely much longer than these introductory notes, is taken from the Deipnosophistae (Dinner-Table Philosophers) of Athenaeus, written in the third century A.D., and from the Historia of Diodorus Siculus, written about 40 B.C. Both were indebted to the lost work of Ctesias.

3

Sardanapalus, the thirtieth king in succession from Ninus, founder of
the Assyrian empire, outdid all his ancestors in sloth and debauchery. No
one ever saw him outside his own palace, for he lived there cloistered like a
woman of the harem and spent his days knitting wool and spinning the
royal purple garments in the company of his eunuchs and concubines. He
habitually assumed feminine garb, and so smeared his face and indeed his
entire body with skin-whitening cosmetics and emollients that it was more
smooth and delicate than any courtesan's. He also took care to tune and
flutter and wheedle his voice coquettishly even during solemn councils of
state. At his orgies he glutted himself regularly on the most exotic foods and
potions; and he also indulged in sexual revels with catamites as well as
concubines, enjoying them separately or together, according to his fancy,
and showed not the least concern for the disgrace such conduct might bring
upon him.

A certain general of his realm called Arbaces, a Mede by birth, once
engaged in an intrigue with the chief eunuch of the palace to obtain an
interview with Sardanapalus inside the harem. The matter having been
arranged, the King reluctantly gave his consent, and he was admitted into
the royal presence. When the Mede, after prostrating himself, finally looked
up, he was amazed to see Sardanapalus with a face anointed with white
lead, his eyebrows plucked and blackened with kohl, his beard shaved close
but rubbed even closer with pumice, and with hair coiffed and bejewelled
for the occasion. He was reclining among the other women with his knees
uplifted and combing purple wool, seemingly absorbed in the task. Upon
being greeted by Arbaces, however, the King is said to have simpered at
him and rolled his eyes seductively.

It was this same Arbaces who later induced the Medes and Persians to
attack the kingdom, promising that they would thus win their freedom and
share the wealth of Assyria, for he little thought that so depraved and
effeminate a monarch could offer any resistance. But this was not to be the
case. When he learned of the rebellion, Sardanapalus roused himself from
his lethargy and collected a large army at Nineveh to meet Arbaces.
Nineveh withstood a siege of two years, until at last the Medes and the
Persians succeeded in diverting the waters of the Tigris to undermine the
walls of the city. Realizing that his cause was hopeless, the King sent his
three daughters and two sons away to Paphlagonia, placing them in the care
of its ruler, and gave each of them three thousand talents in gold. He then
prepared himself for death.

Sardanapalus heaped up a pyre four hundred feet high, on top of which
he constructed a chamber of cedar wood one hundred feet long; inside he
placed a hundred and fifty gold tables and an equal number of couches,
these also of gold. The King lay down on one couch with his Queen, while
all the concubines of the harem surrounded them on the others. He had
previously roofed the chamber with huge beams and piled thick timbers all

about so that there should be no exit. Upon the tables were loaded ten million talents of gold and one hundred million of silver, vials of perfumes and precious ointments, caskets of jewels, along with purple robes and splendid garments of every description. When all was ready he then gave orders to light the fire, which burned for fifteen days. The people of Nineveh beheld the smoke with astonishment, believing that the King was offering sacrifices. Only the palace eunuchs knew the truth.

And so Sardanapalus, after he had enjoyed pleasure in strange ways, died as nobly as he could.

Just outside Nineveh there once stood a high mound, which was demolished by Cyrus the Persian in his time in order to raise counterwalls against the city for a siege. On the summit of this mound Sardanapalus had caused to be engraved an inscription in Chaldean letters:

"I, Sardanapalus, became King; and whilst I looked upon the sun's light I drank, I ate, I loved, for I knew the time in which mortals live to be short, and moreover hath many changes and mishaps, and that others would have joy of the goods I left behind. Wherefore I have allowed no day to go by unfulfilled while pursuing my own desires."

Two hundred years afterward, Alexander the Great, when marching inland against the Persians, pitched his camp at the city of Anchiale. There he came upon the tomb of Sardanapalus. Outlined against the sky was a huge stone figure of a man mounted on a mule, his right arm upraised, and with the thumb and middle finger of the hand brought closely together as if snapping them. Upon the base of the statue was inscribed:

"Sardanapalus, son of Anacyndaraxes, built Anchiale and Tarsus in a single day. Eat, drink, love; for other things are not worth *that*"—meaning a snap of the fingers.

Shih Huang Ti

Charcoal rubbing from an ancient stone tomb
engraving at Wou Leang Tseu. The only known contemporary
likeness of the Emperor.

What dire offense from amorous causes springs,
What mighty contests rise from trivial things . . .

> Alexander Pope, *The Rape of the Lock*

*M*editating on what sublime or subliminal motives might have impelled the
*Emperor Shih Huang Ti to build the Great Wall of China and decree the
Burning of the Books, Jorge Luis Borges suggests the possibility that he wished,
by this "wall in space and fire in time," to fortify himself against the intrusion of
"a single memory: the memory of his mother's dishonor." For it seems that
while Shih Huang Ti was still a child his mother took as her lover a sexual
prodigy and entertainer in brothels, famed for the polyphiloprogenitive size of
his penis, who (as the following biography relates) used to dance about naked
during palace orgies to "wild music," with his member "filling up the hole of a
wheel made of* t'ung *wood."*

*Should this psycho-historical analysis of the Emperor be correct, it would at
least be inversely commensurate in its mock-heroic bathos with his stupendous
exploits, which have never been surpassed as the most vain (to cite Sir Thomas
Browne) of "the vain enormities of ancient magnanimity." For more than two
thousand years they have continued to appall the conscience and fire the
imagination of mankind:*

> *Far eastward cast thine eye, from whence the sun
> And Orient science their bright course begun:
> One god-like monarch all that pride confounds,
> He, whose long wall the wandering Tartar bounds;
> Heavens! what a pile! whole ages perish there,
> And one bright blaze turns learning into air.*
>
> > Alexander Pope, The Dunciad

*As it turned out, however, copies of the Confucian texts and various other
classic works were secretly preserved by scholars at the risk of death or exile
and transmitted to later generations; and the Great Wall itself, which was*

intended to keep out the savage and marauding horsemen of the Hsiung-Nu, ancestors of the Huns, proved, after successive barbarian invasions throughout the centuries, as permeable as memory.

Though Shih Huang Ti was actually a contemporary of Hannibal in the West, he seems to belong to a far more remote and even mythic past. There is an aura of childhood once-upon-a-time magic about his life, aside from the Wall and the Books, that makes us wonder whether he is a character out of history or a fairy tale. Consider, for instance, the fantastic all-devouring fee-fie-fo-fum of an imperial ogre who built as trophies to his own vanity 270 fully equipped and interconnected palaces, each one the replica of a palace that had once belonged to a defeated king or feudal warlord, forming a belt 70 miles wide around his capital at Hsien-yang; or how he once commanded his soldiers to defoliate and scarify the sides of the mountain of Siang, then paint the bare earth red, because, he believed, it had insolently raised a storm against him while he was traveling past; or, finally, his ceaseless but unavailing quest for the marvelous mushroom tche, from which he might squeeze the elixir of eternal life, and so dwell forever with "the blessed Immortals in palaces made entirely of gold and silver, and where all the birds, beasts and other living creatures are of a pure transparency or flawless whiteness."

Failing that, Shih Huang Ti was compelled by mortality to settle for the kingdom of this world, becoming the founder of a dynasty that he confidently expected would endure for "ten thousand generations." His youngest son and successor, Erh ("Second") Shih Huang Ti, however, was also the last; and following Erh's death and the civil war that then broke out in the empire, the Han dynasty, in 202 B.C., came to power and commenced its long 400-year reign.

Of course in our own times the career of another world-conquering book- and people-burner, the Führer, who hoped to establish a "Thousand Year Reich," might remind us of Shih Huang Ti. But his true alter ego, the ruler with whom he shares a ping-pong affinity across the ages both in personal achievement and in political style, is the Chairman himself. Mao, for instance, also succeeded in unifying China under a single government; also campaigned against Confucianism, family authority, traditional customs, and all the other "olds";

9

*also conceived a grand design to maintain his Communist dynasty for "ten
thousand generations" by means of cultural revolutions in perpetuity; also
devised a strategy for walling off the northern barbarians—Russians this time,
not Hsiung-Nu—and deflect them against the West. In an extraordinary
document smuggled out of China after the failure of the plot [see note on p. 30]
by Lin Piao, former Defense Minister, to kill Mao, the conspirators described
him as "a maniac of suspicion and a sadist," whose "own son went berserk
under his high-handedness"; and then they added:* "In fact, he has become a
Shih Huang Ti of modern times" *(my emphasis). Which would almost make it
appear that the ghost of the ancient Ch'in Emperor has risen from the tomb to
haunt our own world.*

   The biography of Shih Huang Ti that follows has been taken from the classic
Shih Chi *("Historical Records") by Ssŭ-ma Ch'ien (c. 145–85 B.C.). The
author was himself a victim of political tyranny, condemned to suffer
emasculation for having opposed an edict of the Han emperor Wu Ti. As the son
of the court astrologer Ssŭ-ma T'an—who is thought to have commenced the
work—he had access to the imperial chronicles and records of antiquity. It
should also be taken into account that his evaluation of Shih Huang Ti, written
a hundred years after the Emperor's death, must undoubtedly have been swayed
by his own Confucianist sympathies.*

   About half of the Shih Chi *was first translated into French by the sinologist
Edouard Chavannes in his five-volume* Les Memoires Historiques de Se-ma
Ts'ien, *published in Paris from 1895 to 1905, from which I have extracted and
translated into English most of my own version; and I have also made use of
several sections of the* Shih Chi *translated into English by Derk Bodde in his*
Statesman, Patriot and General *(New Haven: American Oriental Society,
1940). Ssŭ-ma Ch'ien composed his immense work as a mosaic of biographies,
in no consecutive order, of rulers, courtiers, scholars, generals, and other
historical personages; it has been necessary, therefore, to select passages here
and there in order to put together a consecutive narrative of the life of Shih
Huang Ti.*

CH'IN SHIH HUANG TI, First Sovereign Emperor of Ch'in, was born in
Han-tan, capital of the kingdom of Chao [in the year 259 B.C.]. His mother
was a beautiful concubine presented as a gift to his father, Prince Tzu-Ch'u
[later King Chuang-hsi], at a time when the Prince was serving in Han-tan
as a hostage. This came to pass in the following way . . .

The Birth and Ancestry of the Emperor

   A certain wily and powerful merchant of Honan named Lu Pu-wei, by
buying cheap and selling dear from one city to the next, had accumulated

thousands of catties of gold. One day while engaged in business in Han-tan, he observed the Prince and said to himself, "Here is some rare merchandise that may be stored up." Prince Tzu-Ch'u was then living in mean circumstances, treated with contempt and discourtesy as a hostage by the feudal lords of Chao, for they hated the warlike people of Ch'in.

Accordingly, Lu Pu-wei went to call on the Prince and said to him, "I am one able to enlarge your gate" [that is, advance your interests].

Tzu-Ch'u smiled and said, "Better enlarge your own gate, sir, and then enlarge mine."

Lu Pu-wei replied, "You do not understand—my gate depends on your gate for enlargement. Consider that you are in a middling place, between twenty older and younger brothers, all of whom are in line for the throne. You have not received much favor from your father, the Crown Prince of An-kuo, and for a long time have been held as a hostage among the feudal lords of Chao. When the great King of Ch'in dies and your father assumes power, you will have no chance to rise above your elder brothers, who are, in addition, always present at court."

Tzu-Ch'u now asked, "What, then, is to be done?"

The merchant replied, "You are poor and a foreigner in this land, with no money to enhance your position. I request that you allow me to travel westward on your behalf to the court of Ch'in with one thousand catties of gold. There I shall try to persuade the Crown Prince and his wife, Lady Hua-yang, who has no children, to establish you as successor."

Tzu-Ch'u bowed and said, "Should it go as you plan, sir, I beg to divide the state of Ch'in and share it with you."

Lu Pu-wei then gave the Prince 500 catties of gold for his own use; and with another 500, he bought rare and beautiful trinkets for making presents, and traveled westward to Ch'in. After obtaining an interview with the elder sister of Lady Hua-yang, a vain but homely woman susceptible to flattery, he offered her gifts, and thus gained the opportunity to praise the devotion and noble character of Prince Tzu-Ch'u.

"The young man," he stated, "thinks tearfully day and night of the Crown Prince and her Ladyship."

When Lady Hua-yang was informed of this, and received her share of the trinkets, she was greatly pleased. Lu Pu-wei continued his courtship of her sister, using all the cunning he had learned as a merchant, and finally persuaded her to make the cause of Prince Tzu-Ch'u her own. At a suitable time, she approached Lady Hua-yang privately and said:

"If a woman charms a man with her beauty alone, after her beauty fades so does his love. At present your Ladyship delights the Crown Prince, who deeply loves you despite the fact that you are without children. Why then do you not promptly attach to yourself one of the royal princes and make him your son, thus establishing him as heir to the throne? During your lifetime you will not only be honored by him, but for a century afterward your adopted son will transmit the royal power to his own sons. This is

known as 'ten thousand generations of benefit resulting from a single word.'
Prince Tzu-Ch'u, now serving as a hostage in Chao, is worthy of such a
favor; and he fully realizes that, as a secondary son in rank, without your
aid he can never aspire to become the successor."

Lady Hua-yang agreed with this counsel. One day, when the Crown
Prince was at leisure and in fine humor, she spoke of his son Tzu-Ch'u and
of the high renown in which he was held by all. Then, sorrowfully, she said,
"I, your concubine, have had the good fortune to occupy a place in your
harem; yet I have also had the misfortune to have given birth to none of
your children. I would feel our love to be fulfilled if you make Tzu-Ch'u
your successor, and I ask also that you entrust him to my care."

The Crown Prince of An-kuo granted her request. He then gave her
Ladyship an engraved jade tablet as a bond that Prince Tzu-Ch'u should be
made his successor. He and his wife also sent gifts to the Prince in Chao
and appointed the merchant Lu Pu-wei to act as his guardian. The fame of
the new heir thus became widespread among the feudal lords.

Now, of the many splendid courtesans of the city of Han-tan, Lu Pu-wei
had chosen one who was extremely beautiful as well as an excellent dancer.
He took her into his household, and soon afterward she became pregnant.
One evening while Tzu-Ch'u was drinking in company with Lu Pu-wei, he
was entranced by this courtesan as she performed for them and desired her
for himself. He arose to offer a toast to his guardian for a long life, and
seized the opportunity to ask for her possession, knowing that as a guest he
could hardly be refused. Lu Pu-wei was angry; but then he reflected that his
expenditures on the Prince's behalf had already brought him close to
financial ruin, so he felt that by this additional bait he might hook
his royal prize securely. Forthwith he gave the concubine to him.

The girl, however, even after she entered the harem of Prince Tzu-Ch'u,
concealed the fact that she was pregnant with Lu Pu-wei's child. At the
expiration of a great period [twelve months], she gave birth to a son, the
future Emperor Shih Huang Ti, whom she named Cheng [meaning
"upright"].

His Rise to the Throne

About two years later, an army was sent by the state of Ch'in to besiege
Han-tan. The people of Chao demanded that their hostage Tzu-Ch'u be
killed along with his family. But the Prince succeeded in bribing their
keeper with 600 catties of gold, and so all escaped to the camp of the
invading army and made their way to Ch'in.

Shortly after they were established at the court, the old King died, having
reigned for fifty-six years. The Crown Prince of An-kuo was now
proclaimed King of Ch'in; Lady Hua-yang became Queen; and Tzu-Ch'u,
in turn, rose to become Crown Prince. Scarcely a year later, upon the death
of his father, Tzu-Ch'u took his place as ruler under the title Chuang-hsi. Lu

Pu-wei was now rewarded by being named the Marquis of Wen-hsin, with revenues from 100,000 households at Loyang and a retinue of 10,000 serving men, and was also appointed Grand Councillor at the court.

After a reign of three years, King Chuang-hsi also died. At the age of thirteen, therefore, Crown Prince Cheng became King of Ch'in [246 B.C.]. Lu Pu-wei, who remained as Grand Councillor, was granted the additional title of "Second Father."

The Queen Dowager's Disgrace

While King Cheng was still a child, and even during the time his reputed father, Chuang-hsi, had been alive, his mother, the Queen Dowager, continued to have secret and illicit sexual relations with her old master Lu Pu-wei. Her behavior was so flagrant that the Grand Councillor feared it might bring disaster upon himself. To prevent this from happening, he sought out a man named Lao Ai, an entertainer in brothels who was famed for the enormous size of his penis, and made the fellow a retainer in his own household. During banquets and orgies he would often command some wild music to be played and have Lao Ai dance about with his penis filling up the hole of a wheel made of t'ung wood. He then brought this man's talents to the attention of the Queen Dowager in order to entice her, knowing that she would surely wish to have sexual relations with such a prodigy. Soon after introducing her to Lao Ai, the wily Grand Councillor then had someone falsely accuse Lao Ai of a crime that entailed the penalty of castration. At the same time he told the Queen Dowager privately that if she merely pretended to have Lao Ai castrated, he could then be allowed to serve her in the women's quarters without fear of detection. Accordingly, she bribed the official in charge of castration to have Lao Ai condemned, to pluck off his beard and eyebrows, and go through the pretense of making him a eunuch. In this way, the man came to enter her service.

The Queen Dowager grew to love Lao Ai passionately. Finding herself pregnant, and fearing that the people might uncover her secret, she announced that an inauspicious divination by the *I Ching* compelled her to retire from the court for a time. She went to live in a palace in the city of Yung, where Lao Ai was constantly in attendance and received from her many rich presents and favors. In his own household there were several thousand servants, while more than a thousand visitors came each month seeking to be made eunuchs so as to become his followers.

In the ninth year of the King's reign [238 B.C.], an informer revealed to him that Lao Ai was not a real eunuch, and was constantly engaged in all sorts of sexual abominations with the Queen Dowager. Furthermore, he said, she had already given birth to two children, both of whom she had concealed, and that Lao Ai was plotting with the Queen Dowager to seize the throne, boasting, "Once the King is dead, we shall make our own children his successors."

King Cheng at once sent an official to investigate the matter, and so learned the entire truth. Upon his being discovered, Lao Ai in desperation started a revolt, which was quickly suppressed. He himself suffered execution by being pulled apart by chariots; all his kindred were exterminated to the third degree [parents, brothers and sisters, wives and children]; and his retainers were exiled to the desolate province of Shu. The two children who had been born to the Queen Dowager were ferreted out and strangled, while she herself was exiled from the court for life.

The King also wished to execute the Grand Councillor Lu Pu-wei, but was persuaded not to apply the law in full. He instead sent him a letter commanding him to go into exile in Shu. "Of what merit, sir, have you been to Ch'in?" the letter said. "Yet Ch'in has given you a fief in Honan with a revenue of 100,000 households. What love, sir, have you borne for Ch'in? Yet you have been given the title 'Second Father.' With your family and your followers, now remove yourself forever to Shu."

Two years after he had been sent into exile, Lu Pu-wei, fearing that he would be seized and tortured by the King, took poison and died.

The Expansion of Ch'in

Long before King Cheng commenced his reign, the warlike Ch'in had already penetrated deeply into the six adjacent states of Han, Chao, Wei, Yen, Ch'i, and Ch'u, devouring its neighbors the way a silkworm consumes a leaf. Feared even by the savage Hsiung-Nu, the warriors of Ch'in were paid according to the number of severed heads of enemies they presented to their commanders after a battle. An extensive system of fortresses and command posts along the borders of Ch'in served to contain the barbarians to the north and to secure the dominions seized from the feudal dukes in the south. But even the geographical position of the kingdom aided its conquests. Behind a natural moated barrier formed by the Yellow River and flanked by high mountains, Ch'in was suspended a thousand *li* above the rest of the world. With an army of 20,000 soldiers it could hold back a million spearmen. And when it poured out its soldiers upon the kingdoms beneath, it was like a man's emptying a cauldron of boiling oil from the top of a battlement.

As was Ch'in, so the King of Ch'in. Cheng's skill and ferocity in warfare soon spread alarm throughout the rest of the empire. An emissary to his court from the feudal principality of Ta-leang thus describes him at the age of 23, ten years after his succession, in a dispatch to his lord:

"King Cheng is a man with a prominent nose, large eyes, the chest of a bird of prey and the growling voice of a jackal. He is cruel, with the natural cruelty of a tiger or a wolf. If he wants something, he finds it easy to dissemble and accommodate himself to others. Once he has achieved his end, it is just as easy for him to devour them. Should he ever realize his ambitions, all the people of the empire will become his slaves."

The Rise of Li Ssu

Now, about this time, there emerged into prominence at the court of Ch'in a former Confucian scholar from the state of Ch'u, named Li Ssu, whose own guile was equal to the King's ruthlessness.

During his younger days Li Ssu had been employed as a petty clerk in his native village of Shang-ts'ai. In the privies behind his official quarters he observed that the rats who lived there ate filth, and that the approach of man or dog would easily frighten them off. But upon entering the granary, he noticed that the rats living beneath the great side galleries ate the stored-up grain freely and displayed no fear or uneasiness. Thereupon, Li Ssu sighed and said, "A man's ability or nonability, success or failure, is comparable to the condition of these rats. It merely depends on where he places himself. There is no greater shame than meanness of position, no deeper grief than poverty."

Li Ssu then became a follower of the Confucian sage Hsun Ch'ing, learning the traditional methods whereby states are ruled. Upon the completion of his studies, he judged that the King of Ch'u was of insufficient worth to be served by him, and that, as the Six States were all weak, there was none but Ch'in that would give him the opportunity of performing great deeds. Whereas in former times the people of Ch'in had been considered rude and barbarous, this was no longer so. Moreover, they were simple and obedient, and stood in deep awe of their officials.

Upon taking his departure for Ch'in, Li Ssu questioned his master, saying:

"Ch'in's armies for four generations have been victorious; it is the strongest state within the seas; it has overawed the feudal lords. This has not been done by 'benevolence' and 'righteousness,' but simply by taking advantage of the course of events."

Hsun Ch'ing replied, "It is not as you think. What you call advantage is an unadvantageous advantage. What I call 'benevolence' and 'righteousness' is the most righteous advantage."

Li Ssu then declared, "I have heard that when the opportune moment arrives one should not be tardy. Now is that moment, when ten thousand chariots are at war, and when the traveling politicians control affairs. The King of Ch'in desires to swallow up the world and rule with the title of Emperor. Anyone nowadays, no matter how lowly in station, who does not seek to better himself, is like a hungry bird or deer that will merely look at food set before it and not dare to approach. . . . Therefore, I intend to go westward to give counsel to the King of Ch'in."

Arriving at Hsien-yang in the first year of Cheng's accession to the throne [246 B.C.], Li Ssu became a retainer of Lu Pu-wei. When the Grand Councillor was dismissed, Li Ssu continued to serve the King as scribe. In the tenth year [237 B.C.], he addressed the King in a Throne Memorial [statement of policy], as follows:

"The small man is one who throws away his opportunities, whereas great deeds are accomplished by taking advantage of the mistakes of others and inflexibly pursuing them. Why is it that in ancient times Duke Mu of Ch'in did not annex the Six States? It was because the feudal lords were still numerous and the power of Chou had not yet decayed. At present these lords are paying allegiance to Ch'in as if they were its dependents. With the might of Ch'in's armies and the leadership of its great King, the conquest of the Six States would be like sweeping the dust from the top of a kitchen stove. Your power is sufficient to crush the feudal lords, to realize the imperial destiny of Ch'in, and to make of the whole world a single state. This is the seed time of ten thousand generations. If you hesitate now and do not press to a finish, the feudal lords will regain their strength and combine in a north-south alliance against you."

The King approved the advice of Li Ssu. He now sent out his agents bearing gold and precious jewels to those warlords in the Six States who swore to ally themselves with Ch'in; to those who remained unwilling to do so, he threatened to send his assassins instead. In retaliation, however, the rulers of the Six States dispatched their own spies into Ch'in to plot against him. When these plots were discovered, the members of the royal family and the chief potentates of the realm, who hated the King's foreign advisers and sought any chance to destroy them, addressed him as follows:

"The men of the feudal lords who come to serve Ch'in are for the most part acting on behalf of their own rulers, and merely travel to Ch'in to sow dissension. We request that there be a complete expulsion of aliens."

The King granted their request, and issued a decree that all foreigners were to be expelled at once from the capital. But Li Ssu, who was himself a native of Ch'u and therefore threatened with banishment, submitted an urgent memorial to the throne:

"At present, your Majesty causes the jade of the K'un mountains to come to him and possesses the treasure of Sui and Ho. From his girdle hang pearls brilliant as the moon, and he wears a sword forged in T'ai-o. He rides Hsiung-li horses and raises banners decorated with green phoenixes. He hears the beat of drums made from the skins of the divine crocodile. And of all these treasures, Ch'in does not produce one. Why, then, does your Majesty delight in them?

"Without the products of foreign states, there would be no utensils of rhinoceros horn and carvings of ivory, the maidens of Wei would not fill the rear palaces, and noble horses would not be installed in the outer stables. Yet you now declare that all foreigners are your enemies and wish to expel them. This being the case, it must seem that the charms of women, music, pearls and jade are valued more highly by your Majesty than sages and warriors. The people you send away are compelled to serve your enemies, the feudal lords, in order to survive. This is what is known as offering weapons to brigands and presenting gifts to robbers."

As a result of this appeal, the decree of expulsion was revoked.

The King now released his armies against the feudal lords of the Six States, attacking each one in turn. Ch'u having already been largely subjugated, he invaded the powerful kingdom of Han. In the fourteenth year [233 B.C.], the King of Han surrendered and asked to become a subject of Ch'in. Two years later, the kingdom of Wei yielded up most of its territory; and three years after that, Chao was occupied and its ruler taken prisoner. King Cheng made a triumphal entry into the city of Han-tan in Chao, his birthplace, seizing all those who had once maltreated his family while they were hostages there, and condemned them to be buried alive.

Since he next planned to invade the ancient kingdom of Yen, adjoining Chao, he set up his bases and massed his armies at the border.

The Plot to Assassinate the King of Ch'in

Crown Prince Tan of Yen had at one time also been a hostage in Chao. In their youth the two princes had been friends, but when Cheng was crowned the ruler of Ch'in, and Tan subsequently became a hostage there, the young King treated Tan with disrespect. Therefore, Tan grew angry and fled back to Yen. On his return he searched for some way to take vengeance on the King of Ch'in, but his state was small and its power insufficient.

Ch'in was now sending forth its soldiers east of the mountains to attack the territories of the feudal lords even beyond the borders of Yen. The lords and ministers of the kingdom all feared that disaster would befall it, and Crown Prince Tan was deeply worried. Not long thereafter, a general of Ch'in named Fan Yu-ch'i, who had fallen into disgrace, fled as a fugitive into the kingdom of Yen, where he was granted refuge by the Crown Prince. The Grand Tutor Chu Wu, alarmed, came into the presence chamber to remonstrate with Tan, saying:

"You cannot do this. When, with all his harshness, the King of Ch'in heaps up hatred against Yen, it is enough to chill one's heart. How much more so when he hears of the whereabouts of General Fan! This is called throwing meat in the path of a hungry tiger. The resulting disaster will be inescapable."

"Well, then," asked the Crown Prince, "what is to be done?"

The Grand Tutor replied, "Let General Fan be handed over at once to the tribes of Hsiung-Nu at the frontier, who will surely put him to death. When the matter becomes known to the King of Ch'in, his rage will thereby be appeased."

But the Crown Prince declared, "General Fan was in great straits in the world when he gave himself to me, and never, to the end of my life, could I, because of pressure from Ch'in, cast aside the bonds of pity and compassion and put him away among the Hsiung-Nu. If I did such a thing, it would certainly be time for me to die. Let the Grand Tutor reconsider the matter."

Rising from his mat, the Grand Tutor then said, "To bind oneself in lasting bonds to a single man, without regard to the great harm that might result to the nation, this is to enflame enmities and to invite destruction. . . . What is there further to talk about?" But before leaving the presence chamber, he added, "I beg the Crown Prince to consult with the sage T'ien Kuang, a man of deep wisdom and great bravery. You can make your plans with him."

Crown Prince Tan then summoned T'ien Kuang before him. When he arrived he welcomed him at the door of the presence chamber, led him inside, knelt, and dusted off the mat for him to sit on. T'ien Kuang settled himself on the mat, and there was nobody around them. The Crown Prince, after explaining his purpose, then leaned toward his visitor and requested him to speak, saying:

"Yen and Ch'in cannot both stand. I should like you, sir, to put your mind on this fact."

T'ien Kuang replied, "The Crown Prince has heard falsely that I am in my prime, and does not know that I have already lost my vitality. Nevertheless, I dare not on that account slight affairs of state. A good person who could be employed would be Master Ching."

This man, Ching K'o, was a wandering scholar who liked to read books and knew how to handle the sword, but he was also fond of wine and mixed with low company. During his sojourn in Yen, he sometimes spent whole days singing to the lute, making merry and getting drunk with his companions in the midst of the marketplace. Afterward they would all weep together, paying no attention to the bystanders. Nonetheless, Ching K'o was a serious man who loved poetry, and the persons with whom he associated during his travels among the feudal lords were all of superior worth and excellence. The sage T'ien Kuang, who had just recommended him to the Crown Prince, had received him as an honored guest into his own home, for he knew he was not an ordinary person.

The Crown Prince then said, "I should like, through you, to make the acquaintance of Master Ching. Can it be done?"

T'ien Kuang replied, "I respectfully obey."

He then arose and departed. The Crown Prince escorted him to the gate and warned him, saying, "What I have told you and what you have said are important state matters. I wish you, sir, not to disclose them."

T'ien Kuang nodded and smiled, saying, "I obey."

Once he had arrived at his home, T'ien Kuang summoned Master Ching and declared:

"I have heard that an old man, when he acts, must not cause people to doubt him. But now the Crown Prince has said to me, 'What I have told you and what you have said are important state matters. I wish you, sir, not to disclose them.' This means that the Crown Prince doubts me. One who acts so as to make people doubt him is not an upright gentleman. . . . I want you to go quickly to the Crown Prince and tell him that I have already died, so as to show him that I have not spoken."

With this, he cut his throat and died.

Ching K'o then went to the palace of the Crown Prince and informed him of what had happened. Prince Tan, deeply grieved, immediately left to pay his last respects to the corpse of the old man. He bowed twice, knelt, moved about on his knees, and wept. After some time had passed, he said:

"The reason why I warned T'ien Kuang not to speak was because I wished to bring the plans of an important matter to fruition. But now he has used death to show that he did not speak. Alas! What intent was it of mine?"

The Crown Prince then followed the last counsel of the sage and opened his mind to Master Ching, saying:

"Ch'in has an avaricious heart and its desires are insatiable. It will remain unsatisfied until it has made subject the kings of all the lands in the world within the seas. Yen is small and weak, and has often suffered from war. Even were I now to conscript the entire country, it would not be sufficient to oppose Ch'in.

"My secret plan, therefore, would be to secure one of the world's bravest men and send him to Ch'in, where he would arouse the cupidity of the King of Ch'in by the promise of great profit. Then, with his strength, he would certainly obtain for us what we desire. If he could actually succeed in carrying off the King and force him to return all the territory of the feudal lords, that would be splendid. But if this were not possible, he could seize the opportunity to stab and kill him."

There was a silence; then Ching K'o replied: "This is an important state matter. Your servant is an inferior nag and fears that his capacities are inadequate for such a trust."

But the Crown Prince bowed before him and urged him not to give up the mission, after which Master Ching finally consented. He was at once lodged in a splendid house next to the palace; and every day the Crown Prince went to his door to present him with rare objects, carriages, horses, and beautiful concubines, freely granting him whatever he desired.

Eventually, Master Ching devised a scheme whereby the capture or assassination of the King of Ch'in might be accomplished. He then approached Prince Tan, stating:

"The King of Ch'in has offered a reward of one thousand catties of gold and a city of ten thousand families for the head of General Fan, who is a fugitive in Yen. Now, if we could actually get hold of the head of General Fan and present it to him, together with a map of the province of Tu-k'ang in Yen, which he covets, then the King of Ch'in would certainly be pleased to see your servant. Thus, I would have an opportunity of avenging the Crown Prince."

But Prince Tan replied, "General Fan came to me in poverty and distress. I could not permit myself, for my own selfish aim, to violate a higher ideal. I should like you, sir, to reconsider the matter."

Master Ching then bowed and left, seeing that the Prince's resolve was

unshakable. Still, he realized that unless he could present these trophies to
the King of Ch'in, his chances of obtaining an audience with him in his
palace at Hsien-yang would be hopeless. Accordingly, without informing
Prince Tan of his intentions, he went directly to the home of the fugitive
general Fan Yu-ch'i. After being admitted, he said to him:

"Ch'in's treatment of you cannot be said to be a generous one. Your
father, mother, and family have all been executed, and now I hear that a
reward of one thousand catties of gold and a city of ten thousand families
has been offered for your head. What are you going to do?"

General Fan looked up to heaven, heaved a great sigh, shed some tears,
and replied, "Every day I think about this and suffer constantly unto my
very bones and marrow. But whatever plan I consider, I know not where it
will lead me."

Master Ching then said, "I have here a single word which can free the
state of Yen from its tribulation and avenge you of your hatred. But how
will you receive it?"

"What is it?" asked General Fan.

"I should like," said Master Ching, "to have your head to present to the
King of Ch'in. Then he would be delighted to see me. With my left hand I
would seize his sleeve, and with my right I should stab his breast, and thus
put an end to the tyrant."

General Fan grasped Ching K'o's wrist, drew nearer to him, and said,
"Day and night I have been grinding my teeth and beating my breast on
this account. But now I have heard my instructions."

And with this he cut his throat.

The Crown Prince, when he learned of the fate of the man he had sworn
to protect, was filled with grief. But since the deed was already done, and
there was no way to undo it, he placed the head of General Fan Yu-ch'i in a
box and closed it. After this, he set about to find one of the world's sharpest
daggers, which he obtained from a swordsman of Chao. Finally, he sought
an accomplice for Master Ching, and chose a young bravo named Ch'in
Wu-yang, who, for some slight offense to his honor, had once killed a man
before he was thirteen years of age, so that no one afterward dared to eye
him contrarily.

Now that all was in readiness, however, Master Ching continued to delay
taking his leave, but remained in his garden with his concubines and
friends, singing songs to the lute and drinking wine. Suspecting that Ching
K'o might have begun to regret his decision, the Crown Prince approached
him and said:

"The day is already done, and what are your intentions? I beg to be
allowed to send Ch'in Wu-yang in advance."

But Ching K'o replied, "This one who will go, never to return, is a mere
boy. And he will be entering an immeasurably powerful Ch'in, carrying
only a single dagger. I have delayed in order to entertain my guests for the
last time. But now that you say I am procrastinating, I beg to bid farewell."

As the two set out on their journey, the Crown Prince and close advisers who knew of their mission put on white clothes and caps [the funeral color of ancient China] and, accompanied by musicians, went to see them off. Ching K'o, followed by his aide, entered his carriage and departed. Not with a single glance did he look back.

When they arrived at the capital of Ch'in, Master Ching at once sought an audience with King Cheng. He bribed a high official to present a petition to his royal master in behalf of the Crown Prince of Yen, and this personage addressed the King as follows:

"Verily Prince Tan trembles with terror before the majesty of the Great King. He dares not raise soldiers to oppose your military might, but wishes instead, offering his kingdom, to become your inner vassal, and thus set an example to the other feudal lords. Being fearful, he does not present himself, but has cut off the head of Fan Yu-ch'i and placed it in a box, together with a map of Tu-k'ang in Yen, which he respectfully presents."

The King of Ch'in was highly pleased when he heard of the death of his enemy General Fan and the abject surrender of the Crown Prince of Yen. He put on ceremonial clothing as if for a state occasion, then summoned Ching K'o and his aide to the palace.

Entering the throne room, where the King of Ch'in sat surrounded by his nobles, Master Ching advanced with the box containing the head of General Fan, followed by Ch'in Wu-yang, who carried the container with the map. When they came to the steps of the throne, however, Ch'in Wu-yang changed color and shook with fear. All the courtiers wondered at this. But Master Ching looked at him with a smile and went forward to excuse him, saying, "He is a simple lad of the northern barbarians, and has never seen the Son of Heaven. Therefore, he trembles with awe. May it please the Great King to pardon him and allow me, his humble emissary, to come forward."

The King said to him, "Bring me the map carried by the boy."

Ching K'o thereupon took it from his aide and went up to the throne to present it. The King of Ch'in took out the map, and when it was entirely unrolled, the dagger was exposed. Ching K'o at once seized the sleeve of the King with his left hand, while with his right he grasped the dagger and struck at him. The point of the weapon ripped through his outer robes but did not reach his body. The King of Ch'in, astonished, drew himself up and jumped back, so that the sleeve held by Ching K'o was torn off. He pulled at his sword, but as it was very long and hung down almost vertically, he could not draw it out of the scabbard in time. He then ran behind a pillar, pursued by Ching K'o. The horrified courtiers rushed forward, jostling and hindering one another in their panic, not knowing what to do.

No one, on pain of death, was ever allowed to bring any kind of weapon into the throne room; and since the officers of the guard were forbidden to enter unless summoned, they were all ranged in the hall outside, unaware of what was happening. In this emergency it would have been useless to call

for them. Thus the assassin pursued King Cheng around the throne room
with his dagger, while the King, still unable to draw his sword, tried to ward
him off with his two joined hands.

At this moment an attendant physician struck Ching K'o with his bag of
medicine, which he was to have presented to the King, temporarily stunning
him. The King meanwhile was dodging round and round the pillars, having
completely lost his head in fear. The courtiers then cried out, "Put your
sword behind you, King!"

The King did so, and so had room to pull it out of the scabbard. He
lunged at Ching K'o, cutting his left thigh. Ching K'o, disabled, then raised
his dagger and hurled it at the King. It missed him, but glanced off a bronze
pillar with such force that it was deflected into the wall up to the very
handle. The King now slashed at Ching K'o repeatedly, inflicting eight
wounds on his arms and chest.

Ching K'o realized that his attempt had failed. He slumped against a
pillar and laughed; then, squatting down, he cursed the King, saying to all
in the room, "The reason my plan did not succeed was that I wished to
carry him off alive. Someone else must now be found to carry out the pledge
to avenge the Crown Prince Tan of Yen."

At this point, those about him rushed forward and killed Master Ching.
His young aide, Ch'in Wu-yang, who had remained trapped in the throne
room, was seized and led away to be tortured.

After this attempted assassination, the King of Ch'in was not at ease for a
long time. As soon as he had recovered, however, he turned all his fury
against the state of Yen. The Ch'in armies, under General Wang Chien,
attacked and laid waste to the country. As they neared the capital, Crown
Prince Tan fled from his palace and tried to conceal himself; but he was
pursued and captured by his father, the aged King of Yen, who then had
him beheaded in order to ingratiate himself with King Cheng. Within five
years, however, all of Yen was occupied and he himself made a captive.

King Cheng Assumes the Title of Ch'in Shih Huang Ti

In the twenty-sixth year [221 B.C.], Ch'i, the last of the Six States to
remain unconquered, refused to pay tribute to King Cheng and sent its
armies to defend its western frontier. Generals Wang Pen and Meng T'ien
of Ch'in then marched through the south of the occupied kingdom of Yen
and inflicted a great defeat on Ch'i, taking its King a prisoner. With this
final conquest, Ch'in now possessed all the empire.

In his court at Hsien-yang, the King proclaimed to his assembled
ministers and counselors:

"It is I, Cheng, in my mortal flesh, who have conquered the kings of Han,
Chao, Wei, Yen, Ch'u and Ch'i, and compelled them to pay the penalty for
their crimes. The empire has now been completely pacified. All rebels and
plotters against the state will be punished by death. For heavenly guidance

and support, I rely as always upon the sacred temple of my ancestors. Henceforth, in accordance with the unprecedented glory I have won and transmit to posterity, let the name by which I am called also be changed. Deliberate, then, on a title worthy of the ruler of the empire."

After consulting with one another, his advisers declared:

"From the times of remote antiquity until the present, the world has been torn apart by invasions of the barbarians and civil wars instigated by the feudal lords. Even the Son of Heaven was incapable of imposing order. But now your Majesty has upraised the forces of justice and put down the outlaws and oppressors. Your Majesty has organized all the territory between the seas into secure and established governments. Laws and decrees now issue from one source. Nothing like this, even during the reign of the Five Emperors, has ever been known before.

"The scholars of vast learning tell us that in olden days there were such titles as Celestial Sovereign, Terrestrial Sovereign, and Great Sovereign. The title of Great Sovereign has always been considered the most honorable. Therefore, at the risk of incurring death for our presumptuous words, we propose that the King be called Great Sovereign."

The King replied, "We reject the word 'Great,' we accept 'Sovereign'; and we add to it the word 'Emperor,' which has served since times immemorial. Our title will thus be Sovereign Emperor [Shih Huang Ti]."

He then issued the following decree:

"In high antiquity, according to tradition, titles were bestowed upon kings during their lifetimes, yet were ignored after they died; and in middle antiquity, it was only after death that kings received descriptive titles befitting their conduct while they reigned. Such practice I refuse to tolerate, for it permits sons to judge their fathers and subjects to criticize their rulers. From this day forward, I suppress the system of bestowing posthumous names and titles. We now declare ourself First Sovereign Emperor. The generations after us will call themselves by number, such as Second Generation, Third Generation, Fourth Generation, and so on, up to the Thousandth and Ten Thousandth Generation, and will transmit this principle without interruption until the end of time."

Shih Huang Ti Remolds the Empire

Soon after his inauguration as First Sovereign Emperor, Shih Huang Ti advanced the evolution of the five Taoist elements—metal, earth, wood, fire, and water—according to their succession in the scheme of things. Since his own dynasty, the Ch'in, had succeeded the Chou, whose element was fire, he adopted water as his element, for water extinguishes fire. Henceforth, he decreed, was to commence the reign of water. He also changed the month at the start of the year from the 11th, which had been that of the Chou, to the 10th, and made all imperial holidays begin from the first day of the tenth month. He also adopted the color black, which corresponds to the Taoist element of water, as the imperial color for flags, pennants, and banners as well as for state robes and other garments. Of the numbers, 6, equated with water, was chosen as the standard of measure: the plaques on which contracts were written, and even the hats worn by public officials, were fixed at six inches. Likewise, six horses were declared to constitute a team. Since water, too, was the most violent and pervasive of all the elements, public officials were told to enforce the laws with the utmost severity and to show no mercy to anyone.

About this time the Grand Councillor Wang Koan, along with other ministers, approached the Emperor, stating: "Now that the feudal lords have been exterminated, it has become increasingly difficult to maintain order in the conquered territories. We propose that the sons of the imperial family be sent to rule in their place. May it but please your Majesty to give his consent."

Shih Huang Ti submitted this proposal to his advisers, who also considered it to be advantageous. But in the midst of the deliberations Li Ssu, then Minister of Justice, arose and said: "Your Majesty, in the days of the Chou dynasty the feudal lords warred with one another, killing, plundering and burning, and not even the Son of Heaven was able to prevent them. Brother attacked brother; families were split asunder by hatred. Now, owing to your divine authority, the world has been united and granted peace. The sons of the imperial family have already been amply rewarded by being made dukes and given much revenue. But to reestablish them in the place of the feudal lords would endanger the peace and unity of your realms."

The Emperor reflected, then handed down his decision:

"If heretofore the whole world has been a prey to unceasing wars, this has been caused by a struggle for power among rival kings. The empire is now at peace for the first time; but if I restored the feudal states, wars would surely break out again. The advice of my minister Li Ssu is correct."

Shih Huang Ti then divided the empire into thirty-six, or six times six, regional administrations, to each of which he apppointed civil governors, military chieftains, and imperial officials directly responsible to himself. At the same time, he codified all the laws and statutes, regulated the standards of weight and measure, and established a single set of written characters throughout the empire. He also promulgated a new name for his subjects: "the black-haired people," to distinguish them from the brown- and fair-haired barbarians.

To make sure his enemies could never rise against him, he collected all their weapons at Hsien-yang and had them melted down and recast into hundreds of bronze bells and tripods. With the metal that remained he also cast twelve gigantic bronze statues in human form, the weight of each one exceeding a thousand *tan* [70 tons], and placed them in the courtyard of the imperial palace. At the same time, the Emperor transported to the capital 120,000 of the most illustrious families of the defeated kingdoms. This had long been planned. For after each conquest by his armies, he had ordered an exact replica of the ruler's palace, with all the halls and gardens, stables, galleries, covered roads and other edifices, to be constructed near Hsien-yang. He had also provided them with similar furnishings, hangings, musical instruments, concubines, eunuchs, and other necessaries so that they would remain content. There were now more than 270 of these palaces stretching for more than seventy miles around the capital.

And when all this had been done, the Emperor held a great banquet to celebrate his achievements.

The Emperor Tours His Realms

In the twenty-seventh year [220 B.C.], Shih Huang Ti commanded his generals to build a system of imperial highways, each road to be 60 feet wide and bordered with trees, that would radiate from the capital and extend east and south to the extremities of the empire.

The next year, he undertook a triumphal tour through the eastern provinces. With his court the Emperor climbed the mountain of I and set up a commemorative stele engraved with verses extolling the conquests of Ch'in. Afterwards he traveled on to the mountain of T'ai, where he also erected a stele and offered sacrifices to his ancestors. On his descent from this mountain, however, a sudden storm sprang up and he was forced to take shelter under a tree. When the storm had subsided, the Emperor bestowed upon this tree the honorary title of *u-ta-fu* in gratitude.

On his return from the tour of the east, he passed by the city of P'ong-cheng on the river Se. There he purified himself and made sacrifices. Then he attempted to recover one of the nine sacred tripods of the Chou dynasty from the bottom of this river, where it had been thrown after their defeat. He sent down a thousand divers to search for it, but without success.

The Emperor now continued his journey toward the southwest along the river Kiang, arriving at a point opposite the temple of the mountain of Siang; but when he tried to sail across the river in order to ascend the mountain, his ship was driven back by a terrific wind. He consulted his magicians and scholars of vast learning, and demanded, "What god rules over Siang?" They replied, "We have heard say that the wives of Choen, the prince of the Chou, are buried here." The Emperor was filled with rage at the effrontery of the mountain. As punishment for sending the gale, he ordered three thousand condemned prisoners to cut down all the trees and to paint the barren slopes in red [the color of the uniform worn by convicts].*

* A similar tale is told by Herodotus (Book 7:36) of the Persian king Xerxes on his way to invade the Greek mainland in 480 B.C. After his engineers had built two bridges, one of flax and the other of papyrus, across the Hellespont, a "storm of great violence smashed them up and carried them away. Xerxes was very angry when he learned of this disaster, and gave orders that the Hellespont should receive three hundred lashes and have a pair of fetters thrown into it. And," adds Herodotus, "I have heard before now that he also sent people to brand it with hot irons."

Just before descending the mountains into the plain of Po-lang-cha, in the eastern province of Honan, the Emperor narrowly escaped assassination by a band of outlaws. These brigands were led by a descendant of the royal family of the conquered state of Han, Chang Leang, who thus sought to avenge his people. Chang Leang had set a trap for the Emperor along a winding pass, stationing his men on the cliffs above with heavy boulders and masses of iron; but when the imperial cortege came through, he was unable to distinguish Shih Huang Ti's chariot from the rest. He merely succeeded in destroying the chariot of one of the lesser officials by hurling down a lump of iron weighing 120 pounds. A grand search lasting ten days was ordered throughout Honan, but Chang Leang and his band managed to escape.

The Quest for the Elixir of Eternal Life

In the twenty-ninth year [218 B.C.], a mariner from the province of Ch'i, known as Siu Che, petitioned the Emperor:

"In the middle of the sea stand the three magic mountains, P'ong-lai, Fang-chang, and Yng-cheou. There, as is well known, reside the blessed Immortals in palaces made entirely of silver and gold, and all the birds, beasts, and other living creatures are of a pure transparency or flawless whiteness. We ask your Majesty to permit us, after we have undergone purification, to depart on a voyage with a company of young men and virgins to search for these mountains in the sea and bring back the elixir of eternal life."

From remote antiquity the legend had persisted that, long ago, certain mariners had succeeded in approaching the abode of the Immortals. While their ship was still some distance away, they saw the mountains from afar shimmering like a cloud; but as they came closer, the mountains appeared, as if in a mirror, reversed under the sea. And then, though the waters were flat and calm, a violent and contrary wind blew their ship away.

The Emperor, in whose presence even the mention of death was forbidden under penalty of the same, longed to find the elixir of immortality for himself. He immediately summoned Siu Che to his throne and equipped him with ships and provisions, plus several thousand young men and virgins to serve as offerings, to make a voyage to the magic mountains.

According to another account, however, the Emperor sent not Siu Che, but a different mariner named Sui Fu, on this expedition, but neglected to provide him with the young men and virgins. When his search proved fruitless, Sui Fu returned to the court and, in order to excuse his failure, told the following story to the Emperor:

"I saw a great god in the sea, who asked me, 'Are you the envoy of the Emperor of the East?' I answered him, 'Yes.' 'What are you looking for?' he asked. I replied, 'I want to ask you for the elixir that bestows immortal life.' The god said, 'The offerings in jewels and raiment by your Emperor are too meagre. You will therefore be able to see this drug but not take it.' So saying, he bore me with him toward the southeast until we arrived at the mountain P'ong-lai, where I saw the golden gate of the palace Che-ch'ang. There was an emissary outside who was the color of copper in the sunlight and had the body of a dragon. His brilliance illuminated the sky above him. I saluted him twice, then asked, 'What offerings can the Emperor of Ch'in make to you so as to receive the elixir that bestows immortal life?' The god of the sea replied, 'Bring me boys and maidens of noble ancestry; also, a company of artisans of every craft; also, specimens of all types of grain that grow in Ch'in.' And so I took ship once more and returned."

Upon hearing this, the Emperor was elated. This time he sent Sui Fu back to sea with three thousand virgins and young men, a band of expert craftsmen, and hundreds of sacks of seed of five varieties of cereal. Sui Fu, however, sailed off with these gifts to a peaceful and fertile island [according to Japanese myth, the island of Honshu], where he declared himself sovereign and was never seen or heard of again in Ch'in.

The Burning of the Books

In the thirty-fourth year [213 B.C.], the Emperor was informed by his ministers of a growing and widespread unrest among the people. His decrees, they told him, were being defied by the lesser officials, legalists, and Confucian scholars who still clung to the old ways. The Emperor therefore summoned Li Ssu, who had now risen to the rank of Grand Councillor, to ask for his advice. Li Ssu submitted the following memorial:

"Your Majesty has set a firm standard of right and wrong and established a single source of power throughout the world. Yet there are those, still clinging to their private teachings and opinions, who conspire with one another to weaken your authority. When they receive your orders at the court, they remain silent but amend them in the light of their own ideas; and once outside, they criticize them openly among themselves and upon the streets. To cast scorn upon their ruler they regard as something worthy of praise. Now, if their activities are not suppressed, the imperial power will decline and factions will form from below. Therefore, it is urgent that they be prohibited.

"Your servant suggests that all books save the records of Ch'in and technical manuals be burned; that all persons in the empire, save those under the control of the bureau of scholars, who dare to preserve the *Shih* and *Shuh* [the classic literary, historical, and philosophical works] be subjected to severe penalty. Books not to be destroyed, of course, are treatises on medicine, pharmacy, divination by the tortoise and milfoil, and works on agriculture and gardening. Those who have not burned the proscribed books within thirty days should be branded and condemned to forced labor. Henceforth let those Confucian ghouls who revere only dead laws and bloodless ordinances learn instead to respect the teachings of the living."

Shih Huang Ti marked this memorial "Approved." A decree for the burning of the proscribed books was then sent throughout the empire.

The Emperor Builds . . .
. . . An Imperial Highway

In the thirty-fifth year [212 B.C.], the Emperor cut a highway through the territory of the northern barbarians that terminated at Yun-yang. Mountains were leveled and valleys filled so that this road could proceed in a straight line. At the same time, rivers were deflected into networks of canals to irrigate the land, which was then colonized with prisoners, vagabonds, and the idle and restless soldiers of the defeated feudal warlords.

. . . And a Great Wall

To keep out the savage tribes of the Hsiung-Nu [Huns], the general Meng T'ien was ordered to commence the building of a Great Wall extending thousands of li.*

. . . And a Palace of Palaces

After returning from a triumphal tour of his empire, Shih Huang Ti now decided that his ancestral palace had become too small for the vastly increased population of the capital. He thus informed his ministers:

"Since King Wen of the Chou had his capital at Fong, and King Ou had his at Hao, therefore the territory between Fong and Hao should become the seat of the emperors of Ch'in."

In a park south of the river Wei, Shih Huang Ti began the construction of a new palace. He first built a main hall on the outskirts of Hsien-yang that was 2,500 feet long and 500 feet wide, capable of holding 10,000 persons. Encircling it was a raised road for chariots. A pavilion at the lower end was situated at the base of a steep mountain, from which a broad highway rose directly up to a triumphal arch on the summit that served as the imperial entrance. A covered bridge leading from the palace crossed the river Wei and proceeded to the capital, thereby symbolizing on earth the bridge of stars that spans the Milky Way.

Inside the region set aside for the court, there were 300 palaces; and just outside it, there were 400 more. Thousands of craftsmen from all over the empire, as well as 700,000 prisoners who had suffered the punishment of castration, were employed in the building of this vast work.

---

* Thus, in passing, the historian Ssu-ma Ch'ien with this brief sentence disposes of the Great Wall that unwound like a blank scroll across northern China for some 2,240 miles, from Kiayukwan at the western end of Kansu Province to Shanhaikwan, now Linyu, on the coast. The close historical association between writing and road-building—in ancient China as in the Roman Empire—may be illustrated by the fact that the general Meng T'ien is also said to have invented the writing brush by soaking goats' hair in limewater. One legend has it that a sorcerer advised Shih Huang Ti that the Great Wall could not be finished unless 10,000 men had first been buried inside it: whereupon he searched for a man whose name contained the character *wan* (10,000), then ordered him to be buried alive in the ramparts.

The "True Man"

Now, at this time, the scholar Lou submitted the following memorial to the Emperor:

"For years your Majesty has been searching for the elixir made from the marvelous mushroom *tche* that bestows everlasting life. The abode of the Immortals has never been discovered, and it seems likely that some malicious spirit not only baffles all your efforts but prevents the Immortals from revealing themselves. In the magic realms, it is said, the Master of Men, the True Man, sometimes hides under an incognito in order to elude the evil spirits; and only when he succeeds in escaping from them can he come forth. For if the residence of the Master of Men becomes known, the gods are alarmed. The Master of Men, the True Man, enters into water without becoming wet, passes through fire without being burned, rises above the clouds, and is as eternal as the earth and sky.

"Now you yourself, your Majesty, govern the empire of Ch'in, yet are unable to find the least repose. We therefore ask you not to permit anyone to know in advance in what palace you are to be found from day to day. Should you do that, then perhaps the elixir of immortality will be granted to you."

The Emperor replied, "I will follow the example of the Master of Men, the True Man." *

Thereafter, Shih Huang Ti referred to himself not by his own title but as "True Man." In order to conceal his whereabouts, he commanded that 270 of the palaces in the environs of Hsien-yang be connected with one another by secret tunnels and walled passageways; and, further, that tapestries, curtains, musical instruments, concubines, furniture, and all other necessaries be supplied in full to each palace to avoid transporting them from one to another.

While the Emperor was favoring a palace with his presence, no one was permitted to disclose it under penalty of death. One day, however, while visiting a palace built on the mountain of Leang, he observed that the chariots and retinues of his ministers in the valley below were far too numerous, and expressed his disapproval. A servant reported this to one of the officials in charge, who immediately reduced the number of chariots and attendants.

When the Emperor next happened to look out and saw what had happened, he fell into a rage, declaring, "Someone in the palace has divulged my words and thus betrayed my presence!"

---

* According to Derk Bodde, in his *China's First Unifier* (Leiden: E. J. Brill, 1938): "It was believed that by returning into nature away from other men, and by withdrawing oneself from the world of human conflict, into a realm where the ordinary distinctions of right and wrong and of 'this' and 'that' do not apply and do not exist, one could gain union with the all-embracing Tao, or Absolute. In such a state one would become a Sage, or, as the Taoists called it, a 'True Man.'"

An investigation was ordered at once, but no one would confess; thereupon, he ordered the arrest of all those servants and courtiers who had been in his company at the time and sentenced them to be buried alive. From then on, nobody dared discuss the whereabouts of the Emperor whenever he moved from palace to palace.

A Revolt in the Court

In conducting matters of state, Shih Huang Ti became more and more suspicious and secretive, refusing to delegate authority to his appointed officials and merely handing them his decrees to be carried out. The ministers Heou and Lu, after conspiring with one another about this, published the following diatribe against the Emperor at the court:

"Though Shih Huang Ti has suppressed the feudal lords and reunited the empire, he is a man who has received from heaven a violent, cruel, and despotic nature. All his plans have succeeded, all his desires have been fulfilled. He believes, therefore, that no one since time began is his equal. Only his judges and executioners can approach him and gain his favor, while his seventy-five scholars of vast learning at the court must content themselves with their empty titles, for they are not employed in any work worthy of them.

"Shih Huang Ti is content to uphold his prestige by tortures and executions; and so his counselors and ministers of state, fearful of being punished and wishing to keep their positions, dare not assert their private beliefs. Even the astrologers and magicians at the court, who number more than three hundred, are afraid to bring up forbidden subjects, preferring instead to flatter the Emperor and conceal his faults from him. Since he never hears any criticism of himself, he becomes more and more arrogant and contemptuous of others. According to the laws of Ch'in, an official is held accountable on pain of death to perform his duties; yet all affairs of state, down to the most minor, are decided by the Emperor alone. He goes so far as to read and examine each night a load of state documents weighing as much as 120 pounds, refusing to go to sleep until he can finish this amount of work. Such is his distrust of others, such his thirst for power. Who then, even if he could do so, would wish to find for such a tyrant the elixir of immortality?" *

---

* There is a remarkable resemblance to this conspiracy at the court of Shih Huang Ti, more than two millennia ago, in the plot by Lin Piao, former Defense Minister of Communist China, and his co-conspirators to overthrow Mao Tse-tung. In a document, stamped "Absolutely Secret" and dated Jan. 13, 1972, which was smuggled out of China to Western intelligence sources, the plotters wrote:

"The masses' worship of B-52 [code name for Mao] is still deep-rooted. As a result of B-52's divisive tactics, there is a serious contradiction within the army ranks, and it would be rather difficult for us to achieve united strength. Furthermore, B-52 seldom appears in public and his residence is heavily guarded. All his movements are shrouded in secrecy. These are difficulties we must face in launching our action. . . .

"At no time has B-52 stopped trying to pit one force against another. Today he may try to win over this force to deal with that, but tomorrow he may pit that force against this. Today

After circulating this indictment among the courtiers, Heou and Lu fled from the capital, then took their own lives so as to frustrate the Emperor's revenge. When the Emperor learned that they had disappeared, he assembled his court and declared: "At one time, I gathered all the books in the empire and destroyed those that were useless, for I desired in this way to establish order and promote a lasting peace. At one time, I asked my magicians to search out and retrieve the drug of immortality. Yet what has been the result? Siu Che, whom I sent to sea to find the magic mountains, has spent a treasure of gold and found nothing. And as for the ministers Heou and Lu, though I loaded them with honors and presents, in return they have slandered and vilified me. Therefore, I resolve to investigate all the scholars and magicians who reside in the capital, for they have spread false rumors in order to arouse the people against me."

He then ordered the royal inquisitors to question them under torture; but when each still refused to confess his own guilt, but instead accused another one, the Emperor chose 460 by lot from their midst and condemned them to be buried alive. All the people saw in this a portent for the future.

Fu-su, the eldest son of the Emperor and heir to the throne, now dared to confront him:

"The empire has hardly been pacified and the people of the most distant regions brought under one rule. The scholars who must carry out the laws all speak of Confucius and accept him as their guide. Yet your Majesty constrains them from studying the works of their master under penalty of severe punishment. As your subject as well as your son, I fear that this will promote unrest and rebellion. It behooves you to pay heed."

Angered by these words, the Emperor banished his son Fu-su to the northern border, there to serve with General Meng T'ien in building the Great Wall.

The Emperor Sinks into Melancholy

In the thirty-sixth year [211 B.C.], a meteor fell to earth near the district of Tong in the form of a black stone. Someone among the people there engraved on the stone these words: "At the death of Shih Huang Ti the empire will be redivided." The Emperor learned of this and sent his inquisitors to look into the incident. Since no one would confess, he

---

his words may drip with honey, yet tomorrow he may put you to death on fabricated charges.

"Looking back over the past decades, how many do you see who were raised to power and fame by him but later escaped political death? What political force could survive coexistence with him? His former secretaries have either committed suicide or have been imprisoned, his very few comrades-in-arms and trusted aides are also mostly behind bars. Even his own son went berserk under his high-handedness. He is a maniac of suspicion and a sadist. . . .

"We cannot deny his historical function of unifying China. But now he has abused the confidence and status given him by the Chinese people. *In fact, he has become a Shih Huang Ti of modern times* (my italics)." (From an article in *The New York Times*, July 23, 1972).

arrested all who lived in the vicinity of the stone and condemned them to be buried alive. Then he obliterated all trace of the stone by fire.

From that time on, Shih Huang Ti began to lose interest in affairs of state and sank into melancholy. He charged the court poets to compose songs for him on the Taoist Immortals and the True Man, then gave these songs to his musicians and ordered them to sing them for him continually.

In the autumn a courier coming through the passes in the east found himself one night on the road of P'ing-chou in Hoa-yn. A man holding a jade ring in his hand stopped the courier and said to him, "Deliver this ring from me to the prince of the lake of Hao." Then he added, "This year the dragon ancestor will die." The courier started to ask for an explanation, but the man suddenly became invisible and disappeared, leaving behind the jade ring. The courier then hastened to present it to the Emperor and report what had occurred.

Upon hearing his story, Shih Huang Ti remained silent for a long time. Finally, he said, "The predictions of a water spirit do not extend with certainty beyond the events of a year." When he retired to his chamber, he sighed and said, " 'The dragon ancestor'—that surely refers to the chief among men, the Emperor himself." He ordered his magicians and scholars of vast learning to examine the ring: it was the same one he had thrown into the lake of Hao eight years earlier to propitiate the spirit there. Determined now to find the elixir of eternal life before the year was up, the Emperor consulted the oracles and received favorable assurances to make a voyage.

The Emperor's Last Voyage

Accordingly, in the thirty-seventh year [210 B.C.], Shih Huang Ti departed with a large entourage of courtiers. While the other ministers of state remained behind in the capital, the Grand Councillor Li Ssu chose to accompany him. The Emperor's youngest son, Hou-hai, also asked to go along on the voyage and his request was granted.

After crossing the land of Ou, Shih Huang Ti traveled north along the sea until he reached Lang-ya. Already many years had passed since Siu Che had set sail in his futile quest for the elixir of eternal life. Since the magicians and scholars traveling with the Emperor feared to be blamed by him if they did not succeed in finding it, they told him:

"It is possible to obtain the drug of P'ong-lai; but we have been thwarted constantly by the great fish *kiao,* which prevents the god of the waters from making his appearance. Therefore, we must first kill the great fish *kiao.*"

That night the Emperor dreamed that he fought with a sea god who had the shape of a man. Upon waking, he consulted a magician famed for his interpretations of dreams, who said:

"The god of the sea, who fought with you in your dream, cannot appear in the flesh because he is surrounded by water dragons and guarded by the great fish *kiao.* Sacrifices must therefore be made to heaven so that the evil spirits may be frustrated and the good spirits evoked. And meanwhile, let your Majesty keep himself in readiness to capture the great fish *kiao* should it decide to strike."

The Emperor immediately prepared the sacrifices; and when they were finished, he ordered his seamen to equip themselves with nets and spears and grapples, while he himself was armed with the crossbow that shoots many arrows in succession. Bands of horsemen searched along the sea from Lang-ya to the mountain of Yong-tch'eng without finding anything; but upon reaching Che-feou, the Emperor caught sight of an enormous fish that came close to shore blowing spouts of steam from its head. While seated upon his throne, he fired his crossbow, striking it with many arrows in succession, and then his men waded into the surf with their spears and killed it. With the fish tied and dragged behind his chariot as a trophy, the Emperor continued his travels up and down the shore, but still the god of the sea did not appear.

Upon reaching the ford of P'ing-yuen in the west, he suddenly fell sick. Since the Emperor had strictly forbidden any talk of death in his presence, no one among his courtiers now dared to broach the subject. However, as he felt his life ebbing away hour by hour, he summoned the high eunuch Chao Kao, chief of the bureau that handled the imperial dispatches, to come at once into his presence. The Emperor then commanded Chao Kao to write a letter to be sent to his eldest son and heir, Fu-su, whom he had banished to the northern regions, stating: "With the soldiers belonging to Meng T'ien, accompany my funeral cortege to Hsien-yang and arrange for my interment."

The letter was already written and sealed, but had not yet been delivered to the messenger, when Shih Huang Ti died.

The Grand Councillor Li Ssu and the chief eunuch Chao Kao, fearing that the other princes might revolt when they heard of their father's death, and thus rend the empire apart, conspired with the Emperor's son Hou-hai to keep the matter secret. The eunuch who had served as personal valet to Shih Huang Ti was ordered to remain with the corpse in the chariot and to bring him his meals and perform other duties for him as if he were still alive. Then the imperial cortege continued on its journey toward the capital. Whenever the local functionaries along the route came with their requests and petitions to the Emperor, as was customary, this eunuch pretended to consult with him inside his closed chariot and relay his approval or disapproval.

Except for five or six other eunuchs in attendance, only Li Ssu, Hou-hai, and Chao Kao knew that Shih Huang Ti was dead. Now these three decided to destroy the sealed letter that the Emperor had written to his eldest son and heir, Fu-su, before his death. They weaved a plot in which it would be claimed that the Emperor had left a testament declaring Hou-hai to be his heir; and to remove the primary obstacles to his succession, they forged a letter from the Emperor to Fu-su and General Meng T'ien accusing them of crimes against the state and ordering them to commit suicide at once.

When this letter reached Fu-su in the northern provinces, where he was helping to build the Great Wall against the barbarians, he obediently swallowed poison and died. But Meng T'ien remained suspicious of the order, and demanded that the emissary return to the Emperor for confirmation.

This emissary, who was in the service of Li Ssu, replied, "I have received the imperial command to apply the law to you, General, and do not dare to report your words."

Whereupon Meng T'ien, builder of the Great Wall, heaved a sigh and said, "What crime have I committed before heaven? I die without fault!" Then, after a long pause, he added, "Indeed I have a crime for which to die. Beginning at Lin-t'ao and extending to Liao-tung, I have dug ramparts and ditches over ten thousand *li,* and in this distance it is impossible that I have not cut through the veins of the earth. This is my crime."

He then swallowed the poison handed to him and died.

By this time the imperial procession was approaching the capital. As it was late summer, the weather during the march was very hot, and the stench of putrefaction became quite noticeable. To conceal the odor, the conspirators commanded that each chariot in the cortege carry a portion of the enormous fish which the Emperor had shot with his cross bow, and which had already begun to stink. Finally, they entered into the capital, where the death of Shih Huang Ti was at last revealed. His youngest son, Hou-hai, was now proclaimed Emperor, under the title Erh Shih Huang Ti (Second Sovereign Emperor).

The Interment of the Emperor

Throughout his long reign Shih Huang Ti had supervised the work of hollowing out and equipping the mountain of Li to serve as his tomb. More than 700,000 soldiers, craftsmen, and condemned prisoners were engaged on the project over the years. To provide sufficient space for this vast undertaking, 30,000 families from the city of Li and 50,000 from Yun-yang had to be uprooted and transported elsewhere. As compensation, however, they were granted a respite from forced labor on public projects for ten years.

After the mountain had been excavated, the soil beneath was dug until the underground streams were reached, and then the entire chamber was sealed off with molten bronze. The dome of the vault was sheathed in copper and set with thousands of rubies, sapphires, and diamonds, intended to simulate the stars and constellations in the heavens. They shone down upon a map in relief of the empire carved upon the floor. Moreover, a system of channels 6 feet wide and 12 deep, representing the Yangtze and

Yellow rivers and their tributaries, had been dredged out and filled with mercury, which was made to flow through the channels by ingenious devices. Along their banks were set models of cities, fortresses, gardens of artificial flowers in jade and precious stones, pavilions, and palaces furnished with exact replicas in miniature of the Emperor's favorite possessions. The body of Shih Huang Ti was then placed inside a sarcophagus in the shape of a royal barge and launched upon the channels so that he could float through his realms forever.*

When the tomb was ready, Erh Shih Huang Ti, who wished to exterminate any possible rivals to the throne, declared, "Only those wives of the Emperor who have not borne him any sons will be given their freedom." All the rest, and there was a vast number, he ordered to join the Emperor inside in death. As the subterranean entrances were about to be sealed off, however, he considered that the many thousands of craftsmen who had been employed in building the tomb might divulge the stupendous worth of its treasures. Therefore, he commanded that they too be led inside and the doors closed upon them. Crossbows were then placed at strategic intervals and triggered to discharge their arrows automatically upon any thieves who might dare to penetrate the enclosure. Finally, trees and grass and flowers were replanted on the slopes of the mountain so that it would look like any other.

---

* According to Leonard Cottrell, author of *The Tiger of Ch'in* (N.Y.: Holt, Rinehart and Winston, 1962): "The tumulus which contained the sepulcher still exists near the town of Lint'ung. Called locally 'The Mound of Ch'in,' it is an artificial hill of sand brought from the river Wei, which flows some miles to the north. South of it rises Mount Li, to which it was said to have been connected by subterranean passages. The tumulus, now worn and weathered by more than twenty centuries, is over one thousand feet along each side, and was oriented, like the Great Pyramid, to the four points of the compass. It was even larger than the pyramid, which measured seven hundred and fifty feet along each base-line."

Elagabalus

Portrait bust, German Archaeological Institute, Rome.

O Nero, your Golden House is but a vile stable compared to the palace I have conceived for myself; and as for you, Elagabalus, my robes of state are far more splendid than yours, my circuses more bloody, my perfumes more piercingly exquisite, my slaves more numerous and more voluptuous. I too have harnessed the most beautiful concubines to my chariot. . . .

Gustave Flaubert, Correspondence, Oct. 29, 1842

*O*n the twenty-ninth of September, 219, the then fourteen-year-old and newly crowned Emperor Elagabalus entered Rome in triumph. Dressed in a tunic of purple silk embroidered with gold, his arms encircled with tinkling bracelets from wrist to shoulder, rubies as large as pigeons' eggs dangling from his earlobes, his face rouged, and his eyes darkened with kohl, he minced and fluttered down the Via Appia behind slaves strewing gold and silver dust in his path as he acknowledged the plaudits of the multitude. Sharing the triumph with him were his grandmother, Julia Maesa; his mother, Julia Soemias; and his aunt, Julia Mammaea; and it was this formidable triumvirate of Julias, not Elagabalus, who wielded the real power in the empire during his reign.*

The founder of the clan, Julius Bassianus, Elagabalus's greatgrandfather, had been hereditary high priest of the Syrian sun-god El-Gabal in the town of Emesa (Homs). His eldest daughter, the brilliant and ambitious Julia Domna, married the Emperor Septimius Severus and thus became the mother of another Emperor, Caracalla. As Empress and then Empress Dowager, she not only dominated state policy but also sponsored and assembled at her court such renowned literary figures as the poet Oppian, the philosophical biographer Diogenes Laërtius, and Philostratus, author of the proto-Christian Life of Apollonius of Tyana. *When Caracalla was assassinated by the usurping Moorish general Macrinus, rather than surrender she committed suicide by starvation. Her role as head of the family was then assumed by her equally talented, ruthless sister, Julia Maesa. By bribing the legions stationed in Syria, this Julia was able to have Macrinus overthrown and her grandson Elagabalus* acclaimed as Emperor. And after he in turn threatened to undermine her authority—not to mention the foundations of the res publica—she contrived to have him assassinated and replaced by his younger cousin, Alexander Severus. But during the brief three years and nine months of his rule, Elagabalus "left a name at which the world grew pale/ To point a moral or adorn a tale."

His prodigality has never been surpassed. Within 50 years of the death in 180 of the Stoic philosopher-king Marcus Aurelius—"when the human race," as Gibbon once wrote, "was most happy and prosperous"—the Roman Empire degenerated and descended, first, to his loutish son Commodus, then to the cruel military dictator Septimius Severus, then to the insane Caracalla, then to the sadistic Macrinus . . . down to Elagabalus. The historian Dio Cassius, searching for a proper epithet to apply to him, came up sputtering "the Assyrian" and "Sardanapalus." If his biographer Aelius Lampridius (the author of the following) is to be believed, he out-Neroed Nero himself. No doubt in their life-style and the warp of their personalities, both of these prodigious dioscuri might have been hatched from the same rotten egg. They shared, for instance, identical sexual tastes and inclinations, Nero even going through a marriage ceremony with his favorite, Sporus, and Elagabalus doing likewise with his Zoticus. Their adolescent pranks and practical jokes were also similar, as well as their passion for hot-rod chariots—Nero once driving a ten-horse team through the sacred precincts of Olympia in Greece, and Elagabalus actually hitching four elephants to his and careening down the Vatican Hill. Finally, Nero's astonishing remark when he first entered his famous Golden House (whose furnishings included a colossal statue of himself 120 feet high, an enclosed lake surrounded by groups of buildings designed to represent cities, dining rooms paved with porphyry and with ceilings of gold and fretted ivory inlaid with jewels): "At last I am beginning to live like a human being," can only be compared in its awesome vainglory to one attributed to Elagabalus, made after his slaves had brought him ten thousand pounds of cobwebs in response to his whim: "From this, one can understand how great a city is Rome."

It is the fairy-tale boundlessness of it all, the daydream transcendence of the usual human condition, that continues to fascinate us groundlings. Ben Jonson, *in his play* The Alchemist, *revels in it when he makes his character Sir Epicure Mammon, who has been schnooked into believing that he is about to obtain the Philosopher's Stone for creating gold, and so become "the master o' the mastery," burst into this paean of ecstatic megalomania:*

> For I do mean
> To have a list of wives and concubines
> Equal with Solomon, who had the Stone
> Alike with me; and I will make me a back
> With the elixir, that shall be as tough
> As Hercules', to encounter fifty a night . . .

And more:

> I will have all my beds blown up, not stuft—
> Down is too hard: and then, mine oval room
> Filled with such pictures as Tiberius took
> From Elephantis, and dull Aretine
> But coldly imitated. Then, my glasses
> Cut in more subtle angles, to disperse
> And multiply the figures as I walk
> Naked between my succubae. My mists
> I'll have of perfume, vapoured 'bout the room,
> To lose our selves in; and my baths, like pits
> To fall into; from whence we will come forth,
> And roll us dry in gossamer and roses. . . .

And more:

> My meat shall all come in, in Indian shells,
> Dishes of agate set in gold, and studded
> With emeralds, sapphires, hyacinths, and rubies.
> The tongues of carps, dormice, and camels' heels,
> Boiled in the spirit of sol, and dissolved pearl,
> Apicius' diet, 'gainst the epilepsy:
> And I will eat these broths with spoons of amber,
> Headed with diamond and carbuncle.
> My foot-boy shall eat pheasants, calvered salmons,
> Knots, godwits, lampreys: I myself will have
> The beards of barbel served, instead of salads;
> Oiled mushrooms; and the swelling unctuous paps
> Of a fat pregnant sow, newly cut off,
> Drest with an exquisite and poignant sauce;
> For which, I'll say unto my cook, There's gold,
> Go forth, and be a knight. . . .

And still more, though this should suffice. In one instance, however, Sir Epicure attempts to cap Elagabalus, who is said to have had all his fish "cooked in a bluish sauce that preserved their natural color, as though they were in the sea-water," by ordering his cooks to make

> *Our shrimps to swim again, as when they lived,*
> *In a rare butter made of dolphins' milk.*

But Jonson wrote The Alchemist *at the peak of his talent and of the High Renaissance, when the universe was almost equal to man's vast appetite, and expanding with it; from which point the true Elagabalian spirit was to decline during the following centuries into the sort of chic diabolism cultivated by J. K. Huysmans and other writers and painters of the* fin de siècle. *It still flares up again, minus any esthetic pretensions, in the secret cults of thrill-killers, such as Charles Manson & Co., and similar gangs of adolescent monsters that are exposed now and then here and there in remote parts of the United States.*

It should be added, however, that contemporary historians have suggested that Elagabalus's exaltation of his own god, El-Gabal, above all others in his Elagabalium, the temple he built on the Palatine Hill to house them, was not merely a further instance of megalomania, but an attempt to unite the empire by establishing a monotheistic religion. This was, of course, to be accomplished a century later by Constantine the Great when he adopted Christianity as the state religion. Elagabalus's aunt, Julia Mammaea, is said to have been converted to Christianity by the Church Father Origen, and her son the Emperor Alexander Severus kept in his private chapel statues of Jesus, Abraham, and Orpheus.

The life of Elagabalus presented here was written by Aelius Lampridius around 323, and dedicated to the Emperor Constantine. Composed in imitation of Suetonius's Lives of the Roman Emperors, *it formed part of a collection of similar biographies, from Hadrian to Carinus, known as the* Scriptores Historiae Augustae, *put together by a variety of authors between 285 and 335, perhaps with a single editor. My version has been adapted from the translation by David Magie published by the Loeb Classical Library in 1921.*

HAD not rulers so depraved as Nero, Vitellius, and Caligula reigned before him, I would never have put into writing the life of Elagabalus Antoninus, who surpassed even them in infamy, so as to spare the Roman people the shame of knowing that he had once been their Emperor. But just as the same earth produces poison as well as grain, not only serpents but also flocks, the Romans may console themselves by recalling that Augustus,

Trajan, Vespasian, Hadrian, Pius Antoninus, Titus, and Marcus Aurelius had also been emperors, enjoying long reigns and dying natural deaths, whereas the tyrants had all been murdered, dragged with hooks through the streets, and even had their names obliterated from the public monuments.

Now when the Emperor Macrinus was slain [in A.D. 218] together with his wasteful and brutal son Diadumenianus, who had shared the power equally with him, the imperial office was bestowed upon Elagabalus. Originally, he had the name Varius, but later was called Elagabalus because he was priest of this god, whom he afterward brought from Syria to Rome, and founded a temple for him.* But when he became Emperor he assumed the name Antoninus, either in order to prove his descent or because he had learned that this name was so dear to mankind.

He was wholly under the control of his mother, Symiamira [Julia Soaemias Bassiana], so much so, in fact, that he did no state business without her consent, although she lived like a harlot and practiced all manner of lewdness in the palace. For that matter, her affair with the Emperor Antoninus Caracalla was so notorious that Varius, or rather Elagabalus, was commonly supposed to be his son. The name Varius, some say, was given him by his schoolmates because he seemed to be sprung from the seed of "various" men, as would be the case with the son of a harlot. When his reputed father, Caracalla, was murdered as the result of Macrinus's treachery, he sought refuge in the temple of the god Elagabalus for fear that Macrinus would kill him also.

Howbeit, soon after obtaining the imperial power he dispatched couriers to Rome, and there all classes were filled with enthusiasm, and a great desire for him was aroused in the whole people merely at the mention of the name Antoninus, now restored, as it seemed, not in an empty title but actually in one of the blood, for he had signed himself son of Antoninus Bassianus [the original name of the Emperor Caracalla]. He had the prestige, furthermore, that usually comes to a new ruler who has succeeded a tyrant. In short, when Elagabalus's message was read in the senate, at once good wishes were uttered for the new Emperor and curses on Macrinus and his son.

As soon as he entered the city of Rome, however, neglecting all the affairs of the provinces, he established Elagabalus as a god on the Palatine Hill close to the imperial palace. There he built him a temple, to which he desired to transfer the emblem of the Great Mother, the fire of Vesta, the Palladium, the shields of the Salii, and all that the Romans held sacred, intending that no god might be worshiped at Rome save Elagabalus. He

---

* El-Gabal, meaning "Lord of the high place," was the patron god of Emesa (the modern Homs) in Syria, where he was worshiped in the form of a phallic-shaped black stone believed to have fallen from heaven. He was popularly regarded as a sun-god, and, after his importation into Rome, was officially called *Deus Sol Elagabalus* or *Invictus Sol Elagabalus*. This identification was responsible for the erroneous form Heliogabalus, applied both to the god and the Emperor.

declared, furthermore, that the religions of the Jews and the Samaritans and the rites of the Christians must also be transferred to this place, in order that the priesthood of Elagabalus might include the mysteries of every form of worship.

When he held his first audience with the senate, he gave orders that his mother should be asked to come into the senate chamber. On her arrival she was invited to a place on the consuls' bench, and there she took part in the drafting of the senate's decree. Elagabalus was the only one of all the emperors under whom a woman attended the senate like a man, as though she belonged to the senatorial order.

He also established a *senaculum*, or women's senate, on the Quirinal Hill. Before his time, in fact, a congress of matrons had met there, but only on certain festivals, or whenever a matron was presented with the insignia of a "consular marriage," bestowed by previous emperors on their kinswomen who had married husbands of a lower social status in order that they might not lose their noble rank. But now, under the influence of Symiamira, absurd decrees were enacted concerning rules to be applied to matrons, namely, what kind of clothing each might wear in public, who was to yield precedence and to whom, who was to advance to kiss another, who might ride in a chariot, on a horse, on a pack animal, or on an ass, who might drive in a carriage drawn by mules or in one drawn by oxen, who might be carried in a litter, and whether the litter might be made of leather, or of bone, or covered with ivory or with silver, and, lastly, who might wear gold or jewels on her shoes.

After Elagabalus had spent the winter in Nicomedia, where he indulged openly in orgies with his catamites, the soldiers soon began to regret that they had conspired to make him their Emperor. For who could endure a ruler with such unnatural lusts when not even a beast of this sort would long be tolerated? And even at Rome he did nothing but send out agents to search for those who had particularly large organs and bring them to the palace in order that he might enjoy their vigor. Moreover, he used to have the story of Paris played in his house, and he himself would take the role of Venus, and suddenly drop his clothing to the ground and fall naked on his knees, one hand on his breast and the other on his private parts, in Venus's characteristic pose, his buttocks projected meanwhile and thrust back before his partner in depravity. He even modeled the expression of his face on that with which Venus is usually painted, and he had his whole body depilated, deeming it the chief enjoyment of life to appear fit and worthy to arouse the lusts of the greatest number.

He took bribes for honors and distinctions and positions of power, selling them in person or through his slaves and those who served his lusts. He made appointments to the senate without regard to age, property, or rank, and solely at the price of money, and he also sold the positions of captain and tribune, legate and general, as well as procuratorships and posts in the palace. Many whose personal appearance pleased him he took from the stage, the circus, and the arena and brought to the palace. Such was his passion for the former slave Hierocles, for instance, that he would kiss him publicly on a place of his body which it is sullying even to mention, declaring that he was celebrating the festival of Flora.

Though defiled by every moral stain, with a company of men equally degraded he once broke into the sanctuary of Vesta, where only Vestal Virgins and anointed priests were allowed to enter. While there he actually violated the chastity of a Vestal Virgin, and, by laying his hands on the holy shrines, profaned the sacred rites of the Roman nation. In truth, he would have liked to extinguish the everlasting fire in the sanctuary, for it was his intention to abolish not only the religious rites and ceremonies of all other peoples but also of the Romans, his one wish being that the god Elagabalus should be worshiped everywhere.

On another occasion he attempted to carry off the shrine of Vesta, but seized instead merely an earthenware replica that the Senior Vestal, having been forewarned, had substituted in its place in order to deceive him. It is related that when he found nothing in the shrine, he threw it down in a rage and broke it. Nevertheless, his agents did manage to steal an image that the Emperor believed to be the Palladium, and, after washing it over with gold, he placed it inside the temple to his own god. At this time, too, he planned to erect a hollow shaft of enormous size that could be ascended from within, then to hoist upon its summit a statue of Elagabalus that would overlook the whole city. However, he could not find stone enough for so grandiose a project, though he sent his barges as far as Thebes in upper Egypt to procure it.

He also adopted the worship of the Great Mother of the Gods and celebrated the rite of the taurobolium*. He carried off her image and the sacred objects of her cult that were kept hidden. The Emperor would toss his head to and fro among the castrated devotees of the goddess, and he infibulated himself [attached a ring or lock to his genitals], and did all that the eunuch priests are wont to do. He also celebrated the rite of Salaambo [a Semitic goddess, probably akin to Aphrodite and Tanith-Caelestis] with all the wailing and the frenzy of the Syrian cult for the dismembered god Adonis—thereby foreshadowing his own impending doom. In fact, he asserted that all gods were merely the servants of his own god, calling some its chamberlains, others its slaves, and others its attendants for divers purposes.

Elagabalus also sacrificed human victims, and for this he collected from the whole of Italy children of noble birth and beauty, with the further requirement that both their fathers and mothers had to be alive, since he probably felt that the grief if suffered by two parents would be doubled. He kept about him every kind of magician to perform these daily sacrifices,

* During this rite to celebrate the Great Mother (Magna Mater), the convert stood naked in a pit above which, on a platform of perforated boards, a bull would be slaughtered. The blood flowing down over his body signified his purification and spiritual rebirth.

himself urging them on; and all the while he would examine the children's vitals [for auspices] and torture the victims after the manner of his own native rites.

When he entered upon his consulship he threw presents to the populace to be scrambled for, no mere pieces of silver and gold, indeed, or confectionary or little animals, but fatted cattle and camels and asses and slaves, declaring that this was an imperial custom. He made a public bath in the palace, and at the same time threw open the bath of Plautinus to the populace, that by this means he might get a supply of men with unusually large organs. He also took care to have the whole city and the wharves searched for *onobeli* [that is, like asses in this respect], as those were called who seemed particularly lusty.

During his reign Zoticus [an athlete from Smyrna brought to Rome by order of the Emperor] had such influence that all the chiefs of the palace departments treated him as their master's consort. This same Zoticus, furthermore, was the kind to abuse such a degree of intimacy, for under false pretenses he sold all Elagabalus's promises and favors, and so amassed enormous wealth. To some he held out threats, and to others promises, lying to them all. With this man, Elagabalus went through a nuptial ceremony and consummated a marriage, complete with bridal matron, after which he exclaimed, "Go to it, Cook!" [Zoticus's father had been a cook, and so he himself was nicknamed "Cook"]—and this at a time when Zoticus was ill. Afterward Elagabalus would ask philosophers and men of the greatest dignity whether they, in their youth, had ever experienced what he was experiencing, and all without the slightest shame. For indeed he never refrained from filthy conversation and would make lewd signs with his fingers and would show no regard for decency even in public gatherings or in the hearing of the people.

On one occasion he invited the nobles of the court to a vintage festival and, after seating himself by the baskets of grapes, began to question the most venerable and dignified among them whether they were still responsive to Venus. When these old men blushed in mortification and remained silent, he cried out in glee, "They're blushing—it's all right!" regarding their blushes as a confession. He then began to narrate his own scandalous doings without any sense of shame; but seeing that they remained silent and were unamused, he turned to the young men about him and questioned them closely on their amorous exploits. Of course they told him what one would expect at their age, and he began to be merry, declaring that a vintage celebrated in such a manner was truly worthy of Bacchus.

He often showed contempt for the senate, calling them "slaves in togas," while he treated the Roman people as the tiller of a single farm and the equestrian order as nothing at all. As prefect of the guard he appointed a dancer who had been on the stage at Rome; as prefect of the watch, a chariot driver named Cordius; as prefect of the grain supply, a barber named Claudius; and to all other posts of distinction he advanced men whose sole recommendation was the enormous size of their privates. At his banquets he preferred to have perverts placed next to him and took especial delight in touching and fondling them, and whenever he drank one of them was usually selected to hand him the cup.

Concerning his life many filthy anecdotes have been put into writing, but since they are not worthy of being recorded, I have thought fit to relate only such deeds as illustrate his extravagance. Some of these, it is said, were done before he ascended the throne, others after he was made Emperor; for he himself declared that his models were Apicius among commoners and, among emperors, Otho and Vitellius.

For example, he was the first commoner to cover his couches with golden spreads, for this was then lawful by order of Marcus Antoninus, who had sold at public auction all the imperial trappings. Also, he would give summer banquets in various colors, one day a green banquet, another day an iridescent one, and next in order a blue one, varying them continually every day of the summer. Moreover, he was the first to use silver urns and casseroles, some over one hundred pounds in weight though spoiled by the most obscene designs. He was the first to concoct wine seasoned with resin and mint and all such mixtures, a habit that our present luxury retains, while rose wine he made even more fragrant by adding pulverized pine cones. He was also the first to make forcemeat of fish, or of oysters of various kinds, or of lobsters, crayfish, and squills. He would strew roses and other flowers, such as lilies, violets, hyacinths, and narcissus, over his banqueting rooms, his couches, and his porticoes, and then stroll about through them. He would refuse to swim in a pool that was not perfumed with saffron or some other well-known essence. And he could not rest easily on cushions that were not stuffed with rabbit fur or feathers from under the wings of partridges.

He had couches made of solid silver for use in his banqueting rooms and bed chambers. In imitation of Apicius he frequently ate camels' heels and also cockscombs taken from living birds, even the tongues of peacocks and nightingales, because he was told that one who ate them was immune from the plague. He served to the palace attendants, moreover, huge platters heaped up with the viscera of mullets, flamingo brains, partridge eggs, thrushes' brains, and the heads of parrots, pheasants, and peacocks. The beards of the mullets that he ordered to be served were so large that they were brought on, in place of cress or parsley or pickled beans or fenugreek, in heaping bowls and disk-shaped platters—a particularly amazing performance. He rarely spent less on a banquet than 100,000 sesterces, that is, 30 pounds of silver; sometimes he even spent as much as 3 million, when all the cost was computed. In truth, he even outdid the banquets of Vitellius and Apicius.

He fed his dogs on goose livers. Among his pets he had lions and leopards, which had been rendered harmless and trained by tamers, and these he would suddenly order during the dessert and the after-dessert to jump up on the couches, thereby causing an amusing panic, for none knew that the beasts were harmless. He sent grapes from Apamea [in Syria] to his stables for his horses, and he fed parrots and pheasants to his lions and other wild animals. For ten successive days, moreover, he served wild sows' udders with the matrices, at the rate of 30 a day, serving, besides, peas with gold pieces, lentils with onyx, beans with amber, and rice with pearls; he also sprinkled pearls on fish and truffles in lieu of pepper. In a banqueting room with a reversible ceiling he once overwhelmed his parasites with violets and other flowers, so that some of them were actually smothered to death, being unable to crawl out to the top. He flavored his swimming pools and bathtubs with essence of spices or of roses or wormwood. As banquet favors he gave eunuchs, or four-horse chariots, or horses with saddles, or mules, or litters, or carriages, or a thousand aurei, or a hundred pounds of silver.

At certain banquets he would also distribute chances inscribed on spoons, the chance of one person reading "ten camels," of another "ten flies," of another "ten pounds of gold," of another "ten pounds of lead," of another "ten ostriches," of another "ten hens' eggs," so that they were chances indeed and men tried their luck. These he also gave at his games, distributing chances for ten bears or ten dormice, ten lettuces or ten pounds of gold. And the performers, too, he invited to what really were chances, giving as prizes a dead dog or a pound of beef, or else a hundred aurei, or a hundred pieces of silver, or a hundred coppers, and so on. All this so pleased the populace that after every occasion they rejoiced that he was Emperor.

He gave a naval spectacle, it is said, on the circus canals, which had been filled with wine, and he sprinkled the people's cloaks with perfume made from the wild grape. He once drove a chariot drawn by four elephants on the Vatican Hill, destroying the tombs that obstructed the way. It is also said that he once collected serpents with the aid of priests of the Marsi [an ancient people of central Italy, famous as snake charmers] and let them loose before dawn, when the populace usually assembled for the greater games, and that many people were injured during the ensuing general panic as well as bitten by the snakes.

Occasionally he would wear a tunic made wholly of cloth of gold, or one made of purple, or a Persian one studded with jewels, and at such times he would say that he felt oppressed by the weight of his pleasures. He even wore engraved jewels on his shoes—a practice that aroused the derision of all, as if, forsooth, the engravings of famous artists could be seen on jewels attached to his feet. He wished to wear also a jeweled diadem to heighten his beauty and to make his face look more like a woman's, and in his own house he did wear one. He once promised a phoenix to some guests, it is said, or in lieu of the bird a thousand pounds of gold, and this sum he handed out in the imperial residence. He constructed swimming pools filled with sea water in places especially far from the coast, and would then bestow them upon his friends. One summer he made a mountain of snow in the pleasure garden attached to his house, having snow carried there from a great distance for the purpose. When on the sea coast he never ate fish, but in places most remote from the sea he regularly served all manner of sea-food, even providing the country folk on his estates with the milt of lampreys and pikes. The fish that he ate were cooked in a bluish sauce that preserved their natural color, as though they were still in the sea.

Elagabalus never had intercourse with the same woman twice, except with his wife,* but he maintained brothels in his palace for his friends, his clients, and his slaves. For amusement, while bathing with his parasites, he would have several of them bound together on a waterwheel and, by a turn of the wheel, plunge them into the water and then bring them back to the surface again, calling them meanwhile "river Ixions." When his friends became drunk he would often shut them up, and then at night let in his lions and leopards and bears—all of them harmless—so that when they awakened at dawn, or worse, during the night, they would find the beasts in the same room with themselves. Some are said to have died of the fright. His humbler friends he would occasionally seat on air pillows instead of cushions and then let out the air while they were dining, so that often these diners were cast abruptly under the table.

When adultery was represented on the stage, he would order what was usually done in pretense to be carried out in fact. He often purchased harlots from all the procurers and then set them free. Once during a private conversation the question arose as to how many ruptured people there were in the city of Rome, and he thereupon issued an order that all should be noted and brought to his baths; he then bathed with them, taunting them, though some were men of the greatest distinction. Before a banquet he would frequently watch gladiatorial fights and boxing matches, and during luncheon he sometimes had a couch spread for himself in an upper gallery to watch criminals exhibited in a wild beast hunt below. His parasites would often be served during dessert with food made of wax or wood or ivory, sometimes of earthenware, or at times even of marble or stone, so that all he ate himself would be served to them too, but different in substance and only to be looked at. And all the while they would merely drink with each course and wash their hands, just as if they had really eaten.

He was the first of the Romans, it is said, who wore clothing wholly of silk, although garments partly of silk were in use before his time. Linen that had been washed he would never touch, saying that washed linen was worn only by beggars.

He once gathered together in a public building all the harlots from the circus, the theater, the stadium, the public baths, and all other places of

* Elagabalus married the Vestal Virgin he had raped, Aquilia Severa, in 221, after divorcing his first wife, Paula. By this marriage he further symbolized the union of his own god, El-Gabal, with Pallas Athene.

amusement, then delivered a speech to them as one might to soldiers, calling them "comrades" and discoursing upon various kinds of postures and debaucheries. Afterward he invited to a similar gathering procurers, catamites collected together from all sides, and lascivious boys and young men. And whereas he had appeared before the harlots in a woman's costume and with protruding bosom, he met the catamites in the garb of a boy who is exposed for prostitution. After his speech he announced a largess of three aurei for each, just as if they were soldiers, and asked them to pray the gods that they might find others to recommend to him.

He also used to play jokes on his slaves, even ordering them to bring him a thousand pounds of spiders' webs and offering them a prize; and he collected, it is said, ten thousand pounds, and then remarked that one could realize from that how great a city was Rome. He would send to his parasites jars of frogs, scorpions, snakes, and other such reptiles, as their yearly allowance of provisions, and he would shut up a vast number of flies in jars of this sort and call them tamed bees.

He often brought four-horse chariots from the circus into his banqueting rooms or porticoes while he lunched or dined, compelling his guests to drive, even though they were old men and some of them had held public office. At odd times he would give an order to bring in to him 10,000 mice, 1,000 weasels, or 1,000 shrewmice. So skillful were his confectioners and dairymen that all the various kinds of food served by his cooks, either meat cooks or fruit cooks, they would also serve up, making them now out of confectionery or again out of milk products. His parasites he would serve with dinners made of glass, and at times he would send to their table only embroidered napkins with pictures of the viands that were set before himself, as many in number as the courses that he was to have, so that they were served only with representations made by the needle or the loom. Sometimes, however, paintings, too, were displayed to them, so that they were served with the whole dinner, as it were, but were all the while tormented by hunger. He would also mix jewels with apples and flowers, and he would throw out of the window quite as much food as he served to his friends. He gave an order, too, that an amount of grain equal to one year's tribute should be given to all the harlots, procurers, and catamites who were within the walls, and promised an equal amount to those without; for thanks to the foresight of Severus and Trajan, there was in Rome at that time a store of grain equal to seven years' tribute.

He would harness four huge dogs to a chariot and drive about within the royal residence, and he did the same thing, before he was made Emperor, on his country estates. He even appeared in public driving four stags of vast size. Once he harnessed lions to his chariot and called himself the Great Mother, and on another occasion, tigers and called himself Dionysus; and he always appeared in the particular garb in which the deity he represented was usually depicted. He kept at Rome tiny Egyptian snakes, called by the natives "good genii," besides hippopotamuses, a crocodile, and a rhinoceros, and, in fact, everything Egyptian that could be supplied. And sometimes at his banquets he served ostriches, saying that the Jews had been commanded to eat them.

The occupations of the day he performed at night, and those of the night in the daytime, and he considered it a mark of luxury to wait until a late hour before rising from sleep and beginning to hold his levee. He received his courtiers every day, and he seldom let any go without a gift, save those whom he found to be thrifty, for he regarded these as worthless.

His chariots were made of jewels and gold, for he scorned those that were merely of silver or ivory or bronze. He would harness women of the greatest beauty to a wheelbarrow in fours, in twos, or in threes or even more, and would drive them about, usually naked himself, as were also the women who were pulling him.

He had the custom, moreover, of asking to a dinner eight bald men, or else eight one-eyed men, or eight men who suffered from gout, or eight deaf men, or, again, eight fat men, his purpose being, in the case of these last, since they could not be accommodated on one couch, to call forth general laughter. He would present to his guests all the silver plate that he had in the banqueting room and all the supply of goblets, and he did it very often, too. He would propose to his guests, furthermore, by way of a feat, that they should invent new sauces for giving flavor to the food, and he would offer a very large prize for the man whose invention should please him. On the other hand, if the sauce did not please him, the inventor was ordered to continue eating it until he invented a better one.

He got himself up as a confectioner, a perfumer, a cook, a shopkeeper, or a procurer, and he practiced all these occupations in his house continually. At one dinner where there were many tables he brought in the heads of 600 ostriches in order that the brains might be eaten. Occasionally he gave a banquet in which he would serve twenty-two courses of extraordinary viands, and between each course he and his guests would bathe and dally with women, all taking an oath that they were deriving enjoyment. It is further related of him that he constructed baths in many places, bathed in them once, and immediately demolished them; and he is said to have done the same with houses, imperial headquarters, and summer dwellings.

He purchased, it is said, a very famous and very beautiful harlot for 100,000 sesterces, and then kept her untouched, as if she were a virgin. Furthermore, he once remarked that he did not wish to have sons, lest one of them should chance to be thrifty. He would have perfumes from India burned without any coals in order that the fumes might fill his apartments. Even while a commoner he never made a journey with fewer than 60 wagons; but after he became Emperor he would take with him, it is said, as many as 600, asserting that the King of the Persians traveled with 10,000 camels and Nero with 500 carriages. The reason for all these vehicles was the vast number of his procurers and bawds, harlots, catamites, and lusty partners in depravity who always went along.

In the public baths he invariably bathed with the women, and he even treated them himself with a depilatory ointment, which he applied also to his own beard, and, shameful though it be to say it, in the same place where the women were treated and at the same hour. He shaved his minions' groins, using the razor with his own hand—with which he would then shave his beard. He would strew gold and silver dust about a portico, and then lament that he could not strew the dust of amber also; and he did this often, as others do with sand, when he proceeded on foot to his horse or his carriage.

He never put on the same shoes twice and never, it is said, wore the same ring a second time. He often tore up costly garments. Once he took a whale and weighed it and then sent his friends its weight in fish. He sank some heavily laden ships in the harbor and then said that this was a sign of greatness of soul. He used vessels of gold for relieving himself, and his urinals were made of murra [a material brought to Rome by Pompey, thought to be Chinese jade] or onyx. And he is said to have remarked: "If I ever have an heir, I shall appoint a guardian for him, to make him do what I myself have done and intend to do." He was accustomed, furthermore, to have dinners served to him of the following kind: one day he would eat nothing at all but pheasant, serving it at every course; another day he would serve only chicken; another some kind of fish, or pork, or ostrich, or greens, or fruit, or sweets, or dairy products. He would often shut up his friends at inns, where he stopped for the night, with old hags from Ethiopia and compel them to stay there until morning, having enticed them beforehand by saying that the most beautiful women were kept in those places.

Sometimes he laughed so loud in the theater that no one else could be heard by the audience. He could sing and dance, play the pipes, the horn, and the pandura, and he also performed on the organ. On one single day, it is said, he visited every prostitute from the circus, the theater, the amphitheater, and all the public places of Rome, covering his head with a muleteer's cap in order to escape recognition; he did not, however, gratify his passions, but merely gave an aureus to each prostitute, saying as he did so: "Let no one know it, but this is a present from Antoninus."

The prophecy had once been made to him by some Syrian priests that he would die a violent death. And therefore he had prepared cords entwined with purple and scarlet silk so that, if need arose, he could put an end to his life by the noose. He had gold swords, too, in readiness, with which to stab himself if a worse fate threatened. He also had poisons ready, concealed in ceraunites [meteoritic stones], sapphires, and emeralds. And he also built a very high tower from which to throw himself down, constructed of boards gilded and jeweled in his own presence, for even his death, he declared, should be costly and marked by luxury, in order that it might be said that no one had ever died in this fashion. But all these preparations availed him nothing.

The soldiers, particularly the members of the guard, could no longer endure to have such a pest clothed with the name of Emperor. They all expressed their views, first one to another, then in groups, turning their thoughts to Alexander Severus, who previously, at the time when Macrinus was murdered, had been hailed by the senate as Caesar [heir to the throne]. Alexander was the cousin of Elagabalus, for both were grandsons of Varia [Julia Maesa], from whom Elagabalus had the name Varius.

The Emperor now gave orders that Alexander, whom he had formally adopted, be removed from his presence, saying that he regretted the adoption. Then he commanded the senate to take away from Alexander the name of Caesar. But when this was announced to the senate, there was a profound silence. For Alexander was an excellent youth, as was afterward shown by the character of his rule, even though, because he was chaste, he was displeasing to Elagabalus. Besides, he was loved by the soldiers and by the equestrian order. Yet the Emperor's madness went the length of an attempt to assassinate his cousin, and that in the following way:

Leaving his mother, grandmother, and cousin in the palace, he himself withdrew to the Gardens of Spes Vetus [where he had built a temple to the god Elagabalus], on the ground that he was forming designs against some new youth, and there he issued an order to slay Alexander. He also sent a dispatch to the soldiers bidding them take away from Alexander the title of Caesar, and commanded agents to smear mud on the inscriptions on his statues in the Camp [of the Praetorian Guard], as is usually done to a tyrant. Furthermore, he sent a message to Alexander's guardians, ordering them, if they hoped for rewards and distinctions, to kill him in any way they wished, either in his bath, or by poison, or with the sword.

But immediately after the inscriptions on Alexander's statues were smeared with mud, all the soldiers were fired with anger, and they set out, some for the palace and some for the gardens where the Emperor was, with the purpose of protecting Alexander and finally ridding the state of this filthy creature full of murderous intent. When they came to the palace they set a guard about Alexander and his mother [Julia Mammaea] and grandmother, and then escorted them with the greatest care to the Camp. Symiamira, Elagabalus's mother, followed them on foot, filled with anxiety about her son. Then the soldiers went to the gardens, where they found the Emperor making plans for a chariot race and at the same time eagerly awaiting the news of his cousin's murder.

Alarmed by the sudden clatter of the soldiers, he crouched down in a corner and covered himself with the curtain that was at the door of his bed chamber, sending one of the prefects still loyal to him to the Camp to quiet the soldiers there and another prefect to placate those who had just entered the gardens. The latter, Antiochianus by name, reminded the soldiers of their oath of allegiance and finally persuaded them not to kill the Emperor—for, in fact, only a few had come and the majority had remained in the Camp with the standard. So much for what happened in the gardens.

In the Camp, on the other hand, the soldiers replied to the entreaties of the prefect by stipulating that they would spare Elagabalus's life on condition that he send away all his filthy minions, his chariot drivers, and his actors, and return to a decent mode of living. He did, finally, dismiss several of his base favorites. The soldiers, furthermore, charged the prefects to keep watch over Alexander, so that no harm might be done him.

But Elagabalus, after the initial danger was past, with earnest entreaties kept demanding back his favorite Hierocles, the most shameless of men, and also renewed his plotting against Alexander.

On the calends of January [A.D. 222], he refused to appear with his cousin in public for their inauguration as joint consuls in the temple of Jupiter Optimus Maximus on the Capitolium. At last, however, when he was told by his grandmother and mother that the soldiers would kill him unless they saw harmony established between himself and his cousin, he put on the bordered toga and, at the sixth hour of the day, entered the senate, inviting his grandmother to the session and escorting her to a seat. But then he refused to proceed to the Capitolium to assume the vows for the state and conduct the usual ceremonies. Accordingly, everything was done by the city praetor just as if there were no consuls there.

Nevertheless, he did not give up the murder of Alexander; but out of fear that if he killed him the senate would only turn to someone else, he gave orders that the senate should at once leave the city. Even all those senators who had no carriages or slaves were commanded to set out immediately, some of them being carried by porters, others using animals that chance threw in their way or that they hired for money. And because Sabinus, a man of consular rank, to whom Ulpian [the celebrated jurist] had dedicated several of his books, remained in the city, the Emperor called a centurion and ordered him to kill him, speaking in a low tone. But the centurion, who was rather deaf, thought that he was being ordered to eject Sabinus from the city and acted accordingly; and so a centurion's infirmity saved the senator's life.

The soldiers, however, either because they knew what evils Elagabalus had in store, or because they foresaw his hatred for themselves, formed a conspiracy to set the state free. First they attacked the accomplices in his plan of murdering Alexander, killing some by tearing out the vital organs and others by piercing the anus, so that their deaths were as evil as their lives. Next they fell upon Elagabalus himself and slew him in a latrine in which he had taken refuge. Then his body was dragged through the streets, and the soldiers further insulted it by thrusting it into a sewer. But since the sewer chanced to be too small to admit the corpse, they attached a weight to it to keep it from floating, and hurled it from the Aemilian Bridge into the Tiber, in order that it might never be buried. The body was also dragged around the Circus before it was thrown into the Tiber.

His name—that is to say, the name Antoninus—was erased from the public records by order of the senate, though the name Varius Elagabalus was left, for he had used the name Antoninus falsely. After his death he was dubbed "The Tiberine," or "The Dragged," or "The Filthy," and many other such names, all of which were meant to signify his reputation and to express the general hatred of the people against him.

With him was also slain his mother, Symiamira, a most depraved woman and one worthy of such a son.* And the first measure enacted after the death of Elagabalus provided that no woman should ever enter the senate, and that whoever permitted one to do so should be declared doomed and forfeited to the kingdom of the dead.

* According to Dio Cassius, Elagabalus was killed in her arms, as she tried to protect him, and her body was dragged about the streets with his. The black phallic-shaped stone of El-Gabal was later returned to Emesa.

Justinian and
Theodora

Mosaic, Church of St. Vitale, Ravenna, Italy.

Vain the ambition of kings
Who seek by trophies and dead things
To leave a living name behind,
And weave but nets to catch the wind.

John Webster, *Vanitas Vanitatum*

W*hat sort of person was Procopius? And how did it come about that he wrote his* Secret History, *the most atrabilious political diatribe ever upspewed, which combines pornography and paranoia so effectively that it has destroyed the reputations of Justinian and Theodora perhaps for all time?*

He was born around the year 500 in Caesarea, Palestine, most likely to a family of Jewish descent that had been converted to Christianity, for he was fluent in Aramaic, then the common tongue of the Semitic peoples in the Near East. After completing his education in Constantinople, in 527 he was appointed legal secretary to Justinian's great general Belisarius, who was stationed in Mesopotamia guarding the eastern frontiers of the empire against the Persians. Procopius accompanied Belisarius on his campaigns in which he defeated the Vandals in Africa and the Ostrogoths in Italy, returning with him to Constantinople in triumph in 540. When Belisarius was removed from his command in disgrace in 542, on suspicion of conspiring against the Emperor, Procopius, too, was dismissed; but even after Belisarius was restored to favor, and set out on his second Italian expedition against the Goths in 544, Procopius had to remain behind.

Meanwhile, he began his classic History of the Wars, *modeled on Thucydides, dealing with Justinian's campaigns from the years 527 to 553. But before the book was finished, in 550, he wrote the* Secret History—*or* Anekdota, *as Procopius called it, meaning "Unpublished"—in which with a gleeful, almost ecstatic, malice he gives us the behind-the-scenes lowdown on the abysmal degeneracy of Justinian, the "Demon Emperor," and his equally diabolical consort Theodora. Of necessity it had to remain "secret" and "unpublished," for its disclosure during his lifetime would have meant death to* the author for lese majesty. However, around 555, he wrote still another book, On the Buildings, *not only praising Justinian for his construction of public works and fortresses and churches, among them the Santa Sophia, but also exalting him as a benefactor of humanity.* The Secret History, *therefore, has to be well salted with skepticism by the reader. As Edward Gibbon declared: "Of these strange* Anecdotes [sic] *a part may be true because probable, and a part true because improbable. Procopius must have* known *the former and the latter he could scarcely* invent."

Judged by his achievements if not his character, the Emperor Justinian (*Flavius Petrus Sabbatius Justinianus*) *must be considered one of the greatest of ancient monarchs. During his unusually long reign he recovered for a time the territories of the western Roman Empire from the German barbarians, who a generation earlier, in 476, had burned and occupied Rome itself. He also checked at the Danube frontier the onslaughts of the Mongolian hordes of Avars, who kept pushing the Bulgars and Slavs into the Balkan peninsula. And, finally, by a series of wars and threats of wars, bribes and skillful diplomacy, he withstood the attempt by the Sassanid Persians under Chosroes I to dominate the trade routes of the Byzantines to the east. As both temporal caesar-spiritual pope in one—self-styled the "Supreme Master of the Universe"—he sought to establish unity of faith as well as unity of law, so that heresy became unpatriotic, political dissent impious. Accordingly, he suppressed all deviant Christian sects, such as the Arians and the Monophysites, that did not conform to the dogma fixed by the Council of Chalcedon in 451; and he also consolidated Roman civil law and scientific jurisprudence, under a commission headed by his minister Tribonian, as well as statutory law into the monumental* Corpus Iuris Civilis *and the* Codex Justinianus. *This last is considered his greatest bequest to posterity.*

Justinian's wife Theodora, *who was 17 years younger and died exactly 17 years earlier, was his co-supreme in formulating state and religious policy. She was a covert adherent of the sect of Monophysites (which held that Christ had a single divine-human nature), and an overt supporter of the "Blue" faction, so that Justinian's own religious and political opinions were somewhat swayed by*

57

hers. Though it was public knowledge that she had been a prostitute in her
youth, after her marriage she lived a strictly moral life as Empress and
remembered her fallen sisters by founding several hospices for them near the sea
of Marmara. Upon her death, of cancer it is said, she was buried in a coffin
made of solid gold.

In the mosaics of the domed octagonal Church of San Vitale in Ravenna are
preserved the most famous contemporary portraits of Justinian and Theodora.
There they are, each in the midst of his/her suite of courtiers, depicted in the
Byzantine style of isocephalic frontality and fixity, staring through glazed,
wide-open eyes back at us. The rigidity of Byzantine society—with its manifold
divisions and subdivisions of caste and class (there were eight distinct grades for
eunuchs alone), its vast pecking-order bureaucracy and priesthood, its elaborate
ceremonial protocol and rigmarole by which court and religious functions were
regulated—a social system, in short, braced against time and change—seems
itself reflected and summed up in the geometrical patterns of these mosaics. The
empire was to last about a thousand years longer, until 1453, when the Ottoman
Turks finally took Constantinople.

Curiously, Procopius, Justinian, and Belisarius all died in the same year 565.
Five years later Mohammed was born.

Procopius's Secret History *lay secret and unpublished until 1623, but since*
then has, of course, been translated into all languages. The translation by G. A.
Williamson, from which the following has been extracted, was published in
1966 by Penguin Books, Ltd., England.

Prelude

What sort of people were Justinian and Theodora? And how did it come
about that they destroyed the greatness of Rome? These are the questions
that I must now answer.

During the reign of Emperor Leo in Byzantium [457–474], three young
farmers of Illyrian origin, Zimarchus, Dityvistus, and Justin of Vederiana
[Justinian's uncle], after waging an endless struggle against poverty,
determined to get away from it all and went off to join the army. They
covered the whole distance to Byzantium on foot, carrying on their
shoulders their blankets in which were wrapped nothing but dry biscuits
baked before they had left home. Their names were entered in the army
lists, and the Emperor Leo picked them out to serve in the Palace Guard, as
they were all men of rugged physique.

Some time later when Anastasius [491–518] had succeeded to the imperial
power, he was involved in war with the Isaurians, who had taken up arms

against him. He sent an army of considerable size to deal with them, the commander being John the Hunchback. This John had locked up Justin in prison because of some misdemeanor, intending to execute him on the following day. He would have done so but for a dream-vision that came to him in time to prevent it. The general said that in a dream he was confronted by a being of colossal size, too powerful in every way to be taken for a man. This being commanded him to release the man whom he had that day imprisoned. On waking from sleep, however, he dismissed the vision from his mind. But when the next night came, he dreamed that he again heard the same words as before; but he remained just as unwilling to carry out the order. Then, for the third time, the vision stood over him, threatening total ruin unless he did as he was told, and adding that one day, a day of wrath, he would need this man and his family.

This occurrence enabled Justin to survive his immediate danger, and as time went on he acquired great power. Anastasius gave him command of the Palace Guards; and when he himself passed from the scene, Justin on the strength of this command succeeded to the throne, though he was by now a doddering old man and totally illiterate besides, an unheard-of thing in a Roman. It was the invariable custom that the Emperor should append his own signature to all documents embodying decrees drafted by him. Justin, however, was incapable of either drafting his own decrees or taking an intelligent interest in the measures contemplated: the official whose luck it was to be his chief adviser—a man called Proclus, who held the rank of quaestor—used to decide all measures as he himself thought fit. But to secure authority for these in the Emperor's own handwriting the men responsible for this business proceeded as follows:

Upon a block of polished wood they carved out the shapes of four letters spelling the Latin LEGI ["I Have Read"]. Then they would dip a pen in the special ink reserved for emperors and place it in the hand of the Emperor Justin. Next they took the block of wood described above and laid it on the document, meanwhile grasping the Emperor's hand, and then guided it along the pattern of the four letters through all the bends cut in the wood. After which, away they went, carrying the Emperor's writing, such as it was.

That was the kind of Emperor the Romans had in Justin. He was married to a woman called Lupicina, a foreign slave who had previously been purchased by another man and had become his concubine. But in the evening of her days she became joint ruler with Justin of the Roman Empire. Justin was not capable of doing any harm to his subjects or any good either. He was uncouth in the extreme, utterly inarticulate, and incredibly boorish. His nephew Justinian, though still quite young, used to manage all the affairs of state, and he brought on the Romans disasters that surely surpassed both in gravity and in number all that had ever been heard of at any period of history. . . .

Not a single person in the whole Roman Empire could escape Justinian's preview. Like any other visitation from heaven falling on the entire human race, he left no one completely untouched. Some he killed without any justification; others he reduced to penury, making them even more wretched than those who had died. In fact, some begged him to put an end to their misery, by any death however painful. Some he deprived of their possessions and of life as well. But it gave him no satisfaction merely to ruin the Roman Empire; he insisted on making himself master of Libya and Italy for the sole purpose of destroying their inhabitants along with those already subject to him. He had not been ten days in office before he executed Amantius, controller of the palace eunuchs, with several others, for no reason at all, charging him with nothing more than an injudicious remark about John, the archpriest of the city. This outrage made him the most feared of men. His next step was to send for the pretender Vitalian, whose safety he had previously guaranteed and with whom he had taken the Christian sacraments. But a little later Justinian took offense through groundless suspicion, and put him to death in the palace along with his closest friends without the slightest justification, making no attempt to honor his pledges, though they were the most solemn imaginable.

The Blues and the Greens

The people had long been divided into two factions, the Blues and the Greens.* Justinian attached himself to the Blues, to whom he had already given enthusiastic support. By doing so he contrived to produce universal chaos and brought the Roman state to its knees. However, not all the Blues were prepared to follow the lead of Justinian, but only the militant partisans. Yet even these, as things went from bad to worse, appeared to be the most self-disciplined of men; for the license given them went far beyond the misdemeanors that they actually committed. Needless to say, the Green partisans did not stay quiet either; they too pursued an uninterrupted career of crime, as far as they were permitted, although at every moment one or another was paying the penalty. As a result they were constantly provoked to commit crimes far more audacious still; for when people are unfairly treated they naturally turn to desperate courses. . . .

Everywhere there was utter chaos, and nothing was ever the same again. In the confusion that followed, the laws and the orderly structure of the state were turned upside down.

To begin with, the partisans now changed the style of their hair to a quite novel fashion, having it cut very differently from the other Romans. They did not touch moustache or beard at all, but were always anxious to let

---

* The rivalry between the Blues and the Greens, so called because these were the colors by which the two factions identified themselves at the circus games, dominated all aspects of Byzantine life. The Blues, it is believed, supported Athanasian orthodoxy in religion, while the Greens were inclined toward Arianism. However, it is difficult for us nowadays to determine the reasons for their passionate, even murderous, hostility toward each other, just as it would be 1500 years hence for historians to understand the issues dividing Democrats and Republicans.

them grow as long as possible, like the Persians. But the hair on the front of the head they cut right back to the temples, allowing the growth behind to hang down to its full length in a disorderly mass, like the Massagetae. That is why they sometimes called this the Hunnish style. Then as regards dress, they all thought it necessary to be luxuriously turned out, donning attire too ostentatious for their particular station. For they were in a position to obtain such garments at other people's expense. The part of the tunic covering their arms was drawn in very tight at the wrists, while from there to the shoulders it spread out to an enormous width. Whenever they waved their arms as they shouted in the theater or the hippodrome and encouraged their favorites in the usual way, up in the air went this part of their tunics, giving silly people the notion that their bodies were so splendidly sturdy that they had to be covered with garments of this kind. They did not realize that the transparency and emptiness of their attire rather served to show up their miserable physique. Their capes and breeches, too, and in most cases their shoes, were classed as Hunnish in name and fashion.

At first the great majority carried weapons at night quite openly, while in the daytime they concealed short two-edged swords along their thighs under their cloaks. They used to collect in gangs at nightfall and rob members of the nobility in the open forum or in narrow lanes, despoiling any they met of cloaks, belts, gold brooches, and anything else they had with them. Some they thought it better to murder as well as rob, since dead men told no tales. These outrages caused universal indignation, especially in those Blues who were not militant partisans, since they suffered as badly as the rest. Consequently, from then on most people wore belts and brooches of bronze, and cloaks of much poorer quality than their station warranted, for fear that their love of luxury would cost them their lives; and even before sunset they hurried back home and got under cover. As this shocking state of affairs continued, and no notice was taken of the offenders by the authorities in charge of the city, the audacity of these men increased.

All this went on no longer in darkness or out of sight, but at any moment of the day and in every part of the city, and the most eminent citizens as often as not were eyewitnesses of what was happening. There was no need to keep the crimes concealed, since the criminals were not troubled by any fear of punishment. In fact, they were moved by a spirit of rivalry, so that they organized displays of brawn and toughness to show that with a single blow they could kill anyone they met unarmed. No one now could expect to live very long amid the dangers that daily threatened him. Constant fear made everyone suspect that death was just round the corner. No place seemed safe, no time could guarantee security, because even in the most revered churches and at public festivals people were being senselessly murdered, and confidence in kith and kin was a thing of the past. For many perished through the machinations of their nearest relatives. . . .

The sons of men in high positions, after associating with these young criminals, compelled their fathers to do a number of things they were most reluctant to do, and particularly to hand over their money to them. Many unwilling boys, with the full knowledge of their fathers, were forced into immoral relations with the partisans; and women who were happily married suffered the same humiliation. . . .

Such were the acts of violence of which at that period the partisans in Byzantium were guilty. But these things cause less misery to the victims than the wrongs that the community suffered at Justinian's hands. Justinian betrayed his subjects not only because he absolutely refused to uphold the victims of wrong, but because he was perfectly prepared to set himself up as the recognized champion of the partisans; for he lavished great sums of money on these young men and kept many of them in his entourage. . . .

A Brief Sketch of Justinian . . .

At this point, I think, it would be well to describe Justinian's personal appearance. In build he was neither tall nor unusually short, but of normal height, not at all skinny but rather plump, with a round face that was not unattractive; it retained its healthy color even after a two-day fast. To describe his general appearance in a word, he bore a strong resemblance to Domitian [Emperor of Rome (81–96), assassinated in a palace plot], Vespasian's son, whose monstrous behavior left such a mark upon the Romans that even when they had carved up his whole body they did not feel that they had exhausted their indignation against him. . . .

Justinian's character is beyond my powers of accurate description. For he was both prone to evil doing and easily led astray—both knave and fool, to use a common phrase. He never spoke the truth himself to those he happened to be with, but in everything that he said or did there was always a dishonest purpose; yet to anyone who wanted to deceive him he was easy meat. He was by nature an extraordinary mixture of folly and wickedness inseparably blended. This perhaps was an instance of what one of the Peripatetic philosophers suggested many years ago—that exactly opposite qualities may on occasions be combined in a man's nature just as in the blending of colors. . . .

Well, then, this Emperor was dissembling, crafty, hypocritical, secretive by temperament, two-faced—a clever fellow with a marvellous ability to conceal his real opinion, and able to shed tears, not from any joy or sorrow, but employing them artfully when required in accordance with the immediate need, lying all the time. He did not lie carelessly, however, but confirming his undertakings both with his signature and with the most fearsome oaths, even when dealing with his own subjects. But he promptly disregarded both agreements and solemn pledges, like the most contemptible slaves, who by fear of the tortures hanging over them are driven to confess misdeeds they have denied on oath. A treacherous friend and an inexorable enemy, he was passionately devoted to murder and plunder;

quarrelsome and subversive in the extreme; easily led astray into evil ways but refusing every suggestion that he should follow the right path; quick to devise vile schemes and to carry them out; and with an instinctive aversion to the mere mention of anything good.

How could anyone find words to describe Justinian's character? These vices and many yet greater he clearly possessed to an inhuman degree; it seemed as if nature had removed every tendency to evil from the rest of mankind and deposited it in the soul of this man. Without hesitation he issued orders for the seizure of towns, the burning of cities, and the enslavement of entire nations, for no reason at all. So that if one chose to add up all the calamities that have befallen the Romans from the beginning and to weigh them against those for which Justinian was responsible, I feel sure that he would find that a greater slaughter of human beings was brought about by this one man than took place in all the preceding centuries.

. . . And Also of Theodora

He married a wife whose origin and upbringing I must now explain, and how, after becoming his consort, she helped destroy the Roman state root and branch.

In Byzantium there was a man called Acacius, a keeper of the circus animals, belonging to the Green faction and nicknamed "The Bear Keeper." This man died of sickness during the reign of the Emperor Anastasius, leaving three daughters named Comito, Theodora, and Anastasia, of whom the eldest had not yet completed her seventh year. Acacius's widow married again, hoping that her new husband would from then on share with her the management of her house and the care of the animals. But the Greens' dancing master, a man called Asterius, was offered a bribe to remove these two from their office, in which he installed his paymaster without any difficulty, for the dancing masters were allowed to arrange such matters just as they chose. But when the wife saw the whole populace congregated in the circus, she put wreaths on the heads of the little girls and in both their hands, and made them sit down as suppliants. The Greens refused absolutely to grant their appeal; but the Blues gave them a similar office, as their bear keeper too had died.

When the children were old enough, they were at once put on the stage by their mother, as they were very attractive, not all at the same time, however, but when each one seemed to her to be mature enough for this profession. The eldest one, Comito, was already one of the most popular harlots of the day. Theodora, who came next, clad in a little tunic with long sleeves, the usual dress of a slave girl, used to assist her in various ways, following her about and invariably carrying on her shoulders the bench on which her sister habitually sat at public meetings. For the time being Theodora was still too undeveloped to be capable of sharing a man's bed or having intercourse like a woman; but she acted as a sort of male prostitute to satisfy customers of the lowest type, and slaves at that, who when accompanying their owners to the theater seized their opportunity to divert themselves in this revolting manner. For some considerable time she remained in a brothel, given up to this unnatural bodily commerce. But as soon as she was old enough and fully developed, she joined the women on the stage and promptly became a courtesan of the type our ancestors called "the dregs of the army." For she was not a flautist or harpist; she was not even qualified to join the corps of dancers; she merely sold her attractions to anyone who came along, putting her whole body at his disposal.

Later she joined the actors in all the business of the theater and played a regular part in their stage performances, making herself the butt of their ribald buffoonery. She was extremely clever and had a biting wit, and quickly became popular as a result. There was not a particle of modesty in the little hussy, and no one ever saw her taken aback. She complied with the most outrageous demands without the slightest hesitation, and she was the sort of girl who if somebody walloped her or boxed her ears would make a jest of it and roar with laughter. And she would throw off her clothes and exhibit naked to all and sundry those regions, both in front and behind, which the rules of decency require to be kept veiled and hidden from masculine eyes.

She used to tease her lovers by keeping them waiting, and by constantly playing about with novel methods of intercourse she could always bring the lascivious to her feet. So far from waiting to be invited by anyone she encountered, she herself by cracking dirty jokes and wiggling her hips suggestively would invite all who came her way, especially if they were still in their teens. Never was anyone so completely given up to unlimited self-indulgence. Often she would go to a bring-your-own-food dinner party with 10 young men or more, all at the peak of their physical powers and with fornication as their chief object in life, and would lie with all her fellow diners in turn the whole night long. When she had reduced them all to a state of exhaustion she would go to their menials, as many as 30 on occasions, and copulate with every one of them; but not even so could she satisfy her lust. . . . And though she brought three openings into service, she often found fault with Nature, grumbling because these were insufficient. Naturally she was frequently pregnant, but by using pretty well all the tricks of the trade she was able to induce immediate abortion.

Often in the theater, too, in full view of all the people she would throw off her clothes and stand naked in their midst, having only a girdle about her private parts—not, however, because she was ashamed to expose these also to the public, but because no one is allowed to appear there absolutely naked: a girdle round the groin is compulsory. With this minimum covering she would spread herself out and lie face upward on the floor. Servants on whom this task had been imposed would sprinkle barley grains over her private parts, and geese trained for the purpose used to pick them off one by one with their bills and swallow them. Theodora, so far from blushing when she stood up again, actually seemed to be proud of this performance. For she was not only shameless herself, but did more than anyone else to encourage shamelessness.

Many times she threw off her clothes and stood in the middle of the actors on the stage, leaning over backward or pushing out her behind to invite both those who had already enjoyed her and those who had not been intimate as yet, parading her own special brand of gymnastics. With such lasciviousness did she misuse her own body that she appeared to have her private parts not like other women in the place intended by nature, but in her face! And again, those who were intimate with her showed by so doing that they were not having intercourse in accordance with the laws of nature; and every person of any decency who happened to meet her in the forum would swing round and beat a hasty retreat, for fear he might come in contact with any of the hussy's garments and so appear tainted with this pollution. For to those who saw her, especially in the early hours of the day, she was a bird of ill omen. As for her fellow actresses, she habitually and constantly stormed at them like a fury, for she was malicious in the extreme.

Later she accompanied Hecebolus, a Tyrian who had taken over the government of Pentapolis [in Libya] in order to serve him in the most revolting capacity, but she got into bad odor with him and was shot out without more ado. As a result she found herself without even the necessities of life, which from then on she provided in her customary fashion by making her body the tool of her lawless trade. First she came to Alexandria; then after making a tour round the whole East she returned to Byzantium, in every city following an occupation that a man had better not name, I think, if he hopes ever to enjoy the favor of God. It was as if the unseen powers could not allow any spot on earth to be unaware of Theodora's depravity.

Such, then, was the birth and upbringing of this woman, the subject of common talk among women of the streets and among people of every kind. But when she arrived back in Byzantium, Justinian conceived an overpowering passion for her. At first he consorted with her only as a mistress, though he did promote her to patrician rank. This at once enabled Theodora to possess herself of immense influence and of very considerable wealth. For as so often happens to men consumed with passion, it seemed in Justinian's eyes the most delightful thing in the world to lavish all his favors and all his wealth upon the object of his passion. And the whole state became fuel for this passion. With Theodora to help him he impoverished the people far more than before, not only in the capital but in every part of the empire. As both had long been supporters of the Blue faction, they gave its members immense powers over state affairs. It was a very long time before the evil was mitigated to any great extent. . . .

As long as the Empress [of Justin] was still alive, it was quite impossible for Justinian to make Theodora his lawful wife. On this one point the

Empress opposed him, though she objected to none of his other actions. For the old lady abhorred anything improper, though she was completely without culture and was of barbarian origin. She was quite incapable of making any mark, and remained utterly ignorant of state affairs; in fact, she dropped her real name, which she felt to be ridiculous, before entering the palace, and assumed the name Euphemia. But some time later it happened that the Empress died. Justin was in his dotage and quite senile, so that he became the laughingstock of his subjects, treated by everyone with complete contempt because of his ignorance of what was happening, and left out of account.

Justinian, on the other hand, was greatly feared and assiduously courted, for he stirred up trouble all the time, producing universal turmoil and confusion. This was the moment he chose for arranging his engagement to Theodora. But as it was impossible for a man who had reached the rank of senator to make a courtesan his wife, such a thing being prohibited from the beginning by the most venerable laws, he forced the Emperor to abrogate the laws by establishing a new one. From that moment he lived with Theodora as his legal spouse, thereby enabling everyone else to get engaged to a courtesan. Then by one bold stroke he seized upon the imperial office, fabricating an excuse to disguise the high-handedness of his action. He was proclaimed Emperor of the Romans, in conjunction with his uncle, by all the aristocracy, whom overpowering fear compelled to vote in this way. Imperial authority was assumed by Justinian and Theodora three days before the feast of Easter, a time when one is not allowed to greet any of one's friends or to wish him good day. A few days later [in 527] Justin died from natural causes, after reigning nine years, and Justinian in conjunction with Theodora became sole monarch. . . .

Sad to say, not even one member of the senate, seeing the state saddling itself with this disgrace, saw fit to protest and to oppose such proceedings, though they would all have to fall down before her as if she were a goddess. There was not even one priest who showed any disgust, and that when they would be obliged to address her as "Mistress." And the people who had previously watched her performances in the theater instantly thought fit to be, in fact and name, her groveling slaves. Nor did one soldier resent being called on to face danger on the battlefield for Theodora's benefit; nor did any other living person oppose her. All of them, I imagine, were subdued by the thought that this was the fate assigned to them, and accordingly lifted no finger to prevent this revolting state of affairs, as though Fortune had given a demonstration of her power. . . .

Now we must sketch the outlines of what she and her husband did in unison, for neither did anything apart from the other to the end of their joint lives. For a long time it was universally believed that they were exact opposites in their ideas and interests; but later it was recognized that this false impression had been deliberately fostered to make sure that their subjects did not put their own differences aside and rebel against them, but were all divided in their feelings about them. They began by creating a division between the Christians; and by pretending to take opposite sides in religious disputes, they split the whole body in two. Then they kept the factions at loggerheads. The Empress made out that she was throwing her full weight behind the Blues, and by extending to them complete authority to assail the opposite faction she made it possible for them to disregard all restrictions and perform outrageous deeds of criminal violence. Her husband replied by behaving as if he were boiling over with suppressed resentment, but was unable to stand up to his wife overtly, and often they confounded the character of their authority and went opposite ways. He, for instance, was determined to punish the Blues as criminal offenders, while she in a synthetic rage would complain bitterly that she had "yielded to her husband under protest." And yet the Blue partisans, as I said before, seemed to be the most orderly; for they were satisfied that it was quite justifiable to go to the limit in doing violence to one's neighbors. . . .

Finally, many were included in this Emperor's list of intimate friends and raised to positions that enabled them to violate the laws and commit offenses against the state to their heart's content. As soon as it was evident, however, that they had made their pile, they promptly came into collision with Theodora and found themselves in disfavor. At first Justinian was perfectly prepared to declare himself their enthusiastic supporter, but later on his sympathy for the poor fellows would dry up, and his zeal on their behalf would become very uncertain. That would be the signal for his partner to damage them beyond recovery while he, shutting his eyes tight to what was going on, opened his arms to receive their entire possessions, thus shamelessly acquired. In practicing these tricks they invariably collaborated, though in public they acted as if they were at daggers drawn; thus they succeeded in dividing their subjects, and in so strengthening their hold that it could never be shaken off.

How They Ruined the State

When Justinian ascended the throne it took him a very little while to bring everything into confusion. Things hitherto forbidden by law were one by one brought into public life, while established customs were swept away wholesale. Long-established offices were abolished, and new ones set up to run the nation's business; the laws of the land and the organization of the army were treated in the same way, not because justice required it or the general interest urged him to it, but merely that everything might have a new look and might be associated with his name. . . .

Of the forcible seizure of property and the murder of his subjects he could never have enough. When he had looted innumerable houses of wealthy people he was constantly on the lookout for others, immediately squandering on one foreign tribe or another, or on crazy building schemes, all that he had amassed by his earlier looting. And when he had without any excuse got rid of thousands and thousands of people, or so it would seem, he promptly devised schemes for doing the same to others more numerous still.

At that time the Romans were at peace with all other nations. So, not knowing how to satisfy his lust for blood, Justinian kept flinging all the foreign nations at each other's throats. Sending for the chieftains of the Huns, though he had no reason at all, with senseless prodigality he flung vast sums into their laps, making out, if you please, that these were pledges of friendship. They for their part, having received this windfall, used to send some of their brother chieftains at the head of their men, urging them to make sudden raids into the Emperor's territory, so that they, too, might be in a position to exact a price for peace from the man who for no reason at all was prepared to pay for it. These chiefs at once began the enslavement of the Roman Empire, and all the time they were in the Emperor's pay. Their example was immediately followed by others, who joined in the pillaging of the unfortunate Romans, and on top of the pillage received as a reward for their inroads the extravagant largess of the Emperor. Thus, in short, from year's end to year's end they all took turns to plunder and pillage everything within their reach. For these native races have many groups of chieftains, and the war was passed from one group to another in rotation as a result of Justinian's inexcusable prodigality. It could never come to an end, but went on circling round itself month after month, year after year. And so no single patch of ground, mountain, cave, or anything else on Roman soil, escaped being pillaged at this time, and many places were actually overrun five times or more. . . .

Throughout the Roman Empire there were many unorthodox beliefs generally known as heresies—Montanism, Sabbatarianism, and numerous others that continually lead men into doctrinal error. All the adherents of these were ordered to renounce their former beliefs under threat of many penalties for disobedience, above all the withdrawal of the right to bequeath their possessions to their children or relations. The churches of these heretics, as they are called, especially those who professed the doctrine of Arius, possessed unheard-of riches. Neither the whole senate nor any other very large body in the Roman state could compete in wealth with these churches. They possessed treasures of gold and silver, and ornaments covered with precious stones, beyond description and beyond counting, houses and villages in great numbers, and many acres of land in all quarters of the world, and every other kind of wealth that exists and is named anywhere on earth, since none of the long line of emperors had ever interfered with them. A great number of people, even though they held orthodox beliefs, depended upon them at all times for their livelihood, justifying themselves on the ground that they were merely following their regular occupations. So by first of all confiscating the property of these churches, the Emperor Justinian suddenly robbed them of all they possessed. The result was that from that moment most of the men were deprived of their only means of support.

An army of officials was at once sent out in all directions to force everyone they met to renounce his ancestral beliefs. In the eyes of country people such a suggestion was blasphemous, so they resolved one and all to stand their ground against the men who made this demand. Many in consequence perished at the hands of the soldiers; many even put an end to their own lives, being foolish enough to think this the godliest course; and the great majority abandoned the land of their birth and went into banishment. But the Montanists, who were established in Phrygia, shut themselves up in their own churches and at once set these buildings on fire, perishing with them for no reason at all. The result was that the whole Roman Empire was one great scene of slaughter and banishment.

A similar law being next passed in respect of the Samaritans, tumultuous disorders descended upon Palestine. All who lived in my own Caesarea and the other cities, thinking it silly to endure any sort of distress for the sake of a nonsensical dogma, discarded their old name and called themselves Christians, managing by this pretense to shake off the danger threatened by the law. Those among them who were at all prudent and reasonable were quite agreeable to remaining loyal to their new faith; but the majority, apparently feeling indignant that in defiance of their wishes they were being compelled by this law to abandon the beliefs they had inherited, very soon defected to the Manichaeans and "Polytheists." But the peasants at a mass meeting resolved as one man to take up arms against the Emperor, putting forward as the Emperor of their own choice a bandit named Julian, son of Savarus. They joined battle with the soldiers and held out for some time, but in the end they lost the fight and were cut to pieces, together with their leader. It is said that 100,000 men lost their lives in this engagement, and the most fertile land in the world was left with no one to till it.

Next Justinian turned the persecution against the pagans, torturing their bodies and looting their property. Many of these decided to assume for appearance's sake the name of Christian in order to avert the immediate threat; but it was not long before they were for the most part caught at their libations and sacrifices and other unholy rites. . . .

After that he passed a law forbidding offenses against boys, not inquiring closely into those committed after the passing of the law, but seeking out men who had succumbed to this moral sickness some time in the past. The prosecution of these offenders was conducted in the most irregular fashion, since the penalty was imposed even where there was no accuser, and the word of a single man or boy, even if he happened to be a slave forced to give evidence most unwillingly against his owner, was accepted as final proof. Men convicted in this way were castrated and exposed to public ribaldry. . . .

There was in Byzantium a man called Zeno, grandson of the Anthemius who had earlier become Emperor of the West. To serve their own ends they appointed this man governor of Egypt and dispatched him there. Zeno packed all his most valuable effects on board ship and got ready to sail, for he had an immeasurable weight of silver, and vessels of solid gold embellished with pearls and emeralds, and with other stones equally precious. Their Majesties then bribed some of those whose loyalty Zeno trusted completely to remove the precious cargo with all speed and drop firebrands into the hold of the ship, after which they were to inform Zeno that the blaze had broken out spontaneously in the vessel and that the entire cargo had been lost. Not long after, as it happened, Zeno died very suddenly, and the two of them promptly took over his estate as his lawful heirs; for they produced a will of sorts, which it was openly rumored was not of his making. . . .

Until the Nika Insurrection* took place, they were content to annex the estates of the well-to-do one at a time. But from then on, they confiscated at a single stroke the possessions of nearly all the senators. On all movable property and on the most attractive landed estates they laid their hands just as they fancied, setting aside those properties liable to oppressive and crushing taxation. These, with sham generosity, they *sold* to their previous owners, who were in consequence throttled by the tax collectors and reduced to penury by the never-ending interest on their debts. . . .

Were They Fiends of Hell?

In view of all this I, like most of my contemporaries, never once felt that these two were human beings: they were a pair of blood-thirsty demons and what the poets call "plaguers of mortal men." For they plotted together to find the easiest and swiftest means of destroying all races of men and all their works, assumed human shape, became man-demons, and in this way convulsed the whole world. Proof of this could be found in many things, but especially in the power manifested in their doings. For the actions of demons are unmistakably different from those of human beings. . . .

It is said that Justinian's own mother told some of her close friends that he was not the son of her husband Sabbatius or of any man at all. For when she was about to conceive she was visited by a demon, who was invisible but gave her a distinct impression that he was really there with her like a man in bodily contact with a woman. Then he vanished like a dream.

Some of those who were in the Emperor's company late at night, conversing with him (evidently in the palace)—men of the highest possible character—thought that they saw a strange demonic form in his place. One

* The Nika Insurrection, in 532, so-called from the cry *Nika!* ("Victory!") of the popular parties, was the last great uprising of the Blue and Green circus factions. Much of Byzantium was destroyed by fire. Justinian was deterred from flight only through the persuasions of Theodora, who took charge of the government and, through her general Belisarius, put down the revolt with much cruelty. Thirty thousand people were massacred; and thereafter the epoch of Byzantine absolutism began.

of them declared that he more than once rose suddenly from the imperial throne and walked round and round the room; for he was not in the habit of remaining seated for long. And Justinian's head would momentarily disappear, while the rest of his body seemed to continue making these long circuits. The watcher himself, thinking that something had gone seriously wrong with his eyesight, stood for a long time distressed and quite at a loss. But later the head returned to the body, and he thought that what a moment before had been lacking was, contrary to expectation, filling out again. A second man said that he stood by the Emperor's side as he sat, and saw his face suddenly transformed to a shapeless lump of flesh: neither eyebrows nor eyes were in their normal position, and it showed no other distinguishing feature at all; gradually, however, he saw the face return to its usual shape. I did not myself witness the events I am describing, but I heard about them from men who insist that they saw them at the time.

It is also related that a certain monk highly favored by God was persuaded by those who lived with him in the desert to set out for Byzantium in order to speak on behalf of their nearest neighbors, who were suffering violence and injustice beyond bearing. On his arrival there he was at once admitted to the Emperor's presence; but when he was on the point of entering the audience chamber and had put one foot inside the door, he suddenly drew it back and retreated. The eunuch who was escorting him and others who were present urged and encouraged him to go on; but he gave no answer, and as if he had suddenly gone crazy he dashed away back to the apartment where he was lodging. When those who accompanied him asked him to explain this strange behavior, we understand that he said straight out that he had seen the King of the Demons in the palace, sitting on the throne, and he was not prepared to meet or to ask any favor of him.

After all, how could this man be other than a wicked demon, when he never satisfied his natural appetite for drink, food, or sleep, but took a casual bite of the good things set before him and then wandered about the palace at untimely hours of the night, although he had a demonic passion for the pleasures of Aphrodite?

We understand, too . . . that a dancing girl called Macedonia, while welcoming Theodora on her return from Egypt and Libya, saw that she was very annoyed and put out by insults she had received and by the loss of her money during that trip. So Macedonia did her best to console her and cheer her up, reminding her that Fortune was quite capable of playing the benefactress and showering wealth upon her. Then, we are told, Theodora declared that actually during the previous night she had had a vivid dream not to worry about money any more, for when she reached Byzantium she would go to bed with the King of the Demons, and would live with him as his wedded wife in every respect, and as a result would become mistress of all the money she could desire.

Such at any rate were the facts as they appeared to most people.

The Cunning and Deceit of Justinian

The character of Justinian was in the round such as I have portrayed; but he showed himself approachable and affable to those with whom he came in contact. Not a single person found himself denied access to the Emperor, and even those who broke the rules by the way they stood or spoke in his presence never incurred his wrath. That, however, did not make him blush when confronting those whom he intended to destroy. In fact, he never even gave a hint of anger or irritation to show how he felt toward those who had offended him; but with a friendly expression on his face and without raising an eyebrow, in a gentle voice he would order tens of thousands of quite innocent persons to be put to death, cities to be razed to the ground, and all their possessions to be confiscated for the Treasury. This characteristic would have made anybody imagine that he had the disposition of a lamb. But if anyone attempted to conciliate him and by humble supplication to beg forgiveness for those who had incurred his displeasure, then, "baring his teeth and raging like a beast," he would seem to be on the point of bursting, so that none of his supposed intimates could nurse any further hope of persuading him to grant pardon.

He seemed to be a convinced believer in Christ, but this too meant ruin for his subjects. He allowed the priests to use violence against their neighbors almost with impunity, and when they looted the estates next to their own he wished them joy, thinking that in doing so he was honoring the Almighty. When he tried such cases he thought that he was showing his piety if anyone for allegedly religious purposes grabbed something that did not belong to him, and after winning his case went scot-free. For in his view justice consisted in the priests' getting the better of their antagonists. And when he himself got possession by unscrupulous methods of the estates of persons living or dead, and gave these as an offering to one of the churches, he would congratulate himself on this cloak of piety—but only to make sure that ownership of these estates should not revert to those who had been robbed of them.

But he went much further, and to achieve his aim he engineered an incalculable number of murders. His ambition being to force everybody into one form of Christian belief, he wantonly destroyed everyone who would not conform, and that while keeping up a pretense of piety. For he did not regard it as murder, so long as those who died did not happen to share his beliefs. Thus he had completely set his heart on the continual slaughter of his fellow men, and together with his wife he was constantly engaged in fabricating charges in order to satisfy this ambition. The pair of them were almost indistinguishable in their aims; and where there did happen to be some real difference in their characters they were equally wicked, though they displayed exactly opposite traits in destroying their subjects. For in his judgment the Emperor was as unstable as a weather-cock, at the mercy of those who at any moment wished to swing him in whatever direction they thought fit—so long as their plans did not point in the direction of generosity or unselfishness—and perpetually exposed himself to gusts of flattery. His fawning courtiers could with the utmost ease convince him that he was soaring aloft and "walking the air."

One day as he sat beside him on the bench, Tribonian [the jurist, chief compiler of the "Justinian Code"] said he was quite terrified that sooner or later as a reward for his piety the Emperor would be carried up to heaven and vanish from men's sight. Such laudations (or were they gibes?) he interpreted according to his own preconceived notions. Yet if ever by any chance he complimented some person on his virtues, a moment later he would be denouncing him as a scoundrel. On the other hand, when he had poured abuse on one of his subjects he would veer round and shower compliments on him—or so it appeared—changing about without the slightest provocation. For his thoughts ran counter to his own words and the impression he wished to give.

What his temperament was in regard to friendship and enmity I have indicated already, evidencing for the most part the man's own actions. As an enemy he was determined and undeviating, to his friends most inconstant; so that he actually brought ruin on numbers of people who had been high in his favor, but never showed friendship to any man he had once hated. Those whom he seemed to know best and to esteem most he soon betrayed, graciously presenting them to his spouse or whoever it might be, to be put to death, though he knew quite well that it was because of their devotion to himself and of that alone that they would die. For he could not be trusted in anything except inhumanity and avarice, as all the world could see; to wean him from the latter was beyond the power of any man. . . .

While he ruled the Romans neither faith nor doctrine about God continued stable, no law had any permanence, no business dealings could be trusted, no contract meant anything. When he dispatched his close friends on some mission, if they happened to do away with a number of those they came up against and collect some booty, his Majesty promptly decided that they deserved both to be and to be recognized as men of real distinction, since they had carried out all their instructions to the letter. But if they treated men with any clemency, when they reported back to the court he was ill-disposed to them from then on, and indeed actively hostile. Writing off men of this kind as hopelessly old-fashioned, he called on them for no further service. The consequence was that many made strenuous efforts to convince him of their villainous character, although their regular behavior was as different as could be. After promising certain people again and again and confirming the promise with an oath or in writing, he immediately contrived to forget it, supposing that such behavior won him admiration. Justinian regularly behaved in this way, not only to his subjects but also to many of his enemies.

He had little need of sleep as a rule, and his appetite for food and drink was unusually small. He did little more than sample a morsel, picked up with his fingertips, before leaving the table. Such things seemed to him irrelevant, as if Nature were trying to make him toe the line. Time after time he went without food for two days and nights, especially when the days before the "Easter Festival" called for such discipline. Then, as I have said, he often went two days without food and chose to live on a little water and a few wild plants, and after sleeping for perhaps one hour he would pass the rest of the night walking round and round the palace. Yet had he been prepared to spend just that amount of time in good works, the nation could have enjoyed a very high degree of prosperity. Instead, he employed all his natural powers for the ruin of the Romans, and succeeded in bringing the whole political edifice crashing to the ground. . . .

The Crimes of Theodora

Let us turn now to Theodora. Her mind was firmly and perpetually fixed upon inhumanity. No one ever once persuaded her or forced her to do anything. She herself with stubborn self-will fulfilled her own purposes with all the powers at her disposal, and nobody dared to ask mercy for anyone who had incurred her displeasure. Neither the passage of time, nor surfeit of punishment, nor any kind of appeal, nor any threat of death [she suffered from cancer], though all mankind lives in expectation that it will fall from heaven, could induce her to abate her wrath in the slightest. Theodora was never once known to come to terms with anyone who had provoked her ire, even when he had departed this life. The dead man's heir inherited the hatred of the Empress like anything else belonging to his father, and bequeathed it to the third generation. For her animosity was ever ready to be aroused to the destruction of other people, and no power on earth could mitigate it.

To her bodily needs she devoted quite unnecessary attention, though never enough to satisfy herself. She was in a great hurry to get into her bath, and very unwilling to get out again. When she had finished her ablutions she would go down to breakfast, and after a light breakfast she would take a rest. But at lunch and supper she indulged her taste for every kind of food and drink. Again and again she would sleep for hours on end, by day till nightfall and by night till sunrise. And though she had strayed thus into every path of self-indulgence for so great a part of the day, she thought fit to run the whole of the Roman Empire! If the Emperor entrusted any business to a man without first seeking her approval, such a change of fortune would come upon that man's affairs that very soon after he would be removed from his position with the utmost ignominy, and die a most shameful death.

Justinian found it easy to cope with everything, not only because of his tranquil temperament, but because, as remarked before, he had little need of sleep as a rule, and was approachable in the extreme. For there was almost complete freedom for people, even if they were obscure or completely unknown, not only to come into the presence of this autocratic monarch, but to converse with him quite freely and be closeted with him in private. But to the Empress's presence even for one of the magistrates there was no admission except at the cost of much time and effort; on every occasion they all had to await her pleasure, waiting like slaves in a small, stuffy anteroom all the time. For it was impossibly risky for any of the magistrates to be missing. Hour after hour they stood on tiptoe, each straining to hold his head higher than those near him in order to catch the eye of any eunuchs emerging from within. At long last, and after days of waiting, a few of them were called for: they went into her presence trembling with fear and hurried out again as quickly as they could, having merely prostrated themselves and touched the instep of each imperial foot with the edge of their lips. To make any comment or request unbidden by her was completely ruled out. The nation had become a community of slaves with Theodora as slavedriver. To such an extent was the Roman state being brought to nothing, what with the monarch's temperament, which seemed too easy-going, and Theodora's, which was harsh and implacable. For an easy-going temperament meant instability, an implacable one made action impossible.

If in their attitude of mind and in their way of life they clearly had nothing in common, they were as one in their rapacity, their lust for blood, and their utter contempt for the truth. Both of them were most practiced liars, and if anyone who had aroused Theodora's ire was alleged to be committing any offense however trivial and insignificant, she promptly fabricated charges that had nothing to do with the accused, and blew the matter up to criminal proportions. The juries impaneled were of Theodora's choosing, and the members were expected to contend with each other to see which of them by the inhumanity of his verdict could succeed better than the others in satisfying the Empress's desire. Thus she saw to it that the property of anyone who had offended her should be immediately pocketed by the Treasury, and after having him most cruelly flogged, though he might perhaps be descended from a long line of noble ancestors, she did not hesitate to punish him with either banishment or death. But if by any chance one of her favorites was known to have committed homicide or any other capital offense, she mocked and ridiculed the efforts of the accusers, and forced them much against their will to keep silence about what had occurred. . . .

Suspicion once fell upon Theodora of a love affair with one of her servants called Areobindus, of foreign extraction but handsome and quite young, whom she had chosen to be her steward. Wishing to refute the charge (though, if report was true, she was madly in love with the man) she made up her mind to have him cruelly flogged for no reason at all. What happened to him after that we have no idea, nor has anybody seen him to this day.

No one who had given offense stood any chance of escaping detection;

an army of spies kept her informed of all that was said or done in the forum and in private houses. In cases where she did not wish the punishment of the offender to be generally known, this is what she used to do: she first sent for the man; then if he happened to be a person of position, she would with the strictest secrecy hand him over to one of her attendants, with instructions to convey him to the farthest limits of the Roman Empire. At dead of night the attendant would put the offender on board ship shrouded and fettered, and go on board with him. Then at the place that the Empress had appointed he would furtively hand him over to someone well qualified for this task, impressing on him that he must keep the prisoner absolutely safe, and forbidding him to say a word to anyone. Only if, after dying by inches and wasting away as a result of the hardships he suffered, the unfortunate creature reached the end of his days, or if the Empress felt sorry for him, could the attendant in charge set off home.

Vasianus again, one of the Greens, a young man of some distinction, made such uncomplimentary remarks about her that she was furious with him. News of her displeasure soon came to his ears, so he took refuge in the Church of the Archangel. She at once detailed the officer in charge of the people to deal with him, not giving him any instructions to charge Vasianus with his uncomplimentary remarks, but accusing him of offenses against boys. The officer soon had the man out of the church and tortured him with an unendurable form of punishment. When the people saw a member of the upper classes who had been surrounded with luxury all his life overwhelmed with such agonies, they were immediately cut to the heart, and their groans and shrieks rose to high heaven as they pleaded for the young man. But Theodora made his punishment even worse: she had his privy member cut off and destroyed him, though he had never been brought to trial, and finished by confiscating his estate for the Treasury. Thus, whenever this harpy worked herself up no sanctuary was inviolate, no law offered any protection, nor was the intercession of a city's entire population sufficient to save the offender from his doom, nor could anything else on earth overcome her determination.

In the same way Diogenes, because he was a Green, roused Theodora's fury. He was a charming fellow, very popular with everyone, including the Emperor himself. That fact, however, did not weaken her determination to charge him slanderously with offenses against male persons. She suborned two of his household slaves, and produced them in court to serve both as prosecutors and as witnesses against their owner. He was not examined secretly and behind locked doors, as was usual with her, but in open court, a large jury being chosen from men with excellent qualifications, in deference to the high standing of Diogenes. The jury, after investigating the case with great thoroughness, came to the conclusion that the evidence of the slaves was not weighty enough to enable them to reach a verdict, especially as the witnesses were mere boys. So the Empress locked up Theodore, one of Diogenes's closest friends, in her favorite cells. There she set about her victim with many flattering enticements, and finally with prolonged physical torture. Since this treatment produced no result, she ordered a strip of leather to be wound round the prisoner's head about his ears and then twisted and tightened. Theodore imagined that his eyes had left their sockets and jumped out of his head, but he resolutely declined to confess anything that he had not done. Accordingly, the jury ruled that the evidence had failed to substantiate the charge, and found the accused not guilty, and the city with one accord kept holiday in honor of the event. . . .

Theodora made it her business also to devise punishments for the sins of the flesh. Prostitutes—more than 500 in all—were rounded up; women who in the middle of the forum sold their services to keep body and soul together. They were then dispatched to the mainland opposite and confined in the convent known as "Repentance" in an attempt to force them into a better way of life. However, some of them from time to time threw themselves down from the parapet during the night, and so escaped being transmogrified against their will. . . .

Now it happened that while she was still on the stage Theodora had become pregnant by one of her lovers, and being unusually slow to recognize her unfortunate condition she tried by all her usual means to procure an abortion; but try as she might she could not get rid of the untimely infant, since by now it was not far from acquiring perfect human shape. So as she was achieving nothing, she was compelled to abandon her efforts and give birth to the child. When the baby's father saw that she was upset and annoyed because now that she was a mother she would no longer be able to employ her body as before, he rightly suspected that she would resort to infanticide; so he took up the child in acknowledgment that it was his and named it John, since it was a boy. Then he went off to Arabia for which he was bound. When he himself was on the point of death, and John was now in his early teens, the boy learned from his father's lips the whole story about his mother; and when his father departed this life, he performed all the customary rites over him. A little while later he came to Byzantium, and made his arrival known to those who at all times had access to his mother. They, never imagining that she would feel any differently from the generality of mankind, reported to the mother that her son John had arrived. Fearing that the story would come to the ears of her husband, Theodora gave instructions that the boy was to come into her presence. When he appeared, she took one look at him and put him in the hands of one of her personal attendants whom she regularly entrusted with such commissions. By what means the poor lad was removed from the world of the living I am unable to say, but no one to this day has ever set eyes on him, even since the decease of the Empress.

At that period almost all women had become morally depraved. For they could play false to their husbands with complete impunity, since such behavior involved them in no danger or harm. Wives proved guilty of adultery were exempt from penalty, as they had only to go straight to the

Empress and turn the tables by bringing a countersuit against their husbands, who had not been charged with any offense, and dragging them into court. All that was left to the husbands, against whom nothing had been proved, was to pay twice the amount of the dowry they had received, and as a rule to be scourged and led away to prison—and then once more to watch their faithless partners showing off and inviting the attentions of their paramours more brazenly than before. Many of the paramours actually gained promotion by rendering this service. Small wonder that from then on most husbands, however shocking their wives' behavior might be, were only too glad to keep their mouths shut and avoid being scourged, conceding every license to their wives by letting them believe that they had not been found out.

The Empress felt herself entitled to assume control of every branch of public affairs according to her own personal ideas. It was she who filled the offices of church and state, investigating one point alone and invariably insisting that no honorable or good man should be a candidate for high office; no one in fact who would be incapable of giving effect to her instructions. Again, she arranged all marriages as if by divine right. In her time no contracts of marriage were voluntarily entered into: a man would suddenly discover that he had a wife, not because he had any desire for one, which is the one thing that matters even in backward countries, but because Theodora willed it. The women thus pushed into marriage found them-selves in the same disagreeable situation: they were forced to live with men when they had not the slightest inclination that way. Often the Empress would even fetch the bride out of the bridal chamber at a mere whim, leaving the bridegroom still unmarried, and merely declaring in a fit of anger that she disapproved of the match. . . .

The Destruction Wrought by a Demon-Emperor

That the Emperor was not a man but, as I have already pointed out, a demon in human shape, could be demonstrated by considering the magnitude of the calamities that he brought on the human race. For it is by the immensity of what he accomplishes that the power of the doer is manifested. To make any accurate estimate of the number of lives destroyed by this man would never, it seems to me, be within the power of any living being other than God. For sooner could one number all the sands than the hosts of men destroyed by this potentate. But making a rough estimate of the area that has been denuded of its inhabitants I suggest that a million million lost their lives.*

Libya, for instance, in spite of its enormous size, has been laid so utterly waste that however far one went it would be a difficult and remarkable

---

* Procopius puts it as "a myriad myriads of myriads," which would, of course, be preposterous. Edward Gibbon suggests that approximately a hundred million lives were lost, "a number," as he says, "not wholly unpermissible."

achievement to find a single person there. Yet the Vandals who took part in the recent armed revolt in that country were 80,000 strong, and the number of their women and children and slaves can hardly be guessed. As for the Libyans who had once lived in the cities and farmed the land or toiled on the sea—as I know only too well since I saw it with my own eyes—how could any man on earth begin to estimate their vast numbers? And even they were few in comparison with the Moorish inhabitants, who perished to a man along with their wives and little ones. Furthermore, many of the Roman soldiers and many of those who had accompanied them from Byzantium lie under the earth. Thus, if one insisted that in Libya alone 5 million people lost their lives, he would, I suspect, be underestimating the facts. Italy, which is at least three times as large as Libya, has been far more completely depopulated than the latter; so proof of the scale of destruction there will not be far to seek.

Before this war began, the Gothic Empire stretched from Gaul to the boundaries of Dacia, where stands the city of Sirmium [near Mitrovica, Yugoslavia]. Gaul and Venetia were for the most part in German occupation at the time when the Roman army arrived in Italy. Sirmium and its neighborhood are in the hands of the Gepidae; but all this region, roughly speaking, is completely depopulated. For some died in the war, others succumbed to disease and starvation, which war inevitably brings in its train. Illyricum and the whole of Thrace—that is to say, from the Ionian Gulf to the suburbs of Byzantium, an area that includes Greece and the Chersonese—were overrun almost every year by Huns, Slavs, and Antes, from the day that Justinian took charge of the Roman Empire. In these raids the local inhabitants suffered untold miseries. I believe that in every incursion more than 200,000 of the Romans residing there were killed or enslaved, so that the whole region was turned into a second Scythian desert.

Such were the consequences of the wars in Libya and in Europe. All this time the Saracens were continuously overrunning Roman territory in the East from Egypt to the frontiers of Persia, doing their deadly work so thoroughly that the whole of that region was left almost uninhabited. I do not think it possible that any human being, however careful his investigations, will ever find out the numbers of those who perished in these raids. Again, the Persians under Chosroes [Sassanian King of Persia (531–579)] thrice invaded the rest of the Roman territory and razed the cities to the ground. Of the men and women they captured in the cities that they stormed and in the various country districts, some they butchered, others they carried away with them, leaving the land completely uninhabited wherever they happened to swoop. And from the time when they first invaded Colchis the destruction of the Colchians, the Lazi, and the Romans has continued to this day.

However, neither Persians nor Saracens nor Huns, nor the Slav peoples nor any other foreign invaders, were lucky enough to withdraw from Roman soil unscathed. During their incursions, and still more during sieges and battles, they came up against many obstacles and their casualties were as heavy as their enemies'. For not only Romans but nearly all the nations outside their borders had the benefit of Justinian's bloodthirstiness. As if Chosroes was not a bad enough character himself, Justinian provided him with every inducement to go to war. For he took no pains to fit his actions to the circumstance of the moment, but did everything at the wrong time. In time of peace or truce he was always treacherously contriving pretexts for aggression against his neighbors; in time of war he slackened off in the most foolish way, showing a woeful lack of energy in preparing for the projected operations, simply because he hated to part with his money. Instead of giving his mind to the task in hand he went in for stargazing and for foolish attempts to determine the nature of God. He would not abandon the war because he was bloodthirsty and murderous by nature, nor could he overcome his enemies because sheer meanness prevented him from tackling the essential problems. Is it surprising that while he was on the throne the whole earth reeked of human blood, shed in an unending stream both by the Romans and by nearly all the peoples outside their borders?

Such, in fine, was the toll of the wars that took place at this time in all parts of the empire. And when I reckon up the toll of the civil strife that took place in Byzantium and every city besides, my conclusion is that as many lives were lost in this way as in the wars. Justice and impartial punishment for crimes committed were hardly ever seen, and the Emperor gave enthusiastic support to one of the two parties; so naturally their rivals did not lie down either. They all took to desperate courses, utterly heedless of the consequences, the one side because they were the underdogs, the other side because they were on top. Sometimes they went for each other *en masse,* sometimes they fought in small groups, or again, from time to time they laid traps for individual opponents. For thirty-two years they never missed one opportunity of practicing frightful brutalities against each other, while at the same time they were constantly being sentenced to death by the magistrate responsible for public order. But even so, punishment for the crimes committed fell almost entirely on the Greens. We may add that punitive action against Samaritans and so-called heretics filled the Roman Empire with blood. . . .

Such were the disasters which in the time of this demon in human form befell the entire human race, disasters for which Justinian as the reigning Emperor must bear the responsibility. For while this man was at the head of affairs there was a continuous series of catastrophes, which as some maintained were due to the presence here of this wicked demon and to his machinations, though others argued that the Deity, hating all that Justinian did and turning His back on the Roman Empire, had given the avenging demons license to work all the mischief that I am about to describe.

To begin with, the River Scirtus inundated Edessa, bringing on the inhabitants calamities without number. Next, the Nile rose in the usual way but failed to sink again at the proper time, bringing upon some of the inhabitants great sufferings. Thirdly, the Cydnus poured almost all round Tarsus, inundated the city for days on end, and did not subside until it had done incalculable damage there. Again, earthquakes destroyed Antioch, the first city of the East; Seleucia, which is its nearest neighbor; and Anazarbus, the most famous city in Cilicia. The number of lives lost in these three cities it is impossible to estimate; and we must not forget Ibora and Amasia, the first city in Pontus, or Polybotus in Phrygia, and the town which the Pisidians call Philomede, or Lychnidus in Epirus, and Corinth, all of which had had huge populations for centuries past. Every one of these cities has been overthrown by an earthquake during this short period, and the inhabitants almost without exception have perished with them. On top of the earthquakes came an epidemic that carried off about half the survivors. On such a vast scale was the loss of life, first while this man was acting as head of the state, and later when he reigned as monarch. . . .

One of these days Justinian, if he is a man, will depart this life. If he is Lord of the Demons, he will lay his life aside. Then all who chance to be still living will know the truth.

Harun al-Rashid

*No contemporary likeness of Harun al-Rashid exists,
but this recently discovered drawing of an oriental king
by Albrecht Dürer seems the ideal image of the
great Caliph of Baghdad as seen in the mind's eye.*

His pride arrived at its height when, having ascended
for the first time the fifteen hundred stairs of his
tower, he cast his eyes below, and beheld men not
larger than pismires; mountains, than shells; and
cities, than bee-hives. The idea which such an
elevation inspired of his own grandeur completely
bewildered him: he was almost ready to adore himself;
till, lifting his eyes upward, he saw the stars as
high above him as they appeared when he stood on the
surface of the earth.

> William Beckford, *Vathek*

S*ometime around the year 801 an embassy from Charlemagne, King of the
Franks and newly crowned Holy Roman Emperor, arrived in Baghdad bearing
gifts of embroidered cloth and offering a pact of friendship and mutual aid to
Harun al-Rashid. The Caliph, after entertaining these envoys lavishly at his
palace, sent them back across the sea in ships laden with presents for the
Emperor, which included an elephant, a pavilion and several other tents of
varicolored linen; bolts of watered-silk Attabi cloth (from whose
brownish-yellow patterns the "tabby" cat gets its name), gazelle musk and
ambergris; an ivory chess set from India; and a clepsydra, or water clock,
though this last was at one time mistaken for a pipe organ.*

*What brought about such an almost other-worldly encounter between the
legendary King of the* Chanson de Roland *and the equally fabled Caliph of the*
Arabian Nights *were the most worldly and practical considerations of state.
For both the Christian "Defender of the Faith" and the Islamic "Prince of
Believers" faced the same hostile powers at their borders: the Byzantine empire
to the east and the Umayyad emirate in Spain to the west.*

*Harun's great-grandfather, the Caliph abu-al-Abbas (who was in turn the
great-great-grandson of al-Abbas, uncle of the Prophet Mohammed), had
overthrown the rule of the Umayyad caliphs in the year 750 and founded the*

*Abbasid dynasty in its place. This abu-al-Abbas, incidentally, adopted the
monstrous though accurate surname "The Bloodshedder" (al-Saffah), which he
lived up to by exterminating the entire Umayyad line—with the exception of the
youthful hero Abd-er-Rahman, who escaped his assassins and later succeeded in
reestablishing the family in Cordova. As collateral descendants of the Prophet,
the Abbasids had a more legitimate claim to the title of Caliph (literally,
"Successor"), and thus could subdue to some extent the religious fanaticism
that had undone the Umayyads. But even so, the more zealous Moslems still
demanded a theocratic state ruled by a direct descendant of Ali, the Prophet's
son-in-law who had married his only daughter Fatima; and these Ali'des, or
Shi'ites as they were called (from shi'a, meaning sect), continued to stir up
rebellion from time to time throughout the empire.*

*Upon the accession of the Caliph al-Mansur, Harun's grandfather, the center
of gravity of the Moslem world shifted from the Umayyad capital of Damascus
in Syria farther east to the city of Baghdad on the Tigris River in Persia.
Al-Mansur is said to have built Baghdad—without the aid of djinns—in four
years' time, from 762 to 766, employing for the purpose more than 100,000
craftsmen, architects, and laborers. It was laid out in a circle (hence its name
"The Round City") and enclosed by a moat and three immense double-brick
walls, the innermost rising 90 feet. The hub of the circle, from which radiated
four highways leading by four equidistant gates in the outer wall to the four
corners of Islam, contained the Great Mosque and the imperial palace. This
palace, almost a city in itself, was sometimes styled the "Golden Gate," after its
gilded façade, or else the "Green Dome," after the dome of its audience
chamber, which rose to a height of 130 feet and was surpassed only by the
179-foot dome of the Santa Sophia in Constantinople.*

*To obtain building materials for Baghdad, the Arabs transported stone from
the ruins of the nearby Persian capital of Ctesiphon; and in a similar manner
they quarried from the ruined civilization of the Sassanid Persians their own
political structure and cultural entablature, so that in the course of time the
would-be assimilators were themselves assimilated. Under the Abbasids the
distinction between Arab and non-Arab Moslems was largely destroyed, and the*

once primitive tribal democracy of the Arab sheikdoms evolved into an oriental-style despotism. The Persian office of vizier, instituted by al-Mansur, wielded power over an immense multinational bureaucracy that effectively united the empire under one law. With his appointment of the illustrious Khaled ibn-Barmak as the first vizier, the office became an almost hereditary possession of the Barmecide family, who lived with a magnificence that rivaled the Caliph's, until they were all destroyed for political as well as personal reasons by Harun al-Rashid in 803.

Astonishing to think that from the death of Mohammed in 632 to the accession of Harun in 786—a period of time less than that which separates the Thirteen Colonies from the contemporary United States—the Moslems were able to conquer an empire that extended from Spain and northwestern Africa through the Middle East and along the steppe gradient of central Asia to the borders of India and China. And all these masses of people of different races and nations were ruled from within the concentric circles of the Round City of Baghdad fixed in the Caliph. It was from this pinnacle of being that Harun—like Beckford's doomed hero Vathek, supposedly based on the Caliph al-Wathiq (842–847), but no doubt inspired by the Arabian Nights *Caliph himself—looked down upon the rest of mankind. Along with his western counterpart Charlemagne, he abides as the very glass and figure of a magnanimous and chivalrous king; and he also (as Beckford says of Vathek) was one who "did not think that it was necessary to make a hell of this world in order to enjoy paradise in the next."*

The story of Harun al-Rashid that follows has been drawn from two main sources: Annals of the Apostles and Kings *by the Persian-born historian al-Tabari (838–923), translated into French by M. Hermann Zotenberg in 1867, and published in Paris by the Asia Society; and from* Meadows of Gold and Mines of Gems *by al-Masudi, sometimes styled "The Herodotus of the Arabs," born in Baghdad around 900 and died in al-Fustât (Old Cairo) in 956. His work was translated into French by C. Barbier de Meynard and Pavet de Courteille from 1861–1877, and published in Paris by the Asia Society. Both historians used the literary form of the* isnad, *in which, according to Philip K. Hitti in his* History of the Arabs, *"Each event is related in the words of eye-witnesses or contemporaries and transmitted to the final narrator, the author, through a chain of intermediary reporters. This technique served to develop exactitude, as did also the insistence on dating occurrences even to the month and the day. But the authenticity of the reported fact generally depended upon the continuity of this chain* (isnad) *and the confidence in the integrity of each reporter rather than upon a critical examination of the fact itself."*

Much of this biography appears in English for the first time.

The Rise of Harun

The Caliph Mohammed al-Mahdi, third of the Abbasid dynasty to rule over Islam, had two sons by his wife Khaizouran: Musa al-Hadi, the eldest by one year and heir to the throne, and Harun al-Rashid. Toward the close of his life the Caliph was troubled by a strange dream; therefore he summoned a wizard, famed as an interpreter of dreams, and told him:

"I dreamt that I gave the branch of a tree to Musa and another branch of the same tree to Harun. Musa's branch produced only some withered leaves near the stem, but Harun's covered itself with foliage from one end to the other."

The wizard replied: "Prince of the Faithful, your dream signifies that both your sons shall rule; but Musa's reign will be short, while Harun's shall exceed in length, prosperity, and glory that of any other caliph."

Not long after, al-Mahdi died suddenly at the age of 43, as the result, it is said, of a harem intrigue. One of his concubines, a Persian slave girl named Hasanah, became jealous of a rival, and sent the girl a present of a dish of poisoned pears. As Hasanah's maid was passing through the courtyard of the palace with the dish, the Caliph saw her from a window of a tower and called her to him. Before the horrified girl could utter a warning, he took one of the pears and ate it. No sooner had he done so than he cried out in agony and fell dead. Hasanah heard his cry and ran to throw herself over his body, wailing, "O my master, I desired you for myself alone, and now I have killed you!"

Just as the dream foretold, Musa now ascended the throne. Musa was a proud and haughty ruler, the first caliph who had guards bearing unsheathed swords, strung bows, and clubs on their shoulders to precede him wherever he went. He was very tall, with a florid and fierce-looking countenance, but his lower lip was deformed, too short to cover his teeth, so that during his childhood he was forever being admonished, "Musa, shut your mouth!" The nickname *Musa Itbiq* [Musa Shut-up] stuck to him all his life. He had a fearful and quickly blazing temper, and delighted in cruelty. Once, while dining with his courtiers, a servant entered hurriedly and whispered into his ear. Whereupon the Caliph arose, telling the company to wait, and was gone a long time. When he returned, breathing heavily, a servant followed in his steps bearing a large silver tray covered by a towel. The Caliph ordered him to uncover it; and the trembling slave obeyed. There upon the tray, amidst the scent of blood and perfume, lay the heads of two of the most beautiful girls in the harem.

"Know ye their offense?" said the Caliph. "I was informed that they were in love, and set my spies to watch over them. I caught and killed them in the immoral act myself."

Now Musa, who hated and feared his brother Harun, wished to deprive him of the succession to the throne in favor of his own son. One of his first acts as Caliph was to imprison his father's grand vizier, Yahya the Barmecide, for he suspected Yahya of being in league with Harun against him; but the vizier, when brought before the throne for sentencing, said to him:

"Prince of the Faithful, do you suppose that if a certain event—which I pray Allah to prevent by granting our Caliph a long life—were to occur, the people would allow your son, who is still a child, to rule over them and conduct the holy war against the infidel? Are you not afraid that someone else might then usurp the throne, and the power thus pass away from the family of Hashim? But if you respect your oath sworn in favor of your brother Harun, and have him in turn swear to recognize your son as next in succession after him, you will be acting with wisdom and prudence."

Musa meditated on this counsel, and soon after called his brother into his presence. "It seems to me," said the Caliph, "that you think too much about the fulfillment of our father's dream and covet something beyond your grasp. Beware, lest you attempt to pluck this flower prematurely, it has sharp thorns."

"Prince of the Faithful," replied Harun, "it is written that the proud shall be brought low, the humble exalted, and the unjust covered with disgrace. If the power of Islam should come into my hands, I promise that your children shall be honored as my own and your sons shall marry my daughters, according to the vow I swore to al-Mahdi."

These words seemed to quench the Caliph's anger. Turning to his treasurer, he ordered, "Carry a million dinars to my brother's palace at once; and as soon as the taxes have been collected, send half the amount to him."

And when Harun got up to leave, Musa even granted him the privilege of having his mount brought to the very edge of the royal carpet.

Yahya the Barmecide, however, suspecting the Caliph of attempting by guile to ensnare his brother in a false security, warned Harun to escape from Baghdad at once. On the pretext of going on a hunting expedition, Harun left with his guard the next day. He followed close by the course of the Euphrates and then turned into the wilderness, where he remained for a considerable time. The Caliph dispatched messengers asking him to return; but when he realized that Harun kept making up excuses for staying away, and that he himself had been duped, his heart seethed with anger. He started after him with a large army, but on the way was taken ill and forced to turn back. An ulcerous malady from which he now suffered became so severe that no one, with the exception of his chief ministers, was allowed to enter his quarters.

It was at this time that Khaizouran, the mother of Musa and Harun, began to intrigue at her palace with the Caliph's own courtiers in favor of her youngest son. When Musa heard about it he summoned her into his presence, and said in rage: "What is the meaning of all these daily processions to your door? Why is your house crowded with officials and ambassadors as if it were the palace of a king? And by what right do you grant and promise favors in my name? Stay in your place, woman, take to your spinning wheel, read the Koran and pray! If I hear once again that you are meddling in affairs of state, I will know what further means to take." Khaizouran, weeping and in disgrace, was then escorted outside by the Caliph's guard and secluded in her own house.

The next day Musa summoned his viziers and courtiers and demanded of them, "Who should behave with more decorum, my mother or the mother of any of you here?"

"The mother of the Caliph," they all replied.

"Well, then," he continued, "would any of you be pleased if your enemies were to gather in your mother's house and conspire against you? And yet I have learned that at private banquets, and even in the bazaar, my mother is the subject of gossip. People say the Caliph's mother has done this, the Caliph's mother has said that. I swear before Allah that whoever approaches Khaizouran henceforth will have all his wealth confiscated and be thrown into a dungeon." From that time on, none of Musa's courtiers dared to send messages to her or be seen entering her door.

When he had recovered somewhat from his illness, the Caliph invited his mother to attend a banquet at his palace. He gave her a plate of rice of which he had already eaten a portion (though the remainder, as he knew, was poisoned), and said to her, "I find this dish of rice excellent—taste some before it turns cold."

At the first mouthful Khaizouran felt faint and spat it out, then threw the rice to a dog under the table, which sickened before her eyes and died. She stood up and denounced the Caliph before the silent gathering, shouting, "Have you no shame or fear of the wrath of Allah to try to poison your mother?"

The Caliph answered, "No, not for that, but only because you have conducted yourself so dishonorably do I feel shame! Never before has the mother of a Caliph attempted so brazenly to rule in his place."

Not long afterward, in the middle of the night, the Caliph Musa al-Hadi died in his bed at the age of 26, having occupied the throne but a year and three months. When Khaizouran was informed of her son's death, she exclaimed, "That is what I longed for!" Some say that the Caliph died of an abscess that had opened in his stomach; others, however, assert that he was strangled while lying drunk in bed by his own slaves, and that they had been bribed to do so by his mother Khaizouran.

The "Honeymoon Years"

On the same day as Musa al-Hadi's death, which occurred in the third week of Rabi I [March] in the year 170 [July 3, 786–June 21, 787], Harun al-Rashid was proclaimed Caliph. He was then 22 years old and of a stern but handsome appearance, with pale white skin and crisp-curled black hair.

After seeing his brother interred within his tomb, the new Caliph summoned Yahya the Barmecide to the throne and told him, "My second father, it is you who have placed me here by your wise counsel and heaven-inspired guidance. Therefore, I invest you with the highest power in my realms."

He then removed the seal ring from his middle finger and gave it to him, together with the insignia of office. However, though he was now once more the grand vizier, Yahya was still obliged to submit all important matters of state for approval to Khaizouran, for she too had regained her old authority upon the accession of Harun.

That very night, in the midst of the inaugural banquet, it was announced that a Persian slave girl in his harem had borne the Caliph a son, whom he named Mamun, thus fulfilling a prophecy once made by a magician to Khaizouran: "A single day of destiny will see the death of one Caliph, the accession of a second Caliph, and the birth of a third Caliph."

Yet another auspicious event occurred during the week when a certain ruby ring, known as the *djebeli,* was recovered from the bottom of the Tigris River where it was thought to have been lost forever. This ring, believed to possess magical properties, had been passed from one king to another among the Chosroes in Persia, though the jewel itself was even more ancient. Any monarch, it was said, who engraved his name on the ring would later die of assassination, so that it was worn by them without any mark of ownership. Placed in a room where there was no light, the ruby blazed like a small red torch and illumined the darkness with its rays; only then could it be noticed that there were mysterious and faintly visible figures in the stone.

Harun rode with his courtiers to the middle of one of the three bridges that spanned the Tigris, and there, displaying the ring, said to Yahya the Barmecide: "My father al-Mahdi gave me this ruby ring. One day, when I was at the court of my brother, Musa saw it and desired it for himself. After I left the palace he sent his guards after me with orders to seize it. I was crossing over this bridge when they approached; and in disgust, I tore the ring off my finger and threw it into the river. For five months the ring remained hidden at the bottom despite all attempts by Musa to recover it. But now, by a stroke of fortune, my own divers have brought it up from this very spot on the bridge."

Harun at this time sent emissaries into all the provinces of the empire announcing his accession and demanding their oath of loyalty. He also compelled Musa's young son and heir to make a public declaration that the rightful Caliph was on the throne and to release from their vows all those who had once sworn fealty to himself.

During the sunrise of Harun's long reign as Caliph—years so filled with hope and splendor that they were known thereafter as the "honeymoon years"—the riches of the whole world poured into Baghdad, including porcelain, silk, and musk from China; spices, dyes, and rare minerals from

India; gold and silver, marble and mercury from Khurasan; ivory and black slaves from Africa; furs and white slaves from Russia and Scandinavia. Each year hundreds of millions of dinars in tribute and revenue from the provinces of the empire replenished Harun's coffers. And he, in turn, lavished this wealth on public works worthy of the ancient Pharaohs of Egypt, building roads and erecting khans and caravansaries for pilgrims to Mecca, establishing new cities and fortresses on the borders of the infidels, dredging a system of canals between the Tigris and Euphrates that made this region bloom and flourish as in the days when it was the site of the Garden of Eden.

The Caliph even planned to divert the waters of the Nile and dredge a canal that would join the Mediterranean and the Red Sea; but his vizier Yahya dissuaded him from this project, declaring, "Let no man join together what Allah has put asunder." He also warned that if the treacherous Greeks should ever become masters of the waterway they would be able to attack the heart of Islam itself and take prisoners even within the sacred territory of Mecca and Medina. The project, therefore, was abandoned.

Harun's palace occupied a third of the Round City of Baghdad, with magnificent gardens, pools and fountains, libraries and laboratories for his astrologers and alchemists, workshops for every craft, banqueting rooms, harems containing hundreds of concubines and eunuchs, as well as halls for assembly and halls of state. In the Hall of the Tree [*dar al-shajarah*] was an artificial tree of silver and gold weighing 500,000 drams, upon whose branches were set ingeniously contrived mechanical birds, fashioned of gold and carnelian, and with ruby eyes and ivory beaks, chirping spontaneously alone from time to time or in responsive duets or in chorus. Within the palace were hothouses that produced rare fruits of every variety in or out of season as well as flowers for the extraction of perfumes; and there was also a grove of dwarfed palm trees from Cathay that yielded dates as small as peas but of a rare savor. Harun was also the first of the Abbasid Caliphs to introduce the sport of polo from India and the first to play the game of chess, bestowing large rewards and pensions on distinguished players.

Harun's wife Oumm-Djafar Zubeida, grand-daughter of the Caliph al-Mansur, added her own grace and luster to the court. It was Zubeida who began the use of dishes of gold and silver inlaid with precious stones at the royal banquets, and the halls where they took place were illuminated by candles that weighed more than 200 rotls [about 240 pounds]. With Harun's beautiful half-sister Ulayyah, she set the styles and fashions of the day. When Ulayyah, for instance, devised a fillet of jewels to conceal a blemish on her forehead, all the other women at the court considered it a blemish not to wear one; and once, when Zubeida wore laced boots decorated with pearls, so as to call attention to her dainty feet, this, too, became the fashion throughout the empire. The most sumptuous *wachi* cloths were woven for

Zubeida's use alone, a single piece of this fabric costing thousands of dinars. Her pet monkey, Abu Khalaf, was girt with a tunic and sword and waited on by 30 slaves; and all who sought an audience with her, be they emirs or generals, first had to bow and kiss the creature's hand. Her palanquins were made of ebony and sandalwood, ornamented with gold and silver hinges, and covered with wachi cloth, sables, and brocades of silk. Wherever she went a troop of bodyguards composed of richly dressed eunuchs and slave girls rode on horseback at her side, executing her commands and conveying messages to and fro as she was carried through Baghdad.

One thing marred her joy in those Honeymoon Years—her inability to conceive a child for the Caliph. But even this was at last granted her when she gave birth to a son, the future Caliph Mohammed al-Amin, in 171 [June 22, 787–June 10, 788]. Zubeida's pregnancy, it is said, came about as the result of a ruse. One day the Caliph consulted a wise physician in his court on his wife's failure to provide him with an heir. The physician suggested the idea of making her jealous, citing the example of the patriarch Abraham *al-khalil* [friend of God]. Abraham's wife Sarah had also been barren; but when Hagar, a comely slave she herself had given to Abraham, became the mother of Ishmael, Sarah was so consumed by jealousy that she later gave birth to Isaac. Harun followed this advice, and lay with the beautiful Persian slave girl who became the mother of al-Mamun; and a year later—no doubt made fertile by jealousy—Zubeida conceived her son al-Amin. To wean the Caliph away from this Persian slave girl, and partly to atone for her jealousy, Zubeida during her pregnancy sent as concubines to him ten of the most beautiful girls from among her own attendants.

Harun Campaigns Against Byzantium

It was as commander of the Moslem army in the holy war against the Byzantines that Harun, in 169 [July 14, 785–July 2, 786], had first received from his father the honorary name al-Rashid [Follower of the Right Cause]. At that time the Empress Irene of Byzantium had been forced to sue for peace and pay an annual tribute to the Caliph of 90,000 dinars. But now it was learned that Irene had been deposed, her eyes plucked out by the usurper Nicephorus, who reigned in her stead.

This Nicephorus not only repudiated the treaty signed by the former Empress but sent a letter to Harun demanding the return of tribute already paid. Enraged by his arrogance, the Caliph called for his writing instruments and, with his own hand, inscribed on the back of the letter:

> In the name of Allah, the merciful, the compassionate, from Harun, the Commander of the Faithful, to Nicephorus, the dog of a Greek: Be assured that I have read thy letter, O bastard son of an infidel mother! As for my response, it shall be for thine eyes to see, not for thine ears to hear. Salaam.

When Nicephorus's spies informed him that the Caliph had drawn up his armies and was ready to march, he took fright and hastened to send him the tribute money, with many rich presents besides. Reluctantly, Harun called off the holy war and disbanded the host of Islam. But the perfidious Greek Emperor took advantage of the truce to send raiding parties across the frontier.

Harun was then suffering from an illness at his palace in Rakka, so no one dared inform him of what had happened. One day, however, a poet presented himself at court and, after receiving permission from the Caliph to speak freely, recited a long poem in which he disclosed Nicephorus's treachery and urged Harun to avenge the Moslems. Startled, Harun demanded of his ministers, "Is it true that Nicephorus has acted in this manner?" And by their silence he understood that they had sought to conceal from him the true state of affairs.

He immediately gave orders to the armies to reassemble; and all the catapults, battering rams, mangonels, and fire throwers, with which to besiege the fortified cities of the Greeks, were drawn up once more. To help devise strategy for the campaign, Harun recalled two of his most skillful generals from the Syrian frontier, Sheik Mokhalled, son of al-Husein, and Sheik Abu Ishak al-Fazari, while he himself rode before the host under the black banners of the Abbasids. After passing into Asia Minor and ravaging the border fortresses, Harun called a halt at the city of Heraclea Pontica [Ereğli] on the Black Sea.

The poet Chibl, who served as interpreter in the Caliph's entourage, relates:

"Heraclea is surrounded by a ditch, with a high front gate that overlooks a ravine. Above this gate I noticed an ornamental stone with an inscription that went back more than 2000 years. I began to translate it aloud, unaware that the Caliph was standing close by watching me do so. Here is what it said: 'O son of man, seize the opportunity of the present moment and abandon the vain striving for things that lie beyond you. Be careful lest the excess of your joy precipitate you into sin. Do not let yourself be overwhelmed by care for a day which has not yet come; for if destiny permits you to see that day, and if your life continues, God will provide for you. How many times has a man accumulated possessions for the future husband of his widow, or imposed privations on himself in order to enrich a stranger.' * Harun was considerably moved by this inscription, and caused it to be written down in his book."

Now that he stood before the gates of this powerful Greek city, the Caliph was perplexed about his course of action. Therefore, he turned to Sheik Mokhalled and asked him, "What would you advise about laying siege to Heraclea?"

"Prince of Believers," replied Mokhalled, "this is the first great city one

---

* This, of course, is a version of the legendary inscription on the tomb of Sardanapalus, here entering into Moslem legend as well.

encounters before Byzantium itself, and it is also the strongest and best defended. If you attack it, and Allah grants victory, no other place will be able to withstand you."

The Caliph then turned to his second general from Syria, Sheik Abu Ishak, who answered in this way: "Prince of Believers, this citadel was built by the Greeks to guard the strategic routes into the heart of their empire. Besides, it is none too rich, so that even if you conquer Heraclea it will not yield sufficient supplies and booty to share among all the Moslems; yet if the city holds out against you, this failure will disgrace your entire campaign. Let the Caliph therefore bypass Heraclea and attack instead one of the cities deeper into the territory of the Greeks."

In the end, however, it was Sheik Mokhalled's strategy that prevailed. Harun besieged Heraclea and for seventeen days carried the war into the surrounding countryside. But still the city held out. And the losses to his army and the growing scarcity of provisions for his men and fodder for the horses filled the Caliph with misgivings. Once again he called Sheik Abu Ishak into his presence and asked for his counsel; and the sheik replied: "Prince of Believers, at the beginning I opposed the plan of attacking this city, but now it is no longer possible to abandon the siege. A retreat at this point would blemish the authority of the Caliph, weaken the prestige of Islam, and encourage other fortified cities to hold out against us. Let us rather proclaim to the Moslems that we will remain beneath the walls of Heraclea until Allah opens its gates to us. Then issue an order to fell trees and gather stone for building a town opposite Heraclea, in preparation for a long siege. But see to it that the army knows nothing of your plans but the decision to remain here. As the Prophet said, 'War is ruse'—especially this war, which is one of stratagems, not of swords."

Without losing time, Harun issued the order, and the host of Islam immediately began to cut down trees and transport heavy stones to construct a citadel opposite Heraclea. When the besieged people saw what was happening, many of them lost heart and escaped during the night, sliding down the walls by means of ropes.

Harun now commanded that the catapults and battering rams and machines for hurling balls of fire be brought up for a supreme assault. At the height of the attack, however, the main gate of Heraclea suddenly opened and a horseman of remarkable beauty, clad in magnificent armor, revealed himself before the astonished gaze of the Moslems and cried out: "Men of Islam, we have faced each other long enough! Let one of you—let ten, let twenty—come measure your strength against me!" But there was only silence. No one dared move before obtaining the consent of the Caliph, who at that moment was asleep in his tent. Contemptuously, the Greek turned his horse about and returned through the gate unchallenged.

As soon as the Caliph awoke and learned of what had taken place, he was filled with rage and blamed his servants for having allowed him to sleep. But they said, "Prince of the Faithful, the silence of our soldiers can only increase his impudence and incite him to come back tomorrow and repeat his challenge." The angry and impatient Caliph paced back and forth in his tent all night. As soon as dawn broke, however, just as had been predicted the main gate of Heraclea swung open and the horseman reappeared. Harun at once addressed his host and demanded, "Who will contest him?"

A great shout arose, and many of the highest officers in the army rushed forward to volunteer. The Caliph was about to select one of these *ghazis* [special champions of the faith] when a delegation of common soldiers from the frontier presented themselves before his tent. Their spokesman then declared: "Prince of the Faithful, your generals are well known for their valor in battle, so that if one of them should slay this barbarian it will add nothing to your glory. But if he himself succumbs, then it may well prove fatal to the fighting spirit of Islam. Therefore, let the Caliph choose instead one among us—a band of ordinary soldiers—to encounter the Greek in single combat."

This course of action pleased the Caliph as much as it did his advisers. A certain Ibn al-Djourzi, whose courage had earned him a great reputation on the Syrian frontiers, was then pointed out to Harun.

"Are you prepared to fight the infidel?" the Caliph asked him.

"Yes," he answered, "and I pray Allah to help me."

Harun wished to give him his own horse and his lance, sword, and shield, but he answered, "Prince of Believers, I have more confidence in my own horse, and this lance I hold seems stauncher in my hand. As for the sword and shield, I accept them as a gift from the Prophet himself." After al-Djourzi had donned his armor, the Caliph kissed him farewell and sent his prayers with him. The ghazi then mounted his horse and went down into the valley before Heraclea escorted by twenty of his comrades.

When the Greek champion saw them approach, he called out in mockery, "We were agreed on twenty men to oppose me, yet you have added one more!" At this, Ibn al-Djourzi separated himself from his escort and rode forward. The barbarian raised his visor and stared at him, at first disdainfully, then narrowed his eyes in seeming recognition, but also in apprehension, and shouted, "Will you answer my question truthfully?"

"Agreed," said the Moslem.

"I beseech you, in the name of God, are you not the Syrian Ibn al-Djourzi?"

"By the heavens, so I am—and also your conqueror!"

Now they took their positions, set their lances, and pounced upon each other. The Greeks, watching from the ramparts of the city, fixed their gaze on their compatriot, while the Moslems, ranged in the thousands upon a nearby hill, cheered for Ibn al-Djourzi. The sun glancing off their polished suits of armor blinded the eyes of the spectators as the two champions charged at each other again and again with their lances. The combat continued for a long time until their weary horses could hardly carry them. Yet so far neither the Moslem nor the barbarian had received a wound.

Then, with one accord, they drove their lances into the ground and drew their swords. Ibn al-Djourzi struck at the barbarian what he thought was a decisive blow, but it was parried by his iron shield, which resounded with a clangor. The Greek then countered with a thrust that pierced through the shield given al-Djourzi by the Caliph, though it was made of Tibetan leather, blunting the point of his sword.

Suddenly, as if in fright, Ibn al-Djourzi wheeled his horse about and rode off, to the immense despair of the Moslem camp. The Greeks from their ramparts sent up a loud cheer of victory. But it was only a ruse by Ibn al-Djourzi. For as the barbarian charged after him with his sword upraised, ready to cut him down, he quickly turned and struck him with such force that he toppled from his mount; and even before he hit the ground, Ibn al-Djourzi, wielding the Caliph's sword, severed his head from his body.

This victory filled the Moslems with exultation and broke the spirit of the barbarians. Harun at once ordered his assembled host to begin their assault. That same night the Moslems succeeded in breaching the walls and wrenching open the gates of Heraclea. The once mighty city was razed and all its people sold into slavery or killed. With the fall of Heraclea, the Emperor Nicephorus hastened to sue for peace. But now Harun not only demanded that the tribute money be paid in full but, as a further humiliation, imposed a personal tax on the Emperor himself and on each member of his family.

The poet Abu Omair relates that among the prisoners captured in Heraclea was a girl of astonishing beauty, the daughter of the Christian patriarch of the city. When she was put upon the auctioneer's block to be sold, Harun's agent kept raising the bid until he had acquired her for his master. This Greek slave girl had such wiles that she captivated the heart of the Caliph. To please her, and to keep her from pining for her homeland, Harun built a city on the banks of the Euphrates that duplicated all the principal sites, monuments, and buildings of Heraclea, then filled it with thousands of his own subjects.

Yahya and His Sons

In the year 173 [May 31, 789–May 19, 790], the Caliph's mother Khaizouran made a pilgrimage to Mecca, but soon after her return to Baghdad fell sick and died at the age of 50. Though born a Persian slave, Khaizouran had helped guide the affairs of Islam through the reigns of three caliphs. All her enormous wealth, which consisted of many palaces, estates, plantations, coffers of jewels, and revenues of over 160 million dirhems each year, was inherited by Harun; and the power she had shared with the grand vizier Yahya the Barmecide was now in his hands alone.

Since Yahya felt himself too old for such a burden, he asked permission of the Caliph to retire to Mecca, where he wished to lead a life of religious devotion. But Harun, who had relied on Yahya's wisdom from his earliest years, refused to let him go, saying, "Either of your sons Fazl and Ja'far is capable of exercising authority as vizier; therefore, give your seal to one of them. He will report to me and receive my decisions, which he can then submit to you to carry out."

Both Fazl and Ja'far were actually foster brothers of Harun, for they had all been reared by the same nurse, Fatimah, a concubine of Yahya's, when the Caliph al-Mahdi had placed his son in the household of the vizier for instruction. Now, bowing to the Caliph's wishes, Yahya elected his son Fazl to take his place, for he was older than Ja'far and had more experience in affairs of estate. Though Harun made no opposition to his choice, he would have preferred Ja'far, whom he loved for his personal beauty, charm, and eloquence. Fazl, on the other hand, was of an ascetic, scholarly, and punctiliously religious disposition. He felt the greatest repugnance while attending Harun's pleasure parties, at which the Caliph amused himself by drinking *nebid* [an infusion of fermented dates] in the company of his dancing girls and musicians. He finally decided to absent himself from these orgies altogether, even at the risk of offending Harun.

Fazl's first important mission was to pacify the restless province of Khurasan in Persia, one of the richest in the empire, and to compel it to yield its full tribute to the Caliph. After completing this task successfully within a year, he was then sent to govern Iraq as emir. But soon after his arrival a revolt broke out in the province of Taberistan. This insurrection was especially dangerous, for it was led by the head of the powerful house of Ali, which had contested with the Hashimite Abbasids for the rule of Islam since the foundation of their dynasty by al-Abbas in 134 [July 30, 751–July 17, 752], and still had numerous supporters even within Baghdad itself. The Ali'de proclaimed himself the true Caliph and soon attracted a large number of warriors to his standard in Iraq.

To help Fazl crush this revolt, Harun sent an army of 50,000 men to his base in the northern Persian city of Rayy. Fazl remained there for more than a year negotiating with the rebel chieftain, and finally persuaded him to accept an amnesty. The one condition demanded by the Ali'de was that the treaty be signed and sworn to by Harun himself. Accordingly, the document was sent to Baghdad, where Harun affixed his own mark and also had it signed by his chief ministers, qadis, and emirs. The Ali'de then disbanded his forces and submitted himself to Fazl, who conducted him in triumph to Baghdad.

Harun was elated that the revolt in Iraq had been suppressed without a war. He greeted his former enemy with great cordiality and full ceremony, prepared a palace for his residence, and ordered his ministers, generals, and all the notables of Baghdad to pay him homage. The Ali'de was gratified, yet somewhat perplexed, for he had hardly anticipated so warm a reception from the Abbasid Caliph. But five months later, without warning, Harun had him arrested and thrown into the Mutbiq, the main prison of Baghdad, on the pretext of having received treasonous messages from his adherents in Iraq.

Ja'far, Fazl's brother, was then secretly commanded by the Caliph to eliminate his rival. But when Ja'far entered the dungeon with his executioners, bearing the silken noose with which to strangle him, the Ali'de exclaimed: "You, Ja'far of the Barmecides, a man of honor, have come to kill me, though you know of my descent from the Prophet and how I have been betrayed! I was sworn and promised safety by your own brother as well as by the Caliph. Yet now that I am in your power, you see fit to break your oath to Allah."

Ja'far, who felt shame at his family's role in this affair, replied: "I give you your freedom—go where you wish. If the Caliph asks me about you, I shall tell him what is necessary." He then ordered the jailers to release him, and the Ali'de fled from Baghdad immediately.

That same night Harun was informed by his chamberlain of the prisoner's escape. At the banquet table he turned to Ja'far and asked, with seeming casualness and affability, what had become of him. Ja'far answered that he was still being detained in the Mutbiq. "Swear!" cried the Caliph. "Swear by my head and my life!"

Ja'far kept silent, then said, "Prince of Believers, I do not wish to swear by your head and your life. It was my conviction that the Ali'de was powerless and you had nothing to fear from him, for he would never again find any followers. Therefore I set him free."

Still showing no displeasure, the Caliph said to him, "You have done well. I feel concerning the Ali'de as you do."

Harun did not speak of it any further that night. Without informing any of the Barmecides, however, he had already sent his personal guards to track down and kill the escaped prisoner. And ever afterward he retained a profound resentment toward Ja'far as a result of this affair.

Harun Chooses His Successor

The time had now come for the Caliph to decide which of his two sons, al-Amin or al-Mamun, would inherit the empire of Islam upon his death. Though inclined to favor his first-born al-Mamun, who most closely resembled him in features as well as in spirit, it was Zubeida's son al-Amin, in whose veins flowed the blood of the Prophet from both parents, who had the strongest claim.

The poet Ali Kisayi relates:

"One day I waited upon the Caliph at his palace in Rakka. After offering my homage and making my vows to him, I was about to withdraw, when he commanded me to approach the throne and sit down. Almost immediately the throng of courtiers moved off, and only a small number of his favorites remained.

" 'Ali,' he said to me, 'would it please you to see my sons al-Amin and al-Mamun?'

" 'Prince of the Faithful,' I replied, 'I cannot experience a keener desire nor feel a greater joy than to know how much Allah has blessed you in these two children.'

"He then ordered them brought before him. The two young princes, charming in their gentleness and gravity of manner, like two lustrous stars of the firmament, moved forward slowly toward the throne with their eyes lowered. Harun bade them approach; and upon his nod they placed themselves on either side of the Caliph, al-Amin to his right, al-Mamun to his left. He invited me to listen to each recite passages from the Koran, which they accomplished in the most impressive manner. Afterward I asked them whether they knew any ancient poetry by heart, and they satisfied me by declaiming in turn from the classics.

"The Caliph was delighted, and did not hide his joy. 'Ali,' he asked me, 'what do you say of their progress?'

" 'Prince of Believers,' I answered, 'these two branches spring from a noble trunk; they grow in fertile soil, where their roots are vigorous and abundant sap nourishes them. Sons of an illustrious father, they will reign with equal wisdom, justice, and felicity.'

"I then made a thousand wishes for their happiness, in which their father joined by saying Amen. He drew them to him with both arms, embraced them for a long time, and when he released them I saw that tears were welling in his eyes.

"Finally, he allowed them to retire, then turned again to me, saying, 'I seem to see these two children when the decree of destiny shall be fulfilled, when doom shall descend from heaven, and the time fixed by the Word of God shall come to pass. Their rivalry will cause streams of blood to flow, the honor of wives and mothers will be violated, and death itself will be longed for by the survivors.'

" 'O my Prince,' I asked him, 'is this the horoscope cast at their birth, or is it a prediction made to the Caliph?'

" 'It is neither,' replied Harun. 'This is an inexorable sentence transmitted by the sages of Islam to the Ali'des, and to these sages by the prophets and wizards of ancient times.' "

The scholar al-Ahmar was summoned to the throne by the Caliph and charged with the education of his son al-Amin. Al-Ahmar relates:

"When I went to see the Caliph he spoke to me in these words: 'Ahmar, the Prince of the Faithful entrusts you with his most precious possession, al-Amin, the fruit of his heart. He allows you absolute authority over him, and makes it his duty to obey you. Teach your student to read the Koran; inform him of the traditions of the Arabs; ornament his memory with classical poetry; instruct him in the sacred customs of Islam. Be neither so strict that his initiative is stifled, nor so indulgent that he gives himself up to laziness and carelessness. Correct him as much as you can with a kind and gentle reproof—but if this has no effect, then do not be reluctant to use force.' "

Zubeida, observing her son al-Amin's pronounced inclinations toward the young pages who waited on him, tried to wean him away from this taste. She chose several young girls from among her attendants who were noted for their charming features and elegant figures, dressing them in turbans and wide trousers, but with belts that cinched in their waists and emphasized the curves of their bodies, and bade them serve her son al-Amin as pages. Seeing them parade by in his presence, the prince was captivated and brought them out in public. As a result, the fashion of having young slave girls dressed as pages was quickly adopted by the court.

One day a Greek captive was brought before the throne to be judged by the Caliph, who then ordered his eunuch Mesrour to strike off his head. The eunuch's sword glanced off; whereupon a second executioner was ordered to complete the task, but he too failed. The Caliph then turned to his son al-Mamun, who was standing nearby, and ordered him to strike. His sword dispatched the victim with a single blow. Proud of his son's performance, the Caliph called in another prisoner; and again al-Mamun struck off his head with one blow. At this, al-Mamun's tutor Yazidi burst into extemporaneous poetry praising the strong arm and the keen sword of his master.

While residing with his court at Rakka, the Caliph once had occasion to teach his son al-Mamun that the magnificence of kings must not be confused with prodigality. Ibrahim, son of al-Mahdi and a half-brother of the Caliph, relates:

"One evening Harun accepted my invitation to dine at my house with his son. He was in the habit of eating the hot dishes before the cold appetizers; and when the latter were served, he filled his plate with what he thought to be a course of *karid* [a sort of fish stew] from a bowl nearby. After praising the sauce, he asked me why my cook had minced the fish into such fine morsels.

" 'Sire,' I answered, 'these are the tongues of fish.'

" 'It seems to me,' replied al-Rashid, 'that there are at least IOO of them in this dish.'

"My valet Mourakib bade the Caliph observe that there were more than 150 tongues. Harun beseeched him to tell how much this dish had cost; and the slave replied that the price had exceeded a thousand dirhems. Pushing his plate away, Harun swore that he would not touch any other food until Mourakib had brought him a thousand dirhems. And when this was done, he ordered the money to be distributed among the poor.

" 'I want,' he said, turning to me, and bidding his son al-Mamun observe, 'to make some amends for your prodigality. A thousand dirhems for a fish stew!' " He then seized the bowl and handed it to one of his valets, saying, 'Leave my brother's palace, wait for the first beggar who passes, and give this to him. But first tell him the price.' "

The poet Asmayi relates the anguish Harun felt in choosing his successor: "Finding myself near al-Rashid at one of his evening gatherings, I noticed that he was in a state of extraordinary agitation: now he sat down, now he stood up, now he lay down. He murmured to himself and his eyes were filled with tears. I had the feeling that he was tormented by some fateful decision.

"At last he ordered his eunuch to go and fetch Yahya the Barmecide; and in a short while, Yahya was in attendance.

" 'Father of Ja'far and Fazl,' the Caliph addressed him, 'the Prophet died without making a testament: Islam was then in the prime of its youth, the faith had just been conceived, and unity reigned among the Arabs, to whom Allah had granted safety after danger of extinction and glory after degradation. But the people were not long in disavowing his father-in-law abu-Bakr—and you know what troubles ensued. . . . The power slipped from the righteous hands that should have grasped it. For my part, I wish to make sure the throne of Islam is occupied by a man who can govern without fear or weakness. Such a man is my son al-Mamun.

" 'However, the family of the Hashimites urges that I choose al-Amin, and this despite his debauchery and his subjection to his passions and pleasures, which seem his only concern. Further, he squanders his fortune and reveals his most private thoughts as well as state secrets to his slaves and favorites. Al-Mamun's character, on the other hand, is sound, and the most important matters can be entrusted to him. But if I designate al-Mamun as my heir, the hatred of the family of the Hashimites will be turned against me; and if I should choose al-Amin, then his follies may endanger and disrupt the empire. Let me know what you think about this, for you are, praise Allah, a man with rare powers of judgment.'

" 'Prince of the Faithful,' replied Yahya, 'every mistake can be rectified except that which concerns the succession to the throne. For such an error in judgment, once made, cannot be corrected from beyond the grave. However, this is neither the time nor place to deliberate over it.' "

"The Caliph understood that his vizier wished to talk with him in private, and ordered me to stand aside. I got up and went to sit in a corner, where I was still able to hear their voices raised in passionate argument. The deliberations lasted the whole night; and the Caliph and his vizier did not separate until after a decision was reached that the throne would pass to al-Amin first, then to al-Mamun."

When the nomination of al-Amin to succeed his father Harun al-Rashid became known, the poet Salin al-Khasir wrote a long poem in praise of the future Caliph in which the name of his mother Zubeida was woven into the last verse of each stanza. In gratitude Zubeida called the poet to the palace and had his mouth stuffed with as many pearls as it could hold.

In the year 186 [802], the Caliph made a pilgrimage to Mecca accompanied by his heirs apparent, al-Amin and al-Mamun. He drew up charters regulating the rights and duties of the two brothers toward one another; and in the presence of the chief imams and potentates of Islam, both swore to abide by his wishes. Harun then commanded the charters to be hung at the sacred stone of the Kaaba. At the moment when they were being hoisted up the walls of the mosque, however, the ropes slipped and the charters fell to the ground.

"I said to myself," writes the poet Ibrahim, who was present at the ceremony, "that just as these writs fell before they could be raised up, so also will this dynasty perish before reaching its height."

It is told that when al-Amin left the Kaaba after the charters had fallen down, he was confronted by Ja'far, who stood in his path and cried out, "May you be cursed by Allah if you betray your brother!" Three times Ja'far repeated these words, and each time he made al-Amin swear to keep his promise to al-Mamun before he allowed him to proceed on his way.

The Fall of the Barmecides

Neither among the ancient kings of Persia nor the caliphs of Islam was there ever a vizier who lived in such splendor or held such limitless authority as Yahya the Barmecide. The wealth of his family amounted to 30 million dinars in revenue each year, besides numerous palaces, farms, libraries, barges, harems, slaves by the thousands. His son Ja'far's palace on the Tigris, with its immense gardens and halls of state, was worthy of the Caliph himself. The gifts bestowed by the Barmecides on poets and men of learning and musicians were so magnificent that even now the word barmaki signifies generosity and greatness of soul.

But power long held always excites envy, and the Barmecides had been close to the throne since the reign of Caliph al-Mansur. Yahya's father Khaled ibn-Barmak, the founder of the family, had adopted his name from his function as chief priest, or barmak, in a Buddhist monastery in the city of Balkh. As a result, the Barmecides were always suspected of impiety toward Islam. Their movements were spied upon by their enemies for the slightest fault or transgression of Moslem law, which would be invariably brought to the attention of the Caliph.

A certain mullah from the city of Rakka, Abu Rabi'a Mohammed, once requested an audience with Harun, at which he said, "Prince of the Faithful, how will you answer to Allah on the day of the Resurrection for having confided the empire to Yahya and his sons? For you must know that in their hearts all the members of that cursed family are atheists."

Harun remained silent at the time, but later summoned Yahya and asked him what he thought of this mullah. Yahya, who had already been informed of the incident, replied that he was a hypocrite and a charlatan who fooled the people by his pious denunciations of the sins of others. Harun then had the man whipped and thrown into prison.

Nevertheless, his words had left their mark on the Caliph; and they also brought to mind how, years before, Ja'far had deceived him when he released the rebel Ali'de from prison. Furthermore, the Caliph was proud of his own authority, and knew that his detractors whispered among themselves that he ruled in name only while the family of his vizier held the real power of Islam. And yet the crucial reason for the downfall of the Barmecides had to do neither with religion nor with matters of state.

Harun had an older sister named Abbassah, a daughter of al-Mahdi, to whom he was devoted. At the time his brother Musa had been Caliph and wished to kill him, Abbassah had risked her own life by attempting to dissuade Musa, saying, "For the sake of Islam, do not harm him! He is your brother and must rule after you." Therefore, when Harun came to the throne he showed his gratitude by sharing all his secrets with Abbassah and inviting her to his private banquets and pleasure parties. Ja'far, who also attended these revels, became fearful as time went on of the dangers that might arise from too great an intimacy with the Caliph's sister. He therefore began to absent himself more and more often until the Caliph, who understood the reason for his discretion, called him to the palace one day and said:

"My dear Ja'far, you have no lower place in my heart than my sister Abbassah. When either one of you is absent, my pleasure is lessened by half. I propose, then, that you marry Abbassah: but on condition that you see her only in my company, that her body never comes close to yours, and that you do not have conjugal relations with her. In this way, you will be able to attend all our parties without fear."

Ja'far agreed, and bound himself by the most solemn vows to accept Harun's conditions. These vows being taken by both, Ja'far and Abbassah then went through a secret marriage ceremony; but whenever they met at Harun's parties, Ja'far lowered his eyes and avoided looking at his wife, out of respect for the Caliph's honor and his sworn oath.

Abbassah, however, who was a beautiful woman and then in her lusty prime, nurtured a strong passion for Ja'far. She wrote him letters filled with reproaches for his indifference to her, but he never responded and shut his doors to all her emissaries.

In her despair, she approached Ja'far's mother, a simple and guileless soul. Abbassah brought her magnificent gifts of jewels and silks and perfumes, everything the royal treasury could provide; and after making sure that she could be twisted to her will, revealed a part of her plans. She let Ja'far's mother imagine how glorious it would be for herself, as well as for her son, to be united with the Caliph by ties of blood. And at last she succeeded in persuading her that the birth of a child, if it should happen, would cancel Ja'far's vows to the Caliph and ensure their safety.

The mother of Ja'far was elated by such a prospect, and promised Abbassah to employ any ruse to help bring it about. Consequently, on Abbassah's direction, she went to her son one day and whispered into his ear: "My child, I have just been told of a certain young slave girl who has not only received a royal education but is gracious and charming and incomparably beautiful besides, with a ravishing figure, breasts like pomegranates, eyes as large and black as a wild doe's, teeth like pearls set in coral, her hair as dark as night and enclosing a face round and white as the full moon—in sum, an ensemble of perfections such as you have never seen. I intend to buy her as a present for you, and have almost completed the arrangements with her master."

Ja'far heard these words with delight; he engraved them on his heart and could think of nothing else. His mother, however, let him wait expectantly for some time, so as to increase his longing and sharpen his desire. The urgency with which he kept reminding her of her promise at last persuaded her that the moment was ripe. She then assured him that he would possess the beautiful slave girl that very night. Abbassah, who was also restless with anticipation, received a message from his mother that all had been arranged.

Though Ja'far was obliged to attend a state banquet that evening at the Caliph's palace, he left early and, with his head still reeling from all the nebid he had drunk, hastened to keep the rendezvous. He was barely inside his house when he inquired eagerly about the new slave girl, whereupon he was told the joyful news that she had already arrived and would soon join him in his bed.

Abbassah, meanwhile, was waiting in a nearby alcove. Upon entering her husband's bed chamber, she took the precaution of at once extinguishing the candles as if in modesty, but this was hardly necessary for she found a man too drunk and too lustful to recognize her features. After his passion had been sated, and he lay in a stupor of contentment at her side, Abbassah calmly asked him what he thought of the cunning wiles of princesses of the royal blood.

"Of what princesses do you speak?" he murmured, still convinced that he lay in bed with his new concubine.

"Of myself," she answered, "your wife Abbassah, the daughter of al-Mahdi."

Ja'far leaped up in dismay, his drunkenness vanished, and his reason returned. Without further word with Abbassah, he hurriedly dressed and then ran at once to his mother's palace. Rousing her, he cried out, "Mother, for what price have you sold my honor? Now let us see how fate resolves this affair!"

As it turned out, Abbassah found herself pregnant after this one night in her husband's bed, and in due course she gave birth to a son. Fearful that her secret might be discovered by the Caliph, she placed the child in the care of two of her most trusted attendants, a eunuch called Rayyah and a nurse called Berrah. She gave them a great deal of treasure and ordered them to leave at once for Mecca, there to bring up the boy as their own. As time went by, and the Caliph's affections toward her and Ja'far remained unchanged, she considered the danger to have passed.

Now Abbassah had among her servants a Persian slave girl who had been present in the room when she gave birth to her child. One day, for having plucked a hair too many from an eyebrow, Abbassah struck her in a fit of rage with a heavy silver comb and threatened to have her whipped. The girl, seeking revenge, ran at once to Zubeida and revealed Abbassah's secret. Zubeida saw in this a means to destroy Ja'far, for she hated him not only because of his intimacy with the Caliph, of which she was jealous, but also for having dared to support al-Mamun's claim to the throne above her son al-Amin's. She waited only for a favorable opportunity to expose him.

This came about when Yahya the Barmecide, who among his other duties was overseer of the royal harem, forbade the women the use of certain recently purchased and highly attractive eunuchs. Zubeida protested to the Caliph, who summoned Yahya and asked, "My dear vizier, what complaints does Zubeida have against you?"

"Prince of the Faithful," replied the aged Yahya, "do you doubt my loyalty as keeper of your harem?"

"Assuredly not," responded the Caliph.

"Well, then," said Yahya, "pay no heed to what she can say against me."

Harun assured him that the matter was closed, and Yahya carried out his duties more rigorously than before. As soon as night fell he demanded that the doors of the harem be shut to all visitors and took the keys with him.

This further inflamed the wrath of Zubeida. The next day she went to the Caliph and asked, "What right does Yahya have to deprive me of my own eunuchs and to treat me in a manner insulting to my rank?"

The Caliph answered that Yahya was a man of great discretion whose wisdom he trusted.

"If that were so," countered Zubeida, "then he would have known how to prevent his own son from committing a crime."

Harun asked her to explain, and she eagerly blurted out the story of Abbassah's affair with Ja'far and the birth of their son.

The Caliph was deeply shaken. "Have you proof?" he asked her. "A witness?"

"Is there proof more certain than the existence of the child itself?"

"Where is he?" he demanded.

"He was here, but his mother was afraid you would learn of the scandal and sent him to Mecca."

"Does anyone besides you know of it?"

"There is not a single slave in the palace who does not know of it," she answered.

At this the Caliph remained silent. Soon afterward, however, he announced that he was about to set forth on a pilgrimage to Mecca. Though filled with rage, he concealed his resentment against the Barmecides so well that he even invited them to accompany him on the first stages of the journey. Abbassah, nonetheless, suspected the real reason for the Caliph's sudden departure. She sent a courier with a message to her eunuch Rayyah and the nurse Berrah in charge of the child, and told them to flee at once to Yemen.

As soon as Harun had arrived in Mecca and fulfilled his religious duties, he sent out his spies everywhere to search for the child. They found him the next day with the two servants, on the road to Yemen, and brought him before the Caliph. He was a beautiful boy, the likely looking son of Abbassah and Ja'far. Harun had at first intended to have him killed, but stayed his hand when he reflected that the boy was completely innocent.

On the way back to his palace, the Caliph paused for several days at a station near the town of Anbar, where he invited Yahya and his sons Fazl and Ja'far to join him. He treated them with a great show of benevolence, giving them all rich presents and robes of honor, which reassured them that nothing was amiss. But secretly the Caliph called in the captain of his guard and ordered him to leave for Baghdad at once and surround the homes of all the Barmecides and their relations, no matter how distant, even those of their secretaries and dependents. He warned that this had to be done with the greatest dispatch and without arousing suspicion, lest his intentions become known before his own arrival in the city.

The Caliph spent the whole day feasting with the Barmecides; and when they parted he paid them the royal favor of accompanying them to their horses. Then he returned and sat brooding alone in his chair amidst the remains of the feast.

Upon his arrival in Baghdad, Ja'far soon became aware of the Caliph's guards surrounding his palace and was filled with dread. Harun himself entered the city the following morning, and at the hour of the afternoon prayer, he called Ja'far into his presence and said, "I would not be without your company this evening, but I want to amuse myself with a new slave whom I favor. You too must take your pleasure with your own concubines."

He then went into his harem and began to drink heavily of nebid. After a while, he dispatched a servant to find out if Ja'far were also celebrating. When he was told that Ja'far's house was dark, and the vizier himself in deep gloom, he sent him a message written in his own hand, stating: "It is essential, I swear it by my head and my life, that you prepare a banquet and give yourself up to joy, for I derive no pleasure from wine if I do not know that you are drinking, too."

Though sick at heart, Ja'far made preparations for a lonely feast. He called in a blind singer, Abu Zakar, to console him. And while the other musicians, hidden behind a curtain, accompanied him on their instruments, Abu Zakar chanted these verses:

What do they want of us? Why do they forever trouble us?
Their only purpose is to reveal what we have kept shrouded.

When the song was finished, Ja'far called the blind singer to him and said, "Abu Zakar, my mind this evening is a prey to fear and anxiety."

"My vizier," answered Abu Zakar, "never has the Prince of Believers shown so much kindness to you as today. Rid yourself of these phantasms and give yourself up to pleasure."

Toward the hour of the evening prayer, one of Harun's servants brought Ja'far bowls of sugar candies, dried fruits, and perfumes from the royal table, with a message from the Caliph again urging him to be light of heart and make merry.

About midnight the Caliph left his harem and summoned one of his guards, a certain Yacir ibn Rikhlah, known for his cruelty and bravery in war, and said to him, "Yacir, I am going to entrust you with a mission that I believe no one else capable of carrying out. Justify my confidence in you, and be careful not to disobey."

"Commander of the Faithful," answered Yacir, "should you order me to run myself through with my saber in your presence, I would obey. Let me know your wish."

"Go at once to the house of Ja'far, take him to your tent, and cut off his head. Then bring it to me."

At these words Yacir shuddered and did not answer.

"Do what I have commanded you to do," said the Caliph, "on penalty of your own life!"

Yacir bowed his head and departed. When he entered the chamber of the vizier, Ja'far recognized him and shut his eyes, as if to drive the vision away, then opened them once more and began to tremble.

"The Caliph calls you," said Yacir.

"Give me time to enter my harem and make certain arrangements," asked Ja'far.

"It is not possible," said Yacir. "The Caliph insists that you come at once. Make your arrangements from here."

Ja'far obeyed, and Yacir then conducted him to his own tent on the palace grounds. Once inside he drew his sword and told him, "The Caliph has commanded me to bring him your head."

"Take care!" Ja'far warned. "It is possible that he gave you the order while drunk, and will surely regret it later."

"No, he was not drunk," said Yacir.

Ja'far then beseeched him to spare his life until the order could be confirmed. "Let me accompany you into the palace," he pleaded, "and if the Prince of the Faithful still demands my head you can carry out your mission at once."

Yacir, who dreaded to perform the deed, allowed himself to be persuaded; and together the condemned man and his executioner went as far as Harun's chamber. While Ja'far remained outside, where he could hear what was said, Yacir entered the room.

The Caliph, seated on a prayer rug, was waiting for him expectantly. He immediately demanded, "Where is Ja'far's head?"

"Oh, my Prince," replied Yacir, "I have brought you Ja'far."

"It is not Ja'far I asked for," said the Caliph, "but Ja'far's head!"

Yacir returned at once to where Ja'far was standing behind a curtain. "Did you hear?" he asked.

"Yes," said Ja'far. "Do what you have been commanded to do."

Taking a silken scarf out of his pocket, Ja'far blindfolded himself and offered his neck. Yacir, with one stroke, cut off his head and brought it to the Caliph, who had it placed before him on a table; then he began to speak to it, tearfully, reciting all his grievances, as if it were still alive. When he had finished, he ordered Yacir to summon his chief eunuch Mesrour.

As soon as Mesrour arrived, he pointed to Yacir and said, "Take this man away and have him beheaded. I can't bear the sight of Ja'far's executioner!"

After this had been done, the Caliph told Mesrour, "Keep the head and body of Ja'far until I ask for them. Now go at once and arrest Yahya and his son Fazl, their families and their aides, and place them in chains in the Mutbiq. Then confiscate all their possessions."

Harun's vengeance extended even to his own sister Abbassah, and she and those of her intimates who had known her secret were strangled with silken cords in the harem that same night. At daybreak the Caliph had Ja'far's head displayed above one of the three bridges of Baghdad, while his body, which was cut in half, was impaled on the other two. Fazl was executed that day by having his throat cut in Harun's presence; and the rest of the Barmecides, when all their wealth had been extracted from them by torture, were similarly disposed of. Yahya himself, however, was kept in chains in prison, so as to suffer the grief of surviving the destruction of his family.

The poet Asmayi relates: "Harun sent for me that night. As soon as he saw me enter, he said, 'I have written some lines that I wish to show you.'

" 'Speak, Sire,' I answered, and he recited the following:

'If Ja'far had feared death, a swift charger, bridled for the trip, would have saved his life.
To avoid death, he would have been able to find a shelter inaccessible to the eagles of the mountain tops.
But his time having come, no wizard would have been clever enough to avoid his fate.'

When Harun's cruelty became known, it aroused widespread indignation and sadness throughout Islam. There were more elegies composed by poets on the downfall of the Barmecides than there had been eulogies addressed to them during the years of their prosperity. Without the guidance of Yahya and his sons, the ties that bound the empire were weakened, its luster dimmed, and even Harun came to repent his actions.

It is said that one day his half-sister Ulayyah, while playing a game of chess with the Caliph, during which he sat inattentive and brooding in silence, dared to ask him, "I have not seen you enjoy a day of happiness since you put Ja'far to death. Why did you do it?"

And he replied, "If I thought that even my innermost garment knew the reason, I would tear it to pieces."

Revolution in Persia

As the Caliph's health began to fail, he removed his court from Baghdad to the more pleasant climate of the resort city of Rakka, on the upper Euphrates, which soon became a second capital. To this court there came one day a delegation of notables from the wealthy province of Khurasan in Persia to lodge a complaint against the emir, one Ali ben Isa. They charged the emir with corruption and debauchery, squandering millions of dirhems on palaces for himself and his favorites in the city of Balkh, money that he had confiscated from the people by oppressive taxes, fraud, bribes, and even violence. They further warned that unless Ali were removed from office, the immense fortune he had accumulated would enable him to revolt against the Caliph and establish a separate kingdom in Khurasan.

Several years before, this emir had brought Harun so many rich presents, including 150 camels laden with wachi cloth, that the astonished Caliph had said to his vizier Yahya the Barmecide, "Where have the treasures of Khurasan been until now?" It was a veiled reproach, for Yahya's son Fazl had once been governor of the same province. Yahya had replied at the time, "Those are treasures that the emir Ali has extorted from his subjects. If you wish, I can have a number of merchants put to the torture and, in a short while, bring you even greater riches."

Now Harun decided to investigate the charges against Ali himself. After dismissing the delegation from Khurasan, he went with a large army to the city of Rayy; and there, to test Ali's loyalty, he summoned him to come at once without his armed escort. Ali soon arrived as ordered, but bearing his usual splendid gifts of merchandise and beautiful slaves; and once again he won the Caliph's favor and was sent back to govern Khurasan. However, the matter did not rest there, for events occurred that opened Harun's eyes.

It seems that a certain high officer of the Samarkand garrison named Rafi al-Laith, a man who loved wine and women to excess, became involved in amorous intrigue with the wife of one of Harun's courtiers. Rafi persuaded her to run off with him to Samarkand and break her marriage vows. Since the woman was not a Moslem at the time, she adopted the faith and, after the proper legal interval, was married to Rafi. The husband appealed to the

Caliph for retribution, and when Harun learned the facts of the case, he determined to make a public example of the miscreant. He therefore wrote to Ali, who had jurisdiction as emir over Samarkand, and ordered him to throw Rafi into prison and compel him to divorce his wife. As a further humiliation, Harun decreed that Rafi was to have his face blackened with soot and then led riding backward on an ass through the streets of the city.

Ali immediately transmitted the Caliph's order to his prefect in charge of the garrison in Samarkand. This prefect, however, was a close drinking companion and old comrade-in-arms of Rafi; and though he put him in prison and forced him to divorce his wife, he otherwise treated him with respect. A short while later, deeming the Caliph's rage already spent, he permitted him to escape. Rafi then fled to the city of Balkh, where he remained in hiding while seeking a pardon from the emir. Ali, as was his custom, extracted a huge bribe from the fugitive before he pardoned him and allowed him to return to Samarkand.

Since he was now a semi-outlaw, Rafi placed himself at the head of a band of rebel warriors and adventurers who lived by plundering the caravans of merchants and kidnapping public officials for ransom. But so much did the people of Samarkand hate the emir Ali and his confederates that he soon grew powerful enough to seize control of the garrison. He then remarried his wife, in open defiance of the Caliph, and even proclaimed himself ruler of Samarkand.

Ali at once sent his own son with a large army to put down the rebellion; but Rafi not only repulsed the attack, adding the soldiers he took prisoner to his own forces, but killed Ali's son and placed his head on a pike above the city gates. The emir himself then marched against Samarkand. After a fierce battle, he too was beaten and had to take refuge in the city of Merv, from which he sent a desperate message to Harun for assistance.

While he was still waiting for a reply, the citizens of Merv also revolted, killing Ali's tax collector, a man hated for his cruel extortions, and looting his house. It is said that more than 30 million dirhems were found buried in the garden. Before Ali succeeded in crushing the rebels, they sent a letter to the Caliph, stating that they were still loyal to the thone but wanted no more of the emir. This letter arrived not long after Ali's own plea for aid.

With these in hand, Harun now summoned one of his most trusted generals, Harthama ibn A'yan, and told him: "I want to send you on a mission whose purpose must remain absolutely secret with you for the time being. Leave for Khurasan and take control of that province as emir. However, should Ali learn that I have invested you with his powers, he would surely resist with arms. Therefore, tell your troops that you are marching to Ali's aid, so as to confuse his spies; and when you are already under way, write to him that you are bringing reinforcements to fight the outlaw Rafi. Once you are in Merv with your army, arrest Ali and place him in chains. He must be forced to give back all the treasure he has extorted from the Moslems. If he refuses to do this willingly, torture him until he does so."

The Caliph then harangued the people, telling them of Rafi's rebellion and letting them believe that Harthama was marching to Ali's assistance. That same day he wrote out Harthama's commission as emir with his own hand, and gave him three other letters besides: one was to the people of Khurasan asking them to obey their new ruler; another was to the army stationed at the various garrisons demanding their allegiance; and the third was to Ali himself. This last letter was phrased as follows:

"In the name of Allah the just and merciful: O son of a whore, I showered you with my generosity, I raised you, from a mere captain of the guards, to be emir of Khurasan, ignoring the advice of my ministers who told me you were unworthy, yet this is the way you repay me! You grind down the people of Islam into such wretchedness and despair as to leave them no course but to revolt. I am now sending my general Harthama with full powers to arrest you and impound your treasure and compel you to give up all you have seized by force and fraud. Hand over your seal as emir to him and obey his orders."

Bearing these commissions, Harthama set out at once for Merv with an army of 20,000 men. The Caliph also sent along his own personal aide to watch over Harthama and make sure he showed no mercy to Ali, for he knew the two men had once been close comrades-in-arms.

When Harthama arrived at the gates of Merv, Ali was already there with a large and brilliantly attired escort waiting to greet him. He wanted to get down from his horse, as an act of homage to the Caliph's emissary, but Harthama prevented him, saying, "If you get down I will get down, too." Riding side by side, they thus entered the city; and when they reached a certain bridge wide enough for only one rider to pass at a time, Ali reined in his horse to permit Harthama to go first, but Harthama said, "You are the emir—I shall not precede you." All these shows of deference reassured Ali about his intentions.

Upon arriving at the emir's palace, Harthama found that a large banquet had already been prepared for him and his officers. After the festivities Ali said to his guest, "I have arranged for you to stay here at my palace so that we can begin our discussions early tomorrow."

Harthama replied, "That will not be soon enough. The Prince of Believers has entrusted me with a letter that I must give to you at once." He then took the emir aside, away from his own cohorts at the banqueting table, and called the master of the post to hand over the letter from the Caliph. Ali broke the seal, and as his eyes fell upon the first words, "O son of a whore . . ." his hand started to tremble. When he had finished reading the letter he said, "The Caliph is right. I am the son of a whore, because at one time he kept me in his palace the way one keeps a concubine."

Harthama summoned his officers to place him in chains, then proceeded to the Great Mosque at Merv, where he announced to all the notables assembled there his commission as the new emir. They received him with acclaim and swore their allegiance to him and to the Caliph. After confiscating Ali's treasure and household possessions, he held court every day in the Great Mosque, with Ali standing shackled beside his throne, so that anyone who had a grievance against him could make his charge and receive indemnity.

Meanwhile, the Caliph learned that Rafi's revolt had already spread to Transoxiana, and that Rafi himself had left Samarkand to take possession of the city of Bukhara. Harun now resolved, despite his continuing illness, to take to the field at the head of an army of 50,000 men. He placed the government in Baghdad in the hands of his son and heir al-Amin, entrusting him also with control of the empire in Iraq between the frontiers of the Maghreb and the heights of Holwan [Sar-i-Pul]; while to his son al-Mamun he gave supreme authority over Khurasan during the time he himself was away, together with the command over the rest of the army.

Learning of this, Zubeida went immediately to the Caliph and declared, "Prince of the Faithful, you are unjust to our son al-Amin, for you give him merely the rule of Iraq, and refuse him subsidies and generals, while to al-Mamun you hand over the army and power in Khurasan."

"Who are you, woman," replied the Caliph, "to dispute our actions and judge our decisions? I gave a peaceful province to your son, but to al-Mamun a province in a state of war. The ruler of a hostile country obviously has more need of arms. And besides, should al-Amin one day be proclaimed the Caliph, it is his hatred against al-Mamun that I fear, but not the reverse."

Now, it was well known in the palace that, even as he was preparing to leave for Khurasan, the Caliph was suffering intensely from his old illness. Al-Mamun's adviser, a man of Persian descent recently converted to Islam, therefore urged him to accompany Harun, declaring, "If you are apart from the Caliph and, may Allah forbid, he should suddenly die, your brother al-Amin will surely attempt to wrest your power away from you." Al-Mamun followed this counsel, and joined the Caliph's expedition with his own force of 30,000 men.

Harun's Last Campaign

Upon reaching the ancient Persian capital of Ctesiphon, on the banks of the Tigris, Harun encamped with his army close by the once magnificent but now ruined palace of the Iwan Kisra. One day he heard an attendant saying to another behind his tent, "This palace was built by a man descended from a family that had the audacity to seek to raise itself from earth up to the heavens." The Caliph at once summoned his guards and ordered them to give the attendant a hundred lashes, saying to those present: "Power establishes a certain solidarity and brotherhood among kings. I have punished this man out of the consideration that kings owe one another, so as to maintain awe of the throne."

At the same time, however, he decided to tear down the remains of the Iwan Kisra, for he felt that it served as a dangerous reminder to the Persians of their vanished glory. But before issuing the decree, he sent a courier with a message to his old vizier, Yahya the Barmecide, who still lay shackled in prison, and asked for his counsel. Yahya, in response, strongly urged him not to do so. Whereupon Harun told his courtiers, "The cult of the Persian magis is still in his heart!" and commanded his army to proceed forthwith in its destruction. But after several weeks, finding the work of demolishing the massive walls and pillars of the palace too difficult and costly, he ordered it stopped; and once more he wrote to Yahya to tell him of his decision, thinking it would please him. But now his vizier wrote back and urged him to spare no effort in tearing it down.

Puzzled by this contradictory advice, the Caliph sent for an explanation, and Yahya replied: "Prince of the Faithful, when I first offered my opinion, my aim was to increase the glory of the Moslems. I wished future nations, seeing the Iwan Kisra, to say, 'The people who conquered a land that could raise such a palace must have been invincible.' But now that I learn the work of demolition has been stopped, I wish to spare the Moslems the shame of having it said that they were unable to destroy what the Persians erected."

When these words were reported to the Caliph, he cried out in admiration, "May Allah curse that man—he is always right!"

Soon after this the Caliph departed with his army from Ctesiphon, and upon reaching the fortress of Nahrewan his illness took a crucial turn. At once he dispatched an embassy bearing rich gifts to the King of Hindustan, with the following message: "I am stricken with a serious ailment while obliged to make a long journey. Send your physician Manka to Khurasan to administer to me; and I will return him to you when I reach the city of Balkh." The King of Hindustan immediately responded to his request, and under Manka's treatment Harun improved enough for him to continue his march.

After crossing the heights of Holwan, the Caliph harangued his army and made the soldiers repeat their oath of loyalty to his sons al-Amin and al-Mamun. He then sent the general Harthama into Transoxiana to war against Rafi, while al-Mamun was ordered to set up a rear base at Merv. Harun himself departed for Rayy, and from thence proceeded to the walled city of Gorgan, where he was to judge the disgraced emir of Khurasan. Ali was dragged before him in chains, and his treasure, amounting to 50 million dirhems, was piled in heaps of silver and gold before the throne. Harun spared his life, but condemned him to perpetual and solitary imprisonment in the Mutbiq.

The Caliph's illness, despite all the efforts of Manka, now grew more severe, so he decided to leave for the more healthful climate of the city of

Tus in Khurasan. His own physician, Bakhtischou, disagreed with Manka on what cure to follow. Once arrived in Tus, therefore, Harun sent for a noted Persian empiric who practiced there to ask his opinion. Several vials of urine, among them one from the Caliph, were presented to him. After examining the Caliph's vial, whose origin he did not know, the Persian declared, "Tell the man that he is lost, and warn him to make his will at once, for his sickness is beyond remedy." Upon hearing these words, Harun wept bitterly and writhed in despair upon his couch.

The weakness of the Caliph compelled him to remain secluded in his palace, where he was visited only by his chief ministers and his physicians. As a result, the rumor that he was already dead began to be whispered among the people. When Harun became aware of this, he immediately determined to show himself before them. After being dressed in his state robes, he ordered an ass to be saddled and brought to him. Once mounted, however, his legs hung down inertly and he could hardly support himself. "Help me to descend," he said at last. "The prophets of doom have told the truth."

That same day he asked for several winding-sheets to be spread before him, chose one, and then commanded that he be carried outside into the garden where he could watch his grave being dug in his presence. After this was done, he peered down into it for a long time, then recited these words from the Koran: "What is the good of all my riches? My regal power has faded away."

While the Caliph thus lay near death, his general Harthama marched against the city of Bukhara and there defeated the armies of the traitor Rafi. Rafi himself was killed in the battle, but his brother, Bischr, was captured alive and sent to al-Mamun in Merv, who in turn sent him to the Caliph in Tus. When the prisoner was brought to his bedside, Harun denounced him, saying, "Enemy of Allah, it is you and your dog of a brother who forced me to undertake this campaign during my illness, and thus brought about my own death. Now I shall inflict upon you the worst punishment that has ever been endured by anyone."

He ordered a butcher from the public slaughterhouse at Tus to be brought in, and commanded him to cut off in his presence all of Bischr's limbs in succession, beginning with the toes of his feet and the fingers of his hands, joint by joint; and then the rest of his carcass was hacked into four pieces.

The next day the Caliph called together all the members of the Hashimite family, and addressed them thus: "All that lives must perish, all that is young grows old. For see what destiny has done with me. I offer you three counsels: keep your promises firmly; be faithful to your imams and united among yourselves; and last, watch over my sons al-Amin and al-Mamun, and should one of them revolt against his brother, condemn his perfidy." Afterward he distributed great sums of treasure, domains, and palaces among them.

The poet Asmayi relates: "That day I found the Caliph deeply absorbed in reading while the tears flowed down his cheeks. I remained standing, waiting for him to calm himself. Finally, he invited me to sit down. He then asked whether I had witnessed his tears. 'Yes, Sire,' I answered. He said, 'You would not have seen them flow for any worldly consideration,' and handed me a paper on which were inscribed these verses:

> Where are all the kings who have lived before your time?
> They have departed where you too shall go in turn.
> O you who crave pleasure, O you who seek flattery,
> Give up your vain illusions, for death draws near.

'Would you not say,' asked the Caliph, 'that these words were addressed especially to me?' "

On the third day of the month of Jumada II [June], in the year 193 [Oct. 25, 808–Oct. 14, 809], the Caliph Harun al-Rashid died in Tus and was buried in the grave that he had seen opened before his eyes. He was then 45 years old and had reigned for 23 years, leaving 13 sons that he acknowledged.

Aftermath: The Prophecy Fulfilled

Al-Amin's first act after being proclaimed Caliph was to send for the charters of succession that Harun had hung on the walls of the Kaaba in Mecca, and tear them to pieces. He then named his own son as heir to the throne, asserting that al-Mamun's nomination had been due to an evil spell laid on his father by Yahya the Barmecide. His brother's wife, Oumm-Isa, and her two sons, who had been left behind in Baghdad when al-Mamun set out for Khurasan with the army, al-Amin now held as hostages; and he also confiscated his brother's share of the 900 million dinars left as their inheritance by Harun in the treasury at Rakka. As a final act of contempt, he ordered his men to break into Oumm-Isa's palace and take from her by force certain rare jewels that his mother Zubeida coveted for herself. The civil war between the two brothers, which had long been prophesied, now became a reality.

As Caliph al-Amin was able to indulge his taste for luxury and unnatural vices without fear of censure. He installed hundreds of eunuchs and ghilmans [catamites] inside the palace and dressed them as girls, dividing them into a troop of blacks, named by him "The Ravens," and of whites, called "The Grasshoppers." For his pleasure parties on the Tigris he built five huge barges of rare woods, ebony, and mother-of-pearl shaped like animals—a lion, an eagle, a dolphin, an elephant, a horse—each one estimated to have cost millions of dinars. He kept about him at all times a hundred singing girls ready to amuse him at a moment's notice with their songs, and to keep it up all night, if need be, in relays of ten. Al-Amin's royal banquets and festivities, and the lavish gifts he bestowed on his favorites, drained even the seemingly inexhaustible riches of Baghdad.

Accompanying him in his escapades was the libertine poet abu-Nuwas, who had been a favorite of his father Harun as well; and once, for having chanted certain verses by this poet celebrating the delights of pederasty, al-Amin is said to have presented a singer at a banquet with the sum of 300,000 dinars.

Meanwhile, at his base in the city of Merv, al-Mamun was gathering to his standard warriors and adherents from every province in the empire. His army was divided into two distinct forces: one led by the veteran Arab general Harthama, who had crushed Ali's revolt, and the other by a Persian commander, Tahir, for al-Mamun's own Persian blood on his mother's side had made him the champion of all the non-Arab peoples converted to Islam.

When al-Amin learned that his brother was in the field, he prepared a great army to meet him. In expectation of an easy victory, Zubeida gave her son a silver chain with which to lead al-Mamun captive through the streets of Baghdad. However, three successive and disastrous defeats by al-Mamun, the last and most decisive at the heights of Holwan, forced the Caliph to retreat behind the walls of Baghdad. When revolts broke out within the city itself, which were put down only with much bloodshed, al-Mamun sent his forces to besiege it.

The blockade continued for nearly two years, during which time famine and pestilence were widespread and criminal bands roamed the streets. Al-Amin, who had taken refuge in his mother's palace, now realized that his cause was hopeless. Zubeida persuaded him to surrender to the Arab general Harthama, rather than risk falling into the hands of the Persian Tahir; for then, she advised, by holding his brother's wife and children as hostages, he might obtain a favorable peace settlement from al-Mamun.

On the night of the twenty-fifth day of Muharram [January], 198 [Sept. 1, 813–Aug. 21, 814], the Caliph attempted to cross the Tigris in a barge with a few close followers to reach Harthama's lines. The barge was so loaded with treasure, however, which al-Amin intended to use as bribes, that it capsized and sank. The Caliph managed to swim ashore, but was seized and beheaded by Harthama's troops, who mistook him for a spy. Al-Amin's head was then sent to al-Mamun, who had it stuck on a spear and displayed before the main gate of the city.

Baghdad itself, ravaged by the siege and the long civil war, never recovered the splendor it had possessed during the reign of Harun al-Rashid.

The Once and
Future King
of Cambodia

Head of a deva-raja, or divinized ruler.

Civilization is hooped together, brought
Under a rule, under the semblance of peace
By manifold illusion; but man's life is thought,
And he, despite his terror, cannot cease
Ravening through century after century,
Ravening, raging, and uprooting that he may come
Into the desolation of reality:
Egypt and Greece, good-bye, and good-bye, Rome!

W. B. Yeats, *Meru*

*I*t might help to justify the ways of God, or history, to man if we imagine that
the Chinese diplomatic mission that departed from Cambaluc (now Peking) for
the distant southern kingdom of Chen-la (Cambodia) in June of 1295, a year
after the death of the great Kublai Khan, had crossed the path of Marco Polo's
caravan heading westward back to Venice about the same time. One of the
members of that Chinese mission was Chou Ta-kuan, author of these
Recollections of the Customs of Cambodia, *who had as childlike a sense of*
wonder as Marco Polo's. But his report may be even more valuable, for it has
survived as the sole eyewitness account of the vanished civilization of the
Khmers.

Though Chou Ta-kuan, as a member of a master race, referred to the
Khmers as "barbarians," not even Kublai Khan had ever decreed at Xanadu a
pleasure dome statelier than the temple-tomb-palace complexes at the capital of
Angkor. The most famous of these, Angkor Wat, comprised a square mile of
sculptured stone, the largest continuous expanse of bas-relief and statuary in
existence, which was surrounded by a moat so as to form a vast mandala
symbolizing the cosmos. ("Heaven is round, earth square," so the Buddhist
scripture affirms.) The vital center of Angkor was the deva-raja, or god-king,
from whom radiated all state power as well as religious and moral authority.
Regarded by the Khmers as the living Buddha, the King carried out even in his
daily life the four-square and logically symmetrical symbolism of the mandala.

118

For instance, he had 4 official wives, one for each point of the compass, plus another for his amusement; 4000 concubines to loll about the palace; and he appeared in public on a golden palanquin supported by 4 palace maidens, one at each corner.

Only the pharoahs of ancient Egypt were so hedged about from birth to death by divinity; and it is likewise only in Egypt that there can be found such prodigious monuments dedicated to the apotheosis of a supreme individual. At the Bayon of Angkor Thom, the greatest of the Cambodian monarchs, Jayavarman VII (1181–1219), constructed around the year 1190 an immense four-sided tower from which he could gaze out at over 250 colossal stone images of himself idealized as the Bodhisattva, or Buddha of the Future, smiling with a wider and more self-satisfied, though no less inward, smile.

At Phnom Bakheng, a natural hill in which the deva-raja, as King of the (World) Mountain, is supposed to have been buried, there was a central shrine composed of five towers on the summit, with 104 smaller towers at the approaches, adding up to 109. This was a sacred number, for it was believed that 108 cosmic revolutions around a single polar axis ($1 + 108 = 109$) comprised the Great Year. "Phnom Bakheng," writes Christopher Pym in his The Ancient Civilization of Angkor, *"is the prime example of a diagram in time and space"—even superior, it might be added, to the Druidic temple of Stonehenge. The mystical Mount Meru of Hindu mythology, posited as the navel of the universe, was thus reproduced in stone at Phnom Bakheng.*

Chou Ta-huan's interest in all these architectural marvels, however, was secondary to his curiosity about the Khmer people, especially the girls at Angkor. In several instances, the customs and mores he describes are reminiscent of our own in the United States nowadays, such as: the gradation in prestige of the types of palanquins supplied to state functionaries, from gold-handled down to silver- and wood-handled, just as we supply our own bureaucrats with conveyances ranging from private jets to free subway tokens; also, the digital ceremonial defloration of virgins by Buddhist priests, not too different from those teen-age "anti-virginity" clubs that flourish secretly in the hinterlands and are exposed from time to time; also, those astonishing muggers of Angkor who used to waylay the unwary at night and extract their gall, so as to provide a jar of the stuff for the King each year. Our own more prosaic muggers merely extract money from the Man to exchange for junk, but if there be any advantage in style or personal dignity, it probably lies with the Khmers. . . .

At the time Chou Ta-kuan sojourned in Angkor, the great period of temple building was already over, the state in decline after a series of disastrous wars with the Thais. Sometime in the fifteenth century, following the conquest of Angkor by the Thais in 1431, the civilization of the Khmers disappeared from history. For centuries the jungles then took possession of the temple palaces of the living Buddha until, around 1850, Angkor was rediscovered by the French explorer and archaeologist Henri Mouhott.

Still, according to the Buddhist doctrine of the cyclical recurrence of all things, the return of "The Once and Future King of the Khmers" may yet take place. Perhaps that awesomely lucky monkey conceived by mathematical theorists of chance—or maybe a whole tribe of such monkeys, who, given the infinite amplitude of time, should be able to reproduce the plays of Shakespeare from start to finish—may even now be banging away, banging away, in a thunderous staccato upon a battery of lost U.S. Army typewriters somewhere along the Mekong River. And when they get to that passage in The Tempest *where Prospero declares:*

> *The cloud-capp'd towers, the gorgeous palaces,*
> *The solemn temples, the great globe itself,*
> *Yea, all which it inherit, shall dissolve*
> *And, like this insubstantial pageant faded,*
> *Leave not a rack behind . . .*

at that moment the jungle will part, and lo! with a blare of conches, the deva-raja himself, brandishing his magic sword, will enter on a golden palanquin borne by four palace maidens, one at each corner.

Chou Ta-kuan's Recollections *was first translated into French in 1902 by Paul Pelliot, under the title* Mémoires sur les coutumes du Cambodge. *What follows has been based primarily on the translation published anonymously by* The Asia Society, Inc., *in 1961.*

T HE country which we Chinese call "Chen-la" is also called "Chan-la"; locally, however, it is termed "Cambodia."

According to our Chinese text, *The Description of the Barbarians*, this country is about 2500 miles in circumference. On the north, Champa

[Vietnam] is about two weeks away. Traveling southwest, one would reach Siam in about the same length of time. On the east lies the ocean.

In past times, this was a country of active trade. When our sacred dynasty [Yüan] received the Mandate of Heaven and spread out over the four seas, General-in-Chief So-tu, in 1281, attempted to bring law and order to Champa. Two officers with their troops were sent, but they were captured and did not return.

In the sixth month of 1295, our Sacred Emperor [Temur Oljaitu, grandson and successor to Kublai Khan] appointed an ambassador to bear an official message, and I was given the duty of accompanying him. In the course of time, eight months and 26 days later, we arrived at Champa. From there we encountered contrary winds, but at long length we reached our destination four months later when it was autumn. We remained there nearly a year and received homage before we went back to our ships. After setting sail, we reached the anchorage of Sseu-ming on the twelfth day of the eighth month, 1297.

Certainly one cannot learn the affairs of a country completely in such a short time, but perhaps I can say something about its principal traits.

The Walled City of Angkor: About 20 miles of walls surround the city, which may be entered by five gates, each of which has two side gates. Two gates open onto the east; and the others have only one. Just outside the walls there is a broad moat, beyond which there are causeways with enormous bridges. On both sides of the bridges there are 54 stone demons, looking like generals, terrible and gigantic. All five gates are alike. The bridges have stone parapets, carved in the form of nine-headed serpents; and the 54 demons hold the serpent in their hands as though to prevent it from escaping. Above the gates there are five heads of Buddha in stone, four of which are turned toward the cardinal points, while the one in the center is decorated in gold. Stone elephants are carved on both sides of the gate.

The walls are constructed entirely of stone blocks, piled on top of each other to a height of about 24 feet. They are carefully fitted and no wild grass appears in the niches. There are no battlements; and certain places on the walls are sown with sago trees. At intervals, there are little empty houses. The inner side of the walls forms a ramp of more than 100 feet, at the height of which there are large gates, closed at night and open in the morning. Only slaves and criminals who have had their toes cut off are not allowed to pass by the gatekeepers.

The walls form a perfect square, at the corners of which rise four stone towers. Marking the center of the kingdom is a tower of gold, surrounded by more than 20 stone towers and hundreds of stone cells. On the east side two golden lions flank a golden bridge, and eight Buddhas of gold are placed at the foot of stone cells.

About a third of a mile north of the golden tower there is a copper tower, even higher, from which the view is magnificent. At the foot there are ten or more small stone houses. Still another third of a mile further north is the residence of the King, where another golden tower exists in his sleeping apartments. It is all these wonders which we think have inspired merchants to speak glowingly of "rich and noble Cambodia" since they first came here.

Leaving by the south gate, a short distance away is the stone tower that Lou-pan [Chinese god of architects] is said to have erected overnight. His tomb is found about a third of a mile away from the south gate, and it is three to four miles in circumference.* There are also several hundred small houses of stone.

The eastern lake lies 3 to 4 miles outside the east wall, and it is about 30 miles in circumference. In the lake there are little stone houses and a stone tower containing a bronze statue of the Buddha sleeping from whose navel there is a continual flow of water. The northern lake is about a mile and a half to the north of the city, and it has small stone houses as well as a square golden tower with a golden lion, a gold Buddha, and bronze statues of bulls, horses, an elephant—nothing is missing!

Dwelling Places: The palace, official buildings and noble homes all face toward the east. The palace, as I have pointed out, lies to the north of the golden tower and bridge; and counting from its outside gate, it contains an area of towers about three miles in circumference. The scale of the buildings is magnificent, with long verandas, covered corridors, and an avoidance of excessive symmetry. The enormous lintels and piles of the bridge are sculptured and painted all over with Buddhas. In the council hall there are golden window frames, on either side of which are square columns with 40 to 50 upright mirrors. On the lower parts are depicted elephants.

I have heard people say that the inside of the palace contains many marvels, but it is forbidden and the defenses are very strict. There is a golden tower in the King's apartment in which he sleeps. All the local people claim that in the tower lies the spirit of a nine-headed serpent, master of the soil of all the kingdom. Every night he appears in the form of a woman with whom the King sleeps and then unites. Even the wives of the King would not dare to come near at this time. Later in the evening, the King can sleep with his wives and his concubines. If, one night, the spirit of the serpent does not appear, the King's death is at hand; and if the King fails to keep his appointment, some tragedy, it is thought, will surely befall the nation.

The homes of the princes and great officers are of a different size and

---

* Here Chou Ta-kuan refers to Angkor Wat as the tomb of Lou-pan, perhaps because of local tradition that the diety, Visvakarman, celestial architect, had constructed it (translator's note).

character from those of the ordinary people. The roof tiles of the palace apartments are of lead; those of other buildings are of yellow clay. All public buildings and special dwelling places are roofed with thatch; only the family temple and private apartment may be roofed with tile. The size of each person's home is determined by his rank.

The homes of ordinary people are roofed with thatch, for they would not dare to use tile. The interiors are meanly furnished, without table, bench, basin, or bucket. For sleeping they use only bamboo mats, and they also lie down right on the floorboards. The common people employ only an earthenware pot for cooking rice, in addition to an earthenware pan for preparing the sauce. They bury three stones for a fireplace, and from a coconut shell they make a ladle. To serve rice, they employ Chinese plates, either earthenware or copper. For the sauce, they employ banana tree leaves, of which they make little glasses; and even when these glasses are full, the liquid does not leak out. In addition, they use the leaves of the *kiao* for making spoons to drain the sauce. When they are finished they throw the spoons away.

Functionaries: Like our own country, Cambodia has counselors, generals, astrologers, et cetera, and below them all sorts of minor officials. Their names are different, that is all. Nobles are usually chosen for the posts, and sometimes those who may have offered their daughters as royal concubines. Their insignia and the number of their attendants depend on their rank.

The highest dignitaries have palanquins with gold shafts and four gold-handled parasols. Those just below them have similar palanquins, but possess only two gold-handled parasols; further below, only one gold-handled parasol; and still further below, merely a silver-handled parasol. The parasols are made of a red Chinese taffeta, and their fringes reach to the ground. There are also oiled umbrellas of a green taffeta with a small fringe.

The Inhabitants: Cambodians are not what we Chinese would call really civilized. They are coarse featured and very black. They look the same in distant villages, on islands in the sea, or on the busiest street. Only among people at the court and in noble homes does one see many who are as white as jade, which must be because they are never in the sun. Both men and women wear only a piece of cloth around their loins, and their upper bodies are bare; the women's breasts are white as milk. Their hair is dressed in a chignon, and even the King's wives go barefoot.

The King has five wives, one for himself, and one for each point of the compass. As for concubines and palace girls, I have heard mentioned that there may be as many as 3 to 5000, divided into various classes, but they rarely come out. The times when I saw the King in the palace, he was always in the company of his first wife, and seated at the golden window of his private apartments. Courtiers ranged themselves on both sides of the window waiting their turn to look at them. I managed to catch a glimpse. Any family blessed with a beautiful daughter brings her to the palace.

There are female palace attendants of lower status; and they number at least 1000 to 2000. They marry, and live where they choose. They shave the front part of their hair in the fashion of northern people, and place there a vermilion mark, as well as one on each temple. This is their distinctive mark. They have access to the palace as ordinary women do not, and they are always passing to and fro on the roads near the palace. These palace women also wear hairpins, combs, and hair ornaments, as well as bracelets and gold rings. Ordinary women do not do so. Both men and women use perfume made from sandalwood, musk, and other scents.

Everyone worships the Buddha.

In this country there are many homosexuals who spend their time in groups of ten or more every day in the market place. They are always trying to lure the Chinese, in exchange for expensive presents. The practice is disgusting and undignified.

Clothing: Everyone—even the Prince, men, and women alike—wears his hair in a chignon and goes bare shouldered. They all wrap a piece of linen around themselves, over which they drape another large piece when they go outdoors. Quality of the material differs; that which the Prince wears is worth three or four ounces of gold. Such material, of course, is the most beautiful in color and workmanship. Although linen is woven here, a highly regarded variety comes in quantity from Siam and Champa, and the most prized of all, of especially fine and delicate workmanship, comes from across the western seas.

Floral patterns, woven into the cloth, are reserved for the Prince. He wears a crown of gold like those on the head of Vajradhara, and when he doesn't wear the crown, his chignon is wrapped with garlands of flowers, perfumed with a kind of jasmine. His neck is hung with nearly three pounds of huge pearls. On his wrists and ankles he wears bracelets, and on his fingers he wears gold rings set with cat's-eyes. The soles of his bare feet and his palms are stained with a red drug. When he appears outside the palace, he carries a golden sword in his hand.

The women of Cambodia dye the soles of their feet and their palms, but the men would not dare to do so. Fabrics with a pattern of thinly scattered flowers may be worn by great nobles and princes; and the palace attendants, clothes are unique in having two clusters of floral design. Only women are permitted to wear such clothes among the ordinary people. Recently, a newly arrived Chinese happened to wear a pattern with two clusters of floral design, but nobody seemed to mind, since he didn't know the local customs.

Emigration: Chinese seamen who come to this country can do very well. Not too many clothes are required, rice is easy to obtain, women are friendly, household needs are not too hard to satisfy, and business is easy to run. For these reasons, many foreign sailors jump ship and remain here.

Bathing and Other Matters: This country is terribly warm and one could not let a day go by without bathing several times. Even at night one is forced to cool off in the water once or twice. Bathhouses and tubs are nonexistent, but there is a kind of family pool, which two or three other families sometimes share, and in which everyone, men and women, enters nude. The young people and their parents and grandparents do not use the bath at the same time, however. But should the young be already in the pool when their elders arrive, they remain and the old ones leave. If everyone is of about the same age, nobody pays any attention. The women simply cover their sex with their hands when they rise to go into the water, and that's that.

Every few days the city women go outside the walls in small groups to the river, where they meet with others by the thousands to swim and bathe. Even the noble women enjoy this sport and have no shame about leaving their clothes on the river bank and going into the water. Everyone can see them from head to toe.

The Chinese, on their days off, often amuse themselves by going to watch. I have heard that some people go into the water and take advantage of the opportunity. The water is always warm, as warm as though a stove were heating it. It only cools off a little during the fifth watch; but as soon as the sun rises, the water heats up again.

As regards personal hygiene, the people customarily dig a trench large enough for two or three families, which they cover with grass; and when it is full, they again cover it and dig another one elsewhere. After they have been to these latrines, they always go into the pool to wash themselves, but use only the left hand. The right hand is reserved for eating. When they see a Chinese man going to the latrines and wiping himself with paper, they make a mock of him and even want to ban him from their houses. Among the women there are some who urinate standing up. This is really absurd.

The Three Religions: There are three main classifications: scholars, monks, and Taoists. I do not know whom the scholars worship. They have nothing that resembles a school or any place of instruction whatsoever; and what books they may read is not known to me. They dress like everyone else, except for a white cord around their necks, which they never remove during their entire lifetimes, and is the distinctive sign of a scholar. They are leaders and have important duties.

The monks shave their heads and wear yellow. The lower part of their body is looped with a skirt of yellow linen, leaving the right shoulder bare.

Their temples are roofed with tile, and contain a single statue exactly like the Buddha Sakyamuni, which they call "Po-lai." It is made of clay, painted red and blue, and dressed in red. The towers contain quite different Buddhas, cast in bronze. Nowhere does one see a bell or a drum, cymbals, banners, a canopy, et cetera.

The monks all eat fish and meat, which they offer to the Buddha, but they do not drink wine. Since the temples have no kitchen, they eat their single daily meal with families who serve them. They recite numerous texts, which have been written in black letters on symmetrical bunches of palm leaves, but since they do not use paintbrush or ink, I do not know how the letters are written. Certain monks have the right to ride in gold or silver palanquins with parasols, and these the Prince consults on serious matters. There are no Buddhist nuns.

The Taoists are dressed in an ordinary fashion, except for a piece of red or white cloth that they wear on their heads. It is rather like the *kou-kou* that Tartar women wear, but here it is worn somewhat lower down. They worship a block of stone, rather like the altar stone of the "god-of-the-soil" [the lingam] in China. I do not know what god these people worship. There are also Taoist nuns, and their temples are permitted to be covered with tile roofs. The monks do not dine with outsiders nor eat in public, and they do not drink wine. I have never seen them recite prayers or perform acts of merit for others. Children of laymen who go to school are taught by monks, and when they are grown they return to secular life. I could not find out too much about this matter.

New Year's Day and the Seasons: Their first month coincides with our tenth month, and they celebrate the New Year with a festival lasting fifteen days.

A grandstand is constructed for more than a thousand people in front of the palace. It is decorated with lanterns and flowers. Across from the grandstand wooden posts are placed end to end about 250 feet around, and in the center is erected a scaffolding like that used for the building of stupas. The whole construction may be 250 feet high, and sometimes they build as many as six each night. On top are placed fireworks and firecrackers, which are paid for by the provincial and palace nobility.

When the sun has gone down, they ask the King to take part in the general festivities, then set off the firecrackers and light the rockets, which can be seen for more than 30 miles. The firecrackers are as large as coconuts, and the explosions shake the whole city. Public officials and nobles take part in lighting them with tapers and hand out presents of betel nuts. To observe the festival, the King invites all the foreign ambassadors.

There is a different festival every month. In the fourth month, they "throw-the-ball." In the ninth, they perform a ceremony called *ya-lieh,* in which the entire population of the kingdom passes in review before the palace. In the fifth month, they "seek the waters of the Buddha"; and in the presence of the King all the images of Buddha, brought from all parts of the country, are bathed. In the sixth, they "make-boats-sail-on-land," during which the King mounts a turret. In the seventh, they "burn the rice." At that time, the new rice is ripe, and it is burned outside the south gate in honor of the Buddha. A great many women take part in this festival, riding in carriages and on elephants, but the King does not attend. In the eighth, they hold a dance called *ngai-lan*. The best musicians and actors are chosen to perform. There are also cock-fights, pig-fights, and contests between elephants. Foreign ambassadors are invited to attend by the King, and the entire festival lasts for 10 days. I don't recall exactly which festivals occurred during the other months.

In Cambodia there are savants, as in our own country, those who understand astronomy and can calculate eclipses of the sun and moon; but they figure the length of their year, with its short and long months, very differently from ours. They, too, must have intercalary years, but for some unknown reason they interpolate the last month.

The hours of darkness are divided into four watches,* and they use a cycle of seven days, analogous to what we Chinese call *k'ai-pi-chien-chou*. As these barbarians have neither surnames nor personal names, and don't celebrate their own birthdays, many of them take their names from that of the day on which they were born. They assign various qualities to the days, such as that the second is unlucky, the third neutral, the fourth a day of mourning. They believe that on one day it is safe to go toward the east, and on another toward the west. Even the women know how to make such calculations. The 12 animals of the zodiac correspond to those of China, but the names are different.

The Young Girls: When a daughter is born into a family, the parents make this prayer: "May your hand in marriage be asked by a hundred thousand husbands!" At a certain age, the girls are ceremoniously deflowered by Buddhist or Taoist priests. This ceremony, known as *tchen-t'an*, is performed on daughters of the rich between the ages of 7 and 9, and on the daughters of the poor by the age of 11.

Each year a night is set aside by a public official during the early summer, and announced throughout the country. Every family with an eligible daughter lets the official know, and he gives them a candle on which he has made a mark. On the appointed evening, when it gets dark, the candle is lit. When it has burned down to the mark, the moment of the *tchen-t'an* has arrived. Meanwhile, a priest of the family's religion has been chosen to perform the ceremony, and some of them have a regular clientele. Well-known monks are preferred by the rich and noble; the poor have to be

---

* Chou Ta-kuan mentions five elsewhere (translator's note).

content with whomever they are given. The monks receive presents of wine, rice, fabrics, silks, betel nuts, and sometimes money up to a hundred picals, which is worth two or three hundred Chinese taels. Less fortunate people give between 10 and 30 picals, depending on their generosity. If a girl reaches the age of 11 without the ceremony, it is only because her parents cannot afford it.

There are priests who refuse to take money, however, and perform the ceremony for poor girls. It is regarded as a good deed. All the more, since a monk may deflower only one girl in a single year; and when he has promised to do so, he cannot promise others.

On the appointed evening, parents and neighbors gather together for a great banquet with music. Outside the door they have built a platform on which are placed a few clay figurines of men, women, and animals. This is an ancient custom, which is now performed only by the rich. The platform remains for a week. Also, they build two pavilions, covered with silk of different colors, one for the girl to sit in and one for the monk. I do not know the names of these pavilions. The music is deafening, but no one is accused on that night of disturbing the peace. As many as ten families on a single street will be performing the ceremony simultaneously.

What I saw occurred in the early summer of 1297, but since a Chinese cannot readily watch the proceedings, it is difficult to know what really happens. It is said that when the time comes, the monk enters the girl's room and deflowers her with his hand. He then dips his hand in wine, and the parents and relatives use the wine to mark their foreheads. Some say they taste it. Some say the monks actually unite with the girls, but others say no.

Before dawn breaks, the monk is led away in a palanquin with parasols, and music plays. Now the young girl must be bought back from the monk with presents of goods and silk. If she were not, her virtue would be gone, and she could never marry. She is free to go wherever she will, but she can no longer sleep next to her parents as she used to.

When a woman marries, cloth is usually given as a token present. Marriage often occurs between a man and his former mistress, to no one's surprise or shame.

Childbirth: When a woman has given birth, she cooks rice, rolls it in salt, and applies it to the affected parts. It reduces any swelling, and after a day and a night, when she removes it, she will keep her youthful appearance. I could hardly believe this, but when a girl in our household gave birth, and on the following day went bathing in the river carrying her baby, I was amazed.

Women in this country are said to be very lascivious. No sooner have they given birth than one or two days later they sleep with their husbands.

They abandon their husband if he should grow cold; and if he travels far away, they may stay faithful for a few nights, but soon they are sure to ask, "How can I sleep alone? I am not a spirit, but made of flesh and blood!" That's how lusty they are! But I have heard that a few are faithful, too.

Women here age very quickly; probably because they marry and have children before they are old enough. At 20 or 30, they look like Chinese women of 40 and 50.

Slaves: Savages are purchased to do the work of servants. Well-to-do families may have as many as a hundred. Even those of modest means have 10 or 20; only the very poor have none at all. These savages are men from the wild mountains, and they form a separate race called "Thieving-Chuangs." They never appear in the streets, and if one man uses the epithet "Chuang" against another, the latter is mortally offended.

Young, strong slaves are worth a hundred pieces of cloth; but when they are old and feeble they are only worth 30 or 40. They sit and sleep under the houses, and when they wish to come inside they must kneel first and make obeisance by prostrating themselves. They call their owners "father" and "mother." When they are beaten for making some mistake, they bend their heads and do not dare to move in the slightest. They couple with each other, but the owner never wishes to sleep with them. If some Chinese, long away from home, sleeps with a slave, the master finds out about it and will have nothing to do with the Chinese. If the servant becomes pregnant, however, the master makes no attempt to find out the identify of the father, because the child will be another slave for his household.

If a slave is captured after attempting to escape, he is often marked with blue on his face. Sometimes he must wear an iron ring around his neck or around his arms and legs.

Savages: Two kinds of savages exist in this country: those who know the language and are sold as slaves; and those who have never adopted any of the ways of civilization and do not understand the language. The latter sort do not live in houses, but roam about in the mountains carrying their provisions in clay jars on their heads. They kill wild animals with spears or bows and arrows, make fire by rubbing stones together, and roast and devour their food at a common meal. Then they all move on again once more. They are also quite fierce, possessing the knowledge of how to make deadly poisons, and have been known to murder people within their own tribe. Recently, some have begun to cultivate cardamom, grow cotton, and weave a rather coarse cloth decorated with bizarre designs.

Silk: The Cambodians weave a cotton cloth, but they do not use silk, and their women are not good at needlework. They make skeins by hand, and do not use spinning wheels or weaving frames, preferring to attach one end of the woven cloth to their waists and continue work at the other end, a piece of bamboo serving them for a shuttle.

Mulberry trees and silkworms are native to Siam, and the Siamese weave their clothes of a kind of dark tussah silk. The Siamese are good tailors; and when a Cambodian's clothes are torn, he hires a Siamese to repair them.

Sickness: Cambodians are often ill, which comes from taking too many baths and washing their heads so frequently. They often cure themselves. One sees many lepers along the roads, but people do not seem to contract the disease even after eating and sleeping with them. They are accustomed to the disease in this country, as a matter of fact; and they say that a former King contracted leprosy. He was not thought the less of for it. In my own humble opinion, I believe they contract the disease because they are so passionate and take too many baths. I have heard that Cambodians bathe immediately after satisfying their desires.

In this country, eight or nine out of ten die of dysentery. Drugs are sold in the marketplace, but they differ from ours; and I do not know them all. They also have sorcerers who practice their arts on the people, and are quite laughable.

The Dead: When people die, coffins are not used, but only a sort of matting; and the corpse is covered with a pall. In the funeral procession the mourners carry banners and musical instruments, and they also take along two plates of fried rice and scatter the grains to the winds along the route. They then proceed to some desolate spot, where they deposit the body, expecting that dogs and vultures will devour it. If this happens immediately, they say that the relatives have been rewarded for their merit. If it does not, they ascribe it to some fault on the part of the same kin. There are a few people who have begun to burn their corpses; they are the local descendants of the Chinese.

After the death of a father or mother, the children do not wear mourning, but the sons shave their heads and the daughters cut their hair quite close. Kings are interred within their towers at their death, but I don't know whether they bury the entire body or merely the bones.

The Harvest of Gall: Every year, in past times, the King of Champa demanded a jar of human gall, collected from thousands of people. During the eighth month, men were sent secretly into the cities and villages to waylay those out at night. People were seized in the dark, their heads covered with a hood drawn tight by a cord, and, with a small knife, gall was then extracted from the right side of their back. They do not attack the Chinese, because one year they waylaid one and all the rest of the gall in the jar rotted. In recent years, however, this custom has been abolished.

A Prodigy: On view outside the east gate of the city are the dead bodies of a brother and sister who were miraculously punished for having had incestuous relations. Despite all their efforts, I was told, and the ministrations of friends who tried to separate them, their flesh remained glued together; and after three days without food in this condition, they perished. My compatriot, Sie, who has lived here for 35 years, says that he has witnessed such a thing on two other occasions. If this be the case, it shows that the people of Cambodia know how to employ the magical power of the Buddha.

Justice: The King listens to all legal disputes, even minor ones. Monetary fines used to be levied in all cases, but nowadays they also beat offenders on the soles of their feet. In cases of a major crime, the criminal is placed in a ditch outside the west gate, and earth and stones are heaped on top of him until he is finished off. Smaller crimes are sometimes punished by amputating noses, ears, toes, and fingers. Debauchery and gambling are not forbidden, but if the husband of an adulterous woman should discover her in the act, he may press the feet of her lover in a wooden vise until the pain forces him to hand over his fortune.

If a corpse is found in the streets, it is dragged by ropes to some waste area outside the city, but no real investigation is made. Whoever catches a robber may punish him himself.

I must commend one of their procedures. If a suspected thief denies his guilt, he may prove his innocence by plunging his hand into boiling oil. If he is indeed innocent, his flesh is untouched. If he is guilty, his hand is completely charred. That's how these foreigners go about things.

But if two families are in dispute; and the case cannot be easily decided for one or the other, they make use of 12 little stone towers in front of the palace. Each of the disputants, accuser and accused, sits on top of one of these towers, and his family gathers at the bottom, keeping an eye on the other family. After a few days, the guilty party reveals himself in some fashion. Either he develops ulcers, or boils, or he catches a cold or some malignant fever. The other person remains perfectly healthy. In this fashion they tell who is right and wrong, calling it "heavenly justice."

Villages: Each village in this kingdom has its own temple or stupa; and no matter how small the population, they have an official called a *mai-tsie*. On the main roads they maintain rest houses, called *sen-mou*, which are very like our own hostels. In the recent war with the Siamese many villages were entirely devastated.

The Army: The soldiers of Cambodia go barefoot and naked, carrying only a lance in their right hand and a shield in their left. They do not use war machines or bullets, helmets or armor, bows or arrows. In the war with the Siamese, the whole population was required to take up arms, but they have no science of tactics or strategy.

The Prince's Appearance in Public: I have heard it said that in past times the King never placed his feet on the ground outside the palace; and if he did so by some mischance, the prints of his feet were avoided. The new King [Srindravarman (1295–1307)] is the son-in-law of the former one [Jayavarman VIII (1243–1295)]. His career has been with the army. His wife, a favorite daughter of the former King, stole his golden sword and gave it to her husband. The King's son, deprived of his succession, began to raise troops, but he was discovered; and the new King put him in prison after cutting off his toes. The new King wears armor made of iron, and knives and arrows cannot harm him. Protected in this fashion, he dares to leave the palace; and during my year or so in this country, I have seen him four or five times.

Cavalry appears at the head of his escort, followed by standards, banners, and musicians. Next come 300 to 500 palace girls, flowers in their hair and wearing flowered cloth. They carry large flares, lighted even in broad daylight. Another group of palace girls follows as a separate troop, bearing the royal gold and silver utensils and also a whole series of ornaments and insignia whose purpose is unknown to me. Next comes a group of palace girls carrying shields and lances, who form the private guard of the King. They are followed by goat- and horse-drawn carriages, all decorated in gold. Ministers and princes follow, riding on elephants and surrounded by innumerable red parasols. They look neither right nor left. Next come more than a hundred golden parasols, elephants, palanquins, and carriages containing the wives and concubines of the King.

At this point in the procession the King appears, standing on an elephant and holding his precious sword in his hand. The tusks of his elephant are sheathed in gold, and other elephants mill around him while the cavalry protects him. He is escorted by more than 20 white parasols, decorated with gold and with gold handles.

At other times, if the King is simply traveling to a nearby spot, he may use a golden palanquin, which is carried by four palace girls. On such occasions, the King has usually left the palace to visit a small gold pagoda with a gold statue of the Buddha in front of it. Those who see the King must prostrate themselves, touching their foreheads to the ground in a gesture called *san-pa.* If they do not do so, they are seized and punished by palace attendants.

Twice a day, for the affairs of government, the King holds an audience. There is no fixed agenda, and those who come to consult him, whether officials or ordinary people, must sit on the ground and wait for him to appear at a golden window. After a short time of waiting, distant music is heard from the direction of the palace, where conch shells are being sounded to herald his approach. I believe that he arrives in his gold palanquin, not having come from very far. Moments later, the curtain of the golden window is lifted by two palace girls, and the King appears with his sword in his hand. Everyone clasps his hands together and beats his head on the ground, even the ministers. They may raise their heads only when the music ceases. The King seats himself immediately afterward. Then, according to the King's wish, they are called forward to sit in a place where there is a lionskin, which is his hereditary royal treasure. When the audience is terminated, the King leaves; and the two girls let the curtain fall. Everyone rises. And so one sees, even though this may be a barbarous land, that the people know full well what it is to be a King.

Tamerlane

By a Persian artist of his period.

Our souls, whose faculties can comprehend
The wondrous architecture of the world,
And measure every wandering planet's course,
Still climbing after knowledge infinite,
And always moving as the restless spheres,
Will us to wear ourselves, and never rest,
Until we reach the ripest fruit of all,
That perfect bliss and sole felicity,
The sweet fruition of an earthly crown.

Christopher Marlowe, *Tamburlaine the Great*

At the time the embassy dispatched by King Henry III of Castile and Léon arrived at Samarkand in 1404, Marlowe's "Scythian shephearde" lad was close to 70 years old and had already plucked several "earthly crowns" in Persia, northern India, Syria, Russia, and Asia Minor. He was even then assembling his horde to "reach the ripest fruit of all," the empire of China half a world away, where the usurping Mongol dynasty a generation earlier had been overthrown by the native Ming; and only two years before the ambassadors' arrival, he had achieved his greatest victory, at the battle of Angora in 1402, by defeating the Ottoman Sultan Bajazet I and taking him captive along with his court.

Though Tamerlane did not, as Marlowe imagined in his "Two Tragicall Discourses," exhibit the Sultan in a cage like a wild beast to the people, he did compel Bajazet to watch while the sultanas and concubines of his harem were paraded naked before the Mongol generals, then distributed among them as prizes. (The legend of the Sultan in a cage, incidentally, has persisted down to our own time, for both Hitler and Mussolini at the end of World War II feared that they would be so punished if they were captured alive; by a perverse kind of poetic justice it was the fate meted out instead to Ezra Pound in a prison camp outside Pisa.) Literature sometimes blurs into fact, and the other way around.

136

However, by castrating the power of the Ottoman Turks at the battle of Angora, and so delaying the fall of Constantinople by fifty years, Tamerlane may be regarded as the savior of western Europe in the early 15th century, though a fearful savior nonetheless. To his friends and allies he was known as "The Splendid," but to his enemies as "The Scourge of God."

His reputation for cruelty is matched only by that of his distant cousin Genghis Khan or by Attila the Hun. To punish a revolt in his army he once embedded 2000 of the rebellious soldiers in a tower of brick and mortar. He also had a macabre passion for erecting obelisks and pyramids of the severed heads of prisoners of war; following the conquest of Baghdad he decapitated 120,000; of Delhi, 80,000; of Isfahan, 70,000. He built numerous lesser pyramids of heads besides, depending on the number of victims available and, most likely, his mood or digestion at the time. As a further refinement, he had all the faces turned outward, so as to discourage any thought of protest by the remainder of the population. Even the idealized portraits of Tamerlane by the Persian artists at his court that have come down to us cannot entirely conceal a certain sadistic Fu Manchu droop to the mouth and a far-off glint in his eyes that might suddenly blaze with apocalyptic fury. By contemporaries he was described as very tall, with a large head and florid complexion, white-haired since childhood, and, of course, with a crippled leg, whence his name Timur i-leng in Turkish, or Timur the Lame. Very like, in fact, his Infernal Majesty Satan himself—a resemblance that must have surely impressed the ambassadors from the little Catholic kingdom of Spain.

Within the century, as it turned out, the military supremacy of the Mongol-Turkic steppe warriors of Tatary who had overrun the ancient civilizations of Asia and the Near East was to recede forever, and the rise of Europe to world dominance to begin. Infantry equipped with field pieces and hand guns firing "bullets, like Jove's dreadful thunderbolts, / Enroll'd in flames and fiery smoldering mists," as Marlowe put it, were able to check the once irresistible cavalry charges of these nomads. Tamerlane's own great victories over the Golden Horde in Russia and the Arab kingdoms contributed unintentionally to this reversal in the balance of power, for he dragooned thousands of captive metalworkers and skilled craftsmen, who might otherwise have helped develop and produce the new weapons, to instead build his capital of Samarkand. Construction was still continuing when Ruy González de Clavijo, the author of the following account, and his fellow ambassadors arrived at the city.

The journey of more than 2500 miles they undertook to get there, from Cadiz to Trebizond on the Black Sea and then overland through Transoxiana in Central Asia to Samarkand, then back again, lasted more than three years, and was about as perilous for those times as a space flight to Mars might be nowadays. The party was still on its way home when Tamerlane, while leading his armies to battle against China, died suddenly, in March of 1405, at the border fortress town of Otrar. His body was embalmed, placed in an ebony coffin, and then sent to Samarkand, where it still lies interred in a tomb called "Gur Amir."

González de Clavijo wrote his account of the mission soon after his return in 1406, the same year in which his master King Henry III of Castile was to die. Clavijo himself lived until 1412. His book was first translated into English by Clements R. Markham, and printed for the Hakluyt Society in 1859, under the title Embassy to Tamerlane: 1403–1406, *from which the following has been excerpted.*

The Meeting of the Twain

The great Lord Timur Beg [Tamerlane], having killed the Emperor of Samarkand and seized upon his empire, where his own dominion commenced; and having conquered all the land of Mongolia and the land of India the less; also having conquered all the empire of Khurasan and reduced to obedience the land of Tagiguinia, with the territory and lordship of a land called Rei; and also having conquered and reduced all Persia and Media, with the empire of Tabriz and of Sultanieh; and also having conquered the lordship of Gheelan, with the land of Derbent; and also having conquered the land of Armenia the less, and the lands of Arsinga, and of Aseron, and of Aunique; and also having reduced to obedience the empire of Merdi and the land of Kurdistan; and also having destroyed the city of Damascus, and reduced to submission the cities of Aleppo, of Babylonia, and of Baldas; and having also overrun many other lands and lordships, and won many other battles, and achieved many conquests, he came against the Turk Yilderman Bajazet in his land of Turkey and gave him battle near his castle of Angora [Ankara], conquering him and taking him prisoner, together with one of his sons.

In this battle there happened to be present Payo de Soto Mayor and Hernan Sanchez de Palazuelos, ambassadors whom the high and puissant Lord Don Henry, by the grace of God, King of Castille and León, had sent to ascertain the power which Timur Beg and Turk Yilderman possessed, and the number of the hosts that they had brought against each other. It happened that in the battle, the great Lord Timur Beg had notice of the presence of Payo and Hernan Sanchez. He treated them honorably, took them with him, entertained them, and gave them certain gifts; and received news of the high and famous King of Castille, and of the great consideration and power he had amongst the Christian kings. To obtain his friendship, he ordered an ambassador, with letters and a present, to be sent to secure an alliance with him.

With the ambassadors there went a certain Chagatayan knight named Mohammed Aleagi, with whom Timur sent his gifts and letters. The said ambassador went to the King of Castille and presented the letters that the Lord Timur Beg had sent, and his presents, and the women that he also sent according to his custom.

His Highness the King commanded that another present and ambassadors should be sent to Timur Beg, to increase the friendship that he had shown. He ordered that Fray Alonzo Paez de Santa Maria, master of theology; Ruy González de Clavijo [the author]; and Gomez de Salazar should convey the present and letters. The mission was very arduous, and the journey very long.

The Arrival at Kesh

On Thursday, the twenty-eighth of August, at the hour of mass, they arrived at the great city of Kesh, which is situated in a plain, traversed in every direction by channels of water, which irrigate many gardens. The Lord Timur Beg, and his father, were both natives of this city of Kesh.

In this city there are great mosques, and other edifices, especially a grand mosque that the Lord Timur Beg has ordered to be built, for as yet it is not finished; within which the body of his father is interred. The firstborn son of Timur Beg, named Jehanghir, is also interred here. This mosque, with its chapels, is very rich and beautifully ornamented in blue and gold, and within it there is a large court with trees and ponds of water. The Lord gives 20 boiled sheep every day for the souls of his father and son.

When the ambassadors arrived, they were conducted to this mosque, and provided with much meat and fruit; and after they had dined, they were taken to their lodging in a great palace. On the top of the palace doorway there was the figure of a lion and a sun, which are the arms of the former King of Samarkand. For this reason, I believe that he must have built the palace, for the arms that Timur Beg bears are three circles like O's, drawn in this manner: O_O^O, to signify that he is Lord of the three parts of the world. The Lord has these three O's on his seals and coins, and he has ordered that those who are tributary to him shall have it stamped on the coins of their countries.

The mosque and palace are amongst the magnificent edifices that the

Lord has dedicated in honor of his father, who was a native of this city. However, he did not belong to the races of this land, but was of a lineage called Chagatai [claiming descent from Chagatai, son of Genghis Khan], which came from the land of Tatary when this country was conquered, as will presently be related to you.

The father of Timur Beg was a man of good family, but small estate, with not more than three or four mounted attendants. He lived in a village near this city of Kesh, for the men of this land prefer living in the villages and in the plains to living in cities. His son, also, had not more than four or five horses. I will now tell you what was told to the ambassadors as certain truth in this city and in other parts.

It is said that Timur, having four or five servants, went out one day to steal a sheep, and on another day a cow, by force from the people of the country. When he had got them, he ate them with his followers; and some because of the plunder, others because he was a brave and good-hearted man, joined him, until he had a force of 300 mounted followers. From that time he traversed the country to rob and steal all he could lay hands on for himself and his companions, and he also frequented the roads and plundered the merchants.

News of these doings reached the Emperor of Samarkand [the Mongol Chagatai Khan Suyurghatmish], and he ordered the robber to be killed, wherever he could be found. But there were Chagatai knights at the court of the Emperor, men of Timur's lineage, who obtained his pardon and brought him to live at court. They say that, when Timur lived there, the Emperor of Samarkand became so enraged against him that he ordered him to be killed; but Timur was informed of it, and fled with his followers, returning to his life of robbery.

One day, when he had plundered a caravan of merchants, he obtained great wealth and went to a land called Seistan, where he stole sheep and horses, for that land is very rich in flocks. And he now had as many as 500 followers. When the people of Seistan knew this, they assembled together; and, one night, when he had fallen upon a great flock of sheep, they attacked him, killed many of his men, knocked him off his horse, and wounded him in the right leg, which lamed him. They also wounded him in the right hand, and cut off two of the fingers, leaving him for dead. As soon as he was able, he got up, and went to the tents of some people who were encamped in a plain, whence he returned to collect his followers again.

The Emperor of Samarkand was not liked by his subjects, especially by the common people, and some of the nobles also wished him ill. They proposed to Timur to kill the Emperor, and declared that they would raise him to power in his place. The conspiracy went so far that the Emperor, being in a city near Samarkand, was attacked and defeated by Timur. He fled to the mountains and called to a man to hide and protect him, promising to make him rich and giving him some valuable jewels. This man, instead of hiding him, betrayed him to Timur, who presently came and killed him, and took the city of Samarkand. Timur married the wife of the late Emperor, named Caño, which means "Great Empress," and she is still his chief wife. Afterward he conquered the land of Khurasan, taking advantage of a quarrel between two brothers, lords of that land. Thus it was that he gained these two empires of Khurasan and Samarkand, and such was his origin.

An Audience with Tamerlane at Samarkand

The ambassadors were in this city of Kesh during the Thursday on which they arrived; and, having departed on Friday afternoon, they passed the night in a village; the next day they reached a large village near Samarkand, called Mecer, where they again passed the night. The noble who conducted them now left the ambassadors, as on that day they could easily reach the city of Samarkand. He said that he would announce their approach to the great Lord, and that he would send a man to report their arrival.

Next day, at dawn, he returned with an edict from the great Lord that the ambassadors, and the ambassador of the Sultan of Babylon, who traveled with them, should be taken to a garden near the village, and remain there until he gave further orders.

On Thursday, the fourth of September, a noble who was related to the Lord came to the garden, and told the ambassadors that the Lord was occupied with the business of some ambassadors from the Emperor Tokatamish [Khan of the Golden Horde], and, therefore, he could not see them yet. But so that they might not be impatient, he had sent some refreshments to them and to the ambassador of the Sultan, that they might make merry for that day. They brought many sheep, cooked and dressed, and a roasted horse, with rice served up in various ways, and much fruit. When they had eaten, they were presented with two horses, a robe, and a hat.

The ambassadors were in this garden from Sunday, the thirty-first of August, to Monday, the eighth of September, when the Lord sent for them; for it is the custom not to see any ambassador until five or six days are passed, and the more important the ambassador may be, the longer he has to wait.

On Monday the ambassadors departed and went to the city of Samarkand. The road went over a plain covered with gardens, houses, and markets where they sold many things; and at three in the afternoon, they came to a large garden and palace outside the city, where the Lord then was. When they arrived, they dismounted and entered a building outside where two knights came to them and said they were to give up those presents they had brought for the Lord to certain men, who would lay them before him, for such were the orders of the private Mirzas of the Lord; so the ambassadors gave the presents to the two knights. The ambassador from the Sultan did the same with the presents that he had brought.

The entrance to this garden was very broad and high, and beautifully adorned with glazed tiles in blue and gold. At this gate there were many porters, who guarded it with maces in their hands. When the ambassadors entered, they came to six elephants with wooden castles on their backs, each of which had two banners, and there were men on the top of them. The ambassadors went forward, found the men who had the presents, which were well arranged on their arms, and then advanced with them in company with the two knights, who held them by the armpits. The ambassador whom Timur Beg had sent to the King of Castille was with them; and those who saw him laughed at him, because he was dressed in the costume and fashion of Castille.

They conducted them to an aged knight, who was seated in an anteroom. He was a son of the sister of Timur Beg, and they bowed reverentially before him. They were then brought before some small boys, grandsons of the Lord, who were seated in a chamber, and they also bowed before them. Here the letter, which they had brought from the King to Timur Beg, was demanded, and they presented it to one of these boys, who took it. He was a son of Miran Mirza, the eldest son of the Lord. The three boys then got up and carried the letter to the Lord, who desired that the ambassadors should be brought before him.

Timur Beg was seated on the ground in a portal, in front of the entrance of a beautiful palace. Before him there was a fountain, which threw up the water very high, and in it there were some red apples. The Lord was seated cross-legged, on silken embroidered carpets, amongst round pillows. He was dressed in a robe of silk, with a high white hat on his head, on the top of which there was a spinal ruby, with pearls and precious stones round it.

As soon as the ambassadors saw the Lord, they made a reverential bow, placing the knee on the ground, and crossing the arms on the breast. Then they went forward and made another, and then a third, remaining with their knees on the ground. The Lord ordered them to rise and come forward, and the knights, who had held them until then, let them go. Three Mirzas, who stood before the Lord, and were his most intimate counselors, named Alodalmelee Mirza, Borundo Mirza, and Nooreddin Mirza, then came and took the ambassadors by the arms and led them forward until they stood together before the Lord. This was done that the Lord might see them better; for his eyesight was bad, being so old that the eyelids had fallen down entirely. He did not give them his hand to kiss, for it was not the custom, but he asked after the King, saying, "How is my son the King? Is he in good health?"

When the ambassadors had answered, Timur Beg turned to the knights who were seated around him, amongst whom were one of the sons of Tokatamish, the former Emperor of Tatary, several chiefs of the blood of the late Emperor of Samarkand, and others of the family of the Lord himself, and said, "Behold! Here are the ambassadors sent by my son the King of Spain, who is the greatest King of the Franks, and lives at the end of the world. These Franks are truly a great people, and I will give my benediction to the King of Spain, my son. It would have sufficed if he had sent you to me with the letter, and without the presents, so well satisfied am I to hear of his health and prosperous state."

The letter that the King had sent was held before the Lord, in the hand of his grandson; and the master of theology said through his interpreter that no one understood how to read the letter except himself, and that when his Highness wished to hear it, he would read it. The Lord then took the letter from the hand of his grandson and opened it, saying that he would hear it presently, and that he would send for the master and see him in private, when he might read it and say what he desired.

The ambassadors were then taken to a room on the right-hand side of the place where the Lord sat; and the Mirzas, who held them by the arms, made them sit below an ambassador whom the Emperor Chuyscan [Ch'eng Tsu], Lord of Cathay, had sent to Timur Beg to demand the yearly tribute that was formerly paid. When the Lord saw the ambassadors seated below the ambassador from the Lord of Cathay, he sent to order that they should sit above him, and he below them. As soon as they were seated, one of the Mirzas of the Lord came and said to the ambassador of Cathay, that the Lord had ordered that those who were ambassadors from the King of Spain, his son and friend, should sit above him; and that he who was the ambassador from a thief and a bad man, his enemy, should sit below them; and from that time, at the feasts and entertainments given by the Lord, they always sat in that order. The Mirza then ordered the interpreter to tell the ambassadors what the Lord had done for them. This Emperor of Cathay is called Chuyscan, which means "Nine Empires"; but the Chagatais called him "Tangus," which means "Pig Emperor." He is the Lord of a great country, and Timur Beg used to pay him tribute, but he refuses to do so now.

As soon as these ambassadors—and many others, who had come from distant countries—were seated in order, they brought much meat, boiled, roasted, and dressed in other ways, and roasted horses, and they placed these sheep and horses on very large round pieces of stamped leather. When the Lord called for meat, the people dragged it to him on these pieces of leather, so great was its weight; and as soon as it was within 20 paces of him, the carvers came, who cut it up, kneeling on the leather. They cut it in pieces, and put the pieces in basins of gold and silver, earthenware and glass, and porcelain, which is very scarce and precious. The most honorable piece was a haunch of the horse with the loin, but without the leg, and they placed parts of it in 10 cups of gold and silver. They also cut up the haunches of the sheep. They then put pieces of the tripes of the horses, about the size of a man's fist, into the cups, and entire sheep's heads, and in this way they made many dishes. When they had made sufficient, they placed them in rows. Then some men came with soup, and they sprinkled salt over it and put a little into each dish as sauce; and they took some very thin cakes of corn, doubled them four times, and placed one over each cup or basin of meat.

As soon as this was done, the Mirzas and courtiers of the Lord took these basins, one holding each side, and one helping behind (for a single man could not lift them), and placed them before the Lord, and the ambassadors, and the knights who were there; and the Lord sent the ambassadors two basins, from those which were placed before him, as a mark of favor. When this food was taken away, more was brought; and it is the custom to take this food, which is given to them, to their lodgings; and if they do not do so, it is taken as an affront.

Another custom is, that when they take any food from before any of the ambassadors, they give it to their retinue; and so much food was placed before them that, if they had taken it away, it would have lasted them for half a year. When the roast and boiled meats were done with, they brought meats dressed in various other ways and balls of forcemeat; and after that, there came fruit, melons, grapes, and nectarines; and they gave them drink out of silver and golden jugs, particularly sugar and cream, a pleasant beverage, which they make in the summertime.

When dinner was finished, the men who bore the presents on their arms passed before the Lord, and the same was done with the presents sent by the Sultan of Babylon; and 300 horses were also brought before the Lord, which had been presented that day. After this was done the ambassadors rose, and a knight was appointed to attend upon them and see that they were provided with all that they required. This knight, who was the chief porter of the Lord, conducted the ambassadors, and the ambassador from the Sultan of Babylon, to a lodging near the place where the Lord abode, in which there was a garden and plenty of water.

When the ambassadors took leave of the Lord, he caused the presents that the King had sent to be brought, and received them with much complacency. He divided the scarlet cloth amongst his women, giving the largest share to his chief wife, Caño, who was in this garden with him. The other presents, brought by the ambassador from the Sultan, were not received, but returned to the men who had charge of them; they kept them for three days, when the Lord ordered them to be brought again, because it is the custom not to receive a present until the third day.

The Feasting Begins

On Monday, the fifteenth of September, the Lord went from that palace and garden to another, which was very beautiful. It had a very lofty and handsome entrance, made of bricks, and adorned with tiles in blue and gold arranged in various patterns. The Lord ordered a great feast to be prepared, and sent for the ambassadors and many other people, both men and women.

This garden, where the feast was to take place, was very large, and contained many fruit trees and other trees that give shade. Amongst them there were avenues and wooden terraces, on which the people walked. There were many tents set up and awnings of red cloth and various colored silks, some embroidered and others plain.

In the center of the garden there was a very beautiful house built in the shape of a cross and richly adorned with ornaments. In the middle of it there were three chambers for placing beds and carpets in, and the walls were covered with glazed tiles. Opposite the entrance, in the largest of the chambers, there was a silver gilt table, as high as a man and three arms broad, on the top of which there was a bed of silk cloths, embroidered with gold, placed one on the top of the other, and here the Lord was seated.

The walls were hung with rose-colored silk cloths ornamented with plates of silver gilt, set with emeralds, pearls, and other precious stones, tastefully arranged. Above these ornaments there were pieces of silk a palmo [about 8.6 inches] broad, whence hung tassels of various colors, and the wind moved them backward and forward, which caused a very pretty effect. Before the great arch, which formed the entrance to the chamber, there were ornaments of the same kind and silk cloths raised up by spear poles, kept together by silken cords with large tassels, which came down to the ground. The other chambers were furnished in the same way, and on the floors there were carpets and rush mats.

In the center of the house, opposite the door, there were two gold tables, each standing on four legs, and the table and legs were all in one. They were each five palmos long and three broad. Seven golden vials stood upon them, two of which were set with large pearls, emeralds, and turquoises, and each one had a ruby near the mouth. There were also six round golden cups, one of which was set with large round clear pearls inside, and in the center of it there was a ruby, two fingers broad, and of a brilliant color.

The ambassadors were invited to this feast by the Lord, but they had to wait for their interpreter; therefore, by the time they arrived the Lord had already dined. The Lord said that, on another day, when he sent for them, they were to come at once, and not to wait for the interpreter, but that this time he would forgive them. He had made this feast for them, so that they might see the house and the people. The Lord was in a great rage with the Mirzas because the ambassaders did not come in time for the feast, and because the interpreter was not with them.

He sent for the interpreter and said, "How is it that you have caused me to be enraged and put out? Why were you not with the Frank ambassadors? I order that a hole be bored through your nose, that a rope be passed through it, and that you be dragged through the army as a punishment."

He had scarcely finished speaking when men took the interpreter by the nose to bore a hole in it. But the knight who attended upon the ambassadors by order of the Lord asked for mercy, and he was pardoned, escaping the infliction of his sentence. The Lord sent to the ambassadors at their lodging to say that as they had not been at the feast, they should have a part of it; and he sent them five sheep and two great jars of wine.

On Monday, the twenty-second of September, the Lord went to another house and garden, which was surrounded by a high wall, and at each corner was a high round tower. In the middle there was a house, called "Bagino," in the shape of a cross, with a great pond in front. This house was larger than those in any of the gardens they had yet seen, and the work in gold and blue was the richest.

The Lord ordered a great feast to be prepared, and the ambassadors were invited to it. In this feast, the Lord gave an order that wine should be drunk, for the people are not allowed to drink wine publicly, nor in secret, without permission. The wine is given after dinner, and they serve it out in such quantities, and so often, that it makes the men drunk; and they do not consider that there is either pleasure or festivity without being drunk. The attendants serve the wine on their knees, and when one cup is finished, they give another; and these men have no other duty except to give another cup as soon as the first is finished. When one attendant is tired of filling the cups, another takes his place; and you must not think that one attendant supplies all, but he confines himself to one or two guests, so as to make them drink more; and those who do not wish to drink the wine are told that they insult the Lord, at whose request they drink. They give the cups full, and they must not leave any wine in them; and if they leave any, the attendants will not take the cup from them, but make them drink it all. They drink from one cup once or twice, and if they are called upon to drink by their love of the Lord, or by the Lord's head, they must drink it all at one pull, without leaving a drop. They call the man who drinks the most wine *Bahadur*, which is as much as to say "a valorous man"; and he who does not drink is made to do so, although he does not wish it.

On this day, before the ambassadors came to the Lord, he sent one of his Mirzas with a jug of wine and a message, asking them to drink the wine before they came, so that they might arrive in a jovial mood. Before the Lord arrived, they were seated according to the order observed at the previous interview; and the drinking lasted a long time. The food consisted of many roasted horses, boiled and roasted sheep, and rice cooked in their mode. After they had eaten, one of the Mirzas of the lord came with a silver basin, full of their silver coins, called *tagaes*; and they scattered them over the ambassadors and over the rest of the company. After they had done this, they put what was left into the skirts of their clothes. The Lord then caused the ambassadors to be clothed in robes; and they bowed their knees to him three times, according to the custom; and he said that they should come and dine with him again on another day.

On the next day, which was the twenty-third of September, the Lord went to another house and garden, near the former one, called "Dilicaya." There he again gave a great feast. At this feast such a multitude of people were assembled that, when the ambassadors came near to the Lord, they could not get on, except by the help of the guards appointed to make way for them. The dust was such that people's faces and clothes were all one color.

Tamerlane's Horde Assembles

In front of the gardens of the Lord there was a vast plain, through which a river flowed as well as many smaller streams. The Lord ordered many tents to be pitched on the plain for himself and his women, and commanded that all his host, which was scattered in detachments over the land, should be assembled, together with their women, to be present at the festivals and marriages that he wished to celebrate. Each man knew where his own tent should be pitched, so that the work was done without confusion or noise. After three or four days, 20,000 men were assembled round the tent of the Lord, and a day did not pass without many arriving from all parts.

In this horde there are always butchers and cooks who sell cooked sheep, others who sell fruit and barley, and bakers who sell bread. Every division of the horde is provided with all that the troops require, and they are arranged in streets. There are even baths and bath men who pitch their tents and make their huts for hot baths, with boilers for heating the water, and all that they require.

The Lord ordered that the ambassadors should be conducted to a house and garden near the encampment.

On Monday, the twenty-ninth of September, the Lord went to the city of Samarkand, and lodged in some houses near the entrance, which he had ordered to be built in honor of the mother of his wife Caño, who was interred in a chapel within these houses. These houses, though very rich, were not yet finished, but every day there were men working at them. On this day the Lord gave a great feast, and sent for the ambassadors. He gave this feast at the reception of some ambassadors who had come to him from a land that borders on the territory of the Emperor of Cathay.

These ambassadors arrived on that day, and were dressed in the following manner: the chief amongst them had on a dress of skins, with the hair outside, and these skins were the worse for wear. On his head he wore a small hat, with a cord to fasten it to his breast, and the hat was so small that his head would scarcely go into it. All those who came with him wore dresses of skin, some with the hair outside and others with it turned inside, and they looked like a party of blacksmiths. They brought presents to the Lord, of skins of martins and sables, white foxes, and falcons. They were Christians, after the manner of those of Cathay.

The object of the embassy was to ask the Lord to give them a grandson of Tokatamish, who was formerly Emperor of Tatary, to be their ruler. On this day the Lord played at chess for a long time with some "Zaytes," or men who were of the lineage of Mohammed. He would not receive the presents from the ambassadors, but they were brought forward, and he saw them.

On Thursday, the second of October, the Lord sent the ambassadors to a garden, where a knight lodged who was his chief porter; and the knight told them that the Lord had ordered him to say that he knew well that the Franks drank wine every day, but that they did not drink at their ease before him. He had therefore sent them to this place, that they might eat and drink at their ease. And he sent them ten sheep and a horse to eat, and also a load of wine. When the food was eaten and the wine drunk, they dressed the ambassadors in robes and gave them shirts and hats and also horses.

On Monday, the sixth of October, the Lord ordered a great feast to be given at the place where his horde was encamped on the plain. He summoned his relations and women, all his sons and grandsons who were near, his counselors, and all the people who were scattered round to assemble at this place. The ambassadors were brought to the plain and, when they arrived, they found many handsome tents pitched close together, most of them on the banks of the river. It was a very beautiful sight. The ambassadors went through some streets of tents, where tradesmen sold all that was required by this great host. When they were near the tents of the Lord, they were placed under an awning made of white linen ornamented with cloths of various colors. There were many awnings of this kind on the plain, and they make them long and high so that the sun may be screened off and air may enter freely.

Near these awnings, there was a great and lofty pavilion, which was like a tent, only square, and three lances high. It was a hundred paces broad and had four corners, and the ceiling was round like a vault. It was pitched against 12 poles, each as large around as a man, measured around the chest. They were painted gold and blue and other colors, and from corner to corner there were poles, three fastened together and making one. When they pitched the tents, they used wheels, like those of a cart, which were turned by men, and they have ropes fixed in various directions to assist them. From the vault of the ceiling of the pavilion, silken cloths descended between each of the poles, which were fastened to them, and when they were fastened they made an arch from one side to the other. Outside this square pavilion, there were porticoes joined to it and supported by 24 poles, not so large as the central ones, so that the whole pavilion was supported by 36 poles. From the pavilion at least 500 red cords were extended, and inside there was a crimson carpet beautifully ornamented with silken cloths of many colors and embroidered with gold threads. In the center of the ceiling there was the richest work of all; and in the four corners were the figures of four eagles with their wings closed.

The outside of the pavilion was lined with silk cloths in black, white, and yellow stripes. At each corner there was a high pole with a copper ball and the figure of a crescent on the top, and in the center there was another tall pole with a much larger copper ball and crescent. On the top of the pavilion, between these poles, there was a tower of silken cloths, with turrets and an entrance door. When the wind blew the pavilion about, or made the poles unsteady, men went on the top and secured anything that was loose. This pavilion was so large and high that, from a distance, it looked like a castle; and it was a very wonderful thing to see and possessed more beauty than it is possible to describe.

The pavilion contained a chamber in one part covered with carpets for the use of the Lord; and on the left hand there was another carpeted chamber and another beyond that. Round this pavilion there was a turreted wall, like that of any castle or city, made of silken cloths of many colors and ornamented in various ways. It had cords, inside and out, to draw it straight, and inside there were poles that supported it. The wall was round, encircling a space about 300 paces across, and it was as high as a man on horseback. It had a broad gate made like an arch, and on the top of it there was a tower with turrets; and the wall, as well as the tower and turrets, was ornamented with patterns and devices of very beautiful workmanship. They call this wall *Zalaparda.*

Within the wall there were many tents and awnings pitched in various ways, amongst which was a high tent not drawn out by cords; and nearby there was another, drawn out by cords of red velvet. In addition, there were four other tents close to each other, so that there was a passage from one to the next, and the street between them was covered over. The first section of tents was for the use of the chief wife of the Lord, Caño; and the other was for his second wife, Quinchicaño, which means "The Little Lady." Each had its own color, and in each there was one of these high tents without cords all covered with red cloth. Between the walls separating the tents there was only a narrow passage, and they were placed in rows, so as to look very beautiful. These enclosures were for the women of the Lord and of his grandsons, and during the summer they were as good as houses.

At noon the Lord came out of one of these enclosures, and went to the great pavilion. He caused the ambassadors to be brought in, giving them a great dinner of roasted sheep and horses.

Two of the most confidential friends of the Lord, who regulated his household, named Xamelique Mirza and Nooreddin Mirza, gave the Lord a present of many silver stands with long legs, on which were sweetmeats, sugar, raisins, and almonds; and on some of the stands there was a piece of silk. These presents were brought in nines; and such is the custom when presents are brought to the Lord, that they should be in nines, or consist of nine things. The Lord divided this present amongst the knights who stood before him; and he ordered the ambassadors to be given two of those which contained the silk. When they rose, they scattered pieces of money and small chaplets of thin gold amongst the people.

Drinking with the Ladies

On Thursday, the ninth of October, Hausada, the wife of Miran Mirza, the eldest son of the Lord, gave a great feast, to which she invited the ambassadors. It was given in the enclosure of tents set apart for her use.

When the ambassadors came near the tents, they found a very long row of jars of wine placed on the ground. The ambassadors were admitted into a tent, and ordered to sit down at the door under an awning. The said Hausada, and many other ladies, were seated at the door of a large tent.

On this day there was a marriage of one of her relations. Hausada herself was about 40 years of age, fair and fat, and before her there were many jars of wine and of a beverage of which they drink much, called *bosat,* made of cream and sugar.

There were also many knights and relations of Timor Beg, and jugglers, who were performing before her. When the ambassadors arrived, the ladies were drinking, and the way they drink is this: an old knight, a relation of the Lord, and two small boys, his relations, serve the cup before Hausada and the other ladies. They hold white napkins in their hands, and those who pour out the wine pour it into small golden cups, which they place on flat plates of gold. Those who serve the wine then come forward, with the pourers behind; and when they have got halfway, they touch the ground three times with their right knees. When they come near to the ladies, they take the cups with their hands wrapped in the white napkins, so that they may not touch the cups, and present them, kneeling, to the ladies who are going to drink. When the ladies have taken the cups, those who bring the wine remain with the flat plates in their hands and walk backward, so as not to turn their backs to the ladies. As soon as they are at a little distance, they bend their right knees again and remain there. When the ladies have finished drinking, the attendants go before them, and the ladies place the cups on the plates which they hold. You must not think that this drinking is of short duration, for it lasts a long time, without eating.

Sometimes, when these attendants are before the ladies with their cups, the ladies order them to drink, and they kneel down and drink all that is in the cups, turning them upside down to show that nothing is left; and on these occasions they describe their prowess in this respect, at which all the ladies laugh.

Caño, the wife of Timur Beg, came to this feast, and sometimes the company drank wine, and at others they drank cream and sugar. After the drinking had lasted a long time, Caño called the ambassadors before her and gave them to drink with her own hand. She importuned Ruy González for a long time to make him drink, for she would not believe that he never touched wine. The drinking was such that some of the men fell down drunk before her; and this was considered very jovial, for they think that there can be no pleasure without drunken men.

Hangings and Other Jollifications

On Thursday, the ninth of October, the Lord ordered a great feast to celebrate the marriage of one of his grandsons, to which the ambassadors were invited. It was given in a very beautifully ornamented enclosure containing many tents, and Caño, the chief wife of the Lord, Hausada, and many other ladies and knights were present.

There was an enormous supply of cooked horses and sheep, according to their custom. Much wine was drunk, and they made very merry. For the sake of more merriment, the Lord sent orders to Samarkand that all the traders in the city, the cooks and butchers, bakers and shoemakers, and all other people should come to the plain where the Lord was encamped with his horde, pitch their tents, and sell their goods there instead of in the city. He then ordered that each trade should play a game, and go through the camp, that his people might be amused. All the tradesmen, therefore, came out of the city, with all their goods, and peopled the plain, each trade in a different street of tents. An amphitheater was covered with carpets, where there were masquerades. The women were dressed like goats, others like sheep and fairies, and they ran after each other. The skinners and butchers appeared like lions and foxes, and all other tradesmen contributed specimens of their skill.

In the place where these traders had pitched their tents, the Lord ordered a great number of gallows to be set up; and declared that, in this festival, he knew how to be merciful and kind to some, and how to be severe to others.

The first piece of justice was inflicted upon a chief magistrate, whom they call Dina, who was the greatest officer in all the land of Samarkand. Timur had left him in the city as his magistrate when he departed for six years and eleven months, during which time this man had neglected his duties, so the Lord ordered him to be hanged, and confiscated all his goods. The justice inflicted upon this great man caused terror amongst the people; and the same punishment was ordered to be inflicted upon another man, who had interceded for this magistrate. A counselor of the Lord, named Burado Mirza, asked for his pardon if he paid a sum of 400,000 bezants of silver, each bezant being equal to a silver rial. The Lord approved of this, and when the man had given all he had, he was tormented to give more, and as he had no more, he was hung up by the feet until he was dead.

Another piece of justice was inflicted upon a great man who had been left in charge of 3000 horses when the Lord departed. Because he could not produce them all, he was hanged, although he pleaded that he would produce not only 3000 but 6000 horses if the Lord would give him time. In this, and other ways, the Lord administered justice.

He also ordered justice to be executed upon certain traders who had sold meat for more than it was worth; and shoemakers and other traders were fined for selling their goods at a high price. The custom is that when a great man is put to death, he is hanged; but the meaner sort are beheaded.

Tamerlane's Grandson

On Monday, the thirteenth of October, Timur Beg gave a feast, and sent for the ambassadors. When they approached near the great pavilion where the Lord was to dine, they found that two fresh enclosures were set up with tents like the others that I have described to you, except that these were more splendid than any that had been pitched before.

In front of these enclosures a great pavilion was pitched, made of white silk; it was ornamented, both inside and out, with many patterns in various colored silks. The ground near the pavilion of the Lord was covered with jars of wine, which were placed in a row, a stone's throw in length. No man was allowed to pass beyond these jars toward the pavilion, and mounted guards were placed to watch the line with bows and arrows and maces in their hands. If anyone passed the line, they shot arrows at him and gave him such blows with their maces that some men were taken outside the gates for dead. A great assemblage of people was waiting in the camp for the time when the Lord should come forth and go under the great pavilion.

Near this pavilion there were a great number of awnings, and under each awning there was a very large jar of wine, so large that one would hold 15 ordinary jugs of wine. After the ambassadors had been waiting for a long time, they were told to go and pay their respects to a grandson of the Lord who had come from India the day before. Timur Beg had sent for him to see him, as it was seven years since they had met.

This grandson was a son of Timur's firstborn son, who was dead, and whose name was Jehanghir. Timur loved him very much, and he was fond of this grandson, whose name was Peer Mohammed, for his father's sake. The ambassadors found him in a tent of red cloth seated on the floor, with many knights standing round him. When the ambassadors approached the tent, two knights came and took them by the arms, and made them kneel on the ground, they then took them a little nearer, and made them kneel again. When they came into the tent, they made their reverence, which was this: to kneel with the right knee on the ground, cross the arms on the breast, and incline the head. The knights who conducted them then raised them and led them out.

This grandson of the Lord was very richly dressed, according to his custom. He had on a robe of blue satin embroidered with golden wheels, some on the back and others on the breast and sleeves. His hat was adorned with large pearls and precious stones, with a very brilliant ruby on the top; and the people who stood round him treated him with great reverence and ceremony. In front of him there were two wrestlers dressed in leathern doublets without sleeves; but they neither of them could throw the other. At last one of them threw the other, and held him down for a long time, for they all said that if he got up the fall would not be counted.

On the same day all the ambassadors who were there went to do reverence to this grandson of Timur Beg, who was about 22 years of age. He was dark and beardless, and they call him Lord of India.

Wedding Festivities

The ambassadors waited until noon, when the Lord came forth from his tent and went under the pavilion. The ambassadors, a great number of his relations, and other people sat with him, according to the order that had been previously arranged. On this day there were many games, played in various ways. The elephants of the Lord had green-and-red-painted castles on their backs, and they were made to perform. The noise made by the drums during these games was so great that it was quite wonderful; and near the pavilion, where the Lord sat, there were many performing jugglers.

There were 300 jars of wine placed before the Lord on the ground; and there were also large skins full of cream, into which the attendants put loaves of sugar and mixed it up; and this was what they drank on that day.

When the people were all arranged in order around the wall that encircled the pavilion, Caño, the chief wife of the Lord, came forth to be present at the feast. She had on a robe of red silk trimmed with gold lace, which was long and flowing but without sleeves or any opening, except one to admit the head and two armholes. It had no waist, and 15 ladies held up the skirts of it to enable her to walk. She had so much white lead on her face that it looked like paper; and this is put on to protect it from the sun, for when they travel in winter or summer all great ladies put this on their faces. She had a thin veil over her face, and a crested headdress of red cloth, which hung some way down the back. This crest was very high, covered with large pearls, rubies, emeralds, and other precious stones, and it was embroidered with gold lace, on the top of which there was a circlet of gold set with pearls. On the top of all there was a little castle, on which were three very large and brilliant rubies, surmounted by a tall plume of white feathers. One of these feathers hung down as low as the eyes, and they were all secured by golden threads; and, as she moved, they waved to and fro.

Her hair, which was very black, hung down over her shoulders, and they value black hair much more than any other color. She was accompanied by 300 ladies. An awning was carried over Caño, supported by a lance borne by a man; it was made of white silk, in the form of the top of a round tent, and held over her to protect her from the sun.

A number of eunuchs, who guard the women, walked before her, and in this way she came to the pavilion where the Lord was, and sat down near him with all her ladies. Three ladies held her headdress with their hands, so that it might not fall on one side.

As soon as she was seated, another of the wives of the Lord came out from another enclosure, with many ladies dressed in the same way, and sat down in the pavilion a little below Caño. She was the second wife, Quinchicaño. Then, from another enclosure, came another wife, and sat down a little below the second; and in this way nine wives came out, and sat around the Lord, eight of them being his own, and one the wife of his grandson.

When they were all seated in order, they began the drinking, which lasted a long time. They gave the women their wine, with the same ceremonies that have been described to you, when I told you of the entertainment given in the tents of Hausada. The Lord called the ambassadors before him, and gave the master of theology a cup of wine with his own hand, for he now knew that Ruy González never drank wine. Those who took drink from the hand of the Lord observed the following ceremonies: first, they knelt down with their right knees, then they went forward a little, and knelt with both knees. They then took the cup, got up, and walked backward a little so as not to turn their backs, knelt down again, and drank so as not to leave a drop in the cup.

Each of the ambassadors was held under the armpits by two knights, who did not leave them until they had returned to the place where they were before. Near the great pavilion there were many tents and awnings for ambassadors who had come to the Lord, and under each awning there was a jar of wine for those to drink who sat there. The Lord ordered two of his own jars to be sent to the retinue of the ambassadors. Before the Lord there were certain poles and cords, on which men climbed and performed.

The Lord also had fourteen elephants, and each one had a wooden castle, covered with silk, with four yellow-and-green banners; and in each castle there were five or six men; and on the neck of each there was a man with a goad, who made the elephants run and perform tricks. These elephants were black, and had no hair except upon their tails, which were like those of camels. The animals were very large, equal in size to four or five great bulls, and their bodies were quite shapeless, like a full sack. Their legs were very thick, the same size all the way down, and the foot round and without hoofs, but with five toes, each with a nail, like those of a black man. They had no neck whatever, and their heads were fixed, so that they could not touch the ground with them. Their ears were very long, round, and scalloped, and their eyes very small. A man sat across their ears, who guided them with a goad in his hand and made them go where he liked. Their heads were very large, and, instead of noses, trunks came out of their heads and reached down to the ground. These trunks are pierced, and they drink through them. When an elephant wants to drink, he puts the trunk in the water and brings it up to his mouth. He also browses with his trunk, as he cannot do so with his mouth. He takes the grass in this trunk when he wants to eat and, turning it up, tosses the food into his mouth. He is thus supported by this trunk, and he winds it about like a serpent, so that there is no part of his body that he cannot touch with it. Under this trunk is the mouth; and he has jaws like a pig and two tusks as thick as a man's leg and as long as an arm. When they make them fight, they bind their trunks with spikes of iron, and fasten swords upon them.

The elephant is a very intelligent animal, and obeys very readily what his guide wishes him to do. The man who guides him sits on his neck, with his legs across the beast's ears. He carries a goad in his hand, with which he scratches its head and makes it go where he wishes, for when he makes a sign with the goad, it goes in the direction pointed out. When it fights, the guide is armed as well as the elephant. It walks like a bear, in jumps, and at each jump it wounds with the swords. When they wish these elephants to fight, the guides hit them on the forehead with the goad and make great wounds; and when they feel the wounds, they give loud grunts like pigs and, with open mouth, rush on in the direction pointed out by the guide. The wounds heal in the night if they leave the beasts in the open air, but if they are put under a roof, they will die. When the guide orders the elephant to take anything off the ground, however heavy it may be, it raises it with its trunk and gives it to the men who are in the castle on its back; and when those in the castle want to come down, they order it to stoop, and it stretches out its fore and hind legs in opposite directions, and touches the ground with its belly, while the men descend by cords that hang from the castle.

On this day they had much entertainment with these elephants, making them run with horses and with the people, which was very diverting; and when they all ran together, it seemed as if the earth trembled. I hold it to be true, from what I then saw, that one elephant is worth a thousand men in a battle; for when they are amongst men, they rush about wounding everyone; and when they are themselves wounded, they become more fierce, rush about more wildly, and fight better. As the tusks are too high up for them to wound with them, they fasten swords to them, so that they may wound the people under them. They can go a day or two, sometimes even three, without eating.

After the Lord and his women had drunk a great deal, they began to eat many sheep and horses, roasted whole, which were served up on very large skins, like printed leather, which men carried round; and there was so much that it took 300 men and more to bring it, and there was a great noise when they brought it before the Lord. They then put it into the basins and served it up without bread, according to the custom; and all this time cartloads of meat did not cease to arrive, also camels with panniers full of meat, which was placed on the ground in great heaps and eaten by the rest of the people. Afterward they brought many tables without cloths, on which were dishes of meat cooked with rice, and bread made with sugar. As night came on they placed many lighted lanterns before the Lord, and they commenced eating and drinking again. During the feast, two relations of the Lord were married. When the ambassadors saw that this would last all the night, and they had had as much as they wanted, they returned to their lodgings, while the Lord and his ladies continued their revelry.

Tamerlane's Treasures

On Friday, the twenty-seventh of October, Caño, the chief wife of the Lord, gave a great feast, and invited the ambassadors. The lady gave her entertainment in an enclosure of very rich tents to which a great assembly of people came, ambassadors from various countries as well as friends of her own, both knights and ladies. The enclosure was full of very rich tents, and the outer wall was made of white cloth ornamented and embroidered with letters and figures in a very beautiful design.

The ambassadors, when they came to the horde, were taken to the enclosure by certain knights who were relations of the Lord, and they entered a tent near the gateway of the enclosure. This tent was of crimson cloth, embroidered inside and out with white. Here they sat down, and much meat and drink was set before them. When they had eaten, Caño ordered that they should be shown the tents in her enclosure.

Among them there was one tent very large and high, unsupported by cords, and covered with very beautiful red silk. There were bands of silver gilt plates all round it, and the tent was beautifully adorned inside and out. It had two doors, one within the other. The first doors were made of thin red wands, close to each other, like a hurdle, and covered outside with rose-colored silk, beautifully woven. These doors were made in this way so that when they were shut, the air might enter freely, and those inside might see the people outside, while those outside could not see the people inside. The second doors were so high that a man might go through them on horseback, and they were covered with silver gilt, consisting of many square plates. They were ornamented very skillfully and in a variety of patterns, amongst which were blue and gold knots; and the workmanship was so cunning and so excellent, that it could not be equaled either in that country or in Christendom.

On one door was the figure of Saint Peter, and on the other that of Saint Paul, with books in their hands, which were covered with silver; and they say that Timur Beg found these gates at Bursa, when he pillaged the treasury of the Turk. Opposite these gates, in the middle of the tent, there was an ornamental cabinet or chest, containing silver. It was made of gold and very rich enamel work, and as high as a man's breast. The top was flat, and surrounded by small turrets in green and blue enamel, with many precious stones and large pearls. In the center of one of the sides, amongst these jewels, there was a stone as large as a small nut, and round, but not very bright. This cabinet had a small door, and within there was a shelf full of cups, above which there were six golden balls covered with pearls and precious stones.

At the foot of this cabinet there was a small golden table, about two palmos high, around which were many precious stones; and on the top there was a very clear and brilliant emerald, flat and four palmos long, which covered the whole table, being also a palmo and a half broad. In front of this small stand, or table, there was a golden tree, made to resemble an oak; with the trunk as big as a man's leg, from which many branches spread out in all directions, with leaves like those of an oak. It was as high as a man, and overshadowed the table, which stood near it. The fruit of this tree consisted of rubies, emeralds, turquoises, sapphires, and wonderfully large pearls, selected for their shape and beauty. On this tree there were many birds, made of enameled gold of various colors, which were seated on the leaves of the tree, with their wings spread out, and in the act of picking the fruit.

In front of this tree,* against the wall of the tent, there was a wooden table inlaid with silver gilt, and near it there was a bed of rich silk, embroidered with golden leaves and flowers and many other devices. On the opposite side of the tent there was a similar table and bed, and the ground was covered with rich silken carpets.

In this horde that the Lord had assembled there were as many as 14 or 15,000 tents, which was a beautiful thing to see; and besides these tents there were many others in the gardens, meadows, and fields around the city. The Lord had caused all the Mirzas and nobles in the land of Samarkand to come to this festival; amongst whom was the lord of Balaxia, which is a great city, where rubies are procured.

The ambassadors went to this lord of Balaxia and asked him how he got the rubies; and he replied that, near the city, there was a mountain whence they brought them, and that every day they broke up a rock in search of these jewels. He said that when they found a vein, they got out the rubies skillfully by breaking the rock all around with chisels.

Another lord also came to the festival, who held the city of Aquivi for Timur Beg, whence they procure the blue mineral, and in the rock they find sapphires. This city is also ten days journey from Samarkand, in the direction of India.

The Wealth of Samarkand

On Thursday, the thirtieth of October, the Lord left the encampment and went to the city of Samarkand, where he lodged at a mosque that he had ordered to be built for the burial of one of his grandsons, Mohammed Sultan Mirza, who had been killed in Turkey when Timur Beg conquered the Turk. This grandson, whom the Lord loved dearly, had himself taken the Turk prisoner, but later died of his wounds.

The Lord went on that day to celebrate a vigil feast, and invited the

---

* Again a golden tree bedecked with golden singing birds. One like it is said to have stood in the "Hall of the Tree" at the Caliph's palace in Baghdad; another, before the Emperor's throne in Byzantium. Concerning the latter, W. B. Yeats wrote the famous lines in "Sailing to Byzantium":

> Once out of nature I shall never take
> My bodily form from any natural thing,
> But such a form as Grecian goldsmiths make
> Of hammered gold and gold enamelling
> To keep a drowsy Emperor awake;
> Or set upon a golden bough to sing
> To lords and ladies of Byzantium
> Of what is past, or passing, or to come.

Perhaps the tree described here is the one that once belonged to the Abbasid caliphs, fell into the hands of the Mongols after the sack of Baghdad by Hulagu in 1258, then passed, in the course of time, to Tamerlane. Since no mention is made of the birds singing, this may indicate that the mechanism had already broken down, and was beyond the competence of his craftsmen to repair. The Greek scientist Hero of Alexandria (third century A.D.) is reputed to have been the inventor.

ambassadors. When they came they were shown the chapel and tomb. This chapel was square and very high, and was covered, both inside and out, with blue and gold ornaments. When his grandson died in Turkey, the Lord sent the body to be interred in Samarkand, and ordered this mosque to be built. But when the Lord arrived, he said the chapel was too low, so he ordered it to be pulled down and rebuilt in 10 days. They worked day and night, and he himself came twice to the city to watch the progress; and the chapel was finished in 10 days. It is a wonder that so great a work could have been completed in so short a time.

When the Lord saw that this work was completed, he ordered another to be built in the city, being moved by a desire to ennoble the city of Samarkand; and this new work was built for the following purpose:

In the city of Samarkand there is much merchandise, which comes every year from Cathay, India, Tatary, and many other parts; and as there is not a place for the orderly and regular display of the merchandise for sale, the Lord ordered that a street with shops should be made in the city. This street was commenced at one end of the city and went through to the other. He entrusted this work to two of his Mirzas, and let them know that if they did not use all diligence to complete it, working day and night, their heads should answer for it. These Mirzas began to work by pulling down such houses as stood in the line by which the Lord desired the street to run; and as the houses came down, their masters fled with their clothes and all they had. They made the street very broad, and covered it with a vaulted roof, having windows at intervals to let in the light.

As soon as the shops were finished, people were made to occupy them and sell their goods; and at intervals in this street there were fountains. A great number of workmen came into the city, and those who worked in the daytime were relieved by others who worked all night. Some pulled down houses, others leveled the ground, and others built the street. Day and night they made such a noise that they seemed to be like so many devils.

This great work was finished in 20 days, which was very wonderful. The owners of the houses that were pulled down went to certain cadis, who were friends of the Lord; and one day, when they were playing at chess with the Lord, they said that as he had caused those houses to be destroyed he ought to make some amends to the owners. Upon this he got into a rage, and said, "This city is mine! I bought it with my money, and possess the letters for it, which I will show you tomorrow. But if you are right, I will pay the people, as you desire." When he had spoken, the cadis were afraid, and they were surprised that he did not order them to be killed or punished for having thus spoken. They replied that all that the Lord did was right, and that all his commands ought to be obeyed.

The city of Samarkand is situated in a plain and surrounded by an earthen wall. It is a little larger than Seville, but, outside the city, there are a great number of houses joined together in many parts, so as to form suburbs. The city is surrounded on all sides by many gardens and vineyards, which extend in some directions a league and a half, in others two leagues, the city being in the middle. In these houses and gardens lives a large population, and there are people selling bread, meat, and many other things, so that the suburbs are much more thickly inhabited than the city within the walls.

Amongst the gardens outside the city, there are great and noble houses, and here the Lord has several palaces. The nobles of the city also have their houses amongst these gardens, and they are so extensive that, when a man approaches the city, he sees nothing but a mass of very high trees. Many streams of water flow through the city, and through these gardens, which contain numerous cotton plantations and melon grounds. The melons of this land are good and plentiful; and at Christmas time there is a wonderful quantity of melons and grapes. Every day so many camels come in, laden with melons, that it is a wonder how the people can eat them all. They preserve them from year to year in the villages in the same way as figs, taking off their skins, cutting them in large slices, and then drying them in the sun.

Outside the city there are great plains, which are covered with villages peopled by the captives that the Lord caused to be taken from the countries he conquered. The land is very plentiful in all things, as well bread as wine, fruit, meat, and birds. The sheep are very large, and have long tails, some weighing 20 pounds, and they are as much as a man can hold in his hand. These sheep are so abundant in the market that, even when the Lord was there with all his host, a pair was worth only a ducat. Other things are so plentiful that for a *meri*, which is half a rial, they sell a *fanega* [bushel] and a half of barley, and the quantity of bread and rice is infinite.

The name of Samarkand, or Cimes-quinte, is derived from the two words *cimes*, great, and *quinte*, a town. The supplies of this city do not consist of food alone, but of silks, satins, gauzes, taffetas, velvets, and other things. The Lord had so strong a desire to ennoble this city that he brought captives to increase its population from every land he conquered, especially all those who were skillful in any art. From Damascus he brought weavers of silk and men who made bows, glass, and earthenware; so that of those articles Samarkand produces the best in the world. From Turkey he brought archers, masons, and silversmiths. He also brought men skilled in making engines of war; and he sowed hemp and flax, which had never before been seen in the land.

There was so great a number of people brought to this city from all parts, both men and women, that they are said to have numbered 150,000 persons of many nations, Turks, Arabs and Moors, Christian Armenians, Greek Catholics, and Jacobites, and those who baptize with fire in the face, who are Christians with peculiar opinions. There was such a multitude of these people that the city was not large enough to hold them, and it was wonderful what a number lived under trees and in caves outside.

The city is also very rich in merchandise that comes from other parts.

Russia and Tatary send linen and skins; China sends silks, which are the best in the world (more especially the satins), and musk, which is found in no other part of the world, rubies and diamonds, pearls and rhubarb, and many other things. From India come spices, such as nutmeg, ginger, mace and cinnamon. The merchandise that comes from China is the best and most precious brought to this city, and they declare that the people of China are the most skillful workmen in the world. They say of themselves that they have two eyes, the Franks one, and that the Moors are blind, so that they have the advantage of every other nation in the world.

There are many open places in Samarkand where they sell meat cooked in various ways, fowls and other birds very nicely dressed; and they are always selling, day and night, in these places. There are also many places for killing meat, fowls, pheasants, and partridges. At one end of the city there is a castle, defended on one side by a stream flowing through a deep ravine, which is very strong. The Lord kept his treasure in that castle, and no man entered it except the magistrate and his officers. In this castle the Lord had as many as a thousand captives who were skillful workmen, and they labored all the year round at making headpieces and bows and arrows.

In honor of his grandson, the Lord gave a feast on this day at which many people were present. After they had eaten, a counselor of the Lord named Xamelique Mirza took the ambassadors before the Lord and dressed them in robes of honor and in furs, which they wear here in cold weather, lined with silk. These robes had two marten skins, one on each side of the neck. They also put hats on their heads, and gave them a bag containing 1500 bits of silver.

They then made their obeisance to the Lord, according to the custom. The Lord said that they should come to him on another day, when he would speak with them, and dismiss them, to return to his son the King of Spain.

A Hurried Departure

On Friday, the first of November, the ambassadors went to see the Lord, according to his order, expecting that he would dismiss them. They waited from morning until noon, when the Lord came out of a tent and sat down on a carpet, where they brought him much meat and fruit. He sent to the ambassadors to say that they must excuse him that day, as he could not speak with them, having much business with his grandson Peer Mohammed, the Emperor of India, who was about to return to his own territory. On that day the Lord gave him many horses and robes, arms and knights, to accompany him on his return.

On the following Saturday, the ambassadors returned to the Lord, as he had commanded, but he did not come out of his tent, because he felt ill. The ambassadors waited until noon, but some of his courtiers told the ambassadors to go away, as he would not see them, so they returned to their lodgings.

On Sunday the ambassadors again went to the Lord, to see if he would order them to be dismissed, and they waited a long time. The three confidential Mirzas asked them what they wanted, and told them to return to their lodgings, as the Lord would not see them. The Mirzas then sent for the knight who had charge of them, asking him why he had let them come, and ordered his nose to be pierced through; but he proved that he did not send them, nor had he seen them that day, and he thus escaped with only a sound flogging. The Mirzas did this because the Lord was very sick, and all his women and attendants were running about in a state of bewilderment.

The ambassadors returned to their lodgings, and neither went to the Lord nor did he send for them; but a Chagatai came and said that the Mirzas had sent him to tell them they were to prepare to start on their journey the following day, in the morning, with the ambassadors from the Sultan of Babylon, from Turkey, and with Carvo Toman Oghlan, who was to accompany them as far as the city of Tabriz and supply them with food and all that they required. He added that, at Tabriz, Omar Mirza, the grandson of the Lord, would dismiss them to their own land.

The ambassadors answered that the Lord had not yet dismissed them, nor sent any compliments to their King, and they desired to know how this could be. He told them that he had nothing more to say, and that the Mirzas had ordered him to give this message to them and to the other ambassadors. The ambassadors then went to the Mirzas at the palace, and told them that they knew very well what the Lord had said to them the Friday before with his own mouth: that they should come to him, and that he would speak to them and dismiss them; but now the Mirzas had sent a man to them to tell them to prepare to start the next day, at which they were very much surprised. The Mirzas answered that they could not see the Lord, and that they must prepare to start the next day, as they were now dismissed.

The Mirzas did this because the Lord was very ill, had lost the power of speech, and was at the point of death, as the ambassadors were told by those who knew it for certain.* The Mirzas wished them to be gone before his death became known, so that they might not publish the news in their own countries. To the remonstrances that the ambassadors constantly urged upon the Mirzas, that they ought not to be dismissed in this way without any message from the Lord to their King, the Mirzas answered that they had nothing more to say, further than that the ambassadors were to go.

On the eighteenth of November, the Mirzas sent the Chagatai, who was to accompany the ambassadors, to say that they were to depart. They replied that they would not go without either seeing the Lord or receiving a letter from him; but he said that they must either go at once, with all the

* Timur did not die until February 17, 1405, at Otrar, beyond the river Jaxartes, when he was marching to invade China. He was, however, subject to very severe attacks of illness, and he was then seized by one of those attacks. He recovered in a week (translator's note).
Perhaps all that feasting and partying may also have had something to do with it.

supplies due to their rank, or stay and go at another time without them. On that day, therefore, they left the place where they were lodging and went to a garden near the city with the ambassador from the Sultan of Babylon, where they were ordered to wait for the ambassadors from Turkey. They remained in this garden until Friday the twenty-first of November, when they all assembled and departed from Samarkand.

Pope Alexander VI

Anonymous painter. Uffizi, Florence.

O yes thy sinnes
Do runne before thee to fetch fire from hell
To light thee thither.

John Webster, *The White Devil*

*C*oncerning *Pope Alexander VI humanity might claim in self-defense that he was as much a "christian" as, say, Stalin was a "socialist." He appears to us now like some mafia-style godfather, the Boss of bosses, surrounded by a murderous conclave of no less ruthless and ambitious "capo"-cardinals, each with his own territorial rights and private family of "soldier"-assassins, against whom he had to maintain himself in power by the use of fear, treachery, violence, and guile. "When we consider," writes the nineteenth century historian Ferdinand Gregorovius, "the utter abandon with which Alexander VI committed his crimes, we are forced to conclude that he was an atheist and materialist. . . . For how could Alexander reconcile his sensuality and his cruelty with the consciousness that he was the High Priest of the Church, God's representative on earth? There are abysses to the human soul," concludes Gregorovius, "to the depths of which no glance can penetrate."*

To those of simple faith who lived at the time, the explanation was equally plain and simple: the Pope had signed a Faustian pact with the devil. Not long after the death of Alexander in mid-August of 1503, the Marquis of Mantua wrote in a letter to his wife as follows:

> *When the Pope fell sick, he began to talk in such a way that anyone who did not know what was in his mind would have thought he was wandering, although he was perfectly conscious of what he said; his words were: "I come; it is right; wait a moment." Those who know the secret say that . . . he made a compact with the devil and purchased the papacy from him at the price of his soul. Among the other provisions of the agreement was one which said that he should be allowed to occupy the Holy See twelve years, and this he did with the addition of four days. There are*

some who affirm that at the moment he gave up his spirit seven devils were seen in his chamber. As soon as he was dead his body began to putrify and his mouth to foam like a kettle over the fire, which continued as long as it was on earth.

Perhaps only an atheist Pope could have been so suited to such a superstitious age. But the age was changing.

In the same year 1492 of Alexander's accession, the world was literally to be turned round by Columbus's voyage of discovery to America. And during the Jubilee Year of 1500, the Prussian Copernicus, who was destined to put it firmly in its place around the sun, resided in Rome and was lecturing on mathematics and astronomy. Within living memory, too, was the conquest of the ancient Byzantine empire by the Ottoman Turks in 1453 and the downfall of Constantinople, which resulted indirectly in the diffusion of Greek learning throughout Europe and the humanist rediscovery of classical art and literature. And concurrently, the invention of the printing press by Gutenberg around 1450 allowed the Bible to be read and studied by the people without benefit of clergy for the first time. Then employed as a military engineer and architect for Cesare Borgia was Leonardo da Vinci; likewise the poet Ariosto received the patronage of the Pope's daughter Lucrezia; and the young Michelangelo by 1499 had completed his "Pietà" for Saint Peter's. In sum, it was an age "pregnant with futurity," which is to say, our present.

Alexander VI, who presided over Christendom at that time, was born Rodrigo Lanzol in 1431 at Xátiva, a small town near Valencia in Spain. His uncle Alfonso Borgia was elected Pope in 1455, taking the name Calixtus III, and adopted Rodrigo into the Borgia family. Rodrigo became a cardinal in 1457, at the age of 26, and a year later assumed the lucrative post of vice-chancellor of the Church of Rome. He was described in those years as being unusually handsome, forceful, and magnanimous—and also as flagrantly addicted to wenching. He took as his official mistress in 1467 Vannozza dei Catanei, a member of one of the lesser noble families in Rome, and by her had four (some say five) children: Cesare, in 1475; Giovanni, 1476; Lucrezia, 1480; and Joffré, 1482. In order to legitimize his children, he married off Vannozza (in name only) three times to various noblemen in exchange for money and

*other benefits, the last time in 1486 when she was in her mid-forties. With the
immense wealth he had accumulated as vice-chancellor, he was able to grease
and simonize his way into being elected Supreme Pontiff by the College of
Cardinals upon the decease of Innocent VIII.*

*A generation after Alexander's death in 1503, the Florentine historian
Francesco Guicciardini wrote in his classical* Storia d'Italia:

> *As his first accession to the Papacy was foul and shameful—for he
> bought with gold so high an office—so similarly his government was in
> agreement with its vile foundation. There was in him, and in full
> measure, all vices both of flesh and spirit. . . . He had no care for
> justice, since in his days Rome was a den of thieves and murderers.
> His ambition was boundless, and such that it grew in the same
> measure as his state increased. Nevertheless, his sins meeting with no
> punishment in this world, he was to the last of his days most
> prosperous. In one word, he was more evil and more lucky than,
> perhaps, any other Pope for many ages before.*

*The account of the life and times of Pope Alexander VI that follows has been
taken from the* Diary *of Johannes Burchard, Bishop of Orta and papal Master
of Ceremonies, who served under five popes, from 1483 until 1506, and kept a
detailed record of what went on in Rome. Gregorovius says of him: "That
Burchard was not friendly to the Borgias is proved by the way the* Diary *is
written; yet it is absolutely truthful. . . . Even the little which he did write
concerning events of the day would have cost him his head had it come to the
knowledge of Alexander or Cesare Borgia. It appears however, that the diaries
of the Masters of Ceremonies were not subjected to official censorship."*

Church historians have always maintained a more or less official policy of
omertà *regarding Burchard's* Diary, *though copies of the complete manuscript
were preserved at the Vatican Library. In 1906 a full edition in the original
Latin was released for publication in Italy, edited by E. Celani. It was partly
translated into English in 1921 by Dr. F.L. Glaser (New York: N.L. Brown),
and in 1963 by Geoffrey Parker (London: Folio Society), from both of which I
have extracted and arranged the selections in this book.*

His Accession

In the year of the Lord 1492, on Saturday, the eleventh of August, at
noon, Rodrigo Borgia, vice-chancellor and the nephew of Calixtus III, was
created Pope and named Alexander VI.

On the twenty-seventh of August Alexander was crowned in Saint Peter's. Then he went through triumphal arches in the customary manner to the church of Saint John in the Lateran while the greatest honor was done to him throughout the city by the Roman people, more than there was ever done to other popes.

In the first consistory he held, on September first, he created the archbishopric of Monreale and named as cardinal his nephew [Giovanni de Borgia-Lanzol, called "il Maggiore," to distinguish him from another nephew of the same name, known as "il Minore," who also became a cardinal] from his sister Giovanna. And on the same day he created his son Cesare, then 16 years old, Bishop of Valencia. [Cesare was named a cardinal a year later.]

After the Pope's coronation it was brought to his knowledge that from the day of the last illness of Innocent VIII [died July 25, 1492] until his accession more than 220 men had been assassinated in various places at various times. It was also brought to his knowledge who the murderers were.

At the beginning of his reign the greatest danger facing Pope Alexander was the hostility of the French Valois King Charles VIII, who threatened to invade Italy and assert his claim to the throne of Naples by force. In this he was supported by the hereditary rivals of the Borgias, the Sforza family of Milan and the Colonna and Orsini families of Rome, who saw in the invasion an opportunity to depose the new Pope on the grounds of simony and elect one of their own. They also held out to the French King the possibility that, with Naples as a base, he could organize a new crusade to wrest the Holy Land from the Turks. The reigning King of Naples, Ferrante [Ferdinand I], therefore dispatched his son Federigo to confirm his alliance with the Pope.

On Monday, the tenth of December, 1492, I rode at daybreak to Marino to instruct the noble lord Federigo of Aragon, Prince of Altamura, second son of King Ferrante of Naples, with regard to the ceremonies at his reception before his arrival in Rome.

The next day, about 2 o'clock in the afternoon, the Prince continued on his way to Rome with his suite until he reached the church of Saint John in the Lateran, firstly, in order to avoid the mud, and then because two cardinals who were to meet him at the church had not yet arrived. The Prince waited about an hour for the arrival of the two cardinals who had been despatched and who arrived finally after 6 o'clock, namely Giovanni Borgia and Ascanio Sforza. They received him in the usual way and escorted him in their midst.

After the arrival at the place of Saint John in the Lateran, where one sees the bronze statue of a horseman, there came the prelates of the palace with the suite of the Pope. Together with the Prince seven other ambassadors had been sent to swear the oath of loyalty to the Pope. I assigned every one his place in due order of precedence, and in this order we rode straight on to the apostolic palace near Saint Peter's. I assume the reason for the cardinals' lateness was that the Pope endeavored in this way to prevent the Prince from continuing on the same day to the palace, and to divert him to the inn, Ad Apostolos, where he was supposed to take his quarters. Behind the barons, nobles, and the whole retinue of the Prince rode the shield bearers of the Pope and our barons with the captain of the palace. There were two pages before the armed men of the Prince and six before those of the Pope: the first with crossbow and quiver of gilded silver in French dress and on a French horse; the second in Turkish dress on a Berber horse; the third clad in Spanish fashion with a long lance on a small Spanish hack; the fourth with the rain-coat of his master; the fifth with a valise of a crimson color; the sixth with a sword sheathed in its scabbard with a handle studded with pearls and precious stones estimated at 6000 ducats in value [approximately $150,000, 1974]. There were several riders mounted on very magnificent horses, dressed in gold brocade and wearing jewels of great value on their breasts and in their hats and birettas. The Prince wore a garment of violet velvet, a chain of pearls and jewels, worth 6000 ducats, and a belt with a sword of the same value. His bridle was studded all over with pearls and precious stones, worth 3000 ducats, and the whole harness was gilded before and behind. The suite was preceded by 200 sumpters all covered with red cloth, and the whole suite included 700 to 800 people, as I was told.

Having arrived at the palace they went up to the Pope, who awaited the Prince in the last of the nine chambers, besides the secret chamber. Five cardinals were with him. After Federigo had been permitted by the Pope to kiss his foot, his hand, and his mouth, they too kissed the foot of the Pope while the Prince was kneeling on a cushion at the left of the Pope. Federigo then declared that King Ferrante of Naples humbly committed himself to worship his Holiness, and presented the Pope with letters written by his father.

Prince Federigo finally left Rome on Thursday, January tenth. He crossed through the city, escorted by Cardinals Caraffa and Piccolomini, to the river side, where his galleys were waiting to transport him back to Naples. Eight of the Prince's pages preceded, dressed in differing national styles, German, Hungarian and Bohemian, and carrying bows, targets, swords, and other weapons, all studded with pearls and precious gems.

*

On the twenty-seventh of December a royal letter from Barcelona was brought to the Pope, by the bishops of Badajoz and Astorga as ambassadors, that King Ferdinand V of Spain had been severely wounded in his neck by a peasant on the steps of his palace on the seventh of December, so that six stitches had to be applied. The criminal had received two wounds from the men of the King and had been seized.

A few days later the additional news arrived that the King was out of danger and that the peasant had acted under a vision from the devil. The devil had appeared to him 20 years ago in the form of an angel and had commanded him to kill the King in order to become king himself, but he had forbidden him to tell anybody of this. After that he had appeared to him again and again urging him on. The peasant had been forced to a confession by the promise of reward. Then the scales fell from his eyes, as it were, and he had repented immediately from the depth of his heart and considered himself worthy of the most cruel death. Whereupon he was condemned to be executed after the following manner, namely, that all his limbs or extremities of every limb should be cut off one after the other and at intervals of time but on one and the same day. In order, however, that he should not be driven to despair he was given at the beginning a heavy blow on the head by order of the Queen so that he might die more quickly and would suffer less while his limbs were being cut off, his consciousness being thus dimmed.

The Pope decided to have a mass said in honor of the glorious Virgin Mary for the recovery of the King on the twenty-ninth of December, in the chapel of Santa Maria della Febbre beside the basilica of Saint Peter. Afterward the face of Our Lord and the spear should be shown to the people and the day should be celebrated as a feast day by all craftsmen and others. And he ordered that all this ought to be proclaimed in public and be made known through placards in the various quarters of the city.

On Monday, June tenth [1493], Don Giovanni Sforza, the Count of Cotignola and Vicar of Pesaro, betrothed and took as his lawful wife Donna Lucrezia Borgia, the Pope's daughter, and still only a girl of thirteen. While still a cardinal, the Pope had married her to a Spaniard [Don Gasparo, son of the Count of Aversa]. As Pope, however, he wished to improve the position of his daughter and therefore dissolved the marriage, bestowing 3000 ducats upon the Spaniard as compensation. Now he married her to the aforementioned lord while her first husband was still living, but the latter remained silent on account of the money and yielded.

Don Giovanni Borgia, Duke of Gandia, was commanded by the Pope to escort Lucrezia from the residence of Cardinal Zeno, where she was living. He brought her in as far as the last room, a Negro girl carrying her train, and she was followed by Donna Battistina, the granddaughter of Pope Innocent VIII of blessed memory, and her train too was borne by a Negress. Donna Giulia Farnese, the Pope's concubine,* and many other Roman ladies, numbering in all about 150, followed Lucrezia and Battistina.

* "La Bella Giulia" Farnese was only 16 years old in 1489 when she became the Pope's favorite, and he was then 57. Among other benefits bestowed upon her family as a result, he appointed her young brother Alessandro Farnese a cardinal; and Alessandro, though regarded with contempt at the time as "The Petticoat Cardinal," was later to be elected Pope Paul III, during whose reign (1534–49) the Society of Jesus was founded, and the Council of Trent, which inaugurated the Counter-Reformation, was convened.

In the palace, the Sala Reale and all the apartments, except the first adjoining it, were prepared with most elaborate decorations of velvet coverings and tapestries. At the end of the Sala Reale and to the right of the entrance, a throne was placed, with four steps as an approach to it across the width of the room. On learning of their arrival, the Pope entered, proceeding from the room above the palace gate through all the apartments to the room by the Sala Reale, where he sat on his throne officially to greet the ladies. They passed in turn before him, but despite my admonishments, none of them genuflected except for the Pope's daughter and a few others close to her. His Holiness, dressed in a rochet and crimson hood, was accompanied by 10 cardinals who took their seats by his throne, 5 priests on the right and 5 deacons on the left. Then the Duke of Gandia approached with his sister, the bride, to kiss the Pope's foot, and they were followed by the ladies.

When all the ladies had kissed the Pope's foot, Don Giovanni Sforza with Donna Lucrezia on his left, knelt on two cushions before the Pope. Don Camillo Beneimbene, a Roman citizen, stepped forward as notary in front of them, and said to Don Giovanni, in the vernacular:

"Illustrious Sir, are you prepared to pledge yourself to, and to receive pledges from, your lawful spouse, and to marry the illustrious Donna Lucrezia Borgia, who is here present and promises to become your wife?" To this question, Don Giovanni replied, "I do, most willingly." Then the notary addressed the bride with a similar question, and she also answered, "I do, most willingly."

Don Leonello, the Bishop of Concordia, next stepped before the Pope and, kneeling beside the bride and bridegroom, placed one ring—the bridegroom's gift—on the ring finger of the bride's left hand, and another ring on the second finger. Meanwhile, the Count of Pitigliano, the captain general of the Holy Roman Church, held a naked sword outstretched over the heads of the bridal pair, beginning to do so as the bishop fitted the rings on the bride's fingers, and lowering the sword when once they were in place.

Afterward, all the ladies who were in the room followed the bride as she was escorted by her brother into the Sala Reale. There Donna Lucrezia and her husband sat on the stools prepared for them, whilst all the rest found places on the cushions scattered around the platform. Shortly afterward the Pope joined them, and when he was seated on his throne, they all enjoyed a series of entertainments. Four grooms of Cardinal Colonna's household dressed up as gentlemen visiting Rome and recited some verses about love, after which two of the sons of Master Andrew, who had a school in the city, also dressed up in fashionable clothes with a number of their friends and performed a comedy with such eloquence that everyone loudly applauded them.

After this, an assortment of all kinds of sweets, marzipans, and drinks of wine, in about a hundred basins and cups, were brought in and carried round with napkins by chamberlains and grooms. They first served the Pope and the cardinals, then the bride, bridegroom, and ladies, whilst others went to the clergy and the rest, and finally they flung what sweets remained amongst the people outside, in such abundance that I believe that more than a hundred pounds of sweets were crushed and trampled underfoot.

King Charles VIII in Rome

Upon the death of King Ferrante [Ferdinand I] of Naples in 1494, his son Alfonso was crowned by Pope Alexander. This provoked King Charles VIII of France to begin his long-threatened invasion of Italy and make good the Anjou claims on Naples. He entered Milan in September with an immense army, where he was greeted by his ally Ludovico Sforza, then proceeded down the boot to conquer Florence by November and drive out the ruling family of the Medici, subduing Pisa and neighboring towns along his way, to reach the outskirts of Rome in triumph by the end of the year.

On Thursday, December eighteenth, all the Pope's possessions, including even his bed and daily credence table, were assembled for removal by road from the Vatican Palace to the Castel Sant' Angelo. The vestments from the Apostolic Chapel, all the money chests from the sacristy, the palace weapons, and stores of food, and all the papal belongings were sent to the castle, whilst the cardinals also prepared to leave, loading packhorses and furnishing their mounts for the road. Next day, Cardinal Sanseverino was released from detention, and on the Pope's instructions, and in his name, rode to the King of France to discuss particular matters with him. Prospero Colonna [of the powerful Roman family, which had sided with Charles VIII] was also set free, and was said to have promised to restore the fortress of Ostia to the Pope and to have changed sides to serve him and the Church.

From December nineteenth onward, the French troops were breaking into the city suburbs by Monte Mario and penetrating as far as the church of San Lazzaro and the fields close to the Castel Sant' Angelo. In these positions they remained throughout a whole night so that, with treacherous help, they could attack the city from that side. It was planned that the Colonna should assault the walls from the other direction, with the aid of a force of a thousand Frenchmen who were to cross the Tiber near Ostia and advance from there. But this part of the scheme was abandoned because such a strong wind sprang up that they could not cross the river.

It was said that they intended putting their evil designs into operation by entering through the Porta San Paolo, and then burning and pillaging the city and committing other crimes. Some people further alleged that Cardinal Peraudi had planned all this, but that on that same night he had found his way barred as he approached the city gate, and had therefore withdrawn. He was nevertheless the greatest single factor in expediting

King Charles's progress toward Rome, for it was he who had persuaded Acquapendente and the inhabitants of other lands of the church to allow the entry of the French, by praising to the skies the honesty and lawful conduct of the King and his troops. The cardinal claimed that they would not take a hen or an egg or the smallest item from anyone without fully paying for it, and he asserted that the Pope himself had promised to secure a passage through the Church's territories for the King. Thus, with these and other lies, he induced the people to admit Charles VIII and his forces, completely against the wishes of his Holiness.

On Friday, the twenty-sixth of December, 1494, on the feast of Saint Stephen, Cardinal Cibo celebrated the solemn mass in the main chapel of the palace in the presence of the Pope. After the Pope had entered there came also three ambassadors of the King of France, who had arrived during the night before, namely the grand marshal of France; Jean de Ganay, the president of the parlement of Paris; and a third one, all laymen. To the first I assigned a seat on the steps of the throne before and above the senator, and the two others were assigned to the bench of the lay ambassadors, where there were seated already two ambassadors of the King of Naples. These would not have anything to do with the newcomers, explaining that they were not aware that they were ambassadors, and they left their seats.

By special order of the Pope, I informed them that those were ambassadors of the King of France, whereupon they yielded and returned to their seats. Many Frenchmen had appeared with the three ambassadors, a large number of whom pushed themselves forward without any consideration near the prelates and sat down on their benches. When I showed them away and assigned them to their proper seats, the Pope summoned me and said angrily that I had ruined his intentions, and that I should permit the Frenchmen to remain where they wanted. I replied to his Holiness that for God's sake he should not get excited as I now knew his intentions, and would not say anything more to them wherever they should stand.

On Wednesday, the thirty-first of December, 1494, I rode out by order of the Pope quite early in the morning to meet the King of France.* Near Galera, after two miles' journey, we met the Cardinals Giuliano della Rovere, Gurck, and Savelli, to whom I made obeisance without dismounting from my horse. Soon afterward came the King, to whom we also made our obeisance without dismounting, on account of the dirt and the rain as well as his fast approach.

---

* The Florentine historian Francesco Guicciardini, who as a boy of 11 witnessed Charles VIII's invasion of his homeland, describes him as follows in the *Storia d'Italia*: "His stature was short and his face very ugly—if you except the dignity and vigor of his glance. His limbs were so disproportioned that he had less the appearance of a man than a monster, and not only was he ignorant of liberal arts but he was virtually illiterate." The King is also said to have had six toes on each foot, which he hid by wearing splayed shoes, thereby setting the fashion for elegant foot gear in the French court at the end of the fifteenth century.

I explained to his Majesty what I had been charged with by the Pope. The King replied he wished to come to Rome without any display whatever. I received his answer, and after me Hieronymus Porcarius, in the name of the Roman authorities, placed the citizens and their possessions at the disposal of the King. The King replied in a few words without entering into this matter. The Romans withdrew, and the King called me at his side and conversed with me for about four miles continuously, asking me about the ceremonies, the condition of the Pope, the rank and position of Cesare Borgia, and a number of other things, so that I found it almost impossible to give proper answers to every particular question.

The whole way to the Palace of San Marco was one mud puddle. In all the streets there was an illumination of fires and torches at 11 o'clock in the evening, and all the people shouted: *"Francia! Francia! Colonna! Colonna! Vincula! Vincula!"*

Beginning next day and continuing through the days that followed, all the cardinals in Rome in turn visited the French King, as was customary, with the exception of Cardinals Caraffa and Orsini, who had permission from his Holiness to remain in rooms in the Vatican. During our conversation as we rode toward the city, I had explained to King Charles how the cardinals would come to welcome him and that he was to receive and accompany them to the steps of Saint Peter's, always giving them his right hand and performing other details of this sort. But matters fell out far differently, for none of the cardinals came thus to meet or escort him, and indeed much less than due courtesy was shown by either the King or the cardinals.

At the Palazzo Venezia, the hall and the best or first apartment were set aside for housing the ambassadors and other Frenchmen. They were provided with plenty of straw beds, but I observed that at no time were the sacks of straw cleaned. Tallow candles were hung over the doors of the rooms and in the fireplaces, and although there were most beautiful tapestries decorating the walls, everything was like a pigsty.

On Friday, January second [1494] the Colonna seized two horses outside Cardinal Sanseverino's house, two more belonging to Geremia Contugi above the Ponte Sant' Angelo, and yet another horse that was the property of Cardinal Riario; their riders were roughly thrown down on the public paths. Other horses were seized from Don Mario Mellini's stable, where many Frenchmen had their quarters. Next day, the Colonna and the French sacked and pillaged the houses of the late Bishop Nicola Grato de' Conti and of Don Bartolomeo de Luna, the Pope's chamberlain. On their way, the French forced an entrance into houses on either side of the road, ejecting their owners, horses and other goods, setting fire to wooden articles, and eating and drinking whatever they found there without paying anything. As a result, wild rumors began to spread amongst the people, and King Charles had a public proclamation made in the city that under penalty of death nobody was to enter a house forcibly.

On Thursday, January eighth, the house of Paolo Branca, a Roman citizen, was plundered and pillaged by the French, and his two sons were killed, whilst others, including Jews, were murdered and their homes ransacked. Even the house of Donna Vannozza Catanei, the mother of Cardinal Cesare Borgia, did not escape being pillaged. Five thieves were hanged the following day in the city, three from one window and a fourth from the other window of the corner house opposite the palace of Cardinal de' Medici and facing the Tiber over the Campo di Fiori. The other thief was hanged from the window of the house of Bonadies, also on the corner of a street and next to the Ponte Sant' Angelo.

Next night, a great part of the outer wall of the Castel Sant' Angelo collapsed over a length of about 30 feet, that is, from the tower to the gate, and with the fall three people, including the keeper, were killed, all crushed by the wall. It was at this time, if I remember rightly, that his Holiness left the Vatican after supper on January sixth and was carried through the cloisters to the Castel Sant' Angelo to stay for greater safety.

*

Within the fastness of the Castel Sant' Angelo, the Pope could hold out against the French and negotiate with Charles VIII for a settlement. One of the strongest pawns in the Pope's possession was a certain. Djem, the youngest brother of the Turkish Sultan Bajazet II, who had fled to Rome during the papacy of Innocent VIII for safety after an abortive rebellion. Bajazet had paid Innocent, and now paid Alexander, 40,000 gold ducats yearly to keep his brother Djem confined in the papal household. But when the invasion by Charles began, the Pope, being in urgent need of funds, had written to the Sultan offering to assassinate his brother for the sum of 300,000 ducats, warning him that Charles intended a crusade on the Holy Land which would depose Bajazet and put Djem on the throne. The Sultan's reply, revealed when the French captured the Pope's messenger returning from Constantinople, was as follows:

Sultan Bajazet Chan, son of Sultan Mahomet Chan, by God's grace Emperor and Lord of Asia, Europe, and all seas, to the Father and Lord of all Christians by Divine Providence, Alexander VI, worthy Pontiff of the Roman Church.

It would be good, We judge, that the original sentence of death on Our brother Djem, who is held in Your Highness's hands, should be carried out, for this would be a release into life for him, useful for Your authority and most convenient and gratifying to Our position. If Your Magnificence is agreeable to please Us in this matter, and indeed We trust that You will be prudent to be so, then for Your greater security and Our deeper satisfaction, You should execute the deed as quickly as possible. Thereby Your Highness will be the better pleased and Djem will more quickly be delivered from the straits of this world so that his soul will have peace in the next. Furthermore, if Your Highness will undertake to fulfill this agreement, and will command that Djem's body should be delivered to Us at any point on our coasts, We, Sultan Bajazet Chan, promise to hand over 300,000 ducats at any place pleasing to Your Eminence, with which sum You may buy possessions for Your sons. These ducats We shall have consigned to any person Your Highness appoints before the body is handed over to Our servants. Moreover, We promise that during the lifetime of each of Us, We shall always maintain a deep and lasting friendship with Your Highness, aiding You as much as possible without any deceit.

However, with the French armies occupying Rome the Pope found himself in a new situation, which altered these plans for Djem.

After much discussion, the Pope and Comte Philippe de Bresse—who was acting for the French King, his nephew—reached agreement on Sunday, January eleventh, concerning Prince Djem. It was arranged that Sultan Bajazet's brother should be handed over by his Holiness to the King of France for six months, and that the latter should pay the Pope 20,000 ducats and provide security in Florentine and Venetian trading bonds to guarantee the immediate restoration of Djem at the end of six months. Furthermore, it was agreed that the Pope should crown Charles VIII King of Naples, without bringing harm to Alfonso, and that he should guarantee the safety of Cardinals della Rovere, Peraudi, Savelli, and Colonna. In order to confirm the papal reconciliation with these cardinals, it was decided that it should be publicly declared on the same evening in the presence of witnesses.

On Sunday, January eighteenth, I was summoned to the Pope's presence by his groom, and told by his Holiness that on the following day there was to be a public consistory to receive the King of France, and that he was going to carry out the reception himself. I replied that such an arrangement as ordered by his Holiness was unique and came outside the usual ceremonial order, but that we could conduct proceedings according to the same form as that adopted when the King first came into Rome.

As we were talking these matters over, King Charles approached the Sala dei Pontefici, and the Pope, somewhat unfittingly dressed in his white cloak and biretta and his decorated stole, went out to meet his Majesty at the entrance. The King had come to review the articles earlier concluded and subscribed to by himself and the Pope, and in discussion over them there arose one matter for dispute. This related to the sureties to be given by his Majesty against the safe restoration of the Turkish Prince Djem to the Pope after six months. The relevant article stated that the King should provide as sureties a number of French nobles, lords, and prelates, according to the Pope's particular wish, but whereas his Holiness wanted the number of such persons to be between 30 and 40, the president of the Paris parlement sought to restrict it to 10, and around this point they argued for about three hours. Finally, the articles of the settlement were read out, sworn to, and signed, the terms being written out in French for his Majesty and in Latin for the Pope.

On the Monday, the Sala Reale in the Vatican was prepared in the traditional way for the public consistory in which the French King should take his oath of obedience. When the Pope was ready to appear, he commissioned me to go to the King of France to instruct him in what to do and say in kissing his Holiness's foot and in swearing allegiance to him. I said nothing to the Pope as to where the King's place should be, whether between the cardinals or immediately behind them, since his Majesty, I knew, had decided with his own advisers not to sit in any such position at all, but rather to stand with the Pope at his throne, and there give his oath of allegiance as briefly as possible.

At the King's arrival in the consistory, the Pope put aside his ordinary miter and replaced it once more with his ornate one. King Charles duly knelt in acts of reverence, first at the entrance to the consistory chamber, the second time in front of the papal throne, and lastly at the throne immediately in front of the Pope, whose foot and hand he knelt to kiss and who lifted him up for the kiss on the cheek. As the Pope resumed his seat, Cardinals San Giorgio and Carvajal came up in turn to pay him reverence and then stand there, whilst the King also remained standing at the Pope's left hand. I reminded his Majesty that he should next recite his oath of obedience, and he replied that he would immediately do so.

In the meantime, however, Jean Ganay, the president of the Paris parlement, stepped forward into the Pope's presence and, kneeling down, declared that the King had come in person to swear allegiance to his Holiness, but that, like any vassal before taking his oath, he wished to seek three favors from the Pope. He desired first of all that every privilege given to him, the Most Christian King, to his wife, and to his eldest son, together with all specified grants in deeds, should be confirmed by the Pope; secondly, that he should be invested with the kingdom of Naples; and thirdly, that the article signed on the preceding day concerning the sureties for the safe return of the brother of the Grand Turk should be struck out and destroyed.

The Pope said in answer to the first petition that he would immediately confirm all requests of such a nature in so far as they could be held to be valid. The second he dealt with by stating that it involved the welfare of another person, and that for this reason he needed to deliberate more seasonably about it with the advice of his cardinals. He wanted with them, so he said, to give the King satisfaction as far as was possible. His answer to the third request was that he wished to be in complete harmony with his Majesty and the Sacred College of Cardinals alike, and did not doubt but that they would all reach agreement.

When the Pope had made this reply, the King, standing at his left, declared, "Most Holy Father, I have come to render homage and reverence to your Holiness in the same way as my predecessors the Kings of France have done."

On Tuesday evening a week later, Prince Djem was escorted from the Castel Sant' Angelo to the Palazzo Venezia, and there handed over to King Charles. Next day, when his Holiness was conferring with thirteen of the cardinals in the first Sala Ducale, the French King, accompanied by his princes and soldiers, all armed, came from the Palazzo Venezia to see the Pope. King and Pope remained closeted together for a short while, and were then joined for a further quarter of an hour by Cardinal Cesare Borgia, after which his Majesty was escorted by the Pope and cardinals through the halls as far as the passage leading to the upper apartments of the palace. There the King knelt down bareheaded, and the Pope, removing his biretta, kissed him, but refused quite firmly to allow him to smother his feet with kisses, which his Majesty seemed to want to do. The King then departed, mounting horse at the steps of the gate of the private garden, after waiting for a brief period for Cardinal Cesare Borgia to join him. [Cesare went with the King as a hostage.]

On that same evening, his Holiness learned that King Alfonso had fled from Naples, taking a great amount of his treasure in four galleys in order to sail to Sicily and Spain and to recruit forces against the French King.

*

On Wednesday, the twenty-fifth of February, 1495, Djem, alias Zizim, brother of the Grand Turk, whom his Holiness had surrendered recently by reason of a treaty with the King, died in Naples, that is to say, in Castro Capuano, through eating or drinking something disagreeable to which his stomach was not accustomed. His corpse was then sent to the Grand Turk at his urgent request together with all the household of the deceased. The Grand Turk is said to have paid or given a large sum of money on this account, and to have received this household with favor.

Life in Rome Under the Borgias

The following incidents drawn from Burchard's Diary *cover several years, but are not in any fixed chronological order.*

At the beginning of April, a courtesan named Cursetta was thrown into prison because she had a Moor as a friend who went around in women's clothing, under the name of "the Spanish Barbara," and had relations with her. Both of them, therefore, as a punishment for this outrage, were led around together through the city, she clad in a loose black velvet dress open from neck to ankle, the Moor in a woman's dress which was taken up to the shirt, that is to the navel, in order that everybody might see his private parts and recognize the fraud he had perpetrated. During this his arms were tightly bound together above the elbows behind his back.

After the procession in public Cursetta was let go, but the Moor was put in prison and finally led out on Saturday, the seventh of April, from the prison of Torre di Nona together with two other brigands with a *sbirre* [constable] riding before them on an ass carrying on the point of a stick two testicles, which had been cut out from a Jew because he had had intercourse with a Christian woman. They were brought to the Flora field where the two brigands were hanged. The Moor was placed on a pile of wood, and was killed on the pole of the gallows, a rope being tied about his neck whereby he was strung fast to the pole. Then the pile was lighted, but on account of a downpour of rain it did not burn well and only his legs were charred.

*

A certain Baron René d'Agrimont, ambassador of the King of France, while on his way to Rome with his sumpters and about thirteen horses and servants was robbed completely by 22 highwaymen and brigands in the mountains of Viterbo. One of his noblemen together with a servant was wounded severely.

The ambassador entered Rome on May thirteenth without pomp and escorted only by his men. The Pope, indignant at the incident, sent out the papal guard to capture the malefactors, and wrote numerous *breve* to Fabrizio Colonna, from whose territory the brigands had come. Fifteen of them were apprehended and brought to Rome.

On Wednesday, May twenty-seventh, the day before Assumption, 18 men were hanged at noon while the cardinals passed over the Sant' Angelo Ponte, nine on each side of the bridge. The hanged men fell down with the gallows on the bridge, but were immediately set up again so that the cardinals when they returned from the palace could see all of them hanged.

The first of the eighteen was a doctor of medicine, physician and surgeon at the hospital of Saint John in the Lateran, who had left the hospital every day early in the morning armed with a crossbow and had shot everyone who happened to cross his path and then stolen their money. It was also said that the confessor of the hospital communicated with this physician whenever a patient confided to him during confession that he possessed any wealth, whereupon he would give an efficacious remedy to the patient, and they divided the money between them. Thirteen belonged to the 22 who had robbed Baron d'Agrimont. The four others had committed various misdeeds.

*

A papal musician, Thomasius of Forli, was arrested with his accomplices and incarcerated in the Castel Sant' Angelo. This Thomasius had come to Rome with a poisoned letter which he put into a reed to give to the Pope, pretending that he had come from the community of Forli, which wanted an agreement with his Holiness. Had the Pope accepted the letter, he would have been poisoned and fallen down dead within a few days or hours. In order to obtain access to the Pope, he had approached a friend, a musician in the household of Giovanni Borgia, and then bribed a guard of the papal palace, whom he initiated into his undertaking. This came to the knowledge of the Pope, and they were imprisoned by his orders.

When questioned they immediately admitted everything. The leader was especially questioned as to whether he had thought that he could ever get away with his life after having perpetrated such a misdeed. He answered that he had had the firm hope that through the death of the Pope, Imola and Forli might be freed from the blockade of Cesare and that peace and tranquillity might thus be restored to the ruler of these cities, the widow of Count Girolamo, his patroness, who had aided him from his youth. If he could die for her ten times, he declared, he would be ready to suffer death and would not be afraid.

*

There was found on the ninth of June in the Tiber, strangled with a crossbow around his neck, the Signor of Faenza, a young man of about 18 years, and of such handsome figure and appearance that his like could hardly have been found among a thousand young men of his age. There were also found two young people bound to each other by the arms, the one 15 years of age and the other 25 years, and with them a woman and many others.

*

On the first day of Christmas, 30 masked men with long thick noses in the form of enormous phalli proceeded after dinner to the place of Saint Peter. Before them a cardinal's chest was borne, to which was affixed a shield with three dice. Then came the masked fellows and behind them someone rode in a long coat and an old cardinal's hat. The fellows rode also on donkeys, some of them on such small ones that their feet touched the ground and they thus walked astride together with the donkeys. They went up to the little place between the portal of the palace and the hall of audience, where they showed themselves to the Pope, who stood at the window above the portal in the Loggia Paulina. Then they made a procession through the whole city.

*

During the night of Friday, the twenty-ninth of January, the brother of the poet Giovanni Lorenzo of Venice was arrested, on the charge of having translated into Latin and sent to Venice a pamphlet against the Pope and Cesare Borgia written in Greek by his brother. His whole goods and belongings, including those Giovanni had left behind, books and other things, were dragged out of his house and nothing was left within. This was reported immediately to the Signoria [governing council] of Venice, which wrote back and instructed its ambassador to make representations to the

Pope with a view to his liberation. In pursuance of this instruction the ambassador presented the letter together with the request for his liberation to the Pope.

The Pope is said to have answered that he had not realized that this was of such great interest to the Signoria, and consequently it was a matter of regret to him to be unable to grant its request, because the man for whom it petitioned had already been disposed of. According to report, he had been strangled as the Pope came back to Rome, and thrown into the Tiber.

*

On Sunday, the twenty-ninth of July, a large and spacious platform was erected before two porticoes of Saint Peter's Church. A hundred and eighty maranoes [Jews who, in order to escape the Inquisition, professed to be Catholics while secretly practicing their own religion] were admitted in order to be reconciled to the faith. There they were cowering down on the floor in their everyday garments; and there sat also the Archbishop of Reggio and Governor of Rome, Pietro Isuagli; the ambassador of the King and Queen of Spain, Juan Ruiz de Medina; the Bishop Octavius de Monte Marano, referendary of the Pope; the auditors Dominicus Jacobatius and Jacobus Dragnatius; the professors of theology, Paul de Modia of the order of the Predicants and Johannes de Malcone of the order of the Minorites, both papal penitentiaries in Saint Peter's church for the Spanish nation, also in their everyday garments. A master of theology of the order of the Predicants preached a sermon on the faith in Italian and reproached the maranoes, who were all Spaniards, among them a Franciscan monk, for their errors in faith, reprimanding and instructing them.

After the sermon the maranoes asked for a remission of sins and absolution. Thereupon Paul de Modia admonished them in a Latin address to adhere to the right faith and to lead a righteous life, and told them of the punishment they all deserved. This admonition he explained to them in a few words in Spanish. Then, while they were all down on their knees, he pronounced the punishment upon them, namely, that they should walk two and two to the church of Saint Peter in a garment prescribed and worn for this purpose. The Pope observed all that was going on from the new chambers and gave them the benediction.

The garment in which the maranoes were clad looked as follows: over their everyday clothes they wore coverings of red and peacock-blue cloth, which were hung down over the shoulders upon the breast and down to the legs behind, with a yellow cross four fingers in width and of the length of the cloth. Before the altar in Santa Maria sopra Minerva everyone put down his cloth. The monks then hung up the cloth in the church in memory of the event.

*

On Thursday, February seventh, there was a fete on the Agone that was well prepared according to Roman custom. Even the papal privy chamberlain, John Marades, had masked himself and sat on the back of a horse. The beast knocked slightly against some Romans, whereupon he came into danger of being wounded, unknown as he was, had not those who stood around intervened. It was prohibited, therefore, on the following day to mask oneself, but this was not observed by anyone.

On the same Thursday or Friday there was also a Spanish priest killed by masked men. The priest had killed the brother of one of the masked men in Spain.

*

On the first of March, the Pope and his son Cesare Borgia went on a pleasure trip, each on his own ship with his suite.

For four days the two ships continued their journey, in spite of the stormy sea and weather, to Corneto, in the neighborhood of which they put in. Cesare, apprehending greater danger, left the ship at the dinner hour, entered a small boat and rowed for the shore. There he sent to Corneto for horses and rode to the city. The Pope, however, was not able to make the harbor with his ship, whereupon all on board were stricken with fear by the stormy sea and cast themselves down here and there on the floor of the boat.

The Pope alone remained sitting firm and unafraid in his armchair on the quarterdeck and looked on at everything, and when the wild seas dashed against the ship, he said: "Jesus!" and crossed himself. He frequently addressed the sailors, ordering them to prepare food for the meal. But they excused themselves, on the plea that they were unable to make any fire on account of the continuous tempest. When after a time the sea had subsided somewhat, they fried fishes, which the Pope ate. The Pope then returned by ship with his whole retinue to Porto Ercole.

The Murder of Giovanni Borgia

On Wednesday, the fourteenth of June, 1497, Cardinal Cesare Borgia and Giovanni Borgia, Duke of Gandia, the favorite sons of the Pope, dined at the house of Donna Vannozza, their mother, who lived in the neighborhood of the church of Saint Peter in Chains. Their mother and various other people were present at the dinner. After the meal, when night had fallen, Cesare urged his brother to return to the Apostolic palace. And so they both mounted the horses or mules with a few attendants, as they had not many servants with them, and rode together until they approached the neighborhood of the palace of Vice-chancellor Ascanio Sforza.

At this point Duke Giovanni declared that he would like to find entertainment somewhere and took leave of his brother. He dismissed all his servants except one and retained further a masked man who had already presented himself before the dinner and had visited him in the Apostolic palace almost every day for a month. The Duke took him up behind him on his mule and rode to the Square of the Jews, where he dismissed the one groom and sent him back to the palace. He instructed him, however, that he should wait for him about 8 o'clock in the square, and if he had not appeared at the end of an hour he should return to the palace. Thereupon the Duke departed from the groom, with the masked man behind him on the back of the mule, and rode no one knows whither and was murdered.

The corpse was thrown into the river at the point beside the fountain where the refuse of the streets is usually dumped into the water, near or beside the hospital of Saint Hieronymus of the Slavonians, on the road which runs from the Ponte Sant' Angelo straight to the church of Santa Maria del Popolo. The groom who had been dismissed on the Square of the Jews was hurt seriously and wounded unto death. He was mercifully taken into the house of someone unknown to me and cared for. Unconscious as he was, he could tell nothing about his instructions and the expedition of his master.

When the Duke did not return to the palace on the next morning, which was Thursday, the fifteenth of June, his trusted servants became uneasy and one of them carried to the Pope the news of the late expedition of the Duke and Cesare and the vain watch for the return of the former. The Pope was much disturbed at the news, but tried to persuade himself that the Duke was enjoying himself somewhere with a girl, and was embarrassed for that reason at leaving her house in broad daylight, and he clung to the hope that he might return at any rate in the evening. When this hope was not fulfilled, the Pope was stricken with deadly terror and set on foot all possible inquiries through a few of his trusted men.

Among those who were questioned was a Slavonian dealer in wood by the name of Giorgio, who had unloaded his wood on the bank of the Tiber near the above-mentioned fountain and who had spent the night on his boat guarding his wood to prevent it being stolen. The question was put to him whether he had seen anything thrown into the river during the middle of the night just past, to which he made answer that at about 2 o'clock in the morning two men came out of a lane by the hospital onto the public road along the river. They looked about cautiously to see whether anyone was passing, and when they did not see anybody they disappeared again in the lane. After a little while two others came out of the lane, looked about in the same way and made a sign to their companions when they discovered nobody. Thereupon a rider appeared on a white horse who had a corpse behind him with the head and arms hanging down on one side and the legs on the other, and supported on both sides by the two men who had first appeared. The procession advanced to the place where the refuse is thrown into the river. At the bank they came to a halt and turned the horse with its tail to the river. Then they lifted the corpse, one holding it by its hands and arms, the other by the legs and feet, dragged it down from the horse and cast it with all their strength into the river.

To the question of the rider if it was safely in, they answered, "Yes, Sir!" Then the rider cast another look at the river and, seeing the cloak of the corpse floating on the water, asked his companions what that black thing was floating there. They answered, "The cloak," whereupon he threw stones at the garment to make it sink to the bottom. Then all five, including the other two who had kept watch, and now rejoined the rider and his two companions, departed and took their way together through another lane that leads to the hospital of Saint James.

The servants of the Pope asked Giorgio why he had lodged no information of such a crime with the governor of the city, to which he answered:

"In my day I have seen as many as a hundred corpses thrown into the river at that place on different nights without anybody troubling himself about it, and so I attached no further importance to the circumstance."

After this, fishermen and boatmen were summoned from all Rome and ordered to drag the corpse out of the river, with the assurance of a large reward for their pains. Three hundred fishermen and boatmen, as I have heard, came together and dragged the bed of the river, and finally brought up the corpse of a man. It was just before vespers when they found the Duke still fully clad, with his stockings, shoes, coat, waistcoat, and cloak, and in his belt there was his purse with 30 ducats. He had nine wounds, one in the neck through the throat, the other eight in the head, body, and legs. The Duke was laid in a boat and carried into the Castel Sant' Angelo, where his clothing was removed. The corpse was then washed and clothed in princely raiment.

On the evening of this day, at 9 o'clock, the corpse of the Duke was brought by his noble retainers, if I remember rightly, from the Castel Sant' Angelo to the church of Santa Maria del Popolo, preceded by 120 torchbearers and all the prelates of the palace, together with the papal servitors and pages. Weeping and lamenting loudly, they proceeded without any orderly formation. The corpse, borne ceremoniously upon a bier in public view, looked more as if sleeping than dead. In the aforementioned church it was consigned to the vault, where it reposes up to the present day.

When the Pope was informed that the Duke had been murdered and thrown into the river like refuse, and there discovered, violent grief overcame him, and in his deep sorrow he locked himself in his chambers and wept bitterly. Only after long pleading, persuasion, and solicitation before his door did the Cardinal Bartolomeo Marti finally succeed after several hours in being admitted with a few attendants. The Pope took no food or drink from the evening of Wednesday, the fourteenth of June, until the following Saturday, and he let no sleep come to his eyes from the morning of Thursday until the next Sunday. Upon varied and ceaseless appeals of his trusted friends he admitted himself to be won over, and finally began to conquer his grief as well as he could. This he did also out of consideration for the risk and danger to his own person.

*

The Downfall of Archbishop Flores and the Burning of Savonarola

An official investigation into the murder of Giovanni Borgia, Duke of Gandia, continued for several weeks, then was abruptly terminated on the Pope's order. It is said that evidence was discovered that incriminated Cesare Borgia himself, who was the most likely to profit by his brother's death.

In his grief after the murder of his son, the Pope resolved to do penance by instituting a grand reformation of the Church. A bull was drawn up in July, 1497, with the aid of his secretary Bartolomeo Flores. It was never published, however, as the Pope soon changed his mind. Many at the time believed that Flores, who was privy to many of the Pope's secrets, was then made the scapegoat in order to suppress what he knew concerning this bull.

On Thursday, September fourteenth, 1497, at about 10 o'clock in the evening, his Holiness sent for his secretary, Bartolomeo Flores, the Archbishop of Cosenza, and had him arrested. The Pope had learned that his secretary had sent out many false and harmful papal briefs, forging their contents and instructions against his Holiness's wish or without his knowledge, and issuing them through his servants. Amongst these briefs was one dispensation by which a Portuguese nun, a legitimate member of the royal family, could lay aside her religious habit and vows and could contract a marriage with the natural and illegitimate son of the late King; another allowed that a person in subdeacon's orders could marry; whilst further briefs in great numbers, amounting in all it was said to around 3000, authorized and provided dispensations and exemptions.

A secret consistory was held on Monday, October ninth, in which the case against Don Bartolomeo was presented and conducted, and a confession made by the accused that contained many details of the dispensations he was alleged to have dispatched without papal knowledge. His Holiness deprived him of his archbishopric and all other benefices, ordered that he should be deposed and degraded from all clerical orders, and delivered over to the secular authorities for punishment.

All Don Bartolomeo's possessions were, on the Pope's orders, carried from the apartment that he had been accustomed to use in the Vatican Palace and set down in the papal storeroom by his Holiness's private servant. It was only at the end of the month that the prisoner in the Castel Sant' Angelo was committed to his final punishment and taken from his room to eat the bread of affliction and drink the water of sorrow in another more squalid dungeon. He was made to put on over his shirt a gown of coarse white cloth that fell in heavy folds to just above his knees, and was provided with a pair of shoes of coarse leather, a loose cloak of rough green cloth that reached to the ground, and a heavy white cap. In his hands was placed the figure and image of Christ, carved in wood, and attached to a cross. Thus attired, he was taken from the room where he had hitherto been kept and led to the Emperor Hadrian's sepulcher, the dungeon called San Marocco. In this cell there was a wooden bed fitted with a head tester as protection against the dampness of the walls, and with a straw mattress and two long cloaks for covering. He was provided with a breviary, a Bible, and a copy of an epistle of Saint Peter. One cask of water, three loaves of bread, one jug of oil, and a lamp for giving light were his other amenities, and thus Don Bartolomeo was incarcerated for the rest of his life.

It is said that the Pope, over a period of time, sent Don Giovanni Marradi, Don Pietro de Solis, and some other close members of his household to his disgraced secretary, and that in playing draughts and chess with him they had been able to entice him to confess that he had sent out many briefs without the Pope's orders. Don Bartolomeo was persuaded to incriminate himself further in this way by the others, who promised that in so doing the Pope would look favorably on him, secure his release, and reward him with greater offices, but once his confession had been secured, they left him, never to return.

On Monday, July twenty-third, 1498, Don Bartolomeo Flores died in the Castel Sant' Angelo, where he had remained in prison.

At his death he had come to a deep understanding and devotion, seeking mercy and forgiveness from Our Savior in the words of the Psalmist, "Against thee only have I sinned and done this evil in thy sight," and he denied that he had ever harmed the Pope. That same evening, his body was carried to the church of Santa Maria in Transpontina, and there buried, without any torches, mourners, church ceremony, or service. May he rest in peace.

*

The Dominican friar Girolamo Savonarola had already earned the enmity of Pope Alexander by welcoming the French King Charles VIII into Florence, during his invasion of Italy in 1494, as the "sword of God" destined to reform the Church. And with the exile of the Medici from Florence that year, Savonarola became a virtual priest-dictator over the morals of the people, denouncing the corruption and venality of the papacy. Thus challenged, the Pope took his revenge when Savonarola's popular support began to weaken.

The news reached Rome on Tuesday, April 10, 1498, that on the preceding Saturday, an ordeal by fire had been prepared in Florence to corroborate or refute the truth of certain conclusions stated by Fra Girolamo Savonarola of Ferrara, the vicar-general of the Congregation of San Marco in Florence and a member of the Dominican Order. The test had been arranged in the Piazza della Signoria in the city of Florence itself, and was to have been undertaken by certain brothers who had offered themselves for the ordeal, but the whole proceeding had been left unfinished.

The incident arose as a result of Savonarola's activities through the preceding years. From the arrival in Italy of King Charles VIII of France, Savonarola had publicly preached in the state of Florence, spreading many lies and falsehoods, and had been in charge of one of the parties in the city, showing it favor and hoping thereby to make himself great. In his sermons, he openly proclaimed that Our Savior Christ had often spoken and revealed many things to him. In practice he employed one certain way for finding out the sins of men through the cooperation of his brethren in the order, six of whom he had instructed and brought into positions of honor and reverence. These men went out to live in different towns in Florence, and whatever of any serious or singular nature was confessed to them, they used to reveal to Savonarola, with the details of the name and condition of the confessed person. From these revelations he was accustomed to preach about the sins of the people, and to assert that God had revealed them to him, so that many believed him to be a prophet and a holy man. He was called to every council where weighty matters were discussed, and the city, reacting to his every wish, arranged its affairs accordingly.

His Holiness, seeing how such a man raged, and recognizing his evil nature, ordered through the general of his order that Savonarola should be restrained from preaching in this way, but the latter refused to comply with such an injunction. The Pope therefore next ordered him to obey under pain of excommunication, but he still refused, claiming that it was better to obey God than man, and using his learning to reason out other conclusions whereby people only believed him all the more. At last he set out certain heretical propositions and published them as articles that he wished to uphold. They were opposed by a certain Franciscan friar who was preaching publicly at the Franciscan Convent of Santa Croce in Florence, and who claimed that he would demonstrate them to be heretical. Savonarola and other Dominican brothers, however, continued to insist that they were true and that they would defend them. In consequence, the point was reached in this dispute between the Dominicans and Franciscans where the former were willing to sustain these conclusions and the latter wished to refute them by a public judgment under penalty of fire and death. It was the Dominicans who chose the ordeal by fire for such a judgment, and this the Franciscans accepted. The conclusions that the Dominicans undertook to prove by reasoning and supernatural signs asserted that the Church of God needed reform, that it would in fact be punished and reformed, and that Florence as well would suffer punishment before renewal and fresh prosperity, whilst the heathen would be converted to Christ. All these events, the Dominicans claimed, would happen in our time. Furthermore, they asserted that the excommunication recently pronounced against Savonarola was invalid, and that it could be disregarded without sin.

Since this dispute had stirred the whole populace, the gonfalonier of justice and the Florentine Signory ordered that a place should be provided and prepared in the Piazza della Signoria on the following Saturday, April seventh, for a trial by fire. Two great pulpits or platforms were therefore erected—one for the lords and leading citizens of Florence, the other for the disputants making the trial—and by them a great pyre was built. The statements by the brothers of each order were published, and they were to be present at 8 o'clock on the morning of the day concerned to provide satisfaction with their claims.

On the appointed day and before the hour arranged, Brother Francesco di Puglia of the Franciscan Order came to the piazza with one companion, climbed on to the platform and sat down humbly to await the Messiah. Then well after 8 o'clock, Brother Domenico da Pescia of the Dominicans arrived in procession with a cross and the Host, and accompanied by all the brethren of his order, including Savonarola, and followed also to the piazza by a great mob of people. On arrival, the appointed members climbed onto the platform made ready for them, and the Signory came out from the palace to take their seats on their rostrum.

When they were all seated, Brother Francesco stood up, and gave a brief speech to their lordships. He stated that he was present there to make the proposed test, but requested further that, although he should be burned to death, the Signory should in no way judge that Brother Domenico thereby was relieved of his commitments or had won the issue, but that he too should make the same experiment and enter the fire, and only if he were not harmed, should he be accounted the victor.

After consulting amongst themselves, the lords of the Signory promised to do what the friar asked, and they then produced two new caps complete with fittings that they gave to the contestants to wear instead of those in which they had come to the ordeal. The Signory suspected that the friars who were to make the test, or possibly one of them, might have some invocation, incantation, or charm hidden in a cap to keep them unharmed from the heat of the fire, and so they wanted to substitute other caps. Brother Francesco readily accepted the Signory's order, and bowed low without any cap on so that they should be the less suspicious, and then made ready to enter the fire with no cap on at all, but Brother Domenico made excuses and refused either to take his cap off or to change it. On hearing this, the Franciscan requested that the others should not argue with Brother Domenico about his cap, but should let him wear what he wished, since it was made of cloth and doubtless would be consumed in the fire with him.

The Signory therefore decided to let the Dominican keep his cap at the other friar's request; but Brother Domenico, fearful about being burned and seeking ways of putting off the whole affair, declared next that he would never enter the fire without the cross. This led the lords to discuss further amongst themselves what to do, but Brother Francesco again intervened to ask that they should let the Domincan have a cross, since it would be of wood and could not defend him from the fire but would rather be burned with him. This request, too, was therefore granted to Brother Domenico, but it did not suffice, as he was desperately afraid of the fire. He therefore asked a third favor, that he should be allowed to enter the fire with the Host, claiming that otherwise the test in which he was engaged would be useless. This request made it fully clear to the Signory that the Dominican would agree to nothing, and so they abandoned the spectacle to return to their own homes.

This news spread amongst the people, whose indignation and suspicion mounted and flourished against Savonarola to such an extent that, on the following Monday, April ninth, they came at dusk in a great mob, wreaking destruction on the convent of San Marco where Fra Girolamo was staying. The brothers of the convent had closely shut and barricaded it, fortifying the building with cannon and other weapons of attack; but these the people dragged outside, after which they forced their way into the convent, killing five defendants before its walls and three others inside, one a brother of Savonarola. He himself was taken with Fra Domenico da Pescia and Fra Silvestro of Florence, and they were all escorted to the Palazzo della Signoria, where they were imprisoned.

Then the mob rushed to the homes of Francesco de Valori and Paolo Antonio Soderini, the main supporters and protectors of Savonarola. They reached Francesco de Valori's house first, but not finding him there, sought further afield and eventually came upon him in the Piazza della Signoria, where they dragged him about most cruelly and finally murdered him. His wife, who tried to defend the house, was also killed, together with everyone staying with her, and all his possessions were pillaged, anyone seizing what he wanted. The people next turned their attention to Soderini's house, where they intended to act in the same way, but the Signory provided Soderini with aid and, with a mixture of threats and promises, they persuaded the mob to desist.

This news was brought to the Pope by the Florentine ambassador on Holy Sunday morning, and his Holiness was petitioned to publish a bull of absolution to send to the Florentine people, as they stood excommunicated for having laid violent hands on the convent of San Marco and its brethren, and had even gravely wounded or killed some priests. The Pope immediately summoned his secretary, and committed to him the order for a bull in these terms without delay.

I learned later on May twenty-fourth more about what had happened to Fra Girolamo Savonarola and his two brethren before their execution in Florence [on May 22, 1498]. In prison, Savonarola was tortured seven times before he pleaded for mercy and offered to say and to commit to writing all the matters in which he had erred. Taken away from the torture chamber and back to his cell, he was given paper and ink, and he wrote down all his crimes and faults, filling, it was said, 80 scrolls or more. Amongst other things, he confessed that he had had no divine revelations, but that he had made an agreement with many of the brethren in the city of Florence and beyond, who revealed to him, with names and details, the confessions made by Christ's faithful people. From this information he had drawn many of his statements, correcting in public meetings those who had in private confessed their sins and crimes, and claiming that the details had been revealed to him by Our Savior. Savonarola also admitted that he had not been confessed for any mortal sin since he was 20 years old, although in fact he had committed many, especially sins of the flesh. He had seemingly performed a daily celebration, but again from the age of 20 had never spoken the words of consecration, and had indeed given communion to many with an unconsecrated Host.

Deaths and Entrances

After the death of Giovanni Borgia, Cesare became even more important to the Pope in furthering the dynastic ambitions of his family. In August, 1498, Cesare put aside his cardinal's robes so as to be able to accept the offer of Louis XII of France, who had just succeeded Charles VIII, of the dukedom of Valentinois and the hand of a French princess in marriage. The first marriage of Lucrezia Borgia to Giovanni Sforza was likewise annulled by the Pope, so that she might be free to marry the nephew of the new King of Naples.

At this time, in August, 1498, his Highness Don Alfonso of Aragon, the Duke of Bisceglia, aged 17 and the natural son of the late King Alfonso II of Naples, came to Rome as the betrothed of Lucrezia Borgia, his Holiness's daughter, formerly the wife of his Highness Don Giovanni Sforza. The Duke of Bisceglia was received and escorted without any public pomp by only a few emissaries sent out by the Pope, and he rode to the palace of Cardinal Zeno, where Donna Lucrezia had her residence. There he was hospitably welcomed, and a few days later the marriage was personally concluded with Donna Lucrezia and consummated. The wedding was celebrated in the Vatican Palace, and the early celebrations were conducted quietly, without any great pomp, though everyone knew of the event.

*

On Saturday, the twentieth of April, 1499, the Pope received a letter from France advising him that the marriage contract had been concluded by the former Cardinal Cesare Borgia and the Lord d'Albret in the name of his daughter, by which, as was reported, and as it was in fact set down in the contract, the Pope was to give a dowry of 200,000 ducats, and the marriage was not to be performed until his Holiness had nominated the brother of the bride a cardinal.

On the twenty-third of May, 1499, a courier arrived from France with the report for the Pope that his son Cesare had contracted the marriage with the Lady d'Albret, on Sunday, the twelfth of May, and had performed it and did take her eight times, one after the other.

*

On Friday, the second of August, 1499, before daybreak, Alfonso of Aragon, Duke of Bisceglia, the husband of Lucrezia Borgia, departed secretly from Rome in order to reach the Colonnese territory. From there he went to the King of Naples, and this without the permission, knowledge, or consent of the Pope.

On Thursday, the eighth of August, 1499, Lucrezia Borgia departed from the city through the Porta del Popolo, to go to the castle of Spoleto, of which she had been appointed governor by the Pope. She was accompanied by Don Joffré Borgia of Aragon, her brother, who rode at her left, and sent many laden sumpters in advance which the Pope inspected from the loggia. When she and her brother had mounted their horses or mules in the place of Saint Peter at the foot of the steps of the church, they made a very reverential obeisance from their horses to the Pope, who stood above, and took their last leave of him. After the Pope had blessed them from the window for the third time they rode away.

Before them there marched in good order the whole palace guard of the Pope and the governor of Rome with his men. In the train was also a mule that had been laden with a stretcher and mattress, a crimson cover strewn with flowers, two pillows of white damask and a beautiful canopy so that Donna Lucrezia could rest there in case she was tired from riding. Another mule bore a saddle upon which was erected a silk-covered and magnificently adorned armchair with back and footstool, in order that Donna Lucrezia might sit in it from time to time and travel more comfortably.

On the first of November, 1499, at 6 o'clock in the morning, Donna Lucrezia was delivered of a boy. This was announced by order of the Pope to all the cardinals and ambassadors and to his other friends even before daybreak in their residences. The messengers received for this from every cardinal and ambassador two ducats, more or less, according to the mood of the giver.

On the feast of Saint Martin, Monday, the eleventh of November, the son of Lucrezia, Rodrigo, was christened by Cardinal Caraffa in the chapel of Pope Sixtus IV in Saint Peter's.

*

Fear of assassination by the Borgias had caused Don Alfonso to flee Rome for Naples the previous August, but he later allowed himself to be persuaded to return. By now, however, his marriage to the Pope's daughter was regarded as politically useless to the Borgias. It was even claimed by Cesare Borgia that the Duke had hired several archers to shoot at him while he was strolling in the Vatican gardens, which assertion was no doubt made in order to exculpate himself for his own subsequent actions.

On Wednesday, July fifteenth, 1500, at about 6 o'clock in the evening, Don Alfonso, Donna Lucrezia's husband, was attacked at the top of the steps before the first entrance to Saint Peter's basilica. He was gravely wounded in his head, right arm and leg, whilst his assailants escaped down the steps to join about 40 waiting horsemen, with whom they rode out of the city by the Porta Portusa. The Duke, badly wounded, was carried to a room in the Torre Borgia, and there was carefully tended to prevent his dying from his injuries. But on Tuesday, August eighteenth, he was strangled in his bed at about 11 o'clock, and later on that same evening, his body was carried to the basilica of Saint Peter and there deposited in the chapel of Santa Maria della Febbre. Don Francesco Borgia, the Archbishop of Cosenza and the papal treasurer, with his household, provided the escort for the funeral procession.

The doctors who had attended the dead man were seized and taken to the Castel Sant' Angelo, together with a certain hunchback who had been accustomed to look after the Duke. But after close questioning, they were soon released, for they were innocent, and the man who had ordered the deed was well known. [Cesare had murdered him with his own hands.]

The same day and almost at the same hour Lucas de Dulcibus, the chamberlain of Cardinal delle Rovere [an ally of the deceased Duke] and master of the Register of Papal Decrees, was wounded to death on the back of his mule before the house of the Roman citizen Domenico de Massimi, and his *membrum virile* was cut off by a man of Reiti whose wife he had kept as a concubine. He was brought into the house of the said Domenico, where he died after three or four hours.

Her Highness Donna Lucrezia, lately of Aragon, left Rome on Monday, August thirty-first, with only a retinue of six horsemen, to ride to Nepi and there seek consolation and relief for her sadness and grief at the death of her husband.

Lucrezia Borgia's Third Marriage

About the hour of Vespers on Saturday, September fourth, 1501, news came of the marriage concluded between Don Alfonso, the eldest son of the Duke of Ferrara, and Donna Lucrezia Borgia, formerly the Duchess of Bisceglia, and earlier the wife of Giovanni Sforza. As a result of these tidings, there was a continual cannonade from the Castel Sant' Angelo from that hour onward into the night.

Next day, after dinner, Lucrezia rode from her residence to the church of Santa Maria del Popolo. She was dressed in a robe of brocaded gold with the veil drawn back, and was escorted by 300 horsemen. Four bishops rode in front of her, and she was followed by her footmen and servants, but she herself proceeded alone; the company returned in the same order to her house. On the same evening from suppertime until 9 o'clock, the great Capitoline bell was tolled and many bonfires were lit on the Castel Sant' Angelo and throughout the city, whilst all the buildings were brightly illuminated and the people became wildly excited, though perhaps shame would have been more fitting.

On the following day, Monday, September sixth, two clowns paraded
through all the principal streets and squares of the city, shouting loudly:
'Long live the most illustrious Duchess of Ferrara! Long live Pope
Alexander! Viva! Viva!" One of these men was on horseback, and had been
given by Donna Lucrezia the golden brocaded dress and veil that she had
worn as new only once on the day before, and was worth 300 ducats or so.
The other man followed on foot and was similarly the recipient of a dress
from the Pope's daughter.

At the end of the following week, the Pope held a secret consistory on the
Friday, and in it, with the consent of all the cardinals present, he remitted
the annual payment of 4000 ducats made by the Duke of Ferrara to the
Apostolic Chamber, canceling it for the Duke and his successors to the
third generation and leaving only a nominal sum of 100 ducats to be paid
each year.

On Sunday evening, October thirtieth, Don Cesare Borgia gave a supper
in his apartment in the apostolic palace, with 50 honest prostitutes, called
courtesans, in attendance, who after the meal danced with the servants and
others there, first fully dressed and then naked. Following the supper, too,
lampstands holding lighted candles were placed on the floor and chestnuts
strewn about, which the prostitutes, naked and on their hands and knees,
had to pick up as they crawled in and out amongst the lampstands. The
Pope, Don Cesare, and Donna Lucrezia were all present to watch. Finally,
prizes were offered—silken doublets, pairs of shoes, hats, and other
garments—for those men who were most successful with the prostitutes.
This performance was carried out in the Sala Reale, and those who
attended said that in fact the prizes were presented to those who won the
contest.

Another incident took place on November eleventh, when a countryman
entered Rome by the Porta Viridaria leading two mares loaded with wood.
When they reached the Piazza di San Pietro, some of the palace
men-at-arms came up, cut through the straps and threw off the saddles and
the wood in order to lead the mares into the courtyard immediately inside
the palace gate. Four stallions were then freed from their reins and harness
and let out of the palace stables. They immediately ran to the mares, over
whom they proceeded to fight furiously and noisily amongst themselves,
biting and kicking in their efforts to mount them, and seriously wounding
them with their hoofs. The Pope and Donna Lucrezia, laughing and with
evident satisfaction, watched all that was happening from a window above
the palace gate.

Before leaving his apartment on Tuesday, December twenty-seventh, his
Holiness summoned the cardinals to inform them that he wanted to send a
sword of honor to Don Alfonso d'Este as the Duke of Ferrara's eldest son
and the husband of Donna Lucrezia. After lunch, some of the traditional
races were held.

Jews competed in a race from the vice-chancellor's clock to the Piazza di

San Pietro, and the older men ran from the pyramid in the Borgo to the same piazza. The winner in the Jewish race was not given his prize because, it was said, the track had not been good or the race fair; but when it was run again on the next day, the same man won and this time took the prize.

On the following day, a race between wild boars was arranged over a course from the Campo di Fiori to the Piazza di San Pietro. The boars were mounted, and those who sat on them used sticks to beat them and kept control of their heads by rings in their snouts, whilst other men guided them along and prevented their running into side alleys. There was also a contest between a great number of prostitutes, and they also ran from the pyramid in the Borgo into the Piazza di San Pietro.

Whilst all these things were happening, the trumpets and all the other musical instruments assembled on the platform above the steps of Saint Peter's basilica began to sound a fanfare, and from her residence abutting the church, Donna Lucrezia emerged, clothed in a robe of golden brocade, decorated in Spanish fashion, and with a long train behind her borne by some girls. They walked in procession to the palace, Lucrezia between Don Ferdinando d'Este and Don Sigismondo d'Este on her right and left, both brothers of her husband, and followed by about 50 Roman ladies most beautifully attired, and by Lucrezia's own ladies-in-waiting. They all mounted to the Sala Paolina above the palace doors, where the Pope, with thirteen cardinals and Don Cesare Borgia, welcomed them.

In the ceremony, the Bishop of Adria delivered the sermon, or address, which his Holiness repeatedly urged him to hurry through more quickly. When at last he had finished speaking, a table or bench was brought out and placed in a suitable position in front of the Pope. Don Ferdinando, as proxy for her husband, brought Donna Lucrezia to his Holiness, and in his brother's name presented her with a golden ring or a gem, so my colleague later told me, for he had been able to observe more closely than myself what had happened. Cardinal d'Este, who was also a brother of Don Alfonso, then brought in four other rings of great value, a diamond, a ruby, an emerald and a turquoise, together with a small box, which was placed on the table and, by the cardinal's order, opened. He took out of it a cap or head ornament studded with 14 adamantines, as many rubies and about 150 pearls or great marguerites, four collars similarly decorated with jewels and pearls, eight bracelets of varied design, a pendant for the breast or head made of larger jewels, still more bracelets of differing designs (four of them of very great value), four long strings of large pearls, four exceedingly beautiful crosses, one in the shape of a Saint Andrew's cross and the other three like the cross of Christ, made of adamantines and other jewels, and finally another cap similar to the first. All these ornaments were valued at 800,000 ducats [about $350,000] and were presented as a gift to the bride by Cardinal d'Este, who most eloquently and graciously asked that she should not despise it.

The Pope then withdrew to the adjoining Sala Paolina, and was followed by Lucrezia with her ladies and many others, who all remained in the palace until 5 o'clock on the following morning.

Whilst these ceremonies were taking place, the races had been succeeded by a spectacle staged in the Piazza di San Pietro, where a wooden castle or screen framework was constructed, and Don Cesare's troops fought a mock battle for its possession. The following night, in the Pope's apartment, a number of comedies were recited and ballets performed, with some singing as well.

On Sunday, January second, the Piazza di San Pietro was barricaded on all sides with tree-trunks and other wooden blocks, from the corner by the house of the palace wardens to the new fountain and thence across to the shops. In that area a bullfight was staged. Altogether, eight bulls and one buffalo were killed, but after this, as night was falling, another buffalo and four more bulls that remained were kept for entertainment on the following day. They were then slaughtered in the Roman fashion, amid considerable feasting and rejoicing.

At about 1 o'clock on Wednesday, January fifth, Donna Lucrezia left the Vatican Palace to set out on her journey to join her husband at Ferrara. She rode out of the city by way of the Porta Sant' Angelo and the streets leading through to the Porta del Popolo, but, since it was snowing, she was not dressed in any costly clothes. On the evening of the fifth of January, 1502, as I have been told, the Pope counted out 100,000 ducats in minted gold in the presence of the brothers of the bridegroom, Ferdinando and Sigismondo, as a dowry for Donna Lucrezia, which he paid over to them in coined money.

The Triumph of the Borgias

Lucretia's third marriage, with the son of the Duke of Ferrara, enabled the Borgias to extend their power into northern Italy. In addition, Pope Alexander now concluded an alliance with France and Spain, rivals for the possession of the kingdom of Naples, in which it was agreed that they would divide it between them. This enabled Cesare Borgia to deploy his armies against those cities in the Romagna that opposed him, and to turn his strength against the families of the Orsini and Colonna, hereditary enemies of the Borgias.

On Sunday, June sixth, 1501, the news spread through Rome that an agreement had been reached between the French and Spanish kings concerning their plans to divide the kingdom of Naples. By the agreement, the King of Spain was going to retain control of the duchy of Calabria and Apulia and the cities of Florence and Siena.

The Colonna, on learning of the pact between the two monarchs, became anxious about what would happen when French forces should march southward against Naples, and they therefore decided to commit their lands and towns into the care of the Sacred College of the Cardinals. The cardinals informed the Pope, but he was completely averse to such a solution and desired instead that the Colonna should hand over the keys of their possessions to himself. To achieve this end, he threatened to punish them unless they did so, and the Colonna leaders consequently decided to surrender control of all their territories into the hands of the Pope and the College. On the morning of June tenth, his Holiness despatched Don Pietro, the Bishop of Cesena, to settle the matter with them.

Eight days later, a proclamation was issued in Rome, that under penalty of a fine of 100 ducats, all were to obey the orders of the 26 stewards appointed and detailed by the Pope to arrange for the supplies of food to the French troops who were approaching on their way to attack the kingdom of Naples. An encampment outside the walls was established on the instructions of these stewards. Those who owned carts, horses, or mules had to declare them to the city governor so that he could use them for relaying food to the soldiers, and nobody else dared to buy anything from them because of the heavy penalties. The reason for these restrictions was that, until then, the French troops had pilfered whatever they could lay their hands on.

*

On the twenty-sixth of July, about the fifth hour of the night the Pope received the news of the capture of Capua by his son Cesare, the Duke of Valentinois. The capture of this city was achieved through treason by a certain Fabrizio, a citizen of Capua, who let the men of the Duke enter in secret. But Fabrizio himself was the first one to be killed by them, and after him there were about 3000 soldiers on foot and 200 horsemen slain, as well as citizens, priests, monks, and nuns in churches and convents, and women as many as there were found of them, without any pity. And the girls that were captured were given as a prey to the soldiers, who treated them with great cruelty. The number of all that were killed has been estimated at about 4000.

On the morning of the twenty-seventh of July, the Pope went from Rome to Sermoneta and the places of the Colonnas with 50 horsemen and 100 soldiers on foot, in the midst of all his confidential retainers and the cardinals who accompanied him. With him rode the Cardinals Serra and Borgia, each of them with 12 servants, who are comprised in the aforesaid 150. The Pope took luncheon in the Castel Gandolfo and afterward went down to the lake, where he amused himself during the whole day in a gondola while his men shouted continuously "Borgia! Borgia!" firing off their blunderbusses.

On the following Thursday, the Pope rode to Rocca di Papa and returned in the evening during a heavy rainstorm to the Castel Gandolfo. Before leaving Rome he handed over his room, the whole palace, and the current affairs to his daughter Lucrezia, who also occupied the papal rooms during his absence. He charged her also to open the letters sent him, and, in case any difficulty should arise, to consult Cardinal Costa and the other cardinals.

It is said that at one occasion Lucrezia sent for Costa and explained the order of the Pope and a pending case. Costa considered the case as being without importance and said to Lucrezia that when the Pope brought up these affairs before the consistory there was the vice-chancellor or another cardinal who kept the record for him. It would be proper, therefore, if there were someone present who would note down the conversation.

Lucretia answered: "I understand quite well how to write!"

Costa asked: "Where is your pen?"

Lucrezia understood the meaning and joke of the cardinal. She smiled, and they brought the conversation to an end in good humor.

At about 3 o'clock on Saturday afternoon, July 23, 1502, the news was brought to the Pope that Don Cesare Borgia had taken over the fortress of Camerino without any fighting. To celebrate this event, a great salute was fired from the Castel Sant' Angelo whilst later in the evening bonfires were lit, rockets sent off, and a magnificent feast was held in the Piazza di San Pietro. On Sunday evening following, the great Capitoline bell was rung, still larger fires were lit, and a more splendid spectacle and triumphal procession arranged than on the previous night. A short while before, Don Cesare had negotiated a peace treaty with the ruler of Camerino for a specific period of time; but then, knowing that he had nothing to fear from him during that truce, had astutely entered and seized the city. Having captured the ruler with all his children, legitimate and otherwise, Don Cesare held them prisoner.

On Wednesday, August third, and in company with Cardinal Ludovico Borgia, and some others, Don Cesare Borgia left Rome disguised as a Knight of Saint John of Jerusalem and bearing the cross. They rode on post horses to Ferrara, where they remained until August twenty-fourth, and then left accompanied by Don Alfonso d'Este, the Duke's brother-in-law, and three other nobles. They dined in the town of Borgo San Donnino [Fidenza] on the following day, feasting in great splendor upon chickens and squabs, and in their riotous way shocking and insulting the local inhabitants.

At two o'clock on the night of the third of January, 1503, the Pope made known to the Cardinal Orsini and to Jacobus de Santa Croce that Cesare Borgia had now taken the strategic castle of Sinigaglia. Therefore, in order to congratulate the Pope, the cardinal rode in the morning to the Vatican, and with him the governor of the city, who made as if he accompanied him by accident. After the cardinal had alighted in the palace, all his horses and mules were brought to the papal stables and he found himself suddenly surrounded by armed men in the Camera Papagalli, whereupon he fainted. He was brought immediately to the Torre di Nona prison, behind the garden or arbor of the Pope into the room of the Bishop Gamboa, and with him afterward the Prothonotary Orsini, Jacobus de Santa Croce, and the Abbot Bernardo de Alvino, who were all kept there in confinement.

The secretary and treasurer of the Pope, Adriano Castelli, who had on the preceding night read the letter of Cesare to the Pope in which he notified the Pope that he should arrest the Cardinal Orsini and Jacobus in the morning, did not want to leave the papal chamber that night so that if Cardinal Orsini should be warned, the Pope might not suspect that he had done it. The same Adriano sent for the Archbishop Rinaldo Orsini of Florence on the morning that the cardinal rode to the Vatican and had him arrested and placed under guard in his room in the Vatican. After the arrest of the cardinal, the governor rode with all his men to his house on the Monte Giordano, locked it, placed guards before it, and took up his residence there himself. While this was happening in Rome, Cesare had apprehended in Sinigaglia Vitelozzo Vitelli, Paolo Orsini, Don Francesco, the Duke de Gravina, and Liberotto de Ferma; and of these he caused Vitelozzo and Liberotto to be strangled within a few hours by Micheletto. The Duke de Gravina, Paolo and Don Francesco he kept under strict guard. The son of Paolo, Fabio Orsini, prudently fled with all possible haste when he saw the arrest of his father and the others. After the apprehension of the Cardinal Orsini, the rumor spread in Rome that the Pope was dead and that Naples had been taken by the Spaniards, but there was nothing in it. This day and the following night Carlo Orsini was held a prisoner in the chamber in the Torre di Nona. The next day he was brought into the rooms above the main chapel and kept there under guard until vespers of the next Thursday. Then he was transferred to the Castel Sant' Angelo, where the majordomo received him in his room.

In the evening of this same day, the governor stayed in the apartment of the Archbishop Orsini of Florence; and after dinner he had all possessions of the Cardinal Orsini and of the archbishop brought in their carriages and other vehicles to the Vatican or to his own house, according to his pleasure. Many things were also taken by the soldiers and others and carried away. Meanwhile, Jacobus de Santa Croce rode with Prince Joffré, the son of the Pope, to Monte Rotonca and in the name of the Pope took possession of it as well as of all land of the Orsini and also of the abbey of Farfa.

At the usual hour the papal vespers were said in the main chapel. Mass was conducted with the Cardinal San Giorgio officiating. The Pope was not present. After this the cardinals went to the Pope to intercede for the Cardinal Orsini. The Pope told them of the conspiracy of Vitelozzo, of the Orsini, of Baglioni and Pandolfo and their accomplices for the assassination of Cesare Borgia, who wanted to take revenge on them. Their intercession was of no avail.

Cesare Borgia had seized the prisoners mentioned above in the following way. When he was lying before the castle of Sinigaglia with Vitelozzo, Paolo, and the others, he pretended that he did not want yet to advance against the castle, but preferred rather to take a meal first and he invited those mentioned to partake with him. The Duke entered the house followed by Paolo, to whom he had extended a special invitation. Then came Vitelozzo, whom Paolo had caused to be called, and the others came behind them. When they were all within the courtyard, the Duke went into one of the rooms, whereupon Michelotto and many others surrounded Vitelozzo as well as Paolo, with the words: "You are under arrest." Thereupon Vitelozzo snatched out his dagger and wounded several who had thrown themselves upon him. This was in vain, for he and others were put into prison and treated as has been told.*

On Wednesday, January eighteenth, Paolo Orsini and the others, who had been kept under close guard since their arrest at Sinigaglia, were all strangled at Città di Pieve in Siena on the command of Don Cesare. The rumor spread through Rome on the following Monday that Don Cesare had recently captured the cities of Chiusi and Pienza and the towns of Sarteano, Città di Pieve, and Santa Quirica. In the last place, it was said, they found only two old men and nine old women. Don Cesare's men hung the women up by their arms and lit fires under their feet, intending by such torture to make them confess where they had hidden their wealth, but the women, not knowing or not wishing to tell where such treasure was, died under this torture. The soldiers then ransacked the houses, tearing down roofs and beams, breaking through doors and coffers, and splitting open casks to spill the wine on the ground before finally setting everything on fire. They seized and raped any woman they found in the places through which they passed, even in the larger communities like Acquapendente, Montefiascone, and Viterbo.

On Tuesday, January thirty-first, the rumor spread through the city that Pandolfo Petrucci, the ruler of Siena, had fled to Lucca. It was also rumored that Don Cesare was returning to Rome.

During the following days, early in February, Don Antonio de Pistorio and his colleague were denied access to Cardinal Orsini, to whom each day they had been accustomed to take food and drink sent by his mother. This change took place, it was said, because the Pope was trying to obtain 2000 ducats from the cardinal, which had been left to him by a relative, and also to secure a pearl that he had bought for a similar amount from Virgilio Orsini or his heirs. Learning of this, the cardinal's mother paid the Pope 2000 ducats to help her son; and his mistress, who had the pearl, dressed up as a man, gained an audience of the Pope and gave him the jewel. When these things happened, his Holiness commanded that the other two men should as before take food and drink to the cardinal, who in the meantime,

---

* Concerning this coup, Machiavelli, who was then the Florentine envoy to Cesare Borgia, noted with admiration:

"He dissembled his aims so well that the Orsini made their peace with him, being represented by Signor Paolo whose suspicions the Duke disarmed with every courtesy, presenting him with robes, money, and horses, so that in their simplicity they were induced to come to Sinigaglia and fell into his hands. Having thus suppressed these leaders and made their partisans his friends, the Duke laid a very good foundation to his power."

it was commonly said, had drunk "what had been specially prepared," on the Pope's orders.

On Monday, February thirteenth, the report spread through Rome that Giovanni Giordano Orsini had surrendered his lands and himself into the hands of the Pope so that his Holiness and Don Cesare could do as they wished with him, whilst it was also rumored that Pandolfo Petrucci of Siena and Baglione of Perugia had been captured in the state of Florence. The Pope dispatched a battery from the Castel Sant' Angelo on the following Thursday to join Don Cesare in his attack on the fort of Bracciano. Some of the supporters of the Orsini had gathered there for a final stand against Don Cesare, and, in a secret consistory, his Holiness told the cardinals that the Orsini were plotting secretly to enter Rome in order to seize the houses of the cardinals and the court. He therefore warned them all to take care of their houses and to fortify them.

On Wednesday, the fifteenth, the Cardinal d'Este departed from Rome after the consistory in which he had taken part. He was in haste to return to Ferrara on account of the resentment Cesare Borgia bore toward him because he loved his sister Lucrezia, and had had intercourse with her, as also had had Cesare.*

Cardinal Orsini, it is said, offered the Pope 25,000 ducats for his release. His Holiness consoled and admonished him to be of good cheer, and before all to take good care of his health, since everything else was of secondary importance; and he told him that he had ordered all the physicians to take the greatest care of the welfare of the cardinal. On Wednesday, the twenty-second of February, the Cardinal Orsini died in the Castel Sant' Angelo. [The cardinal, it was generally acknowledged, had been poisoned by order of the Borgias.] May his soul rest in peace! Amen!

The Pope commanded my colleague, Bernardino Gutterii, to arrange the funeral of the deceased. I will not, therefore, attend the ceremony myself nor have anything to do with it, as I have no wish to learn aught that does not concern me.

The Death and Funeral of Alexander

On Saturday, the twelfth of August, 1503, the Pope fell ill in the morning. After the hour of vespers, between 6 and 7 o'clock, a fever appeared and remained permanently.

On the fifteenth of August 13 ounces of blood were drawn from him and the tertian ague supervened.

* Numerous scandalous rumors circulated in Rome at the time that Lucrezia Borgia had committed incest not only with her brother Cesare but with her father Pope Alexander as well. After her death in 1519, the following couplet by the poet Giovanni Pontanus appeared:

> Hic jacet in tumulo Lucretia nomine, sed re
> Thais: Alexandri filia, sponsa, nurus.

> *Here lies Lucretia, chaste by name, but Thais lewd by life,*
> *Who was to Alexander Pope both daughter and his wife.*

On Thursday, the seventeenth of August, at 9 o'clock in the forenoon, he took medicine.

On Friday, the eighteenth, between 9 and 10 o'clock, he confessed to the Bishop Gamboa of Carignola, who then read mass to him. After his communion he gave the Eucharist to the Pope, who was sitting in bed. Then he ended the mass, at which were present five cardinals, Serra, Giovanni and Francesco Borgia, Casanova, and Loris. The Pope told them that he felt very ill. At the hour of vespers, after Gamboa had given him extreme unction, he died. There were present, in addition, only the datary and the papal grooms.

Cesare, who was lying sick in bed, sent Michelotto with many men, who locked all doors to the entrance to the residence of the Pope. One of them drew a dagger and threatened Cardinal Casanova: if he did not give him the keys and the money of the Pope, he would stab him and throw him out the window. Whereupon the frightened cardinal surrendered the keys to him. One after the other they entered the room behind the chamber of the Pope and took all the silver they could find, as well as two chests with 100,000 ducats each. At 8 o'clock they opened the doors again, and the death of the Pope became known. In the meantime, Cesare's servants had appropriated whatever was left in the wardrobes and they left nothing but the papal armchairs, a few cushions, and the rugs on the walls. Cesare did not appear during the whole illness of the Pope, not even at his death. Nor did the Pope mention him or Lucrezia with one word.

After 7 o'clock my colleague arrived at the Vatican, and was recognized and admitted. He found the Pope dead and had him washed by the servant of the sacristy, Balthasar, and a papal servant. Then they put on him all his everyday garments and a white coat without a train, which he had never worn while alive. Over this they put a surplice. And thus they laid him on a bier in the antechamber of the hall, where he had died, with a crimson silk and a beautiful carpet over him.

After 8 o'clock my colleague sent for me and I came. The cardinals in the city had not yet received any announcement, but during the time that I went to the Vatican, it was communicated to them. But none of them made any move, nor did they meet anywhere else. I suggested to Caraffa that he ought to prepare for imminent dangers, and after 9 o'clock he notified all the cardinals, through his secretary, that they should deign to appear the next morning in Santa Maria Minerva. There, in the middle of the sacristy, four benches were placed for the cardinals in a quadrangle. When I came to the Pope I dressed him in red robes all of brocade, with a short fanon, a beautiful chasuble, and with stockings. And as there was no cross on the shoes, I put on instead his daily slippers of crimson velvet with the golden cross, which I bound with two strings to the back of the heels. His ring was missing and I could not recover it.

Thereupon we carried him through the two rooms, the Hall of the Pontiffs, and the audience room, to the Camera Papagalli, where we prepared a beautiful table of one rod in length with a crimson cover and a beautiful rug over it. We obtained four cushions of brocade and one of crimson velvet. The one of old crimson velvet we did not use, but of the others we laid one under the shoulders of the Pope, two beside and one beneath the head, and over this an old carpet. And so he lay throughout the night with two torches, quite alone, although the prothonotaries had been invited to read the burial service.

On the following Monday, the nineteenth of August, 1503, I had the coffin brought to the Camera Papagalli and laid the body in it. The subdeacon, in his cloak, stood ready to carry the cross, but we could not find the papal cross. During the night they sang the requiem, sitting on the window bench and laying their hands on the bier of the Pope, which was then carried by the poor who stood around in order to see the Pope. I then put a double mattress into the coffin and over it a beautiful new bishop's cloak of brocade of pale mauve with two new veils, on which were embroidered the arms of Pope Alexander. I then laid the Pope on this and covered him with an old rug, placing an old pillow beneath his shoulders and two cushions of brocade beneath his head. Two new crimson hats with golden strings I took home with me. The body, thus wrapped up, was borne by our servants.

When the coffin was deposited in the center of the church, the *Non intres in judicium*, et cetera, should have been recited, but there was no book there. While we were waiting for it in vain, the clergy intonated the responsorium: *Libera me, Domine*. During the singing some soldiers of the palace guard attempted to appropriate several torches. The clergy defended itself against them, and the soldiers turned their weapons against the clergy, who left their singing and fled to the sacristy. The Pope was therefore left lying almost alone. I took up the bier together with three others, and we carried him up to the main altar and the papal throne and placed him with the head toward the altar, closing the choir behind the coffin.

The Bishop of Sessa feared that if the people came near to the dead, there might be a scandal—that is, someone whom the dead had injured might take revenge upon him. Therefore, he had the coffin taken away again and deposited it at the entrance of the chapel between the stairs, the feet so near to the rails and the door that one could touch them easily with the hand through the railing. There it remained the whole day through behind the well-closed railing.

In the meantime, 16 cardinals had assembled in Santa Maria Sopra Minerva after 9 o'clock. They appointed Archbishop Sachis of Ragusa as governor of Rome and assigned 200 soldiers to him.

After dinner the cardinals, together with the clerics of the Camera, took an inventory of the silver and costly furnishings. They found the papal crown and two precious tiaras, all the rings that the Pope used at the mass, and the whole service of vessels used by the Pope when officiating, as much as could be packed into eight large chests. There were, furthermore, silver vessels in the first chamber behind the papal apartment, which Michelotto Neri had overlooked, and a box of cyprus wood that was covered with a green cloth and had also not been discovered. In this box were precious stones and rings to the value of about 25,000 ducats, many papers, among them the oath of the cardinals, the bull of investiture of the kingdom of Naples, and various other documents.

Meanwhile, the Pope, as has been told before, stood between the rails of the main altar. Beside him there burned four torches. The decomposition and blackness of his face increased constantly so that he looked at 8 o'clock, when I saw him, like the blackest cloth or the darkest Negro, completely spotted, the nose swollen, the mouth quite large, the tongue swollen up, doubled so that it started out of his lips, the mouth open, in short so horrible that no one ever saw, or declared to know, of anything similar.

In the evening, after 9 o'clock, he was brought from there to the chapel of Santa Maria delle Febbri and deposited in the corner on the wall at the left of the altar by six porters, who made jokes and allusions to the Pope all the while. The two carpenters had made the coffin too narrow and too short. They laid the miter by his side, covered him with an old carpet, and helped with their fists to fit him into the coffin. All this without torches or any other illumination, without a priest or any person who took care of his body!

*

Cesare Borgia's severe illness at the time of his father's death left him incapable of interfering in the events that followed. The surviving members of the Orsini and Colonna clans returned to Rome, recovered most of their old power and possessions, and exacted revenge on the followers of the Borgias. The College of Cardinals elected as the new Pope the aged Cardinal Piccolomini, who reigned for less than a month as Pius III before dying; and following him, the Cardinal della Rovere, an ancient enemy of the Borgias, became Pope Julius II on November 1, 1503.

In return for the support of the Spanish faction in the College of Cardinals, Julius II permitted Cesare Borgia to retain his position of Captain-General of the Church after his recovery. Before Cesare could gather his forces, however, the Pope had him arrested and kept him imprisoned in Rome until mid-1504. Upon his release he joined the Franco-Spanish armies at Naples, but was again arrested, this time by the King of Spain, and sent to prison in Seville. Cesare escaped in 1505, then joined the forces of his brother-in-law, the King of Navarre, and was killed fighting in a skirmish during the siege of the castle of Viana, at the age of 31, in 1507.

Lucrezia Borgia remained in Ferrara as the wife of her third husband, Alfonso d'Este, never returning to Roman life and politics. Her court, as Duchess of Ferrara, became one of the most celebrated in Europe. She died in 1519, at the age of 39, soon after giving birth to a stillborn child.

Ivan the Terrible

Collection of the Stockholm Museum, Sweden.

> . . . so shall you hear
> Of carnal, bloody, and unnatural acts,
> Of accidental judgements, casual slaughters,
> Of deaths put on by cunning and forc'd cause,
> And, in this upshot, purposes mistook
> Fall'n on the inventors' heads. . . .
>
> William Shakespeare, *Hamlet V:2*

At Stalin's nod the famous Soviet film director Sergei Eisenstein made a movie during World War II based on the life of Ivan IV, a czar once termed by Eisenstein "the sixteenth century poet of the state," but better known to posterity as Ivan the Terrible. The first section of the movie, shown in 1945, won a Stalin Prize; but the second, which was previewed in 1947 and then summarily suppressed and condemned, provoked the rage of the dictator. "In Part II," declared an article in Pravda issued anonymously by the Central Committee of the U.S.S.R., but most likely inspired by Stalin himself, "the director Eisenstein displayed his ignorance of historic fact by showing Ivan's progressive army of oprichniks [the czar's private military and political forces] as a band of degenerates in the style of the American Ku Klux Klan; and Ivan, a man of great will power and strong character, as a weak and feeble being, a sort of Hamlet."

In February of 1947, when the so-called "personality cult" of Stalin was at its most intense, Eisenstein was summoned to meet with him in the Kremlin to discuss the matter. Present during this symposium of the Higher Criticism were, it is said, Stalin's pince-nezed executioner Beria; the robotized golem Molotov; and, of course, the Secretary himself, whose lips must have twisted throughout in a sneer at human fatuity and pusillanimity, though concealed beneath what the poet Ossip Mandelstam once referred to—and paid with his life for so doing—as a "cockroach moustache." Anyway, Eisenstein found their arguments irresistible, and after shriving himself of his ideological sins by the required penance of public confession, agreed to remake the movie. He died, however, early the next year, in 1948, before it was finished.

When Part I and the remnant of Part II were shown at last in 1956, as a result of the Khrushchev "thaw," the reason for Stalin's anger became apparent. There was not only a historic parallel between Stalin's Soviet Union and the Holy Russia of Ivan the Terrible—threatened from without by powerful and hostile neighbors and from within by the hatred of their own subjects—but the close personal resemblance of both tyrants, especially in their sadistic fury and cruelty, was also unmistakable. Yet Eisenstein's work, though widely acclaimed as a masterpiece, was in many ways an apologia for the czar, with the ghastly events of his reign somehow refined and aestheticized into a choreography of horrors, a cinematic Dance of Death, presented in a series of black-and-white tableaux that might have been so conceived by Aubrey Beardsley.

By contrast the imagery in the account of Ivan that follows, written by an English adventurer and agent for the Russia Company named Jerome Horsey, might have sprung fully realized from the paintings of a Matthias Grünewald or Hieronymus Bosch. What the author's contemporary Giles Fletcher, who served as Queen Elizabeth's ambassador to Russia, described in his own Of the Russe Common Wealth (1591) as the "strange face of a tyrannical state . . . without true knowledge of God, without common justice, without written law," Horsey observed close-up, delineated in the features of the Czar himself. For a final macabre touch to his portrait, Horsey remarks that even after Ivan's death, with his body "sumptuously entombed in Michael Archangel Church [in the Kremlin], and guarded day and night, he remains a fearful spectacle in the memory of those who pass by and hear his name spoken, and they are content to cross and bless themselves against his resurrection amongst them again, etc."—an almost uncanny premonition, as it turned out, of the scene nearly 400 years later, in Moscow's Red Square, when the mummified corpse of Ivan's even more terrible avatar was displayed on his bier before silent crowds of Russian unbelievers crossing and blessing themselves against "etc." as they filed past.

English merchants, diplomats, and adventurers such as Horsey had established themselves in a pre-eminent position at Ivan's court in the years following the voyage of discovery by Sir Richard Chancellor, who first opened *the White Sea route to Muscovy in 1553. Queen Elizabeth's Russia Company was granted a monopoly on northern trade with Russia as well as exemption from all customs duties in 1569. Besides cloth, which was England's principal export, its merchants supplied Ivan with metal products and chemicals, such as saltpeter and sulphur, for the manufacture of munitions. These last were a vital necessity to Russia in her ongoing wars with Sweden and Poland in the west and with the khanate of the Crimean Tatars in the south. For at that time the very survival of Russia as an independent state was as precarious as was England's before the defeat of the Spanish Armada in 1588. The Czar's own grandfather, Ivan III, who finally shook off the dominion of the Tatar Golden Horde in 1480, until then had been forced to pay tribute and to humiliate himself every year by feeding the Khan's horse inside the Kremlin, kneeling before him with the oats held in his cap, as a sign of his submission; and during earlier centuries the Slav people had been herded and driven like cattle by these fierce nomads from the southern steppes, who often used them as a buffer in their periodic assaults against the outlying cities of the Byzantine Empire. They were also an easy prey to Scandinavian pirates and Teutonic knights, thousands of Slavs being sold yearly in the slave markets of Europe and Asia, where their ethnic name became identified with slavery. Ivan's military victories against these ancient enemies abroad, and his success in crushing the power of the Orthodox priesthood and of the feudal boyars at home, enabled him to establish Russia as a modern autocratic state. Furthermore, his assumption for the first time of the title of Czar, the Russianized form of "Caesar," implied that Moscow was the imperial successor to Rome and Byzantium, the "third Rome," destined for world dominion.*

Horsey's Travels, *from which the following has been excerpted, was begun by him soon after his return from Russia. He was brought back to England under arrest, in 1591, to answer charges against him by disgruntled rivals that he had been engaged in double and shady dealings while in Moscow. After a long trial, as a result of which he was exonerated by the Privy Council, Horsey became an M.P. and also High Sheriff for his home county of Buckinghamshire. It took him apparently 30 years of fits and starts to complete these memoirs, though they give the impression of having erupted in a single burst of vituperative indignation. In editing and abridging the book for modern readers, I have made no attempt to dam his sometimes torrential prose.*

The original manuscript, in the British Museum, was first edited by Edward A. Bond in 1856 and published in London for the Hakluyt Society. I am indebted to Lloyd E. Berry and Robert O. Crummery's excellent notes and introduction to Horsey's Travels *in their* Rude and Barbarous Kingdom *(Madison: University of Wisconsin Press, 1968).*

The Early History

This great Duke of all Russia, Ivan Vasilievich, grew up comely in person, endowed with wit, excellent gifts, and graces fit for government of so great a monarchy. He married, at 12 years, Anastasia Romanova, daughter to a gentleman of good rank. The Empress was wise and of such holiness and virtue that she was honored, beloved, and feared of all her subjects. He being young and riotous, she ruled him with such affability and wisdom that, calling on the prowess and courage of his princes, bishops, and council, he cast off the yoke of homage his predecessors had always paid unto the Scythian Emperor of the Crimea; conquered the empires of Kazan and Astrakhan 2700 miles from his city of Moscow, down the great river Volga, near the Caspian Sea; conquered, in a short space after, all the princes and their country of Tatary of divers sorts; and brought a vast host of people under his subjection, whose devastation is to this day most mournfully sung and spoken of among those nations. Through which conquests he was crowned and styled the Emperor, great monarch, and great Duke of Kazan, Astrakhan, Moscow, Vladimir, Novgorod, Russia, and a great rabblement more of the names of his provinces. Yet he had continual wars with the Crimean Tatars, who did sore annoy him and his subjects with their yearly incursions.

As he grew in years and greatness, so did his conquests increase and augment. He got from the King of Poland the famous cities of Polotsk, Smolensk, Dorogabuzh, Viaz'ma, and many other towns, with much riches and infinite numbers of people captives; also, Byelorussia and Lithuania, goodly towns of traffic, and countries yielding commodities of wax, flax and hemp, tallow, hides, corn and cattle in abundance; also, many nobles, gentry, and merchants oought and sold and put to ransoms, so that he grew very proud, mighty, cruel, and bloody in his conquests. And when his good Queen, Empress Anastasia, died [in 1560]—he having by her two sons, Ivan and Fëdor—then he married [in 1561] one of the Circassian princesses [Mariia, daughter of Temriuk, Prince of Kabarda, in the Caucasus] by whom he had no issue that he would be known of. The manner and solemnity of this marriage was so strange and heathenly as credit will hardly be given to the truth thereof.

Having strengthened himself not only by his conquests of those empiredoms but also, by this late marriage, gotten an invincible power from his alliance with the Tatars, he made use of them to suppress such of his princes and nobles as he perceived were in discontentment and mutiny against him. Swelling in ambition, boasting beyond all sense what conquest he intended, he then set forward with an army of 100,000 horse and 50,000 foot toward Livonia and Sweden.

The Emperor first builds a strong castle at the Narva [river in Estonia], called Ivangorod, afterward commanding the eyes of the builder to be bored out for his so rare architecture [so that it could never be duplicated]. From Pskov he enters the confines of Livonia, sends Knez Mikhail Glinskii with the cannon to besiege the first castle, called Newe Howse [Neuhausen], takes it and the soldiers captives, and puts in 300 soldiers for garrison thereof, to whom he gave the spoil and pillage. He takes over small towns and castles on his way to Dorpat, a great and strong town of traffic, batters and besieges it: the citizens yield with a dejective flag of truce. Four thousand Tatars carry away 8000 captives, men, women and children, the treasure and merchandise of the city being sent away to Novgorod for the Emperor's use. He then goes forward, severing his army into four parts, with 10,000 men to guard and draw his ordnance over rivers frozen hard and lakes of ice, taking without resistance many castles, towns and villages, riches, cattle and people.

Oh the lamentable outcries and cruel slaughters, drowning and burning, ravaging of women and maids, stripping them naked without mercy or regard of the frozen weather, tying and binding them by three and by four at their horses' tails, dragging them, some alive, some dead, all bloody through ways and streets already full of carcasses of aged men, women, and infants! Some among these victims were goodly persons clad in velvet, damask, and silks, with jewels, gold, and pearl hid about them; and they were besides the fairest people in the world, by reason of their generation and the climate, cold and dry. There was an infinite number of slaves thus sent and dragged into Russia. The riches in money and merchandise and other treasure carried out of the cities and surrounding country, and out of 600 churches robbed and destroyed, were inestimable.

Thus the Emperor and his cruel and hellish Tatars, having ranged and ransacked the land and its miserable people, came at last to the capital. This city, called Reval [Tallinn] stood very strong upon a high rocky mountain at the edge of the Baltic Sea, over against Stockholm in Sweden. The Emperor besieged it with 20,000 men and battered it with 20 cannons. The soldiers and men and women within the town made up the breaches in the night that were battered in the day, carrying and casting cauldrons of hot and cold water, which continually froze so thick that the Emperor, after six weeks' siege and 20,000 cannon shot, did little prevail. Wherewith, after the loss of 6000 men, he hasted his retreat and left Reval with shame.

The sudden thaw and inundation of the great land waters made him lose a great deal of his artillery, booty, and baggage, and at least 30,000 men in his retiring; so that, being overcome with fury and madness, the Emperor determined to put in execution the most bloody and cruelest massacre that ever was heard of in any age. He came to the Narva, robbed and spoiled the town of all its riches and merchandise, killed and murdered all the men, women, and children, and gave the spoils to his Tatar army. Thence the Emperor sped to Pskov, where he intended to do the like, because he was incensed and easily made to believe that this city, along with Novgorod, had conspired treacherously with his enemies to destroy him at Reval and overthrow his armies.

Outside this city there met him an impostor or magician, but whom the people held to be their oracle, a holy man named Nikola Sviatoi. This man called the Emperor to his face bloodsucker, devourer, and eater of Christian flesh, and swore by his angel that he should not escape death by being struck by a thunderbolt if he or any of his army did touch a hair of the least child's head in that city. He warned him to depart before the fiery cloud, God's wrath, broke upon his head, there being in truth a very great and dark storm forming in the skies at that instant. (I [Jerome Horsey] saw this impostor or magician, a foul creature, who went naked both in winter and summer; he endured both extreme frost and heat, and did many strange things through the magical illusions of the Devil, but was much followed, feared, and reverenced both of prince and people.) His words made the Emperor to tremble, so that he desired prayers for his deliverance and forgiveness of his cruel thoughts.

But soon after his return to the great city of Novgorod, where all his captives and prisoners remained, he felt mightily displeased against this city above all others. He charged it with 30,000 Tatars and 10,000 gunners of his guard, who without any respect ravished all the women and maids, ransacked, robbed and spoiled all that were within it of their jewels, plate, and treasure, murdered the people young and old, burned all their household stuff, merchandise, and warehouses of wax, flax, tallow, hides, salt, wines, cloth, and silks, set all on fire, with the wax and tallow melted down the gutters in the streets together with the blood of 700,000 men, women, and children slain and murdered, so that their very carcasses did stop the stream of the river Volga by being cast therein. No history maketh mention of so horrible a massacre.*

With the city of Novgorod left desolate and wasted, he returned with his army and Livonian captives toward Moscow. Along the way he commanded his captains and other officers to drive and take out of the towns and villages within 50 miles compass all sorts of people—gentlemen, peasants, merchants, and monks, young and old, with their families, goods, and cattles—to go cleanse and inhabit the ruinated city of Novgorod. He thereby exposed them to a new slaughter, for many of them died with the pestilence of the infected and noisome air.

His cruelty bred such a general hatred throughout his kingdom that there were many who practiced and devised how to destroy this tyrant; but he still did discover their plots and treasons by ennobling all the rascalliest and most desperate soldiers in his army to peek out and spy upon them. He employed these soldiers to ransack and spoil and massacre the nobility and richest officers and the best sort of his merchants and subjects. With his

---

* Horsey's figures throughout are bombastically inflated. Modern scholars estimate the number of victims in Novgorod at about 40,000.

hands and heart now so hardened and imbrued, the Emperor put many of them to most horrible and shameful deaths and tortures. And now, distrusting the fidelity of his Tatar army, he placed them in garrisons upon the confines of his last conquered towns and castles in Livonia and Sweden. Suspecting some insurrection at home, and especially fearful of the approaching power of his ancient enemy the Scythian Khan, Emperor of the Crimea (incited and stirred up, as he found out, by his own nobility and subjects), he levied out of his provinces, even the most remote, a huge army consisting of Poles, Swedes, and his private 100,000 horse and 50,000 foot.

In the meantime he discards his Circassian wife, Mariia, shears her [hair] a nun and puts her in a monastery, then chooses out of his own subjects Natalia, daughter to Knez Fedor Bulgakov, a chief lieutenant, or *viovode,* of great trust and experience in his wars. But this man soon after lost his head, and his daughter within a year was also shorn a nun.

The time approaches; news comes that his enemy, the Crimean Khan, is in the field.* Though fearful to the Emperor, this is pleasing news to most of his princes and people who live in thralldom and misery. The Scythian Emperor Chigaley Mursoye [Devlet Geray] now enters the confines of Russia and stands with an army of 200,000 soldiers, all horsemen, within 50 miles compass of the river Oka, facing Ivan's army of 100,000 gallant generals and soldiers. The Russians keep the fords and passages very strong with great artillery, munitions, men at arms and a plentiful supply of victuals and all other provisions. But upon secret intelligence, the Scythians are encouraged to venture out, and so cross the river without repulse. For upon strict orders Ivan's army dare not stir (and it is death for them to exceed their commission) beyond their lines, of 25 miles compass, to defend the approach.

The enemy, being come at this side of the river without opposition, speeds toward Moscow, but 90 miles off, where the Emperor Ivan thinks himself secure. But at the Scythians' near approach he turns and flees with his two sons, treasurer, household servants, and personal guard of 20,000 gunners toward a strong monastery, Troitsa, 60 miles farther off, upon Ascension Day [1571].

Inside Moscow the enemy fired the high steeple of Saint John's Church, at which instant happened a wonderful storm wind, through which the city and suburbs of 30 miles compass, built most of fir and oak timber, were set on fire and consumed within six hours' space, with infinite thousands of men, women, and children burned and smothered to death by the fiery air. Even within the stone churches, monasteries, vaults, and cellars, as well as the three walled castles of the city, very few could escape. The river and

---

* According to Giles Fletcher's *Of the Russe Common Wealth,* "The principal cause of this continual quarrel betwixt the Russe and the Krym is for the right of certain border parts claimed by the Tartar but possessed by the Russe. The Tartar allegeth that besides Astrakhan and Kazan (that are the ancient possession of the East Tartar), the whole country from his bounds north and westward as far as the city of Moscow itself, pertaineth to his right. . . ."

ditches about Moscow were stopped and filled with the multitudes of people, many laden with gold, silver, jewels, chains, earrings, bracelets, and treasure, who tried to save their heads above water.

Notwithstanding, so many thousands were either burned or drowned that the river could not be cleansed of the dead carcasses 12 months thereafter. Those who remained alive in Moscow, and from many other towns and places as well, occupied themselves every day within a great circuit to search and fish, as it were, for rings, jewels, plate, bags of gold and silver, by which many were enriched. The streets of the city and the churches, cellars, and vaults lay so thick and full of dead and smothered carcasses that no man could pass through long after because of the noisome smells and the putrefaction of the air.

The Scythians Taunt Ivan

The Scythian Emperor Chigaley Mursoye lodged and solaced himself in a fair monastery four miles from the city by the river side, called Simonov monastery, where he and his army beheld this goodly fire. Though little the better for the burning of Moscow, they rejoiced in their exploit, then soon returned with their captives and booty to Crimea.

Ivan now fled with his two sons and his treasurer to a great town called Vologda, 500 miles off, where he thought himself more secure. Much amazed and perplexed by the great disaster that had befallen him, he summoned to a council the metropolitans, bishops, and clergyman as well as his chief princes and nobility. As soon as he learned the enemy had left his kingdom, he dissolved his army that had fought not a stroke for him. He examined, racked, and tortured many of the viovodes and chief captains, put some to death, confiscated their goods and lands and destroyed their race and families. He then set a course for cleansing, repairing, and replenishing the city of Moscow, which was an infinite labor.

In the midst of these proceedings, the Scythian Emperor sent him an ambassador attended with many noblemen, all well horsed, and clad but in sheepskin coats girt to them, with black caps also of sheepskin, bows and arrows, and with curious rich scimitars by their sides. They had a guard to keep them in dark rooms; stinking horseflesh and water was their best food, without bread or beer or bed. Much disgrace and base usage was offered them, but they endured, puffed, and scorned it.

The time was come when the Emperor must grant an audience. With his three crowns before him in his royal estate, and with his princes and nobles standing about him, he commands that the sheepskin coat and cap be taken off the ambassador and a golden robe and rich cap be put on him instead. The ambassador, well contented, enters his presence; but his Scythian followers are kept back in a space with grates of iron between the Emperor and them, at which the ambassador chafes with a hellish, hollow voice, looking fierce and grimly.

Four captains of the guard now bring him near the Emperor's seat. A most ugly creature, without reverence he thunders out his taunts, saying his master Chigaley Mursoye, great Emperor of all the kingdoms the sun did spread his beams over, had sent to Ivan Vasilievich, his vassal and duke over all Russia by his permission, to ask how he liked the scourge of his displeasure by sword, fire, and famine. But Chigaley Mursoye had sent Ivan for remedy (pulling out a foul rusty knife as he spoke) this to cut his throat withal. The guards haste him forth from the room without answer, and would have taken off his golden gown and cap, but he and his company strive with them so stoutly that they are unable to do so.

Soon after they left his presence, the Emperor Ivan fell into such an agony that he sent for his ghostly father and tore his own hair and beard for madness. The chief captain prayed his Majesty's leave to cut them all in pieces, but had no answer. After he had kept this Scythian ambassador and his fellows some time, and with better usage than formerly, the Emperor sent him away with this message: "Tell the miscreant and unbeliever, thy master, it is for my sins and the sins of my people against my God and Christ that he hath been granted, though a limb of Satan, the power and opportunity to be the instrument of my rebuke."

But the ambassador replied: "I would not do you so much service as to carry any such message to him."

The Emperor was loath to come to the city of Moscow, though he sent for the chief merchants, craftsmen, and tradesmen from all other towns within his kingdom to build and inhabit there and draw traffic thither. He took away all impositions from them and gave them freedom of customs. He also set 7000 masons and workmen to build a stone wall round about Moscow—very strong and beautiful and furnished with goodly pieces of brass ordnance—which they finished in four years' space. Ivan's officers of justice and governors were settled therein. Himself he kept much at Vologda, upon the river Dvina, and at Sloboda Alexandrovskaia. There he conferred each day with Eleazar Bomelius, a doctor of physic [Ivan's confidant, an adventurer and sometime astrologer who had studied medicine in London before entering the Czar's service]; and he sent for skillful builders, architects, carpenters, joiners and masons, goldsmiths, physicians, apothecaries, and such like out of England, having some purpose in his head that will shortly discover itself. And he built at Vologda a treasure-house of stone, along with great barks and barges to transport upon sudden occasion his treasure to Solovetskii monastery, standing upon the north seas, the direct way into England.

Ivan "Abdicates"

The Emperor had so fleeced his merchants by seizing their commodities, with little or no payment, and exchanging them with foreigners for cloth-of-gold, dollars, pearls, jewels, etc., that he had exhausted all their wealth. The empire, as a result, seethed with discontent. In such a desperate case, he had made [in 1565] a division of his towns, offices, and subjects, taking one part, the *oprichnina,* as his private domain, and appointing to it those officers in whom he had complete confidence, so as to frustrate and annihilate all treason. But now [in 1575] Ivan established a new King or Emperor, Czar Symeon [Bekbulatovich], son of the ruler of Kazan, whom he crowned with his own hand, but with no solemnity nor consent of the peers, and caused his subjects to address themselves and their affairs, petitions, and suits to him.

Czar Symeon, sitting in majesty, coins money, receives customs, and collects fines and certain revenues for the maintenance of his house, officers, and servants. Pleas in all courts of justice are conducted in his name, and he is liable to all debts and matters concerning his office of treasurer. The old Emperor Ivan comes and prostrates himself before the throne, commanding his metropolitans, bishops, priors, noblemen, and officers to do the like, though some refuse, and directing all ambassadors to resort before him. He is even married, by Ivan's order, to the daughter of a prince of the royal blood.

All state matters being thus contraverted and changed, Ivan refused to take notice of debts owing in his time; letters patents and privileges to towns and monasteries were all declared void. His clergy, nobility, and commons must now petition Ivan that he would be pleased to take the crown and government upon him again. He was contented; at which infinite gifts and presents from men of worth were bestowed upon him, amounting to a great treasure. He was also freed of all old debts and former charges whatsoever . . . but it is too tedious to recite any more of this tragedy.

No doubt the device of his own head might have set him clear beside the saddle if it had continued but a little longer, but he is soon happily invested again *in statu quo prius.* He regrants privileges, jurisdictions, charters to towns, monasteries, and noblemen and merchants, for which great sums and fines are obtained. With his power restored, he now sends an army of Tatars, governed by his own captains, to reconquer the towns in Livonia that King Stephen [Báthory of Poland] had lately taken from him. [At the close of the Livonian War (1579–82) Stephen Báthory retook Polotsk and advanced victoriously to Pskov.]

The Emperor was jealous of his brother Knez Andrew [Vladimir Andreevich], for he himself had ruled so tyrannically that he incurred the hatred of his subjects, while his brother had gotten their hearty affections, which Ivan well perceived. He now propounded a marriage betwixt Duke Magnus [of Livonia] and his brother's daughter, and sent for his brother out of his province of Vaga to come to the court.

When Knez Andrew came into his presence, he laid himself prostrate at his foot, but the Emperor took him up and kissed him. "O cruel brother," declared Knez Andrew with tears (so goes the story), "this is a Judas kiss.

Thou hast sent for me to no good end. Take thy fill," he finished, and so parted for that time. Knez Andrew died the next day, and was buried in Micholsea crest [probably the Cathedral of the Archangel Michael in the Kremlin] in Moscow, solemnly. [He was poisoned at Ivan's command on Oct. 9, 1569.]

Soon after this, the Emperor sent throughout his kingdom for his nobles' and gentlemen's fairest daughters, and chose out among them a wife for his eldest son, Czarevich Ivan. Her name was Natalia, daughter to Ivan Sheremetev, a viovode of a good family. Great feastings and tournaments were held at the solemnizing of this marriage.

But I fear I shall fill my discourse with too much of this narration, so I will therefore go onward with the story of the Emperor's life.

Ivan's Cruelties

The Emperor lived in great danger and fear of treasons, which he daily discovered; and he spent much time in the examination, torturing, execution, and putting to death of such noble captains and officers that were found conspiring against him. Knez Ivan Kurakin being found drunk in Wenden [Tsesis], a town in Livonia, when King Stephen [Báthory] besieged it [in 1578], he was stripped naked, laid in a cart, and whipped through the market with six whips of wire, which cut his back, belly, and bowels until his death. Another, as I remember, Ivan Obrossimov, a master of his horse, was hanged on a gibbet naked by the heels, while the skin and flesh of his body from top to toe was cut and minced into small gobbets by four swordsmen. One of them, wearied of his long carving, thrust his knife somewhat far into his bowels, the sooner to dispatch him. This man was immediately taken to another place of execution and his sword hand cut off, which being not well seared [to staunch the flow of blood], he died the next day. Many other victims were knocked in the heads, then cast into the pools and lakes near Sloboda, their flesh and carcasses fed upon by huge overgrown pikes, carps, and other fishes, so fat that hardly any other thing but fat could be discerned upon them.

Knez Boris Tulupov, a great favorite of that time, after being discovered to be a treason worker against the Emperor and confederate with the discontented nobility, was drawn upon a long, sharpened stake, which entered his fundament and passed through his body and out at his neck; upon which he languished in horrible pain for 15 hours alive and spoke unto his mother, the Duchess, who was brought to behold that woeful sight. And she, a goodly matronly woman, upon like displeasure was given to 100 gunners, who defiled her to death one after the other, her body lying naked and swollen in the place. The Emperor then commanded his huntsmen to bring their hungry hounds to eat and devour her flesh and bones, which they dragged in morsels everywhere. At the sight, Ivan exclaimed, "Such as I favor I have honored, and such as be traitors will I have thus done unto!"

The Emperor's hands and heart being thus inbrued in blood, he made it his chief exercise to put in execution new torments, tortures, and deaths upon such as he took displeasure against, especially those of the nobility most beloved by the people, of whom he was exceeding jealous. He countenanced the most desperate captains and soldiers and decayed gentry to affront them and breed faction; whereby, indeed, there grew such suspicion among them as they durst not trust one another, though they longed to ruin and displace him. All of which he perceived, and knew that his throne grew every day more desperate and in danger.

Troubled how to shun and escape the same, he was very inquisitive with one Eleazar Bomelius, as you have already heard mention (a cozening impostor, once doctor of physic in England, also a rare mathematician and magician), asking how old Queen Elizabeth was, and what likely success there might be if he should be a suitor of her for himself.* And though he was much disheartened, not only because he had two wives living, and that many kings and great princes had formerly been suitors to her Majesty and could not prevail, yet he magnified his person, his wisdom, greatness, and riches above all other princes. Presently he put the Empress, his last wife, into a nunnery, to live there as dead to the world. And having had it in his thoughts long before to make England, in case of extremity, his safest refuge, he built and prepared many goodly barks and barges at Vologda. His plan was to pass down the river Dvina with all his treasure by the English ships, leaving his eldest son, the Czarevich Ivan, to govern his so troubled estate. For that purpose, he devised a plan to raise a new treasure to leave unto him, the better to establish his strength.

A high provincial convocation was then called by him in the great consistory of the Holy Ghost. The Emperor's spies had long brought him full intelligence that the chief bishops, priors, and abbots assembled and dissembled often times together with the discontented nobility on how to make a war of resistance against him. But there wanted a head or general that had courage sufficient to lead such an army; and they were altogether unprovided both of horses and arms. The Emperor now took advantage and opportunity of the convocation to proclaim the heads of all those religious houses to be traitors. And to make them appear more hateful, he summoned 20 of the principal members and charged them with odious and horrible crimes and treacheries.

Now come we to the merry tragedy to requite your patience all this while. The Emperor commands his great bears—wild, fierce and hungry—to be brought out of their dark caves and cages, kept on purpose for such delights and pastimes in a spacious high-walled place at Sloboda Velikaia. About seven of those principal rebellious big fat friars are brought forth, one after another, each with his cross and beads in his left hand and, through the

---

* Ivan contemplated taking refuge in England about this time. In 1567 he had sought formal guarantees from Queen Elizabeth that either could find asylum in the other's domains, but she did not respond.

Emperor's great favor, a boar spear five feet in length in his right for his defense. A wild bear is let loose, ranging and roaring up against the walls with open mouth. Scenting the friar by his greasy garments, and made more mad by the cries and shouting of the people, the bear runs fiercely at him, catches and crushes his head, body, bowels, legs, and arms, as a cat doth a mouse, tearing his clothes to pieces till he comes to his flesh, blood, and bones, and so devours the first friar for his prey. The bear is then shot and killed by the gunners firing pell-mell. And so another friar and another bear are brought forth, till seven are devoured in the same manner as the first was; saving one friar, more cunning than the rest, who bestirs his boar spear so nimbly, setting the end thereof in the ground and guiding it to the breast of the bear, which runs itself through upon it. Yet even he does not escape devouring after the bear is hurt, both dying in the place. This friar is later canonized for being a valiant saint by the rest of his living brothers of the Troitsa monastery.

The metropolitans, bishops, monks, and friars were all duly impressed by this spectacle, and resorted with petitions and prostrations to pacify the Emperor's fury. They presented unto his Majesty a true inventory of all their treasure, and had to meet his resolute demand of 300,000 marks sterling, besides many precincts, villages, towns, and lands.

Ivan Seeks an Alliance with England

Having thereby raised a standing treasure for his son without diminishing any part of his own, the Emperor still had an eye and an aim to England. His mind was prepared. But his ambassador, Andrei Sovin, could not altogether discern his intention, which was darkly expressed by word of mouth, since the Emperor durst not commit it to paper; nor did Mr. Jenkinson and Mr. Randolph [Queen Elizabeth's envoys to Moscow from 1567 to 1572 who at that time discussed granting asylum to the Czar in England] in their particular negotiations, so thoroughly understand, move, or break the matter as he expected. But he himself kept it not so secret but that his eldest son, the Czarevich Ivan, and several favorites and nobles, took notice of it. Which the Emperor perceiving, and to put out all jealousy thereof from their minds, he married again his fifth wife, the daughter of Fëdor Nagoi, a very beautiful young maiden of a noble house and great family, by whom he had a third son, called Dmitri Ivanovich.

The Emperor now spent his time still in pacifying his discontented nobles and people. He kept two armies afoot, yet at small expense, for his princes and nobles went mostly upon their own charge. One army consisted mostly of Tatars, which he employed against the kings and princes of Poland and Sweden, by whom he was environed; and the other consisted commonly of 100,000 horse, most of them his own natural subjects, saving some few Poles, Swedes, Dutch, and Scots employed against his great enemy in Crimea.

The Emperor was expecting some return of his letters to Queen Elizabeth and news from England by Daniel Sylvester [the Queen's courier]. Sylvester arrived with the Queen's letters at Saint Nicholas, then went up to Kholmogory where he set about preparing and making clothes fit for him to be presented to the Emperor with those letters. The tailor, while in his lodgings, had scarce gone down the stairs to fetch a yellow cotton jacket when a thunderbolt came through the window and struck Sylvester dead, piercing down the collar inside his new coat and out the right side of his body, though the wound was not outwardly seen. The flash of lightning killed also his boy and dog beside him, and burnt his desk, letters, house, all at an instant. The Emperor was much amazed when he heard of it, saying, "God's will be done!" but raged and was in a desperate case.

The difficulty was in how to convey his letters to the Queen, as his country was surrounded by enemies and the passages shut up. He sent for me, and told me he had a message of honor, weight, and secrecy to employ me in to her Majesty, the Queen of England, perceiving that I had attained familiarity in his language as well as in the Polish and Dutch tongues. (Though but a plain grammarian, having some smattering of Greek, I attained by the affinity thereof in a short time to a ready knowledge of their vulgar speech, the Slavonian, the most copious and elegant language in the world.) The Emperor questioned with me of divers things, liked my ready answers, and asked me if I had seen his great vessels and barks built and prepared at Vologda. I told him I had.

"What traitor hath showed them to you?"

"The fame of them was such, and people flocking to see them upon a festival day, I ventured with thousands more to behold the curious beauty, largeness, and strange fashion of them."

"Why, what mean you by those words, 'strange fashion'?"

"For that the portraiture of lions, dragons, eagles, elephants, and unicorns were so lively made and so richly set forth with gold, silver, and curious colors of painting."

"A crafty youth—he commends his own countrymen's artifice!" said the Emperor to his favorite standing by. "It is true. It seems you have taken good view of them. How many of them?"

"It please your Majesty, I saw but 20."

"You shall see 40 ere long be, and no worse. I commend you. No doubt you can relate as much in a foreign place; but much more to be admired if you knew what inestimable treasure they are inwardly to be beautified with. It is reported your Queen, my sister, hath the best navy of ships in the world."

"It is true, and please your Majesty."

"Why have you dissembled with me then? Speak."

"The Queen's navy is built for strength and greatness to break out and cut through the great ocean and turbulent seas."

"How framed so?"

"For art, sharp-keeled, not flat-bottomed; and so thick and strong-sided that a cannon shot can scarce pierce through."

"What else?"

"Every ship carries cannon and 40 brass pieces of great ordnance, bullets, muskets, powder, chain shot, pikes, and armor of defense, wild fireworks, stanchions for fights, a thousand mariners and men at arms, soldiers, captains, and officers of all sorts to guide and govern; discipline and daily divine prayer; beer, bread, beef, fish, bacon, peas, butter, cheese, vinegar, oatmeal, aquavitae, wood, water, and all other provisions plentiful, fit and necessary for food and maintenance of men; anchors, cables, tackles, masts, five or six great sails spread, ancients, flags, costly silk banners displayed with the Queen's ensigns and arms, to which the ships of all other kings bend and bow; drums, trumpets, tabors, pipes, and other instruments of warlike designs and defiance to the enemy. Her ships are able to assault and batter the strongest maritime towns and castles, and are most terrible and warlike for the aid and defense of her Majesty's alliance and friends."

I had the grace and spirit and speech in the essential delivery of this, as he often cast his head and eye aside upon the hearers and standers-by to attend.

"How many such ships has the Queen as you describe?"

"Forty, and please your Majesty."

"It is a good 'navy royal,' as you term it. It can transport 40,000 soldiers to a friend."

He then charged me to prepare myself, and be silent and secret, and daily to attend till he could provide for my dispatch. He also commanded Eleazar Vyluzgin, his private secretary, to take from me in writing the description I made of the Queen's navy; unto whom I presented a ship curiously made, set forth and drawn, with all its sails spread, banners and ensigns displayed, ordnance gilt, and all things in a warlike fashion.

At this time the Emperor was very much busied in searching out a notable treason against him by Eleazar Bomelius and also the bishop of Novgorod and some others. He discovered from their servants, tortured upon the rack, letters written in Latin and Greek ciphers and sent three manner of ways to the kings of Poland and Sweden. The bishop, upon examination, confessed. But Bomelius denied all, hoping to fare the better by means of some of his confederates—favorites near about the Emperor whom he had appointed to attend his son Czarevich Ivan. Bomelius was then examined upon the rack—his arms drawn back disjointed, his legs stretched from his middle loins, his back and body cut with wire whips—where he confessed many things more than he was willing the Emperor should know. The Emperor sent word they should roast him. He was taken from the rack and bound to a stake, when his bloody back and body were roasted and scorched till they thought no life in him. He was then thrown into a sled and brought through the castle. He cast up his eyes, naming Christ, after which he was dragged into a dungeon where he died.

This Bomelius lived in great favor and pomp. He was a skillful mathematician, but a wicked man and practicer of much mischief. Most of the nobles were glad of his dispatch, for he knew much concerning them. He had conveyed great riches and treasure out of the country, by way of England, to Wesel in Westphalia, where he was born, though brought up in Cambridge. Notwithstanding, he was an enemy always to our nation.

Bomelius had deluded the Emperor, making him believe the Queen of England was young, and that it was very feasible for him to marry her, whereof the Emperor was now out of hope. Yet he had heard that she had a young lady in her court of the blood royal, the Lady Mary Hastings, of which we shall speak more hereafter.

The bishop of Novgorod was condemned for his treason, for coining money and sending it and other treasure to the kings of Poland and Sweden, for buggery, for keeping witches and boys and beasts, and for other horrible crimes. All his goods, horses, money, and treasure, which was much, were confiscated by the Emperor. He himself was condemned to everlasting imprisonment in a cave, where he lived on bread and water, with irons on his head and legs, and spent his days painting pictures and images. Eleven of his confederate servants were hanged at his palace gate in Moscow, and his women witches shamefully dismembered and burned.

The Emperor was loath to take notice of all those who were joined in this treason, but passed it over with admonitions. At this time, his eldest son having no issue, he declared his pleasure and intent to marry off his second son, the Czarevich Fëdor, to a beautiful young lady named Irina, out of a famous and powerful family most trusty to the Emperor. All in the court prostrated themselves to his sacred Majesty, desiring God to bless his holy purpose. After the solemnities, feastings, and triumphs, the Emperor dismissed all his nobles and prelates with good words and a more favorable countenance, which was held for a mutual reconciliation and forgiveness of all.

The Author Goes on an Embassy to Queen Elizabeth

The Emperor's letters and instructions for me to present to her Majesty, Queen Elizabeth, were now ready. He himself and Sava Frolov, chief secretary of state, closed them up in one of the false sides of a wooden bottle filled full with aquavitae, not worth 3d., to hang under my horse's mane. He also gave me 400 Hungarian ducats in gold to be sewn into my boots and quilted in some of my worst garments. The Emperor then said:

"I forbear to tell you of some secrets of my pleasure, fearing that in your passage through my enemies' countries, now in combustion, you may fall into their hands and be forced to disclose what I would not have known. What thou shalt say to Queen Elizabeth, my loving sister, the bottle thou carriest with thee shall declare unto thee when thou comest in a safe place to open it. In the mean and always, be thou trusty and faithful, and thy reward shall be my goodness and grace from me hereafter."

I fell prostrate and laid my head on his foot, but with a heavy heart to be thus exposed to possible misery and not avoidable danger. A gentleman of good rank attended me. My sled and horses posted that night 90 miles to Tver [Kalinin], where victuals and fresh horses were prepared; then on to Novgorod and Pskov and to Newe Howse [Neuhausen], traveling 600 miles in three days.

Entering into Livonia, my gentleman and servants took their leaves, desiring some token of my safe arrival thither. I bade them hie themselves away, lest the enemy round about us might take them and hinder my service. The sentinel then brought me to the *stadtholder,* or lieutenant of the castle, and there he and his accomplices strictly examined and searched me. Coming from their enemy's country, they could not but suspect me. I told them I was glad to come into their hands out of the vale of misery which was Russia. They laid their heads together, and on the third day they appointed me a guide and suffered me with more humanity to pass. The guard and attendants expected some reward, but I prayed them to spare me, as my purse was not answerable to my willingness.

I took three days in passing with great danger over land and frozen marsh to Oesel [Sarema] in Livonia, which was a large island that belonged to the King of Denmark. Then I was conducted by some ragamuffin soldiers, who used me very roughly, to Sonneburg [Kuressare], and on to Arensburg, the chief town and castle in those parts. There they delivered me to the stadtholder's lieutenant, a sick, aged, and crabbed man. I attended his pleasure, knowing I was suspected as a spy. The snakes [worms, that is] in my lodgings crept in at bed and board, hens and other poultry pecking at them in the flour and in the milk pans, a noisome sight, but fear of what might become of me made me think less of that.

The time came when I was called before the governor. This chief was a very grave gentleman in good favor with the King. Soldiers stood about him with halberds and swords while he questioned me. I told him that I was a subject of the Queen of England, who had peace and amity with all Christian princes, especially with his Majesty of Denmark.

"Yes, but that will not serve," he replied, "for the English confederate most with the Muscovite against Christendom."

Asked my name and quality, I framed him an answer, and he then committed me to the custody from whence I was brought, and dismissed me from his company.

Afterward he sent his son, a proper fine gentleman, to convey me to him in private. He had a letter in his hand, and asked my name again. When I told him, he said, "I have received sundry letters from my friends, and one of late from a beloved daughter I have, captive with the Emperor in Moscow. She writes of much Christian favor she has found at an English gentleman's hands, a man named after your name, that negotiates in that court for the Queen of England."

"Is your daughter called Madelyn van Uxell?" I asked.

"Yes, indeed, sir," says he.

"I am the same she writes of. I know her well, and she was in good health within the last ten days."

"Oh, sir, she is my dear and beloved daughter, whom I cannot have ransomed, though the Majesty of Denmark has written in her behalf." He then clapped me about the neck, crying, and his son behaved in like manner. "God's angel has brought you to me," he declared, "so that I might render you thanks for your benevolence toward me and mine. What this island can afford, you shall command."

It seems he was very joyful, and I no less glad of this good hap. He caused me to be brought to a pleasant lodging; and his son next day showed me his stables of great horse, his armor, munitions, and library. The governor also sent for divers of his friends, feasted me, and made ready his letters and passports with many ceremonial loving entertainments. On my departure he gave me a fair German clock, asked his son and servants to guide me out of all danger, and, with prayers and tears, asked that I would continue my goodness toward his daughter in Russia.

I hasted on my way. A *domherr* [canon] met me along the road, a man of good account in Livonia, who marveled that I was so meanly attended. This man knew me, and told his company of my quality, which might have done me hurt—and my aquavitae bottle too, which was girded close under my cassock by day and served by night as my best pillow under my head. Past all danger, as I thought, I came to Pilten, a strong castle upon the Baltic Sea, where King Magnus [of Holstein] lay. He used me but roughly, by reason I could not drink excessively with him. The King had already spent riotously and given away to his followers and adopted daughters most of his towns, castles, jewels, money, horses, and plate that he had received as dowry with the Emperor's niece. (Not long after he died miserably [in 1583], leaving his Queen and his only daughter in very poor estate.)

I went thence through the Duke of Courland's country, and after that to Königsberg, Elbing, and Danzig in Poland, then on through Pomerania and Mecklenburg, and so to the imperial town of Lübeck, where I was known and exceedingly well and honorably entertained.

By now I had gotten some better attendance, four or five Dutch and English servants, which I had hired at Elbing and Danzig. Here in Lübeck the burgomeister and lords of the town sent me by their recorder a present of fish and flesh and wines of all sorts, with a long oration of the favors I had done and showed to them and theirs. The next day divers now worthy merchants also came with their thanks and acknowledgments that I had been the means of their redemption from captivity in Moscow. They presented me with a fair bowl of silver gilt, with a like cover, filled with rix-dollars and Hungarian ducats of gold. I poured out the gold and silver, returning it unto them again—more prodigal than wise—but kept the bowl and gave them my thanks. They then brought me their town book, and prayed me to write therein my name and place of birth and abode, to the end that they and their posterities might honor my name forever.

Afterward I departed from Hamburg, but 10 miles from Lübeck. The Hamburgers having heard of my entertainment at Lübeck, those who had been in the same predicament in Russia and were helped by my means out of their captivity, presented me their thanks and remembrances. The burgomeister and *raetzheren* [aldermen] feasted me; and the others gave me a fair tablecloth of damask work, two dozen of napkins, and a long towel of the same.

Arriving at last from Hamburg into England, I opened my aquavitae bottle and took out and sweetened the Emperor's letters and directions as well as I could. But yet the Queen smelled the savor of the aquavitae when I delivered them to her Majesty; and for her satisfaction, I then related the cause.

I had access to the Queen's presence and some discourse with her three or four several times, by means of the Lord Treasurer and Sir Francis Walsingham and also of my lord of Leicester; but most by the love and countenance of my noble good friend and kinsman Sir Edward Horsey. The company trading with Muscovy gave me good entertainment and presents; and they also provided, by her Majesty's order, all those things that the Emperor had requested in his directions, but in no wise were they acquainted with any secret matter. After which her Majesty commanded me to be sworn Esquire of her body, and gave me her picture and her hand to kiss.

The Author Returns to Russia

I departed [in 1581] in the company of thirteen tall ships. At sea we met with the King of Denmark's navy near the North Cape, fought with them and put them to the worst. Arrived at Saint Nicholas, I posted over Vaga and came to Sloboda Alexandrovskaia, where I delivered the Queen's letters to the Emperor and told him her pleasure in secret. He commended my speed and the business done for him, gave me an allowance, and promised his great goodness for recompense when he came to the city of Moscow. He took there all those commodities that we had carried on our ships into his treasury, consisting of copper, lead, powder, saltpeter, brimstone, and other things, to the value of 9000 pounds sterling, and paid ready money for them.

On his arrival at Moscow, the Emperor cast his displeasure upon some noble men and governors of the city. He sent a parasite of his with 200 gunners to rob Mekita Romanovich, the brother of his first wife, the good Empress Anastasia, and took from him all his armor, horses, plate, and goods to the value of 40,000 pounds sterling. The Emperor also seized his lands, and left him so poor and needy that he sent to the English house the next day for sufficient coarse cotton to make gowns to cover himself and his children withal, and for some other relief. The Emperor next sent Semen Nagoi, another of his instruments of mischief, to rob and spoil one Andrei Shchelkalov, a great bribing officer, who was forced to bring out his fair young wife, repudiate her, and cut and gash her naked back with his scimitar. Shchelkalov's trusty servant Ivan Lottish was killed in his presence, and he himself was beaten and compelled to yield 5000 rubles in money.

At this time the Emperor also turned against those Dutch and Livonian people whom he had planted and placed with their wives and children and families outside the city of Moscow. He sent several thousand gunners in the night to rob and take the spoil of these people; and they stripped them naked, most barbarously ravished and deflowered both young and old women without respect, carrying divers of the youngest and fairest maids to serve their wicked lusts away with them. Some escaped to the English house, where they were covered, clad, and relieved, but we were in danger of the Emperor's displeasure in so doing.

Well! God would not leave such cruelty unpunished. Not long after, the Emperor fell out in a rage with his eldest son, the Czarevich Ivan, for having some commiseration for these distressed poor Christians, and also for commanding an officer, without the Emperor's leave, to give a gentleman a warrant for five or six post horses. The Emperor struck him in his fury a box on the ear and thrust at him with his pikestaff; and the Czarevich Ivan took it so tenderly that he fell into a burning fever and died within three days after [in November, 1581]. Whereat the Emperor tore his hair and beard like a mad man, lamenting and mourning for the death of his son.* But the kingdom had the greatest loss, the hope of their comfort, a wise, mild, and most worthy prince of heroical condition and comely presence, 23 years of age, beloved and lamented of all men. The Czarevich Ivan was buried in Michaela Sweat [Saint] Archangel Church, and jewels, precious stones, and pearls worth 50,000 pounds were put into the tomb with his corpse.

Now was the Emperor more earnest than ever to send into England about his long conceived match and marriage. He commissioned one Fëdor Pisemskii, a noble, grave, wise, and trusty gentleman, to request of the Queen the Lady Mary Hastings, daughter to the noble Henry Hastings, Earl of Huntington, whom he had heard was her kinswoman and of the blood royal. He also asked that it would please her Majesty to send some noble ambassador to treat with him about it.

---

* Horsey's contemporary Giles Fletcher, who served in Moscow as ambassador for Queen Elizabeth, wrote in his *Of the Russe Common Wealth* that "he [Ivan's son] died of a blow given him by his father upon the head in his fury with his walking staff, or (as some say) of a thrust with the prong of it driven deep into his head. That he meant him no such mortal harm . . . may appear by his mourning and passion after his son's death, which never left him till it brought him to the grave." Another contemporary authority, Antonio Possevino, in his *Moscovia*, declares that the quarrel began when the Czar criticized the manner in which his son's pregnant wife was dressed, and, in reproving her, beat her so severely that she had a miscarriage. When the son protested, the Czar then gave him the fatal blow with his staff.

Fëdor Pisemskii arrived in England [1582-83], was magnificently received, had audience of the Queen, and delivered his letters. Her Majesty then caused the Lady Hastings to be attended with divers great ladies and maids of honor and young gentlemen, so as to be seen by the Russian ambassador in York House garden. She put on a stately regalia accordingly. The ambassador with his attendants were brought before her Ladyship; at which he cast down his countenance, fell prostrate at her feet, rose, ran back from her with his face still toward her, she and the rest much admiring at his manner. He then declared, by an interpreter, it sufficed him to behold the angel he hoped would be his master's spouse, and commended her angelical countenance, state, and admirable beauty. She was afterward called by her familiar friends in court "the Empress of Muscovia."

Sir William Russell, the Earl of Bedford's third son, was chosen her Majesty's ambassador to the Emperor. But he and his friends, after better considering of it, made his unwillingness the means for another to receive this honor. The company of merchants [of the Russia Company] then entreated for Sir Jerome Bowes (though they repented afterward), and he was well set forth at their charge.

These two ambassadors, the Queen's and the Emperor's, were dispatched from her Majesty with leave and letters, well shipped, and arrived at Saint Nicholas in Russia. The Russian ambassador posted overland and delivered his letters and an account of his embassage to the Emperor, which was joyfully received. The other, Sir Jerome Bowes, embarked by the merchants, passed slowly up the river Dvina a thousand miles to Vologda. The Emperor sent one Michael Protopopov, a pensioner, to meet him and to make provision of victuals, carts and post-horses for himself and his company. At Iaroslavl another equerry of the stable met him with two fair ambling geldings, one for himself to mount whenever it pleased him. He was very honorably received at Moscow by a duke, Knez Ivan Sitskii, attended with 300 well-appointed horse, and brought to his lodgings. The Emperor sent his secretary, Sava Frolov, to welcome him, providing him also with many dishes of meat for his supper and promising he would be well accommodated.

The next day the Emperor dispatched a nobleman, Ignatii Tatishchev, to visit Sir Jerome Bowes to learn his needs and to tell him he longed to see him; and, if he were not overwearied with his journey, he should have his audience upon Saturday, following two days' respite. Bowes answered that he hoped to be able to attend his Majesty.

Accordingly, about nine of the clock upon that day, the streets were filled with people; and a thousand gunners, clad in red, yellow, and blue garments, set in ranks by the captains on horseback, stood with bright pieces and arquebuses in their hands from the ambassador's door to the Emperor's palace. Knez Ivan Sitskii, attended with 300 richly furnished gentlemen on horseback, was mounted upon a splendidly clad and bedecked jennet; and he also led before him a fair gelding that had been sent for the ambassador. But Sir Jerome Bowes, displeased that the duke's horse was better than his, mounted instead one of his own; and with his 30 livoried footmen, each carrying a piece of his present to the Emperor, consisting mostly of plate, marched onward to the palace. There he was met by another duke, who told him the Emperor waited for him; at which the ambassador replied that he had come as fast as he could. Along the way the people, partly guessing at the message he brought, which was generally disliked, cried *"Carluke!"* at him in mockery, which means "Crane's legs." The passages, terraces, and rooms of the palace he was conducted through were all beset with merchants and gentlemen with golden coats. His men, entering the throne room before him, placed their presents at one side.

The Emperor sat in his majesty, richly clad, with his three crowns before him. Four young noblemen, called *ryndy,* shining in cloth of silver, and bearing four scepters or bright silver hatchets, stood on each side of the Emperor, while the prince and other of his great dukes and the noblest of rank sat round about. The Emperor stood up; the ambassador made his speech and delivered the Queen's letters. Upon receiving them, the Emperor took off his imperial cap and asked how his sister Queen Elizabeth did. The ambassador answered, then sat down upon a bench at one side covered by a carpet. After some little time of pause and view of each other, Sir Jerome Bowes was dismissed in the same manner as he came, and his dinner of 200 dishes of meat was sent after him by a gentleman of quality.*

Some secret meetings and conferences, and also some public, were later held. A great allowance of provisions was daily made to the ambassador, all things were granted him, yet nothing would please him, which caused the Russians some annoyance. A reconciliation of accounts between the Emperor's officers and the company of merchants was made; all their grievances were heard and remedied and their privileges granted. The Emperor also resolved to send a nobleman as his ambassador to the Queen. If Sir Jerome Bowes had taken advantage of this opportunity, the Emperor, so inflamed with effecting his desire for the Lady Hastings, would have yielded to anything propounded; yea, he would have promised that if the marriage did take effect, her issue should inherit the throne. The princes and nobles, especially those of the family of the Godunovs, were much grieved and offended by this, and plotted a remedy to cross and overthrow the Emperor's designs.

The Emperor, most distracted and doubting what he must do, caused many witches and magicians to be sent for out of the north, between Kholmogory and Lapland, where there are many. Threescore were brought post to Moscow, placed and guarded, and daily visited and attended by the Emperor's favorite, Bogdan Belskii, who alone was trusted by him to

---

* Horsey's scathing description of Sir Jerome Bowes' reception at Ivan's court may be attributed to the fact that Bowes was later to become his chief accuser during his trial in England. But Bowes was also a bearer of unwelcome tidings to Ivan—Lady Hastings' refusal of his offer of marriage.

receive their oracles and divinations. But his favorite was now revolted in his faith to the Emperor, wholly seeking and serving the turns of his son Fëdor Ivanovich, for he was wearied and tired with the devilish tyrannical practices and wicked devices of this Elagabalus. The soothsayers told Belskii that the best signs and strongest planets of heaven were against the Emperor, which would produce his end by such a day. But the favorite feared to tell him so, and instead fell into a rage and warned these witches and magicians that they were all very likely to be burned that very day.

The Death of the Emperor

The Emperor began grievously to swell in his cods, with which he had most horribly offended above fifty years together, boasting of a thousand virgins he had deflowered and thousands of children of his begetting destroyed.

He was carried every day in his chair into his treasury. One day the Prince [Fëdor Ivanovich] beckoned to me to follow. I stood among the rest venturously, and heard him [the Emperor] call for some precious stones and jewels. He then told the Prince and nobles present about him the virtue of such and such; and I pray I may a little digress to declare out of my own memory what was said:

"The lodestone, you all know, hath great and hidden virtue, without which the seas that compass the world are not navigable, nor the bounds nor circle of the earth cannot be known. Mohammed, the Persians' prophet, in his tomb of steel hangs suspended by this means in their *ropata* [mosque] at Derbent most miraculously." He then caused the attendants to bring a chain of needles touched by this lodestone, and they hanged all one by the other. "This fair coral and this fair turquoise you see. Take them in your hand. Of their nature they have orient colors. Now put them on my hand and arm. I am poisoned with disease. You see they show their virtue by the change of their pure colors into pale, which declares my death. Reach out my royal staff, made of a unicorn's horn garnished with very fair diamonds, rubies, sapphires, emeralds, and other precious stones that are rich in value. It cost 70,000 marks sterling of David Gower, from the Fuggers at Augsburg. Now, seek out for some spiders."

He caused his physician, Johannes Eilof, to scrape a circle upon the table; then put within it one spider and now another, both of which died, and then some others without the circle that ran alive apace from it. "It is too late; it will not preserve me. Behold these precious stones. This diamond is the orient's richest, and more precious than any other. I never affected it; it restrains fury and luxury and [promotes] abstinence and chastity; the least parcel of it in powder will poison a horse given to drink, much more so a man."

He pointed at a ruby. "Oh, this is most comfortable to the heart, brain, vigor, and memory of man, and clarifies congealed and corrupt blood."

Then at an emerald. "The nature of the rainbow. This precious stone is an enemy to uncleanness. Try it. Though man and wife cohabit in lust together, having this stone about them, it will burst at the spending of nature. The sapphire I greatly delight in; it preserves and increases courage, joys the heart, pleasing to all the vital senses, precious and very sovereign for the eyes, clears them, takes away bloodshot, and strengthens the muscles and strings thereof." Then he took the onyx in hand. "All these are God's wonderful gifts, secrets in nature, and yet He reveals them to man's use and contemplation as friends to grace and virtue and enemies to vice. . . . I faint—carry me away till another time."

In the afternoon the Emperor peruses over his will and yet thinks not to die, for he has often been bewitched and oftentimes unwitched again. But now the devil fails. The Emperor commands his apothecary and physicians to prepare a bath for his solace and to attend him there. And as he still looks for a good sign from the stars, he sends his favorite, Belskii, to his witches again to know their calculations.

Belskii comes and tells them the Emperor will bury or burn them all quick for their false illusions and lies, as the day predicted for his death has already come, yet he is as heart-whole as ever he was. They reply, "Sir, be not so wrathful. You know the day is come and ends with the setting of the sun."

He hastes him back to the palace, where there is great preparation being made for the bath. About the third hour of the day the Emperor goes into it, solaces himself, and makes merry with pleasant songs as he used to do. He comes out about the seventh hour well refreshed, sits down upon his bed, calls Rodion Birkin, a gentleman whom he favored, to bring the chess board. His chief favorite Bogdan Belskii, and Boris Fëdorovich Godunov and other nobles, stand about him as he sets his men. The Emperor, in his loose gown, shirt and linen hose, faints and falls backward. Great outcry and stir. One sends for aquavitae, another to the apothecary for marigold and rose water, another to call his ghostly father and the physicians. In the meanwhile the Emperor lies strangled and stark dead [March 18, 1584].

Some show of hope was made for his recovery, so as to still the outcry. Bogdan Belskii and Boris Fëdorovich Godunov—unto whom the Emperor had bequeathed the government—went out upon the terrace, accompanied so suddenly at hand with so many of the nobility and a multitude of familiar friends as it was strange to behold. The prince protector Boris Fëdorovich cried out to the captains and gunners to keep their guard strong, with their pieces and matches lighted, and to shut the gates about the palace. I offered myself, men, powder, and pistols, to attend the prince protector: he accepted me among his family and servants. Passing by with a cheerful countenance upon me, he said, "Be faithful and fear not."

The metropolitans, bishops, and others of the nobility flocked into the castle, holding it as a day of jubilee for their redemption. It was a matter of who could press first to the book and cross to take oath and vow faith to the new Emperor, Fëdor Ivanovich. With what admirable dispatch, in six or seven hours, the treasuries were sealed up and new officers added to the old! Twelve thousand gunners, with captains over them, were set as a garrison about the walls of the great city of Moscow.

Ivan's Legacy

Boris Fëdorovich, now lord protector by the old Emperor's will, began to manage and dispose of all affairs. He took inventories of all the treasure everywhere, gold, silver, and jewels; made a survey of all the offices and books of revenues; placed new treasurers, new counselors, new officers in all courts, and new captains and lieutenants in all the garrisons; and in the castles, towns, and countries of most importance, he rewarded such out of those families as were best to be trusted. And so likewise the attendance about his sister, the Empress, was increased, by which means he and his family became exceeding safe and strong.

The natural disposition of this nation was so wicked and vile that if the old Emperor Ivan Vasilievich had not held so hard a hand and severe government over them, he could never have lived so long. But he reigned above fifty [51] years. He conquered Polotsk, Smolensk, and many other great towns and castles, 700 miles southwest from the city of Moscow, into the lands of Lithuania, belonging to the crown of Poland. He conquered also as many towns and castles eastward in Livonia, and other dominions of the kings of Sweden and Poland; and he conquered the kingdom of Kazan and the kingdom of Astrakhan, and all the regions and great people of the Nogai and Circassian Tatars inhabiting above 2000 miles on each side of the famous river Volga, southward even to the Caspian Sea. He freed himself from the servile tribute and homage that he and his predecessors had yearly paid and performed to the great Scythian Emperor, the Khan of Crimea. He conquered the kingdom of Siberia and all those adjacent countries northward above 1500 miles, so that he had mightily enlarged his country and kingdoms in every direction. So spacious and large are now the dominions of this empire that it can hardly be held within one rule, but must be divided again into several kingdoms and principalities.

One deed of charity I may not omit, one memorable act, to shut up his devotion with. In *anno* 1575 a great famine followed a pestilence among the people. The towns, streets, and ways swarmed with rogues, idle beggars, and counterfeit cripples; no riddance could be made of them in the time of scarcity. Proclamation was made that they should resort to receive the Emperor's alms upon such a day at Sloboda. Out of some thousands that came 700 of the most vile and counterfeit were knocked in the heads and cast into the great lake, for the fish to receive their dole there; the rest and most feeblest were dispersed to monasteries and hospitals to be relieved.

This Emperor, among many other such like acts, did build in his time 155 castles in all parts of his kingdoms, planting them with ordnance and garrisons. He built 300 towns in waste places and wildernesses, of a mile or two in length, and gave every inhabitant a proportion of land to keep so many speedy horses for his use as occasion requires. He built a strong and spacious stone wall about Moscow, placing ordnance and officers to maintain his garrisons. And he also built in his time above 40 fair stone churches, richly bedecked and adorned within, and the turrets all gilt with fine pure gold; also, above 60 monasteries and nunneries, and endowed them with bells and ornaments and maintenance to pray for his soul; also, a goodly steeple of hewn stone in the inner castle of Moscow, with 30 great sweet-sounding bells in it, which serve all the churches standing round about it, ringing all together every festival day and very dolesomely at every midnight's prayers.

Thus, to conclude with the Emperor Ivan Vasilievich: he was a goodly man in person and presence, well favored, with a high forehead and shrill voice, a right Scythian in his appearance, and full of ready wisdom in the management of state affairs. But he was cruel, bloody, merciless. Though sumptuously entombed in Michael Archangel Church, and guarded day and night, he remains a fearful spectacle in the memory of those who pass by and hear his name spoken, and they are content to cross and bless themselves against his resurrection amongst them again, etc.

Akbar the Great

*Portrait of the Mogul Emperor by a Persian
painter, 16th century. Louis Cartier Collection, Paris.*

Where the land is kingless the cloud, lightning-wreathed and loud-voiced, gives no rain to the earth. . . .
A river without water, a forest without grass, a herd of cattle without a herdsman, is the land without a king.

Ramayana, ii, 57

W*ho, and how great, was Akbar? His grandfather Babar, the founder of the Mogul (or Mughal) dynasty in India, was the great-great-great-grandson of Tamerlane, which would therefore make Akbar himself "great" to the seventh power by direct descent from the world-conquering "Scythian shephearde lad." But aside from that, his life had about it that numinous aura, "huge cloudy symbols of a high romance," by which destiny swaddles its own.*

He was born in the province of Sind, in northern India, in November 1542, at a time when his father Humayun was driven from his throne by the Afghan forces under Sher Shah and compelled to seek refuge in Persia. With the aid of the Persians, Humayun reassembled his horde and, by the year 1555, succeeded in establishing Mogul sovereignty once more at Delhi and Agra. Upon Humayun's death in 1556 Akbar (also known as Jalal-ud-din Mohammed) at the age of 14 became the third of the Mogul emperors.

Within the next two decades he consolidated and extended the empire to the whole of northern India, a part of the Deccan, and the northwestern frontier region as far as Kabul and Kandahar. To administer these vast conquests, containing a diverse population of tens of millions, Akbar relied not on terror (in Delhi in 1398 his ancestor Tamerlane had once slaughtered 80,000 people and then erected a pyramid of their severed heads) but on justice and magnanimity. Under his reign the local Hindu lords, or Rajputs, were allowed to continue their jurisdiction, and though a Moslem he tolerated native religious practices and customs in the villages and countryside. His system of government, incidentally, proved so successful that it served as a model for the pukka sahibs of the British Colonial Office two centuries later when it came their turn to civilize India.

But Akbar's chief claim to greatness, from the modern point of view, lies in his attempt to reconcile all the sacred creeds of mankind within a higher syncretic religion that would enable his subjects to worship their god or gods in peace. In his time the religious civil war within Islam, between the Sunni and Shi'a factions, rivaled in its ferocity and blood-thirsty fanaticism the struggle between Catholics and Protestants then taking place in Christian Europe. In 1575 he built a magnificent House of Worship (Ibadat-khana) at his capital of Fatehpur Sikri, near Agra, where he promulgated this new religious faith (Din-i-ilahi), based on the scriptures and traditions of all faiths, with himself presiding as the infallible imam under Moslem law. He then instituted public debates on religion open to Hindus, Jains, Buddhists, Zoroastrians, Sabaeans, Christians, Moslems, pagans, et al.

Which brings us to the Jesuit mission to the court of Akbar led by Fathers Monserrate (the author of the account in this book), Aquaviva, and Enriquez. Hoping to convert the Emperor to the true faith, they started out from the Portuguese enclave of Goa toward the close of 1579 and arrived at Fatehpur Sikri more than a year later, in February, 1580. And a hard cold coming they must have had of it, "the ways deep and the weather sharp," across most of the length of India, though their journey was still not as arduous as the one undertaken by the diplomatic envoys of King Henry III of Castille who came as humble suppliants to Tamerlane in 1404. The self-confidence and condescension toward the natives displayed by the fathers, in comparison, may provide a measure of the shift in the world's balance of power between East and West that had occurred during the intervening centuries. For all their piety, they were no doubt well aware that the force of their religious arguments might ultimately be backed up by still more persuasive forces.

As for Akbar himself, he appears from Father Monserrate's description to have been not only a shrewd but a merry old soul like Old King Cole, calling now and then for his hashish pipe, his bowl of post (an opiated beverage to which he seems to have been addicted), and his thrice three hundred sitar players. One has the feeling throughout that he must have been slyly amusing himself at the fathers' expense, occasionally letting the air out of their divine

233

afflatus, as, for instance, when he proposed an ordeal by fire between them and the Moslem mullahs to determine which had the stronger magic. "When he laughs," the author remarks, "his face becomes almost distorted." Monserrate also mentions that Akbar "limps in his left leg, though indeed he has never received any injury there"; which suggests that the Emperor, consciously or unconsciously, wished to emulate his illustrious forebear Timur the Lame.

The Mogul empire, whose cultural and political foundations were established by Akbar, is generally regarded as the most brilliant to have arisen in India since the Gupta dynasty some 1,250 years earlier. It was during the reign of his grandson Shah Jahan (1628–1658) that the palace of Khass Mahal and the still more famous tomb of the Taj Mahal were constructed. Only after the Mogul throne was usurped by the rebel Emperor Aurangzeb (1659–1707), who imprisoned Shah Jahan and reversed Akbar's policy of religious toleration, did the empire begin to disintegrate. Thereafter, as we know, India became the prey of European imperialist powers.

The description that follows has been excerpted from The Commentary of Father Monserrate, S.J., *translated from the Latin by J. S. Hoyland (London: Oxford University Press, 1922). The author remained at Fatehpur Sikri, where he served as tutor to Akbar's son Murad. He died in 1600.*

They Arrive at the Capital

When the fathers perceived from afar the city of Fattepurum,* where the great King resides, they gave hearty thanks to the Eternal God who had brought them safe to their destination. They then began to gaze with the keenest delight upon the immense size and magnificent appearance of the city.

The most noteworthy features of Fattepurum are, firstly, the King's audience chamber, which is huge and also very beautiful, overlooking the whole city; secondly, a great building supported on arches, around which is a very spacious courtyard; thirdly, the Circus where elephants fight, gladiatorial displays take place, and a game is played, on horseback, with a wooden ball which is hit by hammers also of wood: fourthly, the baths: fifthly, the bazaar, which is more than half a mile long, and is filled with an astonishing quantity of every description of merchandise, and with countless people, who are always standing there in dense crowds.

To supply the city with water a tank has been carefully and laboriously

---

* Fattepurum, as the fathers called it, was the city of Fatehpur Sikri near Agra in Uttar Pradesh. It was founded by Akbar in 1571 as his capital and magnificently built, but abandoned upon his death.

constructed, two miles long and half a mile wide. By this means not only is a copious supply of water assured, but the discomfort of the climate mitigated. For when the sun gets low in the sky, the heat, which in Fattepurum is very great, is tempered by a cool and pleasant breeze blowing over the tank. Besides this the King descends to the lake on holidays, and refreshes himself with its many beauties.

Passing over the other remarkable features of Fattepurum, I must mention that the citadel is two miles in circumference and embellished with towers at very frequent intervals, though it has only four gates. The most striking is the Circus gate, through which the King frequently descends to the Circus. For there stand in front of this gateway, which they seem to guard, two statues of elephants, with uplifted trunks, and of life-size. These statues are so majestic and so true to life, that one might judge them to be the work of Phidias.

On entering the city the fathers became the cynosure of all eyes on account of their strange attire. Everyone stopped and stared in great surprise and perplexity, wondering who these strange-looking, unarmed men might be, with their long black robes, their curious caps, their shaven faces, and their tonsured heads.

At length they were taken before the King, who, having looked at them from his high dais, ordered them to come nearer to him, and asked them a few questions. Thereupon they presented to him an atlas, which the Archbishop of Goa had sent as a present. This he graciously received. He was greatly pleased to see them, but was not too warm in his greeting, and shortly afterward withdrew, partly in order to hide his true feelings and partly to preserve his dignity. Having retired for a short time into an inner apartment, he ordered them to be conducted to him there (that is, to the hall which is known as Capur Talau), in order that he might exhibit them to his wives. Then he took them to another courtyard called the Daulatqhana, where he seized the opportunity presented by a sudden rainstorm and put on Portuguese dress—a scarlet cloak with golden fastenings. He ordered his sons also to don the same dress, together with Portuguese hats. This he did in order to please his guests. He also ordered 800 pieces of gold to be presented to them; but the fathers replied that they had not come there to get money. Nothing that he could say would persuade them to accept the present, whereupon he expressed admiration at their self-control, and ordering the money to be distributed to certain attendants who had remained behind, he retired to the inner part of the palace.

The fathers were delighted at the King's kindly reception and were conducted rejoicing to their quarters. For they were persuaded that these signs foretold the speedy conversion of the King to the true religion and the worship of Christ.

On the next day we were most kindly entertained by Father F. J. Pereira, who had been summoned by the King from Gangaris, and was then in residence at Fattepurum. As it was Lent, the diet was simple, fish only.

After dinner we inquired from our host what was the state of the King's mind regarding Christianity. He replied that Akbar reverenced Christ and the Virgin, and was not far from paying divine honors to Christ. Moreover he not only approved, but warmly praised those portions of the Gospel story which had been recounted to him. He was astonished that Christians paid so much attention to chastity of life as to forbid a man to have more than one wife and to enjoin complete celibacy on their priesthood. But, as the King himself said, his judgment was dulled and clouded as it were, when he heard that there are three persons in one God, that God had begotten a son from a virgin, had suffered on the Cross, and had been killed by the Jews. He might, however, be led to acknowledge the truth of these doctrines if they could persuade him that the Gospel had indeed come from God. He listened gladly to the story of Christ's miracles, and believed in them.

His sentiments with regard to Mohammed were very different, for he believed him to have been a rascally impostor, who had deluded and infatuated men by his lies. In his dining hall he had pictures of Christ, Mary, Moses, and Mohammed. When naming them he showed his true sentiments by putting Mohammed last; for he would say, "This is the picture of Christ, this of Mary, this of Moses, and that of Mohammed." In brief, this priest's description of the King's state of mind enlightened the other fathers as to the necessity for a more thorough investigation regarding the course they must adopt.

An Ordeal by Fire Proposed

Some days later the haughty pride of Mohammed provided the matter for a debate in which the Mussalmans were beaten and discomforted—whereupon they appealed to an ordeal. "Let us put it to the test," said they, "which Holy Book is true. Let a pyre be constructed and kindled. Then let one of you, carrying the Gospel, and one likewise of us, carrying the Koran, ascend the burning pyre. The book which comes out safely together with its bearer, shall be judged true." The King urged the same course upon the priests, who briefly replied that there was no need of miraculous ordeals in order to demonstrate the truth of Christianity. The King answered that he had had enough of argument, whereupon everyone cried, "Peace be to the King!" This was the end of the discussion.

Now Rudolf, whose leadership his companions gladly followed, was full of religious zeal and fervor, and eagerly sought any opportunity of facing death for Christ's sake. Moreover, he always earnestly sought to obey the dictates of his religious duty; and, hence, if he had been convinced of its necessity, would never have shrunk from the proposed ordeal. But he was in doubt as to its rightness at present, and hence had made no attempt to clinch the matter. However, in order to avoid the appearance of cowardice in refusing the ordeal, he took the first opportunity of making the following declaration to the King:

"Since, O King," he said, "you desire, with regard to the proposed ordeal, to put to the test the constancy of myself and my companions in the faith and religion of Jesus Christ, which we received from our ancestors and drank in with our mother's milk, we will, with a cheerful heart, and fortified by the help of God, most readily ascend not one but a thousand pyres. We are servants of the same God who preserved the three Hebrew children harmless in the furnace, and brought them out of it again without any injury from the flame. Trusting in divine aid, we have no fear of elephants, lions, panthers, leopards, precipices, crosses, stripes, and all manner of tortures. You can prove this by immediate experiment, O King, if you so please.

"However, a similar ordeal was once proposed by the Mussalmans at Marrhoqium in Africa, in the case of Andreas Spoletanus, a Franciscan. They falsely declared that they would become Christians if he came out of the fire unharmed. They beheld Andreas walking about in the middle of the flames and lifting up his hands and eyes toward heaven; but when the Christian people, who were held in captivity there and were present to see the ordeal, began to clap their hands for joy, together with the rest of the common people who were astonished by the novelty of the affair, forthwith the leaders of the Mussalmans and of the Jews, who were also spectators, buried both Andreas and his pyre beneath a hail of stones, lest it should be said that the flames had spared him. His relics—of which the flesh is still as healthy as that of a living man—were taken to Portugal to Queen Catherina of Austria by a certain captive who was exchanged out of his captivity."

At which the King declared, "God forbid that I should have summoned you hither in order that you might suffer any calamity. But there is in my court a certain religious preceptor who boasts that he is a holy man—though indeed he is befouled with many and great crimes—and who has written a new and original commentary on the Koran. I am desirous of punishing him, and wish to use your help in the matter."

"In this," replied Father Rudolf, "we cannot help you; for priests are forbidden not only to kill a man, but also to make any attempts to bring about a man's execution or death, even in a case where express permission is granted by the ruler."

The King replied, "I do not wish you to undergo the ordeal; I only desire that you should say you will undergo it."

"We cannot do even that, O King."

"At least agree to this—I myself will loudly announce that you will ascend the pyre; you yourselves shall be silent."

"If you make this announcement publicly, O King," replied Rudolf, "we shall as publicly declare that we will do no such thing. And indeed if this man deserves punishment, what need is there of adopting this roundabout and disingenuous course in committing him to the flames?"

The nobles who heard this clear and straightforward declaration on the part of Rudolf applauded it with remarkable enthusiasm.

Such was the course of the first meetings and debates with the King and his religious preceptors.

Akbar in Person

Akbar is of a stature and of a type of countenance well-fitted to his royal dignity, so that one could easily recognize, even at the first glance, that he is the King. He has broad shoulders, somewhat bandy legs well-suited for horsemanship, and a light-brown complexion. He carries his head bent toward the right shoulder. His forehead is broad and open, his eyes so bright and flashing that they seem like a sea shimmering in the sunlight. His eyelashes are very long, as also are those of the Scythians, Chinese, Nipponese, and most other north Asiatic races. His eyebrows are not strongly marked. His nose is straight and small, though not insignificant. His nostrils are widely opened, as though in derision. Between the left nostril and the upper lip there is a mole. He shaves his beard, but wears a moustache like that of a Turkish youth who has not yet attained to manhood (for on reaching manhood they begin to affect a beard). Contrary to the custom of his race he does not cut his hair; nor does he wear a hat, but a turban, into which he gathers up his hair. He does this, they say, as a concession to Indian usages, and to please his Indian subjects. He limps in his left leg, though indeed he has never received any injury there. His body is exceedingly well-built and is neither too thin nor too stout. He is sturdy, hearty, and robust. When he laughs, his face becomes almost distorted. His expression is tranquil, serene, and open, full also of dignity, and when he is angry, of awful majesty.

When the priests first saw him he was 38 years of age. It is hard to exaggerate how accessible he makes himself to all who wish audience of him. For he creates an opportunity almost every day for any of the common people or of the nobles to see him and converse with him; and he endeavors to show himself pleasant-spoken and affable rather than severe toward all who come to speak with him. It is very remarkable how great an effect this courtesy and affability has in attaching to him the minds of his subjects. For in spite of his very heterodox attitude toward the religion of Mohammed, and in spite also of the fact that Mussalmans regard such an attitude as an unforgivable offense, the King has not yet been assassinated. He has an acute insight, and shows much wise foresight both in avoiding dangers and in seizing favorable opportunities for carrying out his designs.

Akbar is greatly devoted to hunting, though not equally so to hawking. As he is of a somewhat morose disposition, he amuses himself with various games. These games afford also a public spectacle to the nobility and the common people, who indeed are very fond of such spectacles. They are the following: polo, elephant-fighting, buffalo-fighting, stag-fighting and cock-fighting, boxing contests, battles of gladiators, and the flying of tumbler-pigeons. He is also very fond of strange birds, and indeed of any novel object. He amuses himself with singing, concerts, dances, conjurers' tricks, and the jokes of his jesters, of whom he makes much.

However, although he may seem at such times to be at leisure and to have laid aside public affairs, he does not cease to revolve in his mind the heavy cares of state. He is especially remarkable for his love of keeping great crowds of people around him and in his sight; and thus it comes about that his court is always thronged with multitudes of men of every type, though especially with the nobles, whom he commands to come from their provinces and reside at court for a certain period each year. When he goes outside the palace, he is surrounded and followed by these nobles and a strong bodyguard. They have to go on foot until he gives them a nod to indicate that they may mount. All this adds greatly to the wonderful majesty and greatness of the royal court.

According to the instructions of the worthless Mohammed and the custom of the Mussalmans, the orthodox must wear a long robe coming down to the calf, together with shoes very low at the ankle. Their dress must be made of wool, linen, or cotton, and must be white. The shoes must be of a certain fixed pattern. However, Akbar is so contemptuous of the instructions given by the false law-giver, that he wears garments of silk, beautifully embroidered in gold. His military cloak comes down only as far as the knee, according to the Christian fashion; and his boots cover his ankles completely. Moreover, he himself designed the fashion and shape of these boots. He wears gold ornaments, pearls, and jewelery. He is very fond of carrying a European sword and dagger. He is never without arms, and is always surrounded, even within his private apartments, by a bodyguard of about 20 men, variously armed. He much approves the Spanish dress, and wears it in private. He himself can ride and control elephants, camels, and horses. He drives a two-horse chariot, in which his appearance is very striking and dignified. He generally sits, with crossed legs, upon a couch covered with scarlet rugs. However, he has a velvet throne of the Portuguese type carried with him on a journey, and very frequently uses it.

His table is very sumptuous, generally consisting of more than 40 courses served in great dishes. These are brought into the royal dining hall covered and wrapped in linen cloths, which are tied up and sealed by the cook, for fear of poison. They are carried by youths to the door of the dining hall, other servants walking ahead and the master-of-the-household following. Here they are taken over by eunuchs, who hand them to the serving girls who wait on the royal table. He is accustomed to dine in private, except on the occasion of a public banquet. He rarely drinks wine, but quenches his thirst with *post* [a drink containing opium] or water. When he has drunk immoderately of post, he sinks back stupefied and shaking. He dines alone, reclining on an ordinary couch, which is covered with silken rugs and cushions stuffed with the fine down of some foreign plant.

His Palaces

The splendor of his palaces approaches closely to that of the royal dwellings of Europe. They are magnificently built, from foundation to cornice, of hewn stone, and are decorated both with painting and carving. Unlike the palaces built by other Indian kings, they are lofty; for an Indian palace is generally as low and humble as an idol temple. Their total circuit is so large that it easily embraces four great royal dwellings, of which the King's own palace is the largest and the finest. The second palace belongs to the queens, and the third to the royal princes, whilst the fourth is used as a storehouse and magazine. The roofs of these palaces are not tiled, but are dome-shaped, being protected from the weather on the outside by solid plaster covering the stone slabs. This forms a roof absolutely impervious to moisture.

The palaces are decorated also with many pinnacles, supported on four columns, each of which forms a small covered portico. Not a little is added to the beauty of the palaces by charming pigeon cotes, partly covered with rough-cast, and partly showing walls built of small blue and white bricks. More than 20,000 pigeons, divided into 10 classes, are kept at court. The pigeons are cared for by eunuchs and servant maids. Their evolutions are controlled at will, when they are flying, by means of certain signals, just as those of well-trained soldiery are controlled by a competent general by means of bugles and drums. It will seem little short of miraculous when I affirm that when sent out, they dance, turn somersaults all together in the air, fly in orderly rhythm, and return to their starting point, all at the sound of a whistle. They are bidden to perch on the roof, to conceal themselves within their nesting places, or to dart out of them again; and they do everything just as they are told.

The other buildings erected by the King in various parts of his dominions are of equal magnificence. These have been built with extraordinary speed, by the help of a host of architects, masons, and workmen. For instance, he built a very large peristyle, surrounded with colonnades, 200 feet square, in three months, and some circular baths 300 feet in circuit, with dressing rooms, private apartments, and many water channels, in six months. Here he himself bathes. In order to prevent himself being deafened by the noise of the tools with which stones are shaped and beams and other timber cut, he had everything cleverly fashioned elsewhere, in accordance with the exact plan of the building, and then brought to the spot, and there fitted and fastened together.

Akbar is so devoted to building that he sometimes quarries stone himself, along with the other workmen. Nor does he shrink from watching and even himself practicing, for the sake of amusement, the craft of an ordinary artisan. For this purpose he has built a workshop near the palace, where also are studios and workrooms for the finer and more reputable arts, such as painting, goldsmith work, tapestry-making, carpet- and curtain-making, and the manufacture of arms. Hither he very frequently comes and relaxes his mind with watching at their work those who practice these arts.

It is the duty of various orderlies to manage the water clocks and to strike the time on bronze gongs. These water clocks consist of a brazen vessel filled with water, and a hollow bronze cone of such a size that exactly a quarter of an hour is taken for the water to fill it through a small hole in the bottom. This cone is placed on the top of the vessel filled with water, and the water runs in through the hole in its bottom. When the cone is full, it sinks, and thus shows that a quarter of an hour has elapsed. Everything that goes on in the palace is regulated by this clock. At fixed hours, namely before dawn when the cocks begin to crow, and in the evening, a barbaric din is kept up for the space of a full hour by means of trumpets, bugles, drums, rattles, bells, and the like.

Amongst the dispatch runners are certain couriers who in one day can run on foot as far as a horseman can ride at full speed. They are said to have their livers removed in infancy, in order to prevent their suffering from shortness of breath. They practice running in shoes made of lead, or train themselves by repeatedly lifting their feet and moving their legs (whilst remaining standing still in one place) till their heels touch their buttocks. When their leaden shoes are removed, they are seen to be magnificent runners, by the help of whose swiftness the King can very rapidly and regularly obtain news or send orders on any matter touching the peace of his realm.

And this realm is indeed a vast one. Of late he has added to it partly by force of arms and partly by voluntary surrender. Hence it may well be believed that the circuit of the whole of his dominions is more than 20,000 miles, and that they lie in the heart of what the ancients called "India within the Ganges," the land which, according to the historians of antiquity, was reached by Alexander the Macedonian.

This empire is very beautiful and healthy, although in many places not well provided with fruit trees. On account of the diversity of the climate in different parts it produces many and various types of crops. Rice, wheat, millet, and pulse are produced in great quantities. In many places in the neighborhood of the Indus, flax and hemp are sown. The plant, which is commonly called bhang, and which when used as a drink produces intoxication and stupefaction of the mind and senses, has leaves very similar to those of the hemp plant. It does not, however, grow on one stalk only, but has a low stem, from which spring a number of other branches, like a bush. Indigo and opium are largely grown in the south, and bring no small profit to the royal revenues.

Aspects of Akbar

The King is a great patron of learning, and always keeps around him erudite men, who are directed to discuss before him philosophy, theology, and religion, and to recount to him the history of great kings and glorious deeds of the past. He has an excellent judgment and a good memory, and has attained to a considerable knowledge of many subjects by means of constant and patient listening to such discussions. Thus, he not only makes up for his ignorance of letters (for he is entirely unable either to read or write), but he has also become able clearly and lucidly to expound difficult matters. He can give his opinion on any question so shrewdly and keenly, that no one who did not know that he is illiterate would suppose him to be anything but very learned and erudite.

Akbar receives foreigners and strangers in a very different manner from that in which he treats his own fellow countrymen and subordinates. For he behaves with marked courtesy and kindliness to foreigners, especially to the ambassadors of foreign kings, and to princes who have been driven from their dominions and appeal to him for protection. Such princes he furnishes with troops and resources, on one condition only, namely, that they shall employ only his own weights and measures and money coined by himself. His generosity is such that, when his aunt returned from Mecca, the King had the street pavements covered with silken shawls, and conducted her himself to her palace in a gorgeous litter, scattering largess meanwhile to the crowds.

Yet he behaves so sternly toward the nobles who are under his proud sway that each one of them believes himself to be regarded not only as a contemptible creature but as the very lowest and meanest of mankind. For instance, these nobles, if they commit offenses, are punished more severely and relentlessly than the rest of the people, even those of the meanest degree.

It was the licentious Mohammed who invented and introduced amongst the Mussalmans two forms of marriage: first, that with regular consorts, who may number four; and second, that with those who are merely called wives, and who may be as numerous as a man's resources allow. Mussalman kings employ this sanction and license of the foulest immorality in order to ratify peace and to create friendly relationships with their vassal princes or neighboring monarchs. For they marry the daughters and sisters of such rulers. Hence, Akbar has more than 300 wives, dwelling in separate suites of rooms in a very large palace.

Akbar has seven chief counselors, one for each day of the week. In the same way he appoints four or five secretaries, out of a body of scribes, for duty each day. These secretaries write down all the business transacted by the King, all the measures he takes, and all the orders he issues. They take down what he says with such speed that they appear carefully to catch and preserve his words before they can fall to the ground and be lost. Such is the childish folly of these scribes that the fools think it the act of a boor and a savage even to tread upon the King's shadow.

He has about 20 Hindu chieftains as ministers and counselors to assist both in the work of governing the empire and in the control of the royal household. They are devoted to him, and are very wise and reliable in conducting public business. They are always with him, and are admitted to the innermost parts of the palace, which is a privilege not allowed even to the Mongol nobles.

The following is the method the King employs in deliberation. He asks each counselor privately for his own opinion, and then himself decides upon the course which seems to be supported by the largest number and the most experienced. He asks their advice even about subjects upon which he has already made up his mind, saying to the nobles, "This is what I think should be done, do you agree?" They reply, "Salaam, O King"; whereupon he says, "Then let it be carried out." If, however, any of them do not agree with him, he listens patiently, and sometimes even alters his own opinion.

Men of low birth, upstarts, and (as the Mongols say) "men who have risen," together with those of alien birth, are given posts in the royal household if the King finds them capable and efficient, and are gradually promoted. But if such men practice mean and contemptible tricks or intrigues, he bids them always carry about with them the tools of their original handicraft, lest in their vulgarity and insolence they ever forget the low station from which they have sprung. Akbar also maintains, and provides with a liberal education, many noble boys and youths who have lost their fathers; and in this he might well be imitated by other princes.

The King exacts enormous sums in tribute from the provinces of his empire. He also derives much revenue from the hoarded fortunes of the great nobles, which by law and custom all come to the King on their owners' death. In addition, there are the spoils of conquered kings and chieftains, whose treasure is seized, also great levies exacted and gifts received from the inhabitants of newly subdued districts in every part of his dominions. These gifts and levies are apt to be so large as to ruin outright many of his new subjects. He also engages in trading on his own account, and thus increases his wealth to no small degree; for he eagerly exploits every possible source of profit.

Moreover, he allows no bankers or money changers in his empire except the superintendents and tellers of the royal treasuries. This enormous banking business brings the King great profit; for at these royal treasuries alone may gold coin be changed for silver or copper, and vice versa. The government officers are paid in gold, silver, or copper according to their rank. Thus it comes about that those who are paid in one type of coin need to change some of it into another type.

Akbar is sparing and tenacious of his wealth, and thus has become the richest oriental King for at least 200 years. This fact the chieftains who surround him at his court are continually dinning into his ears, in order to ingratiate themselves with him. With the object of exhibiting his wealth four times every year, he has sacks of minted copper money publicly piled up (I think in the palace courtyard) into a heap 10 feet wide and 30 feet high. By the side of this pile sit the superintendents and tellers of the treasury. They supervise the counting of the money, which is paid out to those who are entitled to receive it, after deduction of the profit which an ordinary banker would have made if it had been deposited with him. Each sack holds about 4000 copper coins.

The King's severity toward errors and misdemeanors committed by officials in the course of government business is remarkable, for he is most stern with offenders against the public faith. Hence all are afraid of his severity, and strive with all their might to do as he directs and desires. By the King's direction all capital cases, and all really important civil cases also, are conducted before himself. He is easily excited to anger, but soon cools down again. By nature, moreover, he is kindly and benevolent, and is sincerely anxious that guilt should be punished, without malice indeed, but at the same time without undue leniency.

The following are the ways in which the guilty are punished. Those who have committed a capital crime are either crushed by elephants, impaled, or hanged. Seducers and adulterers are either strangled or gibbeted. The King has such a hatred of debauchery and adultery that neither influence nor entreaties nor the great ransom which was offered would induce him to pardon his chief trade commissioner, who, although he was already married, had violently debauched a well-born Brahman girl. The wretch was by the King's order remorselessly strangled. Although Mohammed did not forbid unnatural crimes, yet Akbar punished those who are guilty of such crimes by savage scourging with leather thongs.

Ordinary criminals are kept under guard in irons, but not in prison. Princes sentenced to imprisonment are sent to the jail at Goaleris, where they rot away in chains and filth. Noble offenders are handed over to other nobles for punishment, but the base-born either to the captain of the dispatch runners, or to the chief executioner. This latter official is equipped even in the palace and before the King with many instruments of punishment, such as leather thongs, whips, bowstrings fitted with sharp spikes of copper, a smooth block of wood used for pounding the criminal's sides or crushing to pieces his skull, and scourges in which are tied a number of small balls studded with sharp bronze nails (this latter weapon must I think be the one called by the ancients "the scorpion"). However, no one is actually punished with these instruments, which seem to be intended rather to inspire terror than for actual use. For the same reason, various kinds of chains, manacles, handcuffs, and other irons are hung up on one of the palace gateways, which is guarded by the aforementioned chief executioner.

The Fathers Reprove the King

I have already mentioned the high opinion which the King had conceived of the fathers' wisdom and integrity. Lest this opinion should turn out to be ill-founded, they felt it to be their duty to mention freely to him anything which was blameworthy. Hence they very frequently pointed out to him his carelessness and dilatoriness in learning divine things. This they did gently, and after testing the state of his mind.

When he invited them to see a gladiatorial contest, they replied that they could not comply. He forthwith excused their attendance at the contest, but asked why they would not come. They replied that it was absolutely contrary to the Christian discipline and moral standard to organize, or even to look on at, human carnage, and that he who was responsible for the holding of gladiatorial games committed a terrible crime. If he wished to amuse himself with mimic war, he should have the edges of the swords dulled, and make the gladiators wear breastplates and helmets, and let them carry small shields on the left arm, with which they could catch the blows without risk to their lives. The King approved of this advice, and wondered at the holy mercy of the Christian religion. It is the custom at the gladiatorial combats of the Mongols for the various signals to be given by four pairs of drums, of which the first pair leads the music of the others, the second gives a low deep note, the third a gentle sound, and the fourth a high note in contrast to the low one given by the second pair.

The wives of the Brahmans—a famous class of nobly born Hindus—are accustomed, in accordance with an ancient tradition of their religion, called *sati,* to burn themselves on the same pyres as their dead husbands. The King ordered the priests to be summoned to see an instance of this. They went in ignorance of what was to take place; but when they found out, they plainly indicated by their saddened faces how cruel and savage they felt that crime to be. Finally, Rudolf publicly reprimanded the King for showing openly by his presence there that he approved of such a revolting crime, and for supporting it by his weighty judgment and explicit approbation (for he was heard to say that such fortitude could only come from God). Such was his Majesty's kindness and favor toward the priests that he showed no resentment; and a certain chief, a great favorite of his, a Brahman by birth, who held the office of superintendent of sacred observances, could no longer persuade him to attend such spectacles.

The wretched women are rendered quite insensible by means of certain drugs, in order that they may feel no pain. For this purpose opium is used, or a soporific herb named bhang, or—more usually—the herb *duturo,* which is known to the Indians, although entirely unfamiliar alike to modern Europeans and to the ancients. Sometimes they are half drugged and, before they lose their resolution, are hurried to the pyre with warnings, prayers, and promises of eternal fame. On arriving there they cast themselves into the flames. If they hesitate, the wretched creatures are driven on to the pyre, and if they try to leap off again, are held down with poles and hooks.

The nobles who were present were highly incensed at the fathers' interference. They did not dare to gainsay the King, but they grumbled loudly amongst themselves, saying, "Away with you, black-clothed Franks!" But the whole city was filled with praise and admiration when news was brought that the Franks had dared to rebuke the King regarding this affair.

On one occasion the fathers met a crowd of worthless profligates, some of those who dress and adorn themselves like women. The priests were rightly disgusted at this, and took the first opportunity of privately complaining to the King (since he was so favorable to them) about this disgraceful matter. They declared with the greatest emphasis that they were astonished at his permitting such a class of men to live in his kingdom, let alone in his city, and almost under his eyes. They must be banished, as though they were a deadly plague, to his most distant territories. Even better, let them be burnt up by devouring flames. They never would have believed that such men could be found in the court itself and in the royal city, where lived a King of such piety, integrity, and prudence. Therefore, let him give orders that these libertines should never again be seen in Fattepurum, seeing that his remarkable Prophet had guaranteed that good men should never suffer for their good actions. The King laughed at this piece of sarcasm and retired, saying that he would attend to the matter.

Furthermore, they warned him that some day he would be punished because he knew well that the Mussalman teaching was pernicious to the minds of men, and yet he allowed his two sons—boys of great natural ability and intellectual power—to be educated by certain old men whose minds were filled with Mohammed. He replied that he had given orders that these tutors should only teach the history of the reigns of his own ancestors.

Not to go into too many details, the fathers frequently and freely admonished the King; but their conscientious readiness in doing this never lessened, still less put an end to, the kindly friendship of the King toward them. Nay more, when the King perceived that it was the sincerity of their hearts that led them to feel themselves free to correct him, he took it in such good part that he always seemed not only to favor them, but to heap honors upon them in his desire to show his affection toward them.

For when they saluted him, which they did with uncovered heads, he answered with a nod and a bright smile. He did not allow them to keep their heads uncovered when they were in his presence. When a council was being held, or when he summoned them to his private audience chamber for familiar conversation, he used to make them sit beside him. He shook hands with them cordially and familiarly. He frequently left the public audience chamber to converse with them in private. Several times he paced up and down with his arm round Rudolf's shoulders. Once, when he was in camp, he desired another of the priests, in the middle of a crowd of his nobles, to help him fasten on his sword, which service the father performed, amidst the envy and wonder of all the courtiers. He wished the priests to be sharers of his inmost thoughts, both in good and ill fortune—no common mark of love and kindness. He ordered his doorkeepers to grant them entrance whenever they wished, even into the inner courtyard of the palace, where only the most distinguished nobles had the right of entrance. He sent them food from his own table—a mark of distinction which he is said never to have conferred upon anyone before. He visited one of the fathers when he was ill, and greeted him in Portuguese as a sign of respect.

There would have been no end to his gifts, had the fathers not frequently told him that all they needed was food and clothing, and these of the most simple description. This reply pleased him so much that he repeated it publicly, and each month sent them as much money, under the guise of alms, as he thought would be sufficient for their daily expenses. This kindness of the King toward the fathers greatly confirmed and increased the rumor that he had abjured Mohammed, so that it was publicly reported that he wished to become a Christian.

The Father Explains His Faith

One night Akbar summoned a priest [Father Monserrate] in order to ask him certain questions, both religious and secular. First of all, he had an atlas brought and asked where Portugal was, and where his own kingdom was. He wondered how we knew the names of the provinces and cities of India. Then he asked why the priest was a celibate: for was it not a divine command, as it were, that all men should have wives? And he (the priest) appeared either to condemn matrimony or to contradict himself when he said that celibacy was good and matrimony also good.

The priest replied, "Does not your Highness know that, of two good things, one often happens to be better than the other? Thus silver is good, but gold is better, whilst wisdom is better than gold, and virtue than anything else. The moon is beautiful: but the sun is more beautiful, and superior to her." The King agreed to this; whereupon the priest added, "Therefore priests remain celibate and unmarried, that they may follow better things, that they may imitate Christ, and that, free from the cares of a wife, children, and family, they may spend their time apart from all desire. For by the sixth commandment of God all luxury is forbidden to Christians, and indeed to all mankind."

The King here interjected, "You declare, do you not, that Christ is God. Do you not then act rashly and insolently in wishing to be like Him?"

The priest replied, "We do indeed believe and asseverate that Christ is God, but we declare at the same time that He is man. And, being man, He practiced chastity as an example to us, and also praised it highly very many times in the Gospel. As regards His being God, it would indeed be the mark of a proud and insolent mind to wish to be like Christ. It is indeed an impossible ambition, and hence to entertain it shows the height of folly and madness. But on the other hand, it shows piety and devotion to follow His footsteps in practicing the virtues which He himself practiced."

The King then added, "The descent from Adam thus perishes in you."

The priest replied, "What if I had died when I was a boy eight years old, or (as frequently happens) just at the time of my marriage? What if my wife had been barren, or I myself, as many are? What if I had been born, or made, a eunuch, like the many that are in your palace? Let not your Highness mistakenly imagine that marriage is enjoined. God indeed allowed much stress to be laid on the value of matrimony under the law of nature, in order that the human race might be increased."

When the question of celibacy and marriage had been so thoroughly dealt with that the King had no objections left to bring forward, he made detailed inquiries about the Last Judgment, whether Christ would be the Judge, and when it would occur. Having dealt with the other points, the priest said, "God alone knows the time when the judgment will take place, and in His unsearchable wisdom He has desired this to be hidden from us. Christ Himself refused to make it known to His disciples. He did not wish either that we should become negligent through knowing it to be far distant, or that we should be saddened by knowing that it is near at hand. Yet signs shall precede that day which will enable men to conclude with confidence that it is at hand."

The King asked what these signs should be. The priest replied, "Christ mentioned especially wars and rebellions, the fall of kingdoms and nations, the invasion, devastation, and conquest of nation by nation and kingdom by kingdom; and these things we see happening very frequently in our time."

The King listened most attentively to all this. He then asked some foolish and absurd questions about the Gospel, showing lack of faith therein. Gradually, he turned the subject to Mohammed and the differences between the Bible and the Koran. This most wicked impostor Mohammed wrote that he was mentioned in the Gospel, and his coming foretold. For the impious villain and rascally babbler wished to persuade men that Christ had spoken of him under the name of the Holy Spirit. Hence the King asked the priest, "Is it true that Christ does not mention Mohammed in the Gospel, and that his name is nowhere found there?"

The priest replied that Christ made no definite mention of Mohammed by name in the Gospel, but that He spoke in general terms of many false prophets who were to come.

The King then said, "Surely Mohammed cannot be he who is to appear at the end of the world as the adversary of all mankind?" (That is, he whom the Mussalmans call Dijal.)

The priest replied, "No, but many European scholars apply to Mohammed the words: 'His hand shall be against all men and all men's hands against him, and he shall pitch his tent far from all his brethren.' For Mohammed was of the race of Ishmael, and he gainsays the Law and the Gospel, and he declared warfare against all nations that did not accept his teaching."

The priest asked for pardon, in case the Mussalmans present should blame the King for having allowed him to speak so freely and plainly against Mohammed. The King answered with some heat, "By God, I am not the man to have my feelings outraged by these things. I am only seeking for the truth, and by Rhohalcuduz (the Holy Spirit) I conjure you to expound the truth to me, and not to be afraid of exposing the crimes of Mohammed." The priest bowed to the word "Rhohalcuduz," and the King said to those who were near him, "It is Jesus Christ." The priest forebore to explain the distinction between the persons of Jesus Christ and the Holy Spirit; for it was already late at night, and it was neither the time nor the place for discussing so important a question. He merely added that he had in good faith set forth what he believed and knew. The King then rose to retire to rest, and thus the discussion came to an end.

Akbar's Conversion at Stake

In order not to remain inactive, Akbar spent his time partly in artisan work, partly in discussions. His learned men initiated a debate regarding holy books, whereupon he ordered the sacred volumes to be brought and the priest to be called. First, he learned from the priest what each volume contained, and then he gave him an opportunity to say what he liked.

The priest, at the King's command, unrolled the books, and, seizing his opportunity, explained the pictures. He told the meaning of the Ark of the Covenant and of what was kept in it. He explained the golden candlestick and the golden table of unleavened bread. All this he did in a simple manner suited to the understanding of his hearers. The Mussalmans hate idolatry; and hence he discoursed at some length on the images of angels on the Ark and in the shrine. He pointed out that God had only prohibited the making and worship of images of false gods—not the making of statues of saints. For He who said, "Thou shalt make thyself no graven image," also commanded that the figures of angels should be painted and carved in His tabernacle and temple. And, since He is God and cannot change or forget, it is blasphemous to believe that He gives inconsistent and contradictory commands. Religious men, inspired by the divine will, explain by the right interpretation passages of Scripture which appear to conflict. These men declare that the words "graven image" and "idol" denote only the images of demons and false gods; and God, the Creator of the universe, forbids both in Law and Gospel the worship of such images. Wherefore it is wrong to accuse of idolatry Christians who do reverence to the painted or carven images of God and divine beings.

A discussion was also held on the subject of Noah's Ark, which the priest clearly explained to have been a type of the Savior Christ. The King appeared to be no little impressed, and received the teaching quite attentively. But he sometimes pretended to be thinking of other matters, lest his courtiers should imagine him to be attracted toward Christianity. However, he did not hesitate publicly to reverence and kiss a picture of Christ.

The King was always pondering in his mind which nation has retained the true religion of God; and to this question he constantly gave the most earnest thought. He devised the following ingenious method of settling the problem. On a certain night he ordered all the nobles, the religious leaders both of Hindus and Mussalmans, and the Christian priests to be summoned to the inner palace. He placed the nobles in lines according to their rank, bade all the wise men and doctors of religion take their places before him, and then asked them questions on various points. The Christian priests, in accordance with a previous decision, brought up for discussion the following very knotty point: "The Koran says that if this book is taken to a mountain, the mountain will be split in twain. In regard to this we have two questions to ask. Firstly, of what book is this to be understood? Is it the one which is said to have fallen from heaven and to have been given to Mohammed by Gabriel? Or does it apply to all the copies of that original book? If the latter is the case, why is this mountain on which we stand not split in twain, if Mohammed is to be regarded as a true prophet? For there are many copies of the Koran on this mountain. But if the saying is to be understood as applying only to the original book which was brought from heaven, then we ask our second question: "Where is that original book and has it ever split a mountain?"

The doctors readily agreed that the words in question were not to be understood of the copies of the Koran in common circulation. But they dared not acknowledge where the original copy was, though they knew well enough. They tried to evade the question by various devices and fictions. A certain man, who was known as the "Sultan of Mecca" because he had lived for long in that city, was asked by the King whether the original was not kept at Mecca, but he replied unblushingly that he did not know.

The King then remarked to the priests, "Do not suppose, Fathers, that my doctors will answer you accurately according to the genuine words of the Koran. For every one of them answers merely according to his own opinion or prejudice."

The priests then said, "We give all who are here present free leave and opportunity to go and look for that original book, to bring it when found to the foot of this mountain, to retire to some distance on the plain, leaving us on the mountain, and then to send the book up to us on the mountain. We are prepared to run the risk of the mountain splitting. If it does not split, they must confess that the book is a tissue of fraud and lies, and was never sent from God, since it does not fulfill the engagement which it contains, and by which it was to be proved the book of God, nor does it vindicate the good faith of him who made this promise."

Someone then suggested that the saying was hyperbolical. Father Rudolfus replied that if this was so, then that other passage must also be understood hyperbolically in which it was said that Mohammed had caught half of the moon in one of the sleeves of his linen shirt, and had tossed it into the sky by means of the other sleeve, in order that it might be united to

the other half of the moon. This is regarded by the Mussalmans as one of
the chief miracles of Mohammed. Father Rudolfus maintained that if there
is no hyperbole in this latter passage, then none can be suspected in the
former.

At the conclusion of this discussion, the King briefly addressed all who
had been present. He said: "I perceive that there are varying customs and
beliefs of varying religious paths. For the teachings of the Hindus, the
Mussalmans, the Jains, the Jews, and the Christians are all different. But the
followers of each religion regard the institutions of their own as better than
those of any other. Not only so, but they strive to convert the rest to their
own way of belief. If these refuse to be converted, they not only despise
them, but also regard them for this very reason as their enemies. And this
causes me to feel many serious doubts and scruples. Wherefore I desire that
on appointed days the books of all the religious laws be brought forward,
and that the doctors meet together and hold discussions, so that I may hear
them, and that each one may determine which is the truest and mightiest
religion." He then turned to the priests and asked which day is auspicious
and "destined to be good" (as he put it).

They answered that no day is inauspicious and evil, although some may
happen sometimes to be better than others: "For since the light of every
day is bestowed by the mandate of God, who does no evil, no day can be
called evil in itself alone. Yet it is written in the Gospel, 'See to it then,
brethren, that ye walk circumspectly, not as fools, but as wise, redeeming
the time because the days are evil.' The reason for this statement is that the
men of that age were evil, or that being close to the coming of Anti-Christ
the age itself was disastrous to those who believed in Christ. It is a common
saying moreover that he who befouls himself with crimes was born on an ill
day; but in so saying we blame the man, not the day. Christ also said, as if
in paradox, 'Sufficient unto the day is the evil thereof.' By the same figure of
speech days are called good or better from the events which happen to us
on them. When enterprises are to be begun which redound to the praise and
glory of God and to the benefit of souls, there is no need to investigate
whether the day is auspicious and good, or inauspicious and evil. For in
truth there is no such thing as a day which is evil and inauspicious by its
own nature, as the saying is, and not by reason of the deeds done on it."

These views appeared very extraordinary to all who heard them; for they
believe that an inexorable fate has decreed that some days shall be evil and
inauspicious, wherefore they cast lots and take the advice of soothsayers
and diviners with most superstitious zeal and an almost incredible anxiety,
in order to find out whether a given piece of business should be started
today or tomorrow. However, no one dared to oppose Father Rudolfus,
and so the King dismissed the assembly and retired.

On the next day he again ordered several doctors belonging to other sects
to be summoned together with the priests. When they had arrived, he said
to the priest: "I desire that we should now begin to carry out my proposal

of yesterday, and I beg you to do your part readily; for the Most High God has given me the desire to take the step you wish, and which you have so often pressed upon me. God knows that I am sincere in my will and intentions regarding this determination which I have made."

At the moment when he said this his two eldest sons were sitting by his side, and several chieftains and petty kings were standing around him. The priests replied that they would not hinder or delay his satisfying his desire, and at once began the proposed course of lectures and discussions with an exposition of the Gospel. However, the others gradually ceased coming to the appointed place, and the Christians alone gladly obeyed the King's desire. They also brought him what they wrote, on the days arranged, and he asked them a few questions, rather to avoid appearing changeable in his intentions than because he was still interested in his original proposal.

However, the priests began to suspect that he was intending to found a new religion with matter taken from all the existing systems; and hence they also gradually withdrew themselves from the meetings. For at this time the King was daily showing greater and greater favor to the Hindus, at whose request he had forbidden the sale of buffalo flesh in the meat market. Hence the priests did not feel it right to give him the pearls of the Gospel to tread and crush under his feet. Furthermore, he had caused a wooden building of ingenious workmanship to be constructed, and had it placed on the very highest point of the palace roof. And from this he watched the dawn and worshiped the rising sun. Nevertheless, the priests continued to pray for better things.

The Grand Signor

Portrait of Ahmed I. Turkish 17th century miniature.
Metropolitan Museum of Art, New York.

Thus have I had thee, as a dream doth flatter,
In sleep a king, but, waking, no such matter.

William Shakespeare, *Sonnet 87*

T*here is a ghoulish but most likely likely story of how a team of deep-sea
divers, sent to salvage a wreck in the Bosporus about a mile off Seraglio Point,
began within minutes to signal frantically to return and were pulled up,
horror-stricken, refusing ever to go down again. At the bottom of the sea they
had come across an amazing spectacle: hundreds of life-size skull-headed dolls
in the shape of bowling pins, most of them toppled over, but with rows of others,
jammed upright between rocks or stuck in the mud and slime, slightly swaying
to and fro in unison whenever the current moved them, and of course grinning,
"with a lipless grin," as if beckoning the divers to approach. By chance, it
seems, they had blundered upon the exact spot where generations of martyred
concubines from the seraglio, who had either fallen victim to court intrigue or
offended the Grand Signor in some way, were once ritually murdered by being
sewn up alive in sacks weighted with stones, with only their heads protruding,
then towed out at night in barges and dumped overboard. The eerie loreleis who
had so frightened the divers were their skeletal remains.*

*From the time the seraglio was founded in 1454 by Mohammed II (the
Conqueror), on the site of the ancient city of Byzantium, until it was finally
abandoned as the royal residence of the Ottoman sultans by Abdul-Medjid in
1853, there must have been thousands of such executions. How many during
any particular period depended to a large extent upon the character of the
reigning sultan. One of the most depraved and bloodthirsty, Ibrahim I
(1640–48), is said to have drowned his entire harem, consisting of some 1200
concubines, merely because he was bored with the old and wished to start a new
collection. But aside from the cruelty of the Grand Signor, which was personal
and hence unpredictable, there was also the moloch state itself that inexorably
demanded its victims. Mohammed II, in order to prevent civil war at the
beginning of each new reign, had decreed in 1451 the so-called Law of*

Fratricide, or Kanun Namé, *in which he stated:* "To whomsoever of my sons the sultanate may pass, it is fitting for the order of the world he shall kill his brothers." *And this also entailed, as a matter of course, the sacrifice of all the brothers' sultanas and concubines, in the manner previously described. However, since the shedding of blood within the family was forbidden by the Koran, the brothers of the newly crowned sultan would be ceremonially strangled by deaf-mutes using a silken cord, called a* keman-kirisi, *haloed for that purpose.*

The place where the fratricide occurred was once visited by an Englishman named Thomas Dallam, a maker of organs, who was commissioned by Queen Elizabeth in 1599 to install one of these new-fangled instruments inside the seraglio as a gift for the sultan. Dallam seems to have had trouble making up his mind to believe his eyes:

> *Coming into the house whear I was appoynted to sett up the presente or instramente; it seemed to be rether a churche than a dwellinge house; to say the truthe, it was no dwellinge house, but a house of pleasur, and lyke wyse a house of slaughter; for in that house was bulte one little house, verrie curius bothe within and witheout. For carvinge, gildinge, good Collors and vernishe, I have not sene the lyke. In this little house, that emperor that rained when I was thare [Mohammed III, 1595–1603] had nyntene brotheres put to deathe in it, and it was bulte for no other use but for the stranglinge of everie emperors bretherin.*

Queen Elizabeth's organ was perhaps intended not so much to provide a solemn music for the occasion but to drone out the cries of the victims. In later centuries, the Kanun Namé *was modified somewhat, and the sultan's brothers were no longer executed but confined for life in large dark cages, called* kafes, *where they were systematically debauched and debilitated by heavy doses of hashish, opium, alcohol and fornication.*

Nonetheless, Dallam's description of the mysterious concert hall as a "house of pleasur, and lyke wyse a house of slaughter" might apply to the entire seraglio—almost, when you come to think of it, as if it were a sort of Freudian id made real. For within his own domain the power of the Grand Signor, worshiped by his subjects as "the shadow of Allah on earth," was nearly as absolute as that of any ordinary mortal within the artificial paradise—or nightmare alley—of his own dreams. The sultan's sultanas and his concubines were in fact and in flesh like whims that he could indulge or dismiss, embody or disembody, as he pleased.

The private life of such a godling, as might be imagined, could not help but arouse the most universal as well as intensely personal curiosity. Yet here again, like the erotic or murderous fantasies pipe-dreamed in the mind of Everyman, his secrets were just as closely guarded. Throughout the 400-year history of the seraglio, scarcely a half-dozen or so outsiders were ever able to penetrate beyond the so-called Gate of Felicity, where the sultan lived and moved and had his being, and obtain more than a peep at the "unholy holies" of the harem.

*One of these privileged few—if we accept his own account—was Robert Withers, Esq., an English adventurer and, perhaps, agent for the Levant Company in Constantinople (now Istanbul), who resided there from 1610 to 1620. However, it was by chance discovered, by the scholar N. M. Penzer, [The Harem (*London: George G. Harrap & Co., 1936*).] that Withers' book, first published in England in 1625 under the title* A Description of the Grand Signor's Seraglio, or Turkish Emperour's Court, *was actually cribbed from the diplomatic reports of a Venetian* bailo, *or consul-general, named Ottaviano Bon. Bon, as we now know, served at the Ottoman court from 1604 to 1607 during the reign of Ahmed I. By bribing the eunuch then employed as chief gardener of the sultan—and at some peril to his own cod, no doubt, were he discovered—he succeeded in gaining entrance to the forbidden precincts of the seraglio. A summary of his reports, intended only for the Doge at Venice, somehow came into the possession of the English ambassador to Constantinople, and through him was acquired by Withers. He then freely translated Bon's manuscript into the fusty and sometimes hilarious camp of his own prose, adding a few personal observations and making several minor deletions here and there to conceal its true source, and thus plumed himself forth as the author. Howbeit, Withers'* Description, *though secondhand, remains the most detailed and intimate survey in English of all the complex workings and heterogeneous inhabitants of the seraglio during its heyday.*

A Description of the Place, Partitions, and Manifold Conveniences of the Seraglio

The Seraglio—the Turkish word is *serai,* borrowed from the Persian word *seraw,* which signifies a house—wherein the Grand Signor resides with his court is wonderfully well situated, being directly in that place where Byzantium once stood, upon a point of the continent which looks toward the mouth of the Black Sea. It is enclosed with a very high and strong wall, upon which there are divers watchtowers, and is by computation about three miles in compass.

The wall has many gates, some of which open toward the sea side and the rest into the city; but the chief gate (which indeed is a very noble one) is one of those facing toward the city, and by it the people go in and out daily, the others meanwhile being kept shut. If any of the other land gates be opened, it is either when some of the principal offices of the Seraglio wish to sit for their pleasure by the sea side, where they may behold the ships sailing to and fro, or when the King sends privately to put some great man to death, or for the execution of some such secret action; but they are all locked fast in the night again.

In the Seraglio there are many stately rooms suited to the seasons of the year. Most of these are built upon plain ground, a few upon the hills, and some also upon the seaside, which are called *kiosks*—that is, rooms of fair prospect, or (as we term them) banqueting houses, into which the King sometimes goes alone, but most commonly with his concubines for recreation.

Amongst the aforesaid rooms is the chamber into which the Grand Signor repairs when he is to give audience to ambassadors or to his Bashaws on the days of public divan. This room stands in a little court curiously adorned with many very delicate fountains, and has within it a sofa, which is a place raised from the floor about a foot to sit upon. This sofa is spread with very sumptuous carpets of gold and of crimson velvet embroidered with costly pearls, upon which the Grand Signor reclines. About the chamber, instead of hangings, the walls are covered with very fine white stones which have divers forms of leaves and flowers artificially wrought and baked upon them, and make a glorious show. There is also a little room adjoining it, the whole inside whereof is covered with silver plate hatched with gold.

The Seraglio contains as well rooms for prayer, *bagnos* (baths), schools, butteries [pantries], kitchens, distilling rooms, places to swim in, places to run horses in, places for wrestling, butts to shoot at, and, to conclude, all the commodities to be had in a Prince's palace for things of that nature. And besides these rooms, which serve only for the King's own person, there is the women's lodging (in a manner like a nunnery), wherein the Queen, the other Sultanas, and all the King's women slaves do dwell. And it, too, has within it all the commodity that may be of beds, chambers, dining rooms, bagnos, and the like, necessary for the use and service of the women.

On the left side of the court is the King's stable, of about 30 or 35 very brave horses, which his Majesty keeps for his exercise whenever he pleases to run or sport with his gentlemen, the Aghas, in the Seraglio. Over this stable there is a row of rooms, wherein is kept all the equipment of the horses, the which (I having seen both the equipment there and abroad of the best sort) I can affirm to be of extraordinary value. For the bridles, pectorals, cruppers, saddles, pommels of the saddles, and stirrups are set so thick with jewels of divers sorts that the beholders are amazed, they so far exceed all imagination.

Adjoining all the rooms and lodgings of the Seraglio are very fair gardens of all sorts of flowers and fruits that are to be found in these parts. Throughout there are also many pleasant walks, enclosed by high cypress trees on each side, and with marble fountains in such abundance that almost every walk has two or three, such great delight does the Grand Signor and all Turks in general take in them.

Upon the top of a little hill there is a row of summer houses facing the sea, all so well contrived with halls and chambers and so pleasantly seated and richly furnished, that they deserve to be the habitations of so great a Prince. Amongst them there is a hall, underset with very fair pillars, which looks toward the east upon an artificial four-square lake (called by the Turks *Hawoz*) filled by about 30 fountains. These fountains are built upon a kind of terrace of fine marble encompassing the lake, the water jetting from the spouts down into it, and from the lake through divers gutters into the gardens.

Two men may walk abreast upon the terrace, where they hear the continual and sweet harmony which the waters of the fountains make through leaden pipes, insomuch that it is a most delightful place. And in the lake there is a little boat, the which (as I was informed) the Grand Signor oftentimes goes into with his mutes and buffoons to make them row him up and down and to sport with them, sometimes prodding them to leap into the water; on other occasions, as he walks along with them on the terrace above the lake, he throws them down into it and plunges them over head and ears.

Close by the said hall is his Majesty's bed-chamber, the walls of which are covered with stones of the finest China metal and spotted with jeweled flowers of divers colors. The *anteportas* (hangings before the doors) are of cloth of gold of Bursia, and their borders are of crimson velvet embroidered with gold and pearls. The posts of the bedstead are of silver, but hollow, and instead of knobs on the tops there are set lions of crystal. The canopy over it is of cloth of gold, and so are the bolsters and mattresses. The floor of this chamber (as of the other rooms) and the sofas are spread with very costly Persian carpets of silk and gold; and the pallets to sit on, with the cushions to lean upon, are also of very rich cloth of gold.

In the midst of the hall itself hangs a very great round lantern, the bars of which are of silver gilt set very thick with rubies, emeralds, and turquoises, while the panes are of fine crystal. There is likewise a basin and ewer of massive gold, inlaid with rubies and turquoises, which beautify the room.

Thus have I made a brief description of some of the rooms and buildings of this Seraglio, according to the notice I took of them.

Of the Persons Who Live in the Seraglio, Chiefly the Women and Virgins

First then I say, that all those who live in the Seraglio, both men and women, are the Grand Signor's slaves (for so they style themselves), and so, indeed, are all who are subject to his empire. For besides his power as their sovereign, they all acknowledge that whatsoever they possess, or enjoy, proceeds merely from his good will and favor; and not only their estates but their lives also are at his disposal.

Within the third gate, called the King's Gate, are about 2000 men and women; and of these the women, both old and young, including the King's concubines and servants, number about 11 or 1200. Those kept up for their beauty are all young virgins bought or stolen from foreign nations. They are instructed in good behavior, how to play upon instruments, sing, dance, and sew curiously, then given to the Grand Signor as presents of great value by the Tatars, Bashaws, and other great men to secure his favor.

Immediately after their coming into the Seraglio, they are made Turks, which is done by this ceremony only: to hold up their forefinger and say these words, *Law illaheh illalaw Allawh, Mohammed resoul Allawh,* meaning, "There is no God but God alone, and Mohammed is the messenger of God." Afterward they are examined by an old woman called the *Kahiyah Cadun*—that is, as we say, the "Mother of the Maids"—and placed in a large room with others of the same age, spirit, and inclination to dwell together.

Now in the women's lodgings they live just as nuns do in great nunneries, always together, and their bed-chambers will hold almost a hundred of them apiece. They sleep upon sofas built longwise on both sides of the room, with a large space left in the midst for them to go to and fro about their business.

Their beds are very coarse and hard (for the Turks use neither featherbeds nor corded bedsteads) and made of flocks of wool. By every 10 virgins there lies an old woman, and all night long there are many lamps burning, so that she may see plainly throughout the whole room, which both keeps the young wenches from wantonness and serves to provide light upon any occasion which may happen. Near the bed-chambers these virgins have their own bagnos for their use at all times, with many fountains out of which they are served with water; and above their chambers are divers rooms where they may sit and sew, and there they keep their boxes and chests in which they lay up their apparel.

They feed by whole companies, served and waited upon by other women, nor do they want anything whatsoever that is necessary for them.

There are other places likewise for them where to go to school to learn to speak and read (if they will) the Turkish tongue, to sew, and to play on divers instruments. And so they spend the day with their mistresses, who are all ancient women. Some hours notwithstanding are allowed them for their recreation, to walk their gardens, and to use such sports as they familiarly exercise themselves withal.

The King does not at all frequent, or see, these virgins, unless it be at that instant when they are first presented unto him; or else in case he desires one of them for his bed, or to make him some pastime with songs and dancing and other sports. When he is prepared for a fresh mate, he gives notice to the Kahiya Cadun of his purpose. She like a crafty bawd immediately bestirs herself, and places them all in good order in a room, in two ranks, like so many pictures, half on the one side and half on the other, then forthwith brings in the King.

After walking four or five times in their midst and viewing them well, the Grand Signor takes good notice within himself of the one he likes best, but says not a thing; only as he goes out again he throws a handkerchief * into the favored virgin's hand, by which token she knows that she is to lie with him that night.

Being (questionless) exceeding joyful to become the object of so great a fortune, she employs all her wiles and all the art that possibly may be bestowed upon her by the Kahiya Cadun in attiring, painting, and perfuming herself. At night she is brought to sleep with the Grand Signor in the women's lodgings, where there are chambers set apart for that business only. And being in bed together, they have two great wax lights burning by them all night, one at the bed's feet and the other by the door. Besides, there are appointed by the Kahiya Cadun divers old blackamoor women to watch by turns that night in the chamber, two at a time, one by the bed's feet and one by the door; and when they change, two other women supply their place, without making the least noise imaginable, so that the King is not a whit disturbed.

Now in the morning when his Highness rises (for he always rises first) he changes his apparel from top to toe, leaving behind those garments which he had worn for the maiden that he lay withal, as well as all the money he had in his pockets, were it never so much, and so departs to his own lodgings. From whence he also sends her immediately a present of jewels, money, and vests of great value, agreeable to the satisfaction and content he received from her that night. In the same manner he deals with all the women in the Seraglio he makes use of in that way; but with some he continues longer than with others, and enlarges his bounty, according to the extent whereby his affection for them increases by their fulfillment of his lustful desires.

* Here may well be found a clue to the murderous fury of Othello when told by Iago that his precious handkerchief, given to him by his mother, and which he in turn had given to Desdemona, was used by Cassio to wipe his beard withal. ("Pish! Noses, ears, and lips! Is't possible? Confess! Handkerchief! O Devil!") It provides an answer, too, for those nineteenth-century critics who thought that hinging the action of the play on such a trifle was a defect in the plot. Shakespeare is believed to have based the character of Othello on an Italian adventurer named San Pietro di Bastelica, who returned from a mission to Constantinople after learning that his wife had been unfaithful, then strangled her with a handkerchief he had given her.

And if it so fall out that any one of them conceives by him and brings forth his first begotten child, then she is called by the name of Sultana Queen. If it be a son, she is confirmed and established by great feasts and solemnities; and forthwith she has a dwelling assigned to her apart from the other women, with many stately and well-furnished rooms and many servants to attend upon her. The King likewise allows her a large revenue that she may give away and spend at her pleasure. All the other women of the Seraglio must, and do, acknowledge her for Queen, showing duty and respect both to herself and her family and attendants.

The other women (howsoever they bring forth issue) are not called Queens but Sultanas, because they, too, have had carnal commerce with the King. She alone is called Queen who becomes the mother of the first begotten son, heir to the empire. The Sultanas, being frequented by the King at his pleasure, have also the prerogative of living in rooms apart from the common sort, where they are exceedingly well served and attended, in conformity to their degree, with no want either of money or apparel. All these Sultanas resort together very familiarly whenever they please, but not without great dissimulation and inward malice, fearing lest the one should be better beloved of the Grand Signor than the other. Yet notwithstanding their jealousy, they (in outward show) use all courtesy one toward another.

Now if it happens that the first begotten son of the Queen should die, and another Sultana should have a second son, then she is immediately made Queen in her place, while the former becomes a Sultana only and is deprived of a Queen's revenue and royalty. Thus the title of Queen runs from one Sultana to another by virtue of the son's succession.

In times past the Queen was wont to be wedded to the King; but now she passes without the *kebin*, that is, without the assignment of any joint estate or celebration of nuptial rites. The reason why the Queens are not now (nor have been of late years) espoused is so as not to dismember the King's patrimony of 500,000 chicquins a year. Howsoever, married or not married, the mother of the heir is acknowledged by everyone to be the Queen, and she is presented with many rich gifts from all great personages. She has continually at her gate a guard of 30 or 40 black eunuchs, together with their master, the *Kuzlar Agha* (the Master of the Virgins), whom she commands and employs in all her occasions.

The Queen, as well as all the other Sultanas, never stirs out of the Seraglio except in the company of the King himself. He sometimes carries either all or some of them abroad to his other houses for pleasure. In those public ways through which they must pass to go to and fro their *kaiks* (barges), canvas is pitched up on both sides of the streets, and none may come near them but black eunuchs until they are settled and covered close at the stern of the kaiks. Only afterward are the bargemen allowed to come in, so that in fine they are never seen by any men save the Grand Signor and the eunuchs.

The King's daughters, sisters, and aunts also have their lodgings in the

same Seraglio, where they are royally served and live together by
themselves in continual pleasures until such time as, at their request, the
King shall be pleased to give them in marriage. They then come forth from
the Seraglio, each of them with a chest given by the Grand Signor full of
rich apparel, jewels, and money, to the value of (at the least) 30,000 pounds
sterling a chest. That is (as we call it) their marriage portion. They carry
likewise along with them all that they might have hid from time to time,
unknown to any but themselves, which sometimes amounts to a great
matter. And if they be in the Grand Signor's especial favor, and he be
disposed to deal royally with them, then they are suffered to remove out of
the Seraglio such women slaves as they please (provided they do not exceed
the number of 20 apiece) and such eunuchs as they like best for their
service.

The Sultanas also receive so long as they live the same allowance of
money which they had while in the King's Seraglio, some 1000, and some
1500, aspars a day. Their houses are furnished with all necessary provisions
from the King's *hazineh* (treasury) and *begleek* (store), so that indeed they
live far better in every respect without the Seraglio than they did while
within it.

And if it so happens that a Bashaw, having married one of them, be
unable to provide a house fit for her greatness and quality, then the King
gives her one of his, for he has many which fall to him each year by the
death of his subjects. Contrary to the usual custom, it is the husband's part
to provide her with a bill of dowry, ordinarily at least a hundred chicquins
in money, besides vests, jewels, brooches, and other ornaments, amounting
to a great sum. For although the fashion of a Sultana's apparel be no
different from that of other women, yet the substance is far more rich and
costly, which redounds to the great charge and loss of their husbands.

Being thus married, the Sultanas do not at all converse with men (except
with their own husbands) more than they did when they lived in the King's
Seraglio. They may commonly go upon visits to see their old acquaintances
who still remain therein; but because they themselves, at their own request,
came forth, they may not come in again without leave from the Grand
Signor.

These Sultanas, the Bashaws' wives, are for the most part their husbands'
masters, insulting over them and commanding them as they please. They
always wear at their girdle a *hanjar* (dagger) set with rich stones, in token of
their domination over their husbands. And sometimes (though not without
the Grand Signor's leave) they may put one husband away and take
another. This divorce commonly proves to be the death and ruin of the
poor rejected husbands, for the King is apt to give way to persuasion of the
Sultanas, so it behooves them in any case to be very obsequious to their
wives.

Now the other women in the Seraglio who are not so fortunate as to be
beloved by the King, must still live together with the rest of the virgins,

wasting their youthful days among themselves in evil thoughts (for they are too strictly looked after to offend in act). And when they grow old they serve as overseers and mistresses of the new virgins who are daily brought into the Seraglio. They hold it their best fortune, since their former hopes of being bedded with the King are now wholly frustrated, to be sent forth through some accident into the old Seraglio; for from the old Seraglio they may be married (if the mistress of that place gives her consent) and may take with them such money as they have saved from their allowance. They also receive many things from the Sultanas who, having formerly been companions with them, cannot but in some measure let them be partakers of their good fortune.

The Sultanas are likewise presented by the Bashaws and the Bashaws' wives (so that by their means they may continue to find favor with the Grand Signor) with most stately and rich gifts, but especially with money, for this is more acceptable to them than any other kind of present whatsoever. Being very covetous, they hoard up and spend but sparingly, and thus wittily provide against disastrous times which may come upon them unawares, especially in case of the King's death. For then (except for the Sultana Queen, who still remains in the Seraglio as the mother of the succeeding King), all the other poor desolate ladies lose the title of Sultana and are immediately sent to the old Seraglio. They then must leave behind them their sons and daughters (if they have any living) in the new King's Seraglio, there to be kept and brought up under the care of other women appointed for that service. But from the old Seraglio they may then marry with men of reasonable quality, according to the measure of the estate which they possess. Thus, by reason of their being turned out of the King's Seraglio, it is sometimes seen that, though the daughter of the King be married to a Bashaw, yet the mother of that daughter (after the King's decease) must be content with a second husband of small account, far unequal in title and in wealth to her son-in-law.

The Sultanas have leave of the Grand Signor to permit certain women of the Jews to come at any time into the Seraglio for various purposes. Under color of teaching them some fine and curious needleworks, or to show them the art of mixing lotions, oils, and painting for their faces, they make themselves by their crafty insinuations so familiar and so welcome to the King's women that (in a manner) they prevail over them in whatsoever they design for their own ends. Being extraordinarily subtle, they are employed by the Sultanas in their private occasions, carrying out whatsoever they would have sold and bringing in anything they have a desire to buy.

Hence it is that all such Jews' women as frequent the Seraglio become very rich, for what they bring in they buy cheap and sell dear to them; and, on the contrary, when the Sultanas have jewels or the like commodities to sell (and which can be conveyed out of the Seraglio by stealth), they receive a reasonable price for them from strangers, and then tell the simple ladies of the King, who know not their worth and are afraid to be discovered, that they sold them peradventure for half that amount. By this means there come things of great worth out of the Seraglio, to be sold abroad at easy rates. Yet in the end the husbands of these crafty women have but a bad market of it; for being discovered to be rich, and their wealth to be gotten by deceit, they oftentimes lose both goods and life, too. By this means the Bashaws and Defterdars of the King restore to him that which from time to time has been stolen.

Yet notwithstanding, there is scarcely a man of authority among the Turks (and especially the Defterdars) who has not a Jew for his counselor and assistant in the managing of his affairs, such a good opinion have they of their sufficiency and so ready are the Jews to entertain any manner of employment. The Jews' wives are not so great with the Sultanas as they themselves are as intimate with the Bashaws and other powerful officials.

The women of the Seraglio are punished for their faults very severely and extremely beaten by their overseers should they prove disobedient, incorrigible, and insolent. They may, by the King's order and express command, be turned out and sent into the old Seraglio, as utterly rejected and cast off, and the best part of what they possess be taken from them. But if they are found culpable of witchcraft or any such like abomination, then they are bound hand and foot, put into a sack, and in the night cast into the sea. So that by all means it behooves them to be very careful and obedient and to contain themselves within the bounds of honesty and good behavior, if they mean to prosper and come to a good end.

Now it is not lawful for anyone to bring ought in unto them with which they may commit the deeds of beastly and unnatural uncleanness. If they have a desire to eat radishes, cucumbers, gourds, or the like, they are sent to them sliced, so as to deprive them of the means of playing the wantons. For they being all young, lusty, and lascivious wenches, and wanting the society of men (who would better instruct them, and questionless far better employ them), they are doubtless of themselves inclined to that which is naught, and often be possessed with unchaste thoughts.

Of the Old Seraglio and the Women's Lives Therein

Having oftentimes made mention of the *Eskee Sarai* (old Seraglio) which is, as it were, a dependent of the King's Seraglio, it will not be amiss to speak somewhat now touching the same. This is a very large place, seated in the noblest part of the city, and immured with a very high wall surpassing even that of the King's Seraglio. The Eskee Sarai was the first Seraglio, built by Mohammed the Second to dwell in with all his court when he took Constantinople. It has but one gate, made of iron, and that is guarded by a company of white eunuchs who allow no man to pass through unless it be to bring in such necessaries as may be needed, nor can they at such times see any of the women.

Now the women therein are those who have been put out of the King's

Seraglio, viz., such Sultanas who once belonged to the deceased Grand Signor; those women likewise who through their evil behavior have fallen into disgrace with the King; and all such as are infirm or defective in what should belong to women fit for the company and bed of a King. They are governed and looked unto by an old woman, the *Bashiya Cadun* (Mistress of the Maids) who is their overseer and takes care that they be served according to the custom of the house, each one in her degree. All have their diet, clothing, and stipends of money, but far short of what they had when they were in the King's Seraglio. Howbeit, such as have been Sultanas live out of the common rank in lodgings apart; and although they are out of the King's sight and (as it were) out of favor, yet they are reasonably well served.

Most of the Sultanas, if they be rich enough, may (by the Bashiya Cadun's solicitation and the Grand Signor's leave) go forth from thence and marry, carrying with them all they have kept and stolen. But if they have aught of any great value, and that be discovered, the Cadun takes it from them at their departure and restores it again to the Grand Signor; so that, I say, they must warily and cunningly make their worth known abroad, to the end that some men of quality may become suitors to them.

The Bashaws and other great subjects, though by marriage they become uncles, sons-in-law, or cousins to the Grand Signor, may not presume any greater familiarity or freedom with his Majesty, but only as much as befits their place, remaining still his slaves, as are all others. Nay, their servitude is thereby increased, and they lose a great part of their former liberty; for they must be very obsequious to the Sultanas whom they have married, turn away most of their other women and slave girls, and with patience support all their wives' imperfections. For this reason, few Bashaws of worth and judgment seek after such marriages.

The Sultanas in the Eskee Sarai have all the commodity of necessaries that may be, with gardens, fountains, and fair bagnos in abundance. The King himself has some rooms therein ready furnished, since he sometimes goes thither to visit his female kindred and other women who, for some of the aforesaid reasons, have been put out of his Seraglio.

The less favored women of the place have but a mean allowance; and had they not somewhat of their own to help sometimes, they would live in a hard state. Many are fain to betake themselves to their needles, by which they in part sustain themselves and reap a reasonable benefit. And as in the King's Seraglio, the Sultanas are permitted to employ divers women of the Jews about their ordinary occasions, who slyly frequent their companies and sell their labors for them, so likewise do the women of this Seraglio.

Any Turk, be he of the clergy or of the laity, may, if he please, take seven wives at Kebin (but few will have more than one or two at the most, to save charges), and he may also keep as many *halayks* (women slaves) as he will. The children begotten of them are held as legitimate as those of his wives, with as much right to the inheritance.

Now once a Turk takes slaves for his use (to lie withal), he may not sell them again, but they become members of his family and remain such till they die. But if they prove barren, then they may be sold from hand to hand as often as it is their fortune. The Turks may buy slaves of every religion and nation and use them as they please (killing only excepted), but the Christians and Jews have liberty to buy only Christians and Jews.

There is for this purpose a place in Constantinople, near the Bezisten, where every Wednesday in the open street there are bought and sold slaves of all sorts, some for nurses, some for servants, some for their lustful appetites. The buyers who make use of slaves for their sensuality cannot be punished by law, as they should be if taken with free women, and with Turkish women especially.

These slaves are bought and sold as beasts and cattle are, they being viewed and reviewed and felt all about their limbs and bodies, and their mouths looked into as if they were so many horses. They are examined of what country they are and what they are good for, either for sewing, spinning, weaving, or the like. Sometimes the mother is bought with the children, sometimes the children without the mother, sometimes two or three brothers together, and again sometimes taking the one and leaving the rest, using no terms of humanity, love, or honesty, but just as the buyer or the seller thinks will best turn them to profit.

Now when there is a virgin that is beautiful and fair, she is held at a high rate and sold for far more than any other. As security for her virginity, the seller is not only bound to the restitution of the money if she prove otherwise, but for his fraud is fined a great sum of money. And in this Bezisten there sits an *Emeen*, that is, a collector of customs, who receives a tax from the buyers and sellers of slaves, amounting to a considerable sum in a year, for the toll is very great.

Of the Agiamoglans [Ajem-oghlans] and of the Itchoglans [Iç-oghlans]

There are ordinarily about 5 or 700 *agiamoglans* (unexpert or untutored youths) in the Seraglio, from 12 to 25 or 30 years of age at the most, and all of them are Christian children gathered every three years in Morea [in southern Greece] and throughout all the parts of Albania. As soon as they arrive in Constantinople, they are all clothed in coarse Salonichi cloth, it makes no matter of what color, and given caps of felt in the form of sugar loaves and of the color of camels' hair.

The best youths chosen by the vizier are carried by the Bustangee Bashaw into the King's own Seraglio. They are then circumcised and made Turks, and set to learn the Turkish tongue. Those who have a desire are also taught to read and write; but generally all of them are taught to wrestle, to leap, to run, to throw the iron weight, to shoot the bow, to discharge a piece, and, in sum, to perform all such exercises as are befitting a Turkish soldier. Now part of the residue of them are distributed by the chief vizier into all the Grand Signor's gardens and houses of pleasure and, mainly, into such ships as sail for the King, on condition that they be restored again whenever he requires them.

The agiamoglans in the Seraglio have their terms and prerogatives among themselves, preceding or succeeding one another according to their length of service. In process of time they may aspire to the degree of chief steward to the Bustangee Bashaw, or even of the Bustangee Bashaw himself, which is a very eminent place, for he has the keeping of all the Grand Signor's garden houses, steers the King's kaik, and wears a turban upon his head.

These agiamoglans are not altogether debarred from liberty, but may upon good occasion be licensed to go whither they please. The Bustangee Bashaw always takes with him a good store of them when, by his Majesty's order, he is sent to put some great man to death, which is commonly done by the hands of the chiefest and strongest of the agiamoglans.

They never see the King, unless it be when he passes through the gardens, or when he takes to his boat, or else when he goes hunting (for he makes them serve instead of hounds to find out the game). But whenever his Majesty goes into the gardens to take his pleasure or make pastime with his concubines, then all the agiamoglans, being warned by a eunuch who cries aloud "*Helvet!*" (a word commanding absence and retirement, never used but for the King) get out with all speed at the gates by the sea side. They may then walk there upon the banks and causeways, but must not dare to go in again until the King and his women have departed. For none may come near, nor even in sight of the women, but the King and his black eunuchs, and if anyone should but attempt (by some trick in creeping into some private corner) to see the women, and should be discovered, he would be put to death immediately. Everyone therefore (as soon as they hear "Helvet" cried) runs out of sight as far as he can, so as to be free of all fear and suspicion.

The Grand Signor's *itchoglans* (youths reserved for the King's person) also are fed and kept in the Seraglio, but in far better fashion than the agiamoglans, and brought up in learning, in knowledge of the laws, and in military exercises. Though for the most part they are Christian captives or renegades, there are some natural-born Turks among them (who must be youths of very comely aspect) brought in by the Capee Aghas with the King's consent.

Great severity is used in all the orders of their discipline and education. The government of them lies in the hands of white eunuchs, who are very rough and cruel in all their actions, insomuch that their proverb says, when one has come out of the Seraglio and run through all the orders of it, he is without question the most mortified and patient man in the world. For the blows they suffer, and the fastings they endure for every small fault, are to be wondered at. Their masters often give them a hundred blows with a cudgel upon the soles of their feet and buttocks, leaving them sometimes for dead.

Neither are they permitted, while still under instruction, to be familiar with any but themselves, so that it is difficult for any stranger to speak with them or see them. Nay, when they have occasion to go to the bagnos, the eunuchs are always at hand to keep them from lewdness. And in their bed-chambers, which are long rooms holding about 30 or 40 in each upon the sofas, there are night lamps burning and eunuchs lying by them to keep them in awe and from lewd and wanton behavior.

After they are ordained for the Grand Signor's own service, their apparel is changed from cloth to silk and cloth of gold of great price. Now their punishments cease, but they continue still with heads and beards shaven, permitted only to grow some locks of hair from their temples on each side, which hang down below their ears as a sign of their preferment.

Out of these young men the King chooses his Aghas, who are gentlemen in attendance only upon him:

1. The Silihatar Agha: the King's sword-bearer.
2. The Chiohadar Agha: who carries the King's *yagmoorlick* [handkerchief].
3. The Rechinbear Agha: yeoman of the stirrup.
4. The Mataragee Agha: who brings him water to wash his hands and face.
5. The Telbenttar Agha: who brings him his turban.
6. The Kenhafir Agha: who looks after his apparel and the washing of his linen.
7. The Cheshneghir Bashaw: the chief steward.
8. The Dogangee Bashaw: the chief falconer.
9. The Zagargee Bashaw: the chief huntsman.
10. The Turnackgee Bashaw: who pares the King's nails.
11. The Berker Bashaw: the chief barber.
12. The Hamawngee Bashaw: who washes the King in the bagno.
13. The Muhasabegee Bashaw: the chief accountant.
14. The Teskeregee Bashaw: his Majesty's secretary.

These must always in the King's presence hold down their heads (for they may not be so bold as to look him in the face), and stand with their hands folded across their chest before him, in token of reverence and humility. Nor may they presume to speak to the Grand Signor unless bidden, nor in his presence to one another; but should the King command or call for aught, they must be wonderfully speedy and ready to obey.

Of Inferior Persons and Buffoons, Mutes, Musicians, etc., and of White Eunuchs and the Grand Officers of the Seraglio

Besides the women and the agiamoglans and itchoglans of the Seraglio, there are many other ministers who perform all sorts of necessary services. There are also buffoons, such as show tricks, musicians, wrestlers, and many mutes, both old and young, who have liberty to go in and out at the King's Gate by leave only of the Capee Agha. It is worthy the observation that in the Seraglio both the Grand Signor and divers who are about him can reason and discourse with the mutes concerning any matter both easily and distinctly, *à la mutescha*, by nods and signs, as well as they can with words—a thing well befitting the gravity of the better sort of Turks who cannot endure much babbling. Nay, the Sultanas also, and many other of the King's women, do practice it, and have many dumb women and girls about them for that purpose.

It is an ancient custom in the Seraglio to get as many mutes as they can possibly find, and chiefly for this one reason: they hold it unworthy of the greatness of the Grand Signor for him to speak familiarly to any person in his company and to make pleasantries. Therefore he takes this course so that he may the more tractably and domestically jest and talk with the mutes and engage in a diversity of pastimes.

The King besides that makes another use of the mutes. When he resolves within himself to put a vizier or someone of that rank to death, and wishes to see it done with his own eyes in the Seraglio, he first calls the man into one of his rooms and then, holding him in discourse while his mutes are in readiness (the poor man peradventure suspecting nothing), he makes but a sign unto them. At once they fall upon and strangle him, afterward drawing him by the heels out of the gates.

But that which, in my opinion, is admirable in these mutes (who are born deaf and so of necessity must remain dumb) is that many of them can write, and do so very sensibly and well. Now how they should learn without the use of hearing, I leave to others' judgments; but I am sure I have seen it, and have myself made answer unto them in writing.

It follows now that I speak of the white eunuchs. Just as the black ones are for the service of the Sultanas and the keeping of their gate, so the white eunuchs are for the King and his gate. There are four ancient and principal men amongst them, who attend only the most trusty and important employments both about the King's person and his household. The first is the Capee Agha, for he is the head of all the white eunuchs and the chamberlain; the second is the Hazinehdar Bashaw, the treasurer of the house; the third is the Keelergee Bashaw, the chief butler and master of the wardrobe; and the fourth is the Sarai Agasee, the keeper of the Seraglio.

Of these four old eunuchs, the Capee Agha (as I have said) is chief in authority and in greatest esteem with the Grand Signor. For none but he can speak openly with his Majesty without first being addressed, and neither can any messages or petitions be sent in but by his hand and means. He likewise always accompanies the King's person wherever he goes both within and without the Seraglio. And when the King visits his concubines, he waits upon him at the very door that leads unto them; but there he stops and returns to his own lodgings again, leaving somebody to wait at the door to summon him as soon as the King comes out once more.

The Capee Agha's ordinary daily pension is eight sultanees (about three pounds sterling; they are called sultanees because they are coined at Constantinople, where the Sultan lives), besides vests and other necessaries. He also gets a great store of money—indeed more than befits a man who has such small occasion of expense—by virtue of his place. Both those within the Seraglio and those abroad, of whatsoever condition or degree, present him with costly gifts so as to obtain his favor and furtherance in any business.

Should the Capee Agha die, he is succeeded by the Hazinehdar Bashaw, the eunuch in charge of the treasury within the Seraglio. He holds one key to the treasury, and the Grand Signor another, but the door is sealed with the royal seal and never taken off but when the King himself gives the order. This hazineh (treasure house) contains all the riches that have been laid up by the deceased emperors; and into it comes no other revenue of the crown but that from Egypt and the adjacent provinces, amounting to 600,000 chicquins yearly (240,000 pounds sterling). All other revenues go to the outward hazineh, out of which all expenses, both ordinary and extraordinary, are borne. But nothing may be taken out of the inward hazineh unless upon extreme necessity, when the Grand Signor is not otherwise able to appease the outcries and threatenings of the soldiers for their pay, or for the ransom of some captured prince, or for some like occasion.

The Hazinehdar Agha must keep an exact account of all the treasure brought in or taken out; nor may any person go into the hazineh but he himself and such officials as accompany him. And when there is any gold or silver taken out, it is all put into leather bags and brought to the King, who disposes of it as he thinks fit. This Agha also has custody of all the King's jewels, of which he keeps a close record, so that he may know what jewels the King gives away, what are given to the King, and what are likewise for the King's own wearing.

The Keelergee Bashaw keeps his Majesty's wardrobe, into which are brought all the presents given to the Grand Signor, such as cloth of gold, plate, silks, woolen clothes, furs of all sorts, swords, brooches, raw silk, carpets, and whatever else may serve for his Majesty's use. This eunuch has many servants under him, and stays (for the most part) within the Seraglio.

The fourth and last, the Sarai Agasee, has charge of the Seraglio. He must never go out of it, especially in the Grand Signor's absence, and is vigilant not only in seeing all things prepared for its daily service but to look over the rooms and see that they are well kept. Now because he is old and his business of importance, he has liberty to ride within the Seraglio about the courts and gardens and by the sea side, as the three former Aghas are also permitted to do: for which purpose they have a stable of horses in a garden for their use alone.

And although all four eunuchs may wear turbans and ride horses in the Seraglio, since they are the chief next to the King in authority, the three last, viz., the Hazinehdar Bashaw, the Keerlergee Bashaw, and the Sarai Agasee, may not of themselves speak when they list to the Grand Signor, but only answer when anything is asked of them.

All the eunuchs in the Seraglio, in number about 200, what with old, middle-aged, and young ones, are not only gelded but have their yards clean cut off. They are chosen, as aforesaid, of those renegade youths of the Christians presented from time to time to the Grand Signor. But few or none of them are gelded and cut against their will, for then (as the master workmen in that business all affirm) they would be in great danger of death. Wherefore, to get their consent, they are promised many things and given assurance that they may in time become high officials. This must be accomplished when they are very young, at their first coming into the Seraglio, for gelding is a work not to be wrought upon men of years.

They are brought up and instructed in the Seraglio along with the itchoglans. His Majesty likewise employs many of these white eunuchs in the government of all the other Seraglios and seminaries of youth in Constantinople, Bursia, and Adrianople [Edirne], as in divers other places. It happens many times that the Grand Signor sends forth the most ancient, richest, and high-ranking eunuchs to become Bashaws of Cairo, Aleppo, or other cities and provinces in Asia. For the eunuchs, though not of great courage, generally prove subjects of the greatest judgment and fidelity, their minds being set on business rather than pleasure.

Of the Black Eunuchs and Blackamoor Girls and Women; and of the Physicians; and of the King's Children

The black eunuchs, while they are still boys, are kept and taught among the other youths of the Seraglio, just as the white eunuchs are, until they come of age and are fit for service. Then they are appointed for the women and set to serve and wait with others of their kind at the Sultanas' gate.

They receive a pension of 50 or 60 aspars a day and two vests of silk yearly, with linen and other necessaries sufficient for their use, besides divers gifts and gratuities which they receive from visitors, especially from the Jews' women, who are daily conversant with them. The reason why their pension is so great, in comparison with others, is that they can never be sent abroad on any employment, thereby enriching themselves as others can. They must forever stay and serve in the Seraglio.

These black eunuchs are named by the names of flowers, such as Hyacinth, Narcissus, Rose, Gillyflower, and the like. The reason is that, being always near about and serving the women, their own names should be answerable to the women's virginity, sweet and undefiled.

The blackamoor girls are no sooner brought into the Seraglio after their arrival in Constantinople (for they come by ship from Cairo and there- abouts) but they are carried to the women's lodgings. There they are brought up and made fit for all services. The more ugly and deformed they are, by so much the more they are valued and esteemed by the Sultanas. Wherefore the Bashaw of Cairo, who for the most part sends them all, is diligent to get the most ill-favored that may be found throughout all Egypt, or the countries bordering on it, and send them as presents to the Grand Signor, who in turn bestows them upon his concubines. But if they should be disliked because of some infirmity, by the King's order and consent they are transported into the old Seraglio, just as the white women are when they are unfit for service or misbehave themselves.

Since the black eunuchs are often sent with messages to the Grand Signor from the Sultanas, they may pass through the gate to carry notes to the Capee Agha, so that he may deliver them to the King; otherwise they may not dare to go forth from the Seraglio without express license from the Sultana Queen. They likewise go to and fro on all other business for the Sultanas which the white enuchs cannot perform. For the white eunuchs are not permitted to come there, nor can any man that is white (but the King only) see and come amongst the women.

When one of the Sultanas has fallen sick, and it is required that the Hakim Bashaw (who is the King's physician) should come thither, he must necessarily first have leave of the Grand Signor. After being allowed to enter by the Sultanas' gate, he sees none but the black eunuchs (all the other women having retired into some withdrawing rooms), who bring him into the sick woman's chamber. She lies there closely covered from head to foot with blankets, and holds out her arm only, so that the doctor may touch her pulse; and after he has given orders about what should be done, both for her diet and medicines, he takes his leave immediately by the same way that he came.

But if the sick woman be the Queen or one of the Sultanas with whom the Grand Signor has lain but lately, then her skin and hand, which she holds out of the bed for the physician to feel her pulse, is covered with a fine piece of white silk or taffeta sarcenet. For her flesh may not be seen or touched bare, neither may the doctor say anything in her hearing. But once he has left her chamber, he prescribes what medicine he thinks fit; which for the most part (according to the knowledge and custom of the Turks) is only some kind of loosening and refreshing *sherbet* (a potion or drink or syrup). They seldom use any other physic, nor do I hold their skill sufficient to prepare medicine for a grave malady.

In case the diseased woman should have need of a surgeon, she must then suffer the doctor's handling without any scruple, for there is no remedy to conceal her skin and flesh from him. As for those women who are not Sultanas, or at least not well beloved of the Grand Signor, when they are in need of a surgeon they are sent into the old Seraglio to be cured.

The King's sons born unto him by his Queen are nursed and brought up together. If his Majesty have sons by other Sultanas also, those are brought up apart and not with the Queen's, so that every mother cares for her own children, watching over them with great envy and jealousy. Yet all the children may play together till they come to be about 6 or 7 years of age, being made much of, sumptuously maintained and appareled alike at the King's charge.

They live among the women till they come to be 9 or 10 years of age; and then about 14 they are circumcised with great pomp and solemnities throughout the whole city. For the circumcision of the Turks' children is like a Christian wedding, there being great feasting, banqueting, music, and bringing of presents.

From 5 years of age until 10, during which time they live amongst the women, they have their *hojah* (that is, their schoolmaster) appointed them by the King to teach them to read and write, and instruct them in good manners. The hojah comes once a day into the Seraglio, and is then brought into a chamber by the black eunuchs (without ever seeing the King's women at all), where the children come accompanied by two or three blackamoor women slaves. They are taught for as many hours as their tutor is permitted to stay, after which he departs.

As for the Grand Signor's daughters, they are but slightly looked after, nor is the King so tender and careful over them. For as they are not destined at all to serve the state in future times, so likewise are they not much respected. Howbeit, they are well provided for by the King, their father, in case they live to be fit for husbands.

After the *Shawh-zawedeh* (the next heir to the crown) is circumcised, if his father think it unsuitable to keep him any longer with him at home in the Seraglio, he provides him with all means necessary to go abroad and see the world. The Prince may thus learn by experience how best to govern the empire after his Majesty's decease. The King sends along with him a trusty eunuch to be his guide and overseer in all his actions, and supplies also many servants to attend upon him chosen from the Seraglio. He allows him likewise sufficient gold to maintain himself like a Prince. And so, all things having been well ordered and prepared for his journey, he takes leave of his father and mother (who present him with many gifts) and departs for Magnesia, a city in Asia, there to reside and govern the province.

Of the Cooks, Kitchens, and Diet of the King and Queen; of the Manner of Service; and of the Scullery and Provisions of the Seraglio

The victuals in the Seraglio (for the most part) are prepared and dressed by agiamoglans called *aschees* (cooks), brought up to cookery and distinguished from the other agiamoglans by their white caps. Howbeit, there belong to the kitchens of the Seraglio more than 200 undercooks and scullions, besides their principal officers, such as stewards, caters, and the like.

The King's kitchen begins to work ordinarily before break of day. For should his Highness rise early, there must always be something ready for him. He commonly eats three or four times a day, breaking his fast usually at ten of the clock in the forenoon and supping about six at night both in the summer and in the winter.

When the King has a will to eat, he tells the Capee Agha of it, who forthwith sends a eunuch to give notice to the chief steward; and he, having ordered the meat to be prepared, brings it in dish by dish to the Grand Signor's table. He then sits down after the common Turkish fashion, with his legs across, with a very richly wrought towel upon his knees to save his clothes, and another such towel hanging upon his left arm, which he uses as a napkin to wipe his mouth and fingers.

The Grand Signor is not carved unto, as other kings are, but helps himself. He has before him on a piece of Bulgar leather (which is used instead of a tablecloth) some fine white bread of three or four sorts, well relished and always very new, as indeed all Turks love their bread best when it is warm and just come forth from the oven. He uses neither knife nor fork, but only wooden spoons, of which there are two always set before him: one serving him to eat his pottage, the other to sup up certain delicate syrups, made of divers fruits compounded with the juice of lemons and sugar, to quench his thirst. He tastes his dishes one by one, and as soon as he has finished with them they are taken off. His meat is so tender, and so delicately dressed, that (as I said before) he needs no knife, but pulls the flesh from the bones very easily with his fingers. He uses no salt at his table, neither has he any antepasto, but immediately falls aboard the flesh, and having well fed, closes up his stomach with *baklava* (a tart) or some such like thing. His dinner being ended, he washes his hands in a basin of gold, the ewer being all set with precious stones.

His Majesty's ordinary diet (as I have been told by some of the aschees) is half a score of roasted pigeons in a dish, two or three geese in a dish, lamb, hens, chickens, mutton, and sometimes wild fowl, but very seldom. And whatever he has roasted for him, he has the same quantity almost of everything boiled, there being very good sauce for each dish as well as other ingredients very pleasing to the palate. He has likewise broths of all sorts, divers porcelain dishes full of preserves and syrups, some tarts, and also *burecks* (little pies), made after their fashion of flesh covered with paste. Afterward, he drinks one draught of sherbet, seldom or never drinking above once at a meal; the sherbet is brought to him by one of his Aghas in a deep porcelain dish.

All the while he is at table, he very seldom, or never, speaks to any man, according to this saying: *Evel tazavin anden kelawm* ("First victuals and then words"). There stand before him many mutes and buffoons to make him merry, playing tricks and sporting one with another *à la mutescha,* which the King understands very well, for by signs their meaning is easily conceived. And if peradventure he should vouchsafe to speak a word or two, it is to grace one of his Aghas standing by him, whom he might also favor by throwing him a loaf of bread from his own table. This is held for a singular and especial honor from the Grand Signor; and the Agha then distributes part of it amongst his companions, which they likewise accept at secondhand as a great honor done unto them, since it came from their Lord and King.

The dishes for his Highness's table are all of gold, and so likewise are their covers. They are in the custody of the Keelergee Bashaw, who attends at the kitchen at dinner and supper time, and this Bashaw also guards the yellow porcelain dishes (which are very costly, and scarcely to be had for money). The Grand Signor uses these dishes during the Ramazan time, which is their Lent, lasting a whole moon, and the month itself is so called. Now at that time, the Turks never eat in the day, but only in the night, not making any difference at all in the meats consumed, excepting swine's flesh and beasts strangled, which they are forbidden by their law to eat at any time.

The King seldom eats fish, unless it be when he is abroad at some garden house by the seaside with his women, where he may sit and see it taken himself.

The meat which remains from the table of the Grand Signor is immediately carried to the tables of the Aghas who wait upon him, so that they (what with the King's and their own diets together) are exceedingly well provided. While the Aghas are eating, the King passes the time with his mutes and buffoons, not speaking (as I said) at all with his tongue, but only by signs. And now and then he kicks and buffets them in sport; but forthwith makes them amends by giving them money, for which purpose his pockets are always furnished, so that they are well contented with that pastime.

In the women's chambers the meat is carried to them by black eunuchs, first to the Queen, then to the Sultanas, and last to all the rest, observing the same order, as aforesaid, with the King. And in the space of an hour and a half, or two at the most, all is dispatched.

The Queen's service is in copper dishes tinned over, but kept very bright and clean, and also some dishes of white porcelain. However, it is to be understood that she herself may be served as she pleases; and so questionless may all the other Sultanas, although their ordinary allowance of dishes be no other than copper. For oftentimes the King is amongst them a whole day together, eating, sporting, and sleeping. When this occurs they make him delicate and sumptuous banquets, over and above the ordinary meals, of sweetmeats and fruits of all sorts, having an abundance daily presented to them.

They drink their sherbet in the summertime mingled with snow: of which there is a great quantity preserved yearly, at great expense, to serve the Seraglio. The snow costs the treasury more than 20,000 chicquins a year to fetch it from the hills and put it underground in houses made for that purpose.

They do not ordinarily use comfits or cheese, for the Turks hardly know how to make them, especially cheese, and if they do so it rarely proves good. The Sultanas and Bashaws and other great personages eat no other cheese but parmesan, which the *bailo* (ambassador) of Venice furnishes them very plentifully. They love it well and eat heartily of it when they go abroad upon pleasure to take the air.

The Grand Signor's galleons make two voyages yearly to Alexandria, and bring out of Egypt rice, lentils, all sorts of spice, sugar, and a great quantity of preserves and pickled meats. And as for sugar, there is spent an unspeakable deal of it in the making of sherbets and baklavas. True it is that but little spice is used in the Seraglio, nor among the Turks in general (pepper only excepted); for as wine is not an ordinary drink among them, they therefore avoid eating such things as provoke the desire to drink wine.

The Turks are no whit acquainted with fresh butter, there being little or none at all made about Constantinople. Neither do they drink much milk, unless it be made sour, which they call *yoghurt*. Both they and the Christians eat a great deal in the summertime to quench their thirst. They also eat a store of *kaymak* (that is, clotted cream), but that is a dish for the better sort only, being too costly for the vulgar.

Now, as for flesh, every year in the late autumn the Bashaw orders a provision of *basturma* (so called because the flesh is pressed and made flat) to be made for the King's kitchens. Basturma must come of cows great with calf, for then (say they) the flesh is most tender and savory. They use it in the same manner as Christians do swine's flesh, for they make puddings and sausages of it. There are commonly spent 400 cows every year for the provision of basturma in the Seraglio.

The Grand Signor (nor any of his women or servants) cannot want for fruit, for at each season all sorts of fruits are brought to the Seraglio in great abundance, especially figs, grapes, and melons, besides what comes from the King's own gardens. The gardeners sell the remainder at a place in Constantinople where only the Grand Signor's fruit is sold, and bring the money weekly to the Bustangee Bashaw, who afterward gives it to his Majesty. It is called *jebbe akchafee,* that is, the King's pocket money, for he gives it away by handfuls, as he sees occasion, to his mutes and buffoons at such times as they make him sport.

Of Apparel, Bedding, Sickness, Hospitals, Inheritance, the King's Expenses, Recreations, Receiving of Petitions, etc., and of the King's Stables and Byram *Solemnities*

The Grand Signor's apparel is no different in fashion from other men's, except in the length of his vests and their richness; nor are his shoes plated with iron at the heels, like those of other Turks, but rather incised with designs and painted with knots and flowers as are children's shoes. The fashion of his turban is the same as that of the Bashaws, but in his he wears plumes and brooches. No other Bashaw may do so except the Vizier Azem, and that is upon the day when he makes a solemn show at his departure for the wars.

As for his lodging, the King sleeps upon mattresses of velvet and cloth of gold: in the summer in sheets of *shash* (the whole piece, long or short, of fine linen) embroidered with silk sewn to the quilts, and in the winter betwixt coverlets of lynx fur and sable. For a nightcap he wears a *gheje-lick,* or little sash, upon his head.

When his Highness lies alone upon his bed he is always watched by the pages of his chamber, two at a time, changing their watch every three hours. One of them stands at the chamber door and the other by the bedside to cover him in case the sheets or furs should slide off, and also to be near in case his Majesty should want anything or be ill at ease. In the chamber where he lies are always two old women who wait with burning torches in their hands, which they may not put out until the King is risen out of his bed. The use of these lights is for his Majesty to say over his beads and to pray in case his devotions are stirred up at midnight or at *Temcheet namaz,* which is about two hours before daylight.

The clothes of his women are much like those of the men, for they wear *chackfirs* (breeches, from the waist down to heel) and buskins too, and the meaner sort also have their shoes shod with iron at the heels. They likewise sleep as the men do, in their linen breeches and quilted vests, having thin and light ones for the summer and more thick and warm ones for the winter.

The Turks never have any closestools or such like utensils in their chambers; but feeling necessity, they rise and go to the privies, made in places apart, where there always stand pots full of water, so that they may wash when they have done. They use no paper in that service, as other nations do, holding it not only an indecent but an extraordinary absurdity for a Mussulman to put paper to so base a use, seeing that both the name of God and the Mohammedan law are written upon paper. They all remove their turbans when they go about that business; and a Janissary may by no means piss with his *uskuf* (cap) upon his head, but having done, he must kiss it and then put it on again. For they hold the covering of the head to be as honorable in a manner as the head itself.

When anyone dies in the Seraglio, whether it be itchoglan or agiamoglan, his chamber fellows are made his heirs, and that which he leaves behind him is equally divided amongst them. So is it also with the young wenches who never lay with the King. But if any great eunuch die, all comes to the Grand Signor, for they are always very rich by reason of the manifold gifts and gratuities which daily come into their hands.

The expenses of the Seraglio are vast, as one may gather by what has already been said. But there are moreover divers other charges, stipends to the Sultana Queen, to the other Sultanas, to the chief viziers, to the *Serdars* (captains, or generals) of his forces both by sea and land, to the great Defterdars, and to many others, to all of whom he gives gratuities as he sees fit upon sundry occasions. The Hazinehdar Bashaw, who has the keeping of the cloth of gold and silver of Bursia, affirms that for stuff to make vests of alone, there is spent yearly 200,000 sultanees, besides what the King disburses for buying Venetian silks and woolen clothes, of which the Seraglio consumes a large quantity. Were his Majesty not the heir to much of the spoil of the deceased, he could not long continue his liberality, for true it is that the greatest part of what he gives away, in time comes back again into his hands. And so of such things there is a continual ebbing and flowing in the Seraglio.

The King may please to go abroad at any time, either by water or by land. When he goes by water he has a kaik of sixteen or eighteen banks, with a very sumptuous and stately poop, covered over with richly embroidered crimson velvet, under which he himself sits, and none but he, upon cushions of cloth of gold. His Aghas stand all upon their feet, holding with one hand to the side of the kaik; and only the Bustangee Bashaw, who steers the barge, may sit down now and then so that he may handle the helm better. Now the Bustangee Bashaw, because the King talks much with him in the kaik (at which time, lest anyone overhear what they say, the mutes fall howling like little dogs), may benefit or prejudice the King against any person he please.

The kaik is rowed by agiamoglans brought up in that exercise, and indeed they manage the business very nimbly, not sitting when they row but, as they fetch their stroke, stepping up upon the next bank before them, and so after the stroke fall backward flat upon their backs onto the next bank behind them, much resembling the manner of rowing in the galleys.

When the King goes forth by land, he always rides on horseback and leaves by the great gate, especially at such times as he intends to pray in the mosque on a Friday, which is their sabbath. Then he is accompanied by all the Bashaws and other grandees, with divers *Solacks* (bowmen) carrying their bows and arrows preceding him as his guard. And as he rides along the streets, he salutes the people by nodding his head toward them, who in turn acclaim him with loud shouts and prayers for his prosperity and happiness. The King oftentimes puts his hand into his pocket and throws whole handfuls of money amongst them as recompense.

The Bashaws of the Seraglio, who ride along by his stirrup, have orders to take all petitions from the people to his Majesty as he goes either to or from the mosque. Many poor men, who dare not presume by reason of their ragged apparel to approach near so majestic a presence, stand afar off with lit candles on their heads, and hold up their petitions, or *arzes,* in their hands. When the Grand Signor sees them (and he never despises, but rather encourages, the poor), he immediately sends a Bashaw to collect them. Once returned to the Seraglio, he reads them all and then gives an order for redress as he thinks fit.

As a consequence of these complaints, the King sometimes executes the fury of his wrath even upon the highest personages before they are aware, without taking any course in law against them, and either puts them to death or turns them out of their places. For as he styles himself *Awlem*

Penawh (The World's Refuge), so he would have the world take notice that those who lament unto him shall be sure to have redress and succor.

For this reason the Bashaws and other great officers fear to see the Grand Signor stir abroad in public, lest their bad proceedings and injustice come to his ear. Indeed they always live in great danger of losing their lives at short warning (as it has often been observed, few viziers die in their beds), which makes them cite this proverb: "Even the greatest in office is but a statue of glass."

The Grand Signor is bound by canon of the empire to show himself publicly upon the first day of the *Byram,* their carnival, and to let all the great men and the better sort of his own servants to kiss his vest. Upon that day, richly clad and bedecked with jewels, he comes forth early in the morning and sets himself down in a certain place called the *Taht* (a throne), upon a Persian carpet of silk and gold, and does not stir until all who are appointed to do so have kissed his vest.

Every night during the three days of the Byram he orders shows of fireworks by the waterside, which continue until morning while a great drum is beaten by his itchoglans. So that the Sultanas may see them, the King comes of purpose into their company to be merry, and is more free and familiar than at other times. He also gives liberty for mirth and sports both day and night throughout the whole city during those three days. To these great festivals are invited all the Sultanas who live outside the Seraglio, and they give presents to the Grand Signor of shirts, handkerchiefs, linen breeches, towels, and the like, all curiously wrought, which he afterwards makes use of for his own person.

During this feast it is somewhat troublesome and dangerous for the poor Christians and Jews to walk along the streets. For the Turks being then somewhat troublesome and full of wine, putting off the sobriety of the Ramazan, at which time they drink no strong drink at all, do scare them exceedingly, often threatening to mischief them if they deny them money. They count nothing so strange in our garments as our codpieces, which seem to them very dishonest. And if a band of Turks find any Christian man, especially a man of war, in a place where they may overcome him, they cut off his codpiece. For they are very presumptuous, great boasters, and generally so proud that they think no nation in the world to be like themselves; wherefor if God permits their strength to prevail it is because of our sins, not because of their wisdom or virtue.

Charles I

Painting by Edward Bower, 1648. Royal Collection, London, England.

When I consider everything that grows
Holds in perfection but a little moment,
That this huge stage presenteth nought but shows
Whereon the stars in secret influence comment . . .

William Shakespeare, Sonnet 15

The late Duke of Windsor, formerly King Edward VIII, while still in his regal chrysalis at the age of 12 as Prince of Wales, was once forced by his fellow students of the Royal Naval College on the Isle of Wight to undergo a sadistic hazing that must have left a lasting scar on his psyche. "An empty classroom window," he wrote in his memoirs, "was raised far enough to push my head through, and then banged down on my neck, a crude reminder ['Remember!' cried Charles on the scaffold] of the sad fate of Charles I and the British capacity to deal with royalty who displeased."

What makes this reminder even cruder and grimmer is that the incident occurred on the Isle of Wight, for it was there, at Carisbrook Castle, that the Stuart king was finally trapped by the radical regicide faction of the army led by Oliver Cromwell. In an attempt to escape through a narrow window of the castle to the courtyard below, where his agents were waiting with a team of horses to spirit him off to a ship and safety in France, Charles unfortunately got stuck, unable to move backward or forward, and remained half suspended in mid-air with his arms outstretched, which was the same posture he later assumed on the block at his beheading.

But then again, the tragedy of Charles I contains several such seemingly uncanny coincidences, as if the scenario of his doom had been plotted by some malevolent Fate or Hardyesque "Spirit of the Ironies" long before it was actually staged on the Theatrum Mundi. For instance, there was that gruesome but proleptic moment during his trial when, in order to gain the attention of a solicitor, the King laid his staff "gently" upon his arm, whereupon its silver head happened to fall off and roll to the floor. "This," remarks the clerk who was assigned by the court to write The Official Report of the Trial, "by some was considered a bad omen." And, for another, what weird casting director except chance itself would have assigned the role of guards to the King after his arrest to two officers with the preposterous names Colonel Hacker and Colonel Hunks?

"Coincidences," states Aristotle in the Poetics, "are the most striking when they have an air of design." Speculating on the sometimes strange confabulations of art and life, he goes on to cite an event that occurred in his own time, when "the statue of the tyrant Mitys at Argos fell upon his murderer while the man was a spectator at a festival, and killed him. Such events," he comments darkly, "seem not to be due to mere chance." To what then? But he leaves the question dangling without an answer, citing instead a somewhat cryptic epigram by the tragic poet Agathon: "It is probable that many things should happen contrary to probability."

As it happened, the people of England at the time, who were themselves both spectators of, and actors in, Charles's tragedy, were struck by its theatrical nature. His execution at Whitehall seemed to them the inevitable result of an historical course of events that couldn't—because, in retrospect, it didn't—have occurred otherwise. Even more so than the French Revolution a century and a half later, his martyrdom also signaled the decapitation of the Divine Right of kings; and (as the poet Andrew Marvell wrote not long after) it brought "To ruine the great Work of Time, / And cast the Kingdome old / Into another Mold." The ode containing these lines, however, was addressed not to the King but to the victorious Oliver Cromwell, next to Charles himself the chief player in the "memorable Scene":

> Where, twining subtile fears with hope,
> He wove a Net of such a scope,
> > That Charles himself might chase
> > To Caresbrooks narrow case.
> That thence the Royal Actor born
> The Tragic Scaffold might adorn:
> > While round the arméd Bands
> > Did clap their bloody hands.

283

> *He nothing common did or mean*
> *Upon that memorable Scene,*
> > *But with his keener Eye*
> > *The Axes edge did try:*
> *Nor call'd the Gods with vulgar spight*
> *To vindicate his helpless Right,*
> > *But bow'd his comely Head,*
> > *Down as upon a bed.*

Of course, there had to be an Epilogue. Upon the restoration of the monarchy and Charles II's return from exile in France, the new King heeded his father's last word: "Remember!" The royalists now took revenge on all who had participated in the trial and execution of Charles I. The corpses of Cromwell, his son-in-law Henry Ireton, together with that of John Bradshaw, who had presided as Chief Justice during the trial, were disinterred from Westminster Abbey and exposed for a day to the populace on the gallows at Tyburn, after which their heads were cut off and stuck on poles on top of Westminster Hall. Most of those who had signed the parliamentary death warrant for Charles I were still alive at the time of the Restoration; of these several escaped by fleeing to the Continent or to the American colonies, a few were granted amnesty, and many others were tried and either executed as traitors or imprisoned for life. Colonel Hacker suffered the savage punishment of being hanged until half dead, then disemboweled and, it so happened, hacked into quarters. Colonel Hunks, who gave evidence against his former comrades, was spared. Only after a generation had left the scene was there a general catharsis of the emotions of pity and terror aroused by Charles I's tragedy.

As prelude, certain facts about the King should be mentioned. Charles Stuart, second son of James VI of Scotland (afterward James I of England) and Anne of Denmark, was born in Denfermline, Scotland. Small and sickly as a child, he was brought to England in 1604, at which time he could neither walk nor talk. He suffered from a speech impediment and a misshapen leg all his life. Upon his accession in 1625, he married Henrietta Maria, a daughter of Henry IV of France, who was a devout Catholic and celebrated mass regularly in the palace. The King himself was brought up as a Presbyterian, but later joined the Church of England. His three closest advisors, who pushed him toward absolutism, all met with disastrous ends: George Villiers, the Duke of Buckingham, was assassinated in 1628 by a Puritan fanatic, and both Thomas Wentworth (the Earl of Strafford) and Archbishop Laud were executed, in 1641 and in 1645 respectively. Financial difficulties compelled the King to summon Parliament, which attempted to curb his power; and this in turn led to the Civil War that broke out in 1642.

The narrative of Charles I's climactic years in this book has been taken mainly from Sir Thomas Herbert's memoirs, which were first published in 1678 under the title Threnodia Carolina *and reprinted thereafter many times as part of a volume entitled* Memoirs of the two last years of the Reign of the unparallel'd Prince, of ever Blessed Memory, King Charles I. *Herbert (1606–82), a diplomat and world traveler who had spent several years in exploration of the remote parts of Asia and Africa, was one of the commission appointed by Parliament to guard and attend the King after his surrender. According to the historian C. V. Wedgwood, in her* A Coffin for King Charles *(New York: The Macmillan Co., 1964), Herbert was a "sly, hard man with a keen sense of his own advantage." She concludes that Herbert "was not devoted to the King, though he seems to have been efficient and civil." However, he succeeded so well in persuading others of his loyalty to Charles I that after the Restoration he was given a baronetcy by Charles II.*

Charles I in Captivity

With the decisive defeat of the Royalist cause at the Battle of Naseby, on June 14, 1645, the Civil War in England drew to a close. Charles I surrendered himself several months later, in May of 1646, to the Scottish forces that had marched to the aid of Parliament, and was held by them at the town of Newcastle in Scotland. However, he continued to parley and to temporize with Parliament, hoping to profit from the growing breach between the moderate Captain-General Thomas Fairfax and the more intransigent military chieftains, Oliver Cromwell and Henry Ireton. But the Scots, in return for their back pay of 400,000 pounds, were persuaded to yield Charles to Parliament, which then dispatched a commission to take the King from Newcastle to Holmby, in Northamptonshire, on January 30, 1647.

Here he remained for five months, until June 4, 1647, when a detachment of cavalry sent by the army arrived suddenly and without warning.

His Majesty being one afternoon at bowls in the green at Althorpe, it was whispered amongst the Commissioners, who were then at bowls with the King, that a party of Horse, obscurely headed, was marching toward Holmby.

Whereupon the King, so soon as he was acquainted with it, immediately left the green and returned to Holmby, and the Commissioners forthwith doubled the guards for the defense of his Majesty's person. Major-General Browne, calling all the soldiers together, acquainted them with the occasion. They promised to stand by him, and not suffer any attempt upon the King's person or affront to the Commissioners. But the difference is great 'twixt saying and doing, as soon appeared.

For about midnight came that party of Horse, which in good order drew up before the house at Holmby, and placed guards at all avenues. Which done, the officer that commanded the party alighted and demanded entrance. Colonel Graves and Major-General Browne asked him his name and business. He replied his name was Joyce, a cornet in Colonel Whaley's regiment, and his business was to speak with the King.

"From whom?" said they.

"From myself," said he, at which they laughed. "It's no laughing matter," said Joyce.

They then advised him to draw off his men, and in the morning he should speak with the Commissioners.

"I came not hither to be advised by you," said he, "nor have I any business with the Commissioners. My errand is with the King, and speak with him I must, and will presently."

They then bade the soldiers within stand to their arms, and be ready to fire when ordered. But during this short treaty 'twixt the cornet and the colonel, the soldiers had conference together, and so soon as they understood they were fellow soldiers of one and the same army, they quickly forgot what they had promised. For they opened the gates and doors, shook one another by the hand, and bade them welcome. So little regard had they for their promise, either in reference to the King's safety or the Commissioners that attended him.

Entrance being thus given, strict search was made after the colonel, who (though he was faultless, yet was it suggested he would have privately conveyed the King to London) got happily out of their reach. Sentinels were ordered by Joyce to be set at the Commissioners' chamber doors, that he might with less noise carry on his design and find way to the back stairs, where the grooms of his Majesty's bed-chamber attended.

The cornet, being come to the door in rude manner, knocked; those within asking who it was that in such uncivil manner and so unseasonable a time came to disquiet the King's rest. The cornet replied that his name was Joyce, an officer of the army, sorry he should disquiet the King, but could not help it, for speak with him he would, and that presently.

This strange confidence of his, and the posture he was in (having a cocked pistol in his hand), amazed these four gentlemen, Mr. Maxwell, Mr. Mawl, Mr. Harrington, and Mr. Herbert, whose duty it was and care to preserve his Majesty's person, and were resolved to sacrifice their lives rather than give him admittance. They in the first place asked Joyce if he had the Commissioners' approbation for his intrusion. He answered no; for he had ordered a guard to be set at their chamber doors, and that he had his orders from those that feared them not. He still presssed for entrance, and engaged his word to do the King no harm. They on the other side persuaded him to lay aside his arms and to forbear giving disturbance, the King being then asleep, assuring him that the next morning he should have his Majesty's answer to his errand.

The cornet refused to part with either sword or pistol, and yet insisted to have the chamber door opened. But these gentlemen keeping firm to their resolution that he should not enter, the noise was so loud (which in this contest could not be avoided) as, it seems, awakened his Majesty, for he rung his silver bell. At which Mr. Maxwell went into the bed-chamber to know the King's pleasure, the other three gentlemen meanwhile securing the door. The King, being acquainted with the business and uncivil carriage of the cornet, sent word he would not rise nor speak with him until the morning, which being told the cornet, he huffed. But seeing his design could not be effected in the night, he retired. So for a few hours there was silence.

Morning being come, the King arose a little sooner than ordinary; and, having performed his morning exercise, he sent for Joyce, who with no less confidence than if he had been a supreme officer, approached the King, and acquainted him with the commands he had concerning his removal. The King desired the Commissioners might be sent for and his orders communicated to them. The cornet replied that they were to return back unto the Parliament.

"By whose appointment?" said the King. As to that, the cornet had no answer. The King then said, "By your favor, Sir, let them have their liberty, and give me a sight of your instructions."

"That," said Joyce, "you shall see presently," forthwith drawing up his troops into the inner court as near as he could unto the King. "These, Sir," said he, "are my instructions."

The King took a good view of them, and finding them proper men and well mounted and well armed, smilingly told the cornet his instructions were in fair characters, legible without spelling. The cornet then pressed the King to go along with him; but the King replied he would not stir unless the Commissioners went as well. The cornet said that, for his part, he was indifferent.

However, the Commissioners in this interim had, by an express, acquainted the Parliament with this violence. And so soon as they perceived his Majesty was inclinable to go with Joyce, and that it was the King's pleasure they should follow him they knew not whither, they immediately made themselves ready. Nevertheless, they asked several questions of the cornet, whose answers were insignificant. The Commissioners then seeing reason was of no force to dissuade, nor menaces to affright, they were willing to attend the King at all adventures.

This audacious attempt exceedingly troubled the Commissioners, the more so because they knew not how to help it, as well appeared by their countenances. And indeed it saddened the hearts of many. The King was the merriest of the company, having (it seems) a confidence in the army, especially in some of the greatest [of the generals] there, as it was imagined.

The King (then being in his coach) called the Earls of Pembroke and Denbigh, as also the Lord Montague, into it; the other Commissioners (members of the House of Commons) being well-mounted, followed, leaving Holmby languishing. For about two years after, that beautiful and famous structure was, amongst other of his Majesty's royal houses, pulled down by order of the two Houses of Parliament.

"Twining Subtle Fears with Hope"

About the middle of August the King removed to Hampton Court, a most large and imperial house, built by that pompous prelate Cardinal Wolsey in ostentation of his great wealth, and then enlarged by King Henry VIII, so that it became a royal palace exceeded for beauty and grandeur by no structure in Europe, unless it be the Escorial in Spain. Hampton Court was then made ready and prepared with what was needful for the court. And a court it now appeared to be, for there was a revival of that luster it had formerly possessed when his Majesty had had the nobility about him, his chaplains to perform their duty, the house amply furnished, and his services in the accustomed form and state.

The Commissioners also continued their attendance upon the King, and those gentlemen that waited upon him at Holmby were, by his Majesty's appointment, kept in their offices and places. The General [Fairfax, commander in chief of the army, soon to be superseded by Cromwell and Ireton] likewise and other military commanders were much at court, and had frequent conference with the King in the park. No offense at any time passed amongst the soldiers of either party, and there was an amnesty by consent pleasing, as was thought, to all parties.

His Majesty, during these halcyon days, intimated to the Earl of Northumberland that he desired to see his children, who at the time were under the government of that nobleman in his house at Sion, which is about seven miles from Hampton Court, on the way to London. Here the King met the young Duke of Gloucester and Princess Elizabeth, who, so soon as they saw their royal father, upon their knees they begged his blessing. The Earl welcomed the King very nobly, by his behavior expressing extraordinary contentment to see the King and his children together after such various chances and so long a separation. Night drawing on, his Majesty returned to Hampton Court.

Negotiations between Charles and the leaders of the rebellion came to an impasse at Hampton Court when the more radical faction of the House of Commons, led by Cromwell, presented him with certain unacceptable demands. The King therefore determined to escape from the army's control and place himself once more under the protection of Parliament.

At this time some active and malevolent persons of the army, disguised under the specious name of "Agitators," began intermeddling with affairs of state. Several things in design were rumored, which fomented parties and created jealousies and fears.

In the night, and in disguise, accompanied by two grooms, his Majesty passed through a private door into the park, where no sentinel was; and at Thames-Ditton crossed the river, to the amazement of the Commissioners, who had not the least foreknowledge or apprehension of the King's fears or intentions.

After a few days it was known that the King had crossed the sea and was safe landed at Cowes in the Isle of Wight. The Governor, with alacrity and confidence, conducted his Majesty to Carisbrook Castle, attended only by Sir John Berkley and those two gentlemen, his servants, lately mentioned. Sure I am that many who cordially loved the King did very much dislike his going to this place, it being so remote and designed neither for his honor nor safety; as the consequences proved.

"To Carisbrook's Narrow Case"

Carisbrook Castle is the only place of defense within that island, albeit upon the marine it has many forts, or blockhouses. Its name is derived from Whitgare, a Saxon word corruptly contracted to garisbrook.

Thither (so soon as the King's being there was rumored) repaired several of his old servants and some new, such as his Majesty at that time thought fit to nominate. For some weeks there was no prohibition, so that anyone desirous to see his Majesty might do so without opposal. His Majesty had free liberty to ride and recreate himself anywhere within the isle, when and where he pleased; the only want was that his chaplains, Dr. Sheldon and Dr. Hammond, were not long tolerated to perform their office, which was no little grief to him.

Howbeit, this liberty was of no long duration. For about the middle of February, Colonel Hammond, the Governor, soon after the King arose from dinner came into the presence and in solemn manner addressed himself to him. After a short preamble, he said that he was sorry to acquaint his Majesty with the orders he had received the night before from his superiors; and then, pausing awhile, the King bade him speak. The Governor replied that his orders were to forbid Mr. Ashburnham, Mr. Legg, and the rest of the servants who had served him at Oxford any further waiting on his person.

The King, by his short silence, seemed surprised and troubled.

King Charles: "Why do you use me thus? Where are your orders for it? Was it the spirit that moved you to it? . . . Did you not engage your honor you would take no advantage from thence against me?"

Hammond: "I said nothing."

King Charles: "You are an equivocating gentleman. Will you allow me any chaplains? You pretend for liberty of conscience—shall I have none?"

Hammond: "I cannot allow you any chaplain."

King Charles: "You use me neither like a gentleman nor a Christian."

Hammond: "I'll speak to you when you are in better temper."

King Charles: "I have slept well tonight."

Hammond: "I have used you very civilly."

King Charles: "Why do you not do so now, then?"

Hammond: "Sir, you are too high."

King Charles: "My shoemaker's fault, then—my shoes are of the same last. Shall I have liberty to go about to take the air?"

Hammond: "No, I cannot grant it."

Upon hearing of the Governor's orders, his Majesty's servants were much perplexed, yet knew that to expostulate with Colonel Hammond would be to no purpose. The only comfort remaining was that they were not excluded from their royal master's affection, which supported them. Next day, after the King had dined, those gentlemen came all together and prostrated themselves at his Majesty's feet, prayed God for his preservation, and, kissing his hand, departed.

The day following, a restraint began of the King's going any more abroad into the Isle of Wight, his Majesty being confined to Carisbrook Castle and the line without, albeit within the works. It was a place sufficiently large and convenient for the King's walking and having good air, with a delightful prospect both to the sea and land. For his Majesty's solace, the Governor converted the barbican, a spacious parading ground within the line, though without the castle, into a bowling green scarce to be equaled, and at one side built a pretty summer house for retirement. At vacant hours these afforded the King most of his recreation, for the building within the castle walls had no gallery, nor rooms of state, nor garden. However, he carefully observed his usual times set apart for his devotion and for writing.

Notwithstanding this restraint, which the Governor was strict in (probably in pursuance of his instructions), nevertheless several diseased persons troubled with the Evil [the "King's Evil," or scrofula], resorted thither from remote parts to be touched. When the King went out of the castle toward his usual walk about the barbican, they had their wished opportunity to present themselves afore him, and he touched them.*

An Attempted Rescue

(Narrated by Mr. Henry Firebrace, once clerk of the Kitchen to his Majesty Charles I.)

I had the honor to be known to his Majesty by several services I had done him in the time of the Treaty of Uxbridge, at Oxford, and other places; and being at Newcastle when the Scots delivered his Majesty to the

---

* That Charles I was called upon to exercise the numenal power supposedly possessed by kings to cure scrofula (a tubercular swelling of the lymph glands in the neck) by their touch, indicates that, despite his captivity, he was still regarded by the people as their lawful sovereign. The superstition re the king's touch persisted until fairly recent times. Dr. Samuel Johnson, who suffered from the disease, was led up to Queen Anne in 1712 when a small boy to be touched. The last known occasion of royal healing by touch occurred in 1825, when Charles X of France attempted to revive the practice.

English, I did (by his directions, to the end I might serve him with greater freedom and less suspicion of those who had him in custody) make my application to some of the Commissioners, that I be admitted to attend his Majesty, as one of the pages of the bed-chamber, in which I prevailed.

They presently conveyed his Majesty to Holmby, where they kept him under a guard, but very few servants to attend him, especially of such as he could trust, which rendered my services the more useful to his Majesty.

In this interim, the two great factions of the time, Presbyterian and Independent, differed, the latter prevailed, and removed his Majesty to Hampton Court, upon pretense of restoring him to his throne. But having gained their prey, the King soon after discovered their falsehood, and that they intended nothing less than what they pretended. He looked upon his life in danger, to preserve which he put himself upon that journey, when he left Hampton Court privately, in a dark and rainy night, about the middle of November, and was unfortunately brought to the Isle of Wight, whither I am confident (by what his Majesty several times after said to me) he did not intend to go. But what fate brought him thither I could never learn.

So soon as it was publicly known where his Majesty was, having received a private letter from him to hasten to him, and with what intelligence I could get after I had acquainted his most faithful friends about London with my going, as his Majesty had commanded me, I got leave of the Speaker of the House of Commons, and his pass, to go (for I had still kept myself out of their suspicion). My first endeavor after my arrival was how to give his Majesty an account of business, and to put into his hands safely those letters I had for him (for there were continually spies upon him). To which purpose, I found out a very convenient and private place in his bed-chamber, where I left papers, of which I gave him an account that night by putting a note into his hand as he was preparing to go to bed; which paper he found.

Next morning after his retirement at his private devotions (of which he never failed), I found his paper in the same place; by which sign his Majesty was pleased to express his satisfaction in what I had done. He directed the continuance of that way and place for converse, which we made use of (for we had no better) for many weeks. I had settled a very good way of correspondence with his Majesty's friends at London, having two men very faithful and unsuspected constantly going and coming, by which means his Majesty never wanted good intelligence from the Queen, the Prince, and many of his friends.

At length I found favor in the eyes of those men appointed by Colonel Hammond to wait at the two doors of the King's bed-chamber by day when his Majesty was there, and to lodge there by night—their beds being laid close to the doors, so that they could not open until the beds were removed. His Majesty constantly went into his bed-chamber so soon as he had supped, shutting the doors to him. I offered my service to one of those conservators to wait at the door opening into the backstairs whilst the man went to his own supper, I pretending not to sup, which offer he accepted, and so I had freedom of speaking with his Majesty.

Then, lest we might be surprised by anyone too suddenly rushing into the bed-chamber, and so discover the bed-chamber door open (for so it was, that we might hear each other the better), I made a slit or chink through the wall behind the hanging, which served as well as the opening of the door and was more safe. Upon the least noise, by letting fall the hanging, all was well. By this means we had opportunity to discourse often of several ways for his Majesty's escape (for his imprisonment was then intolerable).

Amongst other ways I proposed his coming out of his bed-chamber window, which he said he could do, there being room enough. I told him, I feared it was too narrow. He said, he'd tried with his head, and he was sure where that would pass the body would follow. Yet still I doubted, proposing a way to make it a little wider by cutting the plate the casement shut to at the bottom. He objected that might make a discovery, and commanded me to prepare all things else, for he was confident the window would not impede him.

I planned for this escape with Mr. Worsly (now Sir Edward Worsly, a very worthy gentleman, still living in the island); Mr. Richard Osburne, a gentleman put in by the Parliament to attend the King; and Mr. John Newland of Newport, who all proved very faithful. And thus we were to proceed—I should toss something against the window, this being the sign for his Majesty to put himself out and to let himself down by a cord which I, for that purpose, had given him.

Once down and in the dark night, I was to conduct him through the court (no sentinel being in the way) to the great wall of the castle, where I was to have let him down by a long cord, a stick being fastened across at the end for him to sit on. Beyond this wall was the counterscarp, which was low; beyond that, and quite out of the castle, waited Mr. Worsly and Mr. Osburne on horseback, with a good horse, saddle and pistols, boots, etc., for the King. They were to help his Majesty from the counterscarp, which they could easily do from their horses.

At the seaside, in a convenient place, was Mr. John Newland with a lusty boat, which might have carried his Majesty to what part he thought fit. All things were thus prepared, and everyone well instructed in his part. The King, as he walked, had been often showed the place by me where he was to be let down, and where he was to get over the counterscarp, a plan which his Majesty well approved of.

In the middle of these hopes I gave the sign at the appointed time. His Majesty put himself forward; but then, too late, found himself mistaken, he sticking fast between his breast and his shoulders and not able to get forward or backward.

Yet at the instant before he endeavored to come out, he had mistrusted his efforts and tied a piece of his cord to a bar of the window within, by means whereof he forced himself back.

Whilst he stuck I heard him groan but could not come to help him, which (you may imagine) was no small affliction to me. So soon as he was in again, to let me see (as to my grief I had heard) the design was broken, he set a candle in the window. If this unfortunate impediment had not happened, his Majesty had then most certainly made a good escape.

Now I was in pain how to give notice to those without, which I could find no better way to do than by flinging stones from the high wall, where I should have set down the King, to the place where they were waiting. This proved effectual, so that they went off, and no discovery was ever made. After this I sent for files and aquafortis from London to make the passage more easy, and to help in other designs I proposed.

Before we could effect them, however, a letter came from Derby House to Hammond to direct him to have a careful eye on those about the King, for they had discovered there were some that gave him intelligence. This was a general suspicion; they could point at nobody. Hammond set his engines to work and did pump me; so, I heard, he did others. But at last he took me into examination and, when he could make no discovery, told me the reason.

I acquainted the King with all these passages, at which he was much troubled. He told me that if they had a suspicion of me, they would never leave till they had ruined me. The King would have me gone with his letters to the Prince [of Wales, later Charles II], his son, but I told his Majesty, I was confident they could prove nothing against me, and therefore begged I might stay to see the issue. If the worst happened, they could but put me away, and then I did not doubt but I should be able, some way or other, to serve his Majesty.

After this, Hammond sent for me again and told me he had received other letters, and that he must dismiss me, as he should do others; but that I might stay, if I would, three or four days. This I looked upon as a trap; however, I accepted of it, but carried myself cautiously. I acquainted the King, and settled such a way of correspondence that his Majesty did not want constant intelligence from his friends as before. He had his dispatches brought carefully to me, and sent them away with the like good success as formerly, during the whole time I was from him.

In my absence, another attempt was made for his Majesty's escape by those I had engaged, but it was unhappily discovered in the execution. Mr. Worsly and Mr. Osburne (who waited as before) fled by the help of the boat that was to have carried away his Majesty. They came to me to London, where I obscured and preserved them.

At this time, the King signed a "Treaty"—framed at Newport on the Isle of Wight—in which he largely capitulated to the demands of Parliament while still insisting on his own sovereignty. However, Cromwell and Ireton and the Levellers in England distrusted Charles's intentions, and were determined to bring him to trial. On December 6, 1648, Colonel Thomas Pride and his troops forcibly excluded from the House of Commons all who had voted for the Treaty ("Pride's Purge"), and the Parliament that remained was thenceforth known as the "Rump."

When the Treaty was voted, amongst those his Majesty named to attend him I had the honor to be one; of which he was pleased to give me notice by a letter, and commanded me to make haste to him. I no sooner arrived than his Majesty told me I should attend him as I did before—which was page of the bed-chamber and clerk of the kitchen—for there must be several diets at the Treaty, and he would have me undertake it.

I desired to be excused, as not at all understanding the employment. He was pleased to tell me he would instruct me (which in earnest he did). Within two or three days I heard that a gentleman, one of his Majesty's clerks of the kitchen, was come to Newport, in expectation of waiting in his employment; and then I desired his Majesty that this man might wait accordingly, I being unskillful. The King was pleased to tell me again I should undertake it, and that that gentleman should wait as Clerk Comptroller, as accordingly we did.

The Treaty being begun at Newport in the Isle of Wight, we did all hope for a happy conclusion thereof, his Majesty having granted whatever they could ask, saving his conscience and the damnation of his soul (which his Majesty once told me he thought they aimed at). But our hopes were all blasted when the army, thirsting for his blood, sent a party into the island to secure him; which was so suddenly and privately done that there was no notice or appearance of them until the night they began their horrid tragedy, the twenty-ninth of November, 1648.

The King had commanded me to attend him that night at eight of the clock for a packet he was preparing for me to send to the Queen. But before that hour I perceived some soldiers with pistols in their hands busily prying about the house where the King was lodged. This, together with the news of a party newly arrived, put me into great apprehension of the King's danger. And, therefore, not staying till the time his Majesty appointed me, I knocked at the bed-chamber door, which his Majesty had commanded me to do at any time when I had business with him, using a knock which he knew and had directed me to use. He presently opened me the door, and seeing me appear in a great astonishment, asked me, "What is the matter?"

I answered, "God Almighty preserve your Majesty, for I much fear some dismal attempt upon your person." Then I told him what I had seen and heard.

He was pleased to lay his hand upon mine, and use these or the like words: "Firebrace, be not affrighted, things will be well. You know Hammond is this day gone for London, and he hath appointed three deputies in his absence. These will be trebly diligent, and it may be will set a treble guard upon me, but I am assured there will be no danger."

I replied, "Ah, Sir, I much fear you are deceived. For God's sake, think of your safety. There is yet a door of hope open—the night is dark, and I can now safely bring you into the street, and thence conduct you to your old friend Mr. John Newland, who hath a good boat always ready and a good heart to serve you. Commit yourself to the mercy of the seas, where God will preserve you, and trust not yourself in the hands of these merciless villains, who I fear this night will murder you." Which indeed I feared, and therefore was transported in my passionate expressions.

His Majesty, notwithstanding, took them very well, and used words of great kindness to me, yet still I begged he would forbear and think of his safety. He told me he did not fear, and that even if he did think there was any danger, he should be cautious of going, because of his pledged word (which I supposed he had passed to Hammond not to stir). Then he bade me stay until he could seal up his letters, which he had just finished, and give me that dispatch to send away. Afterward, with a sorrowful heart, I left.

I had not long been gone before he found the beginning of the sad effects of my fears, for those villains came down and set guard in all places within and without the house, even in his bed-chamber, and in this posture they continued till break of day. A little before then, with difficulty I had gotten leave of those bloodhounds to come into the bed-chamber, as I was a page thereof as well as clerk of the kitchen.

The King now said to me, "I know not where these people intend to carry me, and I would willingly eat before I go; therefore, get me something to eat," which I caused the cooks immediately to do. But coming myself in half an hour to tell him it was ready, I met those wretches leading him down the stairs to hurry him away, not suffering him to break his fast.

I kneeled down to kiss his hand, at which he stopped to give me leave so to do. They then pushed him, saying, "Go on, Sir," and so thrust him up into the coach, which was set close to the door.

And then one Rolfe,* who had before attempted to murder him, impudently (with his hat on) stepped up into the coach to him. But his Majesty, with great courage, rose up and thrust him out, saying, "It is not come to that yet. Get you out." The King then called up Mr. Herbert and Mr. Harrington, who at that time waited as grooms of his bed-chamber. Rolfe, thus disappointed, took his saddle horse and got upon him, and so, using insulting words, rode by the coach side, in which they carried him to Yarmouth in the island, and from thence by water to Hurst Castle, and from thence to his martyrdom.

From Hurst Castle and Environs to Windsor
(Sir Thomas Herbert's narrative here continues.)

The coach (by the Lieutenant-Colonel's [Rolfe's] directions) went westward toward Worsley Tower in Freshwater Isle a little beyond Yarmouth

---

* It was later believed by the Royalists that a counterplot, led by this Major Rolfe, had been in effect at the time of Firebrace's attempted rescue, and that Charles would have been shot while trying to climb down the rope from his window. But Rolfe was subsequently brought to trial and acquitted.

Haven. Thereabouts his Majesty rested until the vessel was ready to take
him aboard, a sorrowful spectacle and a great example of Fortune's
inconstancy. The wind and tide favoring, they crossed that narrow sea in
three hours and landed at Hurst Castle (or Block House rather) erected by
order of King Henry VIII upon a spot of earth a good way into the sea, and
joined to the firm land by a narrow neck of sand covered over with small
loose stones and pebbles. Upon both sides the sea beats, so that at spring
tides and stormy weather the land passage is formidable and hazardous.
The castle has very thick stone walls, and the platforms are regular, and
both have several culverines and sakers [small cannon] mounted—altogether a dismal receptacle for so great a monarch, the greatest part of whose
life and reign had been prosperous and full of earthly glory!

The Captain of this wretched place was not unsuitable; for at the King's
going ashore, he stood ready to receive him with small observance. His look
was stern; his hair and large beard were black and bushy; he held a
partizan [a long spear] in his hand, and (*Switz*-like) had a great basket hilt
sword by his side—hardly could one see a man of a more grim aspect—and
no less robust and rude was his behavior. Some of his Majesty's servants
were not a little fearful of him; and that he was designed for mischief,
especially when he vapored [boasted], being elevated with his command
and puffed up by having so royal a prisoner. But being complained of to his
superior officer, the fellow appeared a bubble; for being pretty sharply
admonished, he quickly became mild and calm.

His Majesty (as it may well be granted) was very slenderly accommodated at this place. The room he usually ate in was neither large nor
lightsome, at noonday (in that winter season) requiring candles; and at
night he had his wax lamp set (as formerly) in a silver basin, which
illuminated his bed-chamber. The air was equally noxious, by reason of the
marish grounds that were about and the unwholesome vapors arising from
the sargassos and weeds and by the fogs that those marine places are most
subject to, disposing to diseases, especially aguish distempers.

Nevertheless, in this dolorous place the King was content to walk above
two miles in length, the Governor one time, Captain Reynolds at another,
discoursing, and Mr. Harrington or Mr. Herbert, by his Majesty's order,
ever attending him. That which made some amends was a fair and
uninterrupted prospect a good way into the sea, with the sight of ships of all
sizes daily under sail, with which his Majesty was much delighted.

There were none now left to wait upon the King in his bed-chamber but
Mr. Herbert, and he *in motu trepidationis* [in fear and trembling], who
nevertheless held out, by his careful observing his Majesty's instructions.
About midnight one night there was an unusual noise that awakened the
King out of his sleep. He was in some marvel to hear the drawbridge let
down at that unseasonable hour and some horsemen enter; who, being
alighted, the rest of that night was in deep silence. The King being desirous
to know the matter, he before break of day rung his silver bell, which, with

both his watches, was usually laid upon a stool near the wax lamp that was set near them in a large silver basin. Upon which call, Mr. Herbert opened the bed-chamber door to know his Majesty's pleasure. The King asked him if he had heard the noise that occurred about midnight. Mr. Herbert answered that he had, as also the falling of the drawbridge; but being shut up in the backstairs room, by the Governor's order being bolted without, he neither could nor would, without his Majesty's order, adventure out at such time of night. The King then bade him go and learn what the matter was.

Mr. Herbert, speedily returning to his Majesty, told him it was Major Harrison that came so late into the castle.

"Are you sure it was Major Harrison?" asked the King.

"May it please your Majesty," said Mr. Herbert, "Captain Reynolds told me so."

"Then I believe it," said the King. "But did you see Major Harrison?"

"No, Sir," said Mr. Herbert.

"Would not Captain Reynolds," said the King, "tell you what the Major's business is?"

Mr. Herbert replied he did what he could to be informed, but all he could then learn from the Captain was the occasion of Harrison's coming.

The King said no more, but bade him attend in the next room, and went to prayer. In less than an hour the King opened the bed-chamber door and beckoned to Mr. Herbert to come in and make him ready. Mr. Herbert was in some consternation to see his Majesty so much discomposed, and wept; which, the King observing, asked him the meaning of it.

Mr. Herbert replied, "Because I perceive your Majesty so much troubled and concerned at the news I brought."

"I am not afraid," said the King, "but do not you know that this is the man who intended to assassinate me, as by letter I was informed, during the late Treaty? To my knowledge I never saw the Major, though I have heard oft of him, nor ever did him injury. I trust in God, who is my Helper. I would not be surprised [by another attempt at assassination]; this is a place fit for such a purpose. Herbert, go again, and make further inquiry into his business."

Mr. Herbert immediately went out, finding an opportunity to speak in private with Captain Reynolds. The Captain told him that the Major's business was to remove the King thence to Windsor Castle within three days at the farthest. Mr. Herbert, believing that the King would be well pleased with the exchange, by leaving the worst to enjoy the best castle in England, returned to his Majesty with a mirthful countenance, little imagining (God knows) the sad consequence. And as soon as the King heard Windsor named, he seemed to rejoice at it.

Major Harrison stayed two nights at Hurst; and when it was dark (having given orders for the King's removal) he returned from whence he came, without seeing the King or speaking with any that attended his Majesty.

Two days after, Lieutenant-Colonel Cobbet came and acquainted his

Majesty with the orders he had received for his remove thence to Windsor
Castle forthwith. Windsor was a place his Majesty ever delighted in, and
would make amends for what at Hurst he had suffered.

All things being in short time made ready, he bade solitary Hurst adieu;
and having passed the narrow passage (which reaches well nigh from Hurst
to Milford, three long miles), there appeared a party of horse belonging to
the army to escort him. On the road from Alesford to Farnham, another
troop of horse was in good order drawn up, by which his Majesty passed; it
was to bring up the rear. In the head of it was the Major gallantly mounted
and armed; a velvet monteir [a kind of military cap] was on his head, a new
buff coat upon his back, and a crimson silk scarf about his waist richly
fringed. His Majesty asked who the man was, for it was the first time he had
ever seen him; and being told it was Major Harrison, the King viewed him
more narrowly and fixed his eyes so steadily upon him as made the Major
abashed.

That night the King got to Farnham, where he was lodged in a private
gentleman's house in the town. A little before supper, his Majesty standing
by the fire in a large parlor, wainscoted, and in discourse with the mistress
of the house, the King (albeit the room was pretty full of army officers and
country people that crowded in to have a sight of him) nevertheless
discovered Major Harrison at the far end of the room talking with another
officer. The King beckoned to him with his hand to come nearer him, which
he did with due reverence. The King, then taking him by his arm, drew him
aside toward the window, where for half an hour or more they discoursed
together. Amongst other things, the King minded him of the information
concerning him, which, if true, rendered him an enemy in the worst sense to
his person; to which the Major in his vindication assured his Majesty that
what was so reported of him was not true. What he had said, he might
repeat, was that the law was equally obliging to great and small, and that
justice had no respect to persons. His Majesty, finding his words affectedly
spoken and to no good end, left off further communication with him and
went to supper, being all the time very pleasant.

Next day the King rode to Windsor Castle, where his usual bed-chamber
had been prepared for him. Here the King seemed to take more delight than
at any place he had been since his leaving Hampton Court. He had the
liberty to walk where and when he pleased within the castle and in the long
terrace without that looks toward the fair college of Eton; also, the soldiers
there gave no offense either in language or behavior to the King or any that
served him. The greatest part of the forenoon the King spent in prayer and
other exercises of piety; part of the afternoon he set apart for health, by
recreating himself in walking, usually in the long terrace. Few of the gentry
were suffered to come into the castle to see the King, save upon the Sundays
to sermon in Saint George's Chapel.

One night, as the King was preparing to go to bed, and, as his custom
was, wound up both his watches—one being gold, the other silver—he

missed his diamond seal, which had the King's arms cut upon it with great curiosity and was fixed to the watch. The seal was set in a collet of gold fastened to a gold chain. His Majesty could not imagine either when or where it dropped out; but thought he had it the day before when he looked upon his watch as he walked in the long terrace. He bade Mr. Herbert look there the next morning; therefore, as soon as the King was ready, and Mr. Herbert had given him his George and Garter (which his Majesty never failed to wear), the King went to his devotion, and his servant to search for the diamond. For near an hour's space he walked upon the terrace, casting his eye everywhere, but could not find it. Some officers of the garrison were then upon the terrace, who observed how intent he was. They imagined he had lost something, and were inquisitive to know what it was; but he, apprehending the danger in telling them and the hazard it would run if they should find it, let them know nothing concerning it. He in like manner sought in the presence chamber, privy chamber, galleries, Saint George's Hall, and every room the King had been in, but all to no purpose. The King, perceiving Mr. Herbert troubled at this accident, bade him not vex himself about it.

Next night, a little before his Majesty went to bed, a good charcoal fire being in the chamber and wax lights burning, the King cast his eye to one end of the room and saw something sparkle. Pointing with his finger, he bade Mr. Herbert take a candle and see what it was. By good providence it was the diamond, which he took up, and found his Majesty's arms in it, and with joy brought it to the King.

Soon after this, the Governor acquainted his Majesty that within a few days he was to be removed thence to Whitehall. To this his Majesty made little reply; seeming nothing so delighted with this remove as he was with the former; but turning him about, said, "God is everywhere alike in Wisdom, Power, and Goodness."

The "Net" Tightens

The day prefixed being come, his Majesty took coach near the Keep (a high mount, on which is a tower built in the middle ward betwixt the two great courts within the castle), a guard being made all along of muskets and pikes, both officers and soldiers expressing civility as he passed by. At the great gate a party of horse commanded by Major Harrison followed the coach, which passed to his Majesty's house at Saint James's.

Strict guards were placed, and none suffered to attend in his Majesty's bed-chamber save Mr. Herbert. It is well worth observation that so soon as the King came to his bed-chamber, before he either ate or drank or discoursed with any, he went to prayer and reading in his Bible.

About the latter end of December, his Majesty had private notice that the House of Commons, in a resolve, had declared that by the laws of England it was treason in the King to levy war against the Parliament and kingdom, which resolve they sent up unto the Lords for their concurrence. The Lords, so soon as they had heard it read, rejected it; and after some debate, passed two votes: first, that they could not concur with the House of Commons in their declaratory resolve; and secondly, as to that order for trial of the King, they could by no means consent unto it. Whereupon the House of Commons passed another vote, viz.: that the Commons of England, in Parliament assembled, have the supreme power. And pursuant thereto, the House also passed an act for the trial of the King.

His Majesty believed his enemies aimed at his deposing and confinement in the Tower, or some such like place; and that they would seat his son the Prince of Wales in his throne, if he would accept of it. But as to their taking away his life by trial in any court of justice, or in the face of his people, that he could not believe, there being no such precedent or mention in any of our histories. 'Tis true, his grandmother, the Queen of Scots [Mary Stuart], suffered under Queen Elizabeth; but in England she was no sovereign, but a subject to law. Indeed, that some kings of England have been lamentably murdered by ruffians in a clandestine way, our chronicles inform us; but the facts were neither owned nor approved of by any King. Such were his Majesty's imaginations until he came to his trial in Westminster Hall, for then he altered his opinion.

For about a fortnight after his Majesty's coming to Saint James's, he constantly dined publicly in the presence chamber, and at meals was served after the usual state: the carver, sewer, cup-bearer, and gentleman-usher attending and doing their offices respectively; his cup was given upon the knee, as were his covered dishes; the say [the assay, or public tasting of food or drink to be partaken of by the King] was given, and other accustomed ceremonies of state observed, notwithstanding his dolorous condition, and the King was well pleased with the observance afforded him. But then the case altered; for the officers of the army (being predominant) gave order at a court of war that thenceforth all state ceremony or accustomed respect to his Majesty at meals should be forborne. And accordingly, the King's meat was brought up by soldiers, the dishes uncovered, no say, no cup upon the knee, nor other accustomed court state was then observed; which was an uncouth sight unto the King. But seeing it was come to such a pass, the best expedient he had was to contract his diet to a few dishes out of the bill of fare and to eat in private.

It is well worth our observation that in all the time of his Majesty's restraint and solitude he was never sick, nor took anything to prevent sickness, or had need of a physician—which (under God) is attributed to his quiet disposition and unparalleled patience; to his exercise, when at home walking in the gallery and privy garden, and other recreations when abroad; to his abstemiousness at meat, eating but of few dishes and (as he used to say) agreeable to his exercise; drinking but twice every dinner and supper, once of beer and once of wine and water mixed, and only after fish a glass of French wine. This beverage he himself mixed at the cupboard, so he would have it; and he very seldom ate and drank before dinner, nor between meals.

Upon Friday, the nineteenth of January, 1649, his Majesty was removed from Saint James's to Whitehall, and lodged in his usual bed-chamber; after which a guard of musketeers and sentinels were placed at the door of his chamber. Thenceforth Mr. Herbert (who constantly lay in the next room to the King, according to the duty of his place) by his Majesty's order brought his pallet into his Majesty's bed-chamber to be nearer his royal person, where every night he rested.

The next day the King was in a sedan, or closed chair, removed from Whitehall to Sir Robert Cotton's house, near the west end of Westminster Hall. Guards were made on both sides of King Street, all along the palace yard and along Westminster Hall. At Cotton House there was a guard of partisans—Colonel Hacker sometimes and Colonel Hunks other sometimes commanding them. When all had been prepared, his Majesty was summoned by Colonel Hacker to go to the court that was then in Westminster Hall.

The Arraignment of Charles I
(from *The Official Report of the Trial*)

On Saturday, the twentieth day of January, 1649, the Lord President of the High Court of Justice [John Bradshaw], with near fourscore members of the said court, having 16 gentlemen with partizans, and a sword, and a mace, with their and other officers of the said court marching before them, came to the place ordered to be prepared for their sitting at the west end of the Great Hall at Westminster.

The court being thus sat, and silence made, the great gate of the said hall was set open, to the end that all persons without exception, desirous to see or hear, might come into it. This done, Colonel Thomlinson, who had the charge of the prisoner, was commanded to bring him to the court.

The Sergeant at Arms, with his mace, receives and conducts him straight to the bar, having a crimson velvet chair set before him. After a stern looking upon the court and the people in the galleries on each side of him, his Majesty places himself, not at all moving his hat or otherwise showing the least respect to the court; but presently rises up again and turns about, looking downward upon the guards placed on the left side and on the multitude of spectators on the right side of the said great hall. After silence made among the people, the Act of Parliament for the trying of Charles Stuart, King of England, was read over by the Clerk of the Court.

Silence being again ordered, the Lord President stood up and said: "Charles Stuart, King of England, the Commons of England assembled in Parliament being deeply sensible of the calamities that have been brought upon this nation, which is fixed upon you as the principal author of it, have resolved to make inquisition for blood, and for that purpose have constituted the High Court of Justice."

Mr. Cook, Solicitor of the Commonwealth, standing within a bar on the right hand of the prisoner, offered to speak. But the King, having a staff in his hand, held it up, and laid it on the said Mr. Cook's shoulder two or three times, bidding him hold. Nevertheless, the Lord President ordering him to go on, he said: "My Lord, I am commanded to charge Charles Stuart, King of England, in the name of the Commons of England, with treason and high misdemeanors. I desire the said charge may be read."

The said charge being delivered to the Clerk of the Court, the Lord President ordered it should be read; but the King bid him hold. Nevertheless, being commanded by the Lord President to read it, the Clerk began, and the prisoner sat down again in his chair, looking sometimes on the High Court, sometimes up to the galleries; and having risen again and turned about to behold the guards and spectators, sat down, looking very sternly and with a countenance not at all moved, till these words, viz., "Charles Stuart to be a tyrant and traitor," etc. were read; at which he laughed, as he sat, in the face of the court.

LORD PRESIDENT: Sir, you have now heard your charge. You find that in the close of it, it is prayed to the court, in the behalf of the Commons of England, that you answer.

KING: I would know by what power I am called hither. I was not long ago in the Isle of Wight—how I came there is a longer story than I think it fit at this present time for me to speak of—but there I entered into a Treaty with both Houses of Parliament, with as much public faith as it is possible to be had with any people in the world. I treated there with a number of honorable lords and gentlemen, and treated honestly and uprightly—I cannot say but they did very nobly with me. Now I would know by what authority—I mean lawful, there are many unlawful authorities in the world, thieves and robbers by the highways—but I would know by what authority I was brought from thence and carried from place to place, and I know not what. And when I know what lawful authority, I shall answer. Remember I am your King, your lawful King, and what sins you bring upon your heads, and the judgment of God upon the land. Think well upon it, I say, think well upon it!

LORD PRESIDENT: Sir, I shall speak something unto you. Sir, neither you nor any man are permitted to dispute the jurisdiction of the court. They sit here by the authority of the Commons of England, and all your predecessors and you are responsible to them.

KING: I deny that—show me one precedent.

LORD PRESIDENT: Sir, you ought not to interrupt while the court is speaking to you. The point is not to be debated by you, neither will the court permit you to do it.

KING: I say, Sir, by your favor, that the Commons of England was never a court of judicature. I would know how they came to be so.

LORD PRESIDENT: Sir, you are not to be permitted to go on in that speech and these discourses.

Then the Clerk of the Court read as follows: "Charles Stuart, King of England, you have been accused on behalf of the people of England of high treasons and other crimes. The court have determined that you ought to answer the same."

KING: I will answer the same so soon as I know by what authority you do this.

LORD PRESIDENT: If this be all that you will say, then, Gentlemen, you that brought the prisoner hither, take charge of him back again.

KING: I do require that I may give in my reasons why I do not answer, and give me time for that.

LORD PRESIDENT: Sir, it is not for prisoners to require.

KING: Prisoners! Sir, I am not an ordinary prisoner.

LORD PRESIDENT: Sergeant, take away the prisoner.

The court then adjourned, and met the next day.

The clerk reads: "Charles Stuart, King of England, you are accused in behalf of the Commons of England of divers crimes and treasons, which charge hath been read unto you: the court now requires you to give your positive and final answer, by way of confession or denial of the charge."

KING: Sir, I again say to you, so that I might give satisfaction to the people of England, that I have done nothing against that trust that has been committed to me. But to acknowledge a new court [by answering the charge], to alter the fundamental laws of the kingdom—Sir, you must excuse me.

Upon which, the Solicitor began to offer something to the President of the Court, but was interrupted by the King gently laying his staff upon the Solicitor's arm, the head of which, being silver, happened to fall off. Mr. Herbert (who waited near his chair) stooped to take it up; but falling on the contrary side, to which he could not reach, the King took it up himself. This by some was looked upon as a bad omen.

LORD PRESIDENT: Sir, this is the third time that you have publicly disowned this court, and put an affront upon it. How far you have preserved the privileges of the people, your actions have spoken it. Sir, men's intentions ought to be known by their actions; you have written your meaning in bloody characters throughout the whole kingdom. Gentlemen, you that took charge of the prisoner, take him back again.

Then the King went forth with his guard, and proclamation was made that all persons which had then appeared, and had further to do at the court, might depart into the Painted Chamber; to which place the court did forthwith adjourn, and intended to meet in Westminster Hall by 10 of the clock next morning.

Cryer: "God bless the kingdom of England!" [Not the customary, "God bless the King!"]

At the court session the following day:

KING: I would desire only one word before you give sentence, and that is, that you would hear me concerning those great imputations that you have laid to my charge.

LORD PRESIDENT: Sir, you must give me now leave to go on, for I am not far from your sentence, and your time is now past.

KING: But I shall desire you will hear me a few words to you. Sir, it is very true that—

LORD PRESIDENT: You disavow us as a court, and therefore for you to address yourself to us, and not to acknowledge us as a court to judge of what you say, it is not to be permitted. Sir, we have given you too much liberty already, and admitted of too much delay, and we may not admit of any further. We should not have declined to have heard what you could have said or proved on your behalf excusing those great and heinous charges that in whole or in part are laid upon you. We cannot be unmindful of what the Scripture tells us, for to acquit the guilty is of equal abomination as to condemn the innocent. We may not acquit the guilty. What sentence the law affirms to a traitor, a murderer, and a public enemy to the country, that is the sentence you are now to hear read unto you, and that is the sentence of the court. [*To the Cryer*] Make an O Yes, and command silence while the sentence is read.

Which done, the Clerk read the sentence drawn up in parchment:

"Now, therefore, upon serious and mature deliberation, this court is in judgment and conscience satisfied that he, the said Charles Stuart, is guilty of levying war against the said Parliament and people, for which in the said charge he stands accused. And by the general course of his government, counsels and practices, this court is fully satisfied that he has been and is guilty of the wicked designs and endeavors in the said charge set forth; and that the said war has been levied, maintained, and continued by him; and that he has been guilty of high treason, and of the murders, rapines, burnings, spoils, desolations, damage, and mischief to this nation acted and committed in the said war, and occasioned thereby. For all which treasons and crimes this court doth adjudge that he, the said Charles Stuart, as a tyrant, traitor, murderer, and public enemy to the good people of this nation, shall be put to death by severing of his head from his body."

Which being read, the Lord President added, "The sentence now read, and published, is the act, sentence, judgment and resolution of the whole court." To which they all expressed their assent by standing up, as was before agreed and ordered.

KING: Will you hear me a word, Sir?

LORD PRESIDENT: Sir, you are not to be heard after the sentence.

KING: No, Sir?

LORD PRESIDENT: No, Sir, by your favor, Sir. Guard, withdraw your prisoner.

KING: I may speak after sentence. By your favor, Sir, I may speak after sentence, ever. By your favor—hold! The sentence, Sir—I say, Sir, I do—I am not suffered for to speak. Expect what justice other people will have!

His Majesty being taken away by the guard, as he passed down the stairs the soldiers scoffed at him, casting the smoke of their tobacco (a thing very distasteful unto him) and throwing their pipes in his way. As he passed along, hearing the rabble of soldiers crying out "Justice! Justice!" he said: "Poor soldiers, for a piece of money they would do so for their commanders."

The "Royal Actor" Prepares
(Sir Thomas Herbert's narrative.)

The King was with a guard of halberdiers returned to Whitehall in a close chair [a sedan chair] through King Street, both sides whereof had a guard of foot soldiers, who were silent as his Majesty passed. But shop stalls and windows were full of people, many of which shed tears, and some of them with audible voices prayed for the King, who through the privy garden was carried to his bed-chamber; whence, after two hours' space, he was removed to Saint James's. Nothing of the fear of death, or indignities offered, seemed a terror or provoked him to impatience; nor uttered he a reproachful word reflecting upon any of his judges (albeit he well knew that some of them had been his domestic servants) or against any member of the House or officer of the army.

The King now bidding farewell to the world, his whole business was a serious preparation for death, which opens the door unto eternity. He laid aside all other thoughts, and spent the remainder of his time in prayer and other pious exercises of devotion.

Resolving to sequester himself, so as he might have no disturbance to his mind, nor interruption to his meditations, he ordered Mr. Herbert to excuse it to any that might have the desire to visit him. "I know," said the King, "my nephew, the Prince Elector, and some other lords that love me, will endeavor it, but my time is short and precious. I hope they will not take it ill that none have access unto me but my children. The best office they can do now is to pray for me."

That evening the King took a ring from his finger and gave it Mr. Herbert—it had an emerald set between two diamonds—and commanded him, as late as it was, to go with it from Saint James's to a lady [the King's laundress, Mrs. Wheeler] living then in Channel Row, on the back side of King Street in Westminster, and give it to her without saying anything.

The night was exceeding dark, and guards were set in several places. Nevertheless, getting the word from Colonel Thomlinson (a man so civil both toward his Majesty and such as attended him that the King, in gratitude, once gave him his gold pick-tooth case as he was walking with him in the presence chamber), Mr. Herbert passed through in all places where sentinels were. He was bade to stand many times till the corporals had the word from him. Being arrived at last at the lady's house, he delivered her the ring.

"Sir," said she, "give me leave to show you the way into the parlor," where she desired him to stay till she returned. In a short time she did, and gave him a little cabinet closed with three seals—two of them being the King's arms, the third, the figure of a Roman—praying him to deliver it to the same hand that had sent the ring, which was left her.

The password secured Mr. Herbert's return unto the King. The Bishop being but newly gone to his lodging, his Majesty said to Mr. Herbert that he should see the cabinet opened in the morning.

Morning being come, the Bishop [of London, Dr. Juxon, the King's chaplain] prayed early with the King, and afterward his Majesty broke the seals open and showed them what was contained in it. There were diamonds and jewels, most part being broken Georges and Garters [insignia of these orders]. "You see," said he, "all the wealth now in my power to give my two children."

Next day Princess Elizabeth [Charles's second daughter, aged 14] and the Duke of Gloucester [Charles's third son, aged 9], her brother, came to take their sad farewell of the King their father and to ask his blessing. The Princess, being the elder, was the most sensible of her royal father's condition, as appeared by her sorrowful look and excessive weeping; and her little brother, seeing his sister weep, took the like impression, though by reason of his tender age he could not have the like apprehension. The King raised them both from off their knees; he kissed them, gave them his blessing, and setting them on his knees, admonished them concerning their duty and loyal observance to the Queen their mother; the Prince [of Wales, later Charles II, in exile with his brother in France] that was his successor; love to the Duke of York [Charles's second son, later James II]; and his other relations.

To the boy he then said, "Mark, child, what I say, they will cut off my head, and perhaps make thee a king. But mark what I say: you must not be a king so long as your brothers Charles and James do live; for they will cut off your brothers' heads (when they can catch them) and cut off thy head, too, at last; and therefore I charge you, do not be made a king by them."

The child replied with great firmness, "I will be torn to pieces first."

This answer greatly pleased his Majesty. He then gave them all his jewels, save the George he wore, which was cut in an onyx with great curiosity and set about with 21 fair diamonds, and the reverse set with the like number. Again kissing his children, he had such pretty and pertinent answers from them both as drew tears of joy and love from his eyes; and then praying God Almighty to bless 'em, he turned about, expressing a tender and fatherly affection. Most sorrowful was this parting, the young Princess shedding tears and crying lamentably, which moved others to pity that formerly were hard-hearted. And at opening the bed-chamber door, the

King returned hastily from the window and kissed 'em and blessed 'em; so parted.

That day the King ate and drank very sparingly, most part of the time being spent in prayer and meditation. It was some hours after night e'er Dr. Juxon took leave of the King, who willed him to be early with him the next morning.

The night after sentence had been pronounced in Westminster Hall, Colonel Hacker (who then commanded the guards about the King) would have placed two musketeers in the King's bed-chamber. His Majesty made no reply, only gave a sigh. Howbeit, the good Bishop and Mr. Herbert, apprehending the horror and the barbarousness of such an act, never left the Colonel till he reversed his order by withdrawing these men.

After the Bishop was gone to his lodging, the King continued reading and praying more than two hours. The King commanded Mr. Herbert to lie by his bedside upon a pallet, where he took small rest, that being the last night his Gracious Sovereign and Master enjoyed. Nevertheless, the King for four hours or thereabouts slept soundly, and awaking about two hours afore day, he opened his curtain to call Mr. Herbert. A great cake of wax had been set in a silver basin that then, as at all other times, burned all night, so that the King perceived Mr. Herbert was somewhat disturbed in his sleep; but calling him, bade him rise, for (said his Majesty), "I will get up, having a great work to do this day." However, he would know why Mr. Herbert was so troubled in his sleep.

He replied, "May it please your Majesty, I was dreaming."

"I would know your dream," said the King.

"May it please your Majesty," said Mr. Herbert, "I dreamed, that as you were making ready, one knocked at the bed-chamber door, which your Majesty took no notice of, nor was I willing to acquaint you with it, apprehending it might be Colonel Hacker. But knocking the second time, your Majesty asked me, if I heard it not? I said I did; but did not use to go without his order. 'Why then, go; know who it is and his business.' Whereupon I opened the door, and perceived that it was the Lord Archbishop of Canterbury, Dr. Laud [executed for high treason in 1645], in his pontifical habit, as worn at court; I knew him, having seen him often. The Archbishop desired he might enter, having something to say to the King. I acquainted your Majesty with his desire; so you bade me let him in. Being in, he made his obeisance to your Majesty in the middle of the room, doing the like also when he came near your person; and, falling on his knees, your Majesty gave him your hand to kiss, and took him aside to the window, where some discourse passed between your Majesty and him, and I kept a becoming distance, not hearing anything that was said, yet could perceive your Majesty pensive by your looks, and that the Archbishop gave a sign; who, after a short stay, again kissing your hand, returned, but with face all the way toward your Majesty, and making his usual reverences, the third being so submissive as he fell prostrate on his face on the ground, and

I immediately stepped to him to help him up, which I was then acting, when your Majesty saw me troubled in my sleep. The impression was so lively, that I looked about, verily thinking it was no dream."

The King said, "The dream was remarkable, but he is dead; yet, had we conferred together during life, 'tis very likely (albeit I love him well) I should have said something to him might have occasioned his sign."

He now declared, "Herbert, this is my second marriage day; I would be as trim today as may be; for before night I hope to be espoused to my blessed Jesus." He then appointed what clothes he would wear. "Let me have a shirt on more than ordinary," said the King, "by reason the season is so sharp as probably may make me shake, which some observers will imagine proceeds from fear. I would have no such imputation. I fear not death! Death is not terrible to me. I bless my God I am prepared."

These, or words to this effect, his Majesty spoke to Mr. Herbert as he was making ready. Soon after came Dr. Juxon, Bishop of London, precisely at the time his Majesty the night before had appointed him. His Majesty then bade Mr. Herbert withdraw, and was about an hour in private with the Bishop. When Mr. Herbert was again called in, the Bishop went to prayer, reading also the 27th chapter of the Gospel of Saint Matthew, which relates the Passion of our Blessed Savior. The King, after the service was done, asked the Bishop if he had made choice of that chapter as applicable to his present condition.

The Bishop replied, "May it please your Gracious Majesty, it is the proper lesson for the day, as appears by the calendar," which the King was much affected with, so aptly serving as a seasonable preparation for his death that day.

Colonel Hacker then knocked easily at the King's chamber door. Mr. Herbert, being within, would not stir to ask who it was; but the Colonel knocking the second time a little louder, the King bade him go to the door. He guessed his business.

Mr. Herbert demanded wherefore he knocked. The Colonel said he would speak with the King.

The King said, "Let him come in."

The Colonel, in trembling manner, came near and told his Majesty it was time to go to Whitehall, where he might have some further time to rest. The King bade him go forth, he would come presently.

Some time his Majesty was private; and afterward, taking the good Bishop by the hand, looking upon him with a cheerful countenance, he said, "Come, let us go," bidding Mr. Herbert take with him the silver clock that hung by the bed side.

He then said, "Open the door—Hacker has given us a second warning."

Through the garden the King passed into the park. The park had several companies of foot drawn up, who made a guard on either side as the King passed, and a guard of halberdiers in company went somewhat before, and othersome followed, and drums beat, and the noise was so great as one could hardly hear what another spoke.

Upon the King's right hand went the Bishop, Colonel Thomlinson on his left, with whom his Majesty had some discourse by the way. Mr. Herbert was next the King, and after him the guards. In this manner went the King through the park. Coming to the stairs of Whitehall, the King passed along the galleries unto his bed-chamber, where, after a little repose, the Bishop went to prayer. His Majesty then bade Mr. Herbert bring him some bread and wine, which being brought, the King broke the manchet [a small loaf of fine wheaten bread] and ate a mouthful of it and drank a small glassful of claret wine. He then was sometime in private with the Bishop, expecting when Hacker would the third and last time give warning. Meantime his Majesty told Mr. Herbert which satin nightcap he would use, which being provided, and the King at private prayer, Mr. Herbert addressed himself to the Bishop and told him the King had ordered him to have a white satin nightcap ready, but that he felt himself unable to endure the sight of that violence they upon the scaffold would offer the King. The good Bishop bade him then give him the cap and wait at the end of the Banqueting House near the scaffold to take care of the King's body. "For," said he, "that, and his interment, will be our last office."

Colonel Hacker came soon after to the bed-chamber door and gave his last signal. The Bishop and Mr. Herbert, weeping, fell upon their knees, and the King gave them his hand to kiss, and then helped the Bishop up, for he was aged. Colonel Hacker attending still at the chamber door, the King took notice of it and said, "Open the door," and bade Hacker go, then he would follow.

A guard was made all along the galleries and the Banqueting House; but behind the soldiers abundance of men and women crowded in, though with some peril to their persons, to behold the saddest sight England ever saw. And as his Majesty passed by, with a cheerful look, he heard them pray for him, the soldiers not rebuking any of them, by their silence and dejected faces seeming afflicted rather than insulting.

There was a passage broken through the wall, by which the King passed unto the scaffold.

"That Memorable Scene"
(From the account by John Rushworth)

The scaffold was hung round with black, and the floor covered with black, and the axe and block laid in the middle of the scaffold. There were divers companies of foot and horse on every side of the scaffold, and the multitudes of people that came to be spectators were very great. The King, making a pass upon the scaffold, looked very earnestly on the block, and asked Colonel Hacker if there were one no higher.

He then spoke thus, directing his speech to the gentlemen on the scaffold:

"I would not now speak nothing unto you in this place, were it not that some men would interpret my silence as an argument of guilt. I call God to witness of my innocency (before whose tribunal I must shortly appear). It never entered my thoughts to retrench the just privileges of Parliament; and I raised not any army before such time as they had raised hostile forces against me.

"Meanwhile I acknowledge God's justice, which this day (by an unjust sentence of mine) he hath inflicted a just judgment on me, for as much as I once would not acquit an innocent man [Thomas Wentworth, Earl of Strafford, formerly Charles's chief minister, who was impeached and executed in 1641] when oppressed by a most unjust decree.

"With what charity I embrace my enraged enemies, this good man is my witness (*pointing to the Bishop of London*). I pardon them all from my very heart, and I earnestly beseech the God of all mercies that He would vouchsafe to grant them serious repentance and remit this great sin.

"Yet I cannot to my last gasp but be solicitous of the peace of my kingdom. Herein I perceive you are most miserably out of the way, in that by the title of the sword, without even the shadow of right, you think good to wrest the government to yourselves, and endeavor to establish the kingdom not by the authority of the laws but upon the score of conquest.

"But being out of the way, as you are, can you by no other expedient return into the right path of peace? By no other counsel, believe me, can you hope to divert God's wrath than by restoring to God, the King, the people, respectively, such things as are their dues. You must give God his due by regulating rightly His Church, according to his Scriptures, which is now miserably convulsed and disjointed. A national synod freely called, freely debating among themselves, must settle this. (*Then, turning to a gentleman that touched the axe, he said, 'Hurt not the axe that may hurt me.'*) As for the King—namely, my successor—you will render full right if you restore those things which by the clear letter of the law stand expressed. Lastly, you will put the people in their rights and due liberties by recovering unto the laws their authority and the people's observance; to the abrogating of which, by the enormous power of the sword, I was brought hither to undergo a martyrdom for my people."

Here the King ceased speaking; and the Bishop, prompting him, urged that (if his most excellent Majesty pleased) he would openly profess what he thought touching his religion.

Thereupon the King said, "I die in the Christian faith, according to the profession of the Church of England, as the same was left me by my father of most blessed memory."

The Bishop then put the King's nightcap on his head and unclothed him to his sky-colored satin waistcoat.

Then, turning to the officers, the King said, "I have a good cause, and I have a gracious God. I will say no more." Then, turning to Colonel Hacker, he said, "Take care that they do not put me to pain, and, Sir, this and it please you—" But then, a gentleman coming near the axe, the King said, "Take heed of the axe! Pray, take heed of the axe!" Then, the King speaking to the executioner, said, "I shall say but very short prayers, and then thrust out my hands." Then the King called to the executioner, "Does my hair trouble you?" The man desired him to put it all under his cap, which the King did accordingly by the help of the executioner and the Bishop.

The King repeated the words, "I have a good cause and a gracious God"; then, taking off his George order, handed it to the Bishop, saying, "Remember!" *

"There is but one stage more, Sir," said the Bishop. "This is a turbulent and troublesome and but a short one, but it will soon dismiss you to a way further, even from earth to Heaven, where you are assured of joy and comfort."

"I go," said the King, "from a corruptible to an Incorruptible Crown, where no disturbance can be, but peace and joy for evermore."

After a moment's silent prayer, he laid his head upon the block. It was severed at one blow by the vizarded executioner.

Epilogue: The Burial of the "White King"
(Sir Thomas Herbert's narrative.)

Mr. Herbert, during the King's execution, was at the door lamenting; and the Bishop coming thence with the royal corpse, which was immediately coffined and covered with a black velvet pall, he and Mr. Herbert went with it to the back stairs to be embalmed. Meantime they went into the Long Gallery, where, chancing to meet the General [Fairfax], he asked Mr. Herbert how the King did. Which he thought strange: it seems thereby that the General knew not what had passed, being all that morning (as indeed at other times) using his power and interest to have the execution deferred.

His question being answered, the General seemed much surprised; and walking further in the gallery, they were met by another great commander, Cromwell, who knew what had so lately passed; for he told them they should have orders for the King's burial speedily.

The royal corpse, being embalmed and coffined, wrapped in lead and covered with a new velvet pall, was removed to the King's house at St. James's, where was great pressing by all sorts of people to see the King. A doleful spectacle! But few had leave to enter and behold it.

Where to bury the King was the last duty remaining.

Whereupon, Mr. Herbert made his application to such as were then in power for leave to bury the King's body in King Henry VII's Chapel, among his ancestors; but his request was denied, this reason being given, that probably it would attract infinite numbers of people of all sorts thither

---

* Bishop Juxon was later very closely cross-examined as to what the King meant by the word "Remember," but his questioners gained no information.

to see where the King was buried, which (as the times then were) was judged unsafe and inconvenient. Mr. Herbert acquainting the Bishop therewith, they then resolved to bury the King's body in the Royal Chapel of St. George within the castle of Windsor.

Accordingly, the corpse was thither carried from St. James's in a hearse covered with black velvet, drawn by six horses also covered with black; after which four coaches followed, two of them covered likewise with black cloth, in which were about a dozen gentlemen and others, most of them being such as had waited on his Majesty at Carisbrook Castle and other places, all of them being in black.

The King's body was then brought from his bed-chamber down into St. George's Hall, whence, after a little stay, it was with a slow and solemn pace (much sorrow in most faces discernible) carried by gentlemen that were of some quality, and in mourning. The Lords in like habits followed the royal corpse, with the Governor and several gentlemen and officers and attendants coming after.

This is memorable: that at such time as the King's body was brought out of St. George's Hall the sky was serene and clear, but presently it began to snow, and fell so fast, as by the time they came to the west end of the Royal Chapel, the black velvet pall was all white (the color of innocency), being thick covered over with snow. So went the white King to his grave in the 48th year of his age and the 22nd year and 10th month of his reign.

Louis XV

Painting by Quentin de La Tour. Louvre, Paris.

He knew the anguish of the marrow
The ague of the skeleton;
No contact possible to flesh
Allayed the fever of the bone.

    T.S. Eliot, *Whispers of Immortality*

A*t a masked ball held at the palace of Versailles in 1745 to celebrate the
marriage of his son the Dauphin of France to Maria Theresa of Spain, and
where all the guests were required to wear Turkish costumes, Louis XV as the
Grand Signor made a famous gesture toward the then Madame d'Etoiles, soon
to become the Marquise de Pompadour, to indicate publicly that she had been
installed as his new favorite. "The handkerchief is thrown!" the courtiers* (on
dit) *cried out at the time, alluding to the custom whereby the Sultan selects a
sultana from his harem.*

    *No doubt the role of Grand Signor (as the author of the following memoirs
relates) suited "a man who justly thought himself the handsomest in France,
and who was, moreover, a King." Yet the story goes that upon his own
marriage, to Marie Leczinska of Poland in 1725, when he was 15 years old, he
was so ignorant of what used to be called "the facts of life," having been
brought up in chaste seclusion by the libertine Regent Philippe d'Orléans, that
he had to be coached for his part on the wedding night by being shown erotic
engravings. In any case, the King soon discovered his own natural talent; and
the bored and dissolute court at Versailles, as well as the demimonde of Paris,
kept him supplied with a cornucopious abundance of mistresses. His first official
favorite, Madame de Châteauroux, once induced him to take command of an
army in the field. But he found little pleasure in what is supposed to be the
legitimate sport of kings, nor even in affairs of state, preferring instead those
intrigues and conquests for which he was so well endowed.*

    *After the death of Madame de Châteauroux, in 1743, the place of favorite
was filled by La Pompadour, a highly intelligent and ambitious Parisienne,
born plain Jeanne Antoinette Poisson in 1721. She was already married at the*

time she met the King to a not too reluctant cornuto, Le Normant d'Etoiles; but Louis soon pensioned him off, then installed her in an apartment at Versailles. She presided there for 20 years, at first serving him as mistress, and then, after his passion had waned, as a sort of Kahiyah Cadun, or "Mother of the Maids," overseeing (and overlooking) the succession of odalisques installed by the King in his seraglio at the Parc aux Cerfs. In the manner of Harun al-Rashid, or of the young King Henry V as depicted by Shakespeare, Louis XV sought relief from the psychic burden of being Louis XV by escaping incognito, now and then, out of the stifling Olympus at Versailles into the world of ordinary mortals. During these escapades he would assume the guise of a Polish count. And upon his return, the familiar and Junoesque presence of Madame de Pompadour must have helped him to recover his own self-identity.

Louis's ennui, if that's what it was, an affliction that Baudelaire once described as a "foretaste of oblivion" ("l'avant-goût du néant"), had for the King an aftertaste as well in his almost necrophilic obsession with death. He is said never to have passed up a chance to attend a funeral or browse in a cemetery reading the inscriptions. The age he lived in, after all, was one in which the so-called Graveyard School of poets haunted the salons of Europe and the leading artists painted classical ruins, dilapidated abbeys, and blasted heaths. The author of the memoirs that follow, Madame du Hausset, relates: "Madame de Pompadour once told me that he experienced a painful sensation whenever he was forced to laugh, and that he had often begged her to break off a droll story. He smiled, and that was all." Again, to cite Baudelaire:

> Je hais le mouvement que déplace les lignes,
> Et jamais je ne ris, et jamais je ne pleut.

The King's world-weary ataraxia, by turning a deadpan upon the agitations of the quotidian, thus not only anticipates Baudelaire's "nonchalant" Dandyism by a century but the "cool" style of contemporary Hippyism as well. Not a sparrow falls, etc.

The portrait of Louis XV sketched by Madame du Hausset seems in fact center-fold, as if he were a Playboy millionaire ensconced in a glassed-in

*Penthouse, though on a far grander even awesome scale. For he was, after all,
the King of France, keystone in the genealogical arch of the Old Regime as the
great-grandson of Louis XIV and the grandfather of the ill-fated Louis XVI.
And kings, among other things, kill. Madame de Pompadour once questioned
Louis's personal physician, François Quesnay, concerning his timidity in the
presence of the King, stating: "You always seem so embarrassed . . . and yet
he is so good-natured." Quesnay replied: "Madame, I left my native village at
the age of 40, and I have very little experience of the world, nor can I accustom
myself to its usages without great difficulty. When I am in a room with the
King, I say to myself, 'This is a man who can order my head to be cut off'—and
that idea embarrasses me." An idea, it should be added, that must have
embarrassed most of his other subjects also, as the revolution a generation later
proved. From Louis "le Bien-Aimé," which he was called at the start of his
reign, he came to be hated and despised at the end of it. The famous remark
attributed to him, "After me, the deluge," like Marie Antoinette's equally
famous "Let them eat cake," though never actually made by either, nonetheless
remain indelibly as captions for their historical cartoons or as epitaphs for their
gravestones.*

*Madame du Hausset, the author of what must be one of the most entertaining
as well as royally privileged books of gossip ever written—like a series of
vignettes conceived by Boucher or Fragonard—was Madame de Pompadour's
lady in waiting as well as confidante during her great years. Louis XV is
thereby observed, as he should be, from the point of view of women, in whose
eyes he preened, and in whose arms he proved, himself every inch a King.
Madame du Hausset's Journal was first published in Paris toward the end of
the eighteenth century, and appeared anonymously translated into English in
1827, from which edition the following has been extracted.*

Au Commencement . . .

I was for a long time about the person of Madame de Pompadour, and
my birth procured for me respectful treatment from herself, and from some
distinguished persons who conceived a regard for me. I soon became the
chère amie of Doctor Quesnay [King Louis XV's physician, author of the
bon mot *"Laissez faire, laissez passer"*] who frequently came to pass two or
three hours with me. M. Quesnay was very learned in certain matters
relating to finance, and he was a great *économiste*. But I do not know very
well what that means. What I do know for certain is, that he was very
clever, very gay and witty, and a very able physician.

When I was alone with her, Madame de Pompadour talked of many affairs which closely concerned her, and she once said to me, "The King and I have such implicit confidence in you, that we look upon you as a cat, or a dog, and go on talking as if you were not there."

There was a little nook adjoining her chamber, which has since been altered, where she knew I usually sat when I was alone, and where I heard everything that was said in the room, unless it was spoken in a low voice. But when the King wanted to speak to her in private, or in the presence of any of his ministers, he went with her into a closet by the side of the chamber, whither she also retired when she had secret business with the ministers, or with other important persons. All these circumstances brought to my knowledge a great many things which probity will neither allow me to tell or to record. I generally wrote without order of time, so that a fact may be related before others which preceded it.

Two persons—the Lieutenant of Police and the Postmaster-General— were very much in Madame de Pompadour's confidence; the latter, however, became less necessary to her from the time that the King communicated the secret of the post-office, that is to say, the system of opening letters and extracting matter from them. The plan they pursued, as I have heard, was very simple. Six or seven clerks of the post-office picked out the letters they were ordered to break open, and took the impression of the seals with a ball of quicksilver. Then they put each letter, with the seal downwards, over a glass of hot water, which melted the wax without injuring the paper. It was then opened, the desired matter extracted, and it was sealed again, by means of the impression. The Postmaster-General carried the extracts to the King on Sundays. He was seen coming and going on this noble errand as openly as the ministers.

Doctor Quesnay often, in my presence, flew in such a rage about that *infamous* minister, as he called him, that he foamed at the mouth. "I would as soon dine with the hangman as with the Postmaster-General," said the Doctor. It must be acknowledged that this was astonishing language to be uttered in the apartments of the King's mistress.

The King's Melancholia

The illness of the little Duke of Burgundy, whose intelligence was much talked of, for a long time occupied the attention of the court. Great endeavors were made to find out the cause of his malady, and ill nature went so far as to assert that his nurse, who had an excellent situation at Versailles, had communicated to him a nasty disease. The King showed Madame de Pompadour the information he had procured from the province she came from, as to her conduct. A silly bishop thought proper to say, she had been very licentious in her youth. The nurse was later told of this, and begged that he might be made to explain himself. The bishop replied that she had been at several balls in the town in which she lived, and that she had gone with her neck uncovered. The poor man actually thought this the height of licentiousness. The King, who had been at first uneasy, when he came to this called out, "What a fool!"

After having long been a source of anxiety to the court, the Duke died. Nothing produces a stronger impression upon princes than the spectacle of their equals dying. Everybody is occupied about them while ill—but as soon as they are dead, nobody mentions them. The King frequently talked about death—and about funerals, and places of burial. Nobody could be of a more melancholy temperament. Madame de Pompadour once told me that he experienced a painful sensation whenever he was forced to laugh, and that he had often begged her to break off a droll story. He smiled, and that was all. In general, he had the most gloomy ideas concerning almost all events.

*

The Chevalier de Montaigne fell ill, and underwent an operation called *l'empiéme,* which is performed by making an incision between the ribs, in order to let out the pus; it had, to all appearances, a favorable result, but the patient grew worse and could not breathe. His medical attendants could not conceive what occasioned this accident, and retarded his cure. He died almost in the arms of the Dauphin [Louis XV's son (d. 1765), father of Louis XVI] who went every day to see him.

The singularity of his disease determined the surgeons to open the body, and they found in his chest part of the leaden syringe with which decoctions had, as was usual, been injected into the part in a state of suppuration. The surgeon who committed this act of negligence took care not to boast of his feat, and his patient was the victim.

This incident was much talked of by the King, who related it, I believe, not less than 30 times, according to his custom; but what occasioned still more conversation about the Chevalier de Montaigne was a box, found by his bed's side, containing haircloths and shirts, and whips stained with blood. This circumstance was spoken of one evening at supper, at Madame de Pompadour's, and not one of the guests seemed at all tempted to imitate the Chevalier.

*

An event, which made me tremble, as well as Madame, procured me the familiarity of the King. In the middle of the night, Madame came into my chamber, *en chemise,* and in a state of distraction: "Here! Here!" said she. "The King is dying!" My alarm may be easily imagined. I put on a petticoat, and found the King in her bed, panting. What was to be done? It was an indigestion. We threw water upon him, and he came to himself. I made him swallow some "Hoffman's Drops," and he said to me, "Do not make any noise, but go to Quesnay. Say that your mistress is ill, and tell the Doctor's servants to say nothing about it."

Quesnay, who lodged close by, came immediately, and was much astonished to see the King in that state. He felt his pulse and said, "The crisis is over; but if the King were 60 years old, this might have been serious." He went to seek some drug, and, on his return, set about inundating the King with perfumed water. I forget the name of the medicine that he made him take, but the effect was wonderful. I believe it was the "Drops of General Lamotte."

I called up one of the girls of the wardrobe to make tea, as if for myself. The King took three cups, put on his *robe de chambre* and his stockings, and went to his own room, leaning upon the Doctor. What a sight it was to see us all three half naked! Madame put on a robe as soon as possible, and I did the same, and the King changed his clothes behind the curtains, which were very decently closed.

An hour after, I felt the greatest possible terror in thinking that the King might have died in our hands. Happily, he quickly recovered himself, and none of the domestics perceived what had taken place. I merely told the girl of the wardrobe to put everything to rights, and she thought it was Madame who had been indisposed. The King, the next morning, gave secretly to Quesnay a little note for Madame, in which he said, "*Ma chère amie* must have had a great fright, but let her reassure herself—I am now well, which the Doctor will certify to you."

From that moment the King became accustomed to me; and, touched by the interest I had shown for him, he often gave me one of his peculiarly gracious glances, and made me little presents, and, on every New Year's Day, sent me porcelain to the amount of 20 louis d'ors. He told Madame that he looked upon me in the apartment as a picture or statue, and never put any constraint upon himself on account of my presence. Doctor Quesnay received a pension of 1000 crowns for his attention and silence, and the promise of a place for his son. The King gave me an order upon the Treasury for 4000 francs, and Madame had presented to her a very handsome chiming-clock, and the King's portrait in a snuff-box.

*

The King was habitually melancholy, and liked everything which recalled the idea of death, in spite of the strongest fears of it. Of this the following is an instance. Madame de Pompadour was on her way to Crécy, when one of the King's grooms made a sign to her coachman to stop, then told him that the King's carriage had broken down and, knowing her to be at no great distance, his Majesty had sent him forward to beg her to wait for him. He soon overtook us, and seated himself in Madame de Pompadour's carriage, in which were, I think, Madame de Château-Rénaud and Madame de Mirepoix. The lords in attendance placed themselves in some other carriages. I was behind, in a chaise, with Gourbillon, Madame de Pompadour's *valet de chambre*.

We were surprised in a short time by the King stopping his carriage. Those which followed, of course, stopped also. The King called a groom, and said to him, "You see that little eminence; there are crosses; it must certainly be a burying ground; go and see whether there are any graves newly dug."

The groom galloped up to it, returned, and said to the King, "There are three quite freshly made."

Madame de Pompadour, as she told me, turned away her head with horror, and the little Maréchale de Mirepoix gaily said, "This is indeed enough to make one's mouth water!"

Madame de Pompadour spoke of it when I was undressing her in the evening. "What a strange pleasure!" said she. "To endeavor to fill one's mind with images which one ought to try to banish, especially when one is surrounded by so many sources of happiness! But that is the King's way—he loves to talk about death."

*

The first physician came one day to see Madame; he was talking of madmen and madness. The King was present, and everything relating to disease of any kind interested him. The first physician said that he could distinguish the symptoms of approaching madness six months beforehand.

"Are there any persons about the court likely to become mad?" said the King.

"I know one who will be imbecile in less than three months," replied he.

The King pressed him to tell the name. He excused himself for some time. At last, he said, "It is M. de Sèchelles, the Controller-General."

"You have a spite against him," said Madame, "because he would not grant you what you asked."

"That is true," said he, "but though that might possibly incline me to tell a disagreeable truth, it would not make me invent one. He is losing his intellect from debility. He affects gallantry at his age, and I perceive the connection in his ideas is becoming feeble and irregular."

The King laughed, but three months afterward he came to Madame, saying, "Sèchelles gives evident proofs of dotage in the Council. We must appoint a successor to him."

Some time afterward the first physician came to see Madame, and spoke to her in private. "You are attached to M. Berryer [the Keeper of the Seals], Madame," said he, "and I am sorry to have to warn you that he will be attacked by madness, or by catalepsy, before long. I saw him this morning at chapel sitting on one of those very low little chairs, which are only meant to kneel upon. His knees touched his chin. I went to his house after mass; his eyes were wild, and, when his secretary spoke to him, he said, 'Hold your tongue, pen! A pen's business is to write, not to speak.'"

Madame was very much concerned, and begged the first physician not to mention what he had perceived. Four days after this, M. Berryer was seized with catalepsy, after having talked incoherently. This is a disease which I did not know even by name, and got it written down for me. The patient remains in precisely the same position in which the fit seizes him—one leg or arm elevated, the eyes wide open, or just as it may happen.

Intrigues and Frivolities

I had remarked that Madame de Pompadour for some days had taken chocolate, *à triple vanille et ambré,* at her breakfast; and that she ate truffles and celery soup. Finding her in a very heated state, I one day remonstrated with her about her diet, to which she paid no attention. I then thought it right to speak to her friend, the Duchess de Brancas. "I had remarked the same thing," said she, "and I will speak to her about it before you."

After she was dressed, Madame de Brancas, accordingly, told her she was uneasy about her health. "I have just been talking to her about it," said the Duchess, pointing to me, "and she is of my opinion." Madame de Pompadour seemed a little displeased; at last, she burst into tears. I immediately went out, shut the door, and returned to my place to listen.

"My dear friend," said she to Madame de Brancas, "I am agitated by the fear of losing the King's heart by ceasing to be attractive to him. Men, you know, set great value on certain things, and I have the misfortune to be of a very cold temperament. I therefore determined to adopt a heating diet, in order to remedy this defect; and for two days this elixir has been of great service to me, or at least I have thought I felt its good effects."

The Duchess de Brancas took the vial which was upon the toilet, and after having smelt at it, "Fie!" said she, and threw it into the fire.

Madame de Pompadour scolded her, and said, "I don't like to be treated like a child." She wept again, and said, "You don't know what happened to me a week ago. The King, under pretext of the heat of the weather, lay down upon my sofa and passed half the night there. He will take a disgust to me and have another mistress."

"You will not avoid that," replied the Duchess, "by following your new diet, and that diet will kill you. Render your company more and more precious to the King by your gentleness. Do not repulse him in his fond moments, and let time do the rest. The chains of habit will bind him to you forever." They then embraced; Madame de Pompadour recommended secrecy to Madame de Brancas, and the diet was abandoned.

A little while after, she said to me, "Our master is better pleased with me. This is since I spoke to Quesnay, without, however, telling him all. He told me, that to accomplish my end, I must try to be in good health, to digest well, and, for that purpose, take exercise. I think the Doctor is right, I feel quite a different creature. I adore that man [the King]. I wish so earnestly to be agreeable to him! But alas! Sometimes he says I am a *macreuse* [a cold-blooded aquatic bird]. I would give my life to please him."

*

I one day said to her, "It appears to me, Madame, that you are fonder than ever of the Countess d'Amblimont."

"I have reason to be so," said she. "She is unique, I think, for her fidelity to her friends, and for her honor. Listen—but tell nobody. Four days ago, the King, passing her to go to supper, approached her, under the pretense of tickling her, and tried to slip a note into her hand. D'Amblimont, in her madcap way, put her hands behind her back, and the King was obliged to pick up the note, which had fallen on the ground. Gontaut was the only person who saw all this, and, after supper, he went up to the little lady, and said, 'You are an excellent friend.' 'I did my duty,' said she, and immediately put her finger on her lips to enjoin him to be silent. He, however, informed me of this act of friendship of the little heroine, who had not told me of it herself."

I admired the Countess's virtue, and Madame de Pompadour said, "She is giddy and headlong; but she has more sense and more feeling than a thousand prudes and devotees. D'Esparbès would not do as much—most likely she would meet him more than halfway. The King appeared disconcerted, but he still pays her great attentions."

"You will doubtless, Madame," said I, "show your sense of such admirable conduct."

"You need not doubt it," said she, "but I don't wish her to think that I am informed of it."

The King, prompted either by the remains of his liking or by the suggestions of Madame de Pompadour, one morning went to call on Madame d'Amblimont at Choisy, and threw round her neck a collar of diamonds and emeralds worth between 2 and 3000 pounds.

*

There was a large sofa in a little room adjoining Madame de Pompadour's, upon which I often reposed.

One evening, toward midnight, a bat flew into the apartment where the Count was. The King immediately cried out, "Where is General Crillon?" (He had just left the room.) "He is the general to command against the bats." This set everybody calling out, *"Où étais tu, Crillon?"*

M. de Crillon soon after came in and was told where the enemy was. He immediately threw off his coat, drew his sword, and commenced an attack upon the bat, which flew into the closet where I was fast asleep. I started out of sleep at the noise, and saw the King and all the company around me. This furnished amusement for the rest of the evening. M. de Crillon was a very excellent and agreeable man, but he had the fault of indulging in buffooneries of this kind, which, however, were the result of his natural gaiety, and not of any subserviency of character.

Such, however, was not the case with another exalted nobleman, a Knight of the Golden Fleece, whom Madame saw one day shaking hands with her *valet de chambre*. As he was one of the vainest men at court, Madame could not refrain from telling the circumstance to the King, and, as he had no employment at court, the King scarcely ever after named him on the Supper List.

*

I learned from M. de Marigny [Madame's brother], that the relations of Maréchale [de Mirepoix] had been extremely severe upon her for what they called the baseness of her conduct with regard to Madame de Pompadour. They said she held the stones of the cherries which Madame ate in her carriage in her beautiful little hands, and that she sat in the front of the carriage while Madame occupied the whole seat in the inside. The truth was, that in going to Crécy on an insupportably hot day, they both wished to sit alone, that they might be cooler; and as to the matter of the cherries, the villagers having brought them some, they ate them to refresh themselves while the horses were changed; and the Maréchale emptied her pocket handkerchief, into which they had both thrown the cherry stones, out of the carriage window. The people who were changing the horses had given their own version of the affair.

*

Madame called me one day into her closet, where the King was walking up and down in a very serious mood. "You must," said she, "pass some days in a house in the avenue of Saint Cloud, whither I shall send you. You will there find a young lady about to lie in." The King said nothing, and I was mute from astonishment.

"You will be mistress of the house, and preside, like one of the fabulous goddesses, at the *accouchement*. Your presence is necessary, in order that everything may pass secretly, and according to the King's wish. You will be present at the baptism, and name the father and mother."

The King began to laugh and said, "The father is a very honest man." Madame added, "Beloved by everyone, and adored by those who know him."

Madame then took from a little cupboard a small box, and drew from it an aigrette of diamonds, at the same time saying to the King, "I have my reasons for it not being handsomer."

"It is but too much so," said the King. "How kind you are!" and he then embraced Madame, who wept with emotion.

Putting her hand upon the King's heart, she said, "This is what I wish to secure." The King's eyes then filled with tears, and I also began weeping, without knowing why.

Afterward, the King said, "Guimard will call upon you every day to assist you with his advice, and at the critical moment you will send for him. You will say that you expect the sponsors, and a moment after you will pretend to have received a letter stating that they cannot come. You will, of course, affect to be very much embarrassed; and Guimard will then say that there is nothing for it but to take the first comers. You will then appoint a godfather and godmother—some beggar or some chairman [of a Sedan chair, that is] and the servant girl of the house—and to whom you will give but 12 francs, in order not to attract attention."

"A louis," added Madame, "to obviate anything singular, on the other hand."

"It is you who make me economical, under certain circumstances," said the King. "Do you remember the hackney coachman? I wanted to give him a louis, and the Duke d'Ayen said, 'You will be known'; so therefore I gave him a crown." He was going to tell the whole story. Madame made a sign to him to be silent, which he obeyed, not without considerable reluctance. (She afterward told me that, at the time of the fêtes given on occasion of the Dauphin's marriage, the King came to see her at her mother's house in a hackney-coach. The coachman would not go on, and the King would have given him a louis. "The police will hear of it if you do," said the Duke d'Ayen, "and its spies will make inquiries, which will, perhaps, lead to a discovery.")

"Guimard," continued the King, "will tell you the names of the father and mother; he will be present at the ceremony and make the usual presents. It is but fair that you also should receive yours." And, as he said this, he gave me 50 louis, with that gracious air that he could so well assume upon certain occasions, and which no person in the kingdom had but himself. I kissed his hand, and wept. "You will take care of the *accouchée,* will you not? She is a good creature, who has not invented gunpowder, and I confide her entirely to your direction. My chancellor will tell you the rest," he said, turning to Madame, and then quitted the room.

"Well, what think you of the part I am playing?" asked Madame.

"It is that of a superior woman, and an excellent friend," I replied.

"It is his heart that I wish to secure," said she, "and all those young girls who have no education will not run away with it from me. I should not be equally confident were I to see some fine women belonging to the court, or the city, attempt his conquest."

I asked Madame if the young lady knew that the King was the father of her child.

"I do not think she does now," replied she, "but as he appears fond of her, there is some reason to fear that those about her, who might suspect the truth, will tell her so," said she, shrugging her shoulders. "She and all the other sultanas are told that he is a Polish nobleman, a relation of the Queen, who has apartments in the castle."

This story was contrived on account of the *cordon bleu,* which the King has not always time to lay aside—because to do that he must change his coat—and also in order to account for his having a lodging in the castle so near the King. There were two little rooms by the side of the chapel, whither the King retired from his apartment without being seen by anybody but a sentinel, who had his orders, and who did not know who passed through those rooms. The King sometimes went to the Parc aux Cerfs [the notorious Deer Park] or received those young ladies in the apartments I have mentioned.

Madame de Pompadour said to me, "Be constantly with the *accouchée* to prevent any stranger, or even the people of the house, from speaking to her. You will always say that he is a very rich Polish nobleman, who is obliged to conceal himself on account of his relationship to the Queen, who is very devout. You will find a wet nurse in the house, to whom you will deliver the child. Guimard will manage all the rest. You will go to church as a witness; everything must be conducted as if for a substantial citizen. The young lady expects to lie in in five or six days; you will dine with her, and will not leave her till she is in a state of health to return to the Parc aux Cerfs, which she may do in a fortnight, as I imagine, without running any risk."

I went that same evening to the Avenue de Saint Cloud, where I found the Abbess and Guimard, an attendant belonging to the castle, but without his blue coat. There were, besides, a nurse, a wet nurse, two old menservants, and a girl, who was something between a servant and a waiting woman. The young lady was extremely pretty, and dressed very elegantly, though not too remarkably. I supped with her and the mother abbess, who was called Madame Bertrand. Before supper I had presented the aigrette Madame de Pompadour gave me, which had greatly delighted the young lady, and she was in high spirits. Madame Bertrand had been housekeeper to M. Lebel, first *valet de chambre* to the King [and his procurer]. He called her Dominique, and she was entirely in his confidence. The young lady chatted with us after supper; she appeared to me very naïve.

The next day, I talked to her in private. She said to me, "How is the Count?" (It was the King whom she called by this title.) "He will be very sorry not to be with me now, but he was obliged to set off on a long journey." I assented to what she said. "He is very handsome," said she, "and loves me with all his heart. He promised me an allowance, but I love him disinterestedly. And if he would let me, I would follow him to Poland."

She afterward talked to me about her parents, and about M. Lebel, whom she knew by the name of Durand. "My mother," said she, "kept a large grocer's shop, and my father was a man of some consequence; he belonged to the Six Corps, and that, as everybody knows, is an excellent thing. He was twice very near being head bailiff." Her mother had become bankrupt at her father's death, but the "Count" had come to her assistance and settled upon her 60 pounds a year, besides giving her 240 pounds down.

On the sixth day she was brought to bed, and, according to my instructions, she was told the child was a girl, though in reality it was a boy; she was soon to be told that it was dead, in order that no trace of its existence might remain for a certain time. It was eventually to be restored to its mother. The King gave each of his children 4 or 500 pounds a year. They inherited after each other as they died off, and seven or eight were already dead.

I returned to Madame de Pompadour, to whom I had written every day. The next day the King sent for me into the room; he did not say a word as to the business I had been employed upon; but he gave me a large gold snuff-box containing two rouleaux of 25 louis each. I curtsied to him, and retired.

Madame asked me a great many questions of the young lady, and laughed heartily at her simplicity, and at all she had said about the Polish nobleman. "He is disgusted with the Princess," she said, "and, I think, will return to Poland forever in two months."

"And the young lady?" said I.

"She will be married in the country," said she, "with a portion of 40,000 crowns at the most, and a few diamonds."

This little adventure, which initiated me into the King's secrets, far from procuring for me increased marks of kindness from him, seemed to produce a coldness toward me, probably because he was ashamed of my knowing his obscure amours. He was also embarrassed by the services Madame de Pompadour had rendered him on this occasion.

*

Besides the little mistresses of the Parc aux Cerfs, the King had sometimes intrigues with ladies of the court, or from Paris, who wrote to him. A rich man, who had a situation in the Revenue Department, called on me one day very secretly, and told me that he had something of importance to communicate to Madame la Marquise, but that he should find himself very much embarrassed in communicating it to her personally. He then told me what I already knew, that he had a very beautiful wife, of whom he was very passionately fond; that having on one occasion perceived her kissing a little *portefeuille,* he endeavored to get possession of it, supposing there was some mystery attached to it. One day, when she suddenly left the room to go upstairs to see her sister, who had been brought to bed, he took the opportunity of opening the *portefeuille* and was very much surprised to find in it a portrait of the King and a very tender letter written by his Majesty. Of the latter he took a copy, as also of an unfinished letter of his wife in which she vehemently entreated the King to allow her to have the pleasure of an interview—the means she pointed out. She was to go masked to the public ball at Versailles, where his Majesty could meet her under the favor of a mask.

I assured M. de —— that I should acquaint Madame with the affair, who would, no doubt, feel very grateful for the communication. He then added, "Tell Madame la Marquise that my wife is very clever and very intriguing. I adore her, and should run distracted were she to be taken from me."

I lost not a moment in acquainting Madame with the affair, and gave her the letter. She became serious and pensive, and I since learned that she consulted M. Berrier, Lieutenant of the Police, who, by a very simple but ingeniously conceived plan, put an end to the designs of this lady. He demanded an audience of the King, and told him that there was a lady in Paris who was making free with his Majesty's name; that he had been given the copy of a letter supposed to have been written by his Majesty to the lady in question. The copy he put into the King's hands, who read it in great confusion, and then tore it furiously to pieces. M. Berrier added that it was rumored that this lady was to meet his Majesty at the public ball; and, at this very moment, it so happened that a letter was put into the King's hand, which proved to be from the lady, appointing the meeting. At least M. Berrier judged so, as the King appeared very much surprised on reading it, and said, "It must be allowed, M. le Lieutenant of the Police, that you are well informed."

M. Berrier added, "I think it my duty to tell your Majesty that this lady passes for a very intriguing person."

"I believe," replied the King, "that it is not without deserving it that she has got that character."

*

Madame de Pompadour had many vexations in the midst of all her grandeur. She often received anonymous letters threatening her with poison or assassination. Her greatest fear, however, was that of being supplanted by a rival. I never saw her in a greater agitation than one evening on her return from the drawing room at Marly. She threw down her cloak and muff the instant she came in, with an air of ill humor, and undressed herself in a hurried manner. Having dismissed her other women, she said to me, "I think I never saw anybody so insolent as Madame de Coaslin. I was seated at the same table with her this evening, at a game of *brelan* [a French card game, similar to poker, in which a king and a queen constitute a pair] and you cannot imagine what I suffered. The men and women seemed to come in relays to watch us. Madame de Coaslin said two or three times, looking at me, '*Va tout,*' in the most insulting manner. I thought I should have fainted when she said, in a triumphant tone, 'I have the *brelan* of kings.' I wish you had seen her curtsy to me on parting."

"Did the King," said I, "show her particular attention?"

"You don't know him," said she. "If he were going to lodge her this very night in my apartment, he would behave coldly to her before people, and would treat me with the utmost kindness. This is the effect of his education, for he is, by nature, kind-hearted and frank."

Madame de Pompadour's alarms lasted for some months, when she one day said to me, "That haughty Marchioness has missed her aim. She frightened the King by her grand airs, and was incessantly teasing him for money. Now you, perhaps, may not know that the King would sign an order for 40,000 pounds without a thought, and would give 100 out of his little private treasury with the greatest reluctance. Lebel—who likes me better than he would a new mistress in my place—either by chance or design had brought a charming little sultana to the Parc aux Cerfs who has cooled the King a little toward the haughty Vashti by giving him occupation. Mme. —— has received 4000 pounds, some jewels, and an estate. Janette [the Superintendent of the Post] has rendered me great service by showing the King extracts from the letters broken open at the post-office concerning the report that Madame de Coaslin was coming into favor."

*

This was not Madame's only subject of alarm. A relation of Countess d'Estrades, wife of the Marquis de C——, had made the most pointed advances to the King, much more than was necessary for a man who justly thought himself the handsomest man in France and who was, moreover, a King. He was perfectly persuaded that every woman would yield to the slightest desire he might deign to manifest. He therefore thought it a mere matter of course that women fell in love with him. M. de Stanville had a hand in marring the success of that intrigue; and, soon afterward, the Marchioness de C——, who was confined to her apartments at Marly by her relations, escaped through a closet to a rendezvous, and was caught with a young man in a corridor. The Spanish Ambassador, coming out of his apartments with a flambeau, was the person who witnessed this scene. Countess d'Estrades affected to know nothing of her cousin's intrigues, and kept up an appearance of the tenderest attachments to Madame de Pompadour, whom she was habitually betraying. She acted as spy for M. d'Argenson [Minister of Foreign Affairs, also Madame de Pompadour's enemy] in the cabinets and in Madame de Pompadour's apartments; and when she could discover nothing, she had recourse to her invention, in order that she might not lose her importance with her lover. This Countess d'Estrades owed her whole existence to the bounties of Madame, and yet, ugly as she was, she had tried to get away the King from her.

One day, when he had got rather drunk at Choisy (I think the only time that ever happened to him), he went on board a beautiful barge, whither Madame, being ill of an indigestion, could not accompany him. Countess d'Estrades seized this opportunity. She got into the barge, and, on their return, as it was dark, she followed the King into a private closet, where he was believed to be sleeping on a couch, and there went somewhat beyond any ordinary advances to him. Her account of the matter to Madame was that she had gone into the closet upon her own affairs, and that the King had followed her, and had tried to ravish her. She was at full liberty to make what story she pleased, for the King knew neither what he had said, nor what he had done.

I shall finish this subject by a short history concerning a young lady. I had been, one day, at the theater at Compiègne. When I returned, Madame asked me several questions about the play, whether there was much company, and whether I did not see a very beautiful girl. I replied, "There was, indeed, a girl in a box near mine, who was surrounded by all the young men about the court."

She smiled, and said, "That is Mademoiselle Dorothée. She went this evening to see the King sup in public, and tomorrow she is to be taken to the hunt. You are surprised to find me so well informed, but I know a great deal more about her. She was brought here by a Gascon, named Dubaré or Dubarri, who is the greatest scoundrel in France. He founds all his hopes of advancement on Mademoiselle Dorothée's charms, which he thinks the King cannot resist. She is, really, very beautiful. She was pointed out to me in my little garden, whither she was taken to walk on purpose. She is the daughter of a water carrier at Strasbourg, and her charming lover demands to be sent as minister to Cologne, as a beginning."

"Is it possible, Madame, that you can have been rendered uneasy by such a creature as that?"

"Nothing is impossible," replied she, "though I think the King would scarcely dare to create such a scandal. Besides, happily, Lebel, to quiet his conscience, told the King that the beautiful Dorothée's love is infected with a horrid disease; and, added he, 'Your Majesty would not get rid of that as you have done of scrofula.' * This was quite enough to keep the young lady at a distance."

"I pity you sincerely, Madame," said I, "while everybody else envies you."

"Ah," replied she, "my life is that of the Christian, a perpetual warfare! This was not the case with the women who enjoyed the favor of Louis XIV. Madame de la Vallière suffered herself to be deceived by Madame de Montespan, but it was her own fault—or, rather, the effect of her extreme good nature. She was entirely devoid of suspicion at first, because she could not believe her friend perfidious. Madame de Montespan's empire was shaken by Madame de Fontanges, and overthrown by Madame de Maintenon; but her haughtiness, her caprices, had already alienated the King. She had not, however, such rivals as mine; it is true, their baseness is my security. I have, in general, little to fear but casual infidelities, and the chance that they may not all be sufficiently transitory for my safety. The King likes variety, but he is also bound by habit; he fears *éclats*, and detests maneuvering women. The little Maréchale [de Mirepoix] one day said to me, 'It is your staircase that the King loves; he is accustomed to go up and down it. But, if he found another woman to whom he could talk of hunting and business as he does to you, it would be just the same to him in three days.'"

* The King may once have suffered from the King's Evil, or scrofula, supposedly cured by sovereign touch. In this case, the saying, "Physician, heal thyself!" would be doubly applicable.

*

The Countess d'Estrades, who owed everything to Madame de Pompadour, was incessantly intriguing against her. She was clever enough to destroy all proofs of her maneuvers, but she could not so easily prevent suspicion. Her intimate connection with M. d'Argenson gave offense to Madame, and for some time she was more reserved with her. The Countess d'Estrades afterward did a thing which justly irritated the King and Madame.

The King, who wrote a great deal, had written to Madame de Pompadour a long letter concerning an assembly of the chambers of Parlement and had enclosed a letter of M. Berrier. Madame was ill, and laid these letters on a little table by her bedside. M. de Gontaut came in, and gossiped about trifles, as usual. Madame d'Amblimont also came, and stayed but a very little time. Just as I was going to resume a book which I had been reading to Madame, the Countess d'Estrades entered, placed herself near Madame's bed, and talked to her for some time.

As soon as she was gone, Madame called me, asked what was the o'clock, and said, "Order my door to be shut, the King will soon be here."

I gave the order, and returned; and Madame told me to give her the King's letter, which has been on the table with some other papers. I gave her the papers, and told her there was nothing else.

She was very uneasy at not finding the letter, and, after enumerating the persons who had been in the room, she said, "It cannot be the little Countess, nor Gontaut, who has taken this letter. It can only be the Countess d'Estrades—and that is too bad." The King came, and was extremely angry, as Madame told me. Two days afterward, he sent Countess d'Estrades into exile. There was no doubt that she took the letter; the King's handwriting had probably awakened her curiosity.

This occurrence gave great pain to M. d'Argenson, who was bound to her, as Madame de Pompadour said, by his love of intrigue. This redoubled his hatred of Madame, and she accused him of favoring the publication of a libel, in which she was represented as a wornout mistress, reduced to the vile occupation of providing new objects to please her lover's appetite. She was characterized as superintendent of the Parc aux Cerfs, which was said to cost hundreds of thousands of pounds a year. Madame de Pompadour did, indeed, try to conceal some of the King's weaknesses, but she never knew one of the sultanas of that seraglio. There were, however, scarcely ever more than two at once, and often only one. When they married, they received some jewels and 4000 pounds. The Parc aux Cerfs was sometimes vacant for five or six months.*

* The Parc aux Cerfs in reality indicates a whole quarter of the town. The house was Nos. 2 and 4 rue Saint-Médéric, Versailles, and was not large enough to contain more than one young girl at a time. It was hired by the usher Vallet, on the King's account, Nov. 25, 1755; but it is probable that this house or another in the same street had already served for the pleasures of Louis XV. These authentic details have been considerably amplified by legends (French editor's note).

*

There was universal talk of a young lady with whom the King was as much in love as it was possible for him to be. Her name was Romans. She was said to be a charming girl. Madame de Pompadour knew of the King's visits, and her confidantes brought her most alarming reports of the affair. The Maréchale de Mirepoix, who had the best head in Madame's council, was the only one who encouraged her.

"I do not tell you," said she, "that he loves you better than her; and if she could be transported hither by the stroke of a fairy's wand; if she could entertain him this evening at supper; if she were familiar with all his tastes, there would, perhaps, be sufficient reason for you to tremble for your power. But Princes are, above all, pre-eminently the slaves of habit. The King's attachment to you is like that he bears to your apartment, your furniture. You have formed yourself to his manners and habits; you know how to listen and reply to his stories; he is under no constraint with you; he has no fear of *boring* you. How do you think he could have resolution to uproot all this in a day, to form a new establishment, and to make a public exhibition of himself by so striking a change in his arrangements?"

The young lady became pregnant: the reports current among the people, and even those at court, alarmed Madame dreadfully. It was said that the King meant to legitimize the child, and to give the mother a title. "All that," said Madame de Mirepoix, "is in the style of Louis XIV—such dignified proceedings are very unlike those of our master."

Mademoiselle Romans lost all her influence over the King by her indiscreet boasting. She was even treated with harshness and violence, which were in no degree instigated by Madame. Her house was searched, and her papers seized; but the most important, those which substantiated the fact of the King's paternity, had been withdrawn. At length, she gave birth to a son, who was christened under the name of Bourbon, son of Charles de Bourbon, Captain of Horse. The mother thought the eyes of all France were fixed upon her, and beheld in her son a future Duke du Maine. She suckled him herself, and she used to carry him in a sort of basket to the Bois de Boulogne. Both mother and child were covered with the finest laces. She sat down upon the grass in a solitary spot, which, however, was soon well known, and there gave suck to her royal babe.

Madame had great curiosity to see her, and took me one day to the manufactory at Sèvres, without telling me what she projected. After she had bought some cups, she said, "I want to go and walk in the Bois de Boulogne," and gave orders to the coachman to stop at a certain spot where she wished to alight. She had got the most accurate directions, and when she drew near the young lady's haunt, she gave me her arm, drew her bonnet over her eyes, and held her pocket handkerchief before the lower part of her face. We walked for some minutes in a path, from whence we could see the lady suckling her child. Her jet black hair was turned up, and confined by a diamond comb. She looked earnestly at us. Madame bowed to her, and whispered to me, pushing me by the elbow, "Speak to her."

I stepped forward, and exclaimed, "What a lovely child!"

"Yes, Madame," replied she, "I must confess that he is, though I am his mother."

Madame, who had hold of my arm, trembled, and I was not very firm. Mademoiselle Romans said to me, "Do you live in this neighborhood?"

"Yes, Madame," replied I, "I live at Auteuil with this lady, who is just now suffering from a most dreadful toothache."

"I pity her sincerely, for I know that tormenting pain well."

I looked all around, for fear anyone should come up who might recognize us. I took courage to ask her whether the child's father was a handsome man.

"Very handsome—and if I told you his name, you would agree with me."

"I have the honor of knowing him, then, Madame?"

"Most probably you do."

Madame, fearing, as I did, some *rencontre,* said a few words in a low tone, apologizing for having intruded upon her, and we took our leave. We looked behind us repeatedly to see if we were followed, and got into the carriage without being perceived.

"It must be confessed that both mother and child are beautiful creatures," said Madame. "Not to mention the father—the infant has his eyes. If the King had come up while we were there, do you think he would have recognized us?"

"I don't doubt that he would, Madame, and then what an agitation I should have been in! And what a scene it would have been for the bystanders! And, above all, what a surprise to her!"

In the evening, Madame made the King a present of the cups she had bought, but she did not mention her walk for fear Mademoiselle Romans should tell him that two ladies, who knew him, had met her there such a day.

Madame de Mirepoix said to Madame, "Be assured, the King cares very little about children; he has enough of them, and he will not be troubled with the mother or the son. See what sort of notice he takes of the Count de L——, who is so strikingly like him. He never speaks of him, and I am convinced that he will never do anything for him. Again and again I tell you, we do not live under Louis XIV." Madame de Mirepoix had been Ambassadress to London, and had often heard the English make this remark.

*

I have heard—and, indeed, it is certainly true—that M. de Bridge lived on terms of intimacy with Madame when she was Madame d'Etoiles. He used to ride on horseback with her, and as he is so handsome a man that he has retained the name of "the handsome man," it was natural enough that he should be thought the lover of a very handsome woman.

I have heard something more than this. I was told that the King said to M. de Bridge, "Confess, now, that you were her lover. She has acknowledged it to me, and I exact from you this proof of sincerity."

M. de Bridge replied that Madame de Pompadour was at liberty to say what she pleased for her own amusement, or for any other reason; but that he, for his part, could not assert a falsehood; that he had been her friend; that she was a charming companion and had great talents; that he delighted in her society; but that his intercourse with her had never gone beyond the bounds of friendship. He added that her husband was present in all their parties, that he watched her with a jealous eye, and that he would not have suffered him to be so much with her if he had conceived the least suspicion of the kind.

The King persisted, and told him he was wrong to endeavor to conceal a fact which was unquestionable.

*

Whether it was from ambition, or from tenderness, Madame de Pompadour had a regard for her daughter [Alexandrine, child of her marriage with her husband M. d'Etoiles] which seemed to proceed from the bottom of her heart. She was brought up like a princess, and like persons of that rank, was called by her Christian name alone. The first persons at court had an eye to this alliance, but her mother hoped for something more.

The King had a son by Madame de Vintimille who resembled him in face, gesture, and manners. He was called the Comte du ———. Madame de Pompadour had him brought to Bellevue. Colin, her steward, was employed to find means to persuade his tutor to bring him thither. They took some refreshment at the house of the Swiss, and the Marquise, in the course of her walk, appeared to meet them by accident. She asked the name of the child, and admired his beauty. Her daughter came up at the same moment, and Madame de Pompadour led them into a part of the garden where she knew the King would come. He did come, and asked the child's name. He was told, and looked embarrassed when Madame, pointing to them, said they would be a beautiful couple. The King played with the girl, without appearing to take any notice of the boy. While he was eating some figs and cakes which were brought, his attitudes and gestures were so like those of the King, that Madame de Pompadour was in the utmost astonishment.

"Ah!" said she. "Sire, look at the boy!"

"Why?" said he.

"Nothing," replied Madame, "except that one would think one saw his father."

"I did not know," said the King, smiling, "that you were so intimately acquainted with the Comte du L——[the boy's titular father]."

"You ought to embrace him," said she, "he is very handsome."

"I will begin, then, with the young lady," said the King, and embraced them in a cold, constrained manner.

I was present, having joined Mademoiselle's governess. I remarked to Madame in the evening that the King had not appeared very cordial in his caresses.

"That is his way," said she. "But do not those children appear made for each other? If it were Louis XIV, he would make a Duc du Maine of the little boy. I do not ask so much; but a place and a dukedom for his son is very little; and it is because he is his son that I prefer him to all the little dukes of the court. My grandchildren would blend the resemblance of their grandfather and grandmother; and this combination, which I hope to live to see, would one day be my greatest delight." The tears came into her eyes as she spoke.

Alas! Alas! Only six months elapsed when her darling daughter, the hope of her advanced years, the object of her fondest wishes, died suddenly.

*

Narrow Escapes

The people heard of the attempt on the King's life with transports of fury and with the greatest distress.* Their cries were heard under the windows of Madame de Pompadour's apartment. Mobs were collected, and Madame feared the fate of Madame de Châteauroux [the King's former mistress, dismissed by him as a result of public pressure].

Her friends came in every minute to give her intelligence. Her room was, at all times, like a church; everybody seemed to claim a right to go in and out when he chose. Some came, under pretense of sympathizing, to observe her countenance and manner. She did nothing but weep and faint away. Doctor Quesnay never left her, nor did I. M. de St. Florentin came to see her several times, so did the Comptroller-General, and M. Rouillé; but M. de Machault [Keeper of the Seals, and the King's confidant] did not come. The Duchess of Brancas came very frequently. The Abbé de Bernis [the celebrated poet and diplomat] never left us, except to go to inquire for the King. The tears came to his eyes whenever he looked at Madame.

Doctor Quesnay saw the King five or six times a day. "There is nothing to fear," said he to Madame. "If it were anybody else, he might go to a ball."

My son went the next day, as he had done the day the event occurred, to see what was going on at the castle. He told us on his return that the Keeper of the Seals was with the King. I sent him back to see what course he took on leaving the King. He came running back in half an hour to tell me that

* The King was stabbed by a madman, Robert-François Damiens, as he was entering his coach (French editor's note).

the Keeper of the Seals had gone to his own house, followed by a crowd of people. When I told this to Madame, she burst into tears, and said, "Is that a friend?"

The Abbé de Bernis said, "You must not judge him hastily in such a moment as this."

I returned into the drawingroom about an hour after, when the Keeper of the Seals entered. He passed me with his usual cold and severe look. "How is Madame de Pompadour?" said he.

"Alas," replied I, "as you may imagine!"

He passed on to her closet. Everybody retired, and he remained for half an hour.

The Abbé returned, and Madame rang. I went into her room, the Abbé following me. She was in tears. "I must go, my dear Abbé," said she. I made her take some orange-flower water in a silver goblet, for her teeth chattered. She then told me to call her equerry. He came in, and she calmly gave him her orders to have everything prepared at her hotel in Paris; to tell all her people to get ready to go; and to desire her coachman not to be out of the way. She then shut herself up to confer with the Abbé de Bernis, who left her to go to the council. Her door was then shut, except to the ladies with whom she was particularly intimate, M. de Soubise [marshal of France and a close friend of Madame's], M. de Gontaut, the ministers, and some others. Several ladies, in the greatest distress, came to talk to me in my room; they compared the conduct of M. de Machault with the double-dealings of M. de Richelieu at Metz. [Referring to the intrigue at the court of Louis XIII during the so called *"journée des Dupes,"* when Richelieu trumped his former patron Marie de Médicis.]

Madame having sent for me, I saw the Maréchale de Mirepoix coming in. While she was at the door, she cried out, "What are all those trunks, Madame? Your people tell me you are going."

"Alas! my dear friend, such is our Master's desire, as M. de Machault tells me."

"And what does he advise?" said the Maréchale.

"That I should go without delay."

During this conversation, I was undressing Madame, who wished to be at her ease on her chaise longue. "Your Keeper of the Seals wants to get the power into his own hands, and betrays you. He who quits the field loses it," responded the Maréchale.

I went out. M. de Soubise entered, then the Abbé, M. de Marigny, in order to console Madame. M. de Marigny, who was very kind to me, came into my room an hour afterward. I was alone. "She will remain," said he. "But hush! She will make an appearance of going, in order not to set her enemies at work. It is the little Maréchale who prevailed upon her to stay. Her "Keeper"—so she called M. de Machault—"will pay for it." Quesnay came in; and, having heard what was said, with his monkey airs began to relate a fable of a fox who, being at dinner with other beasts, persuaded one of them that his mortal enemies were about to break in, so that he might get possession of his share of the feast during his absence.

I did not see Madame again till very late, at her going to bed. She was more calm. Things improved from day to day, and M. de Machault, the faithless friend, was dismissed. The King returned to Madame de Pompadour, as usual.

The next day, Madame having ordered her chaise, I was curious to know where she was going, for she went out but little, except to church and to the houses of the ministers. I was told that she was gone to visit M. d'Argenson. She returned in an hour at latest and seemed very much out of spirits. She leaned on the chimney-piece, with her eyes fixed on the border of it. M. de Bernis entered. I waited for her to take off her cloak and gloves. She had her hands in her muff.

The Abbé stood looking at her for some minutes. At last he said, "You look like a sheep in a reflecting mood."

She awoke from her reverie and, throwing her muff on the easy chair, replied, "It is a wolf who makes the sheep reflect."

I went out; the King entered shortly after, and I heard Madame de Pompadour sobbing. The Abbé came into my room, and told me to bring some Hoffman's Drops. The King himself mixed the draught with sugar, and presented it to her in the kindest manner possible. She smiled, and kissed the King's hands. I left the room.

Two days after, very early in the morning, I heard of M. d'Argenson's exile. It was her doing, and was, indeed, the strongest proof of her influence that could be given. The King was much attached to M. d'Argenson, and the war [Seven Years' War, 1756–63] then carrying on both by sea and land, rendered the dismissal of two such ministers extremely imprudent. This was the universal opinion at the time.

*

I must here relate a singular adventure, which is only known to six or seven persons, masters or valets. At the time of the attempt to assassinate the King, a young girl, whom he had seen several times, and for whom he had manifested more tenderness than for most, was distracted at this horrible event. The mother-abbess of the Parc aux Cerfs perceived her extraordinary grief, and managed to make her confess that she knew the Polish Count was the King of France. The girl divulged that she had taken from his pocket two letters, one of which was from the King of Spain, the other from the Abbé de Broglie. This was discovered afterward, for neither she nor the mother-abbess knew the names of the writers.

The girl was scolded, and M. Lebel, first *valet de chambre,* who had the management of all those affairs, was called; he took the letters and carried them to the King, who was very much perplexed as to what manner to meet a person so well informed of his condition.

The girl in question, having perceived that the King came secretly to see her companion, while she was neglected, watched his arrival; and, at the moment he entered with the abbess, who was about to withdraw, she rushed distractedly into the room where her rival was. She immediately threw herself at the King's feet.

"Yes," said she, "you are King of all France; but that would be nothing to me if you were not also monarch of my heart: do not forsake me, my beloved sovereign! I was nearly mad when your life was attempted!"

The mother-abbess cried out, "You are mad now!"

The King embraced her, which appeared to restore her to tranquillity. They succeeded in getting her out of the room, and a few days afterward the unhappy girl was taken to a madhouse, where she was treated as if she had been insane, for some days. But she knew well enough that she was not so, and that the King had really been her lover. This lamentable affair was related to me by the mother-abbess, when I had some acquaintance with her at the time of the accouchement I have previously spoken of.

*

When the King spoke of Damiens [the man who had attempted to assassinate him], which was only while his trial lasted, he never called him anything but "that gentleman."

I have heard it said that he proposed having him shut up in a dungeon for life; but that the horrible nature of the crime made the judges insist upon his suffering all the tortures inflicted upon like occasions.*

Great numbers, many of them women, had the barbarous curiosity to witness the execution; amongst others, Madame de P——, a very beautiful woman, and the wife of a farmer-general of the taxes. She hired two places at a window for 12 louis, and played a game of cards in the room whilst waiting for the execution to begin. On this being told to the King, he covered his eyes with his hands, and exclaimed, *"fie, la vilaine!"* I have been told that she, and others, thought to pay their court in this way, and signalize their attachment to the King's person.

La Pompadour Extends Her Sway

I was surprised at seeing the Duchess de Luynes, lady of honor to the Queen [Marie Leczinska, daughter of the deposed King of Poland], come privately to see Madame de Pompadour. She afterward came openly.

One evening after Madame was in bed, she called me and said, "My dear, you will be delighted—the Queen has given me the place of Lady of the Palace. Tomorrow I am to be presented to her. You must make me look well."

* Damiens's arms and legs were attached to four horses, and he was literally torn limb from limb; after which, since the trunk still showed some signs of life, boiling oil and melted lead were poured into his wounds. The execution took place before an immense crowd at the Place des Grèves in Paris on Jan. 5, 1757.

I knew that the King was not so well pleased at this as she was; he was afraid that it would give rise to scandal, and that it might be thought he had forced this nomination upon the Queen. He had, however, done no such thing. It had been represented to the Queen that it was an act of heroism on her part to forget the past; that all scandal would be obliterated when Madame de Pompadour was seen to belong to the court in an honorable manner; and that it would be the best proof that nothing more than friendship now subsisted between the King and the favorite. The Queen received her very graciously.

*

About that time, she had a quarrel with her brother, and both were in the right. Proposals were made to him to marry the daughter of one of the greatest noblemen of the court, and the King consented to create him a duke, and even to make the title hereditary. Madame was right in wishing to aggrandize her brother, but he declared that he valued his liberty above all things, and that he would not sacrifice it except for a person he really loved. He was a true Epicurean philosopher, a man of great capacity, according to the report of those who knew him well and judged him impartially. [M. de Marigny, a connoisseur and patron of the arts, organized the exhibitions held each year in the Salon of the Louvre by the French Academy.]

He said to his sister at that time, "I spare you many vexations by depriving you of a slight satisfaction. The public would be unjust to me, however well I might fulfill the duties of my office. Kings' mistresses are hated enough on their own account; they need not also draw upon themselves the hatred which is directed against ministers."

*

The King had another mistress who gave Madame de Pompadour some uneasiness. She was a woman of quality, and the wife of one of the most assiduous courtiers.

A man in the immediate attendance on the King's person, and who had the care of his clothes, came to me one day and told me that, as he was very much attached to Madame because she was good and useful to the King, he wished to inform me that a letter having fallen out of the pocket of a coat which his Majesty had taken off, he had had the curiosity to read it, and found it to be from the Countess de ——, who had already yielded to the King's desires. In this letter, she required the King to give her 50,000 crowns in money, a regiment for one of her relations, and a bishopric for another, and to dismiss Madame in the space of 15 days.

I acquainted Madame with what this man told me, and she acted with singular greatness of mind. She said to me, "I ought to inform the King of this breach of trust of his servant, who may, by the same means, come to the knowledge of, and make a bad use of, important secrets. I feel a repugnance to ruin the man. However, I cannot permit him to remain near the King's person, and here is what I shall do. Tell him that there is a place of 10,000 francs a year vacant in one of the provinces. Let him solicit the Minister of Finance for it, and it shall be granted to him. But if he should ever disclose through what interest he has obtained it, the King shall be made acquainted with his conduct. By this means, I think I shall have done all that my attachment and duty prescribe. I rid the King of a faithless domestic, without ruining the individual."

I did as Madame ordered me. Her delicacy and address inspired me with admiration. She was not alarmed on account of the lady, seeing what her pretentions were. "She drives too quick," remarked Madame, "and will certainly be overturned on the road."

*

The King came into Madame de Pompadour's room one day as she was finishing dressing. "I have just had a strange adventure," said he. "Would you believe that, in going out of my wardroom into my bedroom, I met a gentleman face to face?"

"My God, Sire!" cried Madame, terrified.

"It was nothing," replied he, "but I confess I was greatly surprised. The man appeared speechless with consternation. 'What do you do here?' said I, civilly. He threw himself on his knees, saying, 'Pardon me, Sire—and, above all, have me searched.' He instantly emptied his pockets himself; he pulled off his coat in the greatest agitation and terror. At last, he told me that he was cook to ——, and a friend of Beccari, whom he came to visit; that he had mistaken the staircase, and, finding all the doors open, he had wandered into the room in which I found him, and which he would have instantly left. I rang. Guimard came and was astonished enough at finding me tête-à-tête with a man in his shirt. He begged Guimard to go with him into another room and to search his whole person. After this the poor devil returned, and put on his coat. Guimard said to me, 'He is certainly an honest man, and tells the truth; this may, besides, be easily ascertained.' Another of the servants of the palace came in, and happened to know him. 'I will answer for this good man,' said he, 'who, moreover, makes the best bœuf à l'écarlate in the world.'

"As I saw the man was so agitated that he could not stand steady, I took 50 louis out of my bureau, and said, 'Here, Sir, are 50 louis, to quiet your alarms.' He went out, after throwing himself at my feet."

Madame exclaimed on the impropriety of having the King's bedroom thus accessible to everybody. M. de Marigny said, when I told him of this adventure, "It is most astonishing to reflect on what might have happened. The King might actually have been assassinated in his chamber, without anybody knowing anything of the matter, and without a possibility of discovering the murderer."

For more than a fortnight, Madame could not get over this incident.

Affairs of State

I never saw the King so agitated as during the illness of the Dauphin. The physicians came incessantly to the apartments of Madame de Pompadour, where the King interrogated them. Everybody's eyes were upon the Duke of Orléans, who knew not how to look. He would have become heir to the crown, the Queen being past the age to have children. Madame de —— said to me one day when I was expressing my surprise at the King's grief, "It would annoy him beyond measure to have a prince of the blood heir apparent. He does not like them, and looks upon their relationship to him as so remote that he feels humiliated by it."

The people, however, did not show so much joy at the Dauphin's recovery. They looked upon him as a devotee, who did nothing but sing psalms. They loved the Duke of Orléans, who lived in the capital, and had acquired the name of the "King of Paris." The Duke of Orléans paid the most assiduous court to Madame de Pompadour; the Duchess, on the contrary, detested her. It is possible that words were put in the Duchess's mouth that she never uttered; but she certainly often said most cutting things. The King would have sent her into exile, had he listened only to his resentment; but he feared the *éclat* of such a proceeding, and he knew that she would only be the more malicious.

*

An adventure happened about the same time which the Lieutenant of Police reported to the King. The Duchess of Orléans had amused herself one evening, about 8 o'clock, with ogling a handsome young Dutchman, whom she took a fancy to, from a window of the Palais Royal. The young man, taking her for a woman of the town, wanted to make short work, at which she was very much shocked. She called a Swiss, and made herself known. The stranger was arrested, but he defended himself by affirming that she had talked very loosely to him. He was dismissed, and the Duke of Orléans gave his wife a severe reprimand.

The King (who hated her so much that he spoke of her without the slightest restraint) one day said to Madame de Pompadour, in my presence, "Her mother knew what she was, for before her marriage she never suffered her to say more than yes and no."

*

"See what the court is—all is corruption there, from the highest to the lowest," said I to Madame one day when she was speaking to me of some facts that had come to my knowledge.

"I could tell you many others," replied Madame, "but the little chamber where you often remain must furnish you with a sufficient number."

She was referring to the little nook from whence I could hear a great part of what passed in Madame's apartment. The Lieutenant of Police sometimes came secretly to this apartment, and waited there. Three or four persons of high consideration also found their way in, in a mysterious manner, and several devotees who were, in their hearts, enemies of Madame de Pompadour. But these men had not petty objects in view—one required the government of a province; another, a seat in the Council; a third, a captaincy of the guards. And this man would have obtained it if the Maréchale de Mirepoix had not requested it for her brother, the Prince of Beauvau.

*

The King used to say, "My son is lazy; his temper is Polonese—hasty and changeable; he has no tastes; he cares nothing for hunting, for women, or for good living. Perhaps he imagines that, if he were in my place, he would be happy. At first he would make great changes, create everything anew, as it were. In a short time, he would be as tired of the rank of King as he now is of his own. He is only fit to live *en philosophe,* with clever people about him." The King added, "He loves what is right; he is truly virtuous, and does not want understanding."

M. de St. Germain said one day to the King, "To think well of mankind, one must be neither a confessor, nor a minister, nor a lieutenant of police."

"Nor a King," said his Majesty.

"Ah! Sire," replied he, "you remember the fog we had a few days ago, when we could not see four steps before us? Kings are commonly surrounded by still thicker fogs, collected around them by men of intriguing character and faithless ministers. All, of every class, unite in endeavoring to make things appear to kings in any light but the true one."

I heard this from the mouth of the famous Count de St. Germain as I was attending upon Madame, who was ill in bed. The King was there; and the Count, who was a welcome visitor, had been admitted.

I remember that the very same day after the Count was gone out, the King talked in a style which gave Madame great pain. Speaking of the King of Prussia [Frederick II, the Great], he said, "That is a madman, who will risk all to gain all, and may perhaps win the game, though he has neither religion, morals, nor principles. He wants to make a noise in the world, and he will succeed. Julian the Apostate did the same."

"I never saw the King so animated before," observed Madame when he was gone out. "And really the comparison with Julian the Apostate is not amiss, considering the irreligion of the King of Prussia. If he gets out of his perplexities, surrounded as he is by his enemies, he will be one of the greatest men in history."

The King disliked the King of Prussia because he knew that the latter was in the habit of jesting upon his mistress and the kind of life he led. It was

Frederick's fault, as I have heard it said, that the King was not his most steadfast ally and friend, as much as sovereigns can be toward each other; but the jestings of Frederick had stung him.

*

Calling one day at Quesnay's, I found they were talking of M. de Choiseul. "He is a mere *petit maître*," said the Doctor, "and, if he were handsomer, just fit to be one of Henry III's favorites."

The Marquis de Mirabeau [one of the so-called *économistes,* or "physiocrats," father of the statesman Honoré Gabriel Mirabeau] and M. de la Rivière came in.

"This kingdom," said Mirabeau, "is in a deplorable state. There is neither national energy, nor the only substitute for it—money."

"It can only be regenerated," said de la Rivière, "by a conquest, like that of China, or by some great internal convulsion. But woe to those who live to see that! The French people do not do things by halves." These words made me tremble, and I hastened out of the room.

On other occasion, Doctor Quesnay remarked, "Louis XIV liked verses, and patronized poets. That was very well, perhaps, in his time, because one must begin with something. But this age will be very superior to the last. It must be acknowledged that Louis XV, in sending astronomers to Mexico and Peru to measure the earth, has a higher claim to our respect than if he directed an opera. He has thrown down the barriers that opposed the progress of philosophy, in spite of the clamor of the devotees. The Encyclopedia [of Diderot] will do honor to his reign."

I one day found Quesnay in great distress. "Mirabeau," said he, "is sent to Vincennes for his work on taxation. The Farmers-General have denounced him and procured his arrest; his wife is going to throw herself at the feet of Madame de Pompadour today."

A few minutes afterward, I went into Madame's apartment to assist at her toilet, and the Doctor came in. Madame said to him, "You must be much concerned at the disgrace of your friend Mirabeau. I am sorry for it, too, for I like his brother."

Quesnay replied, "I am very far from believing him to be actuated by bad intentions, Madame. He loves the King and the people."

"Yes," said she, "his *L'Ami des Hommes* [Mirabeau's celebrated book, published in English as *The Friend of Man*] did him great honor." At this moment the Lieutenant of Police entered, and Madame said to him, "Have you seen M. de Mirabeau's book?"

"Yes, Madame, but it was not I who denounced it."

"What do you think of it?"

"I think he might have said almost all it contains with impunity if he had been more circumspect as to the manner; there are, among other objectionable passages, this, which occurs at the beginning: 'Your Majesty has about 20 millions of subjects. It is only by means of money that you can obtain their services, and there is no money.' "

"What, is there really that, doctor?" said Madame.

"It is true—they are the first lines in the book—and I confess that they are imprudent. But in reading the work it is clear that he laments that patriotism is extinct in the hearts of his fellow citizens, and that he desires to rekindle it."

The King entered; we went out, and I wrote down on Quesnay's table what I had just heard. I then returned to finish dressing Madame de Pompadour. She said to me, "The King is extremely angry with Mirabeau, but I tried to soften him, and so did the Lieutenant of Police. This will increase Quesnay's fears. Do you know what he said to me today? The King had been talking to him in my room, and the Doctor appeared timid and agitated. After the King was gone, I said to him, 'You always seem so embarrassed in the King's presence, and yet he is so good-natured.' 'Madame,' said he, 'I left my native village at the age of 40, and I have very little experience of the world, nor can I accustom myself to its usages without great difficulty. When I am in a room with the King, I say to myself, 'This is a man who can order my head to be cut off'—and that idea embarrasses me.' "

*

The King, who admired everything of the age of Louis XIV, and recollected that the Boileaus and Racines had been protected by that monarch—who was indebted to them, in part, for the luster of his reign—was flattered at having such a man as Voltaire among his subjects. But still he feared him, and had but little esteem for him. He could not help saying, "Moreover, I have treated him as well as Louis XIV treated Racine and Boileau. I have given him, as Louis XIV gave to Racine, some pensions, and a place of gentleman in ordinary. It is not my fault if he has committed absurdities, and has had the pretension to become a chamberlain, to wear an order, and sup with a King [Frederick the Great]. It is not the fashion in France; and, as there are here a few more men of wit and noblemen than in Prussia, it would require that I should have a very large table to assemble them all at it."

And then he reckoned upon his fingers, Maupertuis, Fontenelle, Voltaire, Piron, Déstoúches, Montesquieu, the Cardinal Polignac.

"Your Majesty forgets," said someone, "d'Alembert and Clairaut."

"And Crébillon," said he.

"And la Chaussée, and the younger Crébillon," said someone. "He ought to be more agreeable than his father."

"And there are also the Abbés Prévost and d'Olivet."

"Pretty well," said the King. "And for the last 20 years *all that* [*tout cela*] would have dined and supped at my table."

Madame de Pompadour Foresees the End

Madame took it into her head to consult a fortune-teller called Madame Bontemps, who had told M. de Bernis's fortune and had surprised him by her predictions.* Madame informed me of this, and asked me how she could disguise herself, so as to see the woman without being known.

I dared not propose any scheme then for fear it should not succeed. But two days later I talked to her surgeon about the art which some beggars practice of counterfeiting sores and altering their features. He said, that was easy enough. I let the thing drop; and, after an interval of some minutes, I said, "If one could change one's features, one might have great diversion at the opera or at balls. What alterations would it be necessary to make in me, now, to render it impossible to recognize me?"

"In the first place," said he, "you must alter the color of your hair; then you must have a false nose and put a spot on some part of your face, or a wart, or a few hairs."

I laughed, and said, "Help me to contrive this for the next ball. I have not been to one for 20 years, but I am dying to puzzle somebody and to him tell things which no one but I can tell him."

"I must take the measure of your nose," said he, "or you can take it with wax, and I will have a nose made. You can also get a flaxen or brown wig."

I repeated to Madame what the surgeon had told me. She was delighted at it. I took the measure of her nose, and of my own, and carried them to the surgeon, who, in two days, gave me the two noses, and a wart, which Madame stuck under her left eye, and some paint for the eyebrows. The noses were most delicately made—of a bladder, I think—and these, with the other disguises, rendered it impossible to recognize the face, and yet did not produce any shocking appearance.

All this being accomplished, nothing remained but to give notice to the fortune-teller. We waited for a little excursion to Paris, which Madame was to take in order to look at her house. I then got a person, with whom I had no connection, to speak to a waiting woman of the Duchess de Rufféc, to obtain an interview with the woman. She made some difficulty, on account of the police; but we promised secrecy and appointed the place of meeting.

Nothing could be more contrary to Madame de Pompadour's character, which was one of extreme timidity, than to engage in such an adventure. But her curiosity was raised to the highest pitch, and, moreover, everything was so well arranged that there was not the slightest risk. Madame had let M. de Gontaut and her *valet de chambre* into the secret. The latter had hired two rooms for his niece, who was then ill, at Versailles, near Madame's *hôtel*. We went out in the evening, followed by the *valet de chambre*, who

---

* La Pompadour had retained a superstitious belief in necromancy from the time in her early youth when an old woman, known for her psychic powers, had hailed her as *"un morceau de roi"* and prophesied that she would some day become the mistress of the king. Upon being installed as Louis XV's favorite, she sought out this woman, who was still living, and lavishly rewarded her.

was a safe man, and by the Duke, all on foot. We had not, at farthest, above 200 steps to go.

We were shown into two small rooms in which were fires. The two men remained in one, and we in the other. Madame had thrown herself on a sofa. She had on a nightcap which concealed half her face, and was worn in an unstudied manner. I was near the fire, leaning on a table, on which were two candles. There were lying on the chairs near us some cloths of small value. The fortune-teller rang—a little servant girl let her in, and then went to wait in the room where the gentlemen were. Coffee cups, and a coffee pot, were set; and I had taken care to place upon a little buffet some cakes and a bottle of Malaga wine, having heard that Madame Bontemps assisted her inspiration with that liquor. Her face, indeed, sufficiently proclaimed it.

"Is that lady ill?" said she, seeing Madame de Pompadour stretched languidly on the sofa.

I told her that she would soon be better, but that she had kept within her room for a week. She heated the coffee and prepared the two cups, which she carefully wiped, observing that nothing impure must enter into this operation. I affected to be very anxious for a glass of wine in order to give our oracle a pretext for assuaging her thirst, which she did, without much entreaty. When she had drunk two or three small glasses (for I had taken care not to have large ones), she poured the coffee into one of the two large cups.

"This is yours," said she, "and this is your friend's—let them stand a little." She then observed our hands and our faces; after which she drew a looking glass from her pocket, into which she told us to look, while she looked at the reflections of our faces. She next took a glass of wine, and immediately threw herself into a fit of enthusiasm while she inspected my cup and considered all the lines formed by the dregs of the coffee she had poured out. She began by saying:

"That is well—prosperity—but there is a black mark—distresses. A man becomes a comforter. Here, in this corner, are friends, who support you. Ah! Who is he that prosecutes them? But justice triumphs—after rain, sunshine—a long journey, successful. There, do you see these little bags? That is money which has been paid—to you, of course, I mean. That is well. Do you see that arm?"

"Yes."

"That is an arm supporting something: a woman veiled. I see her—it is you. All this is clear to me. I hear, as it were, a voice speaking to me. You are no longer attacked. I see it, because the clouds in that direction are passed off (pointing to a clearer spot). But, stay—I see small lines which branch out from the main spot. These are sons, daughters, nephews—that is pretty well."

She appeared overpowered with the effort she was making. At length, she added: "That is all. You have had good luck first—misfortune afterward. You have had a friend who has exerted himself with success to extricate you from it. You have had lawsuits—at length fortune has been reconciled to you, and will change no more."

She drank another glass of wine. "Your health, Madame," said she to the Marchioness, and went through the same ceremonies with the cup. At length, she broke out: "Neither fair nor foul. I see there, in the distance, a serene sky; and then all these things that appear to ascend—all these things are applauses. Here is a grave man, who stretches out his arms. Do you see? Look attentively."

"That is true," said Madame de Pompadour with surprise (there was, indeed, some appearance of the kind).

"He points to something square—that is an open coffer. Fine weather. But, look, there are clouds of azure and gold which surround you. Do you see that ship on the high seas? How favorable the wind is! You are on board; you land in a beautiful country, of which you become the Queen. Ah! What do I see? Look there—look at that hideous, crooked, lame man who is pursuing you—but he is going on a fool's errand. I see a very great man, who supports you in his arms. Here, look, he is a kind of giant. There is a great deal of gold and silver—a few clouds here and there. But you have nothing to fear. The vessel will be sometimes tossed about, but it will not be lost. . . . *Dixi.*"

Madame said, "When shall I die, and of what disease?"

"I never speak of that," said she. "See here, rather—but fate will not permit it. I will show you how fate confounds everything"—showing her several confused lumps of the coffee dregs.

"Well, never mind as to the time, then, only tell me the kind of death."

The fortune-teller looked in the cup, and said, "You will have time to prepare yourself."

I gave her only two louis, to avoid doing anything remarkable. She left us, after begging us to keep her secret.

Madame told the King of the adventure her curiosity had led her into, at which he laughed, and said that he wished the police had arrested her. He added a very sensible remark: "In order to judge," said he, "of the truth or falsehood of such predictions, one ought to collect 50 of them. It would be found that they are almost always made up of the same phrases, which are sometimes inapplicable, and sometimes hit the mark. But the first are rarely mentioned, while the others are always insisted on."

*

Madame had terrible palpitations of the heart. Her heart actually seemed to leap. She consulted several physicians. I recollect that one of them made her walk up and down the room, lift a weight, and move quickly. On her expressing some surprise, he said: "I do this to ascertain whether the organ is diseased; in that case motion quickens the pulsation. If that effect is not produced, the complaint proceeds from the nerves."

I repeated this to my oracle, Quesnay. He knew very little of this physician, but he said his treatment was that of a clever man. His name was Rénard; he was scarcely known beyond the Marais. Madame often appeared suffocated, and sighed continually.

One day, under pretense of presenting a petition to M. de Choiseul, as he was going out I said, in a low voice, that I wished to see him a few minutes on an affair of importance to my mistress. He told me to come as soon as I pleased, and that I should be admitted. I told him that Madame was extremely depressed; that she gave way to distressing thoughts, which she would not communicate; that she said one day to me, "The fortune-teller told me I should have time to prepare myself. I believe it, for I shall be worn to death by melancholy."

Madame's illness increased so rapidly that we were alarmed about her; but bleeding in the foot cured her as if by a miracle. The King watched her with the greatest solicitude; and I don't know whether his attentions did not contribute as much to the cure as the bleeding.

*

Madame de Pompadour died not long after, in 1764, of what was described by her physicians as a "fever." The King is reported to have made the cruel remark at her funeral that he had never loved her, but suppressed his true feelings out of fear that his rejection might prove fatal.

Toward the end of his life, he took as favorite a demimondaine from Paris, Jeanne Bécu, who had become by marriage with a superannuated courtier the Countess du Barry. The King died of smallpox in 1774, at the age of 64, and was succeeded by his grandson Louis XVI. Madame du Barry survived him for nineteen years, when she was guillotined during the Terror in 1793.

Catherine the Great

reminded of sweltering Crete
and Pasiphae's pungent sweat
   Basil Bunting, *Briggflatts*

When *the aging and sagging Catherine, with her by then amoeboid
embonpoint laced and trussed into her corsets, her wrinkles concealed beneath
diamond chokers and a thick impasto of rouge and powder, asthmatic and
toothless besides, and with legs so swollen with dropsy that she swayed and
tottered as she walked, yet still sexually rampant and passionate as ever, took
as her last favorite a 25-year-old lieutenant of the Horse Guards named Plato
Zubov, the wits at court said that Catherine had finally ended her long career of
debauchery with "platonic love." But to those in the know the point of the joke
went even deeper. For it seems that Zubov, with the Empress's consent, kept a
blooming young peasant wench in a side chamber, and then when fully aroused,
but just before the climactic moment, would rush into Catherine's bedroom,
where he would impress the seminal "Idea" of his love upon her.*

*It is this image of the Empress as an imperially demanding and insatiable
virago, "The Semiramis of the North," as Voltaire once dubbed her, that
fascinated her own contemporaries. They also admired her, however, as the
most enlightened as well as politically adroit and ruthless of the despots of
Europe. During the 34 years of her reign she enormously expanded the
territories of Russia by wars of conquest, chiefly at the expense of Turkey and
Poland (installing her lover Poniatowski on the Polish throne in 1764);
established the legal and departmental system by which the nation was governed
until the revolution of 1917; and forwarded the westernization of the country
begun by that other Russian potentate styled "the Great," Peter I. But now that
the history of those times has faded, the Catherine who still glows in the modern
consciousness is the aforesaid imperial beldam—there she goes!—almost like
the Grand Signor himself in drag, stumping painfully on high heels through the
corridors of her palace between a double row of stalwart young guardsmen,
resplendently gold-braided, bemedaled, codpieced and accoutered with spurs*

and plumes, all standing stiffly at attention while she selects a stud for the night.

Her own self-conception was of course quite different. In a letter she once wrote to assuage the jealousy of the most illustrious of her favorites, Potemkin, Catherine confessed that she had had several lovers before him, but then declared: "God is my witness that it was not through wantonness, for which I have no leanings, and had I been destined as a young woman to get a husband whom I could have loved, I would never have changed toward him. The trouble is that my heart is loath to remain even one hour without love." And surely meant every word—notwithstanding that they came from a woman who, with her lover Gregory Orlov, had plotted the overthrow and then acquiesced in the murder of her husband Czar Peter III. Howbeit, though the average male chauvinist cochon, *even in these days of Women's Lib, expects more ("O world, be nobler for her sake!") of the average female chauvinist sow, power still tends to corrupt either sex impartially, and absolute power absolutely. Catherine must have fancied the idea of herself as a faithful and loving spouse, just as she once fervently espoused the revolutionary ideas of Voltaire and Montesquieu, Diderot and d'Alembert, so long as they remained mere ideas; but she turned in the end as reactionary as she was debauched.*

Our own American old glory, Mae West, who has been appositely described as a "female impersonator," crowned her career on the stage in a play called Catherine Was Great, *taking the role of an Empress who was herself something of a "male impersonator." Perhaps only in such a compound travesty of personae, as by the refractions in a double concave-convex funhouse mirror, can we catch a glimpse now and then of the "real" Catherine.* Tel qu'en Lui-même enfin l'éternité le change *("Such as to Herself she is changed at last by eternity"), as Mallarmé would put it; or else John Dryden's great lines, referring separately and in turn to Diana, Mars, and Venus, might serve as Catherine's own composite epitaph:*

> *All, all of a piece throughout!*
> *Thy Chase had a Beast in View;*
> *Thy Wars brought nothing about;*
> *Thy Lovers were all untrue.*

351

'Tis well an Old Age is out,
And time to begin a New.

The account of the life and times of Catherine the Great in this book has been
drawn mainly from two sources: The Life of Catherine II, *by Jean Henri de*
Castera, translated by W. Tooke into English and published in London in 1802;
and Memoires Secrets sur la Russie, *written anonymously and published in*
Paris in 1799. I have also inserted, wherever appropriate, excerpts from the
memoirs of various contemporary observers.

I.

The Early Years

The Princess Sophia Augusta Frederica, afterward Catherine II of
Russia, was born at Stettin in Prussia on the second of May, 1729. Her
father Christian Augustus, Prince of Anhalt-Zerbst-Dornburg, was at that
time a major general in the Prussian service and governor of the town and
fortress of Stettin; and her mother, a woman of parts and beauty, honored
by Frederick the Great of Prussia as a friend and correspondent, was
herself a princess of Holstein.

Burghers are still living in Stettin who remember in their childhood to
have played with the Princess; for she was brought up in the simplest
manner, and was called by her parents, in the common diminutive of her
name, "Fiéke." Good humor, intelligence, and spirit were even then the
striking features of her character. Whatever was the play, she always took
upon herself the principal part, and made her little companions know theirs,
sometimes with the full emphasis of command. A lady of quality, who
frequently saw her, describes her in the following manner:

"Her deportment from her earliest years was always remarkably good;
she grew uncommonly handsome, and was a great girl for her years. Her
countenance, without being beautiful, was very agreeable, to which the
peculiar gaiety and friendliness which she ever displayed gave additional
charms. Her education was conducted by her mother alone, who kept her
strictly and never suffered her to show the least symptoms of pride, to which
she had some propensity, accustoming her from her earliest infancy to
salute ladies of distinction who came to visit the princess with the marks of
respect that are seemly for a child."

She lived till her fifteenth year alternately in Stettin and in Dornburg or in Zerbst; but she always accompanied her mother on several little journeys abroad, which contributed much to the forming of her mind and manners. Her mother caused Sophia to be daily instructed in the doctrines of the Lutheran religion by the court preacher Dovè, who at that time little thought that his illustrious disciple would so soon afterward adopt the very different faith of another church.

For, as it happened, three years after the Grand Duke Peter had been called from Holstein to Russia by his aunt, the Empress Elizabeth, as the heir to her throne, the Empress agreed to marry him with Sophia, who was about one year younger than himself. On embracing the Greek Orthodox religion, she changed her name to that of Ekatarina Alekseevna, a name which she was destined to render illustrious.

All Europe was deceived on the causes of this alliance, which was attributed solely to the intervention of the King of Prussia. It is true that Frederick was desirous of seeing it brought to effect, but had there not been a motive unconnected with politics, the solicitations of that monarch would have fallen to the ground. Long ere she mounted the throne of the czars, Elizabeth had been promised to the young prince of Holstein-Eutin, brother to the Princess of Anhalt-Zerbst [mother of Catherine]; but at the instant when the marriage was about to be celebrated, the prince fell sick and died. Elizabeth, who loved him to excess, became inconsolable; and in the bitterness of her grief made a vow to renounce the nuptial tie, a vow which was, at least to the public, religiously kept. Even if Elizabeth was seen afterward to yield to the gallantries of several of her courtiers, she nevertheless retained a lively tenderness for the object of her first affection. She paid a sort of worship to his memory, and never mentioned him without tears.

The Princess of Anhalt-Zerbst, not ignorant of the tender remembrance preserved by Elizabeth for her brother, resolved to take advantage of it and secure a throne for her daughter. She trusted her plan to the King of Prussia, who applauded her for it, and shortly after supported it with all his might.

The Princess of Zerbst then repaired to Petersburg, where Elizabeth received her with friendship. Her daughter [Catherine], who was handsome and endowed with all the graces of youth, immediately made a pretty forcible impression on the heart of the young Grand Duke; and as he himself was at that time well made, and of a very good figure, the attachment became reciprocal. It was soon the subject of conversations at court. Elizabeth herself remarked them without seeming to be displeased. The Princess of Zerbst, who spied the favorable moment, lost no time, but ran and threw herself at the Empress, represented to her the inclination of the two young lovers as an unconquerable passion, and calling to mind the love that the Empress herself had borne to the Prince of Holstein, her brother, she conjured her to promote the happiness of the niece of that so much regretted prince.

There was, doubtless, no need of all this for determining the Empress to consent to their union. She mingled her tears with those of the Princess of Zerbst; and, embracing her, promised her that her daughter should be Grand Duchess. The day following, the choice of Elizabeth was announced to the council and to the foreign ministers. The marriage was fixed for a day shortly to arrive; and preparations for its celebration were arranged with a magnificence worthy of the heir of the throne of the Russians.

But fortune, which had hitherto seemed so favorable to the Grand Duke, now began to change its course. Catherine was threatened with the loss of her lover, as Elizabeth had been deprived of hers. The Grand Duke was attacked with a violent fever, and a smallpox of a very malignant nature soon after made its appearance. The Prince, however, did not fall under the violence of this disease, though he retained the cruel marks of it. The metamorphosis was terrible. He not only lost the comeliness of his face, but it became for a time distorted and almost hideous.

None were permitted to approach the young Princess from the apartment of the Grand Duke, but her mother regularly brought her tidings of the turns of his distemper. Observing how much he was altered, and desirous of weakening the effect the first sight of him might have upon her daughter, she described him as one of the ugliest men imaginable, but advising her at the same time to dissemble the disgust she must naturally feel at his appearance. Notwithstanding this sage precaution, the young Princess could not revisit the Grand Duke without feeling a secret horror. She was artful enough, however, to repress her emotion, and, running to meet him, fell upon his neck, and embraced him with marks of the most lively joy. But no sooner was she retired to her apartment than she fell into a swoon, and it was three hours before she recovered the use of her senses.

The uneasiness which the young Princess had just experienced, however, did not induce her to defer the period of her union with the Grand Duke. The Empress contemplated this alliance with pleasure; the Princess of Zerbst was passionately desirous to see it concluded; and the suggestions of ambition, acting more powerfully on the heart of Catherine than even the will of her mother and that of the Empress, permitted her not a moment's hesitation. The nuptials were accordingly solemnized; and she and her husband lived for some time in an apparently good understanding, which Catherine supported as long as she conceived it to be necessary.

This Princess, brought up with all possible care under the eye of a prudent mother, and at no great distance from the court of the great Frederick, where reigned such a taste for the sciences and the fine arts, added to the beauty and quickness of understanding which she had received from nature a very extensive knowledge. From her youth she had always been addicted to reading, to reflection, to learning, and to employment, and she had the facility of expressing herself with elegance in several languages.

The Grand Duke too had sense, but his education had been totally neglected; he possessed an excellent heart, but he wanted politeness. Kept at a distance from all business of public concern, he confined himself almost solely to his old friends from Holstein, and to the drilling of his company of German soldiers, in emulation of Frederick the Great, fatiguing his little army in useless maneuvers and painful exercises. And from these he sat down to the excesses of the table, and in the delirium of intemperance would declare that he would one day be the conqueror of the North and rival of the Prussian hero.

In Catherine's own Memoirs, *which recount her life as Grand Duchess in Russia up to 1759, she describes her husband's juvenile passion for playing with soldiers, whether toy or real, as follows:*

"The principal plaything of the Grand Duke while in town consisted of an immense number of little dolls, representing soldiers, formed of wood, lead, pith, and wax. These he arranged on very narrow tables, which took up an entire room, leaving scarcely enough space to pass between them. Along these tables he had nailed narrow bands of brass, to which strings were attached, and when he pulled these strings the brass bands made a noise which, according to him, resembled the roll of musketry. He observed the court festivals with great regularity, making these troops produce their rolling fire; besides which, he daily relieved guard, that is to say, from every table was picked out the dolls that were assumed to be on guard. He assisted at this parade in full uniform, boots, spurs, gorget, and scarf. Such of his domestics as were submitted to this precious exercise were obliged to appear in similar style."

The Grand Duke was of a good stature, but ugly and almost deformed. He frequently blushed at the superiority of his wife, and his wife often blushed at seeing him so little worthy of her. But the alteration that had taken place in the features of the Prince's visage as a result of the smallpox was not the sole cause of the indifference of his young consort: in brief, he was not capable of making her happy.

He had a slight physical imperfection, easy to cure, yet this made it seem even more cruel. Despite all his passionate and repeated efforts, he was not able to consummate the marriage. If the Prince had confided in anyone with the least experience, and then gone to a surgeon, the obstacle between him and his desires would have been removed. But he was too ashamed or too proud to reveal it; and the Princess, who was then even more innocent than he, endured his caresses with repugnance and did not attempt to console him or urge him to seek a cure. Hence arose that mutual dislike which the people of the court were not long in finding out, and which was visibly augmenting from day to day.

The young men who surrounded the Grand Duke did not at all, like that

Prince, resign themselves entirely to the pleasures of the table, to play, and to military parade. There was especially one who distinguished himself as much by his taste for the amiable arts as he was admired for the graces of his person: it was [Sergius] Saltykov, the Grand Duke's chamberlain.

Though scarcely outgrown the boy, he had already the reputation of having obtained the favors of several belles of the court; and his success made him proud. Saltykov, it is true, was held rather deficient in courage with the men, but he was not the less presumptuous or the less bold with the women. The husbands of Petersburg regarded him as the most agreeable and the most dangerous man in town.

Saltykov was not long ere he lifted his eyes even to the spouse of his master; and vanity yet more than love led him to conceive the temerarious design of captivating her heart. He began by sedulously studying the inclinations of the Princess. He perceived that, notwithstanding the constraint in which she lived, Catherine had always a propensity to pleasure. He accordingly procured her some new amusement with every returning day. Catherine was not insensible to such gallant, such continued attentions. The seducing figure of Saltykov, and the vivacity of his wit, had made an impression on her mind, and his assiduities made him master of her affections.

Catherine's Memoirs* *contain an unusually candid description of the inevitable seduction, which occurred during a hunting party:*

"Saltykov seized the moment when the rest were in pursuit of the hares, to approach me and speak of his favorite subject. I listened more attentively than usual. He described to me the plan which he had arranged for enshrouding, as he said, in profound mystery the happiness which might be enjoyed in such a case. I did not say a word. He took advantage of my silence to persuade me that he loved me passionately, and he begged that I would allow him to hope, at least, that he was not wholly indifferent to me. I told him he might amuse himself with hoping what he pleased, as I could not prevent his thoughts. Finally he drew comparisons between himself and others at the court, and made me confess that he was preferable to them. From this he concluded that he was preferred for himself. I laughed at all this, but I admitted that he was agreeable to me. At the end of an hour and a half of conversation, I desired him to leave me, since so long a tête-à-tête might give rise to suspicion. He said he would not go unless I told him that I consented. I answered, 'Yes, yes, but go away.' He said, 'Then it is settled,' and put spurs to his horse. I cried out after him, 'No, no!' but he repeated, 'Yes, yes.' And thus we separated.

"On our return to the house, which was on the island, we had supper,

---

* These *Memoirs*, incidentally, which remained hidden in the archives of the imperial family until the mid-nineteenth century, were first discovered and published by the revolutionary aristocrat Alexander Herzen, in an attempt to discredit the Romanov dynasty. "They prove," wrote Herzen in his introduction to the book, "that the father of the Emperor Paul [Catherine's son and heir] is Sergius Saltykov."

during which there sprang up a heavy gale from the sea; the waves rose so high that they even reached the steps of the house. In fact, the whole island was under water to the depth of several feet. We were obliged to remain until the storm had abated and the waters retreated, which was not until between two and three in the morning. During this time, Saltykov told me that heaven itself had favored him that day, by enabling him to enjoy my presence for a longer time, with many other things to the same effect. He thought himself already quite happy. As for me, I was not so at all. A thousand apprehensions troubled me, and I was unusually dull, and very much out of conceit with myself. I had persuaded myself that I could easily govern both his passions and my own, and I found that both tasks were difficult, if not impossible."

While the Grand Duke and the Grand Duchess were passing the summer at Oranienbaum, the Empress Elizabeth remained at Peterhof, though not without sending, from time to time, for the imperial couple to share in the pleasures of her court. On these little expeditions Saltykov never failed to make one of the party. In order to avoid being present at the entertainments and festivities of the palace, where the prying eyes of indiscreet observers would throw too great a restraint on her conduct, Catherine feigned an indisposition. The Grand Duke was so infatuated in regard to his chamberlain that he even engaged him himself to share in the solitude of his wife, and to exert all the talents of his capacity to amuse and to cheer her. This was exactly what the two lovers desired; and it is not difficult to imagine that they turned the moments to profit.

In the meantime, however, the Grand Duke cohabited with his spouse, and Catherine expected shortly to become a mother [to the future czar Paul I]. For by an operation in a small degree similar to that of the judaical rite, Peter had at last become freed from his obstacle.

Thenceforward Saltykov tasted without disturbance or remorse those pleasures from the consequences of which he had nothing to dread. Catherine herself had no need to be so severe in her precautions: her first success had given her additional boldness. Besides, the example of the Empress Elizabeth, whose manners were growing more and more corrupt, and who engaged in new follies from day to day, seemed to afford some excuse for her passion. The Empress questioned nothing of an intrigue which she might easily have perceived. Nonetheless, certain of her counselors, who were fully aware of the scandal, thought it best to remove Saltykov from court, and he was persuaded to accept the post of minister plenipotentiary at Hamburg.

Catherine preserved for some time the passion she had conceived for her husband's chamberlain; and she wrote to him in Hamburg and frequently received letters in return. Then, all at once, the presence of a stranger whom fortune had brought to the court of Russia caused her to forget the lover whom she no longer saw.

The young Count Stanislaw Poniatowski (whom Catherine was later to raise to the throne of Poland and afterward hurl indignantly from it) became the happy successor to Saltykov. Born a simple nobleman and destitute of fortune, he was endowed with a handsome figure and imbued with ambition. He was by nature gay, witty, and spirited, therefore adapted to succeed at a court where amusement seemed to be the most important concern. Accordingly, it was not long before he perceived the impression he had made upon Catherine.

Poniatowski, bold and even audacious, was yet awed by the high rank of the Grand Duchess; and the observant eyes of the numerous courtiers obliged him to repress his ardor. For some time the two lovers conversed only by their looks; but to these mute conversations at length others succeeded in which they reciprocally declared their attachment, and consulted on the means of indulging their inclinations without restraint.

Already sure of the Grand Duchess's heart, he succeeded soon after with the spouse. He talked English and German with him; he drank, smoked, abused the French, and extolled the King of Prussia with unlimited praise. In addition to so many recommendations, he affected an immoderate pursuit of pleasure. What indeed might not a man of penetration and address have done in those days at that luxurious, intriguing, and profligate court?

The Empress Elizabeth had no esteem for her nephew; she cared but little for the honor of the Grand Duchess, and was in general not more severe toward the conduct of others than careful of her own. Through the years she had insensibly proceeded from moderate pleasures to the extravagance of sensuality. Yet her taste for religious devotion augmented with her voluptuousness. She continued whole hours before the picture of some saint, to which she spoke, which she even consulted, and passed alternately from acts of bigotry to the intemperance of lust, and from scenes of lasciviousness to the opiates of prayer. She would frequently drink to excess; and at such times, too sensual, too impatient for the delays of unlacing, her women used to effect the same purpose by means of the scissors. In what manner such nights were passed, it becomes not the historian to undraw her curtains to reveal.

The Grand Duchess, blinded by her own passion, and consequently unmindful of the lessons of prudence, betrayed a faint imitation of the irregularities of her aunt. Poniatowski was never from her; she devoted to him the whole of her time; and she made so little secret of this intimacy that public report was very loud to her prejudice. As frequently happens, her husband the Grand Duke was the only man at court who knew nothing of what was passing.

Led by the several motives of interest and vanity, some persons perceived that it would be no difficult matter for them to cause hatred and quarrels to succeed to the coldness which for a long time had been visible between Peter and his spouse. The first step was to call the Prince's attention to the frequent conversations of Poniatowski with the Grand Duchess. Their gestures were watched; every little word that escaped them, which might serve as a pretext for some allusion, was carefully laid hold of. One evening in particular, when the Grand Duchess was at table with a numerous company, and seated facing Poniatowski, the discourse fell upon the dexterity with which some women managed a horse, and the dangers to which they exposed themselves in that exercise.

Catherine, who had her eyes fixed on her lover, answered in a lively manner, "There are few women so bold as I am. I am of an unbounded courage." These words were immediately reported to the Grand Duke, accompanied with suggestions that might occasion some sinister application to arise in his mind.

The jealousy of Peter being thus alarmed, they lost no time to foster the surmises of the husband into proofs of the infidelity of the wife. In sum, they revealed her love for the Polander and the criminal correspondence they mutually entertained. The Prince was overwhelmed with grief and consternation. He bewailed his misfortune, and condemned his imprudence. He no longer observed the consideration and respect he had hitherto shown the Grand Duchess, and forbade her to be seen with Poniatowski. He then hastened to the Empress, and besought her to avenge the affront he had received.

Catherine, who thought she had everything to fear from the resentment of her husband, now saw herself abandoned on all sides in this distressing situation. She had at once to support the aversion of the Grand Duke, the indignation of the Empress, and the insulting disdain of a court which, a few days before, had been lavish of its assiduities and smiles. But what afflicted her much more was the dread of losing forever her favorite, Poniatowski.

It was about this time that, whether in compliance with an involuntary passion (for passions are involuntary in such characters as Peter), or whether to avenge himself for the infidelities of his wife, the Grand Duke formed an attachment with one of the three daughters of the senator Vorontsov, brother of the chancellor to the Empress. The eldest of these sisters, Madame Bouttuclin, was justly reckoned one of the handsomest ladies of Russia; the youngest, the Princess Dashkov, was equally handsome, and moreover endowed with extraordinary talents; but as for the third, Elizabeth Romanovna Vorontsov, of whom Peter was so passionately enamored, she was neither witty in conversation, graceful in behavior, nor beautiful in person. Her good humor, so congenial to his own, seduced him, her caprices amused him, and the habit of living with her soon gained her an imperious ascendance over him. The senator Vorontsov, an insipid and ambitious courtier, with abject complaisance contrived at the commerce of the Prince with his daughter.

In the meantime the health of the Empress Elizabeth began visibly to decline. The necessity of indulging repose, in addition to her natural indolence, rendered her more negligent than ever of the affairs of government. Festivities, masquerades, balls, and brilliant shows still yielded her a faint amusement; and dreading to lie down upon a restless pillow, she went to the opera or the play at 11, passed the rest of the night at the card table, and went to bed at 5 in the morning. Business of the gravest import appeared now as trifles to her. Acquainted with the passion of her nephew for the young Countess Vorontsov, to whom she scornfully gave the nickname "La Pompadour," she listened with avidity to the idle tales that were brought to her of the particulars of their amorous revels, seeming to seek in such anecdotes some palliation for her own infirmities.

Catherine, who waited with impatience for a favorable opportunity of reconciliation with the Empress, threw herself at her feet and implored her forgiveness; but the irritated monarch would listen to no accommodation, except on the most mortifying conditions. It was afterward proposed to her, by message, to confess her guilt and to submit to the clemency of her husband and the Empress.

From this moment Catherine summoned up all her pride. She purposely avoided appearing at court, kept close to her apartments, and asked leave of the Empress to retire with her son into Germany, a permission which she was very sure of being refused, because of the extreme fondness of Elizabeth for the young Paul Petrovich.

The stratagem succeeded: an accommodation shortly after ensued. Catherine promised no longer to permit the visits of Poniatowski; and thenceforward she actually held a greater reserve in her conduct. At the very moment when she was thought on the brink of irremediable disgrace, to the great astonishment of the court she made her appearance at the theater by the side of the Empress, who carefully drew upon her the notice of the spectators by the particularity of her attentions.

The Accession of Peter III

Catherine's newfound security, however, was abruptly terminated by the death of the Empress Elizabeth, in the winter of 1762, of a severe attack of the colic.

No sooner had the Empress closed her eyes than the courtiers pressed in crowds to the Grand Duke. This Prince, laying aside at once his weakness and indecision, accosted them with dignity, and received the oaths of the officers of his guard. Delivered on a sudden from the long and servile constraint in which he had been kept by his aunt, he negligently let his satisfaction appear, but without betraying an indecent joy. He took the name of Peter III.

The Grand Duchess, who could not think without dread of the moment when her husband should be invested with the sovereign power, received from him the most flattering salutations, and marks of the greatest confidence. He seemed to forget the wrongs he had suffered, and passed a great part of the day in her apartments, discoursing with her on the most friendly footing and consulting her on all delicate and important affairs. The courtiers, surprised at this conduct, felicitated Catherine on the happiness of her lot. Catherine was almost the only person who was not deceived. She easily saw that her husband was not capable of governing by himself, and she was too well acquainted with his character to mistake that for benevolence which was only weakness.

As soon as the Czar thought himself well settled on the throne, he no longer concealed his indifference, and sometimes even made her experience it in a very humiliating manner. At the time of the celebration of the peace that had just been signed with the King of Prussia, Peter, who during the exhibition of the fireworks was seated by the side of Catherine, on seeing his mistress the Countess Vorontzoff pass by, called to her and made her sit down beside him. Catherine immediately retired, without any endeavor to detain her being vouchsafed on the part of her husband.

The same evening, at supper, he drank the health of Prince George of Holstein; at which all the company rose up, excepting Catherine, who pretended to have got a hurt in her foot. Peter, irritated that the Empress should affect to fail in the respect which she owed to her uncle, launched at her an epithet which, whether or not she deserved it, the Czar ought to have spared his spouse. Catherine was so mortified that she could not refrain from weeping; but her tears interested the spectators, as the harshness of Peter excited their indignation.

It was by scenes of this nature that the Empress felt her hopes revive. She now made it her sole employment to gain those hearts which her husband was losing. Instructed from her infancy in the arts of dissimulation, it was not difficult for her to affect, in the sight of the multitude, sentiments the most foreign to her mind. The pupil of the French philosophers now put on the air of a bigot: she sedulously repaired every day to the churches of Petersburg, praying with all the semblance of a sincere and fervent devotion, punctual in the most superstitious practices of the Greek Orthodox religion, and treating the popes with reverence. As she had hoped, they failed not afterward to go proclaiming her praises from house to house.

In the apartments of the palace, the way of life pursued by this married couple was not less different. While Peter III was shut up with the Countess Vorontsov, and some Prussian officers, and others of his favorites, so far forgetful of his rank as to live familiarly with buffoons and common stage players, even to invite them at times to sit at table with him, the Empress kept her court with such a mixture of dignity and affability as charmed all those that approached her. She particularly made it her study to attract to her such persons as, by their reputation, their courage, or their intrigues might become useful to her.

The Countess Vorontsov, meanwhile, having already been told by interested parties of the first amours of the Empress with Soltykov, took care that the Czar should have no reason to complain that she kept the secret from him. When she apprised him of it, the Czar in his anger resolved on declaring the illegitimacy and the exheredation of his son. He recalled Saltykov from Hamburg, loaded him with caresses and benefits, and put every stratagem in practice to draw from him the authentic avowal of the criminal commerce he had formerly held with Catherine. It was visible to all the court that Saltykov, incited by the hope of glorious rewards or intimidated by the dread of serious chastisements, would do whatever the Czar desired.

Although the Czar lived openly with the Countess Vorontsov, held frequent assignations with a handsome stage dancer of Petersburg, and, in short, gave reason to think that he had various adventures of gallantry, he was not perhaps therefore the fitter for obtaining another heir. Nature had inspired him with an ardent passion for women; his desires were impetuous; but all seemed to prove that his efforts were doomed to be fruitless. Wishing notwithstanding to raise someone to the place of Paul Petrovich, he conceived all at once a very singular project. He determined to adopt the unfortunate Prince Ivan,* who had been dethroned by Elizabeth, and declare him his successor.

In the meantime, however, the indiscretions of the Czar revived from day to day the hopes of Catherine; and the designs he had formed against her emboldened her to run all hazards in order to prevent them. Dismissed to Peterhof, and lodged in one of the least desirable apartments of the palace, she passed her days in meditating a project for precipitating her husband from the throne, and her evenings in the company of a peculiar intimate, one Gregory Orlov, whom she made the most intrepid of her conspirators.

Since the removal of Count Poniatowski, the Empress had had the address to appear, in the eyes of the most attentive of courtiers, faithful to her attachment to him, yet by her intimacy with Orlov she found the means of compensating for his absence. Her very friends were deceived. Even the Princess Dashkov [sister of the Czar's mistress, but Catherine's closest confidante] was unaware that the Empress had any other love than that of study and of Poniatowski. Furthermore, she herself had long been enamored of Orlov without once suspecting that her lover was also known to Catherine. The only person that was in the secret, and, in fact, the manager of the piece, was one of the Empress's women, named Catherine Ivanovna, the most ingenious of intriguers and the least scrupulous of duennas. She behaved with so much address that many of those whom she presented to Catherine enjoyed almost always her amorous favors without knowing who she was.

Gregory Orlov possessed neither the advantages of birth nor those of education; but he had received from nature what are often found more useful, courage and beauty. Count Peter Schuvalov, grand master of the

---

* This Ivan was still in his cradle when the revolution that placed Elizabeth on the throne, in 1741, occasioned him to be shut up, with the regent Anne, his mother, and all his family, in the fortress of Schlüsselburg.

artillery, a vain and pompous man, was desirous of having the handsomest of his officers for aide-de-camp, and so he had selected Gregory Orlov. But Count Schuvalov, as it happened, possessed for his mistress one of the most illustrious and beautiful women of the court, the Princess Kourakin, who was not long in giving the aide-de-camp to understand that she preferred him to the general. Unfortunately the general one day surprised them together, and forbade Orlov any more to appear in his presence, threatening to exert all his interest to get him banished to Siberia.

This adventure made a noise. It was for a time the subject of conversation both in town and country; and the story found its way even into the retreat in which Catherine was forced to do penance. Curiosity, pity perhaps, led her to wish for an acquaintance with the young officer whose disaster was the topic of public discourse. Her woman Ivanovna, with the customary precautions, procured her a sight of him; and Orlov, at first unable to guess who the fair one might be that took such concern in his lot, found her to possess more charms and a fonder affection that the Princess Kourakin. This first and mysterious conversation was succeeded by several interviews in which Catherine was only obliging; but when she thought herself well assured of the boldness and the discretion of her new acquaintance, she unveiled to him her ambitious designs. Orlov now entered into a conspiracy with her, in which he shortly after engaged his brothers.

The Plot to Overthrow the Czar

Princess Dashkov, lately returned from Moscow where her husband had kept her in a kind of exile, was prevented from concurring with the aims of certain of her relations who were desirous of seeing her supplant her sister in the favor of the Czar. That sister was more suitable to the military taste of Peter; and Madame Dashkov would never be satisfied with a lover addicted only to drinking and the fumes of tobacco.

She then formed an intimate connection with Catherine. They passed whole days together in the pursuits of literature and intrigue; and when the Empress was dismissed to Peterhof fortress, Princess Dashkov remained at Petersburg, in order to serve her the better. She kept up a correspondence with the Empress, in which she gave her an account of all that was passing at the court or in the city, and advised her of the means which she ought to employ for preventing the designs of the Czar.

The attachment which Princess Dashkov had vowed to Catherine was not the sole motive for exciting her zeal. She was principally jealous of the glorious elevation that awaited her sister. In the hopes of arriving at the slippery honor of directing a conspiracy, she openly braved the resentment of her family; though only 18 years old at the time, indeed she would have braved every danger, and even looked death boldly in the face. Princess Dashkov had for some time kept about her a Piedmontese named Odart, whom dire penury and the hopes of making his fortune had brought to

Petersburg, and who had confirmed the taste of that lady for French literature and acquainted her with the best writers of that nation. Odart became even more valuable to the princess, for like her, with an aptitude for witty conceits, he possessed a turn for intrigue. She was ever extolling this man, to whom she thought herself indebted for her superiority; and she spoke of him to the Empress in so advantageous a manner as to induce her to offer him the office of her private secretary.

It was not long ere this artful and insinuating secretary became one of her confidants in her ambitious designs. He easily perceived that there was no other way for Catherine to escape from the humiliation that awaited her than by the fall of the Czar. But how to accomplish this fall? How dare to attempt it? Odart saw all the difficulties, all the dangers, with which it was attended; but he also knew that if punishment and death were on one side, honors and riches presented themselves on the other.

Accordingly, Odart and Madame Dashkov began to think of procuring soldiers, and money—which always propagates soldiers, and in Russia more than elsewhere—and a chief whose name and authority might command respect; and, in addition, a man who, accustomed to direct courtiers and manage intrigues, was neither to be embarrassed by obstacles nor dismayed by disappointments. They then turned their eyes on the hetman [Cossack general] Cyril Razumovsky and Count Nikita Ivanovich Panin.

When Princess Dashkov communicated her designs to the hetman, he applauded the scheme; and, without seeming to take a direct part in the business, assured her that in case of need she might rely upon his concurrence. But he went even further. He assembled his friends on the spot, and without disclosing to them precisely the twofold plan with which he had been entrusted, informed them that he knew with certainty that among the troops a plot was hatching to dethrone the Czar. If they neglected for a moment to declare themselves its leaders, he advised, no other alternative would be left them but to submit to becoming the forced instruments of the soldiers or, probably, their victims.

Thus certified of the assent of the hetman Razumovsky, Princess Dashkov and Odart now made it their business to bring over Count Panin to their party. Catherine very well knew that if the name and presence of the hetman would be of great weight in the first openings of the revolt, the experience and ability of Panin were still more necessary for leading it to success. Princess Dashkov then commissioned Odart to propose to Panin his uniting with them; and Panin, prompted by a desire to preserve the throne for Catherine's son, the young Paul Petrovich, promised all they requested.

The archbishop of Novgorod was in like manner brought over. The conspirators had made themselves sure of this prelate even before they disclosed their design. The Czar had just recalled him from exile, to which he had some months before been condemned; but the prelate, more irritated at the severity of the sentence than affected by the Czar's clemency, waited only for an opportunity for signalizing his sacred fury. Inventive superstition furnished him with numerous means. He knew the blind zeal of the Russians for whatever belongs to the Orthodox Greek religion; and the swarms of monks whom he had at his command continued, under the pretense of defending that religion, to disseminate in all hearts their hatred toward the Czar, who so imprudently seemed to have declared himself its enemy.

The Plot Discovered

While these maneuvers were occurring, his Majesty went to pass some days at his country palace of Oranienbaum, taking with him some of the handsomest women of the court. On this occasion a report was spread that he wanted to demand divorces for these women in order to marry them to several of his intimates. It was even added that beds had been ordered for these pretended nuptials; and shame, contempt, and jealousy created him new enemies, and procured as many partisans to Catherine.

The conspirators, who at first had agreed to seize and carry off the Czar on his appearance again at Petersburg, now thought, in consequence of a new deliberation, that it would be too dangerous to wait so long, and that it would be better to execute their design on his coming to Peterhof.

The plan was well concerted: each of the conspirators was reckoning on his own courage and the fidelity of his friends, when all at once the plot was discovered. This discovery, however, was not entirely the effect of chance; and, by a strange caprice of fortune, the very accident which ought to have disconcerted the traitors, emboldened them. And their precipitancy secured their success.

By an excess of diffidence or precaution, Princess Dashkov and Odart had set a trusty person to watch the steps of each of the chiefs of the conspiracy, who regularly brought them an exact account of whatever these chiefs might be likely to do. By such means, if there had been the least tendency toward treachery among them, they would have detected it instantaneously and have taken measures for their security or their vengeance.

A certain Passick, attached to the Princess Dashkov, had won over the soldiers of the guard in which he served as lieutenant. One of these soldiers, imagining that Passick did nothing but in concurrence with his captain, asked the captain on what day they were to take up arms against the Czar. The captain, surprised, had recourse to dissimulation, and answering the questions of the soldier in vague and indistinct terms, drew out of him the secret of the conspiracy. He then went without delay to make report of it to the chancery of the regiment.

It was 9 o'clock at night. Passick was put under arrest; but at first he was shoved into a room, where he had time to write with a pencil on a scrap of paper: *"Proceed to execution this instant, or we are undone."* At that moment the man assigned by the conspirators to watch the lieutenant's actions presented himself at the door. Passick, not knowing him, but seeing that everything was to be risked, gave him the scrap of paper, telling him that if he ran with it in all speed to the hetman Razumovsky, he would be handsomely rewarded.

The spy hurried to the Princess Dashkov, and put the billet into her hand. Panin happened that moment to come in. She proposed to hasten the execution of their project, observing that the only means of saving themselves from the vengeance of the Czar was to prevent it; and that, however weak he might be, if time were allowed him to put himself on his defense, it would be impossible to get the better of him. Panin, hesitating, told her that it would be better to wait till the next day, to know what was fittest to be done; but in the meantime the emissaries of Princess Dashkov were sent off to give intelligence to the other conspirators.

These conspirators, when they learned what had happened, were neither less uneasy than Princess Dashkov nor less impatient for hastening the execution of their plot. The delay till the morrow appeared to them to be big with consequences the most to be dreaded; and it certainly would have been fatal. The time of acting was the silence of the night, without allowing the Czar time to form an inclination to prevent them, nor the troops and people time to arm for the defense of the Czar. The resolution was unanimous. While Gregory Orlov, one of his brothers, and his friend Bibikov repaired to the barracks to tell the soldiers of their party to act on the first signal, another brother of Orlov, Aleksei, took upon himself the perilous commission of going to find out the Empress at Peterhof.

The Czar had at length fixed his departure for the day following the festival of Peter and Paul, which he was, as usual, to celebrate at Peterhof, and at the end of which he intended to arrest the Empress. But Catherine, aware of his design, had already taken measures to prevent it.

Under pretext of leaving the apartments free for the festival that was to be celebrated at the palace, and for enabling herself, in reality, to be more in readiness to escape, Catherine was lodged in a remote summer house, at the foot whereof ran a canal that communicated with the Neva. There she had caused to be fastened a small boat that might occasionally be of service in the secret visits of her favorites, and also to facilitate her own escape into Sweden if the conspiracy should be discovered. Gregory Orlov, having given his brother a key to this summer house, instructed him in the methods he must employ for getting thither; and the Princess Dashkov entrusted him with a short note urging the Empress to come to them without loss of time.

It was now 2 o'clock in the morning. The Empress, not expecting anybody, had retired to rest, and lay in a profound sleep, when she was suddenly roused, and saw standing at the side of her bed a soldier whom she knew nothing of. Without delivering her the note from Princess

Dashkov, the soldier said to Catherine, "Your Majesty has not a moment to lose—get ready to follow me!" and immediately disappeared.

Catherine, astonished, terrified, called her woman Ivanovna. They dressed themselves in haste and disguised themselves in such manner that they could not be known by the sentinels about the palace. Scarcely were they ready when the soldier returned and told the Empress that a carriage was waiting for them at the garden gate. It was a coach which, under pretext of having a change of horses for an excursion into the country, Princess Dashkov had kept in readiness at a house inhabited by one of her peasants a few miles from Peterhof, and which Aleksei Orlov had sent one of his comrades to fetch. At length Catherine, worn out with fatigue and anxiety, but sufficiently mistress of herself to assume a sedate and tranquil air, arrived in the city of Petersburg, on July 9, 1762, at 7 in the morning.

She proceeded to the quarters of the Ismaïlofsky guards, of which three companies had already been won over. But the conspirators would not permit them to leave the barracks till Catherine appeared, for fear of failing in their aim by too great haste. At the report of the arrival of her Majesty, about 30 of the soldiers, half dressed, ran out to receive her with clamorous shouts of joy. Surprised and alarmed at seeing so small a number of soldiers, she kept silence for a moment, then told them, in a tremulous voice, that her danger had driven her to the necessity of coming to ask their assistance, for the Czar had intended to put her to death that very night, together with her son; and she had no other means than by flight of escaping death.

The hetman Razumovsky, their colonel, was not long ere he appeared; and soon other soldiers, led by curiosity, gathered in great numbers about the Empress, and welcomed her as their sovereign. The chaplain of the regiment of Ismaïlof was immediately called. Fetching a crucifix from the altar, he received on it the oath of the troops. Some negative voices were heard in the tumultuous concourse proclaiming Catherine as regent; but these were presently stifled by the threats of Orlov and the more numerous cries of "Long live the Empress!"

The Simeonofsky and the Préobajinsky guards had already imitated those of Ismaïlof. The officers, with the utmost docility, put themselves at the head of their companies, as though they had originally engaged in the plot. Two officers alone, of the regiment of Préobajinsky, had the boldness to counteract their soldiers, but they were immediately arrested.

While the hetman Razumovsky, Prince Volkonski, Counts Bruce and Stroganov, several other general officers, and Princess Dashkov remained about Catherine, and she was completely securing the three regiments of guards, Gregory Orlov ran to the regiment of artillery to draw it into the revolt and march it to the Empress. So many advantages cost the Empress no more than two hours. She saw herself already surrounded by 2000 warriors, together with the inhabitants of Petersburg, who mechanically followed the motions of the soldiers and were eager to applaud them.

The hetman Razumovsky advised her then to repair to the great church at Kazan, where everything was prepared for her reception. She accordingly set out, attended by her numerous suite. The windows and doors of all the houses were filled with spectators, who mingled their acclamations with the shouts of the soldiers. The archbishop of Novgorod, appareled in his sacerdotal robes and accompanied by a great number of priests, whose long beards and hoary heads gave them a venerable appearance, stood at the altar to receive her. He set the imperial crown on her head, proclaimed her in a loud voice sovereign of all the Russias, by the name of Catherine the Second, and declared, at the same time, the young Grand Duke Paul Petrovich her successor. A "Te Deum" was then chanted, accompanied with the shouts of the multitude. This ceremony being over, the Empress repaired to the palace that had been occupied by Elizabeth. The gates were thrown open to all comers. During several hours the crowd flocked thither, falling on their knees before her, and taking the oath of allegiance.

In the meantime the conspirators were unwearied in their visits to the several quarters of the town to put them on alert, stationing guards and placing cannons without meeting any impediment or interruption. Prince George of Holstein, uncle to the Czar, dared to venture out, followed by a few faithful soldiers; but he was surrounded, forced to surrender, loaded with insults, roughly handled, and dragged to prison, whence the Empress delivered him after some hours, in order to put him under arrest in his own house. Not only no resistance was opposed to the partisans of Catherine, but none of the friends of the Czar once thought of informing him of what was passing at Petersburg. All circumstances seemed to concur to favor the plot.

Before the end of the day, Catherine had already 15,000 men of picked troops. The city was in a formidable state of defense. Strict order prevailed there; and by the greatest good fortune, not one drop of blood had been shed. Her partisans aroused the sympathy of the crowd by propagating on every side the rumor that the Czar had destined that very day to put her to death with her son. The atrocious falsehood was believed without examination; and success was the reward of the calumny.

When the Empress arrived at the palace, she sent without delay for her son Paul Petrovich. A detachment of soldiers, at the head of which marched a trusty officer, went to fetch him. The young Prince, then eight years of age, who had often been told of the designs of the Czar against him, on waking from his bed in the midst of the soldiers was seized with an alarming fright. Panin took him in his arms, and brought him to his mother. Catherine then led him onto the balcony of the palace, holding him up to show him to the people, whose acclamations redoubled at the sight of the child, thinking that in him they beheld the new czar.

A rumor suddenly spread that Peter III was no more, and a procession with his corpse was at that moment going by. A profound silence then took the place of the cries from the multitude. Several soldiers in long black cloaks, with torches in their hands, walked on each side of a large coffin covered with a pall; and it was followed by a number of priests chanting their litanies as the procession moved along, while the crowd respectfully fell back on both sides to make room for it to pass. But afterward it was not doubted that this was an additional stratagem invented by the conspirators for deceiving the people and intimidating the partisans of Czar Peter III.

The principal nobles, who for the most part had taken no share in this conspiracy, and had first learned the success of it at their rising in the morning, resorted immediately to the palace. Forced to disguise their astonishment and vexation, they united their homage and their oaths of fidelity to those which the multitude had just taken to Catherine.

The heads of the conspiracy now collected around her and held a council. They resolved to profit from the dispositions of the army by marching in all haste directly to the Czar. But in the meantime, to secure the Empress from any attack by sea—or rather, to quiet the soldiers, who imagined that she was liable every moment to be surprised and assassinated—they conducted her from the palace of Elizabeth into an old palace built of timber, facing a large open place, which they surrounded with troops.

Toward noon her Majesty, entirely sure of Petersburg, ordered that a manifesto, which Odart had secretly printed a few days before, be distributed throughout the city. This notification being made, Catherine then sent a message to the foreign ministers concerning the day when they were to be admitted to pay their court and present their compliments on the event.

While these things were transacting, the new Empress, decorated with the insignia of the order of Saint Andrew and habited in the uniform of the guards, which she had borrowed for the occasion from a young officer, mounted on horseback and rode through the ranks with Princess Dashkov, who was also in uniform. It was then that the young Potemkin, the future favorite of the Empress, perceiving that Catherine had no plume in her hat, rode up to offer his. The horse on which Potemkin was mounted, being accustomed to form into the squadron, was with difficulty brought to quit the side of her Majesty, thereby affording her an opportunity of remarking for the first time the grace and agility of the man who later gained such an ascendancy over her.

The troops, being incessantly supplied with beer and brandy, incessantly likewise expressed their satisfaction by reiterated vociferations of *hourra!* and by tossing up their hats and caps. One regiment of cavalry, of which Peter III had been colonel while yet only Grand Duke, refused to participate in this tumultuous joy. The officers were at once put under arrest, and replaced by those of other regiments; but the soldiers, by their sullen silence, formed a striking contrast with the furious noise and gesticulations of the rest.

However, the party was too strong to have anything to fear from this regiment; and they began now to march the troops from the city to proceed against the Czar. Her Majesty sat down to dinner near an open window, in full view of the soldiers and the multitudes whom curiosity had assembled in the ample place before the palace.

The Czar Is Taken

Peter III had as yet no suspicion of what was passing. His security was so great that he had that morning arrested a faithful officer who, having had some intimations of the conspiracy the night before, had hastened to Oranienbaum, thinking it his duty to inform the Czar. Peter afterward set out in a calash with his mistress, his favorites, and the women of the court for Peterhof. The Czar's carriage was attended by several others; and this numerous train proceeded at a swift pace, the several companies within gaily entertaining themselves with the pleasures they expected, when General Gudovich, the Czar's aide-de-camp, who had galloped on before, was perceived returning at full speed. Gudovich had met on the road one of the chamberlains of the Empress coming on foot to his master to inform him of Catherine's escape. At this unexpected news, Gudovich turned back and, as he approached the Czar's carriage, called out to the driver to stop.

Peter, surprised, and even rather angry, not knowing what could cause his aide-de-camp to ride back with so much speed, asked him if he was mad. Gudovich came close to the carriage, and whispered some words in his ear. Peter now turned pale and, strongly agitated, got out of the carriage, then went aside with Gudovich in order to interrogate him more at his ease. Afterward, returning to the carriage, and having requested the ladies to come out, he showed them a gate of the park, through which he bade them join him at the front of the palace. He then regained the carriage with some of his courtiers, and departed with the greatest expedition.

On coming to Peterhof, the Czar ran to the pavilion that had been occupied by Catherine; and in his confusion, in his extreme concern, he looked about for her as if she might have been concealed under the bed or in one of the cupboards. He overwhelmed all he met with questions; but nobody could give him any satisfaction. Those of greater penetration than the rest already foresaw the whole extent of his misfortune, but were silent, so that they might not increase his despair.

His mistress Countess Vorontsov and the other women, who were now coming up the walks of the garden, were still ignorant of what it could be that had forced the Czar to quit them in the midst of the road. As soon as Peter perceived the Countess, he called to her, "Romanovna, will you believe me now? Catherine has made her escape. I told you that she was capable of anything!"

At length a countryman suddenly came up in the midst of this affrighted concourse, and without pronouncing a single word, drew from the bosom of his caftan a sealed note, which he presented to the Czar. Peter took the note, ran his eyes hastily over it, and then, reading it aloud, informed those who were standing round him that a rebellion had broken out that morning in Petersburg; that the troops had taken arms in favor of Catherine; that she was going to be crowned in the church at Kazan; and that the whole of the populace seemed to have taken part in the insurrection.

The Czar appeared greatly dejected at these tidings. The courtiers did their utmost to communicate to him a courage which they did not themselves possess. Chancellor Vorontsov observed that it was highly possible that Catherine might have attempted to make the soldiers and the people rise, but that this slight fermentation could not be attended with any dangerous consequences; and if the Czar gave his consent, he would haste immediately to Petersburg and bring the Empress back.

The Czar, without hesitation, accepted the Chancellor's proposal, and that minister soon departed for town. On entering the palace, he found the Empress surrounded by a multitude of people in the act of doing homage. He nevertheless had the boldness to represent to her with a blustering confidence the danger to which she was exposing herself. "You may, Madame," said he, "have some success; but it will not be of long duration. Consider that the regiments of the guards do not compose the whole army of the Czar, and that the inhabitants of Saint Petersburg are but a very weak part of the Russian nation."

Catherine calmly replied, "You see how it is—it is not I that am doing anything. I only yield to the ardent sensibility of the nation."

The Chancellor, who actually saw the crowd every moment increasing, and read in the angry looks of some of the conspirators that his remonstrances might be attended with the worst of consequences to him, forgot his duty, took the oath with the rest, and added, "I will serve you in the council, Madame, but I am useless in the field. My presence might even be displeasing to those who have been hearing my address to you; and that I may avoid exciting their jealousies, I beseech your Majesty to let me remain in my house, under the guard of some trusty officer."

To this reasonable request the Empress consented. She sent him home, with orders not to quit his house. By this prudent precaution, the Chancellor was at once safe from the vindictive spirit of the partisans of Catherine and from the suspicions of the Czar.

At 6 in the evening, Catherine a second time mounted her horse; and, with a drawn sword in her hand, and an oaken wreath about her temples, she hastened to put herself at the head of her troops that were already on their march. Princess Dashkov and the hetman Razumovsky rode one on each side of her. A crowd of courtiers followed. Her army was augmented by a new accession of 3000 cossacks well mounted. The Czar had previously ordered them to file off toward Pomerania, but they had been stopped on the way by a messenger from the hetman with directions to join him.

In the meantime, after the departure of the Chancellor, the Czar continued a prey to the most distressing anxieties. He was every instant receiving some news of the progress of the revolt. It was impossible any longer to make it a matter of doubt. Surrounded by women in tears, and by young courtiers incapable of giving advice, he strolled with great strides about the walks of the gardens, forming twenty different plans and adhering to none, then dictating useless manifestos. When the hour of dinner was come, he commanded it to be served up on the margin of the sea, and seemed for some time to have a respite from his sorrowful reflections. But this respite was of short duration. His affrighted imagination soon held up again the danger that menaced him, and he dispatched an order to the 3000 Holsteiners whom he had left at Oranienbaum to come immediately with their artillery.

It was just at this point of time that the venerable Marshal von Münnich [Count Burkhard Christoph, who had served with distinction in the wars against Turkey and Austria] made his appearance. Münnich, whom the Czar respected on account of his great military reputation, was the only man able to give him salutary advice, and he gave it to him. "Your Majesty's troops are arriving," said the veteran commander. "Let us put ourselves at their head, and march straight to Petersburg. You have still many friends there. Immediately on your appearance they will arm in your defense."

This resolution seemed feasible to the Czar, but it was far from pleasing to his timid courtiers. While they were preparing to begin their march, news arrived of the Empress's approach with an army said to consist of 20,000 men. The ladies of the court cried out that it would be better to go back to Oranienbaum. Peter himself now seemed determined not to expose his person.

"Well!" returned Münnich. "If you wish to decline a battle with the rebels, it is not advisable for you at any rate to stay to be attacked by them here, where you have no means of defending yourself to advantage. Neither Oranienbaum nor Peterhof are in a capacity to hold out a siege. But Kronstadt offers you a safe retreat. Kronstadt is still under your command. You have there a formidable fleet and a numerous garrison. It is, in short, from Kronstadt that you will find it an easy matter to bring Petersburg back to its duty."

This advice was unanimously applauded. General Devier was immediately sent off in a boat to take command of Kronstadt. And scarcely were two yachts prepared for the departure of the Czar when an officer came to assure him that he might rely on the fidelity of that place. Peter, who thought he already saw Catherine at the gates of Peterhof, precipitately got on board, followed by his affrighted court and the intrepid Münnich. It seemed as if some dreadful fatality hung over the head of the unfortunate monarch to frustrate all the wisest measures he adopted. Everything in Kronstadt assumed a new face within the space of a few hours. The fleet and the regiments broke out into open revolt; and Devier, not long after he arrived, was deprived of his command and put into prison.

Precisely while this scene was transacting, Peter presented himself before the mouth of the harbor. Admiral Talizin, the leader of the Kronstadt insurrection, had already made the dispositions for preventing his coming on shore. A part of the garrison, under arms, lined the coast. The cannons were leveled, the matches lighted, and at the moment when the foremost yacht cast anchor, the sentinel called out, "Who comes there?"

"The Czar!" it was answered from the yacht.

"There is no Czar," replied the sentinel.

Peter started forward; and, throwing back his cloak to show the badges of his order, exclaimed, "What! Do you not know me?"

"No" ejaculated a thousand voices at once. "We know of no Czar. Long live the Empress Catherine!" Talizin then threatened to sink the yacht if it did not put off in an instant.

In his dismay, Peter would consent to nothing but flight, and ran to hide himself in the cabin of the yacht among the terrified women. They did not even give themselves time to raise the anchor, but cut the cable and went off by the use of their oars. It was 4 in the morning when they reached Oranienbaum. Some of the Czar's domestics, in great alarm, came to receive him. He commanded them not to divulge the news of his return, but shut himself up in his apartment, strictly forbidding any person to be admitted, and secretly wrote to the Empress.

At 10 o'clock he came out with a countenance tolerably calm and serene. Those of his Holstein guards who had come back to Oranienbaum ran and surrounded him, shedding tears of affection and joy. They pressed him to march them against the army of the Empress, and solemnly swore that they were all to a man ready to sacrifice their lives in defense of his. Old Münnich once more tried what influence he might have upon Peter, exhorting him to make a courageous stand in his own defense. But the persuasion of Münnich had no more effect on the Czar than the noble devotedness of his Holstein troops.

At this time the Empress, at the head of her army, had come to a halt at Krasnoë Kabac, a small public house by the roadside, exactly eight versts [about five miles] from Petersburg. There she reposed for some hours on the cloaks which the officers of her suite had made for her into a bed. At 5 in the morning, Catherine again got on horseback, and rode to the monastery of Saint Sergius, near Strelna, where she made a second halt. The Empress was still there when she received the letter from the Czar, in which he told her that he acknowledged his misconduct, and proposed to share the sovereign authority with her. But Catherine returned him no answer, detained the messenger, and soon after set out again.

Peter, learning that the Empress was approaching, ordered one of his horses to be saddled, with the intention of escaping, alone and disguised, toward the frontiers of Poland. But, always pusillanimous, always irresolute, he shortly after gave orders to have his little fortress at Oranienbaum dismantled, so as to convince Catherine that he would offer no resistance. He then wrote to her a second letter, imploring her mercy and asking her pardon in the most humiliating manner. He assured her at the same time that he would resign to her the crown of Russia, and petitioned her only to grant him a pension, with liberty to retire into Holstein.

Catherine deigned no more to reply to this letter than she had done to the former; but after having conversed some time with the chamberlain Ismaïlov, who had brought it, and whom she easily persuaded to betray his master, she sent him back to the Czar to advise him to submit unconditionally to her will.

Ismaïlov returned to Oranienbaum, attended by a single servant. The Czar had then with him his Holstein guard, consisting of 600 men. These he ordered to keep at a distance, and shut himself up with the chamberlain. Ismaïlov exhorted him to abandon his troops and to repair to the Empress, assuring Peter he would be well received and would obtain of her all that he wished. Peter hesitated for some time; but Ismaïlov kept urging him to make no delay, for his life was in danger, and so finally he followed the advice of this traitor. Ismaïlov then helped him into a carriage with his mistress Romanovna Vorontsov and his aide-de-camp Gudovich, and they took the road of Peterhof.

The unfortunate Czar thought that so much resignation might move the heart of Catherine. He was presently undeceived. When the carriage in which he rode passed through the army, the cossack troops whom he first encountered, men who had never seen him before, kept a mournful silence. Then their reiterated vociferations of "Long live Catherine!" completed his despondency. On stepping out of the carriage, his mistress was carried off by the soldiers, who tore off her riband, with which Princess Dashkov, her sister, was then almost instantly decorated. And it has been said by some persons that it was Princess Dashkov herself, not the soldiers, who pulled it off with her own hands.

The Czar was led up the grand staircase. There the attendants stripped him of the marks of his order; they took off his clothes and, on ransacking the pockets, found several diamonds and pieces of jewelry. After he had remained there some time in his shirt, and barefoot, they threw over him an old morning gown and shut him up alone in a room, with a guard at the door.

Count Panin, being sent by the Empress, was admitted to the Czar, and had a long conference with him. He told him that her Majesty would not keep him long in confinement, but send him into Holstein according to his request. To this promise he added several others, probably without the design of keeping any. The unfortunate Czar, moved with the vain hope of life, was then forced to sign a paper declaring his conviction of his inability to govern the empire, either as sovereign or in any other capacity. Having obtained this fatal act, Count Panin left him; and Peter seemed to enjoy a greater composure of mind. In the evening, however, an officer with a strong escort came and conveyed him as a prisoner to Ropscha, a small imperial palace about 20 versts from Peterhof.

Thus was a revolution of such immense importance effected in one day, and without shedding a single drop of blood. The unfortunate Czar had enjoyed the power of which he had made so imprudent and impolitic a use no longer than six months. His wife, without any hereditary title, became sovereign mistress of the Russian Empire, and the most absolute power on earth was now held by an elective monarch.

In the meantime, Petersburg had remained, since the preceding day, in a state of uncertainty and expectation. Nobody had yet come with intelligence of Catherine's successes. Peter III had still some friends in that city, and if he had commanded force enough to attack and repulse the rebels, its inhabitants would have received him with eagerness.

Toward evening the noise of cannon heard from a distance spread a sudden alarm throughout the city. But it was soon remarked that these firings, being heard at regular intervals, could only announce the victory of the Empress. Tranquillity was thenceforward restored, and hope took the place of fear.

Catherine slept that night at Peterhof no longer as a captive but as absolute sovereign. The day following, she received at her levee the homages of the principal nobility, who had joined her the foregoing evening, and those of the courtiers and young women who came from Oranienbaum. Among these were the father, the brother, and several other relations of the Princess Dashkov.

On beholding them prostrate before the Empress, the Princess said, "Madame, pardon my family. You know that I have sacrificed it to you." Catherine then commanded them to rise, and gave them her hand to kiss.

In the afternoon, the Empress returned to Petersburg. Her entry was truly triumphant. She was on horseback, preceded or followed by the chiefs of the conspiracy. The whole army was crowned with wreaths of oak; the shouts of joy and the applause of the populace mingled with the cheers of the soldiers.

Her first care was to have Prince Ivan [whom the Czar had wished to establish as heir in place of her own son Paul] conveyed from the house where he was concealed, and sent back to confinement in Schlüsselburg. She next proceeded to bestow magnificent rewards on the principal actors in the revolt. Nikita Ivanovich Panin was made Prime Minister; the Orlovs received the title of count; and the favorite, Gregory Orlov, was appointed a lieutenant general of the Russian armies and Chevalier of Saint Alexander Nevsky, the second order of the empire.

She made a point of showing clemency toward the officers and the friends of the Czar, and though several of them were forbidden the court, not one was deprived of his property or his life. The Czar's mistress, Countess Vorontsov, who at first had been treated rudely by the soldiers, was sent to the house of her father; and the Empress expressly forbade a repetition of similar affronts to her. She was afterward exiled for some time to a village a thousand versts beyond Moscow.

All the courtiers now eagerly pressed about the sovereign. They endeavored to discover the person on whom her favor would alight, everyone flattering himself that he should obtain the greater share of it, while none suspected that the heart of Catherine had long been fixed on an officer of humble birth. The marks of distinction shown to Gregory Orlov seemed to them only the reward for his services, not the pledges of love. It was Princess Dashkov who discovered it first. Jealousy is more watchful than ambition; it is especially less discreet; and Madame Dashkov, not satisfied with reproaching Catherine for a choice that degraded her, spread the rumor of it among her friends, and thus brought on her own disgrace.

In Princess Dashkov's Memoirs, *she tells how she first discovered that Gregory Orlov was Catherine's lover:*

"When I came back to the palace [following the *coup d'état*] I saw in the room in which Gregory Orlov was lying on a sofa a table laid for three. I pretended not to notice. Presently her Majesty was told that her dinner was served. She invited me to share it, and to my great annoyance I saw it being served by the side of Orlov's sofa. Apparently my face betrayed by emotions, which were those of anger tempered by sadness, for I sincerely loved the Empress. She asked me what the matter was.

" 'Nothing,' I said, 'except that I have had no sleep for the past fortnight and am terribly tired.'

"She then begged me to lend her my support against Orlov, who wanted to leave the service. 'Just think,' she added, 'how ungrateful I should appear if I allowed him to retire.'

"My reply was the opposite of what she wanted it to be. I told her that now she was sovereign she was in the position to reward him in a manner which would make his fame resound far and wide, without compelling him to stay in the service. It was then I realized with a pang that Orlov was her lover, and that never would she be able to keep it a secret."

The chiefs of the revolt now also learned, with displeasure, that they had been working for a man whom they had always regarded as merely the instrument of their own projects.

The Death of Peter III

Despite the fact that the Czar was in their power, the most zealous partisans of Catherine were not without uneasiness. Some regiments murmured, and began to repent the part they had acted against their lawful sovereign. The people, who easily pass from rage to compassion, now pitied the fate of this unfortunate prince. They forgot his defects, his caprices, his infirmities, in the recollection of his amiable qualities and his sad reverse of fortune. The sailors reproached the guards to their face that they had sold their master for brandy and beer. After the first tumult of the revolution was over, they now waked as it were out of a profound intoxication: they contemplated what had happened in solemn silence, and began to consider whether all was right.

In short, apprehensions were entertained of a new insurrection. Nothing was wanting but some resolute leader to have now restored Peter III to the throne as suddenly as but three days ago he had been precipitated from it.

Undoubtedly no great efforts were necessary to determine the conspirators to free themselves from an object of disquietude. They who have taken one step in the road of guilt make no hesitation at taking a second, and the death of the unhappy Czar was now decreed.

On his removal from Peterhof, the Czar was still blind to the fate that awaited him. Thinking he should be detained but a short time in prison, then be sent into Germany, he dispatched a message to Catherine asking her to permit him to have his Negro servant, "Narcissus," who amused him with his singularities, together with a dog he was fond of, his violin, a Bible, and a few romances. At the same time he told her that, disgusted at the wickedness of mankind, he was resolved henceforth to devote himself to a philosophical life. However reasonable these requests, not one of them was granted, and his plans of acquiring wisdom were turned into ridicule. He was conducted to a little imperial retreat at Ropscha.

Here he remained six days without the knowledge of any other persons than the chiefs of the conspirators and the soldiers by whom he was guarded. On the last day Aleksei Orlov, accompanied by an officer named Teplov, came to him with the news that he was soon to be released, and asked permission to dine with him. According to the custom of that country, wine glasses and brandy were brought in previous to dinner; and while the officer amused the Czar with some trifling discourse, his chief filled the glasses, but poured a poisonous mixture into the one intended for the Czar. Without any distrust, he swallowed the potion, after which he experienced the most cruel pains. On his being offered a second glass, on pretense of its giving him some relief, the Czar refused it, with reproaches on him that offered it.

He called aloud for milk, but the two monsters offered him poison again, and pressed him to take it. A French valet de chambre, greatly attached to the Czar, now ran in. Peter threw himself into his arms, saying in a faint tone of voice, "It was not enough to prevent me from reigning in Sweden, and to deprive me of the crown of Russia—I must also be put to death!"

The valet de chambre presumed to intercede for his master; but the two miscreants forced this dangerous witness out of the room, and continued their ill treatment of the Czar. In the midst of this tumult, the younger of the princes Baryatinsky came in and joined the pair. Orlov, who had already thrown down the Czar, was pressing upon his chest with both his knees and firmly gripping his throat between his hands. As the unhappy monarch continued to struggle with that strength which arises from despair, the two other assassins threw a napkin around his neck and put an end to his life by suffocation.

Such is the account of the death of Peter III, as circulated in whispers at Petersburg, and which indeed has never been contradicted.

In her Memoirs, *the Countess Golovine, who was raised at the court of Catherine, relates the following:*

"One evening when we were at the house of the Prime Minister Panin, he told us a number of interesting anecdotes, and one concerned the assassination of Peter III.

" 'I was in the Empress's cabinet,' he said, 'when Prince Orlov came to announce to her that all was over. She was standing in the middle of the room; the word *over* struck her. 'He is gone,' she replied at first; then learning the sad truth, she fell into a dead faint. When she recovered she shed the bitterest tears. 'My glory is departed,' she repeated. 'Posterity will never forgive me for this unintended crime!' The favor in which they were held had stifled in the Orlovs any feeling but that of unbounded ambition. They had thought that, by killing the Czar, Prince Gregory Orlov might step into his place and induce the Empress to crown him.' "

II.

The Empress and Her Court

Under the reign of Catherine the women assumed a pre-eminence at court which they carried with them into society and into their own houses. The Princess Dashkov, for one, masculine in her tastes, her gait, her exploits, was still more so in her titles and functions of *Director* of the Academy of Sciences and *President* of the Russian Academy. It is well known that she long solicited Catherine to appoint her colonel of the guards—a post in which she would undoubtedly have acquitted herself better than most of those by whom it was held. Several other women of the court, as bold as La Dashkov, accompanied the Russian Army against the Turks; and though taking no part in the fighting, they delighted in visiting the fields of battle and admiring the handsome corpses of the Turks as they lay stretched on their backs, their scimitars still in their hands. Indeed, after I had seen the Russian women who surrounded Catherine, the existence of the Amazons appeared to me no longer a fable.

Nowhere did so many women arrogate to themselves the right of making the first advances, and being the active party, in affairs of love. And almost all the ladies of the court kept men who served them as "favorites." I do not say lovers, for that would imply sentiment; while theirs was merely gross desire, or frequently a wish to follow the fashion. This taste was become as common as eating and drinking, or dancing and music. Tender intrigues were unknown, and strong passions still more rare. Debauchery and ambition banished love. Marriage was merely an association, in which convenience alone was considered. And in their restless and continual search for new pleasures, they had the example of the Empress herself, who encouraged and rewarded them for such proclivities.

In her youth Catherine was considered quite handsome, and she preserved a gracefulness and majesty throughout her life. She was of moderate stature, but well proportioned, carrying her head very high so that she appeared rather tall. She had an open countenance, an aquiline nose, an agreeable mouth, and her chin, though long, was not misshapen. Her hair was auburn, her eyebrows black and rather thick; and her blue eyes often affected gentleness, but oftener still a mixture of pride and disdain. However, her expression never revealed what was passing in the soul of Catherine, but rather served her the better to disguise it.

The Empress was usually dressed in the Russian manner, in a green gown (this being her favorite color) cut somewhat short, forming in front a kind of vest, and with close sleeves reaching to the wrist. Her hair, slightly powdered, flowed upon her shoulders, topped with a small cap covered with diamonds. In the latter years of her life she put on a great deal of rouge, for she still desired to prevent the impressions of time from being visible on her face; and she always observed the strictest temperance at table.

But even when almost 70 years of age, Catherine still retained some remnants of beauty, and no head ever became a crown better than hers. Though grown somewhat corpulent, few women of similar embonpoint would have attained the graceful and dignified carriage for which she was remarked. In private, the good humor and confidence with which she inspired all about her seemed to keep up an unceasing scene of youth, playfulness, and gaiety. Her charming conversation and familiar manners placed all those who were admitted to her dressing room or assisted at her toilette perfectly at ease. But the moment she put on her gloves to make her appearance in the neighboring apartments, she assumed a very different countenance and deportment. From an agreeable and facetious woman, she appeared all at once the reserved and majestic Empress.

I saw her once or twice for ten years, and every time with renewed admiration. My eagerness to examine her person caused me successively to neglect prostrating myself before her with the crowd; but the homage I paid by gazing at her was surely more flattering.

She walked slowly, and with short steps; her majestic forehead unclouded, her look tranquil, and her eyes often cast on the ground. Her mode of saluting was by a slight inclination of the body, yet not without grace; but the smile she assumed vanished with the occasion. If, upon the introduction of a stranger, she presented her hand to him to kiss, she demeaned herself with great courtesy and commonly addressed a few words to him upon the subject of his travels and his visit. All the harmony of her countenance, however, was instantly discomposed, and you forgot for a moment the great Catherine, to reflect on the infirmities of an old woman; as, on opening her mouth, it was apparent that she had no teeth. Her voice too was hoarse and broken, and her speech inarticulate. The lower part of her face was rather large and coarse; her eyes, though clear and penetrating, evinced something of hypocrisy, and a certain wrinkle at the base of the nose indicated a character somewhat sinister.

The celebrated Lampi once painted a striking likeness of her, though extremely flattering. Catherine, however, remarking that he had not entirely omitted that unfortunate wrinkle, the evil genius of her face, was greatly dissatisfied, and said that Lampi had made her too serious and too wicked. He must accordingly retouch and spoil the picture, which appeared now like the portrait of a young nymph, though the throne, the scepter, the crown, and some other attributes, sufficiently indicated that it was the picture of an Empress.

Catherine's Favorites

Elizabeth of England, Mary of Scotland, Christina of Sweden, all the Empresses of Russia, and most women who have been their own mistresses, have had favorites or lovers. To consider this as a crime might be thought too rigid and ungallant. Catherine II alone, however, availed herself of her power to exhibit to the world an example, of which there is to be found no model, by making the office of favorite a place at court, with an apartment, salary, honors, prerogatives, and, above all, its peculiar functions. And of all places at court there was not one whose duties were so scrupulously fulfilled: a short absence, a temporary sickness of the person by whom it was occupied, was sometimes sufficient to occasion his removal. Nor perhaps was there any post in which the Empress displayed more choice and discernment, yet it was never twenty-four hours vacant.

Twelve favorites succeeded each other in this place, which became the first of the state. Several of these favorites, confining themselves to the principal duty it presented, and having little merit but the skill to perform that duty well, had scarcely any influence except within the immediate sphere of their peculiar department. Some, however, displayed ambition, audacity, and above all, self-sufficiency; obtained vast influence, and preserved an ascendancy over the mind of Catherine after having lost her heart.

It is a very remarkable feature in the character of Catherine that none of her favorites incurred her hatred or her vengeance, though several of them offended her, and their quitting their office did not depend on herself. No one was ever seen to be punished, no one to be persecuted. Those whom she discarded went into foreign countries, to display her presents and dissipate her treasures, after which they returned to enjoy her liberalities with tranquillity in the bosom of their country, though their terrible mistress could have crushed them in a moment.

Saltykov, Orlov, and Lanskoï were favorites of whom she was deprived by death; the rest, surviving her love, still possessed places or wealth which rendered them objects of envy to the whole empire. She contented herself with dismissing Korsakov, whom she surprised even in her own apartments with one of her maids of honor; and she resigned Mamanov to a young rival. Assuredly these are very extraordinary features, and very rare in a woman, a lover, an Empress. This great and generous conduct is far removed from that of an Elizabeth of England, who cut off the heads of her favorites and her rivals; and from that of a Christina of Sweden, who caused one of her lovers to be assassinated in her presence.

It will be sufficient to relate how Zubov, her last favorite, was installed, to show my indignant readers in what manner these affairs were managed. Plato Zubov was a young lieutenant in the Horse Guards, patronized by Nicholai Saltykov, to whom he was a distant relation. His name led to a witticism often repeated at court, that Catherine had ended her long career of gallantry with "platonic love."

Zubov spoke French fluently; he had had some education; was of a polite and pliant disposition; could converse a little on literary subjects; and had learned music. He was of a middle size, but supple, muscular, and well made. He had a high and intelligent forehead and fine eyes, and his countenance when young had not yet that air of coldness and severity, mixed with vanity, which it afterward assumed.

When the Empress went to Tsarskoë Selo in the spring of 1789, he solicited from his patron the favor of being appointed to command the detachment that attended her, and having obtained it, dined with Catherine. The court had scarcely arrived when the rupture with Mamanov, her previous favorite, took place. Mamanov was married off and dismissed. Zubov was the only young officer in sight; and it appears that he was indebted rather to this fortunate circumstance than to the deliberate choice of Catherine for the preference he obtained.

After some secret conferences, Zubov was approved and sent for more ample information to the Empress's confidante and indispensable aide in all her amours, Miss Protasov [referred to privately at court as *"L'Eprouveuse,"* or "The One Who Tries Out," comparable in function to a wine taster], and then to the Empress's physician, Mr. Rogerson. The account they gave must have been favorable, for he was named aide-de-camp to the Empress, received a present of 100,000 rubles (20,000 pounds) to furnish himself with linen, and was installed in the apartment of the favorites with all the customary advantages. The next day, this young man was seen familiarly offering his arm to his sovereign, equipped in his new uniform, with a large hat and feather on his head, attended by his patron and the great men of the empire, who walked behind him with their hats off, though the day before he had danced attendance in their antechambers. In the evening, after her card party was over, Catherine was seen to dismiss her court and retire, accompanied only by her favorite.

Next day the antechambers of the new idol were filled with aged generals and ministers of long service, all of whom bent the knee before him. He was a genius discerned by the piercing eye of Catherine; the treasures of the empire were lavished on him, and the conduct of the Empress was sanctioned by the meanness and shameful assiduities of her courtiers.

He increased in power, in riches, and in credit solely because the activity of Catherine had been diminished, her vigor abated, and her understanding impaired by age. During the last years of her life, this young man found himself literally Emperor of all the Russias. He had the folly to wish, or to appear, to direct everything; but having no knowledge of the routine of affairs, he was obliged to reply to those who asked him for instructions: *"Sdélaite kak prégedé"* ("Do as before"). Nothing equaled his haughtiness but the servility of those who strove to prostrate themselves before him; and it must be acknowledged that the meanness of the Russian courtiers has always surpassed the impudence of the favorites of Catherine.

All crouched at the feet of Zubov: he stood erect, and thought himself great. Every morning a numerous court besieged his doors and filled his antechambers. Veteran generals and grandees of the empire did not blush to flatter and caress his most insignificant valets. Stretched with indecent negligence on a sofa, his little finger in his nose, his eyes vacantly turned toward the ceiling, this young man, of a cold and vain disposition, scarcely deigned to pay attention to those who surrounded him. He amused himself with the tricks of his ape, which leaped on the shoulders of his degraded courtiers, or else he conversed with a buffoon who wore a cap and bells; while the veteran courtiers, the Dolgoroukys, the Galitsyns, the Saltykovs, and all the rest, distinguished for their exploits or their crimes, waited with profound silence till he condescended to turn his eyes toward them, so that they might again prostrate themselves before him. His vanity and effrontery were such that he scarcely deigned to pay the heir of the crown, the Grand Duke Paul, that exterior respect which the etiquette of the court required. . . .

Perhaps the reader may have some curiosity to peruse a list of those who preceded this popinjay, and who reigned over Russia more or less in the name of their august mistress.

1. Sergius Saltykov

It is whispered that he received Catherine's first favors when she was only Grand Duchess, a happiness said to have been denied by nature to the unfortunate Peter III. Saltykov, however, grew indiscreet, and excited jealousy. The Empress Elizabeth civilly banished him from court, and he died in exile.

2. Stanislaw Poniatowski

Pontiatowski was the Polish envoy at Petersburg. Handsome, gallant, and lively, he engaged the affections of the young Catherine. Peter III sometimes interrupted them, though he was little addicted to jealousy, and preferred his pipe, his bottle, his soldiers, and his mistress to his lovely wife.

It is well known that Catherine, when seated on the imperial throne, rewarded her lover with the crown of Poland [in 1764]. His disastrous reign evinced that love, when it bestows a crown, is as blind as favoritism when it distributes places and honors. Stanislaw was the most amiable of men, but the weakest of kings.

3. Gregory Orlov

Orlov enjoyed such long and distinguished favor, and his history is so intimately connected with that of Catherine's, that he seemed to share with her the throne on which he had placed her. He enjoyed all the power and honors united which were afterward seen to adorn Potemkin and burden Zubov. He also had much of the haughtiness and firmness of Potemkin. Though he was young and robust, his brother Aleksei, a Hercules in strength and Goliath in stature, was associated with him in office as co-favorite. The Empress was then in the bloom of life. She avowedly had a son by Gregory, who was named Basil Gregorievich Bobrinsky, and educated in the corps of cadets. Two pretty maids of honor, whom Protasov, her first *femme de chambre,* educated as her own nieces, are likewise reputed to be Catherine's daughters by Orlov.

Twelve years of intimacy, further abraded by the haughtiness of this favorite, at length wearied his sovereign, who was by then firmly established on the throne; and after a long contest, Potemkin bore off the laurel. The triumph of his rival, and the inconstancy of Catherine, whom he openly accused of ingratitude, had such an effect on him that his health was destroyed, his mind deranged, and the once proud, powerful, and magnificent Orlov died in the most horrible state of insanity and physical infirmity. Many assert that Potemkin poisoned him with a herb which possesses the quality of turning the brain, called by the Russians *piannaïa trava,* or "drunkard's plant."

4. Vasilchikov

Orlov was followed by Vasilchikov, who was introduced to the Empress by Prime Minister Panin. He served to fill up the interval that took place during the contest between the two haughty rivals, Potemkin and Orlov, and was merely the tool of Catherine's pleasures.

5. Potemkin

One day Gregory Potemkin came and boldly seized on the apartments of his predecessor, Orlov, thus making himself master of the field of battle so long disputed against him. His love, his valor, and his colossal stature had charmed Catherine. He was the only one of her favorites who dared become enamored of her and to make the first advances. It appeared that he was truly and romantically captivated by her. He first adored his sovereign as a mistress, and then cherished her as his glory. These two great characters seemed formed for each other: their affection was mutual; and when they ceased to love, they still continued to esteem each other. Politics and ambition united them even when love had dissolved its bands.

I leave to travelers and courtiers the task of describing the pomp of his entertainments, the luxury of his house, and the value of his diamonds; and to German scribblers to relate how many bank notes he had bound up as books in his library, and what he paid for the cherries he was accustomed to present every New Year's Day to the Empress; or the cost of his sturgeon soup, which was his favorite dish; or how many hundreds of miles he would send a courier for a melon, or a nosegay, to present to one of his mistresses. Suffice it that Potemkin had in his suite an officer of high rank, named Bauer, whom he dispatched sometimes to Paris for a dancer, then to Astrakhan for a watermelon, now to Poland to carry orders to his tenants, or to Petersburg to carry news to Catherine, or to the Crimea to gather grapes.

He created, destroyed or confused, yet animated, everything. When absent, he alone was the subject of conversation; when present, he engaged every eye. The nobles, who detested him, and were able to cut some figure at court only when he was away with the army, seemed at his sight to sink into nothingness and to be annihilated in his presence. The Prince de Ligne, who was his tale-bearer and flatterer, once said, "There is something barbarously romantic in his character." And he spoke the truth.

His death left an immense void in the empire, and that death was as extraordinary as his life. It occurred in the following manner:

Potemkin had spent nearly a year at Petersburg, indulging in nearly all kinds of pleasure and even debauchery, forgetting his glory and displaying his wealth and influence with insulting pomp. He received the greatest men of the empire as footmen, scarcely deigned to notice the Grand Duke, and sometimes entered Catherine's apartments with his legs bare, his hair about his ears, and in a morning gown. Old Marshal Nikolai Repnin availed himself of his absence from the army to beat the Turks and force them to demand peace, doing more in a campaign of two months than Potemkin had done in three years.

Potemkin, who wished still to prolong the war, was roused at the news and set off to take command of the army once more. But he carried death in his veins. On his arrival at Jassy, where his headquarters had long been established and was as well his capital and his court, he was gloomy, melancholy, consumed with vexation, and impatient under his disease. He determined to wrestle with it and overcome it by his iron constitution: he laughed at his physicians, ate salt meat and raw turnips. When his disease grew worse, he insisted on being conveyed to Otchakof [in the Ukraine], his beloved conquest; but he had scarcely advanced a few miles before the air of his carriage seemed to stifle him. His cloak was spread by the roadside; he was laid on it, and there expired in the arms of his niece Branicka, who had accompanied him.

Catherine fainted three times when she heard of his death; it was necessary to bleed her, she was thought to be dying. But it was not the lover she regretted; it was the friend whose genius was assimilated with her own, whom she considered the support of her throne and the executor of her vast projects. Catherine, holding a usurped scepter, was a woman, and timid; and she was accustomed to behold in Potemkin a protector.

6. Zavadovsky

Zavadovsky was the man whom Potemkin had presented to Catherine to succeed him in fulfilling the office of favorite. He was young, vigorous, and well made; but Catherine's inclination for him was soon at an end. Zavadovsky had previously served as secretary, so his disgrace made no noise. He continued to be employed in the affairs of the cabinet, and was later made a privy counselor.

7. Zorich

The inconstant Catherine next cast her eye on Zorich, the only foreigner whom she ventured to create favorite during her reign. He was a Serbian who had been taken prisoner by the Turks and confined as a slave in Constantinople, from where he made his escape. Zorich appeared at court for the first time in the dress of a hussar. His beauty dazzled every eye, and the old ladies in Russia still speak of him as an Adonis. Protected at first by Potemkin, he was desirous of shaking off his yoke, quarreled with him, and even challenged him to fight a duel. His mind was not sufficiently cultivated to captivate that of Catherine, who dismissed him at the end of twelve months loaded with favors.

8. Rimsky-Korsakov

A sort of Russian fop, Rimsky-Korsakov was raised to the rank of favorite from that of sergeant in the guards at the palace, where Catherine noticed him. He was either faithless or ungrateful. Catherine herself surprised him in the arms of the handsome Countess Bruce, her maid of honor and confidante. Struck with astonishment, she withdrew, and would never again see her lover or her friend. This was the only vengeance she exercised against them.

9. Lanskoï

Lanskoï, one of the horse guards, had already obtained some reputation at court as a gallant before he was presented to the Empress. All the officers who had, or thought they had, fine persons endeavored on every occasion to throw themselves in Catherine's way. Even at court the nobles would sometimes give place to a handsome man, such as Lanskoï, knowing that nothing pleased their sovereign so well as to traverse her apartments between two rows of handsome youths. It was a situation which men eagerly sought after, and so they exhibited themselves to the greatest advantage. Indeed, many families founded their hopes on some young relation, whom they compelled to throw himself in the way of such good fortune.

Lanskoï was soon the most favored of Catherine's lovers, and appeared most worthy to be so. He was handsome, graceful, and accomplished, an admirer of the arts, a friend to talents, humane and beneficent. Everyone seemed to share the sovereign's predilection for him. Perhaps he would have acquired as much influence by the qualities of his mind as those of his heart secured him partisans. Potemkin feared him, and, it is rumored, gave him poison. He died with horrible pains in his bowels. Catherine in vain lavished on him the most tender cares; her lips received his last breath. She then shut herself up for several days, which she passed in all the violence of grief. She accused heaven, would die, would cease to reign, and swore never to love again. She really loved Lanskoï, and her affliction turned into rage against the physician who could not save him, and who was obliged to throw himself at the Empress's feet and request her pardon for the impotence of his art. A decent and afflicted widow, she went into mourning for her lover and erected for him a superb mausoleum near Tsarskoë Selo. She suffered more than a year to elapse before his place was again filled; but she gave him an unworthy successor.

10. Yermolov

Yermolov was the least amiable and least striking in figure of all she had chosen, but he was able to console her for the handsome, the tender Lanskoï. He displeased Potemkin, however, before he ceased to please Catherine, and the haughty Prince demanded and obtained the dismissal of this favorite, who did not continue two years in office.

11. Mamanov

Mamanov, who had disputed the place with Yermolov, succeeded to it. Mamanov was amiable, and his bust was a perfect model; but he was not well made. Catherine approved and loved him, and would have done so long, but he was soon disgusted with the faded charms of a mistress of 60.

He became enamored of the young Princess Scherbatov, and had the courage to avow it, demanding permission to marry her. Catherine had pride and generosity sufficient to grant his request, without any reproaches. She saw him married at court to the object of his honorable attachment, and sent him to Moscow loaded with presents.

12. Zubov

The rise of this last favorite has already been related. At the time of his accession he was not quite 25 years old, the Empress was upwards of 60. She finished, however, by treating him as much like a child as a lover, took upon herself the care of his education, and grew more and more attached to her own work, which became her idol.

Yet even at this advanced period of her life she was seen to revive the Lupercalia and the orgies which she had formerly celebrated with the brothers Orlov. Valerian, a younger brother of Zubov, and Peter Solikov, their friend, were associated in office with the favorite. With these three young libertines did Catherine spend her days while her armies were slaughtering the Turks, fighting with the Swedes, and ravaging Poland; while her people were groaning in wretchedness and famine, and devoured by extortioners and tyrants.

It was at this juncture that she formed a more intimate society, composed of her favorites and most trusty ladies and courtiers. The society, which adopted the name of Little Hermitage, met two or three times a week. The parties were frequently masked, and the greatest secrecy prevailed. They danced, represented proverbs in charades, played, joked, romped, and engaged in all sorts of frolics and gambols; in short, there was no kind of gaiety which was not permitted. Such foreign ministers as enjoyed the favor of the Empress were sometimes admitted to the Little Hermitage.

But Catherine afterward formed another assembly, more confined and more mysterious, called the Little Society. The three libertines—Zubov, his brother Valerian, and Solikov—along with some confidential ladies of the court and *valets de chambre,* were its only members. In this Little Society the Cybele of the North celebrated her most secret mysteries; and, it is said, Catherine's prize stallions from her stables, and even the mastiffs from the royal kennels, were pressed into her service.

The "Great" Catherine

The generosity of the Empress, the splendor of her reign, the magnificence of her court, her institutions, her monuments, her wars, were precisely to Russia what the age of Louis XIV was to Europe. But, considered individually, Catherine was greater than this Prince. The French formed the glory of Louis, Catherine formed that of the Russians. She had not like him the advantage of reigning over a polished people; nor was she surrounded from infancy by great and accomplished characters. The usurper of a throne which she was desirous to retain, she was under the necessity of treating her accomplices with kindness. A stranger in the empire in which she reigned, she sought to remove everything discordant, everything heterogeneous, and to become one with the nation by adopting and even flattering its tastes and prejudices.

Catherine's ordinary method of life, in which she almost always persevered, was as follows:

About 6 o'clock in the morning the Empress usually rises. To which we may add that frequently, even in the depth of winter (nay, in the latter years of her life almost commonly), she rose earlier. Without calling anyone, she prepares her own breakfast, as in general she is not fond of being much waited on, and accordingly dispenses with all attendance on her person as much as possible. The business of her toilet lasts not long, during which she signs commissions, orders, and papers of various purport. On days when the council does not meet in her apartments, she is busied alone in the cabinet from 8 till 11 of the forenoon. She then usually goes to chapel, where the service continues till 12. From this time till 1, some of the ministers of the several departments have access to her. After the table is removed, to which she sits down at latest at about half after 1, she goes to work again for an hour or two, according as business may require; she then walks, rides on horseback, or goes out in a coach or sledge; and at 6 her Majesty appears at the playhouse, where the performances are alternately in French or Russian. If the Empress takes her supper in public (which happens extremely seldom), it never continues later than half after 10. At other times she retires at 10.

The only court day in the whole week, holidays excepted, is Sunday. On this day in the morning, as the Empress passes from chapel to her apartments, she gives the ambassadors and foreigners of rank who have been presented at court her hand to kiss; likewise such persons as have any petition, or desire to return thanks for bounties received, are presented on this day to the Empress, and kiss her hand, dropping on one knee.

The court begins not till 6 o'clock in the evening. At the same time a ball or concert is usually given. The Empress never dances, but sits down immediately to cards, having previously told the chamberlain in waiting whom she will have of her party. She plays at piquet, or some other game at which she is not obliged to be constantly silent. A semicircle is formed around her card table, which the ladies begin on the left hand and the privy councillors close on the right. When the Empress has finished her game, she gets up and talks indiscriminately with the ladies, generals, and ministers that form the circle. At about 10 o'clock, and often earlier, she breaks up her party, and then retires unobserved through a side door. What has been here mentioned relates only to the winter months, when the court is held at Petersburg. While the Empress is at Tsarskoe Selo, there is no court held except on extraordinary festivals.

Of civil processes, criminal and consistorial causes, the Empress allows nothing to be referred to her in the hours of the forenoon allotted to confer with the minister. Yet no person can be condemned to death without previous information delivered to her: and then this punishment is almost always commuted or mitigated. But all matters relating to the army, the navy, the finances, to foreign affairs, the taxes, and public buildings, must be reported to her by the chiefs of the several departments. Everyone knows that the Empress is made acquainted with whatever concerns the administration of government, and acts for herself in state affairs. As she never interferes in the private matters and family concerns of her household, she has always time enough for business of a public nature; and her mind is tranquil, cheerful, resolute.

The ten last years of her reign carried her power, her glory, and perhaps her political crimes, to their height. When the great Frederick, dictator of the kings of Europe, died, she was left the senior sovereign, the eldest of the crowned heads of the continent of Europe; and yet all those heads taken together were unequal to her own: for she surpassed them as much in understanding as she exceeded them in the extent of her territories. The immense Russian Empire, an empire almost of romance, which she had subjected to her sway; the inexhaustible resources she derived from a country and a people as yet in a state of infancy; the extreme luxury of her court, the barbarous pomp of her nobility, the wealth and princely grandeur of her favorites, the glorious exploits of her armies, and the gigantic views of her ambition, threw Europe into a sort of fascinated admiration.

In the first year of her reign, 1762, when Catherine was 33 years of age,* she began a correspondence with the great Voltaire, who was then approaching 70. She saw to it that his principal works were translated into Russian, thus initiating the cult of *Vol'ter'iantsvo* in her realms. Her enthusiasm for the ideas of the *philosophes* in France, especially of Montesquieu and d'Alembert, was reflected in her own *Nakaz* (or "Instruction"), in which she undertook a defense of monarchy on the basis of natural philosophy; and she also adopted many of the advanced liberal ideas of the Italian reformer Beccaria and the English savant Jeremy Bentham. The noble act of bounty which she showed to the Encyclopedist Denis Diderot, in buying his library at a price far above its value, and then appointing him librarian of it for life, with a large annual stipend, gained her the esteem of all literary men in Europe.

Catherine did much to advance the arts and to refine the manners of her subjects. In the midst of the Turkish war [1768–74], she purchased in Italy a multitude of inimitable curiosities, pictures in France for 15,000 rubles, and pictures in Holland to the amount of 60,000 rubles; but these last were lost when the ship which had them on board was wrecked off the coast of Finland.

Yet the Empress was neither fond of poetry nor of music, and she often confessed it. She could not endure the noise of the orchestra between the acts of a play, commanding it to be silent in her presence. This defect of taste and feeling in a woman who appeared in other respects so happily constituted is astonishing, yet may serve to explain how, with so extraordinary a capacity and genius, she could become so obdurate and sanguinary.

* Catherine may have been two years older than is generally believed. At the time of her engagement to the Grand Duke Peter, the Empress Elizabeth is said to have taken two years off her age, so as to make her appear younger than her nephew, when she first sent for her into Russia. And there are old German calendars which prove that she was born in 1727. This is an opinion, however, which several dispute, and which I have it not in my power to verify (author's note).

At her Palace of Tauris she constantly dined with the two pictures of the
sacking of Otchakov and Ismail before her eyes, in which the painter
Casanova has represented with a most hideous accuracy the blood flowing
in streams, limbs torn from bodies and still palpitating, the demoniac fury
of the murderers and the convulsive agony of the murdered. It was upon
these scenes of horror that her attention and imagination were fixed while
the singers Gasperini and Mandini displayed their vocal powers, or Sarti
conducted a concert in the banquet hall.

Catherine herself, however, tried her hand at the writing of dramatical
pieces, one of which, entitled *Oleg: A Historical Representation*, was of a
new kind, neither tragedy nor comedy, nor opera, nor play, but an
assemblage of all sorts of scenes, best described as nothing more than a
magic lantern show, exhibiting different views in succession to the eyes of
the beholder. Upon the celebration of the peace treaty with the Turks, it
was got up by her direction with extraordinary pomp and the most
magnificent decorations, and upwards of 700 performers appeared upon the
stage. The piece is truly Russian, and particularly emblematical of the
character of Catherine: her design of subjugating Turkey is alluded to even
while celebrating a peace with that country.

In a similar manner, Catherine's own enlightened views as a despot,
drawn from her reading of the *philosophes,* were in basic opposition to the
security of her throne, and in time were abandoned by her. For the power
of the czars, though absolute and uncontrollable in its exercise, is extremely
weak in its foundation. There is not perhaps in Europe a government which
depends so much on the goodwill and affection of those that are governed,
and which requires a greater degree of vigilance and a steadier hand. The
regular succession of rulers so often broken, and the great change of
manners introduced in less than a century, have left in Russia a weakness
amidst all the appearance of strength, and a great facility to sudden and
dangerous revolutions.

The revolt of the Don Cossacks and other subject peoples led by
Emilian Pugachev in 1773, an uprising which caused the death of over
100,000 men and ravaged the eastern half of the Russian Empire before it
could be suppressed, awakened Catherine to the danger of encouraging
liberal ideas. It is said that the striking resemblance which Pugachev bore to
the deposed Czar Peter III took such possession of his mind that he actually
fancied himself to be the Czar, and signed decrees in his name. When
Pugachev was finally trapped, then betrayed by his own followers and sent
in an iron cage to Moscow, in September of 1774, the Empress appointed a
commission for the trial of the rebel, taking care at the same time to
recommend to them to be satisfied with the confession of his crimes without
applying torture and compelling him to name his accomplices. Her Majesty
was doubtless apprehensive lest the declarations of Pugachev might oblige
her to multiply punishments and plunge the empire into new calamities,

which shows that she considered him merely an instrument, and that the sources of the rebellion were to be traced elsewhere.

The sentence passed on Pugachev was that he should have his two hands and both his feet cut off; that they should be shown to the people; and that afterward he should be quartered alive. But this butchering sentence was not fulfilled. By some persons it is said that it was mitigated by a secret order from the Empress, while others declare that the executioner was less inhuman than the judges. What seems to confirm this last opinion is that, after the execution of Pugachev, the wretched hangman had his tongue cut out and was sent to Siberia. However it be, Pugachev was first decapitated; after which his body was cut into quarters, which were exposed in as many parts of the town. Five of his principal accomplices were likewise beheaded; three others were hanged; and 18 more underwent the knout and were sent to Siberia.

The French Revolution, so unfriendly to despots in general, was particularly so to the Empress of Russia. Had Catherine been asked, when her mind was calm, if she had not herself considerably advanced and helped to strengthen this revolution by her aid to Voltaire and Montesquieu, d'Alembert and Diderot, what would she have answered? Yet such is the fact. Having composed herself in her youth to sleep on laurels, she awoke on the carcasses of the dead. Glory, which in illusion she embraced, was changed in her arms to one of the furies; and the legislatrix of the North, forgetting her own maxims and philosophy, was no longer anything more than an old sybil. Her dastardly favorites, everywhere pointing out to her in her own court Brutuses, Jacobins, and incendiaries, succeeded in filling up the measure of her suspicions and terrors.

The blaze which suddenly emerged from the bosom of France, as from the crater of a seething volcano, poured a stream of light upon Russia; and injustice, crime, and blood were seen where before all was grandeur, glory, and virtue. Catherine trembled with fear and indignation. In her delirium she ordered the bust of Voltaire to be taken from her gallery and thrown into the rubbish. Even the Americans, at this epoch, became hateful to Catherine. She condemned a revolution which she had formerly pretended to admire, called Washington a rebel, and said publicly that a man of honor could not wear the Order of Cincinnatus.

Catherine's Last Days

The visit of King Gustavus Adolphus of Sweden to Petersburg in the autumn of 1796, and the entertainments to which it gave rise, undoubtedly hastened the death of Catherine.

For six weeks she had given herself up to a round of amusements, and subjected herself to continual fatigue. The going up and down the stairs of the palace, the business of dressing and appearing in public, had long been a wearisome task; and the more so as she was still desirous of looking young and healthful, and was always averse to the use of her sedan. Aware of the first of these difficulties, several of her courtiers, upon occasion of the balls and entertainments that were given by them in honor of the King, contrived for her ease that the stairs of their houses should form a gentler ascent, and so they were richly carpeted.

At this time, Catherine had so increased in size as to be an object almost of deformity. Her legs, which were always swollen, and often ulcerated, had entirely lost their shape, and she could no longer boast that handsome foot which had formerly been so much admired. The noted pirate Lambro Canziono (who acted in the quality of buffoon, after having previously served her as corsair in the Black Sea) was desirous also of prescribing as her physician. He accordingly persuaded her that he had an infallible remedy for her legs; and he himself was even at the pains of fetching water from the sea for the purpose of a cold bath, to be used once a day for her feet. The application succeeded at first, and she joined with Lambro in ridiculing her physicians; but the swellings soon returned, and from late hours and fatigue her disorder greatly increased.

When the King's refusal [to marry her granddaughter, the Grand Duchess Alexandra, unless converted to the Lutheran faith] was announced to the Empress, and she was obliged to dismiss her court after having summoned it to celebrate the betrothal, she experienced a slight stroke of apoplexy. From the constraint which for several days after she imposed on herself, that she might appear with her accustomed serenity and betray no symptom of the vexation she felt, the blood and humors crowded still more to the head. Her face, which was before highly inflamed, became at this period additionally red and livid, and her indisposition returned with greater frequency.

I should not perhaps have mentioned here the signs and tokens of her death; but as miracles are still in fashion in Russia, it may not be amiss to observe that, on the evening of her visit with the King, a bright star shot from the sky over her head and fell into the Neva; and for the honor of truth and funeral tokens, I must add that this fact was the common talk of the whole city. Some would have it that this beautiful star was a prognostic of the young Grand Duchess's journey into Sweden; while others, remarking that it made its descent near the spot where the citadel and tombs of the sovereigns were situated, tremblingly whispered that it was the harbinger of the approaching dissolution of the Empress. I say "tremblingly whispered," for in Russia death and the Empress were words that could not be coupled together without danger of punishment.

But waiving this, it is certain that on the fourth of November, 1796, Catherine, having what was called her Little Hermitage, or small party, displayed an uncommon share of spirits. She amused herself greatly with Leon Narishkine, her *grand écuyer* [master of the stables] and first buffoon, trafficking with him for all sorts of baubles which he usually carried in his pockets to sell to her like an itinerant pedlar, whose character he attempted to personate. She rallied him with great pleasure upon the terrors to which he was subject upon hearing of any obituary intelligence, by informing him of the death of the King of Sardinia, which she had just learned; and she spoke of this event in a free and jocular manner. She retired, however, somewhat earlier than usual, assigning as a reason that too much laughing had given her slight symptoms of colic.

The next morning she rose at her accustomed hour, and, sending for her favorite [Plato Zubov], gave him a short audience. She afterward transacted business with her secretaries, but dismissed the last that came, bidding him wait in the antechamber, and she would presently call for him. The valet, Zachary Constantinowitz, waited for a while; but, uneasy at not being called, and hearing no noise in the apartment, he at last opened the door, when he saw, to his surprise and terror, the Empress prostrate on the floor between the two doors leading from the alcove to her water-closet. She was already without sense or motion. The valet ran for the favorite, whose apartment was above; physicians were sent for; and consternation and tumult prevailed about the Empress. A mattress was spread near the window; she was laid upon it; bleeding, bathing, and all the means usually resorted to upon such occasions were employed, and they produced their ordinary effect. She was still alive; her heart was found to beat; but there was no other perceptible sign of motion.

The favorite, seeing her in this alarming state, sent to the counts Saltykov [not Catherine's first lover, but of the same family] and Besborodko, and others of the nobility. Everyone was eager to dispatch a messenger to the Grand Duke Paul; and the person employed in this service by Zubov was his own brother Valerian.

Meanwhile, the imperial family and the rest of the household were ignorant of the situation of the Empress, which was kept secret. Till 11 o'clock, her accustomed hour of summoning the Grand Dukes [Paul and his eldest son, later Czar Alexander I], it was not known that she was at all indisposed; and the circumstance of her being seriously ill did not transpire till 1 o'clock, and was then mentioned with a timid and mysterious caution, through fear of the consequences of mistake. You might see two courtiers meet each other, both perfectly acquainted with the circumstance of the apoplexy, yet questioning one another, answering in turn, watching each other's looks, and cautiously advancing step by step, that they might arrive both together at the terrible point, and be able to talk of what both already knew. It is necessary to have frequented a court, and especially the court of Russia, to be able to judge of the importance of these things.

Five or six couriers arrived nearly at the same instant at his residence at Gatschina, but the Grand Duke was absent. He was gone a few miles with his court to inspect a mill which he had ordered to be constructed. Upon receiving the intelligence, he appeared extremely affected. He soon, however, recovered from his emotion, asked a thousand questions of the messengers, and gave orders for his journey, which he performed with such expedition that in less than three hours he was at Petersburg, which is twelve leagues from Gatschina. He arrived at 8 in the evening with his wife, and found the palace in the greatest confusion.

His presence attracted about him some courtiers and ministers, while others disappeared. The favorite, Plato Zubov, a prey to grief and terror, relinquished the reins of empire. The great, occupied with the consequences of this event, arranged their affairs in private; and all the intrigues of the court were disconcerted in a moment.

Paul, accompanied by his whole family, repaired to the chamber of his mother, who gave, however, no sign of recognition at the appearance of her assembled children. She was lying on the mattress, perfectly still, and without any appearance of life. The Grand Duke Alexander, his wife, and the young princesses burst into tears and formed round her a most affecting group. The Grand Duchesses and the gentlemen and ladies of the court were up all night, awaiting the last sigh of the Empress. The Grand Duke and his sons were frequently by her side to witness this event; and the next day passed in the same anxiety and expectation.

Paul, whose grief for the loss of a mother by whom he had hitherto been so little beloved could not be expected to be extremely overwhelming, was occupied in giving directions and preparing everything for his accession. Catherine still breathed, although nothing was thought of but the changes that were about to take place, and the individual who was on the point of succeeding her.

By degrees the apartments of the palace were filled with officers who had come with expedition from Gatschina, and were dressed in a manner so different from that which prevailed at Petersburg that they appeared to belong to some remote age or to have arrived from another world. In the pale and haggard countenances of Catherine's old courtiers, wherever they were seen, mortification, terror, and grief were depicted; and they successively retired, to give place to the newcomers. The palace was surrounded, and all the streets that led to it were crowded with carriages; and he who could claim the slightest acquaintance passed the day there, awaiting the effect of this sudden event. Orders were given that no person should quit the city, and no courier was suffered to pass the gates.

It was generally believed that Catherine had died the preceding evening, and that her death, for reasons of state, was still concealed. The fact, however, is that she was all this time in a kind of lethargy. The remedies which were administered produced their natural effect, and she had even moved one of her feet and pressed the hand of one of her women; but, happily for Paul, the power of speech was gone forever. [Catherine, who despised her son Paul, had indicated that she wished to remove him as heir to the throne.] About 10 in the evening she appeared suddenly to revive, and began to rattle in the throat in a most terrible manner. The imperial family hastened to her; but this new and shocking spectacle was too much for the princesses, who were obliged to withdraw.

At last she gave a lamentable shriek, which was heard in the neighboring apartments, and died, after having continued for 37 hours in a state of insensibility. During this period she gave no indication of pain till the moment before she expired, and her death appears to have been as happy as her reign.

A Summing Up

Catherine had two passions which never left her but with her last breath: the love of man, which degenerated into licentiousness; and the love of glory, which sank into vanity.

Tsarskoë Selo is an immense and dreary palace, yet the monuments with which it has been adorned by Catherine are so many emblems of her character. By the side of obelisks, rostral columns, and triumphal arches erected to Russian warriors, are seen tombs consecrated to some of her favorite dogs; and not far from these is the mausoleum erected to the amiable Lanskoï, the most beloved of her favorites, and the only one whom death tore from her embraces. These are records, certainly, of very different services, most familiarly placed together. Are we from this to imagine that a dog, a lover, and a hero were all of equal importance in the eyes of the imperial Catherine?

Napoleon I

*Drawing by a British officer who accompanied
Napoleon to St. Helena.*

Yes, here he is, the champion and the child
Of all that's great or little, wise or mild;
Whose game was empires, and whose stakes were thrones,
Whose table earth, whose dice were human bones.
Behold the grand result, in yon lone isle,
And, as thy nature urges, weep or smile.

Lord Byron, *Napoleon*

*A*fter the destruction of the Grande Armée *at Waterloo, Napoleon fled with his aides to his palace at Malmaison, where he remained in seclusion for several days, pondering the alternative of either surrendering to the British or attempting to escape incognito to the United States. His mind was still undecided when he and his party had to leave hurriedly for the port city of Rochefort, on the western coast of France, only to find the harbor blockaded by British men-of-war; at which point they took up residence at a nearby house to make further plans.*

One day, while these discussions were in progress, a bird flew in through an open window, and was caught by General Gaspar Gourgaud, Napoleon's aide-de-camp and the author of the following Journal. *Gourgaud cried out, "It is an omen of good fortune!"*

But the Emperor responded, "There are enough unhappy things in the world. Set it at liberty." As Gourgaud did so, Napoleon had an afterthought, and added, "Let us watch the augury."

The bird, which must surely have been an English sparrow, flew to the right, in the direction of a British cruiser anchored in the bay, and this helped persuade Napoleon to surrender, fully expecting that he would be granted asylum in England and accorded all the honors due a former Emperor of France. Instead, at the Duke of Wellington's insistence, he was sent into permanent exile to Saint Helena, a semitropical speck of an island in the mid-South Atlantic.

But even if Saint Helena had been as large as Australia it wouldn't have mattered: henceforth that napoleonic ego, which had once been allowed to expand throughout the universe, as a sort of ubiquitous huis clos, *was to be shut up entirely within himself. "Which way I go," said Milton's Satan, "am Hell, myself am Hell." In a marvelous little poem by Walter de la Mare, the Emperor, on the retreat from Moscow, similarly solipsistically soliloquizes:*

> *"What is this world, O soldiers:*
> *It is I:*
> *I, this incessant snow,*
> *This northern sky;*
> *Soldiers, this solitude*
> *Through which we go*
> *Is I."*

Napoleon, during the years spent at Saint Helena, is described by Gourgaud from day to day pacing back and forth in memory like a condemned man in solitary confinement, sometimes blaming Fate and other times the deceit of his enemies or the mistakes of his aides, revising this and rehearsing that, but always nonetheless himself, with his self-esteem still intact. Who else, for instance, but Napoleon could have chastised a general for displaying too much pride, with the remark: "You still believe yourself to be the chief ordnance officer of the Master of the World." (Madhouses even nowadays still admit several Napoleons each year.) Though he apparently hoped up to The End that he would some day return to the world stage in triumph, he also (as the historian Sir Lewis Namier once wrote of him) "above all men, knew the value of time," and so must have realized that his time was past. Napoleon was destined to die at Saint Helena, on May 5, 1821, six years after his arrival there, of what could only have been terminal ennui, complicated by cancer of the stomach.

Somewhere in the Journal, *Napoleon recalls with pride a compliment that had been paid him by the revolutionary Corsican patriot Pasquale Paoli in 1790, when he was hardly 21 years old: "You, Bonaparte! You are all Plutarch. You have nothing modern about you." And in truth he was the last of the great imperial monsters, of the same breed as Alexander and Caesar and Hannibal;*

and yet, at the same time, the precursor of the ideological tyrants who have arisen in our own century. Napoleon's famous line, "I found the crown of France in the gutter . . ." has been completed for him by his biographers in either of two ways: "and picked it up with the point of my sword," or, "and the people of France placed it on my head." The first would have been worthy of one of Plutarch's heroes, whereas the second is the sort of pious if resounding cant that a Stalin or a Hitler or a Mussolini might have uttered. Whichever, he seemed to his contemporaries, and remains so for us, a colossal figure, towering above the groundlings. From such heights the pathetic dégringolade of Napoleon into the pettiness of everyday life on Saint Helena, as recorded by Gourgaud, provides us with scene after scene of a cosmic farce: such as Napoleon's attempt to set up an experimental dairy farm on the island with a single cow; or his pompous declamations, still strutting and fretting before a captive audience, on the meaning of life, women, war & peace, suicide, religion, the class conflict, etc.; or his amorous pursuit of the belle of Saint Helena, sometimes dubbed by him "Rosebud" or else "the Nymph," and the spiteful jealousy he exhibited when she jilted him to marry an English sea captain. After all, it might be said, even Zeus chased after milkmaids . . . but Napoleon?

General Baron Gaspar Gourgaud, who served as the Emperor's straight man throughout this farce, was born in Paris in 1783, the son of a violinist at the Chapel Royal and the grandson of an actor. He joined the army at the age of 18, gradually working his way up the ranks, and participated in Napoleon's most important campaigns. At Moscow Gourgaud twice was instrumental in saving his life: the first time in 1812, when he discovered a bomb hidden in the Kremlin, for which act he was made a Baron of the Empire; and again in 1814, when he struck down a Cossack who was about to thrust his lance into the Emperor. Gourgaud never failed to remind him of these incidents. When Napoleon was placed on board the Northumberland to be sent into exile, he pleaded with him to be allowed to join his staff at Saint Helena, and was reluctantly accepted.

Concerning his Journal, Hilaire Belloc wrote in a preface to the English edition that "we have here something living, immediate, right from the heart of reality, and of a different quality from the other evidence upon Napoleon's last years." But Sir Lewis Namier, though valuing the book itself, says of the author: "How . . . could Napoleon let General Gourgaud be one of the few companions allowed to him at Saint Helena? It is enough to look at the man's picture, his garrulous, wide-open eyes, at his blabbing, argumentative mouth, at his forehead of a half-wit, at the excitable stupidity of his face, to see what Napoleon let himself in for; it 'portrays a man who would have tried the patience of Job.'" Even so, it is through the lucid vacuity of Gourgaud's

*extraordinary diary, undimmed by self-reflection, almost like a see-through
mirror, that we can observe Napoleon himself in the round.*

The St. Helena Journal of General Baron Gourgaud 1815–1818, *from
which I have extracted what seem to me the most interesting entries, first
appeared in France as late as 1899. It was translated by Sidney Gillard and
edited with an introduction and notes by Norman Edwards in 1932 (London:
John Lane The Bodley Head, Ltd.).*

F OLLOWING *his surrender to the British at Rochefort, on July 15, 1815,
Napoleon was taken on board H.M.S.* Bellerophon *with a small staff and
transported to Torbay in England, anchoring in the harbor on July 24, and then
to Plymouth. Though he had requested the Prince Regent in a letter to be
allowed to place himself "at the hearth of the British people," he was refused
permission to go on land. On July 31, an Admiral and an Under Secretary of
State came on board and summarily informed the Emperor that the government
had decided to send him into exile at Saint Helena.*

*Accordingly, despite his protestations that he had been tricked and betrayed,
Napoleon was transferred to H.M.S.* Northumberland *for the more than
two-month-long voyage to Saint Helena. Voluntarily joining him in exile were,
in addition to General Gourgaud: Count Bertrand (General Henri Gratien),
former Grand Marshal of Napoleon's palace, accompanied by his wife and three
children; the Marquis de Montholon (General Charles Tristan), a member of
the old Corsican nobility and a boyhood friend of Napoleon, who was also
accompanied by his wife; the Marquis de Las Cases (Emmanuel August
Dieudonné), who was to serve Napoleon as secretary; and Dr. Barry Edward
O'Meara, an Irish naval surgeon and former double agent for both the French
and the British, who was permitted to join the Emperor as his physician.*

The Northumberland *sighted Saint Helena on Oct. 14, 1815.*

October 15, 1815

After lying to from 9 P.M. until 6:30 A.M., we cast anchor at midday. I was
in the Emperor's cabin as we approached the island. When he saw it, he
exclaimed, "It's not an attractive place. I should have done better to remain
in Egypt. By now, I should be Emperor of all the East."

The pilot's cutter comes alongside, with an officer from the island. At
2:30 the Admiral returns with the Governor, Colonel [Mark] Wilks
[Governor of the island from 1813–16, replaced by Sir Hudson Lowe], who
seems a very gallant man, and presents him to the Emperor. To his
Majesty's questions, Wilks replies that the island has 2 or 3000 inhabitants,
two-thirds of whom are slaves. There are no Catholics among them.

October 21

I go with Bertrand to the Emperor, who orders him to write saying that we are very uncomfortable. "This is a disgraceful island," he says. "It is a prison. You must all complain very strongly."

I walk with the Emperor in the garden, and we discuss women. He maintains that a young man should not run after them.

October 30

The Emperor speaks to me of his campaigns. He cannot understand his defeat at Waterloo. "It isn't for me," he adds, "it is for poor France." His Majesty tells me again that, with 20,000 men less, he ought to have won the battle. It is fate which made him lose it.

November 5

We find his Majesty in the small garden, playing chess. After the usual compliments, the Emperor speaks about the situation, complaining that no one has written weekly, expressing our grievances as he desired, and that no freedom has been granted us.

The Grand Marshal [Montholon] is angry because the Emperor told him that he was nothing but a ninny. "Your Majesty errs in not believing in my opinion. Your Majesty would have done well to do so." He raises his voice.

The Emperor, amazed at this, imposes silence on him with these words: "At the Tuileries you would not have said that to me! Everything I did there was right."

The Emperor tells me that I must come and sleep in the tent at the door of his chamber. He talks and strolls with me, discusses his love affairs with Madame D—— and Mademoiselle Gallienne; and tells me that in going to Lyons he had *bonne fortune* with Mademoiselle Pellaprat. His Majesty adds that women are often good to consult; that if he were ever restored to the throne, he would devote two hours daily to conversation with women. He learned many secrets from Madame de Rovigo and Madame de Montebello.

Las Cases tells his Majesty that it is very probable he will sit on the throne again, and that Russia will help. The Emperor declares that that is possible only if the Jacobins become masters of Europe. "It is only I who can crush them, and that involves great risks, for I envisage secret assemblies. Deliberative assemblies are a terrible thing for a sovereign."

His Majesty discusses Egypt with me. "If I had stayed there, I should now be Emperor of the East. At Acre, the whole population was declaring itself for me. I should have been able to go to India."

November 19

His Majesty is sad. We dine with him. He makes me read some Molière. He is rather feverish.

November 29

There had been shouts of: "Long live the Emperor!" beneath the King's windows. His Majesty remarks: "I shall need much strength and courage to tolerate life in my position."

I stroll with him in the garden, and we speak of Waterloo. He doesn't understand this battle, regrets not having put Clausel or Lamarque in his War Ministry, and repents of having appointed Fouché to the Ministry of Police. "I ought to have had Fouché hanged. That was indeed my intention. If I had been conqueror at Waterloo, I would have had him shot immediately. I was perhaps wrong in creating Chambers [of Deputies], but thought they would be useful to me. I was wrong to waste valuable time bothering about the constitution, all the more so since it was my intention to dissolve the Chambers once I saw myself victor and affairs settled. But my hopes of finding resources in the Chambers were vain. I was deceived. They injured me before Waterloo, and have abandoned me since."

His Majesty is roused, becomes sad and melancholy.

December 3

The Emperor dictates on the decimal system, which he criticizes without understanding. I stroll with him in the garden. He tells me that what the English ought to do would be to raise an insurrection in Paris as a pretext for burning the city. "It would be a great coup for England to destroy our capital. The English could probably sink our fleet, overwhelm our ports—especially Cherbourg, Brest, Toulon. After this they would have nothing to fear from France for a long time."

December 6

Montholon announces that sentries will be placed round the house at 9 P.M., and that we won't be allowed to walk in the garden after 11 o'clock. His Majesty flies into a rage, and cries: "You can be certain they have instructions to kill me. They will find some excuse or other for running me through with a bayonet. Oh, I know the English!"

December 16

His Majesty strolls with me, and speaks about the constitution. "We must not have deliberative assemblies," he remarks. "The men on whom one believes one can rely in these assemblies change their opinions too easily. Waterloo! Waterloo! The English constitution is useless for France."

In the town I inquire after a Negress. *Reversi* [a game played with counters on a checkerboard] after dinner, and bed at 10 o'clock.

December 22

I am sad. It is raining. The English troops are maneuvering near

Plantation House. The Emperor speaks to me about my mother: "You are mad to dote so on your mother. Do you think that I didn't love mine? One must be reasonable. Every dog has his day. How old is she?"

"Sixty-seven, Sire."

"*Parbleu*! You will never see her again. She will be dead before you get back to France."

I weep. Bed at 11. Wind and rain the whole night.

January 1, 1816

At 10 o'clock, we all go to his Majesty to wish him a Happy New Year. He receives us in the drawing room and remarks: "A year ago I was at Elba."

This reflection saddens him. We lunch together, and then drive in the park in an open carriage. The Emperor rides around the valley and is nearly thrown into the stream. He meets Miss Robinson [Rosebud] and finds her very pretty.

January 5

His Majesty rides with the Grand Marshal in the valley, visits a freed slave, and Miss Robinson. We go all over the island, breaking down hedges and fences. At Mr. Pey's, the Emperor accepts a glass of wine and allows Mrs. Pey and the children to be presented. He discusses forestry and agriculture. They give us a branch of a coffee plant. His Majesty says that he has never seen one before. He then brings the conversation around to Miss Robinson, whose face he finds charming. Las Cases, who usually agrees with the opinion of his master, does not think her so pretty.

January 7

Mr. Porteous brings Rosebud to lunch. Madame Montholon, who believes Rosebud to be His Majesty's mistress, flatters her intensely, and takes her arm. The Emperor goes into the garden, meets them, talks to Porteous, and declares that Madame Walewska is much more beautiful than Rosebud. He orders me to harness the horses to take the ladies back, and I am to accompany them. On the ladies' return, his Majesty salutes them, and we observe that Madame Montholon is no longer the same to Rosebud, since she sees that his Majesty doesn't find her so beautiful after all!

Later on, the Emperor talks to us of his love affairs, and asserts that nothing has more effect on a woman than a good-looking boy. "Isn't that so, Madame Montholon?" he asks.

January 11

The Emperor strolls with Las Cases and me until 8 o'clock. The conversation turns on Corsica: "The Corsicans hate traitors. I could have gone from Malmaison to Corsica; that would have been quite possible. But the United States tempted me. Even London would have been a great opportunity for me. I would have been welcomed there in triumph; all the populace would have been on my side, and my own reasoning would have convinced the Greys and the Grenvilles."

January 16

His Majesty dictates on Egypt, does not go out riding, but drives around the park in the open carriage. He then strolls, plays chess with me, and asks me how we are to spend our time. It would be nice to fall asleep and not wake up for a year or two! We would then find big changes. O'Meara makes a dubious joke by declaring that we may be taken to Botany Bay. This rumor does nothing but sadden us. At dinner the Emperor talks mathematics like a professor.

January 18

His Majesty tells us that, on his return from the Italian campaign, Madame de Staël * did everything possible to please him. She went to the Rue Chantereine, but was ejected. She had written numerous letters to him in Italy and Paris, and had invited him to a ball. But the Emperor had not accepted. At a party at the Talleyrands she came and sat by his side, spoke to him for two hours, and finished by shamelessly asking:

"Which is superior—the woman of antiquity or the woman of the present day?"

The Emperor replied, "The one who has had the most babies!"

January 28

I go shooting, and kill seventeen turtle-doves. The Emperor wishes to go to camp, and asks me to prepare a route. Then he orders me to buy a pretty slave for myself. I reply that I intend to do so.

January 30

His Majesty rides at 4 o'clock, and goes along the valley. He attempts a few words in English, but cannot master the pronunciation. We visit the Nymph [Rosebud], who hints that she goes out walking every morning, alone. The Emperor is in good spirits. Dinner and chess.

February 7

Dr. O'Meara brings the *Gazette*, and informs us that Murat [Joachim, brother-in-law of Napoleon and deposed King of Naples, captured trying to

---

* Madame de Staël (1766–1817), the celebrated social and literary critic as well as bluestocking champion of women's rights, offended Napoleon's own cocksure opinions on the status of the sexes. In 1803 he banished her to a distance 40 miles from Paris as a result of her liberal agitations with her then lover Benjamin Constant; and in 1810 he ordered the French edition of her *De l'Allemagne* seized and burned, declaring it disloyal to France.

regain his throne] has been shot. I announce the fatal news to his Majesty, who preserves a calm countenance, and says that Murat must have been mad to risk such an enterprise. I assure his Majesty that it grieves me to see a man as brave as Murat, who had faced death so often, perish at the hands of such people. The Emperor declares that it is hideous. I contend that Ferdinand [reigning King of Naples] need not have had him executed in this way.

"That is the way young people think," says the Emperor. "But one does not trifle with a throne. Could one regard him as a French general? He was one no longer. As a king? He had never been recognized as such. Ferdinand had him shot as he has had scores hanged."

The dinner is a sad one. No one speaks. We read the English gazettes. His Majesty, sad and preoccupied, plays mechanically with some coins during the reading. He is obviously suffering.

February 8

The conversation turns on women. "When I told Josephine," says his Majesty, "that I wished to divorce her, she employed all the tactics that tears can possibly suggest. If 50,000 men were to perish for the welfare of the state, I would mourn them, but reasons of state must come before everything else. So in spite of Josephine's tears, I said to her: 'Will you accept this decision willingly, or is it to be by force? My mind is made up.' The next day Josephine sent word that she consented. But later, sitting at table, she uttered a cry and fainted. Mademoiselle d'Albert had to lead her out.

"It's the marriage with the Austrian [Marie Louise] which ruined me. Could I believe that the Austrian Emperor would ever act as he has done? But let's speak of other things. It was Talleyrand who procured Mademoiselle Walewska for me. She has not denied it. Louis XVIII is in an embarrassing position. I don't know what I would do in his place. France is in a wretched state. Gauls! Gauls! It isn't in the French character to insult kings."

February 13

Montholon, who yesterday had reported to the Admiral that a ghost had been about the house, had foolishly requested the sentries to be posted nearer. During the night one of them comes to my window. I get up, and find another at my door. In the morning, I tell Montholon that it is extreme foolishness, and that if he is afraid of ghosts coming through his window, he has only to shut it. We are too hemmed in as it is!

The Emperor tells me that Montholon has spoken to him about a ghost. I reply that that is why the sentries were placed beneath my windows. The Emperor summons Montholon, who, under pressure, and in my presence, confesses to his Majesty that he asked for the sentries.

"You must have a very wicked mind to make yourself our jailer," exclaims the Emperor. "Soon, if this continues, there will be sentries in my bedroom. Why do you pretend that I am exposed to danger, that the sailors and inhabitants are annoyed at my living on the island, and that they wish to assassinate me? It is foolishness! Moreover, if necessary, one of my officers could sleep near my room. But, for God's sake, don't take care of my safety by using an English sentry! You say that girls are being brought here at night. If that becomes a scandal, you can prevent it without the English helping. Do you wish this to be a convent? Come now, leave me alone."

February 17

I go riding, and remark that even if his Majesty were once again on the throne of France, his power would not be dreaded by the English. His Majesty replies to the effect that in six years he would place France on the same footing as formerly.

"Bavaria, Saxony, Italy are discontented," he says. "Belgium would soon declare herself for me."

"Your Majesty saw," I remark, "that at Waterloo the advance guard of the English consisted of Belgians, and they fought well."

"One always fights well," replies the Emperor, "when one's heart is light. But the Belgians are for me. If I hadn't been foolish enough to let myself be beaten at Waterloo, all would be well. I can't even now conceive how that defeat happened. But don't let us talk any more about that!"

February 19

The meat sent us is rotten. The Emperor declares we must write and complain, because everything is inadequate. In the morning, while out riding, we discuss our position. We should have been better off in the United States. I consider that the Prince Regent, yielding to public opinion, could get us brought back to England. We are also fortunate in that Princess Charlotte, on her accession to the throne, will wish to have us back.

April 4

The Emperor asks for me. He is in his bath. He says that he has a mind to spend his time thus—to stay at home each day until 4 o'clock, undressed, reading and working at his English; from 4 to 6 o'clock, walking; from 6 to 8 o'clock, working with Bertrand; dinner and conversation till 10; and from 10 P.M. to midnight, working with me on the campaigns of 1812, '13, and '14.

The Emperor discusses these campaigns with me. He recounts that the Turks, learning that the French had entered Moscow, predicted that the army would perish in the cold. His Majesty's plan was to return to

Smolensk; from Smolensk he intended to return to Vitebsk; but having learned that this town was occupied by the Russians, he altered his mind.

April 20

Mr. Wilks, with his charming daughter, and Mr. Younghusband, arrive at midday. The Emperor dresses to receive them, enters the drawing room, and says to Laura Wilks that he will not repeat to her all the kind things he has heard said of her. Then his Majesty talks with the ex-Governor on the methods of commanding men, whether by persuasion, honor, force, or the lash. His Majesty finds English discipline rather too rigorous; it doesn't leave sufficient to one's honor.

The ex-Governor asserts that 10 Englishmen are as difficult to command as 100 Irishmen, 1000 Scotsmen, or 10,000 Sepoys! However, he has often employed persuasion with success.

The Emperor declares that distinction between officers and men is wrong, and that instead of proposing to the government to abolish the lash, it would be better to propose equality between men and officers. The ex-Governor and the ladies depart, enchanted.

April 23

The Emperor talks about his expedition to Egypt: "Had I taken Acre, I would have gone to India. My intention was to wear the turban at Aleppo. I was sufficiently beloved for that, and I would have found myself at the head of an army of 200,000 men. The East only awaits a man! Now that I am no longer there, Czar Alexander will march on Constantinople. He fears nothing from Poland, and the Greeks are all for him. At Erfurth, he asked me for Constantinople, but I wouldn't consent. I put him off. If the Russians had not burned Moscow, I would have been Master of Russia. I would have allowed the peasants to return, to bring food and horses. Moscow being burned, I would have had to stay there for only a fortnight at most; but I was deluded. Waterloo is cast in my teeth. . . . I ought to have died at Moscow!"

I maintain that in France public opinion is all for his Majesty; that it asserts itself daily; that it behooves us only to live. If they recall Napoleon II [his son by Marie Louise, nicknamed by him the "King of Rome"], our return is imminent. Europe is in a state of ferment.

May 6

I go into the valley to see the Nymph [Rosebud]. Her house is poverty itself. Her father tells me that the Governor is a very good man; he has harangued the three hundred militia men and told them that, to show his appreciation of their services, he is going to give them fresh meat six times a year! The Nymph's father thinks we are very fortunate people, because we have sufficient to eat. He is a simple rustic. At seven, the Emperor summons me, and discusses the Nymph.

May 10

The Emperor declares that I am a young man; that I let my imagination run away with me. I maintain that I have one great fault, that of always telling the truth. This annoys the Emperor, to whom I remark that the tone of the conversations I had heard last evening made me conscious of a certain lack of respect for his Majesty. But the Emperor interrupts me with these words: "You still believe yourself to be the chief ordnance officer of the Master of the World."

May 11

His Majesty sends for me early. He dictates notes on Waterloo. This dictation rends my heart by reminding me of our defeat. The Emperor is very calm when dictating. He asks me: "Is that well?"

"Ah, Sire," I answer, "it is only too well!"

May 16

His Majesty goes for a drive with Bertrand, and seems very moved. He doesn't utter a word. On his return, he tells me about the visit of the Governor [Lowe], whom he made feel ashamed.

Lowe said: "I haven't come here to receive lessons."

"It isn't for the want of needing them," retorted his Majesty.

His Majesty told Lowe that he was nothing but a jailer, who had once wished to enter his presence by force, adding that nobody could do that. He defied the Governor to do it. If the Governor were to employ the brave 53rd Regiment for this task, it would only be over the Emperor's corpse that they would enter his house.

After this rating, Hudson Lowe hastened to O'Meara. He was puzzled, and declared to Bertrand that the Emperor had seen an imaginary Spain, an imaginary Poland, and that he now sees an imaginary Saint Helena.*

May 19

After dinner, we discuss ladies of honor, and the Emperor remarks that Marie Louise, at her confinement, was afraid of being sacrificed for the sake of the child. She had cried out: "I am the Empress, yet above all they would save my son!" This poor young woman, isolated as she was from all her family, very justifiably complained. She thought herself lost. She held the Emperor's hand throughout her delivery.

---

* It has been suggested—and with good reason, if the above conversation with Napoleon is any example—that the real "martyr" of Saint Helena was Sir Hudson Lowe. For carrying out his directives from London, he was the recipient of much abuse from Napoleon's sympathizers for the rest of his life. In 1822 a volume of memoirs by Dr. O'Meara, entitled *Napoleon in Exile, or A Voice from St. Helena*, depicted him as a sadistic villain who delighted in persecuting the Emperor, and Lowe's reputation was thenceforth never entirely cleared.

May 29

The Emperor speaks to me about Corsica. The General of the Insurrection, Paoli, said to him in 1790, when showing him the place where 150 Corsicans had beaten 1500 Genoese: "You, Bonaparte! You are all Plutarch! You have nothing modern about you!" [Paoli, who fought for Corsican independence against the Genoese and then the French, in 1793 banished Napoleon's family from the island.]

May 30

The Emperor speaks to me about my mother. He has received a letter from his mother saying she wishes to come and see him. "I am very old," she says in her letter to the Emperor, "to undertake a voyage of 2000 leagues. I shall probably die on the way, but what does it matter? I shall die near you."

She is with his sister, Princess Pauline. His Majesty tore the letter up.

June 13

I persuade the Emperor to dress, and to breakfast in the garden. He speaks of Waterloo: "The men of 1815 were not the same as those of 1792. The generals had become timid. It would have been better to have waited another month in order to have given the army more stability. I needed someone to command the guard. If I had had Bessières, or Lannes, in command of the guard, I would never have been defeated. I thought I had the Horse Grenadiers in reserve. Their charge would have retrieved the day, for there was only a brigade of cavalry which caused all the disorder. An officer had given General Guyot the wrong order to charge. Soult had not a good staff. My ordnance officers were much too young—for example, Regnault and Montesquieu. They were only aides-de-camp. Ney did me a lot of harm by his attacks on La Haye Sainte, and by changing the position of the artillery. When I left Quatre Bras, I ought to have left just Pajol with the troops of the Sixth Army Corps to pursue Blücher, and to have brought the rest with me.

"On the night of the seventeenth, I sent three orders to Grouchy, but in his report, he says he only received the order to advance on Saint Lambert at 8 P.M. on the eighteenth. It was fate, for, in spite of all, I should have won the battle. . . . I didn't want to declare war on Russia, but I believed that Russia wanted it. I knew the difficulties of such a campaign. The destruction of Moscow did great harm to Russia; it put her back 50 years."

June 16

His Majesty strolls with me, and we lunch under a tree. "It was after entering Moscow that I should have died," he says. Las Cases protests that all his Majesty has done since would have been lost, but I think as the

Emperor does. Death at Moscow, or at Waterloo, would have been best, for the campaign of Dresden had nothing extraordinary about it, whereas the return from Elba was one of the Emperor's most remarkable performances. The culminating point of his reign was his stay at Dresden. [It was at Dresden, in 1813, that Napoleon was able to regroup his armies following the debacle in Russia and win what was to be the last great victory of the First Empire over the Allies.]

August 18

The Governor arrives with the Admiral and his staff, and insists on seeing his Majesty, who is in the garden. The Emperor tells him all that is in his mind. Sir Hudson Lowe replies, "But, Sir, you do not know me."

"Eh, *pardieu!*" replies the Emperor. "Where should I have known you? I have never seen you on the battlefield. You were only fit to hire assassins."

The Governor then threatens to stop sending food supplies. His Majesty answers: "Do you see the camp yonder, where the troops are? Well, I shall go there and say, 'The oldest soldier in Europe begs to join your mess, and I shall share their dinner.'"

The Governor is taken aback, and assures the Emperor that he did not apply for his present post, and that he wishes to be recalled. The Emperor interrupts, "I know—I, who have been Master of the World—I know the type of man such positions as yours are given to. It is only the dishonored who accept them. You do well to ask to be recalled. It would be to our mutual advantage."

With these words his Majesty leaves Hudson Lowe, bids the Admiral a polite good-bye, and comes to my room.

December 7

The Emperor speaks to me about anatomy. He assures me that no one has ever heard his heart before; it is as if he never had one. I reply, as a real courtier, that the Emperor has his in his head. His Majesty thinks that a man can be dead and then restored to life; that there is a certain interval of time in which that is possible. I express the opinion that, once life is extinct, it cannot be revived: one may have seen people who were believed to be dead restored to life, but, really, they had only fallen into a state of coma.

The Emperor continues with these words: "I know that my opinion is that of the materialist, for one might ask: 'What happens to the soul in the interval which elapses between death and the return to life?'"

December 11

After dinner, the Emperor (who is in a good humor) tells me that, after Marengo he had "sent for" Mme. Grassini. She refused to come, because she had not been summoned during previous campaigns, when she was much prettier. She followed the Emperor to Paris, thinking she was his titular mistress; but she was not treated as such, which vexed her considerably. She spoke everywhere of the Premier Consul as an "ingrate"!

December 15

The Emperor says that the massacres of September [during the Terror] were almost entirely the work of old military men who, before leaving for the frontier, didn't wish to leave any enemies behind them. "It was Danton," says the Emperor, "who conceived this plan. He was a remarkable man. He could have done almost anything. It is impossible to understand why he separated from Robespierre and got himself guillotined. It seems that the 2 millions he acquired in Belgium had changed his character. It was Danton who said: 'Boldness, then boldness, still more boldness.' Marat had intelligence, but was also a bit of a fool. What won him great popularity was his prophecy, in 1790, of what would happen in 1792. He fought everybody alone. He was a very curious man. Such men are the makers of history. However much people may try, one cannot belittle them. Few men have made such an impression as these two. Robespierre will never be remembered in history. It is certain that Carrier, Fréron, Tallien, were much more sanguinary than he. Danton has left many friends, among whom are Talleyrand and Semonville. He was a real party leader, beloved of all sectarians. Robespierre ought to have appointed himself Dictator, but that was not so easy for him as it was for a general.

"Soldiers are not republicans. They are accustomed to obey, and are satisfied to see the bourgeoisie submitting likewise. At the camp at Boulogne, all the soldiers wished to see me Emperor, for armies are essentially monarchist, and you will see this spirit in England. While surrounding myself with the old aristocracy—which is the real aristocracy —I gave the premier place, the command of the armies, to plebeians, such as Duroc.

"In one of my travels in Italy, I was on foot with Duroc, when we met an old woman who said she would like to see the Premier Consul. I said to her, 'Bah! Tyrant for tyrant—it's all the same thing.'

" 'It is not,' she replied. 'Louis XVI was the king of the nobility, but Napoleon's the king of the people.' "

December 24

Dinner, then chess. His Majesty asks just this: "What's the time?"
"Ten o'clock, Sire," I reply.
"Ah! how long the nights are."
"And the days, Sire!" I reply.

December 26

The conversation turns on Egypt. "In Egypt, what astonished the natives most was our uniforms and our hats," says the Emperor. "I had already altered several features of the French uniform. The sheiks always said that if I wished to become a patriarch, the army would have to become Mussulmen and assume the turban. That, indeed, was my intention; but I didn't want to take any step unless I was certain of success. Otherwise, I would have made myself a laughing-stock. But I could have done what I wished with the army; it was devoted to me. Any other general at the head of such troops—accustomed as they were to the delights of Italy—would have failed in this expedition. . . .

"Perhaps the destruction of the French fleet was advantageous in that it removed from the army, for the time being, all idea of returning to France. With our fleet I should have been master of everything. The Mamelukes would have joined forces with me, but the loss of the fleet prevented all that. The Arabs only wanted a man. They regarded me as an extraordinary being, especially in view of the absolute obedience of my generals to me. I was careful to convince them that, were I to die, another would take my place and receive the same obedience—although, probably, he might not be so well disposed in their favor as I was!"

January 1, 1817

At about 5:30, his Majesty sends for me in the drawing room. He is with Bertrand and the children, who are playing with the billiard balls. As I enter, his Majesty says to me: "Well, Gourgaud, what are you giving me for a New Year's present? I hear that you're giving everybody something."

"Sire," I answer, "I can only give you what I have always given—my life."

The Emperor sends for a box of sweets, which Pauline (his sister) had once given him. He offers the sweets to Hortense Bertrand, and says the box is worth 50 louis. He then sends for another box, and asks me what it is worth, as he believes it is very expensive. I answer, that the jewel is certainly pretty, but it is only an agate. His Majesty assures me that it is very beautiful, and then asks for all his snuff-boxes. He displays them, valuing them highly. He sends for some lorgnettes, which have just arrived from the Queen of Naples, and says: "Gourgaud, I give you these. They are very good lorgnettes."

After this, he sends for a trunk given by Mr. Elphinstone, and distributes the contents among the ladies—shawls, robes, etc. To Bertrand, he gives a set of chessmen; to Montholon, a mosaic cross; to the children, Tristan and Napoleon, a drum each. The New Year begins well!

January 2

Talking after dinner, his Majesty says that in France many women will cherish a fond memory of him. "I speak of the young girls who, in the various towns, were chosen to make me presentations of bouquets, etc. I always gave them some present or other, and I never failed to pay them a compliment, which flattered them extremely. At Amiens, one of these young ladies who, on a previous occasion, had presented me with a bouquet, rushed at me crying, 'Ah, Sire, how I love you!' I told the mother and father of this young lady that I was deeply appreciative! All these young girls would easily have provided me with a harem—if my tastes had been in that direction!"

January 4

At 8:30, I am informed that the Emperor is in the drawing room. During conversation he says: "At San Miniato, one of my relations, who was a Capucine—Brother Boniface Buonaparte—died in an odor of sanctity. On my arrival in Italy, the Capucines begged me to have him recognized as a saint. That would have cost a million! When, afterward, the Pope came to Paris, he proposed that I should have this brother sanctified. Such an event would have won over to my side many monks and peasants. Nevertheless, I sought advice on the matter, but it was thought that it would lend itself to ridicule, and so Boniface was never made a saint!"

January 9

In conversation with me, the Emperor says: "I did all I could to better the fate of bastards, of the poor innocent wretches thus dishonored; but one cannot do much for them without injuring the institution of marriage, otherwise few people would marry. In the olden days, besides having a wife, a man had concubines, and bastards were not despised as they are today. I think it ridiculous that a man can have, legitimately, only one wife. When the wife is pregnant, it is as if the husband were unmarried. One no longer has concubines, it's true, but has mistresses, who upset fortunes very much more! I speak of people in easy circumstances, for the poor wouldn't be able to maintain more than one wife.

"In France, women are considered too highly. They should not be regarded as on a plane of equality with men. In reality, they are nothing more than machines for producing children. During the Revolution, they rose in insurrection, instituted assemblies for themselves, and were even desirous of organizing themselves in battalions. They had to be stopped. Disorder would have been introduced into society had women abandoned the state of dependence which is their rightful position. There would have been struggles, and continuous warfare. One sex must be subordinate to the other.

"One has seen women wage war as soldiers; then they are dangerous, overexcitable, and capable of committing unheard-of outrages. At Orgon, a young and pretty woman was so infuriated with me that I am certain she would have drunk my blood! If ever there were war between the sexes, it would be very different from that between rich and poor, or white and black. Divorce is entirely to the disadvantage of women. If a man has had several wives, he shows no sign of it, whereas a woman several times married fades completely.

"In the event of war, pregnancy is the only thing which would give inferiority to women. One has always decried loose women, and yet they are a necessity. Without them, men would attack respectable women in the streets. When a pretty woman prostitutes herself, it does much harm to her sex; it lowers it; and particularly does it reduce the charm which the presence of a beautiful woman should produce in society."

January 14

Dinner, with trivial conversation on the superiority of stout over thin women.

January 15

I remark to the Emperor that what was said about the Jewish race has been confirmed, and still continues to be confirmed. They wander about the earth—it is a constant miracle. His Majesty retorts that it is a curious thing, but equally amazing is the fact that there remain in France a million Protestants, after all the persecutions they have had to suffer; yet there are not more than two million Jews. Madame Montholon thinks that the Jews ought to reconquer their own country. The Emperor adds: "The Christians are much more numerous, and they haven't been able to do it! I regret very much never having visited Jerusalem, but this would have delayed my expedition to Acre two or three days, and time was precious." *

His Majesty speaks of populations. We discuss that of Amsterdam. He requests me to verify the number in the library, and I fetch the *Imperial Almanac*. The Emperor looks up the ages of his brothers. "My mother can live a long time yet," he says. "Josephine faked her age—according to the entry. Eugene must have been born at the age of twelve!"

Then, taking the *Almanac* again, the Emperor looks at the names of the ladies of his court. He is moved. "Ah! it was a fine Empire. I had 83 million human beings under my government—more than half the population of all Europe."

To hide his emotion, the Emperor sings, and scans the *Almanac*, turning over the pages of names of members of the Institute. He is obviously

---

* In 1799, at the time Napoleon's revolutionary army was besieging the city of Acre in Palestine, he issued a proclamation calling on the Jews of Asia and Africa to rally to his flag for "the restoration of ancient Jerusalem." This proclamation, headed "General Headquarters, Jerusalem, 1st Floreal, April 20, 1799, in the year 7 of the French Republic," read partly as follows:

"Israelites, unique nation, whom in thousands of years lust of conquest and tyranny have been able to deprive only of their ancestral lands, but not of name and national existence! . . . Arise, then, with gladness, ye exiled! A war unexampled in the annals of history is being waged in self-defense by a nation whose hereditary lands were regarded by its enemies as plunder to be divided . . . avenging its own shame and the shame of the remotest nations, long forgotten under the yoke of slavery, and also the almost 2000-year-old ignominy put upon you."

touched, although he wishes not to appear so. He reads several articles, as one not understanding what he reads. What a man! What courage! What a fall!

January 20

"You are under no obligations to me," says the Emperor. "Yes, Gourgaud, you are the most fortunate of all here. If I die at Saint Helena, though poor, I still have a few millions. I have no other family at present besides you all. My works will be yours, and no one does justice to your merit and ability more than I. But while I am here, it is everyone's bounden duty to please me, and to brighten my days—but you are always gloomy."

I reply, "If Your Majesty were to treat the Montholons for two or three days in the same way as you have treated me this last month, you would see whether they would patiently bear such treatment. You lavish honey on them, and absinthe on me."

The Emperor declares that it isn't right that I should be paid as much as the Montholons put together, to which I reply that I ask for nothing. I can last out for some time yet, by selling my watch and scarf-pin. His Majesty urges me to show respect to Madame Montholon. Finally, the Emperor, in a kinder vein, adds that Bertrand is to bring about a reconciliation between Montholon and myself.

"Let it all finish now," says the Emperor. "Do you think that when I lie awake at night I haven't my bad moments, when I think of what I was, and what I am now? When I came to Saint Helena, I would have given you my sister, or Madame Walewska, but now—no, you are too suspicious, and given too much to idle imaginings."

January 21

At 7:30, I go into the drawing room. His Majesty is busy, reading to Bertrand and O'Meara the *Amours Secrètes de Buonaparte*. He is laughing heartily, and says he knows none of the women mentioned.

"They make a Hercules of me!" he exclaims.

January 27

The Emperor thinks that if Nelson had run into the French fleet, the English Admiral would have been beaten. The French possessed a three-decker, whereas the English hadn't anything of the sort. Besides, the English had no frigates, and could not have pursued the convoy.

"Nelson was a brave man," says the Emperor. "If Villeneuve, at Aboukir, and Dumanoir, at Trafalgar, had had a little of his blood, the French would have been the conquerors."

We read *Paradise Lost*. The Emperor wants to buy a cow, but where shall we keep it?

January 28

The Emperor sends for me to dine with him. He remarks: "The day on which the Empress was delivered, she had been out walking with me for some time, although she had already felt the first pains. It was thought that nothing would happen before 4 o'clock. I went to my bath. Soon, [Doctor] Dubois came running to me, quite distracted, and as pale as death.

"I cried, 'Well, is she dead?' for I am accustomed to crises. It isn't at the time that they affect me—it is afterward.

"Dubois answered, 'No, but the child is being born askew.'

"That was very unfortunate, for such a thing happens only once in 2000 cases. I hurried to the Empress. Another bed had to be got for her, so that the Doctor could use the instruments. She didn't want to be moved, but Madame de Montesquieu assured her that that had happened to her twice and encouraged her to allow the operation. The Empress cried horribly. I am not sensitive, but to see her in such agony moved me. Dr. Dubois, not knowing what he was doing, wanted to wait for Dr. Corvisart, who would give him courage. The Duchess of Montebello was also there, behaving like a madwoman.

"The 'King of Rome' [Napoleon's intended heir, who became the Duke of Reichstadt, and died at the age of 21] was born and remained for at least a minute without a murmur. He was lying on the carpet, as if dead. It was only by dint of much rubbing and massage that the child showed signs of life. He had a slight scratch on his head, caused by the instruments. The Empress sacrificed for the child—though, as a matter of fact, that was the reverse of what I had ordered. What a wonderful thing medicine is! . . .

"Mange is a terrible malady. I got it at the siege of Toulon. Two artillery men who had it, were killed under my very nose, and their blood covered me. I was only partially cured, however, for it recurred in Italy and Egypt. On my return, Corvisart completed the cure by inoculating me in the chest. Before the inoculation I had been emaciated and yellow; after it, I became robust. I have often joked with Corvisart about the number of people he has killed, and asked whether, after their death, he never wondered whether he ought to have treated them differently in order to save their lives. Corvisart replied, 'Yes, once or twice.' But I could only make him confess by comparing him to the general who, by issuing a certain order, had brought about the destruction of 3 or 4000 soldiers. . . .

"I believe that a man is the product of the earth's clay, heated by the sun and fused with electric fluid. What are animals—an ox, for instance—if not organic matter? When one sees that men have a constitution almost similar, isn't one justified in believing that man is only matter more highly organized; perhaps in an almost perfect state? The day will surely come when human beings will be constituted of matter even more perfect. Where is the soul of a child, or of a fool? The soul follows the physical. It waxes with childhood and wanes with old age. If it is immortal, it must have existed before us. It is thus devoid of memory. On the other hand, how can one explain thought? At this very moment, as I talk with you, my thoughts go back to the Tuileries. I see the Palace, I see Paris. . . .

"It is thus, in the old days, that I used to explain presentiment. I used to think that the hand rebuked the eye for lying, when the latter declared it could see a league off. The hand objected: 'I can see only two feet—how can you see a league?' So, presentiment is the eye of the soul. Nevertheless, the idea of God is very simple. Who has made everything? There is a veil which we cannot lift; it is outside the perception of our soul and of our understanding. It belongs to a superior plane. The simplest idea is to worship the sun, which fructifies everything. I repeat, I think that man is the product of the atmosphere, plus the heat of the sun, and that, after an allotted time, this faculty ceases to be productive. I wonder if soldiers believe in God? They see death on all sides. Religion can purify and pacify them."

January 29

The Emperor discusses a book on the Revolutionary Tribunal. "An excessive hatred exists between master and man, and between the masses and those who possess the world's wealth," he remarks. "The masses ask: 'Why do they have everything, and we nothing?' The populace always rejoices when they see those who possess more than they perish. The servant is the most implacable enemy of his master. Ah, my God! Even here, if there were to be a total change in my position, my own people would torment me for having been my servants! It is human nature! Lords who treated their peasantry in the best possible way have been most maltreated. The peasants say: 'They have done only what they ought to do, and they remain more fortunate than we are. Why have they lands and we nothing?' Well, the best way to make everyone poor is to insist on equality of wealth!"

February 3

The Emperor says priests ought to be able to marry, because it is difficult to do without women. I interrupt, saying, "Let the priests come to Longwood—they would do without women, all right!"

His Majesty continues: "I think I should have no wish to confess to a priest who would probably go and tell everything to his wife. Formerly, all the priests had servant girls and nieces. At the Council of Constance, the older priests were in favor of marriage, while the younger ones, because of their ambition, were against it."

February 4

A few days ago, at the request of his Majesty, Mr. Balcombe sent a cow and her calf. They were brought into the stable, although nothing was said to me about it. After much trouble, the cow was tethered; but in the evening, she broke loose and got away. Two days later, she was brought back and tethered again in the stable, and Montholon announced that she was to be fed at the expense of the horses. Whether by accident, or whether because the grooms had no wish to look after the cow, in the evening they found the rope broken again, and the beast gone! The next day—that is to say, yesterday—I told Montholon about it. This morning, Montholon related the incident to the Emperor in such hectic colors that the Emperor became very angry and sent word that if the cow was not brought back again to the stable, he would deduct the value of it from Archambault's [Napoleon's coachman] wages. Also, he threatened that he would kill all the chickens, goats, and kids that were in the yard!

Later, Bertrand calls on me. The Emperor is in a very bad humor, and full of the cow incident. At dinner, the Emperor asks Archambault, "Did you let the cow get away? If it is lost, you'll pay for it, you blackguard!"

Archambault assures his Majesty that he caught the cow again at the other end of the park; that she twice broke her rope; and that she gives no milk. I hold my tongue throughout the meal.

His Majesty, in a very bad humor, retires at 10:30, muttering, "Moscow! Half a million men!"

February 7

After dinner, his Majesty remarks that he could live very comfortably in France on 12 francs a day, dinner costing 30 sous. He would frequent literary salons and libraries, and mingle with the public at the theatre. A louis a month for a room. "But I should have to have a servant," he muses. "I am so accustomed to one—I can't dress myself. I should enjoy myself very much in the company of people of my own fortune. *Eh, mon Dieu!* All men have the same share of happiness. I was certainly not born to live the life I am living now. *Eh bien!* As M. Bonaparte, I would have been just as happy as I am as Emperor Bonaparte. The common workman is as happy as the next—everything is relative. I have never experienced the pleasures of good living, because I have always been well served; but the private individual, who does not dine as well, is quite as happy as I. Certainly, that sort of life would have been far happier than the one we are living at Saint Helena. Yes, with one louis a day, one can be very happy—it is only a question of knowing how to limit one's desires.

"For instance, if I were able to go about incognito, I should travel through France with three carriages drawn by six horses. Thus, I should make little excursions, accompanied by three or four friends and three or four women, stopping wherever I liked, visiting everything, chatting with farmers and farm laborers. Agriculture is man's real profession. I should have letters of introduction to all the principal places. I ought, when

Emperor, to have traveled in France thus, but with 4 or 500 horses, and a part of my guard, sending on ahead of me a carriage with servants to prepare a royal chamber wherever I proposed to stay. In this way, I should have done some good—not only to others but to myself. To have stayed a few days in a place would have enabled me to become beloved of all the inhabitants. If I had been in America, I should have traveled extensively, with three or four carriages and friends.

"I repeat, money and honors do not make for happiness. The sort of life I live here—if I were not a prisoner, and provided I lived in Europe—would suit me down to the ground. I should love to live in the country and see how land is farmed, for I never could understand farming. It's a fine existence. A sick sheep provides subject matter for conversation. Also, one is happy in Paris, mixing in a society of folk of a rank inferior to one's own. One takes one's share in conversation as others do. One gets genuine respect for one's intelligence. I am convinced that, among the middle classes, there is more real happiness than among the upper classes. At Elba, with money, living among the savants of Europe (of whom I would have formed the center), I would have been very happy. I would have built a palace to receive people who came to visit me. I would have lived a life befitting the castle, surrounded by people of merit."

February 8

I am told that the cow has produced a bottle of milk, and that she may produce a second! Noverraz [Jean Abram, third valet to Napoleon, who remained with him until his death] is going to make some butter.

At 9 o'clock, we were informed that the Emperor, indisposed after bathing, is dining in his own room.

February 12

The Emperor sends for me in the reception room, treats me well, asks for champagne, and gives me a glass to drink the health of my mistress in France.

I leave the Emperor at 5 o'clock, half-satisfied, half sad. He has spoken kindly to me; but he does not appreciate real devotion. When I declared that he considered all humanity false, he replied, "I am not paid to find it better."

February 13

At 7 o'clock, his Majesty sends for me in the reception room. He is extremely sad and depressed. He wants to play chess but can't, because he is so taken up with his own thoughts.

February 16

The conversation turns on Fouché. "Fouché," says the Emperor, "presumed to speak to Josephine about my divorce—as if I required his help! He did it out of self-importance. When I had made up my mind, I said to Josephine, 'You have children. I haven't. You must appreciate my necessity for thinking of consolidating the dynasty. For this reason I must divorce and remarry. That would be to the advantage of your children. Your tears are vain. Reasons of state have the greater claim. You must submit with a good grace for, come what may, my mind is made up.'"

February 24

His Majesty is extremely affable to me. He passes into the reception room, promising to take both Bertrand and me on at chess until dinner time. Conversation: "Ney," [Marshal of France under Napoleon, condemned to death and executed after the Restoration], says the Emperor, "defended himself badly [at his trial]. He ought to have been more noble in his answers, and relied for support on the Convention of Paris. He could not justify himself. He was sincere, until March fourteenth, and I believe everyone was convinced of his sincerity. . . . But Ney only got what he deserved. I miss him as a valuable man on the field of battle, but he was too immoral, and too much of a fool, to succeed. . . . I am convinced that it is through him that we are here; instead of remaining quiet, as I asked him, he attacked the Austrians just when the Emperor Francis was declaring himself for us. Then there was no remedy, for it was said immediately that I should want to start my 'system' again and risk 'everything for everything.' In vain I protested that Murat's attack was contrary to my wishes. It was believed to be a put-up affair between Murat and myself. . . .

"The rabble is nothing; it can do nothing on its own. From all that is going on in France today, I can see clearly that the rabble would have shot me, if they had been able."

BERTRAND: "I should never have believed it."

NAPOLEON: "Yes, they would have shot me—if they had caught me."

GOURGAUD: "It is like the trial of the King of Naples [Murat]. . . ."

NAPOLEON: "If I had delayed my attack [at Waterloo], I should have had 12,000 extra men, drawn from the Vendée; but who would have guessed that the Vendée could have been so easily pacified? Moreover, my plan had been well executed. It is fate that beat me at Waterloo. The campaign ought to have succeeded. The English and the Prussians were taken by surprise in their cantonments."

February 25

We speak of Elba. "I was very well there," says the Emperor. "I should have sent for artists from Italy. I was more independent than a prince in Germany. I should have remained there, if the King had had good ministers, and I was feared so little that they didn't even send a *chargé d'affaires* near me. I was insulted in all the public newspapers. *Ma foi!* I am a man. I wanted to show that I was not yet dead!"

March 4

His Majesty speaks to us about Paris, and the improvements he contemplated making there: "I should have preferred my capital at Lyons, but everything had still to be prepared there, whereas Paris was far in advance of any other town in France. I wanted this capital to overwhelm with its splendor all the capitals of the world. . . .

"Ah! If I had been able to govern France for 40 years, I would have created the most illustrious empire the world has ever known."

MADAME MONTHOLON: "Who knows, perhaps your Majesty will some day build a vast empire in America?"

NAPOLEON: "Ah! I am an old man."

March 10

The Emperor urges me to be gay, and maintains that I am a big baby. He asks why it is I grieve. I do not reply. He makes me play chess, and treats me with kindness. At dinner, his Majesty speaks to me frequently, and does for me what he has done only once before, and then for Las Cases—namely he places the spoon in the macaroni, and offers to serve me with some! "May I serve you with some macaroni?" He repeats this, and then inquires how I like it.

"Excellent, Sire," I reply. "I have never tasted such excellent macaroni." The servants are amazed. I receive unheard-of attentions!

March 16

We must write up the story of Waterloo. There is a way of sending it to England, where it can be printed, both in French and English. It will earn me a great reputation, and bring in large sums of money. The Emperor dictates his memories of Waterloo. It appears that he couldn't see the battle very well. He wanted to make a perpendicular attack, and to lead it himself; but Bülow's arrival forced him to remain in a central position. Ney didn't understand this attack.

March 17

We discuss confessors. The idea of having one here has never occurred to me. I have nothing with which to reproach myself. My conception of God is such that I can speak to Him myself. I have the greatest confidence in His loving-kindness. It is believed that I am always reading the Bible. "I don't know why your Majesty thinks I am a hypocrite," I remark.

"Yes, I do think that you are, rather," replies the Emperor.

"I confess that I believe steadfastly in God, and cannot justify the existence of atheists," I retort.

"Bah!" says the Emperor. "Laplace is an atheist, likewise Berthollet. At the Institute, everyone was an atheist; yet Newton and Leibnitz believed in God."

"I confess, Sire," I answer, "that this very evening, I was considering the stars, and was wondering how people could pretend to imagine that all such mechanism was merely a string of matter. Who, then, created matter, if not a Superior Being, like God? Laplace himself cannot explain the sun, the stars and the planets; yet he dares to declare there is no God!"

"Atheists compare man to a watch," replies the Emperor. "A watchmaker is the superior intelligence; they agree that it is the effect of matter, just as heat is the effect of fire. I would believe as steadfastly in Christ as Pope Pius VII does, if religion were to go back to the beginning of the world, and if it were the universal religion."

The Emperor says that, in time of war, he has seen so many people disappear suddenly, and pass so rapidly from life to death, that he has become familiar with death. "Matter, matter," he says.

Madame Montholon declares herself a materialist.

NAPOLEON: "It is cowardice to commit suicide. The English often kill themselves. It is a malady caused by their damp climate."

March 18

The Emperor asks for the Bible, which he believes is often in my room. He wishes to read the books of Saul and David, to find out what the Scriptures say about legitimacy.

"There are many Napoleons in Corsica," says the Emperor. "I call myself Bonaparte. Bonaparte is the same as Bonarotti, or Buenarotti. I made a mistake in not allowing my relative, Brother Boniface, to be canonized."

March 23

The Emperor regrets he never established good prisons in Paris. He would have interned 5 or 6000 people, and accommodated them as in a furnished hotel, each prisoner according to rank. He doesn't know why he allowed himself to be dissuaded from doing this. He is sorry now. He has just been reading the observations of an Englishman on the prisons of Paris.

April 7

His Majesty believes that, in England, he would have had many amusing adventures; and he asks me whether, in order to marry a rich girl, I would consent to remain 10 years in England.

"Yes, certainly," I reply. "I am 34, and the longer I delay my marriage, the less likelihood there is of my marrying at all!"

His Majesty married the second time very much later in life. He says, if he were to lose Marie Louise, he would not marry again.

"At fifty," says the Emperor, "one can no longer love. Bertrand always loved, but I have a heart of bronze. I have never loved anyone for love's sake, except, perhaps, Josephine—*a little*. But then I was only 27 when I knew her! I have some affection for Marie Louise. I share the view of

Gassion, who once told me that he didn't love life sufficiently to give it to others."

April 11

At 8 A.M., the Emperor sends for me in the billiard room. He is still in his night attire, and wants to know all I heard yesterday. The Emperor is so weary, so dispirited and sad, that his mind is incapable of work. He cannot go out; he is in prison. In the United States, it would have been very different. He would have had plenty of books to read and Frenchmen with whom he could associate, but here, he has nothing. At the same time, it would be very useful to write up certain things—for instance, scarcely anything has been written about Louis XIV.

"Louis XIV," says the Emperor, "was the greatest sovereign our country has ever possessed.

April 13

The Emperor sends for me. He is naked. He dictates notes, dresses, and passes into the reception room. Four vessels bound for China sail tomorrow. Possibly through fear lest someone should escape, the Governor redoubles the sentries. . . .

During dinner the Emperor addresses me: "Isn't it true, Gourgaud, that there is happiness in being egoistic and hard-hearted? If you were hard-hearted, you wouldn't worry about your mother and your sister."

"Ah, Sire," I reply, "I prefer to suffer, and to have an affectionate disposition."

April 27

I speak of English history, of the great similarity existing between the reigns of Charles I and Cromwell and the French Revolution. The Emperor promises to read this history again.

He asks if the Protector had great talent. Wasn't he a bully? He had one excellent quality—dissimulation: but also, great political talent. He saw, and judged things, to perfection. There is no deed in his whole life in which he can be accused of exercising bad judgment. The Emperor thinks he was an extraordinary man.

May 6

According to Madame Bertrand, the Emperor will not live two years here. If he wakes up during the night, he can never go off to sleep again, but turns over in his mind all his mistakes, and compares his present position with the past. Yes, the Emperor is very unhappy. Later on, he sends for me. I thought it was to dictate notes. No, it is for some calculations on fire pumps, and the Nile. He asks me at what period I think he was happiest. I reply, "At the time of your marriage, Sire."

Madame Montholon says, "When you were Premier Consul."

Bertrand replies, "At the time of the birth of the 'King of Rome.' "

"Yes," says his Majesty, "I was happy as Premier Consul, also at my marriage, and at the birth of the 'King of Rome'; but on those occasions, I was not quite sufficiently balanced. Perhaps it was at Tilsit. I had just experienced vicissitudes and cares at Eylau, but amid all, I was victorious, dictating laws, etc., and emperors and kings were paying me court. Perhaps, too, I was most happy after my welcome in Italy. What enthusiasm! What cries of 'Long live the Liberator of Italy!' At 25 years of age! From that time, I foresaw what I could become. I saw the world floating under me, as if I were borne on air."

His Majesty sings an Italian air.

May 12

Dinner. We read *La Nouvelle Héloïse.*

"Let us see the letter about the suicide," says the Emperor, who then remarks, "It is cowardice to commit suicide."

"Religion forbids it," I said, "but apart from this, there are two pains—the one physical, and the other, moral. I find it easy to believe that a man suffering from an incurable illness might commit suicide."

The Emperor repeats that it is cowardice.

"Yes," I remark, "but only in the case of a man who has friends, or a family to maintain. In a word, it is cowardly for a man who can still be useful, but I find in other cases, when a man suffers, he is justified in destroying himself."

According to his Majesty, a man must not be swayed by the desire of the moment. He might repent of what he has already done. Men who have succeeded only in administering self-inflicted wounds have often later thought that moment absurd in which they made the attempt on themselves.

May 14

The Emperor is sad. At 6 o'clock, he abandons his chess, passes into the billiard room, and discusses dancing. Before his second marriage, the Queen of Naples, Pauline, and Hortense all tried to teach him the waltz, so that he might dance with the Empress, but he could never master it. His Majesty tries a few quadrille steps, but he no longer has the legs for this sort of thing. He leans on me after attempting a few steps. The Emperor treats me as a youth, although I shall soon be thirty-four. "I am only fourteen years older than you," remarks the Emperor. "Differences in ages," he adds, "are big when one is young, but the difference diminishes the older one gets."

We dine. His Majesty doesn't like dueling with pistols—it's English! Duels with swords, he says, are all right: "I like to see blood drawn. It maintains politeness."

The Emperor talks about his mother. "Madame has had thirteen children," he says, "and I am the thirteenth. On the fifteenth of August, 1769, she was returning from church, when she was seized with birth pains. She only just had time to get home and drop me on the rug. My father died in 1785. Had he lived, my mother was capable of bearing 20 children. She was a superior woman, was Madame—a woman of resource!"

May 21

According to the Montholons, there is a rumor prevalent in town that were are to be transferred to Botany Bay.

May 22

Great boredom. All Longwood seems depressed. We tremble at the thought of Botany Bay.

May 30

During the night, the Emperor sleeps first on the big bed, then on the small one, and, finally, abandons both for the sofa.

June 9

I am sad, thinking of what the Emperor said to me two days ago, that the rioters in England were speaking of no one but his Majesty; that they had a tricolor; and that they were crying out for the Emperor to lead them in defense of the rights of the people. They might seize several vessels and come and rescue us, after which they would go to France and expel the Bourbons. His Majesty believes that it would be quite possible for them to commandeer a few English ships, and come here and rescue us.

June 11

The Emperor declares: "This is not the moment to leave me. Within three years, the King of France will die. There will be a crisis, and if the princes succeed the King, France will be tranquil and consolidated. If the Prince of Orléans, or Napoleon II, succeeds, you will be well received. Furthermore, everything is now in a state of ferment; and you must await the crisis with patience. I have still a great many years to live. My career is not yet finished!"

June 19

The Emperor says I ought to go to the camp and visit the ladies more frequently. "Make promises, but don't keep them; that's the way of the world," says the Emperor. Seeing my downcast look, he asks me whether it is in consequence of the letters I have received. He gets up from his couch, struts about animatedly, and repeats that I need have no qualms as to my future. I am to trust in his promises!

Shortly afterward the Grand Marshal arrives to say that the Admiral and Lady Malcolm are at his house, with two officers, and request an audience with the Emperor. The Emperor dresses, and receives them in the billiard room, then ushers them into the reception room. I remain with Bertrand, Montholon, and the two officers in the billiard room. His Majesty talks with the Malcolms for two hours, and as the door of the billiard room is open, and the Emperor speaks in a high voice, we hear a great deal of the conversation.

The Emperor relates all his complaints against Hudson Lowe [the Governor]. After 20 generations, his descendants will disclaim their relationship to such a man. When one takes a prisoner, one considers him according to the rank he held.

"I was Emperor," says Napoleon, "but I am treated as General Bonaparte. It is ridiculous in the extreme. If they preach legitimacy, then remember that your reigning family has usurped the throne. Consult the Holy Scriptures, and you will see that Saul and David reigned because they were the Lord's anointed. I was chosen Emperor by the French nation, and I was consecrated by the Pope. Your country recognized the republic at the Treaty of Amiens. Their object in keeping me at Saint Helena is that I may fall a victim to its devouring tropical climate. It would have been more generous to finish me off with a single blow. Why do they bring me here, if it is not to give me more liberty than in a prison? As it is, I cannot leave my room. Haven't they any prisoners in England then?"

June 27

The Emperor dines with Bertrand, and I call at the house about 8:30. "Well, Gourgaud," the Emperor greets me. "One doesn't see much of you."

"*Ma foi,* Sire," I reply, "I thought your Majesty had escaped."

The Emperor is disconcerted at this, and says to me, "Bah! Well, anyhow, sit down."

His Majesty agrees that I do really need a wife, for to be without one at my age is indeed a great privation. The Emperor adds that I ought to make friends with Madame Bertrand's mulatto servant.

Now, I have never spoken a word to this girl, because the Grand Marshal had begged me not to. Even so, the Bertrands' behavior is very extraordinary; whenever I arrive at the house, the maid is sent out. The Emperor laughs, and asks Bertrand whether this is so. The latter excuses himself on the grounds of his wife's delicacy of mind!

June 28

When dinner is served, his Majesty calls for me, and says: "If you haven't dined, will you do so with me?" He makes me sit down, but I eat very little, and the wine has a disagreeable taste. After dinner, the Emperor talks about his love affairs. It appears that Mademoiselle D—— would never accept anything from him—not even a diamond necklace.

"I made love also," says the Emperor, "to Mademoiselle Mathias, a Piedmontese lady, who was staying with my sister Pauline. I gave her presents, because she wasn't very rich. Her father, who lived at Turin, believing that she was contracting debts, wrote and requested her to come home. She went home, but no sooner had she told her father the real facts when he, too, came back with her. He reckoned on making a thing or two out of me! It was at Lyons that I saw her again, and she told me that her father had scolded her for not telling him sooner . . . !

"At Vienna in 1805," continues the Emperor, "Murat said to me, 'I want to introduce you to a charming lady who is madly in love with you. She wants only you.'

"Although this appeared rather suspicious, I asked Murat to bring her along. She didn't speak a word of French, nor I of German. She pleased me so much that I spent the night with her. She was one of the most attractive women I have ever met. At daybreak, she woke me up, and I have never seen her since. I never knew who she was. Only, in 1809, the Chief of Police at Vienna told Savary that her name was Judith. A woman must be pretty and amiable to please me."

June 29

I am melancholy and unwell, and oppressed with boredom. The Emperor dines with Montholon, and sends me a bottle of wine. It is tainted. Then he sends for me. "This rogue Reade [English Deputy Adjutant-General]," he says, "is quite capable of trying to poison me. He has the key to the wine cellar, and he can change the corks."

I think his Majesty would be well advised not to be the only one to drink wine. They would not dare to poison the whole lot of us. It would cause too great a sensation. The Emperor shakes his head.

"All the same, the fact remains—I should be dead."

June 30

The Emperor again assures me that I am very fortunate. In England, where we shall be within a year, he will get me married to some young lady from the city who, in her enthusiasm, will bring me 7 or 800 thousand francs.

"Ah, a little girl is what you need," says the Emperor. "If I were to give you a portfolio containing 4 millions, you wouldn't be happy."

The Emperor repeats that he will find me a bride. He says he will come and visit us, and enjoy fox hunting.

July 18

His Majesty thinks the English are a savage race, but they fear death less than we do. They are more philosophical and live more from day to day. All this, if you please, because it is said that the Nymph [Rosebud] is to marry a merchant sea captain who proposed to her only two days ago!

July 26

After lunch, we all take a stroll in the park, and on our return, meet the Nymph with her husband, Mr. Edwards. The Emperor asks the husband whether he has *avantagé* his wife. He gets no reply! The Emperor then asks whether the husband knew that, before his marriage, an officer of the 53rd courted his wife. The husband blushes horribly!

We return to the reception room, where the Emperor drinks to the health of the Nymph's first baby. The weather is superb. There are only four such days in the whole year.

"As Warden says," remarks the Emperor, "the Nymph is a real Marie Jeanne. She looks like a *religieuse*. In London, she will be much sought after. Everyone will want to have her at their parties. All that is necessary is for people to know what *I* thought of her." The Emperor continues to speak about the Nymph.

"Pillet [a French novelist] has painted the English well, although he has rather exaggerated his picture. He says that the English practice incest. That's probably because they read the Bible too much. The Pope often told me that one ought not to make the reading of the Bible too common. And it's true."

August 22

Madame Bertrand has just seen a midshipman from the *Conqueror* who seems well disposed toward us. He expresses his conviction that the Emperor will soon be on the throne again. It appears, also, that many people in England are of the same opinion.

His Majesty gets up on hearing this, caresses Madame Bertrand, and alludes to her height, whereupon we all measure ourselves by the door. The Emperor is 5 feet 2 inches in height, Madame Bertrand 5 feet $4\frac{5}{12}$ inches, and I, $\frac{5}{12}$'s more, when measured in my boots. Bertrand is $\frac{4}{12}$'s shorter. His Majesty would like to know how much he weighs.

August 30

When I call on the Emperor, he prevails on me to play chess; after which, we again discuss Jesus Christ. We assure his Majesty that he will end his days a devotee, but he replies: "When the body becomes enfeebled, one's intelligence goes with it, and one never becomes a devotee without that happening."

It appears that at the time of the Emperor's marriage, Madame de Bassano wrote to her husband saying she hadn't slept, because she found Marie Louise so ugly. She was convinced that the Emperor, accustomed as he was to seeing pretty women in Paris, would never get used to Marie Louise's face. But, later, she wrote again saying that she was wrong in her previous estimate, for Marie Louise was really well made and quite pretty.

"When I went to meet her," remarks the Emperor, "I had her carriage stopped, as I didn't want her to know who I was. But the Queen of Naples, who was in the carriage with her, cried, 'It's the Emperor!' Whereupon, I threw myself into the coach and embraced Marie.

"The poor child had learned a long speech by heart, which she hoped to deliver on her knees. I had asked Metternich and the Bishop of Nantes whether I might sleep the night under the same roof with her. They removed all my fears by assuring me that she was the Empress, and not an archduchess. Only the library separated Marie Louise's room from mine. I asked her what she had been told before leaving Vienna. She replied that her father had said to her: 'As soon as you are alone with the Emperor Napoleon, obey him in everything he requires.'

"Marie Louise was a charming child . . . yet I think that, although I loved her, I loved Josephine more. But that is natural. I had been brought up with Josephine, and she was a real wife—the one of my choice. She was the epitome of elegance, both in the bed chamber and in her toilet. But just as Marie was sincere, so Josephine was a liar. She would always say 'No' at first, in order to give herself time to reflect. She contracted debts which I was obliged to pay. Every month she would break out, revealing everything that was in her heart—just like a real Parisienne. If she could have borne me a baby I would never have left her, but, *ma foi!* . . ."

Madame Montholon remarks, "Ah, it would have been a happy thing for her!"

I add, "And for France, too!"

The Emperor looks at me with pleasure. "Yes, certainly," he remarks. "If it hadn't been for my marriage with Marie Louise, I would never have made war on Russia. . . ."

September 1

At 4 o'clock, 27 officers of the 66th Regiment call on Bertrand, who, shortly afterward, introduces them to the Emperor. The room is full. His Majesty asks his usual questions: To the paymaster: "How much do you steal?" To the surgeon: "How many arms have you amputated?" Later on, he sends for me. He is in his study. Apparently the officers were pleased. The way to make them laugh is always to ask the surgeon and the paymaster questions such as the Emperor asked them.

September 8

At 10 o'clock, the Emperor sends for me, and asks me for my notes and researches on Waterloo. It appears that Las Cases also did a good deal of work on the campaigns of Italy, but his Majesty, having added a few of his own observations, claimed it as *his* work! "You make a mistake if you think that this work belongs to you," he remarks. "Disillusion yourself."

I point out that I have taken great pains over the manuscript of Waterloo.

I have studied the subject thoroughly, so I contend I have some right to ownership.

"No," replies the Emperor. "A comma, or a full stop by me, changes everything."

September 10

The Montholons come to dinner, and afterward we read *The Death of Cæsar.*

"It is true that Cæsar himself was a failure," remarks the Emperor. "Otherwise, he would not have died at the hands of assassins."

September 12

While I am visiting the Montholons, the Emperor and the Grand Marshal arrive. We discuss the idea of finding ourselves on a desert island. His Majesty says he would like to found a colony of 2000 people, with rifles and cannons. He himself would be King, and *we* would constitute the Chamber of Peers. The mob would play the part of the Chamber of Deputies. If we had gone to America, we would have established a kingdom. . . .

After discussing the means we would employ to suppress insurrection on our desert island, the Emperor suddenly cries out, "Bah! We are better off here."

On the way home, the Emperor again talks about the desert island. "You would all require me as chief," he says. "We should have to build a citadel, and obtain powder and guns. Each of us would need a wife, for it is horrible to see oneself die without children."

September 16

Sadness. Boredom. After dinner, his Majesty sends for me, and, in the course of the conversation, declares that he prefers blondes to brunettes. "When I saw that Marie Louise was a blonde," remarks the Emperor, "I was very pleased."

September 17

I dine with the Emperor, and he tells me that in his younger days he won a prize offered by the Academy of Lyons for an essay on the following question: *"What principles and truths should be inculcated in man to advance his own happiness?"* The Emperor says he received a gold medal worth 50 louis, which he sold later.

September 26

In the evening, after dining alone, the Emperor sends for me. He tells me that he has drunk a bottle, to calm himself. Later, he remarks that he thinks Madame Bertrand is a beautiful woman. Apropos of this, he adds:

"Josephine almost invariably lied, but intelligently. I can tell you, she was the woman I loved most. She knew me well, and never asked anything from me for her children. She never solicited me; but her debts ran into millions! She had bad teeth, but she was so careful that this defect was hardly ever noticed. Marie Louise was innocence personified—the very antithesis of Josephine. She never lied. She loved me. She always wanted to be with me. If she had been well advised, and had not listened to that scoundrel Montebello or to Corvisart, who I am now sure was a wretch, she would have come here with me. But they told her that her aunt had been guillotined, and I suppose the circumstances were too much for her."

Later on, the Emperor talks about his mother: "My mother was a superb woman, and of great intelligence. Even when she was carrying me, she followed the army in the Corsican War. The French generals took pity on her, and instructed her to return home for the accouchement, where she was given a triumphal welcome."

October 2

His Majesty complains of his liver, and makes me feel his legs.

"Sire, when I heard how ill you were, I was stricken with sorrow," I remark.

"What!" exclaims the Emperor. "You speak of sorrow—*you!* What sorrows have I not had? What things to reproach myself with! You, at any rate, have nothing to regret."

October 4

In a few days, the Emperor is going to ask for a medical examination, which, he hopes, will be the means of getting us away from Saint Helena. That is, if the doctors are honest. His Majesty is sure of O'Meara, and of his devotion. In my opinion, the Emperor's liver trouble would be his strongest claim for removal, for his legs have been swollen ever since he left Moscow.

His Majesty speaks about the Corsicans: "I am not a Corsican. I was brought up in France. I am, therefore, a Frenchman, as all my brothers are. I was born in 1769, Corsica already being joined to France. At Lyons once, the Mayor, wishing to pay me a compliment, said to me, 'It is amazing, Sire, that, although you are not a Frenchman, you love France so much, and are doing so much for her.'

"It was," remarked the Emperor, "as if he had given me a big blow with a stick. I turned my back on him."

October 7

His Majesty goes out with Montholon, visits the stables, and later, calls on Madame Bertrand. He asks her why she looks so upset. She replies, because her husband is such a poor fish.

"At night, or during the day?" asks the Emperor.

"Ah, *ma foi!*" replies Madame Bertrand.

"Ah," says the Emperor, "you forget that woman is but one rib—she is the slave of the husband."

Yes, and it is true that here we are all slaves! Shortly afterward, I meet Bingham [Brigadier-General of the British forces at Saint Helena].

"How is his Majesty?" he asks.

"Well," I reply, "he is suffering from his liver, his legs and his gums."

Later, the Emperor sends for me. He is in his bath: he says he wants to have a saltwater bath. He asks me whether Bingham really believes that he is ill. He invites me to dinner, and talks of women.

October 15

His Majesty is tired, and unable to walk. He says he would have lived until he was 80 if he had not come to Saint Helena. Here, he will never make old bones.

October 20

In the morning, the Emperor dictates to Montholon on Marlborough's Italian campaigns. Later, he sends for me and discusses war:

"Waterloo was lost because Grouchy [the French general ordered by Napoleon to attack the Prussians under Blücher] failed to join us. Poor France—to be beaten by those rascals! But it's true—they had already beaten us at Crécy and Agincourt. I felt too confident of beating them. I had guessed their numbers, but probably I ought to have waited another fortnight. Perhaps I was wrong in attacking. Russia and Austria would certainly not have acted against me."

November 1

The Emperor assures me that he has only a year to live. We shall all be freed from his service soon. Prisoners remain in their cells. After all, exercise isn't necessary. Then the Emperor adds that he will go out in the morning if the Governor is changed. By remaining indoors he preserves his dignity. He is still Emperor. He couldn't live otherwise. His Majesty recognizes that he has his faults.

"Now that I am far away, I see them," he remarks. "I will not hasten the end of my life by one minute; but I will not tolerate insolence from anyone, nor will I allow my privacy to be violated."

November 13

It appears that his Majesty was sad, suffering from a toothache and a swollen face. In the evening, the Emperor asks the time, and then announces that he isn't dining. He retires with the remark: "The weather has been bad today, Monsieur Gourgaud."

"Pardon, Sire," I reply, "but it has been excellent."

"I don't think so," says the Emperor.

And that's the end of the conversation!

November 16

His Majesty has had a wisdom tooth out. He sends for me in the reception room.

"*Eh bien!*" he exclaims. "You have been talking to the commissioners."

He embraces Madame Bertrand, who is all dressed up, caresses her, and begs her to play chess, although she doesn't even know the moves. At dinner, he has eyes for no one but her.

He told us that O'Meara made him sit on the ground when he pulled his wisdom tooth out. The operation caused vomiting. The doctor used his forceps. O'Meara was quite proud of the operation. It was a back tooth, and had two cavities above the gum, one on the outside, and the other at the back of the tooth.

November 19

The Emperor sends for me in the reception room, where he is playing chess with Montholon. Madame Montholon is on the sofa, and she remarks that the Emperor's extracted tooth is worth at least a thousand louis. The Emperor plays until 7 o'clock, and then says: "Ah, what a villainous country!"

November 22

In the reception room, the Emperor remarks: "I've been reading Hume. What a fierce nation the English are! What crimes in their history! Look at Henry VIII, who married Lady Seymour the very day following that on which he had Anne Boleyn executed. *We* would never have done such a thing in France!"

December 11

When his Majesty sends for me, he says he hears from a reliable source that everyone is in a state of terror at Plantation House, as the Governor is expecting to be recalled. He hears, too, that it was Lord Wellington who insisted on his Majesty being sent to Saint Helena.

The Emperor remarks: "Miss Hamelin says that Wellington has no courage. He acted out of fear. He has had one stroke of fortune, and knows that such fortune never comes twice. He doesn't wish to risk losing his reputation. He knows well enough what would happen in a year or two if I were at the head of 200,000 Frenchmen . . . !"

December 17

Conversation with the Emperor on God: "Why I cannot believe in a just God punishing and rewarding is because good people are always unfortunate, and rogues always lucky. Look at Talleyrand! You will see—he'll die in his bed. When I see that a pig and a dog have stomachs and eat, I say to myself, 'If I have a soul, they must have one also.' Give a watch to a savage. He will believe that it has a soul."

"Just so, Sire," I remark, "but the watch proves the existence of God, for to make a watch requires a watchmaker."

Replies Napoleon: "If a man thinks it is because his nature is more perfected than that of, say, a fish. When my digestion is bad, I think differently from when I am well. Everything is a question of matter. Besides, if I had believed in a rewarding God, I should have been afraid of war."

December 27

At the Governor's request, O'Meara visits Plantation House. When the Emperor summons me, he discusses the Deity. He says that he can hear my confessions, as he has been anointed.

"Montholon will die first," he remarks, "then you, and then I." He continues: "I believe that the most religious countries are those in which most crimes are committed. On the other hand, religion offers great consolation. Man is less unhappy when he believes in God. I confess that having seen so many men pass instantaneously from life to death on the battlefield, this has made me a materialist. When a man is asleep, or when a man is mad, where is his soul? I believe Voltaire contributed most to the Revolution. Everyone read his books."

January 7, 1818

The Emperor declares that, nowadays, people only play at fighting. "Formerly, the vanquished were either massacred, or reduced to slavery, and their women folk violated. Had I done that at Vienna, the Russians wouldn't have reached Paris as easily as they did! War is a serious thing."

I reply that, if our armies had "massacred everything," conquests would have been more difficult, as people would have defended themselves better. The rifle has established equality among men. Take Spain, for example. We behaved there in the old traditional way, with the result that the entire population rose as one man and cleared us out.

His Majesty is vexed at this, and assures me that, if he had remained in Spain, he would have conquered the country. He ought to have stayed there another month, in 1809, and driven General Moore into the sea. The English would have been disgusted, and would never have set foot again in Spain.

"It is because of Austria that I am here," remarks the Emperor.

January 16

In the evening, we play chess. The Emperor exclaims, "What a bore life is! What a cross!"

How it grieves me to see a man who had once commanded Europe talk like this!

January 19

After dinner, I walk round the garden with the Bertrands. The Emperor sees me, but says nothing. Bertrand remarks that the great man is losing his hair.

"Cæsar," I reply, "covered his with laurels."

January 25

The Emperor confesses that his greatest strength, when in France, lay in his ability to withstand mental strain; and that he never knew anyone superior to him in this respect. "I could discuss a question for eight hours," he remarks, "and, immediately afterward, begin another discussion with the same energy as the first. Even today, I could dictate for twelve hours on end. . . .

"You must confess, it requires tremendous courage to live here. My God! I am as calm here as I was at the Tuileries. I have never made a trouble of life. I have never taken, nor will I ever take, steps to avoid death."

After quarreling with the Marquis de Montholon—whom he wished to challenge to a duel but was prevented from doing so by Napoleon—General Gourgaud left Saint Helena on March 14, 1818. It has been suggested by some historians that this quarrel was merely a pretext employed by him to receive permission from Governor Lowe to return to Europe, where he then organized a campaign for the Emperor's release.

Not long after his departure, Napoleon remarked to the Russian commissioner on the island, Count Balmain: "Speak to me no more of that man; he [Gourgaud] is mad. He was jealous, in love with me. Que diable! I am not his wife, and can't sleep with him. I know he will write things against me, but I don't care. If he is received in France, he will be shut up, or hanged, or shot."

In his History of the Captivity of Napoleon at St. Helena, Based on the Letters and Journals of Sir Hudson Lowe, *by William Forsyth, the author writes that Gourgaud was once told by Napoleon in a fit of anger to put an end to his life by suicide. Gourgaud had then replied that they should both commit suicide by shutting themselves up in a room with a pan of burning charcoal. Napoleon's response to this suggestion to emulate Sardanapalus is unrecorded.*

During the last slow three years of his life, the Emperor became more and more despondent, complaining of the bad treatment accorded to him until the end, which fell on May 5, 1821. The French believed that he had died of hepatitis, brought about by a poor diet and the unhealthy climate of the island; but it was later determined that his death was due to cancer of the stomach, the same disease that had killed his father.

In 1840 General Gourgaud was appointed a member of a secret commission by King Louis-Philippe to dig up Napoleon's remains from his grave at Saint Helena and take them back to France. He was present at the Emperor's second interment at the Invalides. His own death occurred in 1852. The Journal *was kept secret by his family and not published until 47 years later.*